1,2,3,4,5

5 DECADES OF DEVOTION TO LUTON TOWN FC

My Life Story

By

Alan Adair

First published in 2012 by Guideline Publications

2nd version updated in May 2013

Copyright 2022 Alan Adair

The right of Alan Adair to be identified as author of this work has been asserted under the Copyright Designs and Patent Act 1988.

ISBN-13: 9798412067254

This book is dedicated to my daughters Georgina and Mollie &
in memory of my late parents Allan & Miriam.

Thank you to my Father for taking me to my first game in 1966 against Exeter City in the FA Cup.

My sincerest appreciation to Roger Wash, the LTFC Historian for his assistance with historical data on our beloved Club.

Finally to my friend, the Official Club Photographer, Gareth Owen, for his photography of myself at Kenilworth Road and our Wedding.

CONTENTS

FOREWORD

I was born in April 1958 at St Mary's Hospital in Luton, one of 3 children to Allan & Miriam Adair. I was the only boy with 2 sisters. Older sister Ann was born 18 months earlier than myself & younger sister Michelle was born 7 years later.

A background to both my Mum & Dad's families is as follows:

Mother Miriam was one of five children. She had 2 Brothers & 2 Sisters to Annie and Bill Roberts. Grandma Annie was born in Silver Town London & Granddad Bill was a Scot from Clydebank, near Glasgow.

He was a bit of a traveller and had left Scotland at the young age of 19 to work in Detroit USA as a toolmaker in the car industry. After leaving Detroit for London, he met Annie in a café in the East End. Within 6 weeks of meeting he had proposed marriage, she accepted & they were married until he died in 1978.

My Mum was born in Ilford, as was her elder brother Billy pre-war. The Roberts family were evacuated during the Blitz. They had a choice of either Coventry or Luton to move to. Luckily it was Luton they chose, as Coventry was heavily bombed in WW2. The Roberts had 3 more children after moving to Luton. A son, named Malcolm & two girls, Ann & Joan. Malcolm, the youngest boy, had to have his leg amputated at the age of 4 after catching gangrene. He had a false leg constructed & fitted. It never bothered him throughout his life.

The Roberts settled in Luton, Bill worked at Vauxhall as a toolmaker until retirement & Annie was a housewife.

My Dad was born in Blantyre, Scotland one of 2 boys born to Isabel & Tom Adair. Tom was a Glaswegian and Isa from Burn Bank, Lanarkshire. The older brother by 4 years to Dad was also called Tom.

Granddad Adair left Glasgow on his own initially, to look for work down South. He travelled down with the intention of heading for London but befriended someone on the journey that had a job set up at Vauxhall in Luton.

Tom decided to disembark at Luton & take his chances there. After getting digs arranged thanks to his new friend on the train, he was also fortunate to gain employment at Vauxhall too. The plan was for Tom to give it 6 months & if successful, Isa & the boys would join him. Tom settled in immediately at Vauxhall so they followed on & moved in to a rented house in Stopsley, Luton. Granddad Adair, a tall articulate man, was evidently so talented at school, his teachers wanted him to go to Cambridge or Oxford University. In those days of course, only wealthy boys were given that chance, working class lads like Tom had no such opportunity.

At Vauxhall he was a pioneer of the Trade Union movement and became a Shop Steward. He played a major part in getting the Union fully established & was responsible for securing the rights & conditions that many workers benefited from in later years. He was also deemed too valuable to go to war, as he was involved in the Churchill Tank Production at the Vauxhall plant. Indeed, when Winston Churchill toured Vauxhall he met my Granddad.

Tom being ultra left wing politically had the Hammer & Sickle flag flying above his workplace.

"What's the Soviet flag for?" asked Winston.

"In celebration of our brave comrades winning the Battle of Stalingrad against the Nazis," was his reply.

A famous war artist by the name of Eric Kennington painted a huge portrait of Tom and it hung in the director's boardroom at Vauxhall Motors for many years until given to Tom on his retirement in the 1960s.

Although he had an English accent, my Dad ALWAYS classed himself as Scots. Grandma Isa Adair was a lovely woman, as was equally Grandma Roberts. I adored them both in different ways.

Isa worked in a clothes shop even after retirement age.

Mum & Dad met on a bus in Luton coming home from a Dance in the town. They married in 1956.

Allan was a painter & decorator by trade. Eventually running his own successful business with a partner called Gwynne James, a Welshman.

He employed many men who have since told me they worked very hard & played VERY hard & were rewarded handsomely. Of course like any true Scot, he did much of his trading in the pub & loved a bet too.

Miriam was a machinist in the clothing trade, but also did other jobs throughout her life - selling insurance for the Provident, working on the track at Vauxhall, in security at Luton Airport for example.

So this is a little taster of my family history. There will be bits & bobs throughout this book, which I hope you will find interesting. It's mainly about my life story of being a Luton football fan and not a book about hooliganism, although that's not to say I was never involved in any trouble. I was what the hooligans describe as a shirt, or a beer monster, which although I never looked for trouble, sometimes you got in a situation where you could not avoid it.

My earliest memory of football in any shape or form was at a very young age when watching a game on TV - the F.A. Cup Final in 1965 - Liverpool v Leeds. It was in the next year when something happened in that summer, which was to shape my life for years to follow. The 1966 World Cup!

CHAPTER ONE

THE SIXTIES

1966 and all that

The World Cup was this year to be held in England. I only have vague memories of the opening ceremony, even less of the first game, England v Uruguay.

It was the second England match which started it all off for me. I remember when Bobby Charlton of Man Utd got the ball in his own half, ran past 2 or 3 Mexican defenders as though they weren't there & hit the ball with such power from about 25 yards, it nearly burst the net. What a goal, to this day still one of my favourite goals. Another memory was hearing Mexican fans singing, "Mechico, Mechico Ra Ra Ra." A feat I was to repeat with one of them 32 years later at the France '98 World Cup.

Game 3 v France a 2-0 win again, with Roger Hunt of Liverpool scoring.

We progressed in to the Quarter Finals against Argentina. This match was played on a Saturday afternoon and I remember watching this on our B&W TV set in our house at Swifts Green Close in Stopsley. The abiding memories are Geoff Hurst of West Ham, rising majestically to head home the only goal of the game & Antonio Rattin being sent off for Argentina & refusing to leave. I also recall the Fulham player George Cohen, being stopped by Alf Ramsey from swapping shirts with an opponent.

The Semi-Final was between England v Portugal, another Bobby Charlton screamer and Eusebio's humility & sportsmanship were my main memories as we beat them 2-1. We were to play West Germany in the final after they were victorious over the USSR in the other Semi. West Germany took the lead from Haller, before West Ham's Geoff Hurst & Martin Peters gave us a 2-1 lead. The Germans equalised in the last seconds and I vividly remember it taking FOREVER to go in. Naturally, the rest is history. In ET Hurst scored the 3rd - OF COURSE IT CROSSED THE LINE! Then to top it off, he scored again for his hat trick - still the only player today to have achieved this feat.

This triggered off the first insane moment of my football fanatical life. I ran out of the house with little Union flag in hand into the street screaming out, "We've won the Cup! We've won the Cup! Ee aye Adio - We've won the Cup!"

My Mum cited, "Oh my god, look at him, we've created a lunatic."

This was the moment that would take me on a life's journey of incredible elation & absolute desperation too. Unless you are a true football fan NOBODY can comprehend this feeling. I actually feel pity for people who have no interest in football. Of course they will say that we are stupid, immature, etc. but it is THEY who are missing out. The feeling we get when our team scores a goal, wins a game, wins promotion, wins a trophy, it's something that money, drink, drugs, anything, you simply cannot buy. So to non-football fans - IT'S YOUR LOSS!

1966-67

In the winter of 1966 on 1st December, my Dad asked me if I wanted to go and watch a real game, at Luton. From the moment we arrived at the Kenilworth Road ground my life was about to begin in earnest.

It was a Thursday night & the match was between Luton & Exeter City in the FA Cup 1st Round Replay. We arrived at the ground and went up the stairs into the Main Stand into our seats. I was mesmerised at the amount of people there. I could smell pipe smoke, Bovril, onions. The boy sitting next to us had a big rattle. When the game started I had already sussed out that Luton were in white shirts & black shorts because of the scarves many folk were wearing.

Then when we scored, the noise seemed deafening but I wasn't scared at all - I LOVED it! Although I can't remember how the goals were scored, we won 2-0. Dad bought me a programme and I was studying some of the names. Bruce Rioch, Alan Slough, Graham French & a player who attracted my attention the most during the game, a little man on the left wing called Ray Whittaker. For the record, the crowd that night was 7,079 but to me it sounded like 70,000. When the match had finished & on our way home, my Dad knew I didn't need to be asked again for it was me who had pleaded, "When can we go again Dad?"

"Well Luton are away next Saturday, but hopefully we can make the next home game," he replied.

On this night against Exeter, although I can't remember it, our goalkeeper suffered an injury. At the time we were second from bottom of Div 4. Only one team were below us, Lincoln City and we had to play there at Sincil Bank 2 days later. We lost 8 (EIGHT) - 1! Luton have never conceded 8 goals in a match since then to this very day, as I write.

Nobody could accuse me of being a glory supporter following this result. Luton did not play at home on a Thursday night again for over 44 years, or indeed have not lost so heavily - to date!

Our next home game was v Chesterfield but alas, my Dad had to work & we could not attend. I remember watching Grandstand on TV & reading the Tele printer with the result Luton 3 Chesterfield 2, the announcer said, "Well that should cheer the Luton fans up after losing 8-1 last week."

The following month we played at Bristol Rovers in the 2nd round of the FA Cup & again watching Grandstand, I found out we were 2-0 up at half time.

Unfortunately, Rovers recovered & we lost 3-2 to exit the Cup.

Boxing Day came & it was off to the match v Tranmere Rovers. I was decked out in my new Luton scarf & rattle in hand, Xmas presents from Santa. This was my first league match and considering we were still 2nd bottom, over 9,000 turned up on a very foggy day. We won 2-0 again. For the remainder of the season I was taken to a further 6 matches.

Southport was next, a 0-0 boring draw. My school friend Steve Toyer sat with his Dad next to us, this was Steve's first ever Luton game.

Exeter were the visitors again for the next league match and we romped home 4-0, with one goal I do remember in particular, a fantastic one from Graham French - who scored it from near the corner flag!

Next was a 1-0 win v Chester.

So my record was quite impressive 5 games - 4 wins and a draw, with no goals conceded. It was with bated breath we attended the next home game on Easter Monday v Hartlepool, their manager at the time, was Mr Brian Clough.

This was the first time we didn't sit in the Main Stand, Dad chose to stand on the terrace in the Enclosure at the Kenilworth Road end. Maybe for this reason, it was to be my first time of seeing us lose. All I remember of this game, apart from losing 2-0 was seeing a Black player for them called Tony Parry.

It was back up to the Main Stand for the next match in a 2-1 win against Lincoln, slight revenge for that 8-1 defeat.

The last match of the season was against York City knowing if we won, we would be safe from having to apply for re-election. Happily we thrashed them 5-1.

Our manager then was Allan Brown, who took charge of Luton just a month before my first game. He was a Scot who used to play for us in the 1950s & was in the Luton side that reached the FA Cup Final in 1959 against Nottingham Forest.

The season had ended and I had completely got the bug. I had by now, started taking more notice of our players. Ray Whittaker of course, Tony Read the goalkeeper, who could also play up front - he once scored a hat trick! Graham French & 2 players, who I would pay particular attention to as they were fellow Stopsley boys, Alan Slough & Bruce Rioch.

Rioch was my favourite player then & could hit the ball as hard as Bobby Charlton.

At this time, we lived in Swifts Green Close, Stopsley, having moved there from Stanford Road in 1965.

At the end of term I left Stopsley Juniors & was to attend a brand new school the next term, Putteridge Junior School. I was the very first person to be registered there - so have my own little piece of history!

My very first Luton game attended Programme cover.

This tattered old book is still just about going today. A record of every single football match I've attended.

Champions

After our annual Summer Holiday to Butlins, this particular year at Minehead, it was then countdown to the new season.

The first game we went to was a League Cup 1st round tie with Charlton Athletic, who were two leagues higher than us. We drew 1-1, a creditable result I thought, in front of over 9,000 fans. In the replay at the Valley, Luton won 2-1.

In the next round, Luton were drawn away to the mighty Leeds Utd. A 3-1 defeat was no disgrace and we held the eventual winners of the Cup to 0-0 at half time. Dad had a painting business to run & couldn't just go to games at the drop of a hat.

For this reason, it was the end of September before my next game v York.

A fine 3-1 win occurred, this had now put us in 6th place. We repeated this score on the Wednesday night against Southend to go 4th, in front of our best crowd to date 13,332. We then had 3 away matches, before the visit of Chesterfield. I remember making his debut for us that day was Ian Buxton, who scored the only goal. He is the only Luton player in my supporting lifetime that was also a professional cricketer (Derbyshire).

The following week whilst watching Grandstand - we won 5-0 at Exeter! It would take over 36 years to match this away result in a league game.

On the Wednesday night I watched a classic in the pouring rain. We beat Doncaster Rovers 5-3 and in an awesome first 30 mins - saw us go 5-1 ahead! This was by far the best I had seen Luton play in my short time as a Hatter. The noise by the near 14,000 in attendance was incredible & I was now well & truly hooked. Another 2 home games followed, both 4-0 wins against Workington & Swansea Town.

Although my Scots Dad was born a Rangers fan, he was now loving see Luton play in such glorious fashion. He was a general football fan and used to go to watch big matches in London too, having a liking for Arsenal.

As Luton were due to play away at Lincoln the next week, he decided to take me to a 'big' game. It was Arsenal v Spurs.

We travelled by train & I remember inside Highbury I was passed down to the front of the terrace, as was common in those days. The noise of the crowd had me in awe - as nearly 63,000 were there! Arsenal won 4-0 & I enjoyed it, but when Dad asked if I wanted to go again the next week, I replied, "No - WE are at home to Halifax!" Luton v Halifax it was, and a 2-0 win had us now up to 3rd place in Div 4.

In the FA Cup, we were drawn away to non-league Oxford City but it was postponed because their floodlights weren't up to the required standard. The game was switched to Luton midweek.

I recall being shocked when Oxford went 1-0 up after half time. Luton did not play well, but we scraped home a 2-1 win.

In the 2nd round, we lost 3-2 at Swindon.

After another tight home 2-1 win v Wrexham we had now won 8 League games in a row, which ended in a draw at Barnsley.

On Boxing Day in second place, we played bottom club Bradford Park Avenue. Along with sister Ann & cousin Bobby Adair joining Dad & I, a so far best of the season crowd of 16,599, resulted in a 2-0 Hatters win. My little idol Whittaker scoring and missing a penalty.

It was nearly a month before my next game, as we played 5 out of 6 games away & I missed the Newport County home match. In those 6 games we lost 3 & drew 3. Winning upon my return, against Rochdale 4-1.

Ann & Bobby came with us again to see Luton beat Lincoln 4-2 - and go top of the league! Next up was a rearranged game v Darlington. The original fixture was abandoned after just SEVEN minutes, due to torrential rain. My Granddad Adair joined us & we stood on the open Kenilworth Road terrace for the 1st time to watch a 3-1 win, including a Bruce Rioch screamer. A new spot again at the next match followed (the Bobbers Stand) v Port Vale, resulting in another win 2-0. Another trip to the Bobbers stand was for the next game v Aldershot. This was a birthday party for one of my school friends John Cubis. I was intrigued by his parents as they were deaf & both, lovely people. John was tragically killed in a car crash 9 years later, aged only 18. We won 3-1.

A boring 0-0 followed v Chester.

We then clinched promotion the following week at Halifax. To my disappointment I missed the next 2 home games because of Dad's work commitments. Losing our 1st home game of the season to Bradford City, this coming after our biggest crowd of 1967-68, nearly 19,000, in a Championship clinching performance, winning 4-0 v Crewe.

For the last home game v Brentford Dad had to work again. There was no way I could miss seeing Luton get the Div 4 trophy presented, so Granddad Adair took me to see us win 2-1 with Rioch & Whittaker (his 45th & last goal for Luton) the scorers.

By now I was an official member of the Bruce Rioch fan club. At the end of the season I met my hero as he was awarded Player of the Season. This was held in the Bobbers Supporters Club, underneath the Bobbers Stand. It was called the Bobbers, as that was the original admittance fee (a Bob - one shilling - 5p) when the stand opened in 1935. I would spend many more times in later years there. We had recently moved to a brand-new house at the top of Putteridge Road in Stopsley. There was no doubt Dad's business was going well. He was now employing more than a dozen Painters. Some names I recall were: John Common, Tony Green, Alfie German, Pat Watts & Del Mash. Del eventually became a good friend of mine too & would represent Dad at my Stag party in 1986.

He sadly died a few years ago. – RIP Del boy.

As I wrote earlier, I was now at Putteridge Junior School & the 2 years there were to be the happiest times of my educational life.

I was captain of the school team and used to actually look forward to going to school! At the end of this term Mr Isles our teacher, a Welshman, had arranged a trip to Wembley Stadium to see England Schoolboys v Wales.

This was my first of 67 (to date) trips to the home of football. We won 3-0 in front of over 75,000 fans.

I also remember one day during that term Mr Isles asking me if I had a relation called Ken. "Yes, he's my cousin, why Sir?" He said he had been to watch Bedfordshire schoolboys play at LTFC the night before & he thought that the winger was magnificent. Looking at the team sheet - he noticed the name Adair! Ken was evidently a brilliant player as a schoolboy. He signed in 1969 as an apprentice at Luton. He spent one season in the youth team, had one reserve game at Highbury & came on as sub in a 1st team friendly at Aldershot. Like many boys at that level, he had the talent, but not the dedication or professionalism to make the grade. He was released by Luton after just 12 months. Looking back & this is not an excuse, but one of the factors was his Dad, my Uncle Tom, had a terrible illness called Motor Neurone Disease which he was diagnosed with at the age of 36. I'm sure Ken tried to use his Dad's condition as a motivator, but I recall how this dreadful disease took its toll on Uncle Tom.

MND is a condition that affects all the muscles, leading to an eventual breakdown in speaking, swallowing, breathing & general movement of the body. It started in his hands, then spread to his arms, legs, until he couldn't move anything in his body. He became wheelchair bound and tragically died on 17th August 1969 aged only 40 years. My Dad was distraught & God only knows how Grandma & Granddad Adair felt losing a son, at a young age.

I was the very first person registered at Putteridge Junior School for 1967-68. Here I am as captain of the first school football team, in goal.

1968-69

The new season began with Oldham Athletic the visitors on a glorious sunny August afternoon. I was now 10 and was allowed to go to the match with just a friend for the first time. We stood on the Kenilworth Road terrace and watched Luton win convincingly 4-0.

Three new signings made their debuts, Brian Lewis, Laurie Sheffield & with the biggest thighs I had ever seen, Mike Harrison.

The following Wednesday night accompanied by Granddad Adair, Dad and I watched Luton thrash our local rivals Watford 3-0 in the League Cup 1st round. This was my first derby and there were over 20,000 there. Because of the occasion & result, Luton fans ran onto the pitch at full time including yours truly. My granddad was not amused - and told me off!

I watched the next four home games, all wins, against Rotherham 3-1, Barnsley 5-1, Brighton, 4-2 in the League Cup & Tranmere Rovers 3-1.

After these matches, came a night to savour.

In front of 19,315, Mansfield came to town on a manic Wednesday night - this match had EVERYTHING!

Hero Bruce Rioch, was sent off for fighting in the THIRD minute. Mike Harrison scored a penalty to lead us 1-0 at half time. Mansfield equalised early 2nd half, then the place erupted. The Stags had a player sent off we went 2-1 then 3-1 up, with just under 15 mins left, what happened next is folklore. Everybody who was there will remember and agree.

Graham French, who was often called the poor man's George Best, got the ball in his six yard box, ran the whole length of the field beating nearly every Mansfield player including rounding their keeper before slotting the ball home. The crowd went ballistic. For individual skill & talent - there will NEVER be a better goal scored at Kenilworth Road! Although I have to write, Scott Oakes came pretty close nearly 26 years later. The real shame, is there is no footage of this wonder goal for any modern Hatter to share with.

Luton's first defeat of the season followed at Brighton and then a dull 1-0 home win v Torquay.

A new journey in my football following career was to follow, with my first away game. It was to be at the enemy Watford & we decided to make it a family day. Mum & two sisters were to go shopping & it was off to the match for Dad & I. We stood on the open Vicarage Road terrace and I can't remember too much from the game, except for Brian Lewis having a goal disallowed by punching the ball into the net. We lost 1-0, at this point it was the largest crowd I had experienced watching Luton, over 22,000.

Prior to these games Luton had drawn mighty Everton away in the League Cup 3rd round, however we were thrashed 5-1 by the Toffees.

Next was a 3-0 home win over Hartlepool, a pattern was now emerging of winning at home, but not winning away.

It was at this point I was now allowed to attend games on my own. So, against Northampton in the next home match I decided to go into the big boys' end where all the singing came from - THE OAK ROAD - we won 2-1. I missed the next 2 Home games v Swindon & Ware (in the FA Cup 1st round).

The erratic league form continued, 5 successive Home wins & 5 away defeats. We then drew 1-1 with Bournemouth, one of only THREE dropped points at home ALL season. After thrashing Ware 6-1 (when Keith Allen created LTFC history by becoming the first ever substitute to score a hat trick) we had Gillingham at home in Round 2 of the FA Cup & beat them 3-1.

Our manager Allan Brown had done a fantastic job so far. He had saved us from re-election in his first season, champions the next & contending for promotion this season, despite our poor away record. Brown had gone for an interview at top flight Leicester after they had sacked their boss. The Luton Board of Directors took exception to this - and promptly fired him! He also failed in the Leicester interview.

Alec Stock, the ex-QPR boss, was unveiled as our new manager shortly after and he carried on the good home form in a 2-0 win v Plymouth. He then stopped the away bogey, when we won 2-0 at Northampton on a freezing bone hard pitch.

Alas, it was away day blues again as we lost the next 2 matches. In the FA Cup 3rd round, it was no disgrace to lose 1-0 at League Champions Man City, who eventually went on to win the Cup.

While we were valiantly losing at Maine Road, Dad took me to see Mum's relatives in London. They lived near Upton Park & as Dad had found out West Ham were at home to Bristol City in the FA Cup that day, we attended the match. A fine game it was too, 3-2 to the Hammers.

My second away day with Luton followed, another family outing to Swindon, where we were a touch lucky to get a 0-0 draw. Upon arrival back to Putteridge Road I watched it again as this was Luton's very first appearance on Match of the Day.

I then missed the next 2 Home games v Walsall & Reading. The latter, was because it was the annual Trade Union Children's Party, which Granddad Adair had always organised at Stopsley Junior School. We won both of these & the next 3 home games, before our 2nd dropped home point v Gillingham. At this stage, we were still in 3rd Position. (Only 2 promoted in those days.) I missed the mid-week 5-1 thrashing of Barrow, but was back in the Oak Road on Saturday for a 2-1 victory over Orient.

We were now only 2 pts behind the leaders, our foes Watford. Easter followed & 4 winless games severely hampered our promotion chances. These were draws at Bristol Rovers & Torquay, another defeat at Mansfield on Easter Monday (while we were having a family day at Huntingdon Horse Races) & then our last dropped home point v Southport, in which Brian Lewis ended up in goal after an injury to goalkeeper Sandy Davie.

We could still mathematically gain promotion after beating Brighton 3-0 at home, a 0-0 draw at Southport, & a rare away victory at Tranmere. With only 2 games remaining, on a Friday night we beat Stockport 4-1 with 2 things that spring to mind that night. I remember all us kids at the front of the terrace having some real good fun & banter with the Stockport keeper called Ogley. The other was Keith Allen, picking the ball up in his area upon hearing the ref's whistle. Unfortunately, it was not the ref's whistle but it was from an Oak Road Ender & Stockport scored from the spot. This was to be ultimately, Bruce Rioch's 52nd & final goal in a Luton shirt. Swindon also won the next day & that was the end of our promotion dream.

The final match was a rearranged one against Watford, the new champions. The original Boxing Day game was postponed because of a frozen pitch & the first rearranged match abandoned at 1-1 because of heavy snow.

There was NO WAY I was allowed to see this match in the Oak Road, Dad was with me in the Enclosure. We saw a game that was a battle both on & off the pitch. Although we knew our promotion hopes were gone, because this was a local derby & they were champs, a never to be beaten astonishing league crowd of 25,523 attended. This KR attendance has never been beaten (in the league) since.

Three players were sent off, Alan Slough for us, & Walley & Endean for them.

This was my very first experience of seeing football hooliganism. Watford fans were trying to take the Oak Road & over 100 of them were injured, many of them actually hospitalised with vicious wounds. Luton fans battered them & there were stabbings and all sorts of injuries. This was in revenge for our Skinheads taking a severe beating on Watford's Rookery end at their place.

We beat them 2-1. If only our away showings of just 5 wins could have been improved? The home record that season has never been bettered (& probably never will be). 20 wins, 3 draws and NO defeats.

Although we did remain undefeated at home (league again) for the entire campaign exactly 50 seasons later in 2018-19 at the same 3rd tier level, with 16 wins and 7 draws.

Here with young Peter Jack, we were members of the Alan Slough fan club. I was aged 10/11.

The late great Alan Slough RIP, scoring a late equaliser v Shrewsbury in 1969 after having scored an own goal earlier in the match.

Promotion Again

In the summer of 1969 I remember crying when I saw the headlines in the Evening Post – RIOCH SOLD TO ASTON VILLA – My favourite player, who we all used to chant for in the Oak Road, "Rioch for England," (ironically, he went on to captain Scotland in the 1978 World Cup), had been transferred, along with his young brother Neil. We received £100,000, a huge amount of money at the time + £10,000 for Neil, to keep him company at Villa.

Our holiday to Butlins resumed, this time Skegness & my abiding memory was my first flight in a plane - just one of those light aircraft that lasted about 10 mins!

This holiday caused us to miss the opening game of the season at home to Barrow, in which Luton won 3-0.

Before our holiday we watched a pre-season friendly against an Italy Under 21 side. A 3-2 victory no big deal, but that night I saw a new signing from Fulham playing at left back. During the game, Alec Stock experimented & changed things a bit by slotting him upfront. He was to become my all-time favourite Luton player, who went on to play for Newcastle & Arsenal, and is the only post-war England player to score 5 goals in a full international (v Cyprus in 1975). MALCOLM MACDONALD.

With my cousin Ken Adair now signed on at the club as an apprentice, if I didn't love Luton enough already, Ken being there was even more reason to now.

After the Barrow game, Macdonald was to score his 1st LTFC goal at Bournemouth & Boscombe Athletic (as they were known then).

The next day, Sunday August 17th was the day Ken's Dad, my Uncle Tom, died. RIP Tom.

My first game of the season followed 2 days later against Peterborough in the League Cup 1st round replay. Dad, in his sad circumstances, took me to see a cracking game in a 5-2 victory for the Town.

Next up, 2 home matches in a row v Orient & Halifax Town respectively.

You will see occasionally throughout this book that I have a liking for statistics, especially attendances and this is a classic example. The crowd v Orient was 13,761 & then 13,759 three nights later. I wonder who the 2 people were that missed the Halifax game?

The Orient match was a belter, at 2-0 down with only 15 minutes left, one of our new signings John Collins pulled one back.

Then a superb equaliser from Graham French (which can be seen today on YouTube) & with 4 mins left showing on the big SKF clock on the Bobbers stand, my new hero Macdonald then scored a brilliant winner.

All I can remember about the Halifax game was signing their centre half after the match, Chris Nicholl, who became a future Northern Ireland International.

A 2-0 win at Gillingham put us top after 5 games.

Next, was my 2nd experience of seeing crowd trouble in the League Cup 2nd round tie at home to Millwall. Dad knew about their reputation even then & we watched from the Enclosure as the Londoners fans were scrapping away in the Oak Road. This of course, would be the first of many times I would witness trouble & Millwall go together like peas in a pod, leading to scenes that all of Europe would witness over 25 years later.

We drew 2-2.

The start of the new school term had seen my leaving Putteridge Juniors for the big school Stopsley High.

The early Hatters pacesetters next thrashed Bristol Rovers 4-0, with the normal Macdonald strike and a debut goal from new signing Matt Tees.

Millwall at The Den followed for the replay, naturally I was not allowed to go but Dad & his painting gang did.

I remember him telling me years later that the whole evening was nothing but Aggro. They had to fight their way out of the pub pre-match, in the ground after Luton had scored & post-match in a restaurant. These were grown men in their 30s. Keith Allen scored the only goal 3 mins from the end of extra time.

We were still top, following a draw at Bradford City and a 3-0 win at Southport. Luton Town then came up with a brilliant idea of running cheap, chartered football special trains because of the ever growing away following we were experiencing. My Dad went on the very first one, a midweek trip for the League Cup 3rd round at Sheff Utd. The cost for this was only 25 shillings (£1.25) return. We lost to the highflying Div 2 Blades 3-0.

On the Saturday, over 1,000 fans filled 2 trains for the same price to see us win 3-1 at Home Park, Plymouth in Devon. How much would that cost today?

The table topping Hatters continued this fine run with another away win at Walsall & a 2-0 home victory v Stockport. Then, in front of the biggest home crowd of the season, 18,065, we drew 0-0 with Bournemouth. It was mid-October before we finally lost our unbeaten run, going down 2-0 at Doncaster in front of 17,380. Anybody who had been to Belle Vue - can you imagine how packed that crowd must have seemed!

Next up was my 1st away game of the season at Brighton and Hove Albion. Dad & I went on the train and this was a brilliant day. The skinhead movement at the time was in full flight and I remember the police at the Goldstone Ground taking the laces out of the Oak Road boys Doc Marten boots. It failed to stop loads of trouble in the Brighton end though. We stood on the open side terrace in glorious seaside sunshine and earned a fine 2-1 win.

Then, in front of the ITV cameras a 1-1 draw at home to Torquay, where I managed to secure Brian Moore, the commentator's autograph.

Another away family trip followed, saw us drive up to Rotherham in Yorkshire & a 1-1 draw cost us top spot. A third 1-1 in a row v Barnsley at home, followed by yet another, as we drove to Bournemouth for the FA Cup 1st round. We took care of the Cherries in the replay by winning 3-1.

The TV cameras were back at Kenilworth Road, this time BBC's Match Of The Day & our home debut on that programme saw us beat Rochdale 2-0 followed by a home 1-0 win against Fulham. The floodlights kept breaking down on this night in a treacherous snowstorm.

Then an embarrassing 2-1 exit in the FA Cup followed, to non-league Hillingdon Borough. Thankfully we didn't attend.

My first full England International at Wembley was with Stopsley High School against Eusebio's Portugal. A Jack Charlton header won it in front of 100,000. After the Hillingdon debacle, we thrashed Bradford City 5-0 with my hero Macdonald getting his first hat trick for Luton. The other thing that bears to mind with this match was the attendance of less than

12,000, our lowest of the season at that point.

Boxing Day at Orient in London was my 4th away game in a row. We drove in Dad's van to see Luton lose 1-0, the first of 4 successive defeats. This was the first genuine wobble we encountered since I started following the Town (the first of many I'm afraid).

I missed a 4-0 home win v Doncaster, which saw us return to top of the league. My cousin Ken was in a LTFC youth team photograph in the match programme that day and also, a well known more modern Luton fan & good friend of mine Freddy Dann, this was to be his first Town game attending.

Because I missed the Donny match, it meant I hadn't seen Luton for over a month. This was partly due to having 5 long distance away games.

A mixture of results meant that when Brighton visited, we were 4th. In a 1-1 draw there was more trouble on the Oak Road terrace that day.

One abiding Oak Road memory from those days, was the chant for an Italian steward who used to walk up & down in front of the masses. The chant used to go up, "Mussolini, Mussolini, Mussolini, Mussolini."

Our lowest crowd of the season, 11,368, saw us beat Tranmere 2-0.

It was on to my first football special for a mid-week game at Reading - 15 bob (75p), the weather was awful, it lashed down all night. The big crowd of nearly 19,000 was never bettered at Reading's Elm Park in the league. Macdonald got the winner in the last minute. This was such an important goal, as we had slipped down to 4th again. In the pandemonium that followed the goal I was separated from Dad & got lost. I couldn't find him anywhere & as I was still not yet aged 12, I admit to being a little scared.

However, I made my way to the Main Stand found a policeman & after an announcement, met Dad in the Reading Supporters Club Bar post-match after being treated to Lemonade & crisps by the locals.

In between the Tranmere and Reading game Luton played a friendly at home to Greenock Morton and we won 5-1. The Cappilow Park men were the very first Scots side I saw play live.

I missed the next home 2-2 draw v Mansfield and then saw a boring 0-0 v Bury. A 3-2 away defeat at Tranmere meant we were 4th again. Two home Easter matches followed, winning 2-1 v Rotherham on Good Friday, & Macdonald's 2nd hat trick for us the next day v Reading, winning 5-0.

On Easter Tuesday night we lost 2-1 at Barnsley.

A school trip to Paris (my first venture abroad) along with older sister Ann, meant I was away for the 2 games at Halifax & Fulham. Of course there were no mobile phones, Internet or Sky in those days & so it wasn't until upon my return that I discovered we drew 0-0 at the Shay, but vitally won 1-0 at Fulham.

FA Cup Final day was Chelsea 2 Leeds 2 on a terrible Wembley pitch after they had stupidly, held the Horse Of The Year Show jumping event there recently.

After watching that on TV, we headed to Kenilworth Road. Oddly, but looking back, a great bit of marketing we played Walsall on the Sat evening (strangely it has never been repeated since). A healthy crowd of over 17,000 saw a 3-0 win & left us 3rd with three games left.

The last home game was a MUST win against Southport. We managed it in a real tense game, with Viv Busby netting the only goal.

Six nights later, Dad & I went to Mansfield to see us gain the point needed to win promotion in a 0-0 draw. There were thousands of Luton fans celebrating in a crowd of over 10,000. It was to be over 41 years before I returned to Field Mill. The final match was at Spotland, Rochdale. I didn't go, but my mate Chris McEvoy did with his older brother Clive, who was a known Skinhead face in the Oak Road then. He told me there was lots of trouble that day with Man Utd fans, as Luton took over the place.

We finished runners up to champions Orient, two points behind them and four points clear of third placed Bristol Rovers. Malcolm Macdonald had scored 25 of our 77 league goals. A new decade was to follow with Luton now in Div 2.

Hatters fans arriving at Sheffield train station for our League Cup tie at Sheff Utd. It was the first LTFC special train of my era. My Dad was on it – only £1 5s (£1.25) RETURN!

CHAPTER TWO

THE SEVENTIES

2nd Division Football

Before our summer holiday a major shock at LTFC was to occur. Graham French, our mercurial winger, was jailed for a shooting incident in a pub called the Unicorn in Lewsey Farm. He served over 2 years before trying to make a comeback in 1972-73 scoring 1 goal in 8 appearances, but to no avail.

The summer of 1970 was to be our final Butlins holiday at Ayr, in Scotland. I remember an old fellow coming up to me there, as I had a Luton Town hat on. He told me that he used to play for Luton and his name was Tommy Kiernan. When I arrived home, I asked Granddad Adair & it was true. He played for us in the late 1940s & scored 15 goals in 60 apps.

After Butlins we stayed & visited various relations in Dad's hometown Blantyre & nearby Hamilton. One of his Uncles had told us that Motherwell were playing Aston Villa in a pre-season friendly. Dad & I joined him at Fir Park to see them beat Bruce Rioch's Villa 2-1.

In another friendly I saw 1st Division Burnley win 2-1 at Kenilworth Road. Our first match in Div 2 was at Bolton where sadly we lost 4-2.

We got off to winning ways in the League Cup by winning 1-0 at Gillingham. My first 70-71 game was a 0-0 home draw with Norwich and my first away trip followed at St Andrews, Birmingham. The family females went shopping as we stood on a massive side terrace to see us draw 1-1. This was to be my first 30,000+ crowd watching the Town, the noise when Blues took the lead was deafening. Macdonald equalised with a penalty late on.

3 home wins in a row followed without conceding a goal against Oxford, Middlesbrough & Workington (League Cup).

Next was a trip to Filbert Street, Leicester, and we were unlucky to lose 1-0. My mum and sisters were really enjoying their shopping trips around the country & of course I loved visiting all these different grounds too.

Four clean sheets followed, thrashing Orient 4-0 at home, a family day at Swindon 0-0, winning 1-0 midweek at QPR (I missed) and a good 3-0 home victory over Bristol City.

The next game was huge. We were drawn at home in the League Cup 3rd round to the mighty Arsenal and I have many memories of this evening. The colossal crowd of 27,023 has and never will be, beaten at Kenilworth Road. There were also over 5,000 fans locked out. I stood on the Bobbers Terrace, which at that time had become a regular spot & witnessed for the first time, the Oak Road End being taken by visiting fans.

Bob Wilson, Arsenal's keeper, denied Malcolm Macdonald a hat trick with 3 outstanding saves before George Graham scored the only goal for the Gunners. Ask any fan that was there and they will tell you Luton played brilliantly against a team who that season, went on to become only the 2nd team of the century to win the League/FA Cup double, along with their rivals, Spurs.

Following that exceptional performance, it was off to Hillsborough, Sheff Wed on our familiar family outing. Macdonald was now in scintillating form and carried this on as he scored his third hat trick for Luton in an amazing 5-1 win. I saw myself on the TV highlights the next day standing in the same area on the Leppings Lane terrace that was to bring such tragedy, nearly 20 years later.

After collecting Mum & the girls from the shops, we headed from the city centre towards the M1. As we travelled with Luton scarf proudly flying from the window, a group of lads threw a brick at our car. Fortunately it didn't smash the window, only hitting the angle. Dad stopped, got out of the car & chased after them to no avail. After this incident - the females never came with us by car again!

Two 2-0 home victories over Lancashire's Bolton & Blackburn saw us go top. These really were great times, in the space of 4 years I had witnessed us go from 2nd bottom of Div 4, to top of Div 2.

The Adair family travelled to Charlton by train. While the girls visited relations, Dad & I watched a 1-1 draw at the Valley.

Our unbeaten league home record came to an end in a 2-1 defeat to Sunderland. I missed the away 2-0 win at Hull but later saw it on Match of the Day.

The next home match was unbelievable, v Carlisle in torrential rain. We had been disgracefully booed off the pitch by some fickle fans at half time losing 2-0. I was shocked to hear this and was arguing with some friends about loyalty, when Carlisle scored a third. With only 20 minutes remaining one mate commented, "Are we going? I'm not watching this rubbish any more."

My response was, "Piss off then. Call yourself a supporter?"

Soon after, Jim Ryan, one of our 4 summer signings from Man Utd pulled one back. Then, Alan Slough made it 3-2. In the last minute super hero Macdonald equalised & the crowd were going ballistic, we even nearly won it but their keeper stopping the comeback of all comebacks. To this day as I write in November 2021 over 50 years later – I have yet to see us come back from 3 goals behind to get a result.

A 2-1 home victory against Portsmouth kept us 2nd.

Next up was high flying Sheff Utd, again winning 2-1 in front of nearly 20,000. Then, it was away to foes Watford. Captain Mike Keen scored the only goal.

Just before Xmas, we started leaving in Dad's works van for the Norwich away game. Dad spotted my mate Chris McEvoy playing football on the street corner. "Do you want to come to Norwich?" he shouted. With that Chris sprinted home to ask his Mum & he was in the van in less than 2 minutes.

Macdonald nearly scored with a looping shot straight from the kick off, such was his confidence then. He did score in the 1st half but the Canaries equalised with a last minute penalty. On the way home we stopped in a restaurant for a slap up meal. I know Chris enjoyed that day & still talked about it for many years after.

We were due to play equally high flying Cardiff on Boxing Day but snow postponed it. It's a shame, because Cardiff were meant to be bringing 9,000 fans, which would have seen a capacity 27,000 crowd that day.

Bloody White Xmases - you can stick them!

Straight into the 3rd round of the FA Cup now being in Div 2, we were drawn away to 1st Division Nottm Forest. Dad & I went on one of the two football special trains and we took Chris McEvoy again. Crossing the Trent Bridge I was eagerly awaiting this match. Forest had been struggling in Div 1 and I fancied our chances of a result. Sadly, in the first 30 mins they battered us and led 1-0. Then Macdonald hit the post, collided with it and actually BROKE the frame. The delay in repairing the post had stopped the deluge & we gradually got back into the game. I recall the ball fiercely heading towards us on the terrace, before Dad punched it with such force I thought the ball would burst. It brought roars of laughter from the crowd. Macdonald equalised deservedly, to end it 1-1 & we eagerly awaited the replay.

When we returned to Luton that night we met a Scottish friend of Dad's. He said to Dad, "Have you heard about the tragedy at Ibrox?"

Rangers were playing Celtic and losing 1-0. Near full time, Rangers fans were heading for the exits at their end & Colin Stein equalised to make it 1-1. In the confusion, fans fell over on Stairway 13 and were trampled, as crush barriers buckled. 66 Rangers fans tragically perished that day. I must stress, that at the official enquiry it was stated that Colin Stein's goal was NOT the cause of this terrible accident. The Stairway was just too steep & narrow with far too many people on it.

At school on Monday I decided I was going to raise funds for the victims' families. The Nottm Forest replay was postponed due to bad weather, so it gave myself more time rattling my tin for the fund raising appeal. I gave all the money I collected to Dad, who sent off a cheque (doubling my contribution) to Rangers FC, with a letter telling them what I had done. It was with enormous pride, that I received a thank you letter from Rangers FC. This was also noted in my end of school report, which meant more to me than any exam result. RIP the 66.

We drew 0-0 at home to QPR next after an immaculate minutes silence for the Ibrox victims.

The replay against Nottm Forest followed 2 days later and it was a thriller.

We went 1-0 down, then Macdonald equalised. In the 2nd half, two goals were scored in a minute for the Reds - & we thought that was it! But my hero was not surrendering, he scored a second, then his hat trick to make it 3-3. With only three mins left Roger Hoy made a mistake, lost possession & their winger Rees scored a 4-3 winner.

In those two days, Luton were watched by 45,507 people at Kenilworth Road. It took us EIGHT games 40 years later to reach that figure in 2010-11!

A hangover followed, as we lost 1-0 at bottom club Blackburn.

Dad & I then returned to Sheffield, this time to Brammall Lane, losing 2-1 in front of 30,986 the biggest crowd to watch Luton all season.

Four winless games saw us drop to 5th, but a local derby was what was needed and an only goal by Macdonald put us back on track. This was the first of many doubles over Watford - lovely!

I missed Portsmouth away (1-0 win) and then went with Dad on the special train to Sunderland. Roker Park (capacity of over 50,000 then) seemed empty with only 12,000-odd there seeing a 0-0 draw.

We were now struggling, drawing again 1-1 at home to Charlton, then again on the special, travelling the long haul to Carlisle for the new decimal price of £1.25 return. Macdonald missed a penalty as we lost 1-0.

The next game was a must win match at home to Hull. Macdonald missed a penalty again, but it came good as we won 3-1.

In between those two games Dad took me to see Arsenal beat Leicester 1-0 in the FA Cup Quarter Final replay in front of over 57,000.

We lost 2-1 at Middlesbrough & then drew 1-1 with Millwall at home. Surprise, Surprise, there was trouble in the Oak Road that night with Lions fans.

Birmingham visited next and they had a new star, a young 16-year-old by the name of Trevor Francis, who had astonishingly scored 15 goals in 15 appearances for Blues.

A massive crowd of over 25,000 including 10,000 Blues witnessed a great game. Before the match Blues fans took the Oak Road but unlike Arsenal earlier in the season, they could not hold it and were booted off up to the Kenilworth Road end. Birmingham led 2-0, then a great comeback saw us win 3-2, with a fantastic Alan Slough goal as the winner. Trevor Francis failed to score because big John Moore marked him out of the game, he didn't get a sniff.

Easter followed and this finally put paid to our promotion hopes. On Good Friday we lost 3-2 at Ashton Gate, Bristol City. This time Luton were 2-0 ahead. Next day & despite my Dad's previous experience, he took me to the notorious Millwall Den. Maybe he felt it was safer with me going too. I have to write, there were no crowd problems (possibly because I did not see any other Luton fans all day) and maybe, because we were thrashed 4-0.

This was now officially my worst Luton defeat seen to date.

There was absolutely no way of knowing at that time, but this would ultimately prove to be my father's final Luton away game.

Two days later on Easter Monday, another massive away following of nearly 10,000 in a crowd of 24,405, saw us lose 3-1 to eventual champions Leicester.

Easter proved our bridge too far: 3 games, 3 losses, 3 goals scored & TEN against.

Unsurprisingly, our lowest gate at that point of 12,308, saw us draw 2-2 with Sheff Wed, whom we thrashed 5-1 away only six months earlier.

Another Highbury visit with Dad followed, with my mate Pete Brooks, to see Arsenal beat Burnley 1-0. I missed the final 2 away league games at Orient & Oxford.

Our lowest crowd of 1970-71 - 10,205, then watched a 1-1 draw with Swindon. Our family, were now getting excited as we were about to embark on a foreign holiday to Lloret-de-Mar in Spain. This was a big thing in 1971, as I knew nobody at school who went abroad for holidays then.

The night before leaving for Spain, Luton played the final game of the season at home to Cardiff.

This match has good memories standing on the open Kenilworth Road terrace. Everybody knew that Malcolm Macdonald, my hero, was leaving in a big transfer to Newcastle for £165,000. This was his swansong but what nobody knew at that time was pre-match, manager Alec Stock had persuaded the Newcastle boss Joe Harvey that for every goal Mac scored tonight it would add £5,000 to the transfer fee. Macdonald had obviously been affected by Luton's stumbling finish to the season & the transfer speculation. He had only scored 1 goal in his previous 9 games. In front of another low 10,000+ crowd, he went out in style. He put us 1-0 up & then scored a 2nd with five mins remaining. In the last minute, he secured his hat trick to win 3-0 as the crowd went berserk. He and we had finished on a high, earning Luton an extra £15,000 and also qualifying us for a new pre-season tournament called the Watney Cup. This was for the 2 highest scoring teams in all 4 leagues who had not won any promotions, or qualified for Europe.

Macdonald only spent 2 seasons with Luton, but boy did he leave his mark. He was sensational. In 88 league games, he scored 49 goals + another nine in 13 Cup matches. Mac - I Salute You!

Our holiday in Spain was brilliant.

1971-72

Pre-season, Chris McEvoy and I travelled on the Special train to Colchester for the Watney Cup match. I, now being a teenager, was a Smoothie (post-skinhead) and dressed in the latest gear of two tone trousers, loafers & Crombie Coat. I missed a family outing to Yarmouth for the game. We lost 1-0 with former Hatter Brian Lewis, scoring the only goal. Luton fans took their end as over 8,000 in total were at the tiny Layer Road ground. Then came two home friendly matches. Man Utd, including the legends Law, Best & Charlton, incredibly attracted over 16,000 for a 2-0 win to the Red Devils.

This was followed with a 2-1 victory to Royal Crossing of Belgium. We kicked off the new season drawing 1-1 at home to Norwich.

In the first ten league matches of 1971-72 we had drawn seven games.

I went to two away games in London that month by Supporters Coach. Each cost 55p return at Orient (0-0) and Crystal Palace in the League Cup (0-2).

It was very clear that we hugely missed Macdonald & therefore signed a new striker. His successor was Vic Halom. We got off to a reasonable start with him when we won 2 home games in a row. 3-2 vs Middlesbrough and 2-0 v Fulham. Having been knocked out of the League Cup, I went to see Macdonald play for Newcastle at Highbury with Dad. Arsenal thrashed them 4-0.

Luton were really struggling for form. I saw us draw 1-1 at home to Swindon and then lose 2-0 to Carlisle at home again. We had played 15 & won just twice.

During that summer of 1971, us schoolboys decided that we would pick a Div 1 team to follow, as well as Luton. I don't know why, but I opted for West Ham.

When Dad asked me if I wanted to go and see West Ham v Liverpool in the League Cup I leapt at the chance. After purchasing a West Ham silk scarf at Shanks & Turner Sports Shop in Dunstable Road, it was off to Upton Park, via visiting Mum's relations in East Ham & Barking. In front of a packed crowd of nearly 41,000 the Hammers won 2-1.

I must admit I felt a little guilty cheering them on so passionately, as if they were MY team. So at Luton's next home match v Charlton I cheered Luton on just that little bit extra. But to no avail, we lost 2-1 & there was trouble in the Oak Road too. The next week I went with friend Peter Brookes & his Dad to bottom club Watford and the score line was the same. It was only their 2nd win of the season. At this time I had now decided to alternate Luton & West Ham home games (making sure I didn't miss a home Luton match naturally). In succession I went to West Ham 0 Man City 2 then at last a good Luton game beating Portsmouth 3-2 after being 2-0 down, West Ham 0 Arsenal 0 and Luton 2 Cardiff 2.

The crowds at Luton were dropping and went below 10,000 for the first time when we beat Orient 2-0.

On Boxing Day, with Luton drawing 2-2 at Sheff Wed, Chris McEvoy & I went to see West Ham win 1-0 at Spurs. The fighting that day at White Hart Lane was shocking.

West Ham fans were everywhere, they took the Park Lane, were in the Shelf & the Paxton Ends. They were even fighting Millwall fans on the tube on the way back. Speaking of which, it was high flying Millwall next at Kenilworth Road in a good 2-1 win for us. Naturally, Millwall fans fought in the Oak Road.

Luton then had another good win at Preston 1-0 and were at last beginning to show some good form of 8 undefeated games. It would be 50 years before we won at Deepdale again.

FA Cup 3rd round time and incredibly, in the draw was West Ham v Luton.

I couldn't believe it. About six of us school friends travelled to Upton Park by train and I'm ashamed to write, I had a West Ham Scarf on one wrist & Luton Scarf on the other. I'm sorry, but I actually cheered when Geoff Hurst scored in the 1st minute. It is the ONLY time in my life I have actually cheered a goal against the Town. When Clyde Best got a 2nd I just politely applauded, feeling VERY guilty. At half time I said to my friends, "Am I Luton or fucking West Ham?" So off came the Hammers scarf and only ONE team for me from then on. (Apart from Rangers in Scotland of course.) Don Givens pulled one back for us, then Tony Read saved a Hurst penalty. We were knocked out 2-1, but it did me a huge favour and taught me where my loyalties should truly lie.

Off to Craven Cottage, Fulham, the next week and we lost 3-1 but I didn't care, I had regained my Luton passion.

That weekend Mum & Dad dropped a bombshell by telling us kids we were to migrate to Adelaide, Australia - and we were leaving in May! I was shocked but equally quite excited.

Sadly, my parents weren't 100% happy with each other. I can never remember them being romantic or even having a cuddle. I reckon that Australia was their way of finally trying to make things work between them. It must have been a huge decision to leave all their families behind. These were the days of the £20 assisted passage, but my parents paid the full fare. With the assisted passage, you had to stay a minimum of two years. They didn't want to risk that in case either of them could not settle & wanted to return early.

The date for our new voyage was 6th May (FA Cup Final Day) at least I could see out the remainder of the season.

After the Fulham match we drew 1-1 at home to QPR in front of the biggest attendance of 1971-72 17,280 and were in 10th place. A position we would not improve on.

A 2-1 home defeat to Oxford followed and then I went to Carlisle on the special train (£1.25 return) on my own.

Bearing in mind I was still only 13, I'm not sure that I would let someone that age travel alone nowadays. Maybe because Dad had experienced the special, he knew I was safe among my fellow Hatters? The match was a boring 0-0 draw. A couple of things stood out, the Brunton Park ground seemed miles from the train station & the Carlisle lads were all still Skinheads, which had gone out of fashion ages ago down South. Another home defeat to Sunderland 2-1 was followed by my final away game of the season at Charlton, losing 2-0.

My interest was now starting to fade & we couldn't even beat bottom of the table foes Watford in a 0-0 draw. We did defeat Burnley at home 1-0, but a 1-0 loss at Birmingham and a stalemate at Middlesbrough, meant we had only scored 2 goals in the last 7 games. A rare lifting of the gloom followed at home to Sheff Wed. We were 1-0 behind early on and with the home crowd giving almighty stick, only 14 minutes remained. Vic Halom then scored a hat - trick to win 3-1. This was to be my final victory witnessed in a poor season.

Two more home defeats followed, 1-0 v Hull and a 4-1 thrashing by Blackpool. The crowds were now down to 7,000-odd and to be honest I was actually looking forward to my new adventure. On a farewell visit to London relatives, I watched Liverpool win 2-0 at West Ham. It was with a tinge of sadness that I witnessed my final match at Kenilworth Road (or so I thought at the time) a dire 0-0 draw v Bristol City.

The final game of the season was a 1-1 draw at Cardiff.

That day we attended my Aunt Joan's wedding to Mick Hines (his brother Vic was in the same LTFC Youth team as my cousin Ken). This was a very emotional day, as it was also a kind of farewell party for us Adairs. The following weekend we left Southampton for Australia. The previous night we had booked into a local hotel in preparation for the month long voyage. Joan & Mick had left their honeymoon in the New Forest and along with Uncle Malcolm, came to wave us off goodbye. We left on the Greek Chandris Line ship called Britanis amid many tears. The epic journey was a fantastic experience. I met lots of friends on this sailing as everyone was also emigrating to South Africa, Australia or New Zealand. It was on this ship that I had my first taste of alcohol & remember rolling about merry one night when the ship was sailing through turbulent waters. These were in the days when the Suez Canal was closed for entry.

Therefore we had to sail via South Africa across the Indian Ocean. There were only 3 stops on the voyage, Madeira, Cape Town and Fremantle. Madeira intrigued me, as it was the first time that any of us had seen beggars in the streets. Cape Town, my abiding memory was Dad getting told off by a policeman for buying ice creams from a black man. Of course this was in the Apartheid era. The last stop was at Fremantle, for those migrating to Perth. On June 3rd, we arrived in Adelaide & were met by Mum's friend and bridesmaid Rita, who emigrated there from Leagrave with her husband John 8 years earlier.

Mum, Dad and I in Cape Town. May 1972, on our way to a new life in Adelaide, Australia. The Suez Canal was closed to us Brits at the time so we had to sail round the Indian Ocean via South Africa.

Australia

Upon arrival, we rented a place in the North of Adelaide for a month while looking around the suburbs for a destination to settle. Rita & John lived on the south side of the city, they advised us to look in that area as it was nicer in their opinion. We found a place we liked called Morphett Vale, an area about 10 minutes from Christies Beach.

Dad got a job with an Austrian painter who had his own company, a similar size to Dad's in Luton.

Mum decided to be a lady of leisure (housewife) & Ann's first employment, was working in a factory making sunglasses.

Michelle and I attended the local schools. Mine, being Christies Beach High. Australia was a great country to live, everything seemed to be so much larger there. It was a mixture of both the UK & USA. I loved the Drive In Movies for example, so unique & something I'd never seen the likes of before.

Mum & Dad found a builder, for in those days you found a plot of land and had the house built to your own spec. 90% of homes in Oz were bungalows.

While our house was being built, we rented a place in Brodie Road, Morphett Vale. When living there Rita's son John built me a lawnmower & I cut the locals' lawns as a part-time job until we moved into our new place in Timothy Road.

I quickly made new friends at school and would say approximately half of them were fellow migrants. Straight away I clicked with a lad called John Foy, who was from Belfast and lived up the hill. We used to go to his house regularly after school to listen to music and one day I recall seeing a Union Jack on his wall. "Why are you flying the English flag, John?" I innocently asked.

His response in Ian Paisley tone, "That's not the English flag - it's the British flag!" He then went on to educate me about all things Rangers, Ulster, Orangemen & the 12th of July etc. Things I've never forgotten!

He also told me about the 'Soccer' team he played for called Wakefield Wanderers. They played in Acre Avenue a 5-min walk from our rented house. Established by British migrants in the early sixties, they played in all Sky Blue & their Latin motto was 'Nulli Secundus' second to none. This club was to play a huge role in my life in Adelaide.

My first visit was memorable, John played for the youth team. It was a set up, where the youths played at 11am, the reserves at 1pm and first team at 3pm, all against the same opposition. You could actually drive your car into the ground and watch from it if you wished. This was near the end of season 1972 from that first day I was hooked on the club.

As a player, I knew I was not good enough. I did manage to get a trial at Camb Utd the previous summer with Chris McEvoy, but secretly I knew the score.

During that Australian winter, John and I went to see Wolves on an end of season tour play South Australia. Wolves won 3-2.

I went to my first music concert at the Royal Showgrounds to see Lindisfarne & Slade. In my time spent in Adelaide, I also saw The Rolling Stones, Gary Glitter (shush) & Slade again.

There were 2 school trips I went on, one Winter & one in the Summer of '73. The first was an outing to the Snowy Mountains in NSW. I was astonished to learn that there is more snow in Australia than Switzerland. Even though the vast majority of Aussies will never see the white stuff. We travelled by train to Melbourne, then coach to the resort Mt Kosiosko, also taking in a day trip to the capital city Canberra. The summer outing was a camping trip in the outback.

Australian wildlife was amazing, lots of the world's deadliest spiders and snakes are found on this massive continent. I remember opening the front door in Timothy Road one day to see a huge lizard on the doorstep. Opposite our house was a creek & I saw Platypus, Budgies, Parrots, Koalas and one day whilst cycling down there - had a Black snake wriggle through my bike spokes!

I ran & got Dad to get my bike back - without the snake I hasten to add!

Now back to the camping trip. On the first night, we had smuggled in the booze. You could buy cans of readymade mixed drinks in Oz, like Vodka/Coke etc. Alas, our teacher caught us, confiscated the drinks & told us to be prepared to face the consequences on return to school.

He was not wrong, we all received six of the best from the Headmaster.

My only contact with home was by airmail letter from Grandma Adair. She also used to send me out the local Sports Post Newspaper. Initially, my only way to find out the football results from UK was to phone a certain telephone number on Sunday mornings.

I had just one year at school in Oz and then left on my 15th Birthday to start work the next day, as a painter with Dad & Dietmar, the Austrian.

By now I was heavily involved with Wakefield. There was a variety of jobs I used to do there and really enjoyed them, mow the pitch, paint the dressing rooms, generally tidy up the place, gate money collector, Programme seller. I loved anything to do with WWSC.

The biggest crowd we had in 1973 was against Adelaide Juventus in the Cup. I persuaded Dad & all work colleagues to attend and it boosted the crowd to - 620!

Aged only 15 and loving life in Australia I look back now, and think it was my life in Adelaide & all the people I met, that made me the personality I am today.

There was only one real soccer ground in Adelaide called Hindmarsh Stadium that had traditional stands, terraces, floodlights etc. and held about 16,000.

In the summer months they held a floodlit competition called the Ampol Cup. I went on a regular basis, using my favourite mode of travel in Oz, Hitchhiking. At Wakefield Wanderers, it was also a fantastic social scene too. Every Saturday after the game all the players, families & fans used to go to the Morphett Vale Hotel, a pub situated about 500 yards from our house.

These were wonderful memories with great people like John Foy, Jimmy Sakkas, Harry Brown, Keith Dalglish, Gary Jones, Glyn Davis, Joe Foley, Greg Simon, Norman Stewart, Cyrille Austin, Andy McArdle the brothers Brian & Geoff Cartwright.

By now I had bought a short wave radio to listen to the UK matches at 2am. In my first season away 1972-73, Luton had reached the quarter finals of the FA Cup, our best run since reaching the actual final in 1959. I listened to the match commentary intently, as we lost 2-0 at Sunderland. The crowd of 53,151 was never bettered again at Roker Park. I later learnt upon my return to England, that there was a Rail strike, so Luton took 94 coach loads of

Hatters & - a chartered PLANE!

Typical - I move to the other side of the world & Luton had their best Cup run in 14 years!

That same year, John Foy & I watched on B&W TV (no Colour TV in Oz then) as Rangers beat Celtic 3-2 in the Scots Cup Final. I was a Rangers fan anyway, but John had taken me to new heights & I remember this game in particular, because of the huge 127,000+ crowd.

John had told me that all Ulster boys had 3 teams, local, English & Scots. Being the good Protestant that he is, his teams were Linfield, Leeds & Rangers. So it was with great pleasure, all the Wakefield boys watched his Leeds team lose to our conquerors Sunderland 1-0 in the final at his house. Leeds were so unpopular in those days EVERYONE bar himself, was cheering for the Makems. I saw a further 4 matches at Hindmarsh Stadium. South Australia drew with Stoke 2-2. Gordon Banks, the best goalkeeper I have ever seen, was attempting to make a comeback after losing an eye in a car crash in 1972. This was too big an obstacle for him and he retired after this tour. Then, Bournemouth followed & won 2-0 vs South Australia, then the Hungarian team Ferencarvous & also Bulgaria beat Australia 2-1 & 3-1 respectively.

During this season of 1973, Adair Travel sprang into action! I organised a coach to take all the Wakefield players & fans to an away game at Para Hills.

At 15 years of age, this was to be the first of many trips that I organised - the origin of Adair Travel!

As we entered 1974, Wakefield had their traditional end of season ball. At the end of the evening I was dumbfounded when the club secretary called me up on to the stage.

He said to the audience, "This young man Alan Adair, has done more for our Soccer Club in one year than most of us have done since the club started, we feel certain that he is a future Club Secretary & it is with great pleasure, that we give him a token of our thanks." They presented me with a club blazer and a watch. I felt very proud, emotional & was nearly in tears.

Soon after that, Mum & Dad told us that they were planning to return to Luton and then go their separate ways. Obviously, the adventure had failed to make their marriage work.

I was given two choices A) Return with Dad in April by plane or B) Travel with Mum & the girls by boat in June for a month's holiday.

I was confused, I didn't want to leave Adelaide but because I was still too young, I also had no say. If this had occurred a year later, I would have refused to leave. At this time Luton were doing really well in Division 2 and challenging for promotion. There was only one answer – Dad!

I don't think my Mum ever truly forgave me for choosing Dad over her. Some people have since asked, what if your Mum came home first? The answer is probably Mum, but back then, Who Knows?

A couple of days before we were due to leave, some friends decided to have a bit of a leaving party for me round Pete Herman's house. It was on this day April 15th 1974 I had the best farewell present of them all - losing my virginity!

Wendy White from Birmingham - I thank you!

Two days later, Dad & I left Adelaide. Obviously Mum & the girls were there to see us off and I knew that John, Jimmy and a few other friends including my first love Ina Warren, would be there too.

But I was absolutely astounded when everyone from Wakefield turned up. I am not exaggerating to write - that there were nearly 100 people at the Airport!

This time I really was crying, it was so emotional. Without trying to sound conceited in any way, I must have left an impression for so many people there to see me off - and still 9 days short of my 16th birthday!

Australia will always stay in my heart forever and without a doubt, those were 2 of the happiest years of my life, and I would love to retire back there one day.

Here I am just back from Australia aged 16 in Grandma Roberts back garden. L-R Uncle Mick Hines, Mum RIP, 17 year old sister Ann, 8 year old sister Michelle next to me, Grandma Roberts RIP & to my left Uncle Malcolm RIP. This was the longest my hair ever grew – SO 1974!

Peter Anderson who saved LTFC from going bust the next year, scoring in our 2-1 win at West Ham 1974 Texaco Cup.

In With The Big Boys

Promotion To Div 1

Dad & I arrived back at Heathrow Airport on Thursday 18th April and were met by Mum's brother, Uncle Malcolm. Upon arrival back in Stopsley everything seemed so small compared to Aussie. It also felt really good to be home again, seeing all my relatives once more. Everyone had noticed a big change in my appearance. I had left as a 5' 14-year-old and returned at 6' 2" & nearly 16.

Having no jet lag whatsoever, I ran round to Chris McEvoy's house. He had no idea that I was coming home and the look on his face was priceless.

I was off to Kenilworth Road on Saturday in my new Baggy trousers & platform shoes to see us play Millwall.

The only change in the appearance of the ground from when I had left was that the Bobbers Stand had now been seated.

There were 3 matches remaining as we sat 2nd behind already promoted Middlesbrough, but just ahead of Orient.

Back in the Oak Road it felt brilliant, as though I'd never been away. Some things would never change though. Millwall fans were in the Oak Road with lots of trouble occurring - there were 3 stabbings on the terrace that day!

This time Luton stood their ground and also won 3-0 to leave us needing just a single point from 2 games, for promotion.

The final away match was at The Hawthorns, West Bromwich on the day after my 16th birthday. With my new Orange, Blue & White scarf (Luton had changed colours from White & Black while I was away) proudly showing, we travelled on one of the two special trains. Inflation had put the price up to £1.50 return.

This was to be an historical occasion, as we stood on the covered Smethwick End terrace. There were thousands of Hatters fans who had travelled.

A common feature of West Midland clubs in that era was to play the reggae tune 'The Liquidator' by Harry J & The All Stars. What a fantastic spectacle to see and hear all the Luton fans in unison – DoDoDoDoDoDoDoDoDoDo – ClapClapClapClap LUTON sing & clap to that song.

Barry Butlin got us off to a fantastic start, heading in an early goal to send us into raptures. Albion equalised with a penalty and after a tense finish the game ended 1-1. Luton Town were in Div 1, only 7 years after finishing 2nd bottom of the 4th Division. It was fate and right there and then I knew that I had made the correct decision to come home. That night the celebrations in Town were fantastic as we celebrated wildly in the Drill Hall.

The night before our final game I went to see Arsenal draw 1-1 with QPR.

On Wed 1st May v Sunderland, this was THE best atmosphere I have ever been in at the Oak Road and it was to be a fantastic game too, in front of the highest gate of the season 20,285 with only a handful from Wear Side, we lost 4-3.

In the carnival atmosphere in the Oak Road, we were singing our hearts out, as a new song bellowed – "In your northern slums, in your northern slums, you look in the dustbin for something to eat, you find a dead cat and you think it's a treat, in your northern slums." Despite the defeat nothing would spoil our night though as we all poured on to the pitch post-match in our thousands, amid jubilant scenes.

A good friend of mine today though unknown then, Liam O'Connell, managed to get our centre half John Faulkner's shirt and a few years later kindly gave me it. The last game of 73-74 I watched was England 2 Argentina 2 at Wembley with long-time pal Steve Toyer.

I went to the careers office to seek alternative employment, as I did not want to continue painting with the English climate in mind. Only to be flabbergasted - to be told I had to return back to school! Apparently, because I was still 15 when the term began, it was illegal for me to start work until school had broken up in the summer. When I went back, it was too late for me to sit exams & therefore I just went as and when I chose. Pretty daft actually, although I did enjoy it as I was a bit popular with the girls because everyone said I had gained an Aussie accent. After finally leaving school I don't know why, but I fancied going into the print trade. In Australia I was earning the equivalent of £32 a week, but I knew that I wouldn't be earning anywhere near those kind of wages in England.

I decided to pick 10 Printers from the local trade directory. I contacted them all and managed to get interviews with three of them. The one I liked the most was called Roydon Printers. The manager Dave Whitby asked me if I wanted to learn Letterpress or Lithographic printing. Having never heard of neither I plumped for Lithographic - as it sounded more technical! "OK son," he responded, "if you had chosen Letterpress I would have said goodbye, as that is a dying form of print and it will be obsolete soon." Within a couple of days I was offered a 5 year apprenticeship as a machine minder, starting on - £11.60 a week!

He agreed that I could start work after my holiday in Scotland with Grandma Adair.

In June, Mum and two sisters returned from Adelaide. I will never forget Michelle running in the back garden of Grandma Adair's back garden to embrace Dad. The look of joy on his face will live with me forever. He adored her. That summer, it was suggested it would be for the best if I lived with Mum and the girls after my holiday. Reluctantly, I agreed.

Upon my return from Scotland I started my career and was living with Mum, Ann & Michelle in Ashcroft Road, Stopsley, not far from the Roberts family and excitedly, was on countdown to the new season.

Div 1 The Elite 1974-75

Before the new season in the top flight started we had a variety of friendly matches, but first I went to see George Best & Jeff Astle play for Dunstable against Man Utd reserves. A local business entrepreneur signed them up for two games in a publicity stunt. A record Dunstable attendance of 3,858 (to this day) saw the first game, which Dunstable won 3-2. When the match finished I ran onto the pitch and shook the legend Best's hand, this was shown on a local TV news bulletin that night. In my opinion George Best was the greatest player these islands have ever produced, certainly in my time. I have yet to return to Creasey Park.

A pre-season tournament called the Texaco Cup followed. We were drawn in a group with Southampton, West Ham and Orient.

Football Hooliganism was now very much in vogue & there was trouble at all 3 games. We first drew 1-1 at home against the Saints, amid fighting outside in the Oak Road itself, post-match. Next at Upton Park, we hid our scarves standing in the South Bank, but were still sussed out as the Cockney boys started on us. I put on my best Aussie accent explaining I was a tourist and it seemed to work - until we scored and won 2-1! Lastly was Orient at Brisbane Road. Now Orient have never had a hooligan firm and this was the case that day, but a mob of various London thugs called London United gathered on the open terrace that day and preceded to fight with the Oak Road boys as we drew 2-2. Despite not losing a game we failed to qualify, which was a real shame personally, as the winners were due to play Rangers at Ibrox Park.

The first week of the season was incredible as I went on a football feast.

Sat Aug 17th Luton 1 Liverpool 2 – Monday, back at Upton Park where we lost 2-0 to the Irons - the next night I saw Arsenal 0 Ipswich 1 - Wednesday, Chelsea v Burnley a 3-3 draw, after Burnley went three up. The following Saturday we went on the special train to Ayresome Park, Middlesbrough. The whole day was spent trying to avoid scrapping. It was a fair distance from the station to the ground and I will confess, we were too scared to go in a pub pre-match, despite having a good drink on the train. The Boro fans were everywhere and really hell bent on looking for trouble.

We drew 1-1. I missed Barry Butlin's last minute equaliser as I had wisely, already left the ground. In those pre-segregation days it was every man to himself. The long walk back to the station took ages I sensed a mob of Boro fans were behind me and I tried to stay calm.

One of them came up to me with the old favourite, "Got the time on ya man?"

"Dunnoo man," was my response in my best Teesside/North East accent.

I heard him say to his mates, "It's ok, he's one of us." Thinking I had a lucky escape I carried on walking at a brisker pace.

Outside a furniture shop, one of the same lot said to me, "Have yas got the time on ya, ya Cockney Baastad."

Knowing I had ran out of luck, I entered the shop and asked the assistant for help. Explaining there was a mob outside waiting for me, he said, "Don't worry, they won't come in here." – WRONG!

They all came in and gave me a kicking in the shop. Battered & bruised, he put me in a taxi to the station. When I arrived, lots of Luton lads had received similar treatment all day.

There just weren't enough of us and police escorts were simply unheard of in the mid-70s.

As the battered troops left Middlesbrough on the train, we were passing a derelict building site and the Boro boys let fly with a hail of missiles, to smash all the windows on one side of the train. Ah, those were the days!

Our next 2 games were home draws to West Ham & QPR. I had seen 6 matches in 9 days.

There was no special train to Leeds after the Middlesbrough fiasco and we travelled on Tricentrol coaches to face the champions, now managed by Brian Clough. In a service station stop on the way, Luton fans fought with Coventry who were en route elsewhere. Upon arrival at Elland Road, it was every man to themselves, as Leeds had a fearsome reputation. Steve Toyer & I were OK as we got to the ground with no problems. Obviously we hid our scarves and kept quiet throughout the game as Luton drew 1-1 with Barry Butlin scoring his 28th and final goal for us. This was to be the final league game of Brian Clough's reign at Leeds. He was sacked after just 44 days.

When we returned to the coaches - we discovered that three of the Luton lads had their leather coats robbed at knifepoint to their throats before the match!

Six games, no wins, but at least we beat Bristol Rovers 1-0 in the League Cup. The poor league form continued, losing heavily 4-1 at home to Ipswich, a 2-2 draw at Highbury against a poor Arsenal side in front of only 21,649 and a 2-1 defeat at Coventry where our coach window was smashed by a bottle.

Around about this time, the murderous IRA scum had bombed two pubs in Birmingham, killing over 20 innocent civilians. Feelings were running very high around town. On the night after the bombings the windows of the Forrester's Arms pub, a known IRA haunt, were put in by locals from the nearby Rangers Supporters Club.

After 10 games, at last we finally won a league game at home to Carlisle 3-1. Our Australian international Adrian Alston scored a beauty. Some people said I resembled him at the time and called me Aussie because of this, along with my alleged Aussie accent. I'm still called this today by a few folk from back then.

A large Luton following then travelled on the special train away to Leicester. We drew 0-0 at Filbert Street.

If it wasn't for Peter Shilton in goal, we would have won 3 or 4-0, we played that well. There was lots of trouble in the streets pre-match.

I was to miss my first game of the season in a 3-0 defeat at Sheff Utd in the League Cup because of work commitments.

The following night I saw Stoke draw 2-2 at Chelsea in the same competition. Two more home defeats followed, first seeing Birmingham win 3-1 with a Trevor Francis hat trick. There was loads of trouble after this game in the West Side Centre.

The Brummies were ambushed in a subway tunnel, getting trapped in the middle with Luton fans battering them at both ends. At this moment in time Luton fans were no soft touch, certainly at home games.

At the next game midweek, we were looking for revenge against Middlesbrough but none of their fans turned up, we lost 1-0 in front of our lowest home crowd of 1974-75 - 10,464.

We travelled on the very last special train to Maine Road, Man City next. There were several reasons why this was the final excursion. 1) Inflation was rampant - the cost had risen to £2 return! & 2) There was only 200-odd Hatters fans on the train & this trip cost the club a fortune, therefore deciding to call it quits. & 3) One of the directors had links to Tricentrol Coaches (most likely THE true reason behind the club decision).

Sadly, they have never organised one since, if ever I won the lotto big I would bring them back myself, as they were my favourite mode of travel. We lost 1-0 at my first of four Maine Road visits. Next, in front of a 22,000+ Kenilworth Road crowd, we drew 1-1 with Spurs. As was the usual case with the big London teams, their fans were in the Oak Road, but on this day Luton gave as good as they got both on and off the pitch. A long trip to St James' Park Newcastle was next, paying £3 (nearly a quarter of my weekly apprenticeship wage then) with Tricentrol coaches. 1-0 to the Magpies, but at least Macdonald failed to score against us.

Another home defeat occurred v Sheff Utd 1-0, followed by a trip to the Potteries. We were on a terrible run but played well, unluckily losing 4-2 to Stoke. I was certainly getting to see lots of new grounds. Although there was no trouble at the Victoria Ground that day, the Stoke fans had loosened the exhaust pipes from our coaches and they fell off on the M6 homeward bound.

In between those games I went to see the recent new England boss Don Revie's side beat Czechoslovakia 3-0 at Wembley and then Luton play at Wembley Arena in the National 5 a sides tournament.

The week after Stoke, we went to see Hitchin play at home to Cambridge Utd in the FA Cup, as Luton's home game v Everton was postponed. Many Luton fans had the same idea and were involved in a big pre-match punch up with Cambridge and bizarrely Spurs fans in the Hitchin Supporters Club.

We then lost 3-2 at home to Burnley.

A trip to Stamford Bridge, Chelsea, followed.

Many Luton fans had just been released from jail after trouble at the previous season's Luton v Nottm Forest match. There was a lot of talk going around about how there was going to be massive trouble but gladly there was none, we suffered the usual defeat by 2-0.

Up next was my very first visit to Liverpool. We had been told that it was really dodgy for visiting fans at Anfield but I have to write I found their fans were great and very friendly. Their thugs weren't there that day, probably because we were Luton and therefore not a big enough attraction for them. This was the game that a popular modern Liverpudlian Hatters fan Keith Brooksbank, saw Luton play for the first time.

Keith became a devout Hatter, he is a good friend and follows Luton everywhere, he is also a sound bloke because like me, has an affinity towards Rangers.

So, we had played half the season and had won ONE game. Of course we were bottom of the table, but I still loved going. The Saturday before Xmas we were at home to Derby, who ended up as Champions. We won 1-0 and when Jimmy Ryan scored the winner, you would think that Luton had won the FA Cup such was the crowd noise that day. On Boxing Day we travelled to high-flying Ipswich and won again, thanks to Ron Futcher's last minute full debut goal. Despite the Ipswich fans bricking our coach window, it didn't dampen our spirits.

Ron was the twin brother of Paul, who manager Harry Haslam had signed in the summer for £100,000 - at only 16 years of age!

The last match of 1974 was at home to Wolves and it was a fantastic game winning 3-2, with Ron Futcher scoring a hat trick. The atmosphere in the Oak Road that day was one of THE greatest I've ever experienced.

We had previously gone nearly five months with just a single victory and now - had 3 in 7 days! Birmingham returned to Kenilworth Road for the FA Cup 3rd round, winning 1-0.

A real relegation battle both on and off the field against Chelsea followed. Despite being all over them, we could only manage to draw 1-1. The notorious Chelsea fans were fighting in the Oak Road & on their return to London - burnt a train carriage out! The attendance that day of 23,096 was the highest of 1974-75. It has never been bettered at Kenilworth Road.

We then travelled to Turf Moor, Burnley, watched a close game and were unfortunate to lose 1-0, while having the rare luxury of a seat in the Cricket Field Stand behind the goal.

Another away trip followed, another good performance drawing 1-1 at Sheff Utd, where once again, we had a seat behind the goal.

When Malcolm Macdonald returned to Luton for the first time, he was made captain for the day and received a rapturous welcome from us Hatters. 1-0 it was, scored by our Ron Futcher.

The Futchers only started playing for us in December and it was no coincidence that this was when our results began to improve dramatically.

Steve Toyer and I went to Selhurst Park midweek, but not to see C. Palace.

Non-League Wimbledon had a remarkable result at Leeds in the FA Cup where they drew 1-1 at Elland Road. Their Plough Lane ground was deemed too small for the replay and so it was held at Palace's ground. Incredibly, over 45,000 watched as Leeds won 1-0.

With Luton's performances and results much improved, nearly 20,000 turned up for the visit of leaders Stoke. In truth, we were a touch lucky to draw 0-0. Stoke even missed a penalty.

Due to work constraints, I missed my first league match of the season, losing 3-1 at Everton in midweek.

We had a good day and night out in London losing 2-1 at QPR, despite Luton playing superbly. The previous night, I was in enemy territory.

My apprenticeship meant I attended Fridays at Watford Printing College. I went to cheer on Huddersfield at Vicarage Road, alas Div 3 Hornets won 1-0.

In what turned out to be my Granddad Roberts final Luton game, we watched the visitors Coventry win 3-1 in the pouring rain and a very poor Luton performance.

Relegation seemed probable and maybe for this reason, I missed the next away game at bottom club Carlisle, of course I was punished as the Town won 2-1 for only our second away victory.

We then had the mighty Leeds (then) visit us at Kenilworth Road. As previously written, Leeds fans were notorious and there were fights all day long. At the train station and down the road outside a pub called The Plume Of Feathers (THE place to be for a Luton fan in 74-75) there were serious brawls. Before the match had even kicked off, there was a pitch invasion by the Leeds masses in an attempt to take the Oak Road. But as they reached the penalty area they had a shock, not only were Luton's fans not running away, but the Oak Roaders actually climbed over and a full scale battle erupted on the pitch - where I can assure you the Whites came off second best! This might be due to the fact that every Luton face was there that day among the crowd of 23,048. A fine 2-1 win for Luton meant Leeds' title hopes were over.

Another large Luton crowd of over 22,000 was present next, for the visit of Arsenal. My boss Dave Whitby was an Arsenal fan, so we all went from work & stood in the Enclosure, along with my Dad. Our best performance of the season meant we won 2-0 making it three wins in a row and I was thinking, 'We aren't down yet.' Easter followed, on the Saturday we travelled to highflying Derby. I'm sorry to write that we were thrashed 5-0, with their Roger Davies scoring all 5 goals - even having 2 disallowed! This was now my heaviest Luton defeat.

Two days later, we were off to Molineux, Wolves. There was plenty of trouble pre-match, as Wolves fans attacked Luton fans in their notorious subway.

Sensing more crowd problems, we wisely chose seats as Wolves continuously attacked Hatters in the huge South Bank End. This vast terrace alone - held more than the whole of Luton's ground! It was now a do or die, game. We fell behind to an early Wolves goal but new signing John Seasman and then Jim Ryan, put us 2-1 ahead. Alas, two goals from Wolves had them leading 3-2 at half time.

Ending 5-2 to Wolves this result had as good as relegated us. This was my final away game of 1974-75. Paul Futcher was sent off for over protesting what was evidently a BLATANT offside Tottenham late winning goal by Alfie Conn. It proved to be an absolutely crucial decision as far as the final Div One table was concerned - at our cost!

I know it was disloyal, but I just could not bear to go to White Hart Lane and see us lose 2-1 to fellow strugglers Spurs.

Second placed Everton arrived at Luton midweek and unsurprisingly, a low turnout of 13,000 odd turned up after the Easter results. I thought we were going to get thrashed, the Toffees were 1-0 up at the interval and in truth, it could have been 4. However, Peter Anderson scored twice and we held on to a 2-1 win. On the Saturday, we played brilliant by beating Leicester 3-0. One of the goals was the funniest own goal I have ever seen.

Keith Weller, at the edge of his penalty area, passed the ball back to his keeper with such a wicked bend it was almost goal of the season, it was on the ITV highlights the following day.

The last away game of the season I missed and bitterly regretted it. A fantastic 4-1 victory at St Andrews Birmingham, in what I was told was our season's best performance by far. It made for a tense final game at home to Man City on my 17th Birthday. Another pitch invasion, although nowhere near as heavy as the Leeds one, followed. Over 20,000 turned up hoping to get the win we needed at a minimum, but we could only draw 1-1.

Safety was now out of our hands. To stay up we had to rely on Leeds winning at Tottenham two days later, any other result, we were down - Leeds lost 4-2!

I am going to tell a true story about this game.

Over nine years later I met Billy Bremner who was the Leeds captain in 1975. I was ground hopping at Doncaster to see them play Plymouth. Bremner, who was Doncaster manager in 1984, was introduced to me in the Donny Supporters Club after the match. Wearing my Luton shirt I asked him for his opinion on the Spurs v Leeds game in 1975. His response was, "Look, no offence, but Leeds would have rather had a big club like Tottenham in the top flight rather than little Luton and besides - you fucked up our chances of retaining our title when you beat us 2-1!"

So there you have it - Leeds fixed it for us to go down!

Dad

Earlier in 1975, I had moved back into the Adair household in Applecroft Road. The previous year I had joined Stopsley Working Men's Club, commonly known as The Club. Officially the criteria for membership was age 18, but because I was proposed by Dad and seconded by Granddad Adair (a previous treasurer), no questions were asked. For many years the Club was THE place to go in Stopsley. At its peak it had over 3,000 members. I eventually became a life member.

Prior to the new season, Luton had arranged home & away friendly matches against French team Dunkirk. Tricentrol coaches decided to run a day trip to France for the fans at just £9 return. Three coach loads of Hatters fans set off very early one Saturday morning. I might add, that the vast majority of travellers were Oak Road Enders including myself, Steve Toyer, John Canny and the Maxwell twins Sam & Ian. This was to be an eventful day - to say the least! Every one of us was draped in Union Jacks and in full Luton colours, the journey to Dover was relatively quiet. On the ferry much alcohol was consumed, the local paper's Evening Post reporters were all taking pictures joining in with the fun & banter - this was about to change though!

Upon our arrival in Dunkirk, we were confronted by a large mob of angry French fans. This was the first match in France after Leeds fans had caused havoc in Paris in their European Cup Final defeat a few months earlier. Whether this had anything to do with it, I don't know, but the trouble that was to occur that day and night, was the worst I had witnessed as a Luton fan. It was bad enough in the coach park and in the town's bars, but when we arrived in the ground, we had been informed that a Luton female fan called Dot from Markyate, had been attacked by French thugs with Iron bars. I'm afraid it erupted into a huge battle. There were only about 2,000 in total attendance that night, but about 20% of those were involved in the most vicious fighting. Although outnumbered, the Oak Road boys gave more than as good as they got. The match result was a 2-2 draw - I don't think anyone cared!

Leaving Dunkirk, as we passed by the mass graves of fellow Brits, I couldn't help thinking to myself, 'Was their sacrifice worth it?' Here lay thousands of fallen soldiers, fighting for our freedom and some 30 years later, those who they liberated, were battling against US - as though we were the Nazis!

What was particularly galling was that upon our return, the headlines in Monday's Evening Post were, Luton Fans Disgrace Themselves In Dunkirk and there in full front page – was a picture of US five lads! I will be brutally honest and write, there was no way we initiated any of the trouble that day/night, but we certainly did defend ourselves against the brawling French – and some!

The new season started with a 2-0 home victory over Hull, followed by the return match with Dunkirk. Of course there were no French fans at the game, as we thrashed them 6-2 in front of a pitiful crowd of less than 1,500.

We went to the first away game WBA, losing 1-0 at The Hawthorns.

A further repeat of mass crowd trouble was at the next home game v Chelsea. Three times pre-match, Chelsea had tried to take the Oak Road and three times they failed, before their massed hordes were marched up to the Kenilworth Road end. The largest crowd of that season, 19,024 witnessed Luton thrash Chelsea 3-0.

Sam Maxwell and I had decided to hitchhike to Portsmouth for the next match. Unfortunately, having only reached the Hampshire border at half time, we admitted defeat and turned round to begin the trek back. We arrived home late, missing a fine 2-0 Luton win. Adrian Alston scored his 9th & final Luton goal. We have never won at Pompey since.

We were knocked out of the League Cup at lowly Darlington midweek, 2-1, starting a run of seven winless games.

Losing at home to Bolton, was followed by my first trip to Meadow Lane, Notts County, the Magpies won 1-0, we were then held to two 1-1 draws at home to Plymouth & Blackburn and then an away trip I was eagerly awaiting, Blackpool.

This was my very first away weekender trip with the lads. Because I was an apprentice only earning about £13 a week I did not want to be short of cash, so I borrowed £5 from Grandma Roberts. Including the loan, I left with £15 for the weekend feeling like Rothschild. The weekend coach fare was £2.50 return. B&B in the guesthouse £6 for two nights and a pint of Lager then - was 22p! We had a fabulous time, going to the famous Blackpool Mecca Night Club (where I pulled a lass from Sunderland), the boxer Brian London's 007 nightclub, the tourist haunts like the Tower and the Pleasure Beach fairground. Despite leading twice, we lost 3-2.

I would return to Blackpool frequently in the future. One vivid memory from this weekend was getting a newspaper printed with the headline – ALAN ADAIR STREAKS THROUGH BLACKPOOL! When I returned home and showed it to Dad & Granddad, the old boy went mental - until Dad assured him it was just a joke!

I missed the 1-1 draw at Carlisle, due to finances.

We then beat Fulham 1-0 as we welcomed back old friends Alan Slough, Viv Busby & Alec Stock.

Missed away games at Nottm Forest, Sunderland & Southampton were in between a mixed bag of home results, 0-0 v Bristol City, 4-0 v York & a 3-2 defeat by Oldham.

Before we travelled by train to Fulham my Dad dropped a bombshell, telling me that he had been diagnosed with Lung Cancer. He had kept this news secret as long as possible, but he knew that it was terminal. In a strong tone of voice he pleaded with me that morning: "Promise me that you will look after Michelle, and that you will live your life to the FULL - like I have!" I was in shock, I knew that Dad had lost a lot of weight, Uncle Malcolm later told me, "Your Dad had come back from the two years spent in Australia looking like a different person, such was his weight loss."

Perhaps Dad was told over there and that's why he wanted to come home? One thing is for sure, he rapidly went downhill after recently falling off a ladder at work. I refused to believe his analysis of only having months left to live and told him we would battle this illness together.

That day we lost 2-0 but for obvious reasons, the result really did not matter. Luton at this time, were also experiencing financial problems. Something that would occur - on more than a regular basis at our club in the future!

We had money trouble 4 years previously, as the then chairman Tony Hunt's insurance company V&G went bust. We were told that if Malcolm Macdonald was not sold, Luton might have ceased to exist. This time the problems occurred because we were not ready for promotion in 1974. The players were all given handsome contracts upon going up, but unfortunately, when we were relegated all the squad, were still on top wages. This would not be the last time Luton experienced severe mis-management from the top.

We followed up the Fulham defeat by beating Orient at home 1-0. Next was a morale boosting 5-1 victory at Charlton. Peter Anderson scored twice that night, before being transferred to Royal Antwerp in Belgium immediately after the game. We had learnt at a later date - this transfer had saved Luton Town!

There was a fighting fund called 'Save The Town' & I donated £5 (more than a third of my wages) and we played Alan Slough's testimonial against an England All Stars team. He kindly donated a sum of the gate money to the fund. Luton won 4-2.

Bizarrely - I missed 4 of the goals that night in either toilet breaks or getting food!

We were at home to WBA next and showing great humility, the visiting Albion fans donated to the campaign. No trouble at that game I'm pleased to write.

Just before Xmas we won 2-1 at Hull and then on Boxing Day a crowd of over 13,000 saw us beat Oxford 3-2 at home. Despite our financial problems, some Luton fans still fought with Oxford fans on the Kenny terrace.

On Boxing night, it was always a party at Grandma Robert's and this year was no exception. This was the first time I was allowed to drink alcohol there too.

The next day, suffering with a severe hangover, Steve Toyer and I travelled in Steve Marriott's car with his Dad to Eastville, Bristol Rovers. Andy King scored the winner late on before 11,044, to send us home happy.

Despite the financial issues, Luton had now won six games in a row. Number 7 followed at Kenilworth Road, as Portsmouth were dispatched 3-1. This was followed, by beating Blackburn 2-0 at home in the FA Cup, whose fans on a special train had been delayed and did not arrive until past Half Time!

In the 4th round we were drawn to play Rochdale or Norwich away. I had decided to run a minibus to the tie and asked Dad to come with us. He said Rochdale was too far, but would try to make it if it's Norwich. It was the Canaries who won but by then he was very ill, not holding any food down and rapidly losing more weight. On the day of the game, I knew he had no chance of attending and that really made me sad.

Sharing the same bedroom as Dad was tough, so going to the football was also a bit of a release for me and took my mind off it a bit. I hope that does not sound callous, as I adored him.

We travelled to 1st Division Norwich with high hopes and there were over 4,000 Hatters fans with the same view. Unfortunately we lost 2-0 and the winning run was over.

We lost again, midweek at Bolton 3-0. This was a rearranged match, as the original match was postponed much to our annoyance, as we did not find out until arriving at Burnden Park. On that day we had hired a Transit van & when leaving the stadium we opted to attend a local game that had survived the weather. It was either Man Utd v QPR or Liverpool v Ipswich, on the toss of a coin Anfield won. We saw a great game 3-3.

After the Bolton defeat, we drew 1-1 at home to Nottm Forest. The next away match was too far to travel, at York. We won 3-2, but others must have felt like us, because there were only 3,000-odd present.

Two more long journeys followed, as we drew at Oldham and lost to Plymouth. A couple of clean sheets against Sunderland and Southampton at home followed, winning 2-0 & 1-0 respectively. Jimmy Husband got the solitary goal against the Saints, leaving us in 6th place, still in with a slight sniff of promotion.

I then went with Dave Lee in his van to Bristol City. Dave, a good friend, lived in a pub called The Regents Arms in town. I got to know him & a lot more friends from the Farley Hill/Corncastle area, by a work mate called Dave Ventris.

We lost heavily at Ashton Gate, 3-0. More crowd violence occurred on the terraces that day when a Luton fan had stabbed a home supporter. Luckily, it wasn't serious - why anyone carries a knife is beyond me!

After beating Carlisle 3-0 at home, we still had a faint chance to go up.

The following week, to earn some good overtime money I worked a Ghost shift. Starting work at 8am Friday and finished at 8am Saturday. I then travelled on the train to London to watch us lose 3-0 at Orient. I guess, being nearly 18 - meant I had more energy in those days!

By now Dad was gravely ill and the situation was severe. I went to the home match against Charlton drawing 1-1, but my mind was only on Dad. That night I spent my final night with him. On the Sunday morning the Doctor had arrived. He administered morphine to Dad such was his acute pain. He was now so ill that one of his eyes had closed. I could not bear to see such a giant of a man suffering like this. He had gone from a hulk of a bloke at 16 stone - to less than half that weight! It was utter cruelty. Michelle usually came to visit on Sundays, but this time I rang Mum asking her to keep Michelle at home. It was too much for me, let alone a 10-year-old child. After taking Grandma's advice, I stayed at Mum's that night.

After a very sleepless night, I caught the bus to work on Monday 29th March 1976. As I arrived, seeing everyone's faces I just knew the worst had happened.

Dave Whitby called me into his office, explaining, "I'm so sorry son, your Father passed away this morning." Even all these years later, writing this I am tearful. I knew it was coming, but I was still devastated.

Dave told me to take as long off work as I needed to. Everybody was very kind at work. I could see in all their eyes, they were hurting for me too. Before getting a lift to Mum's to tell them I don't know why, but I rang Granddad Roberts first. He was distressed too, saying, "No matter what marital problems your parents had, all of the Roberts family truly loved your Father, he was a colossus of a man." After Dave dropped me off at Mum's I told her the news and even she, had a tear in her eye. I rang Ann at Monarch Airlines where she worked and she came home immediately. Naturally, she was upset too, but I never really felt Ann was THAT close to Dad unlike her relationship with Mum. The one thing I could/would not do, was tell Michelle. I was just not strong enough to do this I'm afraid. I went to Grandma Roberts' house up the road, as I just couldn't bear to be at Mum's when she had to inform Michelle.

Mum collected Michelle from school to give her the heartbreaking news. Michelle told me later in life, that Mum was actually very good and warm to her at this time. I'm sorry to write this, but that example was a rare occasion. Mum never treated Michelle as she should have done. There would be many arguments & troubles between the two of them, ending in much acrimony - especially on Mum's part!

The Roberts family rallied round to help me. I stayed at Aunt Joan & Mick's that night and my mate Pete Woods' the next.

It was a harrowing time. Dad was only 44, but he had lived a short life to the absolute full.

Apart from Michelle, I also really felt for Grandma & Granddad Adair. They had now lost both of their sons. Tom aged 40, then seven years later Dad at 44. You simply cannot comprehend losing your children first - it is not meant to happen this way! I honestly don't know how anyone could cope with that? Perish the thought, but I know I could not. When people used to say to Grandma, "How can you ever get through this?" She replied, "Because I have to live for my Grandchildren."

Old Tom on the other hand, never REALLY did get over it. He maybe just about got over Tom junior, but losing Dad too, eventually would send him over the edge. Who can blame him?

The funeral was arranged for the Thursday, just a day after Grandma Adair's 67th Birthday.

Apart from Dad, I had also lost both my godfathers Uncle Tom & Michael (my Aunty Miri's son, who sadly died in a car crash at only 21, ten years earlier). I was not allowed to attend either funeral because of my age. I agree with this decision, in my opinion, funerals are not the place for children to be. It is upsetting enough, but imagine a child's mind seeing all these grief-stricken adults. It is for this reason, that I did not want Michelle, aged 10, at Dad's funeral. Maybe I'm right, maybe I'm wrong, but I don't regret it.

Of course Michelle tells me to this day it was wrong, but I disagree. The service was packed to the rafters, as he was a very popular man.

Mum did not attend which was correct but she did go after everyone had left, to pay her own private thoughts.

After the funeral, we went back to Applecroft Road. A sign of things to come with Granddad was when he refused Mum's brother Uncle Malcolm entry. Malcolm was not only related to Dad by marriage, but a good friend of his too. I can definitely vouch for that. In his dying days, Dad told me many things - some of which will remain secret, but he really liked Malcolm and would have been mortified at what had happened. Malcolm was OK about it saying, your Granddad is in shock. Malcolm was not only my Uncle, but like he was with Dad, a true friend of mine also. I was to go through much heartache for him, nearly thirty years later.

I worshipped my Dad and granted it was a long time ago, indeed I have now outlived him, but many people still talk fondly of him and say that I'm his double in the way I look, walk and general mannerisms. That's good enough for me.

RIP Dad.

Naturally, I missed the match two days after the funeral where we lost 3-0 at Blackburn. Indeed, I also missed the Easter games at Oxford & Chelsea.

I did watch a Luton v Notts County 1-1 draw, but in a daze.

Luton were still struggling financially at this time - when Everton stole Andy King for a miserly £35,000!

The hottest summer on record was about to begin, with glorious sunshine starting in April, all the way through to October.

On a lovely Easter Monday afternoon the lowest crowd of 1975-76 - 7,646, were there to witness the birth of a legend.

Standing on the sunny open Kenilworth Road terrace against Bristol Rovers, we watched in amazement, as warming up pre-match for Luton, was a black man. Luton had a black player in the 1960s named Williams, but he never played in the first team. This was a big thing in 1976. There were very few black players around at that time.

This player was on the bench and 99.9% of Luton fans didn't know who he was. We were 1-0 down at half time. Paul Price equalised and then five minutes from time he came off the bench to make history. With his first touch, he set up Brian Chambers to give us a 2-1 lead. His next touch a minute later was to score a great goal with a fierce strike. He went on to play for Luton for over 13 years, became our second highest league appearance player EVER and our first full England international in nearly 25 years. His name was RICKY HILL. Not only that, he was to become a friend too. Legend is an understatement. Ricky made his full debut a few days later in the last game of the season at home to Blackpool. An extra 1,000 people turned up on the strength of 5 minutes football.

They were not disappointed, although failing to score, he had a fine game and the Town ended with a 3-0 win.

This was a traumatic year for both Luton Town and myself.

My 18th Birthday had arrived, it was inappropriate to have a party so soon after Dad had died. So Pete Woods and I booked an 11-night holiday in Benidorm for the princely sum of £78 Full Board at the Rio Park Hotel. Unfortunately, after just 2 days in Spain, I was bedridden with Fever and Tonsillitis for three days. Nearly all of my pesetas had gone on Doctors' fees & tablets. I knew that I would get compensation on my Insurance but that would be at a later date. Pete offered to lend me some but I didn't want to ruin his holiday too, by both of us being broke. Of course there were no credit cards or anything like that then. I managed to ring home and plead with Ann to send some money over.

The next night in the Hotel Bar, sitting feeling sorry for myself, despite people buying me drinks I looked up and said to Pete, "I thought I just saw Ann then."

Indeed it WAS Ann, 10 seconds later she ran up to me and shouted, "I can't stop, there's a taxi outside waiting to take me back to the airport, and I have to leave NOW." She handed me the pesetas, gave me a hug & was offski!

I was over the moon to say the least, leading to a fantastic night, and further week of fun & games - ANN I THANK YOU AGAIN!

I stayed with the Adairs during that long hot summer. It would have been wrong to leave them. Shortly after I arrived back from Benidorm, I had a tattoo on my arm, it was a scroll on a cross reading 'In Loving Memory of Dad' costing £3.50! (I guess that would be about £70 now?)

One day, while watching the Montreal Olympics the phone rang; upon answering it, a female with an Australian accent said, "Could you please tell me if an Alan Adair lives here?"

I replied, "This is Alan, who's this?" she screamed excitedly. It was Dawn Jolly, a friend from Adelaide, who married a mate Jimmy Sakkas. I was gobsmacked, she told me that she just took a chance, rang telephone directories guessing there wouldn't be too many Adairs in Luton and bingo, got through.

Dawn was from Leigh in Lancashire and was home, visiting relations. She told me that her and Jimmy had divorced & asked if she could come and visit. It was no problem and she came down the very next weekend.

I fancied her in Australia something rotten but of course she was forbidden fruit, as she was a mate's girl. The two of us went up the Club on the Friday night - within minutes it was blatantly obvious we would be more than just friends! My mate Pete Woods' parents were away that weekend so at a party there on Saturday night, we spent a long hot night of unbelievable passionate sex. It was a fantastic experience. We were at it at every given moment in time throughout that weekend, even when Grandma & Granddad went to the cemetery. She returned up North, then to Australia and we've never spoken since - wonderful memories though!

Also later in that summer, Grandma was to start having Luton players as lodgers. Graham Jones was our first.

A young lad from Manchester who I got on great with, he made his debut on the same day as Ricky Hill at only 16.

I had by now passed my driving test at the second attempt. It wasn't long before I bought a car off a work mate, Barry Tebbutt. A 1965 Vauxhall HA Viva for £135. Another colleague, Ian Bealey (married to Alan Slough's sister) lent me the money and I was to pay him back at £5 a week. I'm sorry to write that tragically, Barry passed away in 2012 with the Big C. He was a lovely man and had a heart of gold. RIP Barry. The car lasted a month! Driving to work one foggy morning, I turned into my work's Street & an Asian taxi driver went straight into me. He never had his lights on. I just didn't see him. Due to turning right, I was guilty of driving without due care & attention, resulting in an endorsement and six months - paying for a written off car!

Oak Road boys on the way to Dunkirk v Luton 1975 pre season 'friendly'. £9 return, three coach loads about 90% Oak Roaders. In all my 55 + years of watching Luton, this by far was the most violent day/night.

Me Aged 10 in 1968.

1976-77

The very little experience of driving the car that I had was to go to work & back, a couple of nights out at a country pub and driving to Watford for a pre-season 1-0 Town Kent Cup win, all in a month.

Luton kicked off the new season at home to Sheff Utd. New signing Dixie Deans scored both goals in a 2-0 victory.

I missed the first two away games, a midweek defeat to Hull, then winning at Burnley. Work timings thwarted Hull and a Bank Holiday weekend in Margate was the reason for missing Turf Moor. Dave Lee, Andy Ormes & I went on the seaside trip and my abiding memory of this was my first sighting of Punk Rockers. Oh - and colliding Dave's van on the M2 while driving it! It would be nearly 6 years before I drove a car again.

We took an early exit out of the League Cup, losing 3-1 at Sunderland.

A 1-1 draw at home to Nottm Forest followed. It was at this moment in time that some Forest fans stood on the Maple terrace next to the Oak Road. No other away fans repeated this then and the Reds lads started this on a regular basis.

Six nights later I went to a rare Friday night game at the Valley. An entertaining match, but we lost to Charlton 4-3.

A big crowd of 19,929 turned up next as George Best was in Town, having recently signed for Fulham. Such was the pulling power of Best this attendance would not be beaten for the rest of the season. Fulham won 2-0.

We then went to Molineux in Steve Marriot's car and saw a great Luton performance. The Hatters deservedly won 2-1, with goals by Dixie Deans and Jimmy Husband, as we watched from the side terrace.

The following weekend, again in Steve's car, we decided to go straight to Plymouth from the Double Barrel pub in Stopsley, after closing time on the Friday night. We got as far as Andover when his car broke down. Having the choice of paying a lot of money to get to Plymouth by train or staying loyal to Steve, we chose the latter and were towed back to Luton. We lost 1-0 anyway. Paul Futcher then scored his sole Luton goal in 142 Town apps at home to Hereford in a 2-0 win.

I missed the next game at Carlisle, before seeing Southampton heavily beat us 4-1 at home.

After losing 1-0 at another missed game away to Blackburn, I watched a very good match when we beat Bristol Rovers 4-2. Because of the recent poor form the lowest home crowd of that season, just 7,066 turned up.

Our lodger, Graham Jones, was in the team for the next match at Millwall & Steve Marriott drove us to the notorious Den. Obviously, we were a little tense & with no colours on, sat in the Main Stand. Having arrived five mins late - Millwall were already 2-1 up!

There was no doubt The Den was one of the most intimidating & scariest places to ever visit. Even in the seats where we thought we would be safe, it was pretty tough.

Luton were awarded a penalty just after half time, we all wisely sat still, not a murmur, as grown men in their forties were standing up looking all round for visiting fans. Steve Buckley scored it - and we just sat there! Millwall then regained the lead and none of us were enjoying this experience at all. When Steve suggested we leave early, everyone agreed and we were offski. We couldn't wait to get to the car and on hearing a Millwall 4th goal, rapidly left South London. So, 6 goals scored, we missed 4 of them & sat in silence for the one Luton goal that we did see - crazy! No wonder so many away fans used to catch 'Millwall flu' and avoid Cold Blow Lane back in the day.

Graham Jones kept his place the next week for the injured John Faulkner, as we took on Cardiff at home, beating the Bluebirds 2-1.

A bizarre game followed as we travelled to Meadow Lane, Notts County. We led 1-0 at half time from an Alan West goal then after the break John Aston made it 2-0. Nothing out of the ordinary occurred until 70 mins. Goalkeeper Keith Barber then got injured in a collision, he was stretchered off and it turned out he had two broken ribs. Our little Scot Dixie Deans went in goal and performed heroics. Jimmy Husband & Steve Buckley added two further goals to romp home 4-0. A short while after, Deans was caught in a Town centre bar drinking instead of training and promptly sacked by Harry Haslam - never to play for us again!

We then watched a stalemate 0-0 draw at home to Blackpool on an icy pitch. There was fighting on the Kenny Terrace - but not involving Luton fans! Man Utd were due to play in London. Their game was postponed so some of them came to Luton to see a game, West Ham fans followed them and battles commenced between the two sets of fans to the Luton fans' amusement.

I missed a 2-1 defeat at Bolton but the day after Boxing Day, we travelled to Orient. Rudi Vallyon, Steve Marriott, Pete Woods, Steve Toyer and I watched us lose 1-0. Two nights later we were at home to Chelsea. We left the Double Barrel pre-match and I vividly remember saying to the lads, "We will beat Chelsea 4-0 tonight."

Now bearing in mind, the Blues were top at this stage. We watched from the Enclosure that night, knowing there would be trouble in the Oak Road as usual - and there was! When Lil Fuccillo scored & then Brian Chambers made it 2-0 the lads said to me, "You may be right." Jim Husband put us 3-0 up and a Steve Buckley penalty completed my forecast. A pity there were no individual match fixed odds back then.

Three away games followed & I missed them all.

On New Year's Day we lost 1-0 at Bristol Rovers. Then we won 1-0 at Halifax in the FA Cup 3rd Rd, followed by a brilliant 3-0 victory at Sheff Utd, seeing the highlights on Match of the Day that night.

Two nights after this, we beat Hull at home 2-1. Hull led 1-0 until the 85th minute. John Aston & Jimmy Husband then turned it around for us.

We were drawn away to Chester in the FA Cup 4th round and I went there with the Windsor Castle lads. The Windsor was my new pub in town that workmate Dave Ventris had introduced me to.

The old Granddad flat caps were the rage then and suitably attired, hundreds of capped Luton fans joined us.

The Oak Roaders took the Chester end and at the opposite open end, were exclusively Hatters fans too. Near the final whistle when Chester scored the only goal, a wall collapsed at the open Luton end. This was because Luton fans had invaded the pitch in an attempt to get the game abandoned. Thankfully, there were no serious injuries.

A 2-0 home victory against Burnley followed.

After Keith Barber's injury, we signed a keeper from Plymouth called Milija Aleksic. He was to become our next lodger at Grandma Adair's. A very nice bloke of Yugoslavian parentage, he was also an extremely good goalkeeper. By now I had got to meet all my heroes regularly in the players bar post-match, via him & Graham Jones. At this time, after the Burnley game we were up against Brian Clough's Nottm Forest away. We won 2-1 - this was no mean feat, as in the next few seasons the bulk of that team won promotion, the Div 1 league title and then the European Cup - twice!

For a month, it was lodger no 3, as David Geddis joined us on loan from Ipswich. Because of these three lodgers - I was now sleeping on the couch!

Geddis made his winning debut for us. Scoring a goal, as we beat Blackburn 2-0 at home. This was now five successive wins and the sequence continued when Ron Futcher scored both as we beat Charlton 2-0 at home.

Now up to 5th place, we had a terrific day and night in London the next week, where we beat Fulham 2-1 making it seven in a row. We celebrated in great fashion that night in the Cockney Pride. This was a Piccadilly pub that was to become a regular haunt for us when playing in London.

Next, a crowd of 19,200 saw us beat high flyers Wolves 2-0 to take us up to only one spot below the promotion places. Two more home games followed, David Geddis scoring the only goal, a late winner v Oldham but sadly, we failed to make it 10 in a row as Plymouth held us to 1-1 at Kenilworth Road.

A last minute winner by Ron Futcher at Hereford had put us back on track and moved us up to 3rd. On our journey back from Edgar Street we stopped at Witney near Oxford for a drink, unfortunately we were involved in an argument with some locals. The police were called and we were taken to the police station for questioning. After being released with a caution we headed home, only to be diverted because of a fatal car crash. It emerged later, that the current Oxford former Chelsea player Peter Houseman was the fatality, although we didn't know that until the following day. RIP.

Carlisle made the long trip south next and were soundly thrashed 5-0.

An old school friend of mine called Michael Bance, commonly known as Baggy started hanging around at this time and became a very good mate. As a schoolboy, he was often bullied. He grew up to become as hard as nails, although you would never guess looking at him. He made a policy of gaining revenge on some of those boys who picked on him at school one by one, sometimes quite savagely. He just loved fighting and for him, I'm afraid there were no rules. At the next match he and I hitched to Southampton. As soon as we arrived inside The Dell, there was trouble on the terraces after Saints had scored on just 2 mins.

He needed no invites and waded in fists flying, loving it. That was the only goal and our superb run of 11 wins and a draw was over.

The next week we travelled to leaders Chelsea at Stamford Bridge. Needless to write Baggy wasn't invited for this trip - we valued our lives too much! We sat in the big new East Stand amid a hostile crowd of 31,911 and lost 2-0.

At home to a very boring Orient team on Easter Monday, we drew 0-0. This was next followed by a visit from the Millwall nutcases. A 2-1 loss meant that Easter had become our nadir once again. We lost at Cardiff, beat Notts County 4-2 at home, lost at Blackpool, then our final home game 1-1 v Bolton & the last away trip to Oldham winning 2-1, to finish in a credible 6th place.

In a bad week, I watched both Wales & Scotland beat England at Wembley, the Scots match in particular was galling, as their hordes ran onto the pitch - and wrecked the goalposts! I must write, it was without any malice, just high jinks. By this time, sister Ann had moved to Amsterdam in Holland. She met a Dutch bloke called Leo on holiday in Tenerife. They fell in love & she decided to move over there. Michelle & I went over & spent a 2-week holiday in the summer.

Cousin Ken Adair (bottom right) in the LTFC Youth team 1969.

Kneeling next to him is the late Vic Hines, my Uncle Mick's brother.

1977-78

Before the new season had started I had attended my second funeral. An old school friend John Cubis was tragically killed in a car crash aged only 18. Steve Toyer and I wrote a letter of remembrance to LTFC - this was printed in the club programme for the first game v Orient. RIP John.

Baggy, Chris McEvoy & I travelled to the first away game, losing 1-0 to Oldham. Following a fine 3-1 win at 1st Division Wolves in the League Cup, we played Charlton at home. Jimmy Husband scored four goals as Luton won 7-1. These were both new firsts for me, a Luton player scoring 4 & also us netting 7 goals. The three of us again then visited Eastville, beating Bristol Rovers 2-1. After a 0-0 draw at home to Blackburn, the terrible trio went to Tottenham next. This was the lone season spent by Spurs in Div 2 in over 50 years. The locals gave us a warm hospitable welcome to White Hart Lane – NOT! Even Baggy could see that we were heavily outnumbered, so kept it cool as we watched from the old West Stand Enclosure.

After the 2-0 Spurs victory we headed off to the Cockney Pride in Piccadilly. We had a great night until closing time then were caught up in a scrap with Sheff Utd fans, they had been to Brighton that day - at least Baggy was happy!

I missed the midweek 3-2 loss at Brighton following this.

At this moment in time, we had now moved from the Oak Road to the Maple, a smaller side terrace by the players' tunnel and where the singers meet today. At the next home game v Notts County, the three of us somehow managed to get arrested. What was laughable was that there was not a County fan in sight. We were arrested for literally celebrating the second goal in a 2-0 win. Charged with threatening behaviour, all we did was jump up and down wildly as we scored.

The following Tuesday night, we kept a low profile as Millwall were in town. Of course elsewhere in the ground, the Lions fans were acting up as normal. We won 1-0, scoring close to the end.

With the court case looming I didn't go to Cardiff, but Baggy did & wildly celebrated at our 4-1 win. We then beat George Best's Fulham 1-0 at home before a weekender in Blackpool. Despite Jimmy Husband giving us an early lead, we lost 2-1 there was lots of street fighting after the game in the resort.

At the court case, we knew we hadn't done anything wrong. Legal Aid and a very good solicitor proved this was fact & the Judge threw the case out of court.

In the League Cup 4th round, we were drawn at home to Man City. A healthy crowd of 16,443 saw us draw 1-1. The replay at Maine Road was also a draw 0-0, with Luton's Gary Heale missing an open goal. In those days, you kept having replays until the outcome was settled.

So the third game was at a neutral venue (Old Trafford, yeah, that was really neutral) in Manchester! Gary Heale atoned for his previous sitter by scoring twice, alas, City won 3-2 AET.

Because of the court scare, I decided to give away games a miss for a while.

We lost at leaders Bolton, then Jimmy Husband scored his 48th and final Luton goal at home to Hull in a 1-1 draw.

The following weekend Mum, Michelle and I flew to Amsterdam for Ann & Leo's wedding. Whilst in Holland, Luton lost 3-1 at Mansfield. I'm glad that Luton were away that day as had we played at home - there would have been a major family row!

I had not missed a single home LTFC match since returning home from Australia and was fanatical & selfish enough in those days to have probably opted to attend a Luton match, rather than my own sister's wedding. Luckily, I didn't have to make that choice.

Our brilliant defender Paul Futcher had been seriously injured in a recent car crash and was actually lucky to pull through alive.

We then lost 2-1 at home to Stoke, some Potters fans were in the Maple as fights broke out there.

A draw at Sunderland was followed by another home defeat to Burnley and the crowd was now down to less than 7,000.

A surprising first win in 8 matches, 1-0 at Southampton followed this.

Just before Xmas we drew 1-1 with Mansfield at home and it now seemed ages since I had last saw us win, the football being played was also pretty poor.

Ann & Leo came over for Xmas and on Boxing Day I took him to Selhurst Park for the C. Palace match. A good crowd turned up of 22,405 (including some Millwall fans in the Luton end), we watched a really good game. I couldn't believe what I was seeing when Luton put in a brilliant 1st half performance, giving us a 3-1 half time lead. Crystal Palace pulled one back, before a brilliant goal ended it 3-3. The next day was even better. I took Leo to Luton and we tore Sheffield Utd apart. Another Luton legend was making his full league debut that day in Brian Stein. He scored the first of his 154 goals for Luton as we thrashed them 4-0.

Leo had definitely brought us a change of fortune, as on New Year's Eve we beat Brighton 1-0 at home in front of the Match Of The Day cameras before a healthy crowd of 13,200.

Leo & Ann returned to Holland and I watched a dire 0-0 draw at Orient. This was the last away game I attended in 77-78.

We played Oldham in the FA Cup drawing 1-1. In the away replay we won 3-1, before playing them again for the third time in a week, losing 1-0 at home in Div 2.

A 0-0 draw at Charlton turned out to be Harry Haslam's final match in charge. Happy Harry was a great character at LTFC. He started off as entertainments manager and was one of the pioneers of the football special supporters' trains. His legacy was getting us promoted to the top league in 1974. He resigned because he felt his hands were being tied and although sorry to see him leave, it was possibly the right timing.

Haslam then became Sheff Utd's new boss.

David Pleat was announced as the new man in charge, at the start of the campaign he was Youth Team manager, then in charge of the Reserves and now the 1st team. He got off to a miserable start, a 4-0 thrashing at Millwall in the FA Cup 4th round.

The lowest crowd of the season 5,913 watched Pleat's league debut as boss in a 1-1 draw with Bristol Rovers. My main memory of that night was the fighting after the game. As we left the Enclosure at the Kenilworth end, the small band of Rovers fans exited at the same time and with not a policeman in sight, a punch up developed with more than 100 blokes, they were at it for a good ten minutes before the Old Bill finally arrived. Bizarrely - the smallest gate of 1977-78 had produced the most trouble of the season!

The football played now, was of a very poor standard and I did not want to waste money following us away. There were 8 away games remaining, we didn't win one, vindicating my decision. To be honest, if it wasn't for the fact I had gone nearly four years without missing a home game, I possibly would have stopped attending some of those too – fickle I know!

Naturally being aged 18/19 I was going to various disco/clubs around the area like Sands, Tiffany's and the California Ballroom in Dunstable.

It was the turn of Spurs to visit us next. Over 8,000 away fans out of a highest of the season crowd 17,024 saw Tottenham win 4-1 although, that score did flatter them as we actually played well.

On 1st March 1978, I lost my first Grandparent when Granddad Roberts sadly died aged 78, succumbing to the same Cancer disease as Dad. He was a quiet, true Scottish Gentleman, who always saw the good in people and I loved him dearly. A classic example of his nature was when he won a considerable amount of money on the Football Pools. He continued to pay his friend's contribution, despite his mate being in hospital seriously ill. When he won the money Granddad took his friend's share to the family, his mate sadly died shortly afterwards. He could easily have kept all of the winnings and no one would be the wiser, but that was not my Grandfather's personality.

RIP Bill.

I took my Uncle Malcolm's son Malcolm Junior, to see Luton beat Cardiff 3-1. Prior to the match I took him in the Bobbers Club, which was now my regular pre-match haunt. The membership fee then was 16 and a half PENCE - a year! I decided to take up the special offer pre-season, of life membership at £1.65. Pretty good value I'd say, considering it's £10 a year today.

I went to the remaining five home games as the season petered out.

Ron Futcher scored his 43rd & final LTFC goal, in a 4-0 win over Blackpool and another good win was against 2nd placed Bolton.

We then lost 4-1 at Harry Haslam's Sheff Utd.

Ann & Leo were back over for Easter and I took Leo, along with Baggy & Chris to our return game with Crystal Palace on the Monday, winning 1-0.

There was nothing too memorable about the match, but after the game the fighting in the West Side Centre was ferocious. Baggy was loving it, but I got Leo well out of it - the last thing I wanted or he needed, was Leo getting nicked and deported!

At the next home game v Sunderland I met some wonderful visiting fans in the Bobbers Club prior to the match. One of them was an old boy known as Sunderland Harry. He was so fanatical, that he painted his house and shed in Red and White stripes, showing me the photographs. We won 3-1. I met him and his family/friends on numerous occasions over the following seasons, both at Luton and up in Sunderland.

The final home game was unusual. Leaders Southampton came to us needing only a point for promotion. They brought a massive following and were in every part of the ground except for the Oak Road. The reason being was because local non-league team Barton Rovers were playing at Wembley that day in the FA Vase Final and it seemed as if half of

Luton went to cheer them on. Not me though, I was staying loyal to the Hatters. Saints won 2-1 and were promoted and after the game I had a chat with Alan Ball their manager, in the players' bar.

Ironic that since 2005 I have lived a mere few hundred yards away from Barton Rovers FC.

I managed to come by a ticket for my first FA Cup Final and saw Ipswich beat Arsenal 1-0.

Then I decided to move out of the Adairs' after taking up a mate's offer. Dave Ventris at work asked me if I wanted to lodge with him and his wife & child. I would have my own bedroom and Maxine would cook & wash for me. The rent helped them and I enjoyed more freedom, so I moved in with them just before the 1978 World Cup in Argentina. It wasn't in the nicest part of Luton, Marsh Farm, but I can honestly write that I never had any problems there. I stayed with Dave and Maxine for about a year.

Leaving Luton to go to Orient away in 1976-77. Myself left & Rudi Vallyon/Steve Marriott holding the other Luton scarf.

21 Years Old

My summer holiday was back in Benidorm with Dave Lee & Andy Ormes. Andy, Dave Ventris and myself are all Beatles fanatics. I have every official Beatles album on vinyl that the Fab Four ever released. My favourite memory from Benidorm was Andy and I serenading these beautiful blonde Swedish ladies with our Beatles repertoire.

Apart from the Beatles I do have other tastes in music as well. I'm a big Tamla Motown fan and saw various groups at the California Ballroom. The Four Tops, Temptations, Martha Reeves & the Vandellas, Jimmy Ruffin to name a few.

I also love dancing to Northern Soul and like the old 60s skinhead reggae, blue beat/Ska.

Before the season started Baggy, Chris and I went to a couple of pre-season friendly games at Oxford away and a home defeat to Coventry.

With David Pleat in charge for his first full season, he went about getting his own team as soon as possible, getting rid of a lot of Harry Haslam's players.

Nine players were shipped out and for the first game of the season at home to Oldham - SEVEN players made their debut! One of them our new LTFC record signing at £110,000, sought after winger David Moss from Swindon. We could afford to splash the money out on these new signings in the summer of 1978 as amongst the departures, we received a record £350,000 from Man City for the Futcher twins (£300k Paul and £50k Ron).

A crowd of 8,043 turned up and after Oldham scored early and led at h/t, it appeared as though not much had changed. How wrong was I? The 2nd half was amazing, debutants Bob Hatton and David Moss both scored twice, Brian Stein and Lil Fuccillo also scored, to give Luton an incredible 6-1 win.

We lost at Crystal Palace and Newcastle, before welcoming newcomers in the league Wigan, beating them 2-0 in the League Cup.

This was followed by another good home win against Charlton 3-0. My first away trip of the season was a 2-0 defeat at Bristol Rovers.

Old Luton keeper Keith Barber returned to Kenilworth Road with Cardiff and wished he hadn't. We walloped them 7-1 and he retired after this match. Lodger Graham Jones came closest to scoring his only Luton goal that day, hitting the post. The Luton players who wore numbers 1 and 2 that day were lodging at Grandma Adair's and I was enjoying getting to meet the team in the Players Bar & Century Club through them. I made some life-long friends in the Century Club, particularly Judy Brown & her family. Her daughter Yvette was to eventually become Commercial Manager at Arsenal and son Tony, a future director on the 2020 board at LTFC.

A week later, we played Cambridge Utd at home. In the absence of Watford, this was now classed as a sort of local derby. There was a lot of trouble pre-match when a mob from Cambridge stopped off at a pub in Round Green called the Royal Oak and caused major problems. Unfortunately for them, Baggy was there. There were skirmishes in the ground too.

I'm pleased to write I was not involved as I was dressed in a velvet suit, white frilly shirt and black - Dicky Bow tie! My cousin Ken Adair was marrying Dee that day in London.

I explained to them that I could not make the church, as Luton were playing at home. Ken & Dee were fine about it and later that night I was carried onto the coach home after the reception, by cousin Bob.

I travelled to Sheff Utd and watched a 1-1 draw on one of those rare occasions in those days, of having a seat at the match.

In the League Cup 3rd round we beat 4th Division Crewe 2-1 at home, followed by another home victory against Wrexham in Div 2 by the same score. Next, was a weekender in Walkden, near Manchester, and I watched a drab 0-0 draw at Blackburn.

A brilliant home performance and 6-0 victory v Notts County, meant we had risen to 4th place. Alas, this was to be the pinnacle point of the season. In the 6 home games played then, we won 5, drew the other and had scored 24 goals.

An eventful day occurred the next week as Dave Ventris and I went to Orient. We travelled by train and lost an absorbing match 3-2. After the game we headed off to our normal London pub The Cockney Pride, in Piccadilly. No problems, a great night and headed back to St Pancras for the last train home. For some drunken reason, we mistakenly sat in the 1st Class carriage. When the ticket guy explained that we were in the wrong place I arose and moved and thought Dave was following. Unfortunately, Dave wasn't budging and despite my pleas, the police were called he was evicted and spent the night in the cell. I travelled home alone and naturally having had a skinful, fell asleep.

The problem for me was, that I was still asleep as the train passed Luton. I woke up when the train stopped and to my amazement - had arrived in DERBY!

Obviously, there were no trains back until Sunday morning. Having been asked to leave the train by rail staff I slept in the waiting room on the platform and got the first train back to Luton in the morning. Having bunked my way back, I headed straight to the Windsor Castle pub and there was Dave. He had been let out after sobering up, with just a caution. Everyone was in stitches at both of our antics.

We had been drawn away at Aston Villa in the League Cup 4th round and I organised a 52-seat Coach from the Windsor Castle for the game. This pub in Albert Road was now my regular drinking establishment as Dave's best mate Eamon Taaffe lived there. It was a smashing pub, only a small one with a tiny lounge, the staff and clientele were brilliant. I made a lot of new friends there through living at Dave's. It was at the Windsor that I started playing Dominoes competitively. At 20, I was always one of the youngest players in the league (I still am today - at 60-odd!). At the end of that domino season, we had won 6 of the 7 trophies available and were Runners up in that other final!

The owners of the Windsor were Doris & Kevin Taaffe, he was a lovely Irishman and Doris a real character with a fiery temper who when angry, swore like a trooper. A favourite of mine was when she used to shout out, "Bloody fucking this and bloody fucking that." They sadly are both no longer with us and also sadly the pub has now been demolished. I have wonderful memories of my times there.

Before the Villa match we were at home to Leicester. We lost this, our first home defeat of the season. After the game I headed off for my usual post-match drinks in the Players Bar (including having a good chat with Leicester boss and ex-Rangers manager legend Jock Wallace - RIP) and the Century Club.

I think David Pleat did not like me, maybe because I was a mate of Graham Jones (who he blatantly did not rate) & Milija Aleksic. Even Milija, a gentleman, thought Pleat was a little strange in his ways. That night, Mr Pleat had asked the doorman in the Century Club to evict me.

The doorman was a jobs worth Welsh prick, who I couldn't stand and he gladly took up Mr Pleat's request. To the astonishment of everyone in the Bar, I was told to leave. Without wanting to cause a scene in front of everyone, I left quietly secretly raging at Pleat and for TWO whole days - I gave up supporting Luton! Of course, that feeling quickly gave way as we left for Villa Park on board the coach, including a massive carry out. We arrived at the ground along with thousands of other Hatters to enjoy a night of splendid magnitude. What a brilliant performance by Luton. Bob Hatton and Brian Stein scored in a thoroughly deserved 2-0 win, witnessed by 32,727 and we were through to the quarter-finals - for the first time in our history! This was the first major cup shock with Luton I had seen, having missed our 2-0 1972-73 FA Cup win at Newcastle when I lived in Oz. It was also the 50th away ground I'd seen us play on.

After this match we were away to Oldham.

Graham Jones had left the Adair household, as he had married a local Luton girl in the summer. At his wedding it was nice to meet all of his family from Walkden, Manchester and I got on particularly well with one of his sisters, Marilyn. We agreed at the time, that as soon as Luton were to play in Lancashire I would come up to visit them and Graham's parents kindly invited me to stay at their house. Marilyn and her young daughter lived there too. So, with a big sign I made at work with Manchester on one side and Luton on the reverse, I left work early on the Friday afternoon and took up my position at Junction 11 on the M1, with thumb out ready to hitch-hike oop north. The arrangement was for me to meet Marilyn and Graham's other sister & brother in their local pub called The Stocks, in Walkden. Obviously, with me hitching it I had no idea when I would get there but hopefully, before closing time. If it was past then, I was to meet them in the Stockade's nightclub next door. Within minutes of standing at the M1 - I struck gold! A lorry driver pulled up and said in his distinct northern accent, "Alright lad, I'm going to Manchester, hop in."

Not only did he take me to Manchester, but dropped me off at a bus stop he knew, which would take me directly outside the pub.

Unbelievably - I was in the Stocks BEFORE the Joneses! When they arrived, they thought I had changed plans and had got the train up. That was until I told them about the lorry man. We had a terrific night in the disco later, I even won a bottle of champagne dancing to Sylvester's You Make Me Feel (Mighty Real).

Marilyn was older (25) than me, after that weekend we became kind of an item. Despite Graham being out of Pleat's team plans, the Jones family still joined me at Boundary Park. This was to be another poor away day, if it wasn't for Milija Aleksic we would have lost by a lot more than 2-0.

Our away record was poor, 2 draws and 5 defeats. Astonishingly, this was to be Milija's last game of the season. I know I'm biased but the man Luton fans christened elastic was at the top of his game. At the next home match v Newcastle, when the teams ran out with no Milija everyone asked me why was he not there? I, like them, assumed he must have been injured. We won 2-0 and the man in goal David Lawson, had little to do. After the game when I saw Milija, I asked him what injury he had. His reply was, "I'm not injured Alan, he dropped me." According to the papers they had a row, but Milija assured me this was untrue. So we'll never know why David Pleat ended the reign of one of the supporters' favourite players.

Sadly, Milija died of Cancer in October 2012 aged 61. He was a lovely guy and friend as well as a top, top goalkeeper. RIP Milija.

Midweek, I went with a bloke called Malcolm Yaxley to Charlton. He was a maniac driver, to say the least - more of that in later chapters! I only recently discovered Malc is the natural father of a certain Tommy Robinson.

We won our first away game in nearly a year. After losing 1-0 at half time, Moss & Hatton turned things around to win 2-1, at the Valley.

Lawson only played 3 games in goal for us, his last being a home defeat to Sunderland 3-0 (another meeting with my Sunderland friends, in the Bobbers). There was obviously no way back for Milija, when Luton paid £100,000 for Aston Villa reserve Jake Findlay. Now I have to give David Pleat credit here, for in my opinion, Findlay was the best keeper at Luton in all my time as a Hatter.

His main strength was that he was so commanding in his area, never flapping or dropping the ball at crosses or corners.

We had been drawn against Leeds at Elland Road in the League Cup Quarter-Final. Before that, we had 2 home matches, a mid-week friendly against Yugoslav team Dynamo Zagreb, winning 5-1 and a 2-1 loss to Preston.

I had once again, organised a coach from the Windsor for Leeds. Nobody was confident, this was proved correct when we lost 4-1 which to be honest, could have been even worse.

In the next game at Brighton, which I missed, we lost 3-1 & Lil Fuccillo suffered a badly broken leg, thanks to a horror tackle from Brighton defender Clark.

It was Xmas time now, not only were Ann & Leo home again, but Marilyn had came down with Graham's Parents to stay with Jonah. On Xmas Eve, Marilyn joined me as we went to a party at my Dad's old mate Del Mash's house. She stayed the night there with me and didn't return until late Xmas morning, much to the family's annoyance - it was the last time I saw Marilyn!

On Boxing Day, Luton played at Millwall - now there was no way I would take Leo there! So we went to see Arsenal 1 v WBA 2 at Highbury. Perhaps as punishment for our 'Millwall Flu' absence at The Den, where Luton won 2-0.

We then travelled to Fulham and standing on the freezing cold open Putney end terrace, watched Luton return to their poor form and lose 1-0. For this reason and the fact we were experiencing a severely harsh snowy winter I didn't travel to York in the FA Cup 3rd Round, where we lost 2-0.

Because of the weather conditions, we only played one match in January, at home to Bristol Rovers. Unsurprisingly, our lowest 1978-79 crowd of 6,002 actually watched a cracking game. We were 2-0 down at HT then completed a great comeback to win 3-2, Ricky Hill getting the winner.

Everybody was looking forward to the next match at Cambridge. I had again organised a coach, this time from The Royal Oak in Round Green.

The night before, I had spent at the California Ballroom dancing myself dizzy. At the end of the night, a punch up occurred in the car park involving Luton and Watford fans. Now while I will write that I never ever started any trouble in my life, I will not deny, that I actually got involved in any. This was the case that particular evening. The police turned up and a few of us spent the night in Dunstable Police Station Cells. Fortunately, we were released without charge the following morning. I headed straight for Round Green & was in the Royal Oak waiting for the coach to arrive. We left for The Abbey Stadium and when we arrived, did the most stupid thing - bearing in mind the night before!

Chris McEvoy, Baggy, a local Millwall mate of ours called Doc and I at Baggy's suggestion, went in the Cambridge end. Yes, that's right - FOUR of us! Naturally, it kicked off straight away. Within minutes, we were carted off to the police station. Even while we were in their end, I thought to myself, "What am I doing?" One pathetic memory from the police station was when an officer asked me if I had been in any trouble recently and if so, when was the last time I was in a police station. Everyone roared with laughter when I replied, "About six hours ago." I know, it's not clever, but it was tame & looking back now, quite harmless.

They charged the four of us with threatening behaviour and told us to expect a court trial date in the near future.

After the weekend's events I definitely needed to calm down. I then decided not to attend an away game for the foreseeable future and also move back in with Grandma & Granddad Adair, to keep me more on the straight and narrow.

I watched a 0-0 home draw v Stoke on a bitterly cold night. Then Harry Haslam received a warm reception from the Kenilworth Road crowd on his first return, as we drew 1-1 v Sheff Utd. Continuing my low profile, I sat in the Bobbers Stand to watch Luton beat Blackburn 2-1. Our biggest crowd of the season and even that was only 14,205 saw West Ham heavily beat us 4-1.

For reasons stated earlier, I missed Notts County away, and then saw us beat Orient 2-1 and lose to C. Palace 1-0 at home.

Everyone who knows me today knows that I am a bluenose. I then missed a 3-1 defeat at Sunderland because I went to see Glasgow Rangers for the first time, beating Aberdeen 2-1 in the Scottish League Cup Final that weekend. It was a great train trip with the Luton Rangers Supporters Club, the return cost - £5! The match atmosphere created by Gers fans was THE best I'd ever experienced at that time. I then watched Luton beat Burnley 4-1.

The court case for the Cambridge 4 was on the 26th April - the day of my 21st! At the next home game v Millwall, there were the usual scraps in and around the ground, though not as serious as on previous occasions.

Of course, I was nowhere near any of this. That night, while dancing in the Hatters Club at the ground I suddenly felt the most excruciating pain in my left knee. I fell down and literally could not get up, as I was screaming in such pain. An ambulance was called - I spent Easter in the L&D Hospital! This was the very beginning of problems with my knees at nearly 21 years of age and was the actual start of my Rheumatoid Arthritis. On Easter Monday from my hospital bed, I listened on the radio as Luton drew at Stoke. I was released from Hospital and we next took on Brighton and drew 1-1. My maniac driving friend Malcolm, that day threw Ketchup at the Brighton player Clark's long blond hair, who had broken Fuccillo's leg earlier in the season.

The night before my court case and 21st Birthday party, Luton lost 2-1 at Cardiff, we were now down to 4th from bottom & in danger of relegation.

I had hired the Hatters Club at the ground for my party on the Thursday night. First though was the Court Case that morning. Thankfully, we were all let off with just a caution and I came back happy and also much wiser.

My apprenticeship had come to an end at Roydon's and I was now a fully qualified Print Machine Minder - with wages of over £100 a week!

The 21st Party was a terrific success, with well over 200 people there. What really pleased me the most thanks to Graham Jones and Milija Aleksic, was the amount of Luton players there.

Ricky Hill, Brian Stein etc. & bearing in mind, they played at Cardiff the previous night & were leaving for Preston in the morning for a vital game. I was humbled by their presence.

Luton earned a point at Preston coming back from 2-0 down, this was chiefly due to the return of the brilliant David Moss after a long injury lay off.

In the final home game, we beat Fulham 2-0 and were officially safe from relegation. The last match was meaningless at Wrexham and we lost 2-0.

This was very much an up and down season. Scoring loads of goals early in the season, reaching the quarter-finals of the League Cup for the first time ever, being the high points. Our wretched away form, winning only twice & some very poor performances post Xmas, being the low.

1979-80

In the summer I went to Ann & Leo's in Amsterdam again, this time with Baggy and Chris. A big mistake, as Baggy caused some problems. Even the Pimps brought him back once - because he was affecting trade in the Red Light District because of his banter with the hookers! But I had learnt my lesson, even though Baggy was a good friend I'm afraid he was also trouble. After the holiday I decided not to hang around with him quite so much - he just loved hassle! I feel bad writing this, but this was the start of Baggy spiralling out of control, things would get far worse for him in the future.

I had also upon my return, decided to gain a little independence. When Chris McEvoy left his bedsit for a bigger flat, I moved in there and took over the rental in my name. The bedsit was in an ideal location for me, at the bottom of Farley Hill/Corncastle in Hillborough Road. This was easy walking distance to work, football, town and the Windsor Castle. Also of course - I was now free to bring home ladies!

At my workplace Roydon Printers, a new guy started as a van driver by the name of Larry Kinloch. He was to become one of my best friends. Lol, his nickname, was a right character, born in Luton to an English mother and American father.

Being a Windsor Castle regular, it was Dave Ventris who got him the job. Starting out as a van driver, Lol would train as a machine minder and become a very competent printer, eventually running his own small business.

Among the new 1979-80 signings was sought-after midfielder Tony Grealish from Orient via a transfer tribunal. Orient wanted £350,000 and we offered £100k. We got a great player for £150,000 and also paid Mansfield a new LTFC club record for Centre Half Mike Saxby.

The first game in 1979-80 was at Gillingham in the League Cup. Larry took us motley mob in his van & we lost 3-0. In those days the League Cup was two-legged, the return leg was a poor 1-1 draw and we were eliminated.

There was fighting on the Kenilworth Road terraces at Luton's first home league game v Cambridge, resulting in another 1-1 draw.

After this match, for some bizarre reason Larry and I applied to become stewards at LTFC. Pre-rigid Health & Safety days, we were immediately accepted and given our passes with said photos. This was great, not only free admission, but touchline seats too.

Lol also liked Ipswich (Lord knows why) we went to see them at Highbury on the Tuesday. He was pleased as they beat Arsenal 2-0, on the same night that we lost 3-2 at Bristol Rovers.

Our first stewarding duties were against Orient. A tame day as Luton won 2-1 in front of what was to be the lowest crowd of 79-80, 6,705.

The following week, Larry drove the Windsor Castle boys to Watford. A couple of the regulars there supported West Ham, so we all went to cheer on the Hammers with them against our foes. Unfortunately, Shitford won 2-0 and perhaps as a punishment for me not going to Filbert Street, Luton had won 3-1 at Leicester the same day. But it was on MOTD that night.

The next game was at home to Swansea and this match had a comical moment.

Luton played superb and we were coasting home 4-0 when in the last minute, we were awarded a free kick just outside the area. From my touchline steward's seat and directly in line, David Moss was preparing to take the free kick.

I shouted to him, "Score from this Mossy & I'll buy you a pint after the game."

He looked at me and replied, "You're on."

Of course, he scored a peach and ran over to me imitating drinking a beer. I kept my word and we chuckled about it in the players' bar after. This victory had put Luton top, the early performances were a joy to watch.

I was amongst a healthy Luton following at Meadow Lane to watch Luton draw 0-0 against Notts County. This was also the score at home to Oldham.

A fair crowd of us then went to London to watch us beat Fulham 3-1, with fighting on the open Putney terrace. This was the day good friends Val & Martyn (Rasher) Bacon first met on that terrace, as fists were flying around them.

Larry and I had already decided at this stage that we had enough of this stewarding lark and gave up after only three games - but kept the passes!

The next away match we took off in his van from The Sportsman pub in Stopsley, heading for Cardiff. This was a morning kick off, as Wales were playing Rugby that afternoon. This was my first meeting of a good friend to be, Mick Dolan. We stood on the side terrace opposite their Bob Bank. How we lost this match 2-1 I'll never know. We were all over them. On the way home, because Luton were due to play Bristol Rovers on the Tuesday, we decided to stop at Eastville and spy on them play Notts County. While all the lads had paid to go in, Larry & I blagged our way in. Covering up the Luton logo - we gained entry via our photographic steward passes! 3 nights later, Bob Hatton scored a hat trick as we beat the Pirates 3-1. The football from Luton that night was scintillating and the playing stature was the best I had seen in four years.

Another excellent display followed, as we beat Sunderland 2-0 after entertaining Sunderland Harry & his friends in the Bobbers Club pre-match.

Next up, Larry drove us Windsor boys to Upton Park. He and others stood in the West Enclosure, while I stood with the West Ham contingent in our party on the North Bank. With us, was a Hammers Stopsley boy called Kevin Beamon. He was as hard as they come, so I knew there would be no problems from their fans that day. Luton put in another great performance and won 2-1, the win left us top.

Pre-match in the Queens Pub, we had arranged to meet up after the game in the Pie 'n' Mash shop in Green Street. Kevin thought that Larry's driving on the way home bordered on the insane - we were used to it! He told Larry, "If I ever need a driver on a bank job – you're the man." Sadly, Kev is no longer with us. RIP.

After three super wins in a row, I was surprised that only 11,648 turned up for the next game v Preston. We drew 1-1.

Back in the mad yank's van, we returned to winning ways at Cambridge. Goals by Bob Hatton and David Moss saw us run out comfortable winners 2-1.

A much better home crowd of 19,619 watched a tight draw 1-1 against QPR.

Leo was to then make his final visit to Luton (not knowing that at the time) and I wanting a peaceful day, took him on the Bobbers coach to Turf Moor. Top-placed Luton played bottom club Burnley, yet we could only manage a 0-0 draw.

It was around this time that the movie Quadrophenia was showing. Larry and I went to see this cult film three times and both decided to join the Mod revival movement. Although he only lasted about a month, I was to get into the Mod scene in a big way, becoming a proper Mod for nearly three years. I went the whole hog buying a white Lambretta 150i, Parka, Two Tone Suits, Fred Perry shirts, Desert Boots, Loafers, etc. I loved every bit of the Mod revival and joined the Route 66 scooter club in Luton, where I would meet many new friends.

Despite this, my support for LTFC never wavered.

The next game at Kenilworth Road I stood in the Kenny amid some fellow Mod Brummies. It was they who were to be the happiest as we lost 3-2 to Blues, our 1st home defeat of 1979-80.

Next, was the first of my two Gay Meadow, Shrewsbury trips. Luton won 2-1.

A top of the table clash followed and nearly 15,000 watched a 1-1 draw at home to Newcastle.

The next night, Andy Ormes, Dave Lee & myself went to see Paul McCartney's Wings at Wembley arena. Dave Ventris would have joined us, but unfortunately was in jail, for stealing a bus and driving it home. – Allegedly!

The concert was absolutely fantastic and was the first of three times I was to see Macca perform. This concert was great, but it was at the 2nd gig at the same venue a few years later, which was the best I have ever attended in my life. Along with Larry, I watched in awe as he closed the show with his band performing the whole of the 2nd side of Abbey Road to perfection.

I closed my eyes and it was as if I was actually listening to the Fab 4. It was truly mind blowing and very emotional.

My first missed away game since 1st Sept followed at Wrexham, we lost 3-1. The last home game before Xmas was played on a Friday night against Charlton. Admittedly, it was on a terrible night played on a Snow-Covered pitch but only 7,277 turned up to see us beat them 3-0.

At this halfway stage, we were in 3rd place, a promotion spot & had lost only four times. Xmas came and went - as we looked forward to the game that mattered to us fans the most.

This was the first time in seven years that Watford & Luton were in the same league. For obvious reasons, the police had made it a mid-day kick off at Vicarage Road on Boxing Day. This did not stop over 5,000 Hatters travelling the short journey. Strangely, the Rookery, which was Watford's end covered terrace previously, was now for visiting Luton fans and the Hornets' singing supporters - had been moved to the opposite open end!

We left straight from a Xmas party in Bedford to Watford. The police had done a good job segregating the fans and keeping the rival mobs apart. It has to be written, that Watford had now become a family club in a big way and they did not have anywhere near their hooligan element as in earlier years. But Watford/Luton matches were still tense affairs. The match itself, never really took off because of the tension.

It was heading for stalemate until the last minute, when our full back Kirk (Basher) Stephens, rose to put a bullet of a header in the Watford net at the Luton end to send us delirious. He only scored 2 goals in his Luton career, but this one was to keep him in folklore.

I met him at a fund-raising dinner, he told everyone he had been living off that goal against Watford ever since. In 2012 I showed him this piece at the Luton v Nuneaton game - and he immediately bought the book!

2 days later, I witnessed us draw 2-2 at Orient.

On New Year's Day there was a classic match on a treacherous icy surface at home v Chelsea. As usual, some of their fans were in the Oak Road causing trouble. There were now fences at both ends of the ground, due in no small part to Chelsea fans' behaviour on previous visits. Chelsea went ahead before Mal Donaghy and Mike Saxby gave us an interval lead. Straight after h/t the Blues equalised. David Moss made it 3-2, before the final score of 3-3. This was about fair, despite 2 incorrect disallowed Luton goals for offside.

We took a surprising exit out of the FA Cup, losing at home to Swindon 2-0. Leicester then came to town and drew 1-1. It was back to winning ways as we won 2-1 at home to Notts County. I missed the next 3 away matches at Oldham, Sunderland & Swansea. In between those games we beat Fulham 4-0, to go top. Now although at this time I was still not that fond of David Pleat because of past occurrences, I had to admit he was now turning into a good manager for Luton. Yet after this Fulham match bearing in mind we were now top of Div 2, he announced that he didn't think that Luton were ready to get promoted – Bizarre! Coincidently, after his announcement we never achieved that position again in 1980.

The largest crowd of that season, 20,040, saw us draw 1-1 with West Ham. The Hammers fans were not only in the Oak Road but a small number, also in the Maple. As the song used to go, "Maple, Maple, do your job, Maple, do your job" – THEY DID!

I then missed a 2-0 defeat at Swansea and a mid-week 1-1 draw at Preston. The following Tuesday, Cardiff did the double over us winning 2-1. The referee that night was truly awful, so bad he had to be protected by the police both coming off the pitch and outside the ground.

We then had a fantastic day and night in London, going to QPR. Despite being 2-0 down, Luton played some terrific football. In the 2nd half, Brian Stein and Ricky Hill levelled matters and in the end it was QPR grateful for the point. Our ex-lodger Graham Jones made his one & only 79-80 appearance that day, it was to be his 43rd and last for LTFC. David Pleat just did not rate him enough. Graham would soon leave for Torquay in search of first team football and then on to Stockport. I haven't heard from Jona for at least 35 years. I believe he split up with his Mrs and lives in Scotland today?

We then made it eight games without a win, drawing 1-1 at home to Burnley. This run was ever since Mr Pleat made the 'not being ready for promotion' statement. Possibly the players' mindset was the same.

Easter was usually Luton's nadir, but not this year. On Good Friday I travelled to the Valley, we beat Charlton comprehensively 4-1. Next day was derby day.

Possibly, because of fears of crowd violence, only 12,783 turned up and there were definitely nowhere near as many Watford fans as they used to bring. Bob Hatton made it a 1-0 win double over them. There WAS much trouble after the game however, as Watford fans were chased out of town. I hasten to add I was not involved having been drinking in the Bobbers Club post-match, as usual.

On Easter Monday, thanks to complimentary tickets from Graham Jones, we sat at the very back row of the huge East Stand at Stamford Bridge Chelsea. The greatest Luton goal scored in 1979-80 was by Tony Grealish that day, with a 30-yard screamer in a 1-1 draw. Tony, otherwise known as Paddy, was one of the friendliest blokes you could wish to meet.

His wife Pip - was truly stunning! Of the players at that time I also got on really well with Ricky Hill, David Moss and Jake Findlay. Jake's wife Sandra was lovely and a friend too.

We drew again, 0-0 at home to Shrewsbury and this near enough put paid to our promotion hopes. But knowing we HAD to win the next game to stand any remote chance, we travelled up to Birmingham City in great numbers.

Yet despite absolutely battering them in the 2nd half, we succumbed 1-0. Blues ended up promoted in 3rd place on goal difference above Chelsea.

The final home game of the season on my 22nd birthday was a satisfying 2-0 win against Wrexham.

For the final game of the season we went in a mini bus with mad Malcolm driving to Newcastle, for a weekender leaving Luton on Friday morning. Although this was well before Newcastle became the popular nightspot it is today, we still had a brilliant time. I am embarrassed to write this, but the only thing I saw and can remember of the actual match was Bob Hatton hitting the bar. The result was 2-2. I missed both Hatton's 30th & 31st final goals for Luton, in his 90th appearance + the 2 from Newcastle. The reason - I was ASLEEP on the terraces! So drunk was I from the Friday night and Saturday morning's sessions. I know - a disgrace! You would get a banning order for that today. The attendance that day was 13,765. Where were the famous Toon Army then? For some reason, a lunatic Sunderland fan had latched on to us. After the game he led about 30 Luton fans and chased Newcastle fans into the City Centre. You had to see it to believe it, unless that was the case, which it truly was, I would never have thought this would be possible.

I attended my second FA Cup Final to watch West Ham beat Arsenal 1-0. This was on the same day that Rangers fans had ran on to the pitch after a 1-0 defeat and battered taunting Celtic fans who had ran up to the Rangers' end, in a huge Scots Cup Final riot.

The late great Tony 'Paddy' Grealish RIP, presenting our Windsor Castle pub team with the Luton Clubs Dominoes Champions trophy. L-R Kevin Taaffe RIP, Me in England shirt, Brian Bland RIP, Tony RIP, Larry Kinloch RIP, Dave Ventris, Pete Taaffe, Micky Murphy.

CHAPTER THREE

THE EIGHTIES

1980-81

After another summer holiday in Holland at Ann & Leo's, I returned and moved out of Hillborough Road. I returned to my Grandparents' in Stopsley. They had been on their own again for a while after the lodgers had moved out. Tom had been suffering mental issues after the death of his two sons, he would never truly get over his grief but I felt that if I was there it might keep his mind occupied a little further, for when they had lodgers that was certainly the case. For this reason, Grandma decided to take in another player as a lodger.

The previous season around Xmas time, Luton had signed a forward from Bristol Rovers named Steve White. After impressing David Pleat when we played them, he signed him for around £175,000, quite a sizeable fee for LTFC. Yet having paid so much - Pleat only started with him twice + 7 subs apps in 1979-80!

When Bob Hatton left in the summer Pleat started with White for the new season as his replacement. Steve moving in was a bonus for me too and we got on well together in the two years he lived with us.

I was still in Holland when the new season kicked off against the FA Cup holders West Ham at Upton Park. We impressively won 2-1 (all 3 goals were penalties). For the first time at LTFC, I had purchased a season ticket. It was in the Bobbers Stand, a brilliant front row seat near the halfway line for just £35. Sitting next to me was a great mate (& still is today), Mick Tearle.

The first home game was against the enemy Watford. In a tense game as usual, our new lodger was to score his first goal for Luton. It was the only goal - what a time to get your first Hatters strike & against the enemy! Making his debut that night was Luton's first foreign signing, a Yugoslav by the name of Raddy Antic.

After getting the winner against Watford, Steve White's reward - was to be dropped by Mr Pleat for the next game at home to relegated Derby! The Rams won 2-1.

Larry Kinloch took me to Reading for the League Cup 1st round. My 2nd & last Elm Park visit. David Moss scored in the 1st minute and Brian Stein added another to give us a 2-0 lead into the return leg.

Two days later and I was off to Geordie land for a weekender.

Malcolm Yaxley hired a car for the trip. He had a mate joining us who worked for the Holiday Inn Hotel group in Aberdeen. One of the perks of that job was an entitlement to have a free weekend at any Holiday Inn Hotel nationwide for 4 people. So he chose the Newcastle one. When we arrived we were delighted to find out he had obtained breakfast, a double bed in a room EACH and use of all the hotel facilities, including the pool & sauna.

Friday night and suitably attired, we ended up in Tuxedo Junction Disco. This was a brilliant club, which had a unique feature, which I had never come across before. On each table, which were numbered, telephones were placed upon them. The idea being to see what talent was sitting where, take a note of the table number and give said lady a ring. This was a brilliant conception.

Of course, it didn't take me long to swing into action and put it to the test. Noticing a lovely little blonde, I put on the charm and pulled her. Her name was Jan Smith and she was from South Shields. When she asked what I was doing in Newcastle, I explained that the four of us were Luton fans and up for the match tomorrow. She was a Newcastle season ticket holder.

We had a brilliant night and me being the gentleman and not wanting to take advantage of her (liar), she didn't come back to the hotel. At the end of the night we arranged to meet again the next evening.

At the match, Brian Stein gave us an early lead, Luton were spraying the ball around nicely. I have to write, I was a bit shocked at the venomous racism levelled at our black players by the Geordies. We were by far the better team, but somehow contrived to lose the game as the Mags came back to win 2-1.

Back in Tuxes in the evening, I was delighted that wor Jan had turned up and not blown me out. We had a fantastic night, one abiding memory was teaching her and the locals the new dance craze from down south, which they had never seen before. It was the rowing boat dance on the floor, to the Gap Band hit 'Oops Upside Your Head'. It's amazing how certain songs always remind you of certain people/places/events. That is one of them. I also still think of Jan when I hear 'One Day I'll Fly Away' by Randy Crawford, which was out then.

Around this time, Larry had started a mobile disco - in which I was his trusted roadie/assistant! He came up with the name San Fran Disco. Boy, did we have some fun in its 2 years of existence.

I was now smitten with Jan and we agreed to keep in touch regularly on the phone and would also meet up again. Life was pretty good at this stage.

In the League Cup 2nd leg against Reading we drew 1-1 and were then drawn at home to 1st Division Man City.

A drab 1-1 draw at home to Wrexham followed. Frankie Bunn scoring his first for Luton in the dying embers.

Mick Tearle had acquired the new Vauxhall Cavalier, a motor in which we would travel extensively that 80-81 season. The first journey was to Blackburn, where we would have a weekender in Blackpool. We lost 3-0.

In those prehistoric licensing hours days, Sunday lunchtime drinking was strictly 12 - 2pm. With this in mind, we left Blackpool straight after Breakfast on Sunday at 9.30 on the dot and arrived in The Sportsman at - 11.58!

Next up was Orient at home. After a goalless first half, Brian Stein gave us the lead only for them to level matters a minute later. A couple of nice memories followed. During a moment in play the ball came over to me and it ended up in my lap. As Ricky Hill came running over preparing to take the throw in I threw the ball to him and with a big thumb up he said, "Cheers Al," to the laughter of the crowd. It got better, as when he scored the winning goal in the dying moments he ran over and gave me a hug.

Man City came in the League Cup & beat us 2-1. Antic scored his first LTFC goal. It wouldn't be Raddy's last against Citeh!

Mick Tearle & I then drove up to Grimsby and saw a 0-0 draw, with David Moss rarely missing a penalty.

We then suffered 4 defeats in a row. In a friendly at home to Tampa Bay Rowdies we lost 1-0. This was repeated against visitors Notts County. I then missed my first match since the opening day, when bottom side Bristol City won 2-1 at Ashton Gate. For Luton's next match at Preston, Jan & I had booked a weekend in nearby Blackpool (told you I loved it there). A weekend of bliss, lust, sex, romance, call it what you want. All I knew was - I had never been so happy!

Steve White had at last been recalled & kindly left Complimentary tickets for the two of us at Deepdale. Sitting in the Main Stand, we watched what could only be described as a pathetic LTFC performance, going down 1-0 in front of only 5,620. Jan was surprised at the difference in Luton's quality since she previously had seen us in August. I was getting stick from the watching lads on the terrace, who were also staying in Blackpool. Amongst Mick Tearle & Steve Toyer was Bob Hills, who to my shame decided to moon in our direction. We all met up in the Blackpool Mecca that night. This was the final time I visited the famous venue, as it sadly closed down shortly after.

Whitey kept his place for the next game at home to Shrewsbury. He rescued us, scoring the equaliser in the 1-1 draw. This result had left us just one spot above the relegation places.

We drew at home again 2-2, but with a vastly improved display v Swansea.

Jan then dumped me! She said she thought the world of me but the distance between us meant it could never work, as neither of us was prepared to move to the other end of the country. This would not be the last time a woman would break my heart and there was no doubt I really was hurting. But we would still stay in touch by phone for a while after.

Needing cheering up I got a boost at the next game away to nearby Cambridge. A stirring performance by the Hatters, but Jake Findlay was stretchered off injured. Mal Donaghy went in goal and we won our first match in nine, 3-1.

Sheffield Wed were the next visitors, with a huge travelling support. In a dogged 1st half Luton upped the tempo after the break and played really well.

Two goals from David Moss and a great goal from our lodger made it a 3-0 victory for the Town. We watched it again that night on Match of The Day. After that win, was the first time that fans started to come round the house asking for Steve's autograph.

Mick & I then travelled to QPR and saw five goals. Brian Stein opened the scoring before QPR equalised, then incredibly, David Moss HEADED us into the lead - from over 20 yards out! Sadly, QPR came back to win 3-2.

Three nights later, Luton played at Watford. Yet again, we beat them 1-0 and just like in August, Whitey scored the only goal. Now I know he was never the most popular player at Kenilworth Road and I would agree he was not the most skilful either, but effort wise he was 100%.

This latest goal was his 4th in nine starts & despite the stick, 2 goals in two 1-0 wins v Watford, certainly cut him some slack in my eyes.

West Ham came next and we watched a thriller. The best attendance that season of 17,031 saw Brian Stein score twice against the Irons. Two Trevor Brooking goals made the score level. Then 5 mins from time, David Moss scored the winning goal. 3-2, a deserved Luton victory and after 18 games we were the only team to beat West Ham - both at home and away!

Mick & I then travelled to South Wales for the game at Cardiff. He had pre-arranged for the two of us to stay overnight at a friend of his. For the match, we sat in the covered stand behind the goal. At half time we had to fight our way out of the toilets, the anti-English bile from the Bluebirds fans was pretty fierce. We lost 1-0 and there isn't much else to comment about the weekend, apart from enjoying the taste of Brains Bitter. I have to write Swansea was a much more welcoming city than its bigger neighbour.

An entertaining game at home to Bolton followed and we drew 2-2.

We drove in Mick's Cavalier to Oldham on a bitterly cold day and froze our nuts off, standing on the open terrace. Just for a 0-0 draw in front of only 4,720 (my first sub league minus 5,000 Luton crowd).

Three days later on 9th December 1980, I went to work as usual. One of my work mates John Corrigan, said to me on my arrival, "Oh, you've obviously heard the news - hence the Black jumper!"

"What news?" I asked and was dumbfounded to hear that one of my musical heroes, John Lennon, had been murdered in New York, shot dead outside his Dakota home in New York by a madman. That day, my mind was not on the job, as I listened intently to the radio playing nonstop Beatles/Lennon music. In the evening, Larry & I went cruising through the town's streets in his van, with Beatles music blaring out full blast.

From that day for many weeks, Beatles & Lennon music made a huge comeback, topping both singles and album charts.

Such was my passion for the Beatles, bizarrely, I even went to church to light a candle for him on the following Sunday, as Yoko Ono had requested a moment's silence worldwide.

A low pre-Xmas turnout of 7,874 witnessed a good game as we beat Preston 4-2. Lil Fuccillo played his first match in 2 years after breaking his leg twice.

I missed the next match at Shrewsbury intentionally. The game at Gay Meadow was played on a Friday night and on that same evening there was a tribute night to John Lennon at Sands nightclub. Sands, was in Gordon Street, Luton. This site used to be the Ritz cinema. The Beatles had performed in Luton on three occasions. The first, when they were unheard of at the Majestic Ballroom, then just as they were getting known a little, at the Odeon in Dunstable Road and finally at the height of Beatlemania in 1964, at the Ritz. So, at the same spot over 15 years later, I had THE best night that Sands had ever had. It was that good an evening - I never had a single drop of alcohol and was on the dance floor the minute I arrived, until the very end of the night.

Anyone who was there (the doors were closed, such was the demand) will tell you it was truly, very special indeed. To round off a perfect night, we had heard Luton won 1-0 at Shrewsbury, Godfrey Ingram scored the goal.

Prior to that evening I had recently decided to change jobs.

A vacancy arose in the print department at BB Kent, a local factory in Biscot Road. Although it was on a smaller press, the job actually paid slightly more. One nice perk was a works canteen, with subsidised food prices.

At the Xmas break, I left Roydon Printers and was grateful to them for giving me the career opportunity. I would start at Kent's in the New Year.

On Boxing Day, we beat Chelsea 2-0 at home, with Brian Stein getting both goals. In truth, 6-0 would have been a fairer result such was our domination. The next day I wanted to go to Bristol Rovers, but Lol wanted to see Ipswich at Arsenal.

Alas, Highbury won. Whilst watching a 1-1 draw there, Brian Stein was scoring a hat trick at Eastville in a 4-2 Luton victory.

In the FA Cup 3rd round we had been drawn to play Orient away, but Larry had a big works function to disco up in Birmingham. He pleaded with me to join him, also knowing that I really wanted to go to the cup game. His persuasive powers (+£20) meant I missed an excellent 3-1 Luton win.

The first game I attended in 1981 was a 2-2 draw at home to Cardiff. We then lost, again at home, to Newcastle. A certain Mick Harford scored the only goal, our first defeat in nine games. We were to play the Geordies again the following week in the FA Cup 4th Round - no way was I missing this one!

Mick Tearle, Keith Stent, Graham Baker & myself, all of us Stopsley W Men's Club boys, had set off for another weekend bash, my 5th so far that season.

A passionate crowd of 29,202 which at the time was a sizable attendance for them, roared on the Magpies to an early lead. When they scored a second everyone thought that was it, but in a frantic Luton finish Godfrey Ingram pulled one back, when Ricky Hill hit the post near the end the Geordies were screaming for the final whistle. They just held on, preventing a replay.

We still had a great night with the locals and in the hotel ordered Champagne to drown our sorrows. The Barman commented, "I would love to see what you guys would be like - had you won!" I met Jan for the final time that night.

Around this time, a new nightclub opened in Luton called The Mad Hatters. The owner was David Bedford, the former athlete. I was at the opening night & became an original member. Jan from Newcastle knew Dave Bedford's wife, a fellow Geordie. This would be a place I would frequent on many occasions in the 1980s.

After the cup defeat, I travelled to Derby to see us earn a point, drawing 2-2. We then beat Blackburn 3-1 at home after trailing at half time.

Mick, Graham Baker and I travelled to Swansea for the next game for another weekender. Unfortunately, the game was postponed due to the weather. This did not stop us having a brilliant weekend though.

We shared the usual champagne, with Luton News Sports reporter Brian Swain in the bar at the Grand Hotel.

As written earlier, the Swansea people were so much friendlier to us than Cardiff folk. We enjoyed the nightlife and also had a very pleasant next day at the Mumbles beach. This was Mick Tearle's final weekender with us, as he then settled down with his good lady June. Larry & I did their wedding disco the next year. They are still happily married today with grown up girls & are grandparents. I attended their 30th Wedding Anniversary Party in 2011.

After over seven years at Luton, Alan West made his 317th and final LTFC appearance against Grimsby at home, in a 2-0 victory to the Mariners. He left us for Millwall. When his playing days finished, he became a church minister. He went on to be Luton's club chaplain in later years before retiring.

I then went to Luton's first ever game on a Sunday, at Orient, in a very drab 0-0 draw. The next game, also away, was at Notts County.

Steve White was recalled for his first game of 1981, as well as Raddy Antic. Brian Stein scored the only goal in a very impressive win, against a team who would eventually gain promotion.

Two home matches followed, after losing an early goal to Bristol City, Steve White helped to turn things round. He scored twice, along with a David Moss penalty to win 3-1. This gave Steve extra delight, being a Bristol Rovers fan. We then drew 0-0 with Cambridge and the same score applied at Wrexham.

As against Notts County, I travelled to Hillsborough with another SWMC mate called Budgie, when we once again went by train. Luton were well beaten 3-1 by Sheffield Wednesday.

Against QPR at home, Luton gave one of the best performances of 1980-81, comprehensively winning 3-0. This was about the only time that season I recall seeing crowd trouble inside the ground. QPR fans tried to take the Maple, but were sent fleeing. In the programme that day, was an advert to see England play Switzerland in Basle for the forthcoming World Cup Qualifier. Three nights in a B&B hotel and the flight was only £55. I booked the trip with a couple of Sportsman regulars, Graham Clay & Mick Knight.

A week later, Luton beat Bristol Rovers 1-0 at home.

On Easter Monday we went to Stamford Bridge. In a late bid for promotion, we secured a 2-0 win double over Chelsea and were in 3rd position. These were in the days when I expected us to beat Chelsea, as they were nowhere near the power of their previous or future glory days, a crowd of less than 13,000 proved this.

In the final home game we lost 2-1 to Oldham, with a full pitch invasion by Luton fans following scandalous refereeing by Mr Gunn and a vicious elbowing incident on Kirk Stephens by Latics Roger Wilde, who scored both their goals when he should have been sent off, really denting promotion hopes. Two nights later, we played at Swansea in the rearranged match.

Graham Baker drove our hired minibus for the game. We were 5th and Swansea 3rd. Luton simply HAD to win. All seemed dead and buried, as we were soon 2-0 down to the delight of Swansea's biggest crowd to date 21,400. However, Ricky Hill scored before the break and then added another shortly after it. As Luton piled forward, Raddy Antic had a winning goal cruelly (& incorrectly) disallowed for offside.

It ended 2-2 but the Hatters had given everything in front of the celebrating Swans fans.

At the final game of the campaign at Bolton, I had another terrific weekend. I decided to make a final swansong and travelled on my own. Early Sat morning I headed to the Junction 11 exit at the M1. As with my previous hitch hiking experience, I struck lucky getting a lift immediately to Watford Gap services.

Having only been there shortly, I was then picked up by Luton fans going to Burnden Park. Pre-match in the pub opposite the ground I met some Bobbers friends inside, Val & Martyn Bacon.

The only VERY slim chance of promotion was if Luton won by at least 3 goals AND Swansea lost at Preston. We kept our side of the bargain, as goals by Brian Stein, Kirk Stephens (only his 2nd and last LTFC goal) & Steve White gave us a 3-0 victory. Alas -

Swansea won and went up instead of us! After the game, I returned to the pub and had more than a few. I then rang Wor Jan from a phone box and went all soppy. It was the last time I spoke to her.

Aided by the alcohol I decided to go back in time and revisit Walkden, not far from Bolton, to the Stocks pub and see if Marilyn was there on the off chance. She wasn't, but I still had a great night.

When I went into the Stockade (the Disco next door), I met a cracking looking girl. After a couple of hours we were getting on great, when out of the blue she said, "OK Lad, two things - 1) You are starting to get too pissed, if you want to stay with me tonight - sober up NOW! & 2) If you do, there's no way we can stay at mine, so it will have to be a hotel." I didn't need telling twice and immediately went on Orange. Not long after, we checked in to the Pack Horse Hotel in Bolton. A fantastic night of lust to see out the season in style, shockingly I forgot her name. Amazing how I can remember crowds from 50-odd years ago - but forget a girl's name the same night!

After watching Scotland beat England 1-0 at Wembley, my final match of 1980-81 was to be at Basle in Switzerland, to see England play there. This was my first England away trip - unfortunately I never saw the game!

We left on Friday morning from Gatwick. The three of us flew to Zurich and then by rail to Basle. After checking in at the hotel for a quick SSS, it was straight out on the lash. What happened over the next three days is something I am not particularly proud of, putting it down to age, immaturity and daftness. On the Friday night, amid hundreds of pissed up Englishmen, I lost Graham & Mick and ended up being picked up off the street by the police, very drunk. I was thrown into the local cells for the night and released without being charged on the Saturday morning. After having breakfast in the hotel & a quick wash, I then went out to do exactly the same thing again (but at least not losing my pals this time). It was a beautiful hot day - I had a swim in a fountain! A crowd of us then headed to the square. Here, we were having a game of football with some local Swiss lads. Everything was OK and we got on fine with our opposing fans. Then the mood changed when one of them said, "Oh no, Italians."

There are evidently a large number of Italians living in Basle. At that time, there was a large amount of hostility between English and Italian fans, due to the serious trouble at Euro 80 the previous year in Turin.

A number of Italian lads headed towards us in a menacing manner. One of them approached and shouted to me, "Ingleesa?"

Now bearing in mind I had a Union Jack Shirt on, England scarf, hat, & was draped in St George flag, I replied, "NAH."

He then spat in my face. I'm afraid I completely lost it, for the first and only time in my life – I totally lost control! Having given him the Glasgow kiss, a full on riot then developed. If I had just left it where he was on the floor, I might have been OK. But because I was so raging, I then picked up a bench & rammed into all of them, completely losing any Self Control. It wasn't long before the riot squad arrived. After being tear gassed in the face and held down on the ground by a large number of police, I was handcuffed, put into the police van then escorted to the cells.

At the game, there were serious disturbances caused by England fans. Gradually, my cell began filling up and in the end - there were 36 English fans joining me in the same cell!

These were various supporters, Charlton, Derby, Oldham & seven Liverpool fans, who coming straight from Paris from their European Cup final against Real Madrid - were arrested for looting a jeweller's shop! Of course I missed the match and spent the night in the jail - amongst all kind of foul smells!

The next day we were all released without being charged, except the Scouse jewel robbers!

Upon my return to the hotel I was greeted with big cheers, such was the lunacy. So, three nights in Switzerland. I had missed the game and spent two nights in a prison cell and fell asleep downstairs in the Disco, so hadn't even slept in my room for any of the three nights.

My abiding memory of the last night was Graham Clay CONSTANTLY singing Yellow Submarine on the stage. Now I'm a HUGE Beatles fan but that song always reminds me of him murdering it and most folk leaving, lol. Sadly Graham passed away in 2016 aged 56, of a sudden heart attack. He was a man who suffered no fools, in fact I'd describe him as not the most popular man in Stopsley & he had more than a few enemies but in the main, he was mostly ok with me. RIP Graham.

Only one word to describe my actions then – PATHETIC!

On a coach leaving the old much missed Rangers Club in Luton, for England 0 Scotland 1 in 1981. I was one of only TWO England supporters on the bus & the only one in colours.

Champions

Due to my new job, the only holiday I took in the summer of 1981 was a works outing day trip to Boulogne in France. A trip I took a few Sportsman mates on. We ended the drunken day swimming in the town centre river. Including a right character and friend, Nigel Doggett - who couldn't even swim!

Chris McEvoy's younger brother Keith drove me to a pre-season friendly at Cambridge, drawing 0-0.

The new season kicked off with a new format of 3 points awarded for a win instead of 2. Our first game was at home to Charlton and after Steve White had been promised a starting run of games, he was leading the attack.

Steve was now very settled in the Adair household and also had a lady friend. I take full responsibility for that occurring. One Friday night pestering him for a lift into town, he eventually caved in. As he was about to drop me off a crowd of girls were heading our way. I started chatting to them, Steve then got out of his car before I headed to a pub. One of those girls, Mandy, was to become his future wife, so my nagging for a lift and fate had brought them together.

We had a new captain in Brian Horton, signed from Brighton, with the popular Tony Grealish heading in the opposite direction.

Luton got off to a fine start beating Charlton 3-0 in front of what would be the lowest home league crowd that season of 8,776. Steve White scored the final goal. He would go on to have a very good campaign, by far his best in a Luton shirt.

Three days later, Chris McEvoy and I had a great day out in London before witnessing history being made. This was the very first league game played on an artificial grass surface, at Loftus Road QPR. Ex-Hatter Andy King, headed them into the lead. The longer the match went on, the better Luton were playing, Mark Aizlewood equalised and then late on, Ricky Hill scored a brilliant winner.

Next it was Burnden Park, Bolton, one of only 2 league games I would miss in 81-82. We beat the Trotters coming from 1-0 down again, to repeat a 2-1 win. Our positive start saw the Match of The Day cameras at the home game with Sheff Wed. Unfortunately the 100% record was brought crashing down to earth with a bang as we lost 3-0. Lots of trouble post-match where the club shop stands today.

When we went to Filbert Street, Leicester took the lead through a penalty. Within six minutes of the 2nd half, Steve White had scored twice to outfox the Foxes, giving Luton another 2-1 win. This was our 3rd successive 1-2 away victory after trailing 1-0.

Cardiff were now becoming a bogey team, they carried on this mantle winning 3-2 at Kenilworth Road. This had become six consecutive wins for the Bluebirds over us, ever since we put 7 past them three years earlier. It would be the 2nd and final home league defeat all season.

The perfect tonic to put things right was to follow, with a home game v Watford. Since being in the same division, we had four victories out of four, all of them by 1-0.

This winning streak continued - only even better! Brian Stein & David Moss each scored twice. After 52 minutes we were 4-0 ahead.

What a shame we couldn't go on further and really annihilate them. Watford ended with a mere consolation. This 4-1 win is still the highest ever victory over them in my Luton supporting life.

In the League Cup 1st leg we surprisingly lost 2-0 at home to Wrexham.

I went on my own to Orient, visiting cousin Ken & Dee Adair in London en route to Brisbane Road. A comprehensive 3-0 Luton win put us top of the table. Apart from one Saturday end of March, we remained top for the rest of the season.

Steve White had scored again and had now hit the net 11 times in his 29 starts. Not bad, for someone who had received a fair amount of stick from more than a few Hatters fans.

We then travelled up to Oldham, having won all four away games. This sequence ended at Boundary Park. Just as it was looking like our first away defeat Whitey scored his finest ever Luton goal, a screamer from over 20 yards to make it 1-1. The day after Mick Tearle's wedding was Grimsby at home. This was to be Steve White's finest moment in a Luton shirt. He silenced many of his critics by scoring FOUR times against the Mariners in a resounding 6-0 win. No Luton player to date, has since scored 4 goals in an official match.

In the driving rain, Malcolm Yaxley drove us up to Wrexham for my first visit to the Racecourse Ground. We were top and they 20th. Goals from Mal Donaghy & Steve White were enough. We even gave Whitey a lift home that day. He had now scored 10 goals in 11 starts this season. He scored again, with the only goal at the same venue on the Tuesday night in the 2nd leg of the League Cup, but the Welsh side went through 2-1 on aggregate.

We then beat Crystal Palace 1-0 at home, although failing to score for the first time in six White did win us the penalty, which David Moss duly obliged. Sadly, Mike Saxby was stretchered off after turning his knee in the turf. It effectively ended his playing career after 7 goals in 91 LTFC apps. He was a fine centre half for whom we paid Mansfield a Luton record transfer fee of £200,000.

Another home victory followed, beating Derby 3-2.

I travelled to Ewood Park to see us defeat Blackburn 1-0.

We then made the long journey to Newcastle. Once again it was Malcolm Yaxley driving, this time in a hired Renault Fuego. It is the return trip that springs to mind the most rather than the match itself.

The Magpies were 2-0 up at h/t. After the break and playing delightful football, we came roaring back. David Moss scored from the spot, then in the 85th minute Mal Donaghy levelled. It looked like our undefeated away record would remain intact, until Varadi scored a peach of a goal in injury time to win it 3-2 for the Mags. We left pretty sharp, reached the car and onto the A1 by 5pm.

Nothing out of the ordinary, but then he never drove under 100mph (told you before about his maniac driving) for the whole journey home, apart from a 15 minute toilet stop. Now I KNOW that Newcastle is a good 240/250 miles from Luton. When we arrived at SWMC someone said to me, "I thought you were going to Newcastle."

After pulling out the match programme, "I did," was my response - the time was 7.40pm!

We soon returned to winning ways, defeating Bolton 2-0 at home. That night we welcomed back old friend Milija Aleksic, on loan from Tottenham.

I then called a truce with Mr Pleat, he had continued to play Steve White (not that he now had any other option) and by calling back Milija due to injuries, he had obviously let past matters drop. Of course not that my splat with Pleatey would have bothered him in the slightest, but he did have the grace to shake my hand at the season's end, even remembering me, by saying, "Ah, Graham Jones' friend."

After beating Rotherham 3-1 at home, we were now TEN points clear at the top. Whitey scored his first in seven. He scored again the next week in a 2-2 draw at Shrewsbury, my 2nd and final visit to Gay Meadow.

We were now experiencing a harsh winter and didn't play again for over 3 weeks. The next game played was after Xmas at Norwich.

Not knowing whether the game would be on or not, we travelled by rail from Hitchin. Despite not playing for 23 days, Luton got off to an astonishing start. Raddy Antic, Brian Stein, followed by Steve White, gave us a 3-0 lead - in just FOURTEEN minutes! We blitzed them. 3-1 was the final score.

Five days later, we beat Swindon 2-1 at home in the FA Cup 3rd round. We were then drawn at home again to 1st Division leaders Ipswich. A season's best crowd of 20,188 watched an even first half. In the second though, Ipswich upped the tempo as the gulf shone through and they won 3-0.

We ended the month defeating Leicester at home. A 2-1 double was achieved as Steve White & Mal Donaghy scored.

My personal life was pretty good at this stage too.

The job at Kents was going fine and I was getting on really well with a girl I had met in the staff canteen, by the name of Sharon Smith. She had been with a steady boyfriend since she was 15 or so, but we were just good friends.

My Mod life was terrific and I particularly loved the Mod night on Thursdays at the Kingsway Arms. Parking up my recently purchased Lambretta li 150cc amongst the dozens of other scooters and dancing myself dizzy to the fantastic 60s Motown & Soul sounds. The next match at Sheff Wed was a real humdinger of a game at Hillsborough. My mate White gave us the lead and they equalised by the interval. We led 2-1 after a David Moss penalty, before the Owls then scored twice to lead 3-2. Gary Megson, their future manager, was nothing but a dirty shitbag that day, constantly fouling throughout and also giving out the verbal too. I've always disliked him, he got his comeuppance at last late on for brutally fouling Brian Horton and was sent off.

Justice prevailed, Brian Stein equalised - oh how we laughed!

On the Monday morning of the 15th February, I received a Valentine's card. The trouble was I genuinely didn't have the foggiest idea who it was from. At first I thought that maybe it was the receptionist at work, with whom I had a little fling at the works Xmas party. I thanked her. "It wasn't from me," she replied, rather sheepishly.

I had no idea until lunch break. Sitting at the table with my lady friends Sharon & Allison, Allison asked, "Get any mail this morning, Alan?"

I replied, "Yes, a Valentine's Card, but I haven't got a clue who from."

Sharon then said with a blushing face, "Well, who would you like it to be from?"

"Please, please tell me it was from you," I replied. From that precise moment, all through the day and night I thought of nothing else but her. When I saw her the next day, I privately asked if we could meet up. We came up with a plan where both of us would take Friday off work as a holiday.

I arranged for Grandma & Granddad to go out and told Whitey, "You MUST go to Mandy's - or anywhere else!" I must admit, after Thursday lunchtime I did wonder if when it came to the crunch, she might bottle out. After all, she had been seeing this bloke for over 5 years, her only real boyfriend. What I failed to write previously was that we very nearly met up about three months or so prior to that, only for her to get cold feet.

On Friday morning to my absolute delight, she arrived. When I told her that I was more than a little worried if she would actually go through with it, she told me after the last opportunity she wasn't going to let me slip away again and that she had wanted this moment for so long - I melted! That day, I will never forget. Out of total respect to her I didn't want this to be just sex & wham, bam, thank you ma'am. We spent the most wonderful day together and I had never felt so close to anyone like this.

I KNEW there and then, I was totally smitten and no doubt about it - in love!

She told me she was going to finish her relationship on the Saturday and asked if she could stay at mine that night, to feel more secure. I told Grandma about it Friday night and she was great, saying she would make up a bed for Sharon in the dining room. I was sleeping in the Lounge, as Whitey had the bedroom. That night, I didn't sleep a wink thinking about Sharon, still worrying if she would ACTUALLY finish with him now that it was crunch time.

The next day of all the games, it was Watford away. Of course I went, but apart from when Brian Stein equalised in a 1-1 draw, I thought of little else but Sharon.

On Sat evening, I was literally sitting next to the phone eagerly awaiting the call. It rang & was Sharon. "I've done it Alan, please can I get a taxi to you - NOW!" As soon as she arrived, I gave her a big hug, introduced her to Isa & Tom then we went out to celebrate up SWMC ending in a night to remember forever. From that night on, we saw each other every single day and night throughout the whole period of our relationship.

Life for me was now perfect bliss, we were hopelessly in love with each other.

I got on fantastically well with all her family, she, with mine - Christ even Mum liked her! I would go to her house on my scooter after work Mon – Thurs nights and she would stay at mine weekends.

It was so much more than sex, 5,6,7,8 times a night sometimes - no word of a lie, I swear! If I had died during my time with Sharon I would have died a happy man. In the period we were together, everywhere we went all my friends loved her, but especially loved seeing me and us SO happy.

Football for the first time ever in my life was almost incidental. I still went to nearly every game of course, but I was just glad there was now something ELSE too.

The following week I watched us beat Oldham 2-0 and then took Sharon to Kenilworth Road for the first time, as we beat Cambridge narrowly 1-0.

Then a time I will remember forever. We spent our first weekend away together. Three days in sunny Cleethorpes to go and see Luton play Grimsby (well that was the excuse). Oh what a weekend of sheer bliss. Just bed, shower, eat, drink, dance, bed, shower, eat, drink, watch Luton in a boring 0-0 draw, drink, eat, bed, dance, bed shower, bed, eat, bed, bed, bed - well I think you get my drift!

The Saturday night we were in a pub chatting to a couple we met, before leaving for the disco. The lady asked us how long we had been together. When we told her two weeks, they were both flabbergasted. The woman said, "I have never in all my life, seen a couple who are obviously so much in love with each other."

When Sharon told them, "That's because - we ARE!" I felt on Cloud Nine.

The following Friday night we played Wrexham at home. A 0-0 draw was the first time we had not won at home since Cardiff ten games prior. I then missed only my second game of the season at Barnsley midweek. Citing not feeling very well as the excuse, spending a night without Sharon, probably being more realistic. Steve White kindly left comp tickets for the lads though.

We lost 4-3, our first defeat since November, only the 4th of the season. Luton would remain undefeated for the remainder of the campaign.

Malcolm Yaxley took us to C. Palace to see a cracking 3-3 draw at Selhurst Park. The once commanding lead at the top was now gradually slipping, as we had not won away yet in 1982. We were still top, but only on goal difference.

A 0-0 draw at Derby cost us that place, the first time since September and thankfully the last. We returned top 3 nights later, beating Orient 2-0 at home. On the Friday night, Sharon and I went to the Baileys Club in Watford, to see Gladys Knight & The Pips. She accompanied me the next day at home to Blackburn. We won 2-0, Steve White netting the second.

The following Friday, Sharon had her 21st party, I was the designated photographer and we had a ball.

Next day I was off to Cambridge. 8,815 watched and the huge Luton contingent made up at least half of that crowd. Wayne Turner scored his only goal of the season a beauty, but Cambridge levelled, 1-1 was the final result.

Our biggest home league crowd to date, 15,061, then attended as Luton were rather fortunate to win 2-0 against Norwich.

It obviously wasn't very cool for Sharon to ride on my Lambretta, so I said farewell to my beloved 2-wheel friend and sold it - to a Modette from Watford! This enabled me to buy a Car to drive her around in. I bought a mustard coloured Mini for £325.

The next game at home to Newcastle was interesting.

After nearly an hour, we were 2-0 down but Brian Stein turned things around, scoring a hat trick, including two poorly taken penalties. We were now within touching distance of promotion.

I took Sharon for what ultimately, would be the final time to see Luton v Chelsea. A great game it was too, in front of 16,185 we watched Chelsea twice take the lead and twice Luton levelling.

I headed off to Rotherham after another unbelievable night & hours of passion with Sharon. Completely oblivious, it proved be our final moments of intimacy. Millmoor was like an old boys' outing. Lots of faces from the past joined us, Baggy being one of them, as thousands of Hatters headed north. Lil Fuccillo gave us the lead before the Millers levelled. When ex-Hatter Seasman scored we did begin to wonder. But a minute later, Richard Money equalised with a cracking goal, his only LTFC one.

In the last minute right in front of where the Luton fans were packed, a penalty was awarded to Rotherham. Alan Judge, standing in for injured Jake Findlay, brilliantly saved it. What followed was hilarious as one of our friends Bob Hills, ran onto the pitch, went up to Judge and shook his hand. The only problem was Bob being a little tipsy to say the least, said to him, "Great save - JAKE!"

We got in for nothing that day too, by scraping through a door in the Rotherham Supporters Club - straight onto the terrace!

Two nights later, Sharon and I went out for a meal to celebrate my 24th Birthday. I honestly thought at that time, life was perfect and could not be better – in less than 24 hours how wrong was that statement!

The following night at her house, she ended our relationship, saying that everything was just too much for her to take in. I had the, "You're a fantastic bloke and I truly do love you, BUT etc., etc., etc." She said after 5 years in a relationship, everything was just happening too quickly for her. By the way, it was HER idea to book a holiday in Spain and it was - HER suggestion that we should get engaged after 6 months! Sharon had told me she came to the decision to end things at the weekend, while I was at Rotherham. If that really was the case, how on earth can you make love to someone multiple times in the night - then want to finish it the next day or so! She also added that she could not be so cruel to finish it on my birthday.

That night I was absolutely distraught, when I got home Steve immediately knew something was very wrong and was concerned for me. I went to work the next day and when I tried to speak, the words just wouldn't come out. At lunchtime, I tried to see if Allison could have any influence but Sharon had taken the rest of the week off.

The timing of all this emotional turmoil was just brilliant.

Three nights after dumping me - Luton were on the verge of promotion to Division 1! Knowing that if Luton beat Shrewsbury on Friday night, we were promoted to Div 1 and yet - I DIDN'T EVEN WANT TO GO! Thankfully, Steve White and my mates talked me round. We won 4-1.

On what should have been one of my happiest nights ever, Luton fans poured onto the pitch in wild jubilation. I should have been celebrating with all the players too in the promotion party, via Steve. – Instead I just went home!

You know what? If Sharon had asked to me to spend that night with her, or one of LTFC's biggest nights in years - Sharon would have won!

After that weekend, with only minimal contact from her to check that I was OK, I just knew that she would not come back to me. I made a quick decision to leave Kent's a s a p, there was absolutely NO way I could continue seeing her at work every day, knowing how close we had become.

There was an advert for a Printer's job in Dallow Road. I applied, got an interview and an offer days later, which I accepted. I managed to get a private lunch date outside of work with Sharon. On telling her this news, she pleaded, "Please don't leave?"

I replied, "I'm sorry Sharon but it hurts too much we are either together, or we are not." Just looking at her face - I knew her answer!

Equally, I also knew that she would soon go back to her bloke, which she did. I believe they are still together today, with two grown up girls. It took me many years to truly get over her. I've seen her only on very few occasions since 1982, fleeting moments. Only meeting by accident, briefly chatting and even that was years ago. Yet to this day, nearly 40 years on, she is still in my heart and always will be the love of my life. One thing is for certain. I have never loved a woman before or since Sharon, with such passion.

So, Luton got promoted to Div One - and I didn't even celebrate it!

The following week at Stamford Bridge, Raddy Antic & Brian Stein scored and led us to a 2-1 win over Chelsea, our first away win of 1982.

We then beat FA Cup finalists QPR, in front of our biggest home league crowd of the season. 16,657 watched as we won 3-2. Steve White scored his 26th and final LTFC goal, not knowing this at that time.

The final home match was very much a case of after the Lord Mayor's show. Against Barnsley, Brian Stein levelled to make it 1-1. Both Barnsley and their fellow Yorkshire rivals Sheff Wed, were the only two teams Luton failed to beat in 1981-82. We travelled for the finale two nights later to Ninian Park in Wales. Luton of course were already promoted as champions. If Cardiff failed to beat us they would be relegated, along with Wrexham and Orient. A victory for the Bluebirds would send Bolton down instead. We even had a Bolton fan standing next to us who had travelled down to support us. Well with less than 10 mins left, he knew The Trotters were safe as Luton were 3-0 up. Despite two late Cardiff goals, the Taffs were relegated.

It had been a fantastic season, my favourite by far, so much style in our great attacking play and the Hatters were a pure joy to watch. Luton had finished eight points above our local foe rivals in 2nd place. Which had made that even sweeter. The final table was listed as: Played 42, Won 25, Drew 13, Lost 4, Goals scored 86, Against 46, Points 88. We had been top scorers both home & away.

I was still pining for Sharon, when my mate Mick Knight the Aston Villa fan, asked me to join him to see Villa play in the European Cup Final in Rotterdam against Bayern Munich. The break was just what I needed and I leapt at the offer. After staying the night in Amsterdam, (we would have stayed with Ann & Leo, but they had recently split, Ann was now back home) we then travelled to Rotterdam.

Standing in the Villa end with my recently acquired Luton Div 2 Champions tee shirt on, I well and truly got into the spirit. Peter Withe had given Villa a very early lead. Despite losing keeper Rimmer pre-kick off, Villa held on to win 1-0.

Celebrating profoundly with Mick and the Villa hordes, I shouted, "Christ, look at me, what would I be like if Luton won the European Cup?"

In the nicest possible tone, a fan standing next to us said, "You might be in for a bit of a wait, son."

Back home in Luton there would be one last trip in season 1981-82.

At the Stopsley Working Men's Club, there were a group of friends that I had got to know well. They were slightly older than myself and were all couples. I had spent a fair amount of time with them in the past, particularly at Xmas/New Year parties. Couples Billy & Kath Smith, Bob & Chris Rumble and Arthur & Kath McGee had invited me to go with them to Scotland for a long weekend, staying in Billy's home village of Cleland near Motherwell at his dad Benny's. They had originally invited me when I was with Sharon, but insisted I still go with them.

We set off early Friday with the intention while there, for Bob & I to attend the Scotland v England game. A crowd of about 12 of us went out on the Friday night to the Cleland

Miners Club & I had noticed Billy's sister was on her own with us. Despite still pining for Sharon, that was all forgotten for a night as she was paying quite a bit of attention to me giving me plenty of t l c - to the point where nature took its course!

Saturday morning Bob and I were given a lift to Motherwell station to get the Glasgow-bound train. Billy's brother Iain cringed, for there was I dressed in England shirt, scarf, Cap & St George flag. The banter from the Tartan Army on the platform was tremendous. I must add it was mild natured without a hint of malice. I spotted a lone policeman standing by the fence and went up to him asking, "OK if we stand next to you, mate?"

He jokingly replied, "No' dressed like that, pal - yous are on ya aen!" Cue them all singing 'Oh Spot The Loony'. This song would be repeated at me many times through the course of the day.

We queued up at the turnstiles without tickets. Upon slipping the turnstile operator a fiver, I jumped over. Bob followed me - only inflation had gone up in seconds and he had to pay £10! In the ground, bearing in mind I had seen TWO other England fans all day, the stick we took was merciless, with no spite. There were Scots fans taking photos, shaking my hand & saying, "Fair play to you lads, we've NEVER seen England fans here before." England won 1-0. There WERE other England fans at Hampden that day, as SWMC pals Chris McEvoy, Graham Clay, Steve Toyer, Mick Knight, Bob Hills all went up with Scots mate Johnny Temporal, staying at his relations' in Greenock. They all sat in the Main Stand - though none of them wore England colours! It was a wonderful weekend, which really cheered me up post-Sharon - especially Billy's sister!

Sadly, Benny, Billy & Iain have all since passed away. RIP.

Division One

My new job was going well, it was a small firm called Impress - there were only 6 of us in total working there. We had an office in the city of London, as well as two other factories in Sundon Park and Slough. These would all merge in 1989 to grow under the banner of CBC Print, employing over 50 staff at its peak.

In July 1982, my mate Larry married Lynne. I was given the honour of being best man. Mind you, Lynne did give Lol an ultimatum - Marriage or San Fran Disco!

To be fair I had taken a back seat with the Disco when I met Sharon anyway, and in truth I think it had run its course too. He sold all his disco gear and they married at Luton Register Office. The reception was at Beech Hill Conservative Club. Larry's dad Wally and his partner Betty came over from the States for the happy occasion and I got on like a house on fire with them. So well, he invited me to his house in Michigan for a vacation. An offer in which I took up and would stay there the following summer.

We said farewell to Steve White in the summer of 1982. Although he was happy at Luton, he left as part of the deal in which Paul Walsh would join from Charlton. Steve went to the Valley & although I was disappointed that he left, his replacement it must be said was different class, a brilliant skilful little wizard. While Steve White lived with the Adairs Granddad's mental health improved dramatically. In fact during that period it was the best I had seen him in years. Sadly, not long after Steve left, his chronic depression returned. He soon locked himself away from life, refusing to go out of the door as slowly but surely, his heartache returned. He became unbearable. I moved out for a final time the next year.

The new campaign with the big boys was about to start. Before that, Keith McEvoy and I went by train to Molineux for a pre-season friendly with Wolves. We won 4-3, Paul Walsh looked dazzling.

We started Div 1 life off at Tottenham, where a coach load of us left Luton Postal's Club and joined 5,000 Luton fans to see Spurs the FA Cup holders, race into a 2-0 lead. Just when I was already beginning to think, is this this too much for us? Spurs defender Lacey scored an own goal. Brian Stein equalised not long after half time, it finished 2-2 & Luton had finished the stronger team, we were more than happy with the point gained.

Two nights later, we kicked off at home to West Ham. The Hammers deservedly won 2-0 and we knew after last season's heroics, this was a different ball game. One other disappointment was the attendance of only 13,403. This got even worse when just 9,071 could be bothered to turn up against Notts County.

Admittedly there were only a few hundred from Nottingham this would be the lowest home league gate of the campaign.

The absentees missed an eight-goal classic. Paul Walsh opened the scoring, County levelled, then scored a brilliant goal. Ricky Hill made it 2-2.

Soon after the break David Moss put us ahead and then Paul Walsh scored one of the best goals I've ever seen at Kenilworth Road. A goal of outstanding skill, he weaved his little body through numerous opposition players, before slotting the ball home. He then got his hat trick to rapturous applause only for Nott's to score again. 5-3 - what a game!

In midweek, we travelled up with Mick Knight to Villa Park. Mick was pleased as Villa won

4-1.

Three days later, one game everyone was looking forward to was at Liverpool away. I decided to make this a weekender & arranged to stay at one of Granddad Roberts' sisters' in Wavertree. I booked the National Bus to leave Luton Bus station at 1am on Saturday. Drinking in The Mad Hatters Club before leaving, I met some other Luton fans that were booked on the same bus. One of these became a good friend and he still is today, his name Gappy. (I still don't know his real name.)

After breakfast in Liverpool I headed to my great aunt's. While waiting at the bus stop, a passing coach from the Luton Labour Club hooted at me. On board were Martyn Bacon, Jimmy Oates & Willie Hood, all Bobbers Club pals.

Upon arriving at my aunt's, we had a chinwag then Uncle Matt joined me en route to Anfield. He didn't want to go to the match but being Scots, did join me for a drink pre match. We went in a pub near Anfield called The Sandon. The Liverpool fans in there were tremendous. I was getting on so well with the company I was in, that they insisted I came in the Kop with them. As I had no colours on and these people were very friendly I went for it. After all, I might never get the chance to stand on the world famous terrace again – and I never did! Luton had over 3,000 fans there that day. I heard one Scouser say, "Fair play to Luton, only Everton and Man United brought more here last season." An incredible match followed. Luton played brilliant football in an enthralling game. Brian Stein had given us a well deserved lead, the style of football Luton had played in that opening spell was as good as I had ever seen them play. It was also being well commented on by Liverpool fans too. Paul Walsh was actually mesmerising. It is my belief that his performance that day was the main reason Liverpool signed him for £700,000 nearly two years later.

Of course Liverpool were one of the best teams in Europe then, certainly in England & Souness soon equalised.

Then Jake Findlay was stretchered off with a rib injury. Full back Kirk Stephens went in goal and the Kop humour shone through as they all sang 'One Shaking Stevens'.

Rush then put the Reds 2-1 up. After the break we changed keepers AGAIN, this time with Mal Donaghy due to his Irish Gaelic football background. David Moss levelled for Luton as I quietly applauded.

Despite our goalkeeper situation, Luton still bravely attacked the mighty Liverpool and the Koppites all around me were really giving Luton praise. However, when Brian Stein had put us ahead I slowly knelt down and went BERSERK - very quietly of course!

Johnston made it 3-3 near the end, the final result of a pulsating match. The Liverpool fans all round me, warmly shook my hand, each of them were saying that's the best away performance they had seen in years, as they gave Luton a great ovation. "You should be very proud of that performance lad" they said – I WAS!

At the end of a fantastic day I somehow in my drunken state, ended up sleeping on a bus in Walton depot, having no idea how I got there. I thoroughly enjoyed my first weekender in the city of my musical idols' birthplace.

The next match at the Kenny saw another brilliant Luton performance. This time we thrashed Brighton 5-0 with Brian Stein netting a hat trick.

Ricky Hill was now playing at the very best level and was at the top of his form. He was rewarded when picked for the England squad by new boss Bobby Robson for the forthcoming international in Denmark. Ricky became the first full LTFC England cap since the 1950s days of Syd Owen and Ron Baynham.

There was no way I was missing out on this historic occasion. Mick Knight & I booked the trip, which entailed train from Luton to London, Liverpool Street to Harwich, then sailing from Harwich to Esbjerg, train to Copenhagen, 2 nights in a hotel, before the return journey. The boat voyage was brilliant. The cost of this trip was £41.60 (excluding hotel) return. England fans were on top form and we met a great bunch of Charlton lads who were complimentary of Steve White.

While we were on the boat, a bunch of West Ham ICF thugs were robbing items from cabins, including fellow England fans, to everyone's disgust. Copenhagen was a lovely city, though very expensive. I'm sorry to write, but England fans again rioted in a big way.

Ricky played as sub in the 2-2 draw - it was his first of only three England caps. A DISGRACE.

We arrived back in Luton on Friday, the next day I travelled to Stoke for another incredibly dramatic game. The Potters opened the scoring. Paul Walsh equalised but after scoring the goal, the Stoke keeper was bizarrely sent off for handling the ball outside his area - despite our goal standing! Stoke then led 2-1, before Brian Stein levelled again. 2-2 at h/t. Stoke took the lead for a third time & Luton equalised AGAIN, through Brian Stein. When Mal Donaghy put the Hatters 4-3 up and we led for the first time, we all thought that would be it. - OH NO! 7 mins from time Stoke made it 4-4 and the drama still had not ended. In injury time Luton were awarded a penalty. Alas, David Moss hit the post then the whistle blew for full time.

This is still, the only time to date I have ever witnessed a 4-4 draw live. Luton had played seven games in the top league and scored 20 goals – we seemed to be on television every week!

17,009 turned up for the next game against Man Utd. Future Hatter, Ashley Grimes gave the Reds the lead, Ricky Hill levelled & it stayed 1-1.

We then played Charlton at home in the League Cup 1st leg. I stood in the away end that night with my recently found friends from the Denmark trip. It wasn't to be a welcome return for Whitey, as we caned them 3-0.

On we travelled to St Andrews, Birmingham. After a goalless first half things livened up in the 2nd period. Stein, Walsh & Moss secured a 3-2 victory in front of only 13,772, which included quite a few from Luton.

Attendances were plummeting nationwide, crowd trouble was one of the key factors and things would get worse, before getting better.

We were now up to eighth, our apex for the season.

I attended Ricky Hill's England Wembley debut, a friendly against West Germany in which we lost 2-1. This was Ricky's only home cap he won one further cap, in Egypt.

We then drew 1-1 at home to Ipswich despite Alan Brazil's goal for Ipswich being blatantly offside. The linesman flagged, yet the Ref allowed it to stand. Then we met an old friend from Switzerland v England the previous year. He was a WBA fan, we called him Brummie Bob and we met him at the Hawthorns, but he went home the happier as the Baggies won 1-0.

At the 2nd leg of the League Cup, I spent an enjoyable evening with our Charlton mates. We drank in the Valley Club pre-match and Charlton won 2-0. Jake Findlay was sent off and in truth, we were a touch lucky to proceed to round 3. These two defeats were the beginning of a poor run of form, which would eventually lead to a relegation battle.

We had our third blank on the trot losing 2-0 at home to Nottm Forest. Arsenal, were our next visitors. After a blank first half, the Gunners scored two quick goals and I was beginning to wonder when we would ever score again.

Then a spirited fight back occurred, we came back to draw 2-2 with goals from Stein & Walsh.

In the League Cup, we had drawn 4th Division Blackpool at home. I arrived pissed straight from a great-uncle's funeral in Forest Gate, East London. We won 4-2. Billy Kellock scored twice, his only Luton career goals.

Another weekender arose. Puff, a Windsor Castle mate and I travelled by train for the Sunderland match. We left King's Cross Friday pm, the intention being to disembark at Newcastle, then stay at his girlfriend's in Sunderland. On the train we found ourselves involved in a card school. The both of us were doing so well and winning, that we decided to stay on the train to its terminal – Edinburgh!

After getting the train back, first thing Saturday, we arrived at her house for breakfast. Before the match at Roker Park I introduced him to my Mackem friends Harry and co in the New Derby pub near the ground. We watched as the Town nearly won it 1-0. Only a hotly disputed late Sunderland equaliser had stopped us achieving our first win in ages.

The following week I drove up to Coventry in my Mini. We lost 4-2 no great surprise there, as the Sky Blues were my jinx team, no doubt about that.

Leaving Highfield Road, I remember thinking how sluggish the car felt as we pulled away. I had put this down to the extreme weight in the car having Puff, big Steve Toyer (who let's say was on the rather large side) and myself. On the journey home we made good time, having not stopped once.

As we were about to exit Junction 11 on the M1 - I went to brake and nothing happened! "Lads," I shouted, "my brakes aren't working!" in a rather alarming tone.

"Put your hand brake on!" Steve roared.

Trying to apply this, I discovered to my horror - it was already on! It had transpired I had driven all the way from Coventry with the hand brake on. What happened next, can only be described as a miracle. As I changed down gears, making a horrendous noise, I shouted, "Get praying lads, if a car is coming round the corner - we are fucked!" I could not stop. Mercifully, it was clear as I swung around the corner, and I somehow managed to get it to a nearby garage.

On a very foggy day, Southampton came to town along with the TV cameras. We came back from 2-0 and 3-2 behind, to draw 3-3 with the Saints. Ricky Hill scored a blinder and that was my best memory of the game.

We had now slid down 10 places since our last victory at Birmingham.

In the League Cup, we were drawn away at Tottenham. It was a close game that either side might have won alas it was Spurs who did, 1-0.

Rain lashed Vetch Field in Swansea, was the next port of call. A thoroughly miserable day occurred, with one exception. We lost 2-0 and on the way home our Bobbers Coach broke down and we waited ages for the replacement to turn up. The exception to this bad day was prior to the breakdown when we stopped at the service station for a food break. I happened to be getting on VERY well with a lovely blonde girl (who shall remain nameless) and we decided to stay on the coach as the rest went and ate.

We were now in mid-December when at last, I cheered a Luton victory. Our first in fully 3 months, we beat Man City at home 3-1. It was at a cost though as post-match it was discovered that Brian Stein had broken a bone in his foot and would miss most of the remaining season.

The following weekend was my first trip to Goodison Park, Everton. On the Friday night, Chris McEvoy & I attended a Vauxhall works fancy dress party at the Rangers Club in Luton. Chris worked at Vauxhall and had arranged with some Scouse work colleagues for the two of us to stay in Birkenhead with them. It was for the Saturday night & return home Sunday. We set off early Saturday, with a severe hangover. On arrival in Birkenhead, we had a bite to eat and then got the 'Ferry cross the Mersey' to Liverpool. We had a great bit of banter with Everton fans in a pub just down the road by Goodison. I'm afraid that was as good as it got though, because Everton tore us apart winning 5-0 in front of only 14,982. This equalled the heaviest Luton defeat I had ever seen to date.

What the doctor ordered, was just the tonic we needed for our next game - Luton v Watford! For a change, Watford had brought a large support as they were in the higher realms in Div 1. A so far best of the season 21,145 attended. Some things would never change though and we beat Watford 1-0. Clive Goodyear getting the winner to send us into raptures. The next day we travelled to Norwich and saw the same 1-0 score, only to the Canaries.

On New Year's Day, my bogey team Coventry beat us at home 2-1. This was now the sixth time I had seen Luton play Coventry - the Sky Blues had won all SIX!

Three days later, it was the Luton of old. We watched a fantastic performance at Upton Park in the Paul Walsh show. Beating West Ham 3-2 with Walsh scoring all three goals.

In FA Cup 3, Fourth Division Peterborough were seen off comfortably 3-0. Tottenham were our next visitors in the league.

Due to the Falklands War in 1982, Spurs Argentine player Ossie Ardiles had been exiled in Paris. This was to be his first match on return to the UK.

A never to be beaten crowd at Kenilworth Road of 21,231, the largest league home attendance in 1982-83, watched an enthralling 1-1 draw.

The next weekend about 16 of us left the Sportsman to the south coast, for our match at Brighton. We arrived at our hotel in Hove on Friday night. After the usual SSS, we went out and had a brilliant night, ending in a club where we saw Brian Stein & David Moss in there. We knew Stein was injured but was surprised to see Mossy there, drinking too. He explained that he had a strain and wasn't playing. After the Friday session, we carried on in the hotel bar Saturday morning as more friends arrived. Freddie Dann, Magnet & his crowd joined us as we went to a pub next to the Goldstone Ground. The pub was mobbed with Luton fans and we were all in great spirits (half of us, still drunk from the previous night). Yours truly did the party piece, leaping on to the pool table and did a strip. I really don't know what made me do such crazy things in those days. We then watched a great 4-2 victory for Luton, with Albion scoring two own goals for us. Equally astonishing, was David Moss actually played - so much for the strain eh Mossy! I recently discovered direct from the legend himself, Mossy WAS genuinely injured - but the next day Mr Pleat pleaded with him to play! Otherwise David would never be clubbing it the night before a game.

In the FA Cup 4th round we had been drawn at home to Man Utd. No cup run I'm afraid, we lost 2-0. The 20,516 in attendance that day, was the last occasion over 20,000 attended Kenilworth Road.

Equally illustrious opposition followed with Liverpool's visit.

Brian Stein had returned after a long injury lay off and when he gave us the lead we had dreams of another classic, like at Anfield earlier in the season. The Reds equalised almost immediately, then took the lead and added another in the 2nd half to finish at 3-1.

Brian Stein was still struggling with his broken foot injury and despite his goal he would miss the rest of the campaign bar the final game.

To my joy, Steve White was signed on a month's loan from Charlton.

We went to Ipswich but lost 3-0. A score that if I'm honest, flattered us. A dull 0-0 draw followed at home to a dour WBA side.

Then a much needed boost by winning at Nottm Forest, Ricky Hill netting the only goal. It would be nearly 39 years - before we won at the City Ground again! Highbury followed and this day became a personal nightmare.

We travelled in a hired Luton box van. A huge drinking session occurred as we went to a pub on the outskirts of London for opening time, on top of the carry out in the van. I was very drunk and remember little of the match while standing in the open Clock End. Post-match, having lost the lads because of the state I was in, I headed for Arsenal tube station.

Still worse for the wear, I embarked on the tube and on the short journey to St Pancras, managed to get badly beaten up by a gang of Gooner thugs resulting in a good hiding, with two teeth knocked out. It would not be the first, or last time - of being in the wrong place at the wrong time! Luton lost 4-1 to Arsenal and this was Steve White's 83rd & final Luton performance.

The next week, another defeat followed, at home to Sunderland 3-1.

I had extremely expensive and I might add, painful dental treatment to get my new crowns sorted out before Easter and decided to keep a low profile.

Easter is not a good period generally for Luton, 1983 would be no exception. We lost our third match in a row at home to Norwich, 1-0.

After a cracking Sunday night out at Batchwood Hall in St Albans, we all left for the Easter Monday clash at Watford. In a blinding 1st half, they took the lead and then Trevor Aylott scored his first Luton goal. He was our latest signing as Stein was still injured and Whitey had returned to Charlton.

When Brian Horton gave us the lead we all thought great - joy again! But that was the Luton finale, Watford then levelled. After the break Antic was sent off and the foe went on to win 5-2. This was our first defeat to them in over 10 years and it hurt. At the end of that day they were 2nd (where they finished - to qualify for Europe!) and we were bottom.

We needed a boost and more importantly, a win.

European Champions Aston Villa came to town. Because of the recent poor form, less than 11,000 turned up. They missed a cracking ending. With the scores level at 1-1 in the last minute, we would have normally been happy to get a point but really needed to win. When David Moss settled it in injury time, you would have thought it was US who had won the European Cup such was the delight and noise from the Luton fans.

Buoyed by the Villa result, fellow Brummies Birmingham City visited us three nights later. A fantastic 3-1 Luton victory occurred and Ricky Hill was sublime. The first half performance by Luton was as good as anything I'd seen all season including Anfield, as we raced to a 3-0 lead.

We then travelled to Nottingham for the visit to Meadow Lane and drew 1-1. In the end we were grateful for a point. Notts County were one up until the dying seconds, then Mal Donaghy struck the equaliser.

We decided to stay in the City of girls that night. At one time, the ratio in Nottingham was six girls to every boy. I think it's down to 3 to 1 now. The hotel we stayed in near the station was a bit of a dive but it had a bed and was cheap, we had a cracking night. It wouldn't be the last time I stayed there.

The recent improved form continued when we beat Swansea 3-1 at home. Paul Walsh scored a hat trick and this sent the Welshmen to bottom of the table.

A well earned point at the Dell occurred next in a 2-2 draw with Southampton. With both Stein and now Walsh out injured, we battled to a hard fought 0-0 draw at home to Stoke.

This wasn't the only battle, as Luton and Stoke fans were involved in heavy fighting both pre, during and post-match. I must add, that while the fans were scrapping away in Beech Path, the alley behind the Bobbers Stand, we just sat drinking merrily oblivious in the Bobbers Club yards away.

The final home match of the season was against Everton. Knowing a win would ensure safety. Ricky Hill's early goal set us up nicely - then it all started to go terribly wrong! Everton scored two quick goals, you could feel the tension rise. Everton counter attacked at will and slaughtered us 5-1. This resulted in the Toffees achieving the double over us - 10-1! And the worst home defeat I had now ever witnessed. More importantly though, was that other results completely went against us and we had slipped from three places above safety to 2nd bottom. We had two remaining games left, both in Manchester.

My first visit to Old Trafford was two nights after the Everton debacle. The odds were stacked against us, we had never won at Old Trafford in our history (and still haven't) and the Red Devils were unbeaten at home all season. Paul Walsh raised our hopes by nearly scoring early on, but hit the bar. That was as good as it got for us. United won 3-0.

The last game of the season had a simple scenario. Brighton and Swansea were already relegated. We were 3rd from bottom with 46 points. Man City our opponents, were 1 point and one place above. If Luton won we were safe if not, we were down - simple as that!

That morning on May 14th, 18 of us set off to Maine Road in a Luton box van. It seemed like every other car that passed us was flying Luton colours.

We arrived quite early but on police advice, weren't allowed go to any local pubs. When we reached the ground we were allocated the same massive Kippax side terrace as City, obviously segregated. The police were astounded at the amount of Luton fans there, saying, "We were told there were 800 Luton fans coming." WRONG – We took 5,000! Boosting the attendance to a mammoth 42,843.

Easily the biggest crowd I had seen Luton play in at that point. Only the Manchester derby bettered that attendance all season.

The atmosphere & singing from Luton fans was simply magnificent, non-stop. It soon appeared that City were quite happy with 0-0, as that would indeed be enough for them. Five minutes remained and it was still goalless. I must admit I thought our efforts had been in vain, then Brian Stein, who had started only his second match of 1983 after breaking his foot, beat a couple of defenders at the far end of the pitch. He crossed a high ball into the area, the City goalkeeper Alex Williams flapped at it and punched the ball out of the area instead of catching it, which he could easily have done. The ball landed at the feet of our Yugoslav substitute Raddy Antic, he caught it perfectly with his right boot and somehow it passed through 2 or 3 defenders and Williams, into the top corner of the City net. Goallllllllllllllllllllllllllllllllllllllllllllllllllllllllllllllllllllllllllllllllllllllllllllllllllll Luton SCENESSSSSSSSSSSSS!

Pandemonium broke out, as us Hatters fans were going ape shit and erupted in joy.

The last few minutes seemed like 40 or 50, as City suddenly realised they were on the verge of being relegated. The final whistle blew and everyone knows what happened next. David Pleat in his beige summer suit and his beige summer shoes did that moronic dance across the Maine Road turf. We knew it was daft, we knew he looked stupid, but we LOVED him.

The past disagreements I had with Pleaty - were all over! Mr David Pleat I salute you, that day you gave me and countless other Luton fans, so much emotion and pleasure & a day to remember eternally. We were kept in the ground for ages for our own safety, but did not care one iota. Their fans invaded the pitch trying to attack the Luton team and then us. This was a huge event Man City were a BIG club, previous League and FA Cup winners, as well as a European trophy 13 years prior.

We were OK coming out of the ground and still on such a high, frankly carefree. We arrived back to the van safe, but the police refused to let us leave yet.

A gang of City fans came round the corner and started charging towards us. All I will write is that two Black gentlemen amongst us were in the van. They were JA & DP, two very good friends of mine from the Windsor Castle days and suffice to write, as anyone who knows them will testify, the City fans come off very much SECOND best. Leaving Manchester we had to go somewhere to celebrate naturally, I chose Blackpool, this was agreed 100%.

We arrived there and I had a word with a guesthouse lady owner. I smooth talked her into letting all 18 of us have a room for the night, guaranteeing that we were well behaved and just here to celebrate our survival. She agreed to take a chance on us. Of course there were no problems, we celebrated well into the night and some Man Utd fans on a stag party, were so pleased at us relegating City - they brought us a round of drinks!

It was the only time I ever saw us win at Maine Road, it's sadly been demolished and they now play in a nice new Eastlands Stadium. Of course today as I write, Man City are a stratosphere away from the likes of Luton (& most English clubs) with their magnitude of wealthy Arab Prince riches, and are far more successful now even than in their late 1960s era.

That never to be forgotten day in 1983 is up there as the No. 2 moment of my Luton Town supporting life.

We carried on celebrating the next day too, stopping at a pub in Stoke on the way home, not wanting the weekend to ever end.

The 1982-83 season was the first one that I attended every single home and away match (until the 2012-13/2015-16 seasons). I doubt I'll now ever add to these 3 campaigns.

I then went to Scotland for the Aberdeen 1 v Rangers 0 Scots Cup Final. Once more I travelled with the Rangers Club from Luton, catching the nightrider train from Euston on the Friday night. Commencing that journey I met a lovely looking blonde lass. I sat next to her for the whole journey and we got along so well - I ended up in a relationship with her for over 5 months! Her name was Jane Smith and she was returning home to Glasgow to stay at her Mum's for two weeks. She had an interesting job, as a children's nanny to the famous singer Gerry Rafferty, in Sussex. He was the Scottish singer of Baker Street and Stuck In The Middle With You fame. I must add, he refused to let me stay with Jane at his place, citing 'I'm having no Orange Bastard staying here' – and they call US the Bigots!

Jane came to stay with me frequently in that summer of 1983. We enjoyed many days and nights in London too, as I would see her off at Charing Cross.

Before I had met Jane, I wrote to Larry's dad Wally in the USA, asking him if his offer to stay there was still on. He wrote back replying, of course it was, 'just say when you want to come, book your flights and we'll make arrangements'. I did just that and booked my summer holiday to the States in the July of '83.

The itinerary was to fly to Detroit via New York City, spend two weeks at Wally's house, fly back to New York, stay at my cousin Bill Robert's for three nights and then fly home.

The weekend before I flew to Wally's, Jane and I had spent a very dirty weekend in Bournemouth.

Flying to America alone, did not bother me at all and I was excited. Wally and his wife Betty picked me up at Detroit Airport & with them was Lol's sister Cheryl, she lived in Luton & was staying at her Dad's for the summer. He lived in a small town called Grand Blanc, which was near Flint in Michigan. His house was incredible, a huge driveway, outdoor swimming pool, his own bar in the lounge and in the bedroom I was to stay in, was the first time I had ever seen, or slept in - a Waterbed! That holiday will live with me forever. Some of the stuff that occurred was mind blowing. It started on the very first night. After spending ages talking with Wally & Betty, they decided to call it a night. Cheryl and I were watching MTV and the drinks were flowing from Wally's bar. Then suddenly, she came over and started kissing me. "What are you doing? Wally's up there, imagine if he came down - and saw this!" I said. So she agreed to stop.

One night, we all went out for a meal. Now what you have to realise, is that most folk in Grand Blanc had never seen, or met English people in their lives. So I played on this, big time. Wherever I went I was the star of the show and loving it. Everyone kept saying, "I just love your accent."

We came home from a restaurant and I noticed there were lots of cars parked in Wally's driveway. "What's happening Wally?" I asked him.

"I've put on a little party for you," was his response. We entered through the back gate and in his garden, there were all these women in his swimming pool - NAKED!

Naturally, me being the reserved type yelled out - "I'll have some of that!" and stripped off to join in. What happened that night must remain private, but a tiny clue begins with O and ends in Y!

During this incredible holiday, I also met Larry's stepbrothers and sisters from Betty, Wally's second wife. One weekend, we all arranged to travel to Sandusky in Ohio. We stayed at a theme park called Cedar Point.

Betty's sons and daughters had brought a female friend along.

Time has faded the memory a touch and I'm sorry, but have forgotten her name. What I do remember is she was of Red Indian origin. What the Yanks today call a Native American. Needless to write, we got it together & - I added a squaw to my list!

Wally and I kept in touch for a while after, but I never saw him again. Sadly he has since died. RIP Wally and thanks for the memories.

I saw Cheryl again at her and Larry's Mum's funeral nearly 30 years later in March 2013. RIP Mary. Then would see her again in 2018 in even more tragic circumstances. Further details to follow in a later chapter.

I left Detroit bound for New York City, to stay with my cousin Billy. He is the eldest son of Mum's brother Bill.

Bill moved to the States in the late 70s to play Soccer. To my disgust, he had spells with W**ford and Wycombe Wanderers, but never made it as a pro. When his football career finished he decided to remain in USA, his English accent was a major selling point in his job as a typewriter sales man. He still lives in the States today, but now in Florida. I had a great time staying with Billy and his first wife. They lived in Long Beach, on Long Island. He took me to the Empire State Building. Being the Beatles fanatic that I am, the must see tourist spot I wanted to visit the most was Strawberry Fields. This is the memorial to John Lennon in Central Park. I also spent a poignant moment at the entrance to the Dakota Building, where Lennon lived and was shot dead by that maniac Chapman.

After I returned home, Jane quickly arranged to visit me the next weekend. I must admit, I did question my loyalty to Jane when in America.

I came to the conclusion that if I was with Sharon, I would never had even dreamed of looking at another woman, so therefore couldn't have loved Jane THAT much. But I saw no point in finishing. Truth is, I wouldn't have dreamt of going to the States had I been with Sharon still.

When Jane visited me she stayed in my room and I on the couch, so sometimes it was difficult for us to get it on but we managed. That first weekend after the States, so desperate for sex was Jane that we went out in my car to find an appropriate place. Because it was raining, there was no suitable venue. I was a key holder of the works premises, so that was there we went. Doing it - on the Bindery bench!

Although I would never say that I was madly in love with Jane, certainly not compared to Sharon, I did really like her. She was exceptionally pretty and the sex was great. Maybe I was just scared of getting hurt again like with Sharon and refused to let myself get too close to her. It's a pity, because looking back I think Jane and I would have been OK.

1983-84

After my mad brilliant summer holiday, I came back home to discover Granddad Adair had sunk into deep depression again. It would get worse, with him continually picking arguments and even fights with me. I knew he couldn't help it, it was an illness but I decided that I had had enough so I began to make plans of finally moving out of Applecroft Road.

Now aged 25 it was the right time to try and get into the property market. After various attempts I managed to locate a 2 bedroomed flat in a perfect location. Despite the high 10% interest rates at that time (0.1% today), I managed to secure a 100% mortgage. From initially looking in August and after all the legal documentation went through I managed to achieve a moving in date of December 9th. The flat was ideal for me, I bought it for £22,000.

It consisted of 2 bedrooms, lounge, bathroom, kitchen, garage and a perfect neighbour in Stopsley Working Men's Club - it was right next door!

The new season began with a trip to Highbury. Thankfully, there was no violent repeat of my last visit. 39,348 were there to see Arsenal win 2-1 in glorious sunshine. We had a new goalkeeper that day and he would become extremely popular with Luton fans, by the name of Les Sealey.

Another away match followed at Leicester. We comprehensively beat them at Filbert Street 3-0. Before the game, some Leicester thugs tried to have a go at us outside the double deck stand behind the goal. But once again we had DP with us, so they received the same outcome as the Man City louts did in May.

Before the season had started (actually it was just after the Man City epic), there had been a shocking major announcement by LTFC. The club were planning to leave Kenilworth Road, which was very much needed, to relocate to a new ground. The shock being that the site chosen was - MILTON KEYNES! This quite rightly provoked a furious reaction from Hatters supporters. How on earth could we be Luton Town playing in another town - in another county! A movement was immediately set up to protest at this, named 'Say NO to MK'. Some fans decided to boycott home games until this decision was reversed. Although after 9 years without missing a home match, I could not bring myself to be one of them. My personal view was that while Luton were in Luton, or at least within the boundaries of Luton, I would continue to follow us. But NO WAY would I, or anyone that I knew, go to MK. The campaign steadily grew. Perhaps this reflected in the attendance of less than 11,000 for the first home game v Sunderland. They missed a treat, as we won 4-1. This was followed by a visit from Norwich. The Canaries led 2-0 but we came back to draw 2-2, with Brian Stein hitting a screamer in the last minute.

I went to Man Utd by coach and as would ALWAYS be the case, we lost at Old Trafford, 2-0. We followed that with a home 4-0 thrashing of woeful Wolves. We then had a day out to Nottingham to see Luton play Forest. A vanload of us left The Sportsman and stopped at a pub on the outskirts of Nottingham en route, although the landlord was slightly sceptical on our arrival.

After having a great time in his pub with us being perfect guests and myself singing the Beatles masterpiece 'Yesterday', we left with him singing our praises. He told us we were welcome anytime and after giving his locals a really enjoyable time, we had restored his faith in football fans. A pity, that sentiment did not include some Forest fans. For as we arrived at the car park by the City Ground, we were attacked by local yobs outside the visiting fans turnstiles.

However, there were enough of us to ensure that we came off OK. In a tight match we lost 1-0.

The same score occurred when Aston Villa (and Tricky) paid us a visit. A David Moss penalty was enough, watched by the best crowd yet of 12,747.

In the League Cup we were drawn against Div 3 Rotherham. The 1st leg at Millmoor I couldn't attend, missing my first game in 18 months. Luton won 3-2.

John Ashton then drove us up to Goodison Park. We had comp tickets through John and sat at the back of their massive three tier stand. We beat Everton 1-0 and Paul Walsh scored. He was now our second modern England International. He also became the only post-war Luton player to ever score for England, in Australia, having toured there in the summer.

We made it three wins in a row, beating Southampton at home 3-1 to go 4th. The 2nd leg against Rotherham produced a shock. Despite a 3-2 lead from the 1st leg, we managed to get knocked out losing 2-0 AET, to exit 4-3 overall.

Three days later Jane and I went to Liverpool for a weekender to see Luton at Anfield. We checked in to the hotel on the Friday, did the necessary and then to my extra delight, visited the Beatles tourist sites. These included the fantastic Beatles museum by the River Mersey.

At the match, we sat in the Kemlyn Road stand instead of in the away fans Anfield Road terrace. There followed a feast of six goals, just the same as my last visit to this famous stadium. Unfortunately, instead of sharing the 6 goals as previous, Liverpool scored them all and Ian Rush - FIVE of them! This was now officially, my heaviest Luton defeat. When Rush scored his 5th, Jane rose & cheered mightily.

"What the fuck are you doing?" I asked, already extremely pissed off.

"That was a greet goal," she replied. We had a furious row and I took the huff. Naturally, back at the hotel, we kissed & made up and took the natural path.

The next day we took in the Anfield tour visiting the trophy room, the famous boot room and of course the tunnel where the sign 'This Is Anfield' is showing. After we had said our goodbyes at Charing Cross Station I don't know to this day why, but I wanted to end our relationship. I took the chicken's way out by sending a letter instead of phoning her. I explained with an element of bullshit, about how I still loved Sharon (even though over a year later, that was true) and that it was unfair to Jane, my feeling this way. I genuinely regret the cowardly way I ended things. Now without sounding boastful, she adored me.

I hope that she found happiness, as she was a decent person. I'm sure she has.

Whoever she ended up with is a lucky man. The following week we were away at QPR.

Our van driver Ted lived in London and was a Hoops fan. I arranged to go to the match with him and we sat together in the Luton end. To my delight and not his, we watched as Paul Elliott scored the only goal on the plastic pitch to make up a little for the Liverpool result.

Next was a 1-1 home draw v Birmingham. There was nothing in particular to remember, apart from before and after the game. Pre-match there was a huge anti-MK rally protest at Popes Meadow which I naturally attended. Post-match whilst in the Bobbers Club as usual, we heard an almighty bang outside. Upon looking to see what had occurred, a car containing Blue's supporters had overturned in the street behind the Bobbers. An ambulance was quickly on the scene and thankfully no one was seriously injured, Lord knows how. It transpired, that the Birmingham fans were fleeing from some Luton thugs, turned into this street but crashed the car in panic, as they realised it was a dead end.

Hooliganism never really bothered me that much, providing they just fought amongst themselves leaving normal innocent fans alone. Incidents like this were just a no for me.

Puff, Mick Knight and I then witnessed much more hooliganism when we travelled to Luxembourg to see England play in a Euro Qualifier. What we witnessed in the tiny duchy was beyond belief. We travelled by rail after having a drink en route in Brussels with no problems, as we entered Luxembourg there must have been every hooligan firm in England there that day. There were no Luxembourg fans to fight, so after England fans had looted the shops and caused mass vandalism, they started fighting the police. The local police couldn't cope - so they brought the Army in! In the ground such was their intent for trouble, the English started fighting with each other on a big scale. The London firms fighting their northern counterparts, it was sickening because this was no small minority. I estimate that of the 12,000 crowd, over half of them were thugs. After the match we actually managed to find a bar that would serve us, only for it to be wrecked within an hour. The hotels refused England fans accommodation later, so we just had to collect our bags with nowhere to stay and leave. There was no doubt this was the worst trouble I had witnessed with England.

Eventually, the Army and police rounded up the England fans and sent them out of the country in specially arranged trains. We were now the vermin of Europe. I recall not long after this, the Eurovision Song Contest was held in Luxembourg. When it was the British act Belle & the Devotions turn to perform you couldn't hear them, such was the booing and jeering from locals. England won 4-0 but were knocked out due to other results and therefore would not play in France 84. Because of our fans at that time - it was probably a godsend!

Our best attendance of 1983-84, 17,275 watched as Tottenham beat us 4-2. Then a very pleasing 2-1 win at the old enemy Watford, pushed us up to 5th. Bogey side Coventry carried on the jinx, winning 4-2 at Kenilworth Road. This was now 7/7 Sky Blue victories I had seen against Luton.

I missed my first league game in 21 months at Stoke, due to my flat move.

We won 4-2 with Paul Walsh scoring his 4th LTFC hat trick.

Town then played WBA at home on a Sunday in a bid to boost the gate. The boycott by some fans was still having an effect though, as only 11,566 watched us beat the Baggies 2-0. Not that good a crowd considering we had never been in the bottom half of the table thus far.

On Boxing Day, a fantastic 3-0 win at Notts County had moved Luton up to 3rd place. This was the highest league position we had been in since the mid-1950s. We were back down to 5th the next day as we lost 1-0 at home to West Ham. I sampled corporate hospitality for the first time that day when the sponsors invited the SWMC secretary and I as guests. From the main stand we watched Hammers fans fighting the Oak Roaders.

Because of the long journey and the fact that it was New Year's Eve, I missed our 2-0 defeat at Sunderland.

The first game of 1984 was at home to Nottm Forest. We had a new player making his debut, a Nigerian called Emeka Nwajiobi. He scored but we lost 3-2. In the FA Cup, we could not believe it as we were drawn at home with Watford. Meka Nwajiobi & Brian Stein gave us a 2-0 lead and we thought game over. But Watford came back to level matters, 2-2 was the final result.

The replay was the best game I ever saw at Vicarage Road. In the opposite to the first tie, Watford led 2-0 then a minute from the break Mal Donaghy pulled one back. When Barnes made it 3-1 we all thought we were out. But Luton came storming back. Paul Walsh scored twice to take the match into extra time. It really could have gone either way but Watford settled it with the final goal, 4-3. Both teams received a standing ovation off the pitch.

There was more trouble in the Oak Road when Arsenal undeservedly won 2-1. We then went to Villa Park, naturally with Mick Knight. After a rather tame 0-0 draw we had a night out in Birmingham with Tricky and his Villa mates. There were no problems involving us at all in the Windsor pub, a Villa stronghold.

Later that night though, Villa and Blues fans clashed as we watched on.

The TV cameras were present for our very first live screening at home to Man United. Unfortunately, it was a humiliating result and we lost 5-0. This was now my heaviest home defeat ever witnessed. The game was also the very first attended by a future work colleague and friend of mine, Pete Morris. What was that song title? – Things can only get better!

I missed the next match at the Dell through illness. The Sportsman boys stayed in Bognor Regis for the night, we lost 2-1 to Southampton.

During the week, England played a friendly against France in Paris. Both Paul Walsh and Brian Stein (his only cap) started. Neither had a good game and we lost 2-0. Once again England fans caused havoc. Fighting in the stadium, rampaging through the streets, overturning cars and mass vandalism.

Luton then drew 0-0 at home to QPR.

LTFC had won only once in 1984 and this was reflected in the size of the gate at our next home game v Ipswich.

Less than 9,000 attended, but we finally stopped the rot winning 2-1. Their neighbours Norwich, were our next port of call. If there is such a thing, this was quite an entertaining 0-0 draw.

On the way home with the Sportsman lads someone asked where we were going out that night. I suggested Dunstable for a change and that received a good response, so we ended up going to a wine bar, which was on the site of the old Aquarius nightclub. When we arrived I noticed two nice looking girls at the bar and naturally gave them the eye. Noticing I smoked, one of them (the tall one) asked me for a light. I responded with my Zippo lighter, which was like a flamethrower, nearly burning her face and we got chatting. It turned out they were sisters by the name of Debbie & Liz Gale. I actually fancied Liz, but it was the tall one Debbie, who seemed the most interested in me. 26 months later, that tall one - became my wife!

On the Tuesday night having the choice of my first date with Deb, or St Andrews to watch Luton at Birmingham, I'm afraid the Hatters lost (my support that is). While Luton were drawing 1-1, we were having our first date at the Vine pub.

We dated a few more times, then it seemed to fade for a while.

The 3rd home 0-0 draw out of the last four, was a dire game against Leicester. We then played at Ipswich and were very poor, heavily losing 3-0.

The same score applied, this time losing at home to Everton. A game that Brian Stein's younger brother Mark, made his debut in.

I was having a ball in my new flat. Every Sunday lunchtime the lads and I would go next door to the Club until closing time, then have a card school at my place, back in the Club at 7 until closing time, then down town to the Sun Do for a Chinese. The Sun Do restaurant was ran by a keen Luton fan, he often had Luton players dine there.

I went to Tottenham next with Wah, one of the Sportsman lads. He is actually a Millwall fan & joined me to see us lose 2-1 at my final away match of 1983-84. Mid-week was another defeat in London, this time 3-1 to West Ham.

The season was drawing to a close when Luton earned a needy win. In front of our lowest crowd of 1983-84 only 8,181, we beat Notts County 3-2.

The next night we went to Ronnelles nightclub to celebrate St George's Day. We all wore roses (something which I never failed to do then, even though I was half Scots and in a minority), entry that night was £5 with all drinks included.

Ronnelles was THE in place at the time & it was to be this night that I bumped into Debbie again. "Where have you been lately?" she asked.

"Well I never heard from you, so I assumed that was it," I replied. We got talking again and had a great night bopping away. After this, we met on a more regular basis.

The win against Notts County was our final victory of the season. What followed was hard to take, as for the very first time I saw us lose at home to Watford, 2-1. To make things worse, they went on to the FA Cup Final matching our achievement of 1959, something that we always held over them.

Raddy Antic scored his 10th and final Luton goal at Coventry in a 2-2 draw.

Typically, I missed the first time the Sky Blues had failed to beat us in my era. Raddy will forever have a place in Luton fans hearts after Maine Road. He tragically died in 2020 aged 71 of pancreatic cancer. Raddy went on to manage both Athletico & Real Madrid, as well as Barcelona - but he'll always be remembered by a generation of Hatters due to THAT goal in 1983. RIP Raddy.

We lost the final home game 1-0 to Stoke, a result that as good as made the Potters safe. Again as in the previous year, there was much trouble between Luton and Stoke fans, before, during and after the game.

The final match was at WBA, a 3-0 defeat in which five players played their last Luton games. Raddy Antic, Paul Walsh, Brian Horton, Trevor Aylott & Clive Goodyear. The first three named players, contributed in a huge way to LTFC. Bob Rumble and I again attended the Scotland v England game at Hampden Park. 1-1 was the result. This was my first visit to Kilsyth, staying at Jim & Sandra Moffat's house and I have returned back untold times since.

On the Monday train journey home (for which we had to bunk back, as our ticket ran out on the Sunday) we learned of some sad news. Eric Morecambe, ex-director and Luton's most famous fan, had tragically died. As a young boy of 11/12, I had the pleasure of meeting this wonderful man on one of the Luton football specials. Bring me Sunshine. RIP Eric.

Before my summer holiday Deb & I attended a pop festival at Wembley. We saw Big Country, Nick Kershaw, Kool & The Gang, & Wang Chung before the main act Elton John. Now I know he is a Watford git but I did like his music. Paul Young was also meant to be appearing, but had to pull out due to throat problems. There is a little piece of family history regarding him.

When we lived at Putteridge Road from 1968 to 1972, he lived around the corner from us in Selsey Drive, Stopsley.

He and my sister Ann actually dated each other for a while when they were aged 15. I remember him coming to our house with his guitar. I got to know him slightly better in the late 1970s when he was in a local band called Q Tips.

Paul had a minor hit called Toast, by Streetband and I remember chatting to him in the Luton nightclubs often. He became nationally famous in 1983 when he had a huge hit with the cover of Marvin Gaye's 'Where Ever I Lay My Hat' followed by a string of other hits in the 80s and he would also sing the first line in the Band Aid song for Africa 'Do They Know It's Christmas'.

My favourite memory of him though, was when he was really famous. One day I was waiting at a bus stop in Park Square. I heard this car hooting continuously and I thought 'Shut The Fuck Up', looked over to see it was Paul shouting - "Do you want a lift Alan, or what?"

Thirteen of us from The Sportsman, headed for the lads holiday to Ibiza as Deb came to the airport to see me off. This was a fantastic holiday, all of us in our 20s, young, free and single (well almost) with long hair and thin. We stayed in apartments at a place near Ibiza Town. The resort was actually quite small with just one main strip of bars and shops, a nightclub and beach of course. We met lots of good people. There were a crowd of girls from Scotland, Bury and a great set of lads from Lewisham who were all Millwall fans. We kept in touch with the Lions supporters for many years after this holiday.

Semi-Final Heartbreak

We started 1984-85 at home to Stoke, a repeat of the final home match from 83-84.

The first major change to the Kenilworth Road ground in 11 years was that the Enclosure had been seated with the total capacity now down to just below 19,000.

Once again there was crowd trouble against Stoke, but nowhere near the scale as on the previous two occasions. This time we won 2-0 only 8,626 turned up to watch 2 teams who would struggle that season, especially Stoke. The Potters would go on to win a total of just 3 League matches and finish bottom.

Two mates from the Bobbers Club, Willie Hood & Jimmy Oates took me to the first away game mid-week, at Ipswich. It was 1-1 David Moss scored a late equaliser.

The following Saturday I travelled alone to see us get thrashed 4-0 at WBA. For my season ticket 1984-85 I had returned to the Oak Road terrace and the next match was a closely fought 2-1 defeat by Liverpool, before returning four nights later with 8,656 other unfortunate souls to watch us draw 1-1 with Southampton in a dreadfully poor match.

There was no doubt at this early stage the squad at Luton was not good enough compared to 1983-84. The new signings were Andy Dibble a keeper who was OK, Ashley Grimes a full back, again OK & forward Steve Elliott - who was not!

Luton had no game the following Saturday, so two girls from Bury who we met in Ibiza, came to visit us for the weekend. They were Bill McKinley & Wah's friends more than mine. We all went with Mick Knight (+ the 2 girls) to support his Aston Villa team at Watford. A good game it was too, 3-3.

I had a lodger by now, but I could not stand him. He was a baldy paedo looking type of guy and I got rid of him after just a month. Sister Ann replaced him and that worked out well. Eventually Tricky took her place.

We then travelled to Nottm Forest and this was a match of two halves. We were by far the better team in the first period, but just could not score. In the 2nd Half Forest were all over us and won it 3-1.

The police made the next home game all ticket with an early kick off against Chelsea to avoid possible crowd trouble. It worked too, as 16,066 well behaved spectators watched a 0-0 draw.

In the League Cup I went to Orient on my own. A bit of history was made this night, as for the first time in English football the majority of a team were black players. Six players, Mitchell Thomas, Paul Elliott, Ricky Hill, Brian Stein, Vince Hilaire & Meka Nwajiobi played in the team that beat Orient 4-1.

We all then enjoyed a great day and night in London again on the Saturday.

The arrangement was to travel by train to see Luton play at Spurs and then meet up with the Millwall boys we met in Ibiza in the evening. We played really well at White Hart Lane despite losing 4-2.

We took the lead twice, only for Spurs to level twice. It was very even in the 2nd period until Tottenham scored twice late on. The long walk up to the tube station post-match was quite intimidating. Spurs fans were continuously trying to have a go at us but were thwarted by the police escort. We met the Millwall lads at their pub The Anchor, in Lewisham and they joined us, now a crowd of about 20 strong, to have a blinding night out at Catford Greyhound Stadium.

The following weekend was another memorable trip though not for football.

I missed the game at QPR as the lads from the Ibiza Summer holiday went on a SWMC coach trip to the Munich Beer Festival. We left early Friday morning with the biggest carry out imaginable. Sharing a coach with a Nottingham WMC, their eyes nearly popped out of their heads such was the amount of drink we took on board. The long journey actually went quite quickly such was the banter. I remember clearly, the beautiful scenery as we drove through Austria. When we reached our destination, a very pretty ski resort/village called Sol I was so drunk that I fell off the coach into the snow on arrival. Sol was simply stunning, so pretty. I have been to Austria twice since then and I think it's the quaintest, most scenic country I have ever visited. The next day we travelled across the border for the short journey to the Oktoberfest in Munich. This was a brilliant day, fantastic fun & obviously drinking lots of wonderful German Beer.

This was my first visit to Germany. I found that the German people were very hospitable and friendly in their own country - well they had been to us! At the festival I was being my usual bashful self, dancing on the tables in my England shirt and Union Jack SHORTS - in October! We met a crowd of Scots boys from Paisley. Any time I meet Scots folk it never takes me long to find out where their allegiances lie. I just tend to be naturally more warm to them if they are Bluenoses, as these guys were.

When we arrived back in Sol after the SSS it was back out to the clubs again.

The next day we were all delighted in finding out that Luton had won 3-2 at QPR ((the last time we won at Loftus Road as I write this in Nov 2021) and prepared for the grand finale last night out. I was sharing a room with Wah (the good looking Stopsley/Millwall lad) and that night we pulled a couple of girls from Cockermouth, Cumbria - I'll write no more!

We left on Monday after the most amazing time but the trip back was the journey from hell. After three days and nights of being on the piss everybody was suffering, this was my worst hangover yet - it felt like the longest coach journey ever! I have never travelled by coach such a distance since, or will again, in future. We arrived home Monday night and I went straight to bed.

Still a bit delicate the next night I watched Luton beat Orient 3-1 in the 2nd leg of the League Cup to succeed 7-2 on aggregate.

I was going away a lot around this time because I had borrowed a large loan from a finance company. I was earning OK money but because of the mortgage etc., I was always broke. I also felt that because of my apprenticeship, I had 5 years of earning peanuts and missed out a touch, so thought I was entitled to have a bit more fun while I was still young enough.

The one sensible thing I did invest in, was a better car. I traded in the Mini and splashed out £1,100 on a Vauxhall 1.6 Cavalier, just a shame about the colour (Brown).

We then lost at home 2-1 to Sheff Wed. This now meant we had only won twice after 10 games and were just one place above the relegation zone. A very welcome 3 points occurred, when we beat the team two places above us. Steve Elliott scored twice and what made it even sweeter was the team we beat were Watford. He only scored 3 LTFC league goals, so these were appreciated.

With my recently acquired wealth I splashed out a bit again to do a spot of ground hopping. On the Wednesday I drove to Peterborough with Keith McEvoy, to see them beat Halifax 2-0. Two days later I travelled from King's Cross to Doncaster. I watched a cracking game at Belle Vue against Plymouth. Argyle had two players with Luton connections. Les Sealey in goal, on loan from us and Clive Goodyear from our 1981-82 title winning squad. Rovers won 4-3 and this was the time I had met Billy Bremner in the Donny Supporters Club after the match, which you have already read about. After a good few in that club I went back to the hotel to sleep and prepare for Saturday.

The next morning I headed to Doncaster station and travelled north for Luton's game at Sunderland. I met a Sunderland fan on the train and we got chatting. He recommended a place to visit pre-match assuring me that I would be OK, called the Barbary Coast Club. He wasn't wrong, it was a cracking place, especially with the strippers on at lunchtime. I then went to meet up with my old Sunderland pal Harry and his chums in the New Derby pub next to Roker Park. An extremely poor showing from Luton, led to a 3-0 defeat.

It was then onwards to Newcastle for a prearranged meet up with Mick Knight. His Villa team had been playing at St James' Park and the prior arrangement was to meet at the station then get the train to Glasgow, via Edinburgh. Mick had met an Edinburgh girl in Ibiza that summer and she joined up with us in Auld Reekie. We travelled to Glasgow, before going to the Glasgow Central Hotel that we had pre-booked.

We met some other Ibiza friends from the holiday that night and spent the evening chatting away into the early hours, reminiscing about the wonderful time we had in Ibiza three months prior.

The real reason we were in Glasgow was because Rangers were playing Dundee United in the Scots League Cup Final on Sunday. Tricky followed Rangers like myself, although he had no Scots links. He was another friend for whom I would be responsible for him meeting his future wife just like I had with Steve White, but that's for later.

In the street leading up to Hampden, we were walking to the entrance when I heard a big shout, "Alan! Ya big Sassanach Luton bassa." Behind me were the Paisley boys we had met in Munich three weeks earlier. Amazing, there were 44,698 at the Cup Final - and we bumped into these guys in the street! After hugs we entered the ground and to our joy saw Rangers lift the cup 1-0.

I had taken off the Monday as a holiday and the next night saw my 5th game in seven nights when Leicester visited in the League Cup. We won 3-1 but at a heavy price. Paul Elliott our centre half, broke his leg and would miss the rest of 1984-85.

We were at home again on the Saturday to Newcastle (drew 2-2). Making his debut for us was ex-England international Colin Todd. It was one of only 2 League games he played for us, this and the next week at Norwich.

I didn't go to Carrow Road, the 1st of three successive away games. We lost 3-0 at Norwich. The reason I was not there was because Deb and I were away on a SWMC weekend outing in Brighton. We stayed at the Butlins hotel.

Although we were by far the youngest couple, the crowd of friends joining us, were brilliant company. It was basically the same couples I went to Scotland with a couple of years earlier + other couples such as Trevor & Jenny Smith and Pat & Jack Gales. Deb and I even won the Mr & Mrs competition, even though we had only been dating 6 months or so. I was now beginning to settle down with Deb more seriously and my feelings for her were definitely growing stronger.

The next weekend I saw our ritual defeat at Old Trafford, losing 2-0 to Man Utd. Mid-week, came the 4th round League Cup tie at Sheff Wed. I wasn't going to go as I had taken a fair bit of time of work lately but when Malcolm Yaxley (the maniac driver) offered to take me straight from work I knew we would make it in time. We even made time to have a drink in the pub by the Sheffield exit on the M1 before entering Hillsborough. I'll never forget the referee from that night, a tosser by the name of Fitzharris. He awarded the Owls THREE penalties and the worst of it was - that NONE of them were valid! It is the only football match I have witnessed that a player has scored a hat trick from the spot. We were 4-0 down, before Steve Elliott scored his final 2 goals for Luton.

Our next game at home to West Ham was a 2-2 draw this result had left us 2nd from bottom.

It was blatantly obvious that the squad needed strengthening. Our chairman at the time David Evans put his hand in his pocket and gave David Pleat money for new signings. Mr Evans would go on to be a controversial chairman and personally, I felt he used our football club for political means, eventually becoming a Tory MP for Welwyn Garden City. His future policies at Luton would make us one of the most unpopular clubs in the country, but that is for later.

What I will give him credit for though, was making these funds available at the right time. If he hadn't we would have certainly been relegated.

The first of four new vital signings was signed in time to play in our next match at Highbury. I went on my own to this game standing on Arsenal's home North Bank terrace. Steve Foster the ex-England centre half, was signed for just £75,000 from Aston Villa.

This transfer was one of Pleat's best signings (and he made many great ones). Although we lost to the Gunners 3-1 Fozzie became one of our best, if not THE finest ever Luton captain in my time. Another new signing made his debut next, at home to Aston Villa.

Only 7,696 watched him score the only goal of the game. He was to become one of the most popular Luton players of all time, even having a stand named after him some 23 years later. His name was David Preece, little by size - immense in heart and ability!

The third signing made his debut the following week at Filbert Street. A name some of you may have heard of - Mick Harford! I went up to Leicester with my boss Dave Kitching, who supported the Foxes and our works manager, who was to become one of my best friends, Gary Hopkins. We sat in the Double Decker stand behind the goal. Mick Harford soon made his mark setting up Brian Stein for the opening goal. To Dave's joy Leicester came back and led 2-1 before the big man made it 2-2 in the last minute. A fair result, in what was an entertaining game. Mick Harford would quickly become a Luton legend, a record signing at £250,000 he would be worth every penny paid and more. He was one of the best strikers in the club's history and would have a total of four spells at the club, twice as a player, once as a coach and twice as manager (inc a caretaker role).

The last game before Xmas was on a Friday night at home to WBA. We lost 2-1 but as I had come straight from my work's Xmas party absolutely slaughtered with drink, the result is my only recollection. This game was watched by the lowest attendance of the season 7,286.

On Boxing Day, we were at home to Coventry. Now even though my record was a 0% total from seven matches against the Sky Blues, I persuaded the SWMC crowd to join me for the match.

It must have worked, the lads brought a change of fortune as we beat Coventry 2-0 and were temporarily out of the relegation places.

Three days later I decided to take Deb to her first football match. We were away to Liverpool and the plan was for Deb to drive us to Milton Keynes station, get the train to Lime Street then return on the last train home. We left early to enable us to visit my favourite Beatle haunts, before heading to Anfield. Pre-match, we went to the pub behind the Kop called the Park. The minute we walked in everyone knew we were from Luton - because we were the only two people not decked out in red! The Liverpool fans were terrific and very welcoming, we got chatting to a group who asked us to come back in after the game. The friendliness of the locals obviously hadn't changed from my Kop visit two years earlier. We lost 1-0 in a rather dull game and headed back to the Park. The crowd we had met before were genuinely pleased to see us again. We sank a few and they asked us what our plans were. On telling them none but we had to get the last train, they insisted on giving us a night out. From there we headed to the Liverpool Supporters Club, then to the City centre. The ale was flowing but because Deb had to drive later, she was on soft drinks. Then one of them suggested we stay at his Granddad's vacant house, as he was away. Deb was astounded, saying, "But we don't even know you." We drank the night away, the lad came back in the taxi, opened his Granddad's house and we stayed the night. He even left the keys with us, then came back Sunday - to make brekkie!

We travelled back Sunday and Deb was mesmerised by what had happened, telling her family and friends about it for weeks on end.

We really should have stayed in Liverpool, as Luton was due to be back playing just two days later at Everton. But Deb wanted to be home for New Year's Eve. I drove Keith McEvoy up to Goodison Park. We lost 2-1, but to be honest that score line flattered us a little, Everton were superb and the rejuvenated Toffees eventually went on to win the league for the first time since 1970.

In the FA Cup 3rd Round we had been drawn to play Stoke at home. The two lowest teams in the table, the Potters being bottom. On a freezing cold wintry day Stoke took the lead late on and we thought we were out. Fortunately, Steve Foster scored after this to force a replay. I did not go to the Victoria Ground such was the amount of snow, plus I thought there was no chance of the match surviving. But indeed, it did and we won 3-2. Because of the bad weather, we didn't play again for 17 days.

The 4th round of the FA Cup was next and we comfortably beat 2nd Division Huddersfield 2-0 at home. This was the first time I ever saw us play the Terriers.

The last of the four new signings was Peter Nicholas, a tough tackling Welsh International signed from Crystal Palace.

This was the final piece of the jigsaw and those 4 transfers made a huge difference to the team. He made his debut in the next game at home to Tottenham. The biggest league crowd of the season 17,511 witnessed a thrilling 2-2 draw. Even better, was the fabulous news announced that the move to MK was now officially finally shelved by LTFC.

Again, due to the bad weather, it was a further 3 weeks before playing once more. I missed a 1-0 defeat at Newcastle. The reason for this was that I was now suffering problems with my knees again, especially the left one. Our next match was at home to their neighbours Sunderland. We met Harry and Co in the Bobbers Club again and they were in fine form for their forthcoming League Cup final v Norwich (which they lost 1-0). Sadly, this was the final time I saw Harry. Sunderland, were to be relegated in 84-85 and by the time we played them again 5 years later, he had passed away. He was a lovely old boy. RIP Harry.

That day we had a sorely needed victory when Mick Harford & Ricky Hill scored in a 2-1 win. Two nights later was the FA Cup 5th round. In a repeat of last season, it was the enemy Watford at home again. We were up for revenge.

18,506 squeezed in to watch a stalemate 0-0. This crowd has never been bettered at Kenilworth Road since.

The draw had already been made for the Quarter-Final because of the backlog of matches the weather had created. So we already knew that the winners would be at home to Millwall. One vivid memory of that night was as we queued to get in the Oak Road. I remember remarking to someone, "It won't be this calm if we get through to play Millwall." – That proved to be the understatement of the century!

Two nights later it was off to Vicarage Road for the replay despite my knees now giving me real jip. On 76 minutes we were 2-0 down and heading out of the cup.

Us Luton fans were now a bit quiet, when suddenly Meka Nwajiobi scored and we were back in the tie. Ricky Hill then sent Luton fans into raptures when he levelled matters. The final whistle blew and 30 minutes of extra time could not produce a winner. At the end, a toss of a coin was to decide at which venue would hold the 2nd replay (no penalties in those days) we went ballistic when it was announced – Kenilworth Road! We and I think secretly even Watford fans KNEW who would finally go through. When I returned home from Watford my knees were in such pain, I did not make it to work the next day. On the Thursday night the pain worsened, such was my agony, Ann had to call the doctor out. When he arrived I was now screaming with pain, he gave me a tiny tablet (Lord knows what) and I was out cold in minutes. I went to the hospital on the Friday morning and they kept me in. They did all sorts of scans, tests etc. for them to diagnose that I was suffering from Rheumatoid Arthritis.

They said that this was a condition that would come and go but would get worse with age. I had to stay overnight and they wanted to monitor me over the weekend. NO WAY was I missing the Watford game, so I discharged myself and headed straight to the ground. I was not that daft to stand on the terrace so bought my seat ticket in the Bobbers Stand. We achieved the result all Hatters fans had craved for, winning 1-0. Wayne Turner scored it, one of his only three LTFC goals, but by far his most important.

The next game occurred that no Hatters fan would ever forget Luton v Millwall in the FA Cup 6th round. This was my first Quarter-Final involving Luton as I was in Adelaide the only other time in my era that we had reached that stage. Now one thing I would like to put to bed once and for all about the shocking violence that occurred on the night, is this popular conception that all kinds of London hooligan/firms were united together.

This is TOTAL AND UTTER BULLSHIT. – As if the likes of Millwall and West Ham would ever join up!

Our Millwall mates we met in Ibiza had rung the day before the game to warn us. "Alan, please be careful EVERY Millwall face known is coming, some have not been on the scene for years and they are coming early to wreck everyone and everything in their way." This was after all, Millwall's biggest match in over 25 years.

I knew as soon as I had stepped off the bus outside the Odeon in Dunstable Road this was a different atmosphere to usual. It was early, but the area even then was heaving with fans. No one had colours on and I did not recognise a single face. I went to the Bobbers

Club. Once inside there I felt safer and was hearing all sorts of things about how Millwall fans had completely taken over the town centre, having arrived from early morning. Baggy was in the Bobbers with his Strawplaiters lads and even HE, was a little edgy. I decided to watch the match with him, knowing that he would NEVER back down - against any odds! We went in the Oak Road and Millwall had invaded the pitch 3 times before kickoff trying to take the Oak Road end, throwing pool balls amongst all sorts of objects.

It was only the high fences and hundreds of police that thwarted them. Baggy had decided it was time to leave the Oak Road and persuaded a steward to let us into the Bobbers. We went back into the Club and decided to all keep together as one unit and sit in the Bobbers Stand. Now this was a pretty handy mob in there, from the Strawplaiters. The Plaiters was a pub in Ashcroft Road that had a large number of locals who lived in Tin Town, a particularly tough part of Stopsley.

The Kenilworth end terrace held 8,000 at the time, but judging by the number of Lions fans in there, I would estimate more like 12,000 were packed in.

It transpired, Millwall fans smashed down a gate and many had gained free entry. After about 40 minutes of mayhem, the game finally kicked off just before 8.30.

Brian Stein scored after 30 minutes and onto the pitch they came again. After their manager George Graham pleaded with them to leave, a number of them came in the Bobbers stand near us. They were also in the Maple and Main Stand. Fights were breaking out everywhere, it seemed as soon as one had stopped, another started in another part of the ground. I have to write though, the Millwall near us, were definitely coming off worse (well we did have JA & Baggy). I hasten to add, that with my acute knee problems I was in no position to fight so I just concentrated on shielding and protecting an OAP in the seat next to me. I had actually heard one of the Millwall boys screaming to his mate, "Go and get some reinforcements, we are taking a bit of a battering from this little Luton firm here." I can definitely confirm to all - it was about the only part of the ground that they were!

Half-time arrived, we went back in the bar and this was literally, the only Millwall free area remaining. We eventually won 1-0. After the final whistle went was when the worst trouble occurred. On the pitch after the final pitch invasion, the police and their dogs were now hopelessly outnumbered and fled for their lives from the Millwall louts. They had now also started to wreck the ground, the Bobbers Stand in particular, literally ripping out seats and using them as weapons against the police and anyone else in their way. This was now anarchy, the worst football violence EVER seen in a stadium in the UK. We managed to scramble in the Bobbers Bar underneath the stand with one fleeing policeman ordering us to lock the door and barricade ourselves in.

One wise wag from the Plaiters shouted, "We'll keep the bar open then?" bearing in mind it had now got to near closing time.

The copper's response, "I don't give a fuck, that's the least of my worries compared to what's happening outside." We kept him to his word and it was well past midnight before the police eventually allowed us to leave.

Millwall fans had caused hundreds of thousands of pounds damage to the ground and property in nearby Bury Park. This was football violence totally spiralling out of control and I'm afraid, the problem was to get even worse. A week or so prior, Chelsea fans had rioted at home to Sunderland.

After the Millwall disgrace, another London team QPR visited the Kenny. Mick Harford scored both goals as we beat the Hoops 2-0.

The next day we queued up with the hordes for the forthcoming Semi-Final at Villa Park against Everton.

Two nights later we were at home to Ipswich.

In a fairly one sided opening it was no surprise when Ipswich took the lead. Mick Harford levelled and then Meka Nwajiobi gave us the lead. Another from big Mick gave us three vital points in a 3-1 win.

I missed the next game, a 1-0 loss at Southampton.

It was time to take Deb again and I drove us up to Stoke. In front of only 6,951 we thrashed woeful Stoke 4-0. The Potters were truly awful and I remember saying to Deb, "Did you enjoy that, better than Liverpool eh?"

Her reply was, "Not really, it was a bit boring, too one sided."

It was the week before the eagerly awaited Semi-Final.

I had organised a 52 seater coach from the Sportsman for Villa Park. Everyone wore colours, a bit of a rarity, as scarves etc. had gone out of fashion by the 80s. Luton had sold out our allocation of over 18,000 tickets against Everton. Mick Knight had arranged a pub in Birmingham pre-match. Food was laid on and we mingled fine with locals and Evertonians in the pub, such was the pleasant atmosphere. We went off to the match and what a game it was. Luton played absolutely brilliant against a side who at that time were one of the best in Europe, certainly the best in England. There was only one team in the game in the 1st half though and that was the Hatters. Ricky Hill scored a cracking goal at the Holte end where we were standing to give us a fully merited interval lead. In honest truth, 3-0 would be a fairer reflection of the score such was Luton's quality dominance. In the 2nd half it was more of the same but as time ticked by I felt one goal was not enough, Everton were top of the league for a reason.

Everybody was dreaming of Wembley and we were counting down the minutes when with just four left, the referee blew for an Everton free kick. The ref was John Martin and he gave the foul against Micky Harford on the edge of the Everton area, when it should have actually - been a free kick to US! The expert free kick taker for Everton, Kevin Sheedy, lined up to take the kick.

He cruelly bent it around Les Sealey and it seemed to take an eternity to hit the back of the net. The Everton fans went absolutely ballistic. If you were to ask any Everton fan there that day, we had honestly played them off the park. It went into extra time. The Toffees fans were buoyant having got out of jail and the extra time period was more even. But just as we thought we had done enough to return to Villa Park for a replay, Mountfield headed in the winner for Everton on 115 minutes.

Nothing previously, or rarely since, had compared to my feelings of utter despair at the result of a football match. Grown men were weeping such was the devastation. If anyone had said to me after that match, "Never mind, it's only a game of football," I think I might have strangled that person!

Every Luton fan felt the hurt, we went back to the coach and not a single one of us wanted to go back to the pub in Birmingham, despite plans that were laid on. We headed home to Luton to drown our sorrows. But after just one pint in the Vine, I sulked off home.

Three nights later, was a vital home game against Norwich. A very subdued crowd of

8,794 (where were the other 10,000?) were still nursing the cup hangover. We fell behind to a goal in the 1st half then a very spirited 2nd half performance followed. When Meka Nwajiobi equalised, the crowd were lifted and now on song. We roared our approval as David Moss gave us the lead with a penalty and then Meka added his second to give us a needy 3-1 win.

On the following Sunday we were at home to Man Utd. A shockingly poor crowd of only 10,320 attended. In fairness, not many travelled from Torquay - I mean Manchester!

When Mick Harford gave us a penalty lead, I thought I was about to witness my first ever victory against the Red Devils. Alas, Whiteside levelled minutes later in front of the live ITV cameras.

Then, a minute from time Luton won a free kick. Steve Foster hit the bar and Mick Harford leapt to head home the rebound and therefore, winner. The scenes of joy were in total opposite to just eight days previous. This result meant two things, we were now out of the bottom three for only the 2nd time since November and I had now seen Luton beat - EVERY single Div 1 team!

The following Wednesday, the opposite score occurred. Our 3rd home game in a row was against Nottm Forest. They took the lead, David Moss scored his 94th and final LTFC goal to equalise and Forest won it in the final minute this time.

I took Deb to London to see her Nan in Wanstead and we then went to see Luton play West Ham at nearby Upton Park. We watched a grim 0-0 draw but strangely, she said she enjoyed it - saying it was a good game!

The next Saturday was an early kick off at home to Arsenal. We won easily. Luton led 3-0 before the Gunners hit a consolation penalty.

It was then back to Villa Park, scene of our heartbreak just three weeks prior. Only instead of 45,289 (the biggest crowd I'd now seen Luton play in front of) there were 14,130 this time against Tricky's team. Again, I took Deb. A lone Brian Stein goal was enough to give Luton the three points and almost certain safety. When I asked Deb how did she like this game, she responded, "Great, I think I have even got a tan." After that lovely sunny day - I never took her to another match! (Apart from briefly when Georgina was mascot v Wycombe in 1999.)

I gave the Chelsea away game a miss and we lost 2-0.

Saturday 11th May 1985 was another sad day for football. We were at home to Leicester and again, Dave Kitching & Gary Hopkins joined me. Much to Dave's displeasure Luton turned on the class and we crushed the Foxes 4-0. When we went in the Bobbers Club after the game, everyone was in stunned silence and glued to the TV screen. The scenes we were all witnessing were horrific.

There was a fire occurring at the Valley Parade home of Bradford City, before our very eyes. City had already been promoted from Div 4 and were playing Lincoln in the last game.

Over 10,000 were there to celebrate the party, their biggest crowd in years.

It transpired, that a lit match or discarded cigarette was dropped through the wooden floor in the old wooden stand. A few minutes later, flames were spotted and then suddenly, the roof caught fire and the whole stand was ablaze. 56 people tragically lost their lives and were burnt to death, with over 200 more people suffering horrific burn injuries. The tragic thing was, that apart from the loss of life obviously, the stand was due to close and be demolished after this game ready to be replaced by a new one being built for 1985-86.

This disaster was to change football stadiums dramatically, just as the Ibrox tragedy 14 years earlier had. All sorts of new safety rules and regulations were to be introduced and many grounds had their stands condemned or closed. One saving grace from the Bradford fire was that mercifully, there were no fences erected in front of that stand. If there were - the fatalities would have been tenfold! RIP the 56 victims (including 2 Lincoln fans).

Unfortunately, it would take another appalling tragedy four years later to happen before the safety of spectators would truly became paramount.

On the same day as Bradford, a serious riot had occurred at St Andrews between Birmingham and Leeds. Such was the ferocity of the fighting it led to a 15-year-old Leeds fan being crushed to death when a brick wall collapsed on top of him. It was only the severity of Bradford, which kept the riot off the front pages. This was indeed a tragic day - only for matters to get even WORSE 18 days later!

Five days after the fire, a benefit match was quickly arranged between Chelsea and Glasgow Rangers, with all proceeds going to the fire victims' families. I went to cheer on Rangers at Stamford Bridge for this good cause, Rangers having experienced their own personal grief in the past. With my Luton/Rangers ski hat on, I was astounded at the amount of Gers fans from Scotland there and indeed so were the Chelsea fans. This match was at a time when Chelsea fans were notorious hooligans, having a firm called The Headhunters. I was slightly concerned and hoped there would be no trouble, bearing in mind the reason for this match. I already knew what Rangers fans stood for and what they are all about. When we started our usual repertoire of songs like God Save the Queen, Rule Britannia and We Hate The IRA etc, the Chelsea fans in the Shed were dumbfounded and started to applaud us wildly. As we came out of the exits after the match, far from fearing trouble, the Chelsea lads were embracing us Rangers fans, singing 'We All Agree Chelsea & Rangers Are Magic'.

This was the very beginning of a bond with Chelsea and Rangers fans called the Blues brothers (along with Linfield in Belfast) that is still relevant today.

The score incidentally was 3-2 to Chelsea, not that it mattered one iota.

I decided not to go to the last away game at Coventry. This was a crucial game for the Sky Blues, they simply had to win this as well as their final game, or else they were down. On 83 minutes Coventry scored the only goal and they were also successful in that last match. This meant that Norwich were relegated instead of the Sky Blues.

Our final match was at home to Everton. Even though they fielded a weakened team, due to already winning the title and 2 Cup Finals on the horizon.

I desperately wanted to beat them to make up in a very tiny way, the heartache of the recent semi-final. We won 2-0. David Moss came on as a sub to make his 245th and final Luton appearance. He was quite rightly, given a standing ovation for his seven years of service with distinction. In my opinion, he was the best crosser of a ball in all my time as a Luton fan. Mossy scored 94 Hatters goals, an incredible amount for a winger - even two more than another legend, striker Mick Harford. David currently stands as the 7th highest all-time LTFC goalscorer. I'm proud to write that we are also good friends on Facebook.

Luton's season was over, very much a roller coaster of a ride. Some huge highs: Surviving relegation, beating Watford & the FA Cup run and some major lows, the semi-final defeat, plus the horrible violent Millwall night.

Man Utd beat our victors Everton in the FA Cup Final 1-0.

On the 29th May 1985 occurred another night of football shame.

Liverpool had reached their 5th European Cup Final against Juventus to be played at the Heysel Stadium in Brussels. The previous year, the Reds had won it in Rome beating the home team Roma on penalties. After the game Liverpool fans were viciously attacked and beaten by Italian fans, with police doing little to protect them. Any Liverpool fan was a target. Hooligans, normal supporters, even women. There were many stabbings and serious injuries to Reds supporters. I knew, like anyone else, that there would be trouble that night in Brussels. I watched on live TV from my flat as pre-match, Liverpool fans attacked the Juve fans in an area that was supposed to be for the neutrals. When the trouble was getting out of hand as Liverpool fans made repeated charges, a wall collapsed. Resulting in 39 Italian fans being crushed to death and scores injured. The start of the game was delayed for ages amid the utter chaos. The match eventually began, much later on. It is not for me to comment but I believe this game should never have started, how on earth could any players play a game of football - knowing that people had DIED! UEFA bottled it by insisting it to go ahead, as they feared it would be worse outside if the match were cancelled. The game finally finished around midnight, with Juventus winning 1-0 from a dubious penalty. But frankly, no one cared. The celebrations from the Juventus team after the game - were disgusting! Their fans had fucking DIED. The team should have gone straight up the tunnel after receiving the meaningless trophy.

This was the classic case of Football Hooliganism reaching its peak and going too far, to say the least. Things would never be the same again.

English football was at its lowest point and our fans were despised worldwide. The fans were staying away in their droves and this disaster could possibly have finished football, as we knew it. Maggie Thatcher the Prime Minister, hated us football fans and was trying to introduce all sorts of legislation to curb this, like membership cards etc. English football clubs were to be banned from European competitions for 5 years, with Liverpool to serve an extra two years on top of that. We were now the pariahs of the world.

While Heysel was happening, the Sportsman lads were in Holland playing a football tournament. The night after the match they were in a pub, when a Dutchman asked Mick Knight, "So what did you think of that disgrace last night then?"

Tricky replied very straight faced, "Well I didn't think it was a penalty."

The Nederlander just sighed, "English," & left. But I agree with Mick - it wasn't! On June 29th Deb & I got engaged and held a big party at the Rangers Club in Luton.

July 13th 1985. While the rest of the universe were rocking all over the world to the sounds of Live Aid at Wembley - Deb joined myself & a coach load from the Rangers Club in Luton, to Corby Rangers Supporters Club for a Sashbash!

The Luton Supporters Special Train. Started in 1969 and
very cheap travel, this pic is of Hatters fans going to Plymouth for £1.5 shillings (£1.25)
return! The first one was to Sheffield United and my Dad was on it.
I was on the final special to Man City in 1974.

Deb and I bopping away at our 1985 Engagement party in the Rangers Club.

Marriage

Our Summer Holiday was in the resort of Lagos in the Portuguese Algarve. Deb and Keith McEvoy's girl Jane were the only two females among a whole crowd of Sportsman lads. We had a ball in the fabulous Golfino Hotel.

LTFC became the 2nd professional team to install an artificial playing surface four years after QPR had and were about to celebrate Luton's centenary year. I changed my season ticket back to the Bobbers Stand.

The first game of 1985-86 was on our new surface against Nottm Forest. Brian Stein made history, scoring the first goal on the Luton plastic in a 1-1 draw.

The first away game was at Newcastle. St James' Park was too far to travel midweek due to work I therefore missed seeing a 2-2 draw.

I travelled alone to Upton Park to see Luton's first win. A Mick Harford penalty was enough to see off West Ham.

A poor crowd of only 10,012 then watched Luton v Arsenal. We led twice through Nwajiobi & Brian Stein, but an own goal from Mal Donaghy and then Woodcock for the Gunners, gave them a point.

We suffered our first 1985-86 loss at Aston Villa, losing 3-1. An example of the reaction to Heysel was an attendance of just 10,524 at Villa Park.

Yet another draw followed, 1-1 at home to Chelsea. We then lost at the Champions Everton 2-0. At last, we achieved our first home win when two headed goals by Harford & Foster, secured a 2-0 victory against QPR. Following on from this was 2 trips to Sheffield.

The first was at Sheff Utd in the League Cup, where we beat the Blades 2-1. Then our third successive away defeat was at Hillsborough, losing 3-2 to Sheff Wed.

After beating Ipswich at home in a narrow 1-0 win, we had played 10 games and sat in 14th place. Man Utd were the next visitors to Kenilworth Road.

The Red Devils had managed a perfect start. They were top of the league with a 100% record of 30 points from ten games. The record opening victories was set in 1960-61 by Spurs double winning side, of eleven straight wins.

The best crowd of the season by far, 17,454 watched an enthralling game. When United took the lead most people thought they would equal Tottenham's achievement. But an equaliser by Brian Stein stopped them. In fact, if Paul Elliott had not missed a sitter near the end Luton would have won.

There was trouble in the Oak Road that day, this is the last time there was fighting on that famous terrace. Perhaps because we halted United's chance of history, there was also serious trouble in Dunstable Road after the match, in which Luton chaps more than played their part and held their own against the Red Army.

Sheff United were easily overcome in the League Cup 2-0, 4-1 on aggregate. For the visit to promoted Oxford I hired a coach from The Sportsman.

Apart from a friendly in 1978, this was my first visit to the Manor Ground. There was a huge Luton following in attendance. Brian Stein gave us the lead, both teams then had a player sent off (Mitchell Thomas for us) before Oxford equalised late on.

Next up, was a never to be forgotten home performance against Southampton. Meka Nwajiobi, Brian Stein and Ricky Hill gave us a 3-0 h-t lead. In the 2nd half, the Hatters performance was truly scintillating. Stein went on to get a hat trick and two more goals were added by David Preece & Ray Daniel. The England goalkeeper Peter Shilton, was voted Saints man of the match - we beat them 7 (SEVEN)-0! Honestly if it had not been for Shilts, I would have witnessed Luton's all time record score. Which would have beaten the 12-0 win against Bristol Rovers when Joe Payne scored TEN for us in 1936. The pity was, that only 8,876 attended.

I drove up to Anfield and when Liverpool led 2-0 (both scored by ex-Hatter Paul Walsh) I had visions of another 6-0 romp similar to two seasons earlier. I was wrong. Steve Foster & Mick Harford made it 2-2. Alas, it was not to last as just a minute later, Molby scored the winning goal for the Reds.

In the League Cup we lost 2-0 at home to Norwich, it was our first defeat on the new artificial surface & to be frank, 2-0 flattered us, we were never in the game. The lowest home crowd of the season, 8,550 watched us beat Birmingham 2-0. At the next match, this was when I felt that Luton had truly made it as a topflight team. I travelled with the SWMC secretary to watch Luton play exceptionally well at Tottenham. Mick Harford & Brian Stein had given us a well earned 2-0 lead. Although Spurs scored on 80 mins I was not anxious at all and a great goal from Ricky Hill in the last moments gave a true reflection of the score, 3-1. This was one of my proudest moments as a Hatters fan when I overheard Spurs fans on our return to Sandy's car being very complimentary about Luton's performance. In a sign of the times, there were less than 20,000 there. Sandy and I drove back to Stopsley and after a quick bite to eat & change of clothes Deb and I joined a coach party from the SWMC. We left for a cracking night out at another WMC in London at - TOTTENHAM! The locals in that club who had been to the match, told me that Luton were the best team they had seen at White Hart Lane that season. It was a great night to end a super day.

Back down to earth with a bump we came, as we lost our first home league match to Coventry 1-0. I should have known better - the jinx team had returned! We made up for it the following week, winning at rivals Watford. Mitchell Thomas scored his first goal for Luton. We never looked in any danger, but then they equalised on 82 mins. Four mins later we, or should I say Watford, scored an own goal to make it a 2-1 Hatters victory.

I had now established a very good spectator record against our rivals, in 26 matches we had lost only five times.

We followed on with two consecutive home wins against Man City 2-1 and Newcastle 2-0. Meaning that after 20 games, Luton had climbed up to 7th place. I missed the next match, a 2-0 defeat at Nottm Forest due to another SWMC weekender in Cliftonville, Margate.

The last game before Xmas was at home to highflying West Ham. They came to Kenilworth Road on a great winning run of nine straight league wins.

A huge West Ham following boosted the crowd to 14,599. In a similar scenario to Man Utd earlier in the season, we also stopped them in their tracks by drawing 0-0. Likewise, we should have won that match too.

On Boxing Day I drove in the pouring rain to The Hawthorns to see us beat bottom club WBA 2-1.

Due to a party at my friend Bob Rumble's house, I missed the final game of 1985 at Ipswich. We drew 1-1.

On New Year's Day we saw off Leicester 3-1 at Kenilworth Road. A superb hat trick by Mick Harford meant that my accompanying boss Dave Kitching the Leicester fan, was not happy.

In the FA Cup 3rd round we were drawn against C. Palace at Selhurst Park. Deb joined us Sportsman lads for a boozy day out. After a skin full at The Duke Of York in Victoria, we set off on the train. Only to find out en route, that the match had been called off due to a waterlogged pitch. The game was rescheduled mid-week but because of work I missed our 2-1 victory over the Eagles. I also missed the next away game at Chelsea, where we lost 1-0.

For our next game at home to Aston Villa, we had a new signing from Wigan. Mike Newell was a striker who would become quite a synonymous name at Luton Town. He only took 16 minutes to score his first Luton goal against Villa. Mick Knight was not pleased when Brian Stein added a second to end it 2-0.

My old mate Steve White rang me up trying to get some info on the current Luton team. The reason being was that we were drawn at home to his team Bristol Rovers in the FA Cup 4th round. I told him it was not worth him and his Pirates turning up as in the form we were in at present, we would thrash them. Indeed thrash them we did, 4-0. A large contingent from Eastville were in fighting mood too, scrapping away on the Kenilworth Road open terrace.

A day out in London followed and we had the usual defeat at Highbury, losing 2-1 to Arsenal. I missed our 2-1 win at Southampton we were now 6th.

In the FA Cup 5th round we had drawn Arsenal at home. The score was 2-2. Another draw occurred at another London side QPR. For the first time we failed to win on their plastic pitch. Mike Newell netted the equaliser in a 1-1 result.

I had a humorous moment at the next game. We beat Sheff Wed 1-0 nothing too special about that. But as I was coming out of the Bobbers Club after half time, the 2nd half had started. With a Burger in one hand and coffee in the other, the ball bounced off the plastic pitch heading in my direction towards my face.

Obviously, I could not protect myself with hands, so without a moment's thought I just headed it back in to play, even the Ref along with the players and crowd laughed.

Two nights later, the FA Cup replay was played at Highbury. I write played, skated would be more appropriate, as the pitch was like an ice rink. Even with their under-soil heating, the pitch was farcical. It was as though the authorities had said to Arsenal, 'We don't need artificial surfaces in this country, go and show them what real pitches are like.'

We stood in the freezing cold on the open Clock End and although both sets of players struggled with the pitch, we were a touch fortunate to gain a 0-0 draw AET. I saw Luton play at Highbury 11 times and never saw us win. This was only my 2nd draw too as we lost all NINE others. When it was announced that the third game would be at Kenilworth Road, you could clearly hear the Gooners groans aloud. Their fears were justified, as two nights later we thrashed Arsenal 3-0. Steve Foster, O'Leary O.G. & Mark Stein netted the Luton goals, but in all honesty 6- or 7-0 would have been a fairer reflection. Arsenal players just were not up for it at all. Evidently there was a lot of trouble post-match between MIGs and Gooner firms, including slashings etc. on Moor Path in town.

Just three days later, we played the Quarter Final at home to Everton – our FOURTH match of that week! But we eagerly awaited our chance to gain revenge over the Toffees, after they so cruelly denied us a Wembley appearance eleven months previous. A crowd of 15,529 turned up and we led Everton 1-0 at ht just as previous, but this time courtesy of

Mick Harford. What changed in 1986 rather than 85, was that we then led 2-0 via Mark Stein and us Luton fans were in raptures. But Everton were not Champions and again leaders at the time, for no reason. Just two mins after little Stein's goal, Sharp pulled one back. I have to write, it was no surprise that Heath levelled the scores. In fact Lineker very nearly won it for them but they were more than happy to take us back to Goodison Park. I drove up for the replay with Keith McEvoy. Lineker opened the scoring. He then missed a penalty as like us in the 1st half at Luton, Everton were controlling the game. As the game went on you could sense the Everton players and especially their crowd, were getting tense. When Ray Daniel hit the post late on, the Scousers were now SCREAMING for the final whistle. It arrived and we were out. We had blown our chance in the initial game. The atmosphere created that night was electric in front of 44,264. This was my final away game of 1985-86.

Back to the league it was and a further hangover occurred when we lost our second home league game next.

Despite David Preece giving us a lead, we went on to lose 2-1 to Oxford. Then the traditional Old Trafford defeat occurred, 2-0 to Man Utd.

Everton were back again for the league visit. Still top of the league, we gained a tiny bit of payback. On 81 mins and Everton leading 1-0 we turned it around to win 2-1. Steve Foster & Mike Newell were the scorers.

I remember meeting some great Everton fans in the Bobbers Club that day too. After missing a 0-0 draw at Leicester, it was a privilege to witness a brilliant Luton performance at home to WBA. We beat the Baggies thoroughly 3-0 and followed this up with a 2-0 win at their rivals Birmingham. Mick Harford haunted his old club, scoring both goals at St Andrews. This old ground, which once had an attendance of over 66,000 - that day had a crowd of just 8,836!

Another cracking game followed. Luton 1 Tottenham 1 and both teams put on a showpiece. Mike Newell gave us a deserved equaliser very late on.

Sandwiched in between the Birmingham and Spurs matches, was a testimonial for Ricky Hill against an England X1.

We lost 3-1 but the result was trivial, a healthy crowd of 7,741 paid their money to show Ricky the esteem with which he was held in by us Hatters.

We lost 1-0 at home to Liverpool and by the same score at Coventry (no surprise there then).

At the last home game against the enemy Watford, it was on my 28th Birthday, we won 3-2. Mick Harford netted a hat-trick. A peaceful end of season pitch invasion followed (Watford fans would not be so stupid to follow) and we then headed back to the Bobbers Club. April 26th 1986 was the last time we ever went in the Bobbers Club as it was. We did not know it at the time, but by next season it was to be relocated.

The final game was at Man City. Nowhere near the importance of the last time we played at Maine Road three years earlier and this was reflected by the size of the crowd 20,361 - less than half of the attendance from that never to be forgotten day in 1983!

We ended 1985-86 in a very respectable 9th position.

I would normally have gone to the final game, but I had other things on my mind – like arranging my Stag Party & Wedding Day! I had two Stag parties. One was in Holland on the weekend before the wedding and a local one, two nights prior to it. Going abroad for Stag do's was unheard of in those days, but I wanted to be a little different. I organised a good package for 36 of us to travel on a minibus from Stopsley and then by boat from Sheerness in Kent, to Vlissingen (commonly known as Flushing) in Holland. Deb was worried from the start and only agreed when my cousin Ken told her he would chaperone me. All of the Sportsman/SWMC lads and some of the Windsor Castle crowd went. I was chuffed when some of my Dad's mates also came too.

Del Mash told me it was an honour to represent Dad and he wouldn't have missed it for the world – I just wish Dad had been there as well!

Larry Kinloch was my Best Man and we had a laugh when I ordered the first round on me, consisting of 36 Beers. We had a fabulous time on the boat and the day in Holland had no problems, except for a tiny blip on the return voyage.

Obviously everyone had been drinking all day and night. Unsurprisingly, I was well oiled, as it was my duty to be. When I fell asleep in the disco it transpired that one of the bouncers took exception to this and was a bit heavy with me (not that I would have known). Ken saw this, went over to the bouncer and gave him the Glasga kiss. Fortunately, everything calmed down and that was the end of it. Unfortunately for Ken - he was to end up being banned from travelling with Townsend Thoresen again! So the irony of it was, there was Ken meant to be minding me - and he ends up banned himself!

At that time Ken was a bodyguard to an Arab billionaire's son in London. One day in the West End, he saw a mugger steal this Arab lady's handbag. Ken chased after the thief, grabbed the bag and gave the mugger a slap, while pinning him down to the ground waiting for the police to arrive.

As a result of this the Arab lady was extremely grateful to Ken, took his personal details and her husband offered Ken a job protecting their son and huge house. When I was having my knee problems the previous year, Ken arranged for me to see the Arab's private Doctor & spend the day at their mansion in Highgate. I've since discovered Beatle Ringo Starr once lived there.

The house was huge. I had a swim in their indoor pool, as well as a Sauna. The thing that fascinated me the most was there being 7 Bathrooms. I recall saying - "You can have a crap every day of the week in a different loo!"

While we were having my Stag do Deb had her Hen night on a boat too, on the Thames in London.

For my local Stag party we met in the Sportsman and ended up in the Flying Club at Luton Airport, a regular popular haunt for late night drinking at the time.

The night before the wedding I stayed at Best Man, Larry's house.

Saturday May 31st 1986 was the wedding day many people didn't think would happen, at St Thomas Church in Hitchin Road, Stopsley, which was where my parents married and most other relatives too, both Adairs & Roberts.

Larry and I were both dressed in hired Top Hat and Tails, as we ventured into the Church I could see many friends & relations, including Scots pals from Cleland and the Moffats from Kilsyth, among them.

Deb walked up the aisle and looked a treat. Upon seeing me, we had our first words at the aisle. She whispered - "I can't believe what you are wearing!" There was no way Luton and Rangers were not going to be represented somehow. I had a brand new pair of BLUE shoes on and a carnation dyed blue for Rangers – I was also wearing a tiny LTFC Lapel Badge!

Our photographer was Gareth Owen who was and remains, the official LTFC photographer today. Despite the teeming rain he did a fantastic job. We left St Thomas Church for the reception in a gold Rolls-Royce (I've never been in a Roller since). There were 2 receptions. The first in the afternoon was a sit down meal at The Green Man in Offley, for 60 relations. After the meal we headed for the evening reception at the SKF Hall in Sundon Park, to be joined by another 250 guests. I always said I wanted a big wedding, so we hired the biggest venue in Luton available for such numbers.

Everyone had a fantastic night as we danced the first dance to 'Sexual Healing' by Marvin Gaye.

Larry had organised a taxi for us to stay at The Wigmore Hotel near the airport for our wedding night. The hotel was owned by a friend of mine, Graeme Gemmell, he used to run the Rangers Club in Luton.

We returned to my flat on the Sunday and the next day flew for our Honeymoon to Gozo. This is an island next to Malta and when Deb's mum Julie told me they are crazy about English football - that was a good enough destination for me!

Gozo & Malta were lovely places to visit. The locals were warm and friendly. I remember being amazed at the number of old classic British Cars that were driven over there. Ford Anglias, Vauxhall Victors & Crestas were ten a penny.

On only the second day of the honeymoon - whilst swimming in the sea I managed to lose my wedding ring! After spending hours looking for it I had to admit defeat but replaced it with a much better one over there.

One memorable night of the honeymoon, was watching the World Cup England v Poland match in a local bar in Marselforn. England had to win this last group match in Mexico, or we were out of the competition. The owner of the bar discovered we were honeymooners and when we won 3-1, treated us to a bottle of champagne, to see out a fantastic night with the locals.

Best Man Larry Kinloch RIP and I at my wedding in 1986.

The Adair family 1972. L to R, Sister Ann, me aged 14,
Dad, Grandma Isa Adair, Granddad Tom Adair, Mum and in front, young sister Michelle.
Just us 3 kids left now.

My wedding to Deb 1986. Note the tiny LTFC lapel badge!

1986-87

Before the new season began there were major changes occurring at Kenilworth Road, both on and off the pitch. On the playing staff front, Mitchell Thomas and Ray Daniel left and we signed Robert Wilson from Millwall.

But the biggest news was that we had a new manager, in John Moore.

After eight years as Luton boss, David Pleat finally left for pastures new. He was at that time a well sought after manager and in recent years had turned down various opportunities. But the lure of Tottenham Hotspur was too big and frankly, nobody could blame him. We totally understood that, but he then left a sour taste by stealing Mitchell Thomas, via a tribunal.

Moore had been promoted within the coaching staff and being an ex-Town stalwart having played 306 games for LTFC, he was not an unpopular choice. There were also noticeable changes to the ground. The Bobbers Stand had been converted into Executive Boxes, resulting in the Club underneath being relocated to under the Oak Road end, which is where it remains today.

The Boxes looked horrendous, like posh Chalets but given the need for Corporate Hospitality in these changing times of football, there really was no alternative given the lack of space, due to the houses behind Beech Path.

The famous Oak Road end was now seated and on top of all this, a roof was erected on to the open Kenilworth Road End, which would help boost the atmosphere. We had more changes to the ground in that summer - than in the previous 80-odd years! The changes didn't stop there.

By far the most controversial of all, was the decision to ban away supporters. The only way you could gain entrance now, was if you were a season ticket holder or a club member. Electronic gates were installed with apparatus fitted to swipe the S/T or Member cards. The away fan ban was introduced by our Tory MP Chairman David Evans, as a response to the Millwall crowd trouble in 1985. While it made him very popular with the Prime Minister Iron Lady Maggie Thatcher, it now made Luton Town one of the most hated clubs in football. The plastic pitch was bad enough, but at least we were not alone on that front. The away ban was a step too far in most people's eyes.

Yes, hooliganism was a major factor and something had to be done to rid football of its cancer, but NOT this. In a short space of time, we had gone from being a very popular club with many nationwide admirers - to one of the most despised! These changes to the ground had now left us with a capacity of less than 15,000. I attended two Pre-Season Matches.

The first was Tottenham 1 Rangers 1 for a Spurs player's testimonial.

The first Luton game played at the revamped Kenilworth Road was a pre-season friendly against Mexican side Monterray. I watched the game from the newly covered Kenilworth Road end, which was where I would have my new season ticket for 1986-87. This was also a 1-1 draw.

One thing I wanted to prove was that just because I was now married, there was NO way my support for LTFC would fade, or diminish in any way.

The first league game of the season was at Filbert Street, Leicester.

Deb's Aunty Gill lived in Loughborough, Leics. So, it was natural that we paid her and husband John a visit before playing Leicester. While Deb was enjoying herself I went to the match with her cousin Laura's boyfriend.

Just 9,801 watched the 1-1 draw at Filbert Street. Leicester scored first and then a stunning equaliser by Brian Stein followed. He beat four Leicester players in a mazy run.

The historic first game to home fans only, was against Southampton. New signing from Millwall Robert Wilson opened the scoring (never to score another Luton goal). Brian Stein added another. When the Saints scored we looked to see if there was any cheering, it was in total silence and ended 2-1.

We then watched Luton absolutely batter Newcastle, only to draw 0-0.

The Newcastle goalkeeper that day was Martin Thomas and he made many outstanding saves.

I drove up to Villa Park with Mick Knight four nights later. The 1st half belonged to Aston Villa, the second Luton and we lost 2-1.

The following Saturday Deb & I took the train to London. While she went shopping in the Kings Road I stood alone in the Chelsea Shed End. I had to keep quiet but thoroughly enjoyed it as we won 3-1. Can you imagine that today? We, beating Chelsea 3-1 at Stamford Bridge and only 13,040 there to watch.

The next match was a sad occasion.

Harry Haslam, our manager from 1972-78, had recently passed away. He died of Cancer aged only 65. Before the game at home to Arsenal there was one of the most solemn minute's silences I have ever witnessed. He was a great character nicknamed 'Happy Harry'. Teams he sent out always tried to entertain. A famous old song I used to love singing in the Oak Road was in our promotion year of 1974 - "You've got your European and you've got your FA Cup, for we are Harry Haslam's boys and we are going up, la la la la la la la la la la la la la la la la la la la."

We drew a poor game 0-0. RIP Happy Harry.

I travelled alone on the Bobbers Coach to see Luton lose 2-0 at West Ham, in which Brian Stein was sent off for punching Alvin Martin. Steiny was mostly known as Bruno after this game.

In the League Cup, we were drawn to play Cardiff at home. The Welsh club insisted on LTFC allowing in their supporters.

David Evans refused to go against his stance and so, we were promptly thrown out by the Football League (not the last time the league would punish our club). I had a programme of this match that never was, probably the most valuable Luton one I possessed. But sadly had to sell it in 2019 because of financial (lack of) circumstances.

It was on this day that my Granddad Adair died. He died in St Mary's Hospital, where I was born.

Old Tom never truly got over the tragedy of losing both his sons. The Adairs had left their Applecroft Road family home after living there for nearly 50 years and had moved to a flat in Lullington Close, off Wigmore Lane in Stopsley. Tom hated it and only lasted less than six months. He missed his beloved garden but in truth, he died mentally many years before.

Tom was a great character, with a brilliant mind. RIP Granddad.

We then beat Man City at home 1-0. Brian Stein scored the only goal. Of the eight goals scored so far, Stein had netted 5 of them.

All of us Sportsman boys travelled to Spurs, in what was now deemed a bit of a grudge match against our old manager David Pleat. A very vocal and large away following gave Luton tremendous support, Tottenham were fortunate to gain a 0-0 draw.

The home crowds were gradually increasing and the first post 10,000 attendance watched us draw 0-0 again against leaders Norwich.

I missed the game at Old Trafford, where we so nearly broke our dreadful duck. We only lost 1-0 but should have got a point against Man Utd, as Brian Stein missed a penalty.

- The next game was incredible!

13,140 watched as Luton tore Liverpool apart, beating them 4-1. Scouser and boyhood Reds fan Mike Newell, scored a hat - trick with Ricky Hill adding the other. With 38 mins still remaining and the Hatters 4-0 up, this could have been a dream to behold. But don't get me wrong even with them scoring a consolation penalty, 4-1 was simply brilliant.

Imagine thrashing Liverpool 4-1 today – the mind boggles!

We followed this up with another home victory over QPR, although the 1-0 win was not quite so exciting. This result had lifted us up to 6th place.

I then organised a coach from the Sportsman to take us to promoted Wimbledon. The Dons had incredibly been a non-league team - just nine years earlier! On the way to their ramshackle Plough Lane ground (it made Kenilworth Road look like Wembley), we stopped at a pub opposite Rossyln Park Rugby ground. When we entered the pub you could sense the nervousness and tension from the Landlord & locals about a crowd of football fans coming into their pub. As always though, we behaved impeccably (though naturally noisy) and by the time we left, they loved us.

It was a freezing cold day on the open terraces and we were glad to get back on the warm coach after Mark Stein netted the only goal of the game.

On the way home, we stopped in St Albans for a drink. It was here, that I was responsible for getting another of my friends hitched up. This time, it was Mick Knight. I introduced him to a Scots lassie I was talking to at the bar. Jackie eventually became Tricky's wife and I'm pleased to write Mr & Mrs Knight are still together living in Round Green, with 2 lovely daughters.

The next home game was another classic. Luton played Nottm Forest who were in 3rd place. After just 16 mins - we were 3-0 up! It eventually finished 4-2.

LTFC was now amazingly - the 4th highest team in the country!

I missed a 1-0 loss at Sheff Wed for a valid reason, as I had moved house. We said goodbye to my bachelor pad next to SWMC and although I only lived there for three years, it had many fond memories. We sold it privately to my mate Keith McEvoy and his girlfriend Jane. Deb was a legal secretary, she did all the conveyancing work for both parties herself. We moved to Turners Road North, still in Stopsley, just down the road from Grandma Roberts and about half a mile from Mum in Ashcroft Road. This was an old 3 Bed Semi, built in 1948, which was cosy. It had a huge back garden of 247 feet, with a garage at the back of it.

The next game was at home to Charlton. I took cousins Richard & Tim Hines (Joan &

Mick Hines' sons) to their first ever Luton match. A one-sided affair saw us beat the Addicks 1-0. Mark Stein, the scorer.

I didn't go to Oxford, but remember keeping up with the score on my new TV, via Teletext. Luton were 3-0 down on 70 mins. Brian Stein pulled one back & when brother Mark scored another three mins later. I thought a late great comeback was on the cards, alas in the final minute it became 4-2 for Oxford.

Our excellent home record continued when Mike Newell headed in the only goal to beat Everton. Which of course being a Reds fan, he enjoyed particularly.

The week before Xmas I travelled to Highbury. Arsenal won 3-0 frankly, that score line flattered us.

On Boxing Day it was derby day, with not a Watford fan in sight. It was a good job too, because those damned Hornets were soon 2-0 up. This was the final result and we even missed a penalty when Peter Nicholas - almost put the ball over the Kenny End roof!

The enemy became the first team to beat us at home since March.

The final game of 1986 was at Nottm Forest. Because of the proximity, it was only right I took Deb to visit Gill & John again. I watched a terrific game at the City Ground. Brian Stein had given us an early lead and it stayed that way until Forest levelled late on. Mick Harford had been out injured all season and this was his first game back.

You could see how his appearance alone, inspired the Luton players. When Mike Newell made it 2-1 late on we thought we would get a great win, but Forest scored an equaliser and if I'm honest, it was a fair result. We ended 1986 in 8th position.

The first game of 1987 was at Coventry. I didn't attend, due to suffering a severe hangover from Bob Rumble's Hogmanay Party. Anyway, we always lost at Highfield Road and I used this as an excuse. Guess What? For the only time in my Luton supporting life and the first time in 56 years - we won at the old home of the Sky Blues! Brian Stein netted the only goal. We never won there again.

A lone Mike Newell goal was then enough to beat Chelsea at home and succeed in doing the double over them.

In the FA Cup 3rd Round we had drawn Liverpool at home. Despite our away fan ban the FA relented and let us stage the tie, due to it being shown live on BBC TV. Although we did permit 200 or so Reds fans seats in the Main Stand as a kind of compromise.

On a snow-swept surface, had it not been for our artificial pitch it would never had started. We drew 0-0 and then mayhem occurred at the replay. The team had decided to fly up from Heathrow on the day of the match rather than travel the previous day, as we should have. Unfortunately, the airport was closed due to snow and Luton failed to reach Anfield. Liverpool FC were furious, in particular Kenny Dalglish. He moaned his head off at our unprofessionalism stating - how come the Luton fans reached Anfield, but not their players? And also said, "What about the wasted pies?" Dalglish hated our pitch, the fan ban and now blatantly, our Club too. The match had to be postponed and was rearranged for Monday 26th January.

Two days before that, we beat Leicester 1-0 at home courtesy of Mike Newell. At the replay, despite Liverpool bombarding our goal, Luton held on and after Extra Time it was still stalemate. When Luton won the toss for the venue of the 2nd replay, you could hear Kenny's moans from here.

A never to be beaten Kenilworth Road crowd of 14,687 attended the third match and watched a thrilling Luton performance. We thrashed them 3-0, with goals from Brian Stein, Mick Harford & Mike Newell. From beginning to end, the Reds players just did not fancy it. Once again, cue the Kenny Dalglish moan show. It was from around this time that the joke did the rounds – What does a Boeing 737 and Kenny Dalglish share in common? – They both whine like fuck when leaving Luton Airport!

Three days later, it was the 4th round and we were at home again, to QPR. When they scored a penalty on 83 mins, we thought it was curtains. But in the last minute Mick Harford levelled with his own spot kick.

A huge Luton following travelled to Loftus Road for the replay and despite Harford scoring again after being 2-0 down, we were out.

I missed a 2-2 draw at bottom club Newcastle.

We then beat Aston Villa at home 2-1. Steve Foster scored a blinder against the team we signed him from.

A 1-1 draw followed at Man City watched by only 17,507 at Maine Road. After beating West Ham at home 2-1, it was back to Anfield again. Kenny Dalglish was happy on this occasion though as Liverpool won 2-0. Their first victory over us in 5 attempts that season.

We then beat Man Utd 2-1 at home and truly, the close score line did not reflect our superiority that day. Brian Stein & Mick Harford each scored.

I went to Norwich with an old school friend and SWMC mate, Phil Francis. I have known Phil for nearly 50 years and I would back him, along with Les Miller & myself - to beat ANY team in a quiz on all matters LTFC!

We sat in the very back row of the new stand behind the goal at Carrow Road and watched a 0-0 draw. The main memory though of that day involved a Luton player getting sent off. Ashley Grimes was shown a red card for spitting at a player, a vile and disgusting act. What made it even worse, was that it was at Rob Johnson - OUR full back!

I didn't attend our mid-week 3-0 loss at Southampton.

The biggest home league crowd of the season 13,447, turned up for the return of David Pleat and Tottenham. Unfortunately, he did not receive the welcome that on looking back, he should have done. Luton played brilliant, almost as if to say to Pleaty, "This, is what you have left behind." Ricky Hill was in mesmerising form and he made all three goals as we beat Spurs 3-1. This victory had pushed us up to third place. Make a note of the date 28th March 1987. The reason being is, I don't think Luton will EVER be theoretically - the 3rd best team in the country again! – Certainly, not in my lifetime anyway!

The following week was another home game, a drab 0-0 draw with Wimbledon. Deb & I took Grandma Adair and Michelle away for a week's break to Lloret-de-Mar, in Spain and therefore missed a 2-2 draw at QPR.

Luton were enjoying a fine season, further proof of this was when we beat our jinx team Coventry 2-0 at home to complete our only ever double over them. Pity this was followed up by a low point. Only two teams had completed the double over us in 1986-87 and I'm sorry to write, Watford was one of them.

They had beaten us 2-0 both home & away and I left Vicarage Road very angry. The next week I upset Deb's family too. Her sister Liz was getting married on Sat 25th April. When I told her that I was sorry, but would be unable to make the Church as Luton were at home to

Sheff Wed she laughed, thinking I was jesting. When she realised I wasn't - she went ape shit!

"Well if you can't be bothered to come to my wedding service just because of a bloody football match, don't bother coming to the reception either."

Totally understandable, I agreed. The thing is I had gone 13 years without missing a single home game. I missed cousin Ken's wedding and if Luton were at home when Ann got married, I probably would have missed hers too. I realise today, that this is stupid and immature, but back then it was a big deal. We drew 0-0 with the Owls in an awful game (my punishment).

In fairness, Liz relented and said, "Alan of course you will be coming to the reception, you are what you are and in a tiny way, I admire your deep loyalty." So, straight from the game in my suit I ordered a taxi to the reception at Redbourne Golf Club, to join in with Liz & Geoff's celebrations. After the reception Deb and her 4 male cousins from Devon joined me to go to Club Tropicana (the old Sands), as it was also my 29th Birthday at midnight.

I'm sorry to write, it did not work out for Liz & Geoff, although they did have a daughter, named Lauren.

My final away trip was at Charlton. Well strictly writing, Selhurst Park. Charlton had been forced to leave The Valley a year or so prior, over ground ownership issues and were now sharing with Crystal Palace. They stayed there from 1985 - 1992 and then at Upton Park for a short while, before returning to their true home The Valley in Dec 1992. This was thanks to non-stop campaigning from the loyal Addicks fans. It took them over seven years of hard work and toil.

We beat Charlton 1-0 with a lone Mick Harford effort and this is still the - ONLY time I have ever seen Luton win at Selhurst Park in 13 visits!

Our final home game was an eventful one against Oxford. They became only the second team to beat us at home, winning 3-2. We were 2-0 down before Mike Newell scored his 19th and final LTFC goal. Mark Stein equalised, only for Oxford to win it at the death.

We also lost the final match at the champions Everton. The 3-1 loss resulted in Luton finishing in 7th place, the highest place in LTFC history.

The pity was, that either a point from the final two games or beating Oxford - would have seen us finish 5th!

The final two games of 86-87 I attended, were both England matches.

A crowd of 92,000 watched a 1-1 draw against Brazil. That attendance has never been bettered since for an England match at Wembley.

Then, Bob Rumble and I travelled up to Scotland for the Auld Enemy Scotland v England 0-0 match at Hampden Park. Staying at Jim and Sandra Moffat's in Kilsyth again, after Jim dropped us off in Glasgow to go to our usual Star Bar pub in the Gorbals - we witnessed scenes that I would NEVER have imagined possible. There were at least 2,000 English in Glasgow and approx. 70/80% of them were 'firms' united as one. They actually took it to the Scots in the streets of Glasgow, creating mayhem. The English ran riot pre-match. So bad, we were forced out of the Star Bar by local 'polis'. This was the 3rd and final time I saw England play at Hampden. Evidently the trouble was even worse at Wembley in '88 and again in Glasgow, 1989. After that, both English and Scots FAs decided to scrap the oldest international fixture in the world - dating back to 1872 - because of the violence.

Wembley-Wembley-Wembley

Before our annual Summer Holiday in Greece there was a shock announcement from LTFC. Our manager of just one season, had announced his resignation after leading the club to its highest ever league position in history. The main reason he quit was that he said he hated the public side to the job and relating with the media etc. John Moore also said he just loved to coach, nothing else. Despite pleas from the Board and supporters alike, there was no going back on his decision.

The new LTFC appointed manager was Ray Harford, the ex-Fulham Boss.

On the playing front Peter Nicholas had left for Aberdeen and his replacement signed from Brighton was Danny Wilson.

We arrived back from Greece on the first day of the season and therefore I had to miss our 1-0 defeat at promoted Derby County. A match, in which Mick Harford was sent off - in the FOURTH minute!

With the Bobbers Club having been under the Oak Road stand for a year, we decided to move our season tickets to that stand (more drinking time pre-match)

LTFC had introduced a new ticketing grading system which although didn't affect us season ticket holders, it had a terrible consequence on any casual fans. The matches were graded Bronze, Silver or Gold, depending on the quality of opposition. It is more than fair to write, this decision along with the continuing away ban, had a detrimental effect on Luton's crowds for the start of 1987-88. The first home game was against Coventry. The jinx returned against the Sky Blues, losing 1-0 and proof of the new grading fiasco was a crowd of only 7,506, lower than for any home game of the previous two seasons. Further evidence of the crazy ticketing system was our next game at home to West Ham. This was classed as category Gold and just 8,073 watched a 2-2 draw.

Results were not going well early season and we lost 3-0 at Chelsea.

Danny Wilson scored his first Luton goal in a 1-1 draw at home to Arsenal. The 8,745 crowd against such major opponents, was proving the point that this new system was a grave error.

I travelled with Phil Francis to the Manor Ground, Oxford for our next game. What a match it was too. Luton led 1-0 via Brian Stein, then Oxford equalised just before h-t. When Tim Breaker gave us an early 2-1 lead in the second period, it was the beginning of some of the best attacking football I had seen Luton perform away from home in years. The Hatters really turned it on with further goals from Nwajiobi, Hill and Harford to give us a 5-1 lead, before Oxford pulled one back. The final score of 5-2 was the first time we had scored five away league goals in nearly 12 years.

We followed that with another victory, 2-1 at home to Everton.

After being thrown out of the League Cup the previous year, Luton were drawn against Wigan.

As the Latics did not protest at the away fan ban, we were allowed to play the ties. I travelled to the 1st leg at Springfield Park (another ground to tick off the list) with the Bobbers Coach. This was on a brand new double deck coach, with all mod cons. The facilities included, toilet, videos and very comfy seating.

We had a new signing from Hibs making his debut that night, in striker Micky Weir. He scored the only goal of the game.

I missed the next two games in London, both defeats at Charlton and QPR.

Final evidence that the ticket grading system failed was against Man Utd. After less than 10,000 watched an even 1-1 draw, the club wisely decided to scrap the scheme after the next home match v Wimbledon.

In the second leg against Wigan, Mick Harford bagged a hat-trick in a 4-2 win to see us proceed into the next round 5-2 on aggregate.

After telling the lads about this wonderful new coach with the Bobbers Travel Club, we all decided to travel to Portsmouth on it. It was another chance of a new ground for me, as I had yet to visit Fratton Park. We purchased a huge carry out and waited in the pouring rain for the wonderful new bus to arrive. When this ramshackle thing arrived I took pelters from the boys - what the fuck is this? It turned out that the Wigan trip coach, was just a one off for that journey. We boarded but before reaching the M1 junction 10, we decided to disembark with the carry out and hailed taxis to Chris McEvoy's flat, for a huge drinking session. Fratton Park would have to wait another near six years before gracing my presence - We lost 3-1 anyway!

The next two games were at home, resulting in a 2-0 win against Wimbledon before only 7,018 and then because the Club at last saw sense re pricing, the largest crowd of the season 12,452 watched us lose 1-0 to Liverpool.

In the League Cup we had been drawn at home to the jinx Coventry. The Sky Blues refused to accept our away fan ban, but rather than have us evicted out of the cup as in the previous year, they agreed to play the tie at a neutral venue.

Originally, the game was to be played at Fulham but was changed to Filbert Street, Leicester - Much nearer to Coventry than us!

Any neutrals attending were to watch a great result achieved by the Hatters as we beat Coventry 3-1. This was the only match in the League Cup 87-88 run that I would miss.

A convincing 4-0 home league win followed over Newcastle. The Stein brothers both scored (Mark scoring 2) plus Meka Nwajiobi's 20th & last ever Luton goal. En route to Hillsborough for the next match, I dropped Deb off at her Aunt Gill's in Loughborough.

At this game I decided to stand in the Sheff Wed Kop end, which recently had a new covered roof erected and was officially opened by Her Majesty The Queen. I saw a fine 2-0 win, but I must admit it was difficult to hide my emotions, especially when the Owls blasted a penalty miles over at the end I stood at.

In the 4th Round of the League Cup, Mick Dolan hired a coach from the Sportsman to Ipswich.

Naturally, we stopped en route to Portman Road for drinks but such was the heavy traffic around Ipswich, we arrived at the game 5 minutes late. By the time we had taken our seats, Luton were 1-0 up courtesy of a Brian Stein goal. We had a team out that was quite inexperienced due to injuries, but managed to hold on to the slender lead and for the first time in nine years, had reached the Quarter Finals.

Luton had a new signing Ian Allinson from Arsenal and it was against their great rivals Tottenham, that he made his debut. He had an excellent home start too.

Allinson scoring both goals, in a fine 2-0 win to lift us up to 11th.

This was followed by a poor 2-1 home defeat to Norwich, despite Brian Stein giving us an interval lead. The biggest disappointment for me was a pathetic crowd of only 7,002 and coming just a week after such a brilliant performance against Spurs.

I drove alone to Watford. After the previous season's double over us by the enemy I wanted revenge. We achieved it when Steve Foster headed the only goal to resurrect our favourite score line against the foe. It should have been 2-0 when Ian Allinson had a shot, which was a mile over the line yet not given.

The week before Xmas we played Southampton at home. The lowest home crowd since being a top flight side of just 6,618 saw a 2-2 draw.

I missed the Boxing Day 2-0 defeat at Everton. A nightmare occurred at this match when Ricky Hill broke his leg on the Goodison Park turf. Two days later, the final game of 1987 saw a lone goal by Danny Wilson beat Charlton at home. My cousin Bill Roberts was over from New York for Xmas, him and his dad Uncle Bill Senior, joined me to watch us comprehensively beat Chelsea 3-0.

Due to our away fan ban the Chelsea chairman Ken Bates refused to attend, giving his complimentary tickets to Chelsea fans in the Directors seats.

In the FA Cup 3rd round we were drawn away to 4th Division Hartlepool. This was another chance of a new ground for me but there was no way I wanted to travel all that distance just to watch a match and return back the same day. For that reason, a crowd of Stopsley boys decided to make a weekend of it in the North Eastern town. Magnet, Freddy Dann, Phil Odell, John Farmer, Martyn Bacon, Mick Dolan, Phil Fensome among others, in what was to become a regular occurrence in Hartlepool. This particular match was the first of many times that when Luton played in the North East, we stayed in Monkey Hanging land. It continues to this day.

For those unfamiliar with why it's called that name it was because legend has it, that during the Napoleonic war locals caught a monkey and believed it to be a spy - so they hung it! It became folklore.

After booking into the Douglas Hotel we met a great set of Poolie lads and stayed in touch with them for many years. Luton won 2-1. Micky Weir scored one of the goals. This was his 3rd and final Hatters goal (all in Cups) in his short stay with us. He was homesick for Scotland and returned to Hibernian.

The following week a 1-0 home victory over Derby lifted us up to 8th place, our highest position that season.

In the Quarter-Final of the League Cup we had drawn Bradford City. There was no way the Bantams would let us play the game without any of their fans (quite right too) so the Luton board had to agree to 2,000 visiting fans or risk elimination again. By allowing them in, this made for an excellent atmosphere at Kenilworth Road once more. Nearly every Luton fan I knew hated the ban and it was after this game, we would try to get any away fans tickets if we could (apart from Watford of course).

In the first half there appeared to be no breakthrough for us but when the Bradford goalkeeper made a howler by picking up the ball in his area for a second time, it resulted in a free kick to Luton in that spot. A pass to captain Steve Foster resulted in a bullet of a shot that hammered into the Bradford net. Mick Harford headed a second and Luton were through to the Semis for the first time in our history. Evidently football violence returned that night in town post-match between warring local Luton 'MiGs' and the Bradford City 'Ointment' firms, with a few Bradford lads slashed, according to the hoolie grapevine.

We were then at home again, this time in the FA Cup 4th round to Southampton. Us Hatters fans were enjoying these home ties, as the board had no option but to allow away supporters entry.

I had decided to have a bet on Luton just before the Bradford City tie. We were 6/1 to win the League Cup and 28/1 the FA Cup. I bet £10 on Luton to win each cup individually + also a win double. Meaning that a £30 outlay would result in over £1,000 if we won both cups.

Against the Saints, there were 2,000 visiting supporters allowed once more. When Southampton took the lead relatively late on, I thought that two of my bets were going tits up already. Then two Luton goals turned things around. Ian Allinson & Brian Stein scored them on 81 and 83 minutes.

In the League Cup Semi-Finals Luton were drawn against Oxford, away first. We first had to play them in Division 1 also, at Kenilworth Road. What an unbelievable epic game this was. I will describe the action as follows: 1-0 via Mick Harford - 2-0 Brian Stein - 2-1 Oxford penalty - 3-1 Darren McDonough a minute later - 3-2 just before half time. Second Half, 4-2 Mark Stein - 5-2 Mark Stein again, - 5-3 61 mins - 6-3 Mark Stein gets his first & only LTFC hat-trick – then 2 mins later it's 6-4 – then 7-4 Mick Harford with still 19 minutes to go.

Alas, there were no further goals but what statistics. I had never seen before or since, 11 goals scored in a professional match. The two league games with Oxford had produced a staggering EIGHTEEN goals (12-6 in favour of the Town).

At work, my career would take a new direction and change my life somewhat. At around that time, I used to sell various items on the factory shop floor like LTFC raffle tickets, Sportsman Tote tickets etc. Any time that guests visited the factory, they were fair game to me and I never hesitated to sell to them as such.

One of these customers said to myself in front of the boss, "You are wasted on a machine, I can't believe you are not in Sales." It was a comment that stuck in my mind for a while and I discussed it at home with Deb.

She agreed with the client and urged me to pursue the matter. I suggested the idea to my boss Dave Kitching and he came up with a plan. "Go out in your car for a month with your suit on, see how you like it, if it doesn't work out you can just return to the press." What had I to lose? I did exactly as he suggested.

Focusing on everyone I knew, I then visited all of the business contacts I could personally meet and took it from there. My first port of call was the Wigmore Hotel (wedding night) ran by a Rangers friend of mine, Graeme Gemmell. He told me my timing was perfect, as he was in the process of beginning to arrange for all his menus, wine lists and stationery to be revamped and printed. I returned back that first day, to get all of the items quoted. The next day he gave me the go ahead. I had my first order at over £2,000, which was quite substantial at the time. I had another two clients in my first week. After the month was up Dave said, "I don't need to tell you, welcome to Sales."

It was in March 1988 that I began my new career. My target and key aim at the time was Vauxhall Motors, Luton's largest employer. A fellow rep at CBC had told me that he admired my enthusiasm, but added that I needed to learn to walk before I could run. He said, "You have NO chance of getting in at a multinational company like Vauxhall, we have been trying for years, it just not happen like that." I had no time for such negativity and had my own plan and was equally determined to prove him wrong.

My Uncle Mick Hines (Joan's husband) worked in IT at Vauxhall. He gave me a contact name for printing tenders. After about 3-4 further enquiries I managed to talk to the person who mattered, his name was Roy Whitworth.

Speaking to him on the phone he told me that my luck was in, as Vauxhall had just reached a decision that they were to close their in-house printing plant and needed further external Printers for contracting print as an outsource. We arranged an appointment and I went to visit him. I just decided to be my natural self and began by telling him about my family history Vauxhall links. When I told him about Granddad Adair and the Winston Churchill episode, I could see he was positively warming to me.

Naturally, we discussed business as well and I left, with him promising that he would be in touch soon.

The next week he rang and asked for my boss and they arranged for the two of them another senior buyer and myself, to show them a tour of our three factories. Everything went well and Dave Kitching told me that Roy had been very complimentary about me. We were to be added to Vauxhall's official list of suppliers within a week and immediately, began to get jobs to tender for. I won my first order within a month - for over £5,000! I have a lot to thank Roy for. He is now retired and lives in the same village as me. We still meet occasionally.

My sales career got off to a flying start, any salesman will tell you that you need three key elements: Contacts, Sales Skills and most importantly, LUCK. I agree with all three views but my philosophy, is that people buy people. 1988 was the dawning of a new era, Print Sales remained as to how I earned a living until 2019.

The 1st leg of the League Cup Semi Final was at the Manor Ground. I drove there alone and sat in the rickety old side stand. There had been snow, sleet and rain all day, but the match went ahead on a soaking wet pitch. Brian Stein gave us the lead just before half - time. A minute into the 2nd period, Mal Donaghy and Oxford's Saunders went for the same ball in the Oxford penalty area. Saunders FELL over and the ref - unbelievably gave a penalty! He made it 1-1. Later on the ref did exactly the same thing again but fortunately for us, Les Sealey saved Saunders penalty. It ended 1-1 evenly balanced for the 2nd leg.

We played a league game at Highbury, which I missed. Arsenal as nearly always, won 2-1.

Back to the cup run, this time in the FA Cup, we were drawn to play QPR in the 5th Round on their artificial pitch. We were the only two teams in the country with plastic pitches, so it would be interesting to see how this would fathom out. A 1-1 draw was the final score and four days later in the replay at Luton, we won 1-0 courtesy of an own goal.

At this stage in late February Luton were 8th in Div 1, in the Quarter - Finals of the FA Cup and one game away - from a League Cup Final!

On Sunday Feb 25th in front of live TV cameras, was the 2nd leg v Oxford at home. Unsurprisingly, the best attendance of the season 13,010, including the now mandatory Cup agreement 2,000 visiting fans, saw us win 2-0. Two goals from Brian Stein and Ashley Grimes sent us Luton fans into dreamland. In all honesty Oxford were never at the races, at the final whistle thousands of ecstatic fans raced on to the pitch in celebration. LTFC had qualified for their first major Cup Final in 29 years – at that time, only the 2nd ever!

Three nights later we were at home again to Stoke, in yet another Cup competition. This was the Simod Cup, a tournament organised for the top two divisions, as some form of consolation/competition to English clubs for being barred from Europe. The big guns treated it with contempt, but we did not.

A convincing 4-1 victory v Stoke meant we were in the Semis of that Cup too. In between the flurry of these Cup games Luton lost 2-0 at Wimbledon in a rare league match, the first for a month. I missed the Plough Lane match because I was in Scotland with Richie Harding watching Rangers win 3-0 at Dunfermline.

Two nights later we beat Swindon 2-1 at home in the Simod Cup Semi-Final and had qualified for Wembley again.

The night before our FA Cup Quarter-Final at home to Portsmouth, I went to a local ground I had still not visited. It was the County Ground, Northampton. I watched a terrible 0-0 bore between the Cobblers and Rotherham & never returned there again.

Against Pompey, once more 2,000 visiting fans stood on the Bobbers side of the Kenilworth Road end terrace, a menacing looking Pompey mob they were too. Goals from Mark Stein, Danny Wilson & Mick Harford were enough to see off Portsmouth 3-1.

Luton were now in the Semi-Final of the FA Cup for the second time in 3 years, along with two other Wembley finals.

I actually started to believe my bet was going to come up.

The first of the finals was played the following Sunday against 2nd Division Reading in the Simod Cup.

Before that in mid-week, we played a catch up league game at Coventry. This match I missed due to being on a Sales Course. The minds must have been on Wembley and the Cup runs, we were thrashed 4-0. Mind - it was my jinx team! My old mate Larry Kinloch who incidentally I helped get a job at CBC (he was now a very able printer) drove us to Wembley. Mick Harford gave us the lead (totally against the run of play) but we ended up getting spanked 4-1 and deservedly so too. The attendance of 61,740 was now the largest I had ever seen Luton play in. It was Reading's first visit to Wembley and their fans outnumbered us 2 to 1. Obviously, if we did not have a much bigger and far more important final coming up, there is no doubt we would have doubled the 20,000 odd fans we took there.

One very amusing story occurred that weekend.

A good mate of mine called Andre Barzilay, (known to all as Barz) had booked into a Hotel at Wembley on the Saturday night. After a drinking session, he was looking at the TV in his room and decided to ring one of the LTFC call lines on the hotel phone. He promptly fell asleep and when he woke up, realised he was still on the line. His phone bill - was £144!

Two nights after the Wembley horror show, we played Portsmouth at home in a league game. Luton owed us a performance after Reading and we certainly got one, beating Pompey 4-1. With all the expense of the Cup runs I missed the away game at Newcastle, where we lost 4-0 for the 2nd successive away match.

Before the FA Cup Semi, we played Sheff Wed at home in another rearranged league match. We drew 2-2 but there was a major injury scare. Les Sealey was stretchered off after being clattered by Sheff Wed's Chapman. Les's season was sadly over.

The Semi-Final was at White Hart Lane, against Wimbledon. Considering the other Semi was Liverpool v Man Utd, the Wombles were definitely our preferred choice of opponents. We travelled on a minibus from SWMC, including mate Bob Rumble. After having a great sing song and drinking session in a pub next to the ground, we took our seats in the East

Stand (the only time I ever sat in that Spurs stand). I was staggered at the low size of the crowd for such a major game. We had almost sold our allocation and took nearly 16,000. Wimbledon - had failed to sell 10,000 tickets! It was embarrassing that such a major event (the Cups were then) attracted only 25,000 in attendance. Only broken in 1995 when a Villa Park FA Cup Semi replay between C. Palace & Man Utd attracted less than 18,000 following a fatal stabbing of a fan at the first tie.

In the 1st half we did not play well at all. Les Sealey's replacement Andy Dibble had so far kept us in it at 0-0. Just after the break Mick Harford broke through and scored to give Luton a rather fortunate lead. The lead only lasted seven minutes and later on Wise scored the 2-1 winner for Wimbledon. I despised the Crazy Gang at the time and their brand of brute hoof ball (just like Watford) but the truth is, they out battled us and deserved to win. The journey home was in silence, just like 3 years prior.

Although I didn't feel quite so bad, because against Everton we played brilliant - this time we were shite!

Thoughts started going through my head that a season which had promised so much, was blowing up in our faces. 2 out of 3 bets were now useless and void. The following Saturday I was back at Wembley AGAIN with Luton.

The Football League was celebrating their centenary and had organised a weekend tournament to commemorate the event. We were drawn to play Man Utd and lost 2-0. Nottm Forest won it, but the club that brought the most fans was definitely Leeds.

We played United a few nights later at Old Trafford in the league and lost 3-0. Before the big final we played QPR at home in mid-week and a much needy 2-1 victory was earned. Equally important, was that one of our major players had returned from injury in David Preece, he had been out since September.

The night before the big match was St George's Day. Deb and I took her parents and sister Liz out for a meal at Wigmore Hotel, as a thank you to Graeme for the recent printing business. It was a lovely warm night and we went up the SWMC to finish off the evening and sink a few for St George.

Sunday 24th April 1988. Arsenal v Luton Town, League Cup Final. As this was the biggest day of my Luton Town supporting life I wanted it to be special, against the reigning holders. After all, who knows when it could happen again? I organised a 52 seat Coach from SWMC. It was to take us direct to Wembley so that we could soak up the atmosphere and bring us straight back after the match. This was a day that I wanted to savour and did not want to arrive at the ground pissed. After the game upon our return I had also arranged a 3 Course sit down meal at The Somerset Tavern for all the Coach Party + Wives & Girlfriends (who didn't attend the match) to join us.

We left SWMC nice and early, most wearing the famous Luton Straw Boaters. When we arrived at Wembley Coach Park I was so nervous with tension that after disembarking off the coach - I had bought SIX programmes! I had brought top priced seats, along with Bob Rumble in the stand opposite the Cameras near the Royal Box. We had a couple of pints in the Bar near that area before taking our seats. All the recent poor performances were forgotten and the sight of 35,000 Luton fans singing their hearts out, will stay with me forever. This amount of support proves a point I have always made, the support for Luton IS there, all we need are decent facilities and of course a decent team and then the supporters WILL come. Some people said that they were just fair weather/cup final fans, but I disagree. I would much rather have this scenario where we sold all of our allocation, rather than our FA Cup victors Wimbledon. They failed to sell their FA Cup final allocation against LIVERPOOL (the biggest club in the land by far, then).

When the teams were announced, there was some major surprises.

Luton's team that historic day was: Andy Dibble, Tim Breaker, Rob Johnson, and to everyone's delight and amazement as he had been out with a broken leg since Boxing Day, Ricky Hill, our captain marvel Steve Foster, Mal Donaghy, Danny Wilson, Brian Stein, Mick Harford, David Preece and a 19-year-old Kingsley Black, who had made only a handful of LTFC appearances. The Subs were Mark Stein and Ashley Grimes.

There were a couple of players very much in our minds, the injured Les Sealey and Darren McDonough, who was badly injured in training just two days prior and broke down in tears. It was with great pride, that I met Darren 21 years later, cheering on his ex-team Luton at another Wembley Final.

The match started at a great tempo and Luton were playing really well, far better than the recent showings. Brian Stein gave us a deserved lead after 13 mins with a lovely goal at the Tunnel (Arsenal) end, from a fine move fed by a sweet pass from Steve Foster. This was the only goal at the interval and biased that I naturally was, it was a thoroughly deserved lead too. In the second half very shortly after the break Brian Stein almost made it 2-0, only for Arsenal's Lukic to make a great save. It almost seemed as if the Gunners had then said, "OK Luton, you had your chance to finish it but failed." Arsenal now began to gradually have much more possession of the ball.

On 70 mins Arsenal turned the match completely on its head in a bewildering eight-minute spell. Hayes equalised and just three mins later, Smith put Arsenal ahead. With 11 minutes left to play, Rocastle fell over Mal Donaghy's challenge in the area. Referee Mr Worrall pointed to the spot. It was never a penalty & I felt physically sick. We had played so well throughout the match, just like the Everton game in 1985. I was actually beginning to think that supporting Luton was a curse. I said to Bob Rumble, "If they score - I'm away, I just can't take it anymore!" Arsenal's Winterburn ran up and hit it low, firmly to the keepers left. Incredibly, somehow, Officer Dibble dived full stretch to get down to his left and managed to push it round the post! We were delirious, as every single Luton fan rose to their feet & cheered wildly. You could see, hear, FEEL, the tension had lifted. Luton found a new sense of belief and faith.

Seven mins from time their defender Caesar, stumbled on the ball and it went everywhere in the penalty box before somehow, Danny Wilson had headed it over the line. We Luton fans jumped for joy amid amazing scenes, I shouted to Bob, "We will win this in Extra Time now." HOW WRONG WAS I?

Seconds from the end, substitute Ashley Grimes raced down the right wing right in front of us to the bye line. Now Ashley only had a right foot for standing on, so he put a cross over with the OUTSIDE of his left boot - Brian Stein met it and crashed it home into the net! I literally jumped out of my seat, ran down the aisle to the front of the stand and lay down with both of my legs kicking in the air like a deranged lunatic, screaming – "YESSSSSSSSSSSSSSSSSSSSSSSSSSSSSSSSSSSSSSSSSSSSS!" I saw my great friend Judy Brown and as we were hugging each other with such sheer delight – the Ref blew the final whistle!

I screamed out looking up to the sky, "God, if you want to take me now I'll understand and I'll die happy."

The celebrations around half of the stadium, as we lifted the Cup were just a joy to behold. We stayed to watch the glorious lap of honour before making our way back to the Coach Park. As we reached our coach, every one of us was in heaven. I knew there was bound to be some unhappy Gooners about and I was about to find out, but NOTHING would spoil my day.

There was a double deck Arsenal bus near our coach and one of their fans was very irate. I sensed something was about to happen and he then lobbed a wine bottle in my direction. Fortunately, I could see this coming and with my old goalkeeping skills, caught the bottle, which still had wine in - then started to drink it! I swear, even some of the Arsenal fans on that bus were laughing, one of them even gave me the thumbs up. It took ages to get out of the Coach Park and just as we were leaving, I spotted my cousin Iain Roberts with a crowd of Arsenal fans.

Iain is a Golf Professional & was then based at Muswell Hill Golf Course in London, he was the lone Hatter amid his crowd and he took some mild stick from his friends upon recognising me.

We arrived back at the Somerset Tavern in Crawley Green Road, to be met by Deb and all the women who didn't attend the match. The night went like clockwork, everyone enjoying their Steak or Chicken Meals (no Vegetarians amongst us in those days) and at the end of the dinner they insisted on me making a speech. I said something along the lines of, "Will everyone raise their glasses please? I would like to toast Luton Town FC for making this THE Happiest - (kick from Deb) - 2nd happiest, day of my life." I'm very sorry Deb, but apart from when my children were born - this day WAS my happiest! After the meal we went back to the SWMC and continued with the wild celebrations.

Half of Luton did not go into work on the Monday and most of them came into Town to see the victorious and memorable Team Bus Parade that night.

Thousands lined the route from the Ground all through the Town Centre to the Town Hall, where the Mayor had a civic reception for the LTFC players & staff. The week after the Wembley euphoria, Luton travelled to Norwich. With only 3 mins remaining, the Canaries had a comfortable 2-0 lead in what had seemed like an After The Lord Mayor's show performance from Luton. But the resilience shown at Wembley was repeated, the Hatters never say die spirit shone through to come back and draw 2-2.

The League Cup trophy was gloriously paraded around the pitch by our victorious heroes, prior to the home game against struggling Watford. We even felt a touch sorry for our foes (NOT), letting them take the lead by allowing Marvin Johnson to score an own goal. But naturally, reality set in and we put a further nail in Watford's relegation coffin by recovering to win 2-1.

I attended my last away game of the season at Tottenham.

The Spurs fans gave us a great ovation and welcome for beating their hated rivals in the Wembley final. Ashley Grimes scored his 4th and final LTFC goal, as we lost 2-1. He will always be remembered for his vital contribution to THAT game.

The next match was a 1-1 draw at the Dell against Southampton in Meka Nwajiobi's 87th and final LTFC appearance and the very credible same result, occurred at Anfield v Liverpool. Bizarrely, the final two games were against the same opposition, Nottm Forest. At home on Friday the 13th we drew 1-1 again. We did not know at the time, but this was to be Mal Donaghy's 21st and final LTFC goal.

The fourth successive 1-1 draw saw the season end at the City Ground. Four Luton players played their final game for us that day. Ian Allinson, Gary Cobb, Andy Dibble & Mark Stein. We ended a remarkable season in a very credible 9th place, considering the Cup efforts involving three epic Cup Runs.

There was one final match that I attended in 1987-88.

The 1988 Euro Championships were held in West Germany and I went to England's first match in Stuttgart, against the Irish Republic. We lost 1-0.

During that summer of 1988 in July, I heard some extremely distressing news. My old mate Baggy - had committed suicide! He was only 28. I hadn't seen him for a while, although we used to bump in to him on the odd occasion. He was at both my Engagement and Wedding celebrations. I knew that he went to the Wembley final, but not with us. He was living with a girl in Lewsey Farm and was a father to a little girl. We had heard through the grapevine, that he was into drugs more and more and that his lifestyle left a bit to be desired (no surprise there) but when I heard the news I was in a state of shock, especially when we learnt how he had killed himself. He went up to the top of the Arndale Multi Storey Car Park in Luton town centre - and DIVED off! His parents had moved to North West London and they arranged for the Funeral at Golders Green Crematorium. There was dozens of Luton folk, including most of the Strawplaiters lads, there to pay their respects. I travelled with Chris McEvoy, for it was us three that had hung around together for most of his teenage/adult life and although Chris and I were both desperately sad, we always agreed that he would one day either end up in prison - or dead!

Deb liked Baggy and so did my sister Michelle and although he was a devil in Amsterdam when we stayed at Ann's nearly 10 years earlier, she was equally shocked at hearing the tragic news.

I don't and never will know what circumstances led to such tragedy, but I will always remember him as a mad & unique special friend.

RIP Baggy Mate.

Who put the ball in the Arsenal net? Bruno, Bruno Stein.

Arsenal 2 Luton 3. League Cup Winners 1988 – THE best LTFC day of my life!

1988-89

Apart from the four written earlier, another player left the Club in the close season. Brian Stein left for Caen in France and he had certainly made his mark at Luton Town. He played nearly 500 times for the Hatters and is the club's 2nd highest goal scorer in history. Steiny or Bruno, as most fans called him now, struck an amazing 151 goals for Luton before returning for a not so successful season in 1991-92 and adding a further three goals to his tally.

Pre-season, I travelled with Dave and Gary from work to Watford for Luther Blissett's testimonial. There's no such thing as a friendly against them, so losing 3-1 still hurt a touch.

Before Luton's season began I travelled to watch Rangers at Ibrox Park for the first time and saw a 0-0 draw with Hibs.

The first Luton league match was away to Sheff Wed. I drove Steve Toyer up to Hillsborough, we played poorly and lost 1-0. Les Sealey returned from his bad injury and gave Steve & I our only bit of joy, when saving a penalty. In the side that day were three new summer signings, in an unusual all red away strip. Our new record fee of £300,000 was paid to Arsenal for ex-England playmaker Steve Williams, a full back from Oxford John Dreyer and a striker from Chelsea few had heard of, Roy Wegerle. Coming out of Hillsborough and getting in the car for the homeward journey I cheered up a bit on hearing the football results. Rangers had thrashed Celtic 5-1.

Luton's first home match was a 2-2 draw against Wimbledon, about the only thing I can recall from that game was Kingsley Black netting his 1st Luton goal. Now that I had a company car I was in more of a position to drive to further away games. I drove alone to The Dell for our next match at Southampton. Steve Foster had levelled scores, only for Saints to score a late 2-1 winner. One memory from then was that I arrived back in the house at only 6.35pm.

During the week Deb & I travelled to Gatwick to wave off my older sister Ann. Ann, her recent 2nd husband Terry and their baby daughter Rachael, had decided to start a new life in Auckland, New Zealand. Amid tears from Mum, Michelle and us all, they flew off to their new life. Ann loved it there and remains in New Zealand today.

The next game was at home to Man Utd and although having the lion's share of the match, we lost 2-0.

The following weekend Deb and I went to Blackpool. At around this era I had constantly told Deb about how brilliant Blackpool was, having had so many great times there over the years. Deb, like many, turned her nose up at Blackpool and wasn't too keen on the idea of going there.

Well with Luton due to be playing at Everton, it was time to convince her. She agreed to give it a try and see the Blackpool Illuminations. If she hated it, well we wouldn't bother again. We had a brilliant time and she was genuinely shocked at how much she enjoyed it there.

We stayed in a lovely hotel called The Claremont. Right on the seafront on the North Shore, with excellent cabaret entertainment and a wonderful SEVEN course menu. It would be the first of our many visits to this lively resort and the Claremont.

While Deb shopped, I headed over to Liverpool for Goodison Park. Luton played great that day and we won our first game of the season, beating Everton 2-0.

Both of our goals came in the final quarter from David Oldfield & Kingsley Black, they were at the Park End in front of the Hatters fans and I had a cracking front row seat. We had a great Saturday night, going to see the wonderful lights (which stunned Deb) and celebrated our win. I never needed to convince Deb again about Blackpool.

The next game was away again to Nottm Forest. We drew 0-0 in a not particularly enthralling match. In between those two away games we began our defence of the League Cup. The first leg was at home to 4th Division Burnley. We only drew 1-1. Rob Johnson scored what turned out to be his only LTFC goal in 126 apps.

Our first home win came against the Champions, Liverpool. An early goal from Mick Harford was enough to see us win 1-0 in front of what would be the best crowd of the season 12,117.

This was to be Mal Donaghy's final Luton appearance, before his transfer to Man Utd. Mal was one of the greatest signings Luton ever made. David Pleat paid only £25,000 to Larne, in Northern Ireland ten years earlier. He scored 21 goals in over 400 appearances and is Luton's record international cap. Mal played for Northern Ireland 58 times while a Luton player, including 2 World Cups. He will always be in my all time Luton team and simply oozed class on AND off the pitch.

In the 2nd leg of the League Cup at Burnley, I listened on the radio as Ricky Hill scored the only goal to send us through.

Two days later, the Stopsley lads were off to the Douglas Hotel in Hartlepool, for one of our great Pool weekenders. Luton were playing at nearby Middlesbrough, so a few of the Hartlepool lads joined us on our minibus to Ayresome Park. I don't know what it is about the Teesside town but of all the North East clubs, Middlesbrough, is definitely the least welcoming I have experienced. I have never felt worried or threatened at Darlington, Hartlepool, Newcastle or Sunderland, but Middlesbrough was menacing and I was always glad to leave the place. Maybe it stemmed from the kicking I received in 1974. This day was no exception and even though we lost 2-1, we still needed a police escort to the A19 to save us from Boro thugs - trying to attack our bus!

The following Tuesday night, we drew 1-1 at home to Arsenal. Luton played really well and stunning goals from both sides made it a great game.

QPR visited next, in complete contrast to the Arsenal match, this was a dull 0-0. In the League Cup we were drawn away to Leeds. I drove up taking Mick Dolan, Steve Toyer & Rasher Bacon. We foolishly made the mistake of having a drink in the pub next to Elland Road, The Peacock. Being the only ones in there with no colours on, therefore Luton, it was blatantly obvious we were not welcome.

After drinking up pretty damned quick, we managed to escape unharmed – JUST! We beat Leeds 2-0, they had been out of the top flight for over six years and their fans had a ferocious reputation. Although only 19,447 were present, it sounded like 199,447. We were glad to escape out of Leeds in one piece.

From one set of nutcases it was straight into another – Millwall!

They had been promoted to the top flight for the first time in their history and this was the first meeting of the two clubs since THAT night, three years earlier. We arranged to meet up with our Millwall mates, whom we met in Ibiza, for the match at the Den. A good number of us from the Sportsman travelled early to meet up in their pub the Anchor, in Lewisham.

It was so funny, as we entered the pub you could see some of the locals were immediately ready to have a pop at us, but once our Ibiza mates assured them that we were their guests, everything was fine.

At that time I was going through a phase of drinking Bitter (I think I have tried every brew going, Guinness, Lager, Snake Bite, Bitter, bottled beer, you name it). Anyway, the normal Bitter was off tap so I drank Abbot Ale. No worries, I thought, I'll drink it just the same as usual - BIG MISTAKE! They nearly had to carry me out of the pub, after 10 pints or so. For safety's sake, we had already agreed to go in their side at the Den with our Millwall mates. It took the rest of Millwall all of 10 SECONDS to suss out we were Luton fans. In my drunken stupor after stupidly shouting for Luton, I deservedly got a slap. That sobered me up a touch. Millwall fans knew we were with their own kind, so thankfully left us alone (I was quiet now and never shouted again). Having written that, Lord knows what would have occurred had we beat them? We lost 3-1.

We returned to the Anchor with them, had a great night and travelled on the last train home. Deb was not amused at all when I arrived home very drunk.

I was meant to be home earlier, as we were going to a firework party - oops! The following week, I sensibly drove to Coventry, taking Dave & Gary from work. The jinx continued at Highfield Road as we lost 1-0.

Our best win to date, was a comprehensive 4-1 home defeat over West Ham. Danny Wilson's goal was the pick of the bunch, a peach of a strike.

When I drove to the next game at the leaders Norwich, we saw a fantastic Luton performance. Two brilliant goals from Roy Wegerle, gave us a share of the points in a 2-2 draw. The Town really deserved victory that day.

In the League Cup, we welcomed back Wembley hero Andy Dibble with his Man City team. He was given a good greeting and it was a great atmosphere that night. There were plenty of City fans with all those Inflatable Bananas, which they introduced to football around then.

The away ban was officially still in force, but Luton had agreed to admit visitors for Cup games again (they had no choice.) Man City took an early lead but after David Oldfield equalised and then Roy Wegerle gave us the lead, there was only one team going to win. Wegerle scored another late on, to end it 3-1 and we were dreaming of those twin towers again. A frustrating 0-0 home draw with Newcastle followed.

Deb and I then went to visit her Granddad in Kingsbridge, Devon the next weekend. It meant missing my first league game of the season at Derby, but I had to try and make up for the fireworks no show. Naturally, while in Devon I took in the opportunity of visiting another ground. I watched a 1-1 draw between Plymouth and Bournemouth. One player who caught my eye that day was Bournemouth's Ian Bishop. He was magnificent and put on a masterful show, he went on to have a good career at Man City and West Ham.

Miles away at the Baseball Ground, Mick Harford scored a blinding only goal, to give us a 1-0 win at Derby in my absence.

The week before Xmas we drew 1-1 with Aston Villa. We managed to secure Tricky and all his Villa mates tickets, but obviously with no colours showing. Roy Wegerle gave Luton the lead, but a ludicrous own goal by Marvin Johnson shared the points.

On Boxing Day I missed my 2nd game of the season at Tottenham. The morning kick-off meant it was a no go after the Xmas party round our house the night before. We drew 0-

0 and Les Sealey saved a penalty.

I promised Deb that I would be back for the traditional Hogmanay party at Bob Rumble's house. Therefore I drove to Wimbledon. I really regretted going as Luton were thrashed 4-0 by the brute force of the Dons. A paltry crowd of only 4,899 (including plenty from Luton) turned out at this poor Luton showing. Two days later, the complete reverse took place.

At home to Southampton, we completely pulverised the Saints 6-1. Mick Harford & Roy Wegerle each scored two, along with Kingsley Black & Ricky Hill. This was by far the best Luton display thus far - just a pity there were less than 9,000 watching!

The first three games of 1989 were all in South London. First up, was the FA Cup 3rd round at Millwall.

After the last drunken carry on, there was no chance of a repeat, so I travelled on the Bobbers Coach. We were 2-0 down quickly, but a spirited Town comeback followed and saw us level it to 2-2. But the Lion's then scored a winner, to see them through to Round 4.

I wondered how the FA would have reacted if there were a replay. One thing is for certain - there is NO WAY LTFC would have allowed away fans in for that one! We will never know.

There would be no repeat of LTFC in the Simod Cup Final in 1989.

Because Selhurst Park is the worst ground in London to drive too, I travelled on the Bobbers Coach again to Palace. Luton were well beaten 4-1.

It was back to the same venue again, this time by train, to see us play Charlton. We lost again, this time 3-0.

In the Quarter-Final of the League Cup we were confident after drawing Southampton at home, after all, we had just put six past them only 16 days earlier. In a terrible game, we drew 1-1.

Roy Wegerle then scored a sublime goal to beat Everton 1-0 at home.

In the League Cup replay at the Dell I drove down. While having a couple of pre- match Shandies in the pub I made a bold prediction to all and sundry. "We will win this 2-1 after Extra Time." – That is EXACTLY what happened!

Harford and Hill scored.

Before the Nottm Forest home match, we played a testimonial game for Brian Stein against his French side Caen. We beat them 4-1 but a disappointing crowd of only 4,012 turned out for Steiny, he deserved much better.

We played Forest on the week before our 2-leg Semi-Final against West Ham. In an end, to end first half each side scored twice. Forest twice took the lead, but Mick Harford & Kingsley Black both equalised. In the 2nd half there was just one goal, a screamer from Clough that resulted in a 3-2 win for Forest.

The 1st leg of the League Cup Semi was at West Ham.

I took Deb to her Nan's in Wanstead and then caught the tube to nearby Upton Park for the Sunday pm match, being shown live on ITV. I had a seat in the West Stand mainly surrounded by Hammers fans, there were a good number of Luton fans packed in the corner of the South Bank Terrace. In the first half, we more than matched West Ham. Then the Hammers keeper McKnight should have claimed the ball, before big Mick Harford headed it into the empty net. Ten mins into the 2nd half, McKnight made another howler, letting Roy Wegerle's tame shot roll under him. The West Ham fans were absolutely slaughtering him and I don't think he ever played for them again. When West Ham full back Dicks inexplicitly assaulted Roy Wegerle in the penalty area, Danny Wilson made it 3-0 from the spot and this was the final score.

There was no way West Ham would come back from this.

Making his debut for Luton that day was David Beaumont, a defender signed from Dundee Utd. He was exceptional in that 1st leg match and I never saw him play a better game for the Town.

The West Ham fans were pretty angry and hostile all around me, although I personally, never felt threatened or in any danger. I obviously kept a low profile on the tube back to Wanstead.

In the next match a Steve Foster header was the only goal at home to Middlesbrough.

We then travelled to leaders Arsenal. After holding out for over an hour, we succumbed to a Gunners goal. We very nearly equalised, only for Smith to then head in a killer second goal.

The 2nd leg against West Ham was a formality. Mick Harford & Roy Wegerle again scored, this time against recalled West Ham veteran keeper Phil Parkes (McKnight had been dropped after the 1st leg) to win 2-0 and 5-0 on aggregate. A good crowd of 12,020 (West Ham failed to sell all their tickets, understandably) watched, as we secured an astounding League Cup Final Wembley return visit.

The next match was against the Hammers hated rivals Millwall, at home.

There was a huge police presence, despite the away ban. Maybe they were looking for a little revenge for that infamous night? We did get our Millwall mates tickets, but only on the proviso they sat with us. A crowd of less than 8,000 watched Millwall win 2-1, to achieve the double over us. In the evening we took the Millwall boys up to our SWMC. They were absolutely as good as gold that night, but unfortunately I ended up getting thrown out and barred for a month, because I was too drunk - allegedly!

With the League Cup Final coming up, I missed the mid-week trip to Anfield. Good decision, as Liverpool thrashed us 5-0.

A fourth loss in a row followed when Sheff Wed won at Luton 1-0, also completing a double over us.

Mid-week I went to QPR straight from our London office (suit and briefcase too) to see us draw 1-1. Ricky Hill gave us the lead, only for QPR to score a minute later. Unbeknown then, this was the last time I saw my mate Ricky score for LTFC. In my opinion, Ricky Hill was one of the most skilful players to ever grace the Kenilworth Road pitch. In the summer of 1989 he left us for Le Havre, in France. I saw the vast majority of Ricky's 507 Luton games and his 65 goals. It was an honour to actually know him too - we will never see the likes of him again! He would be in each Hatters fans all time XI - he certainly is in mine! I am privileged to have met him and been around to witness his skills playing for LTFC. I actually feel sorry for the modern Hatters fans that have missed out on seeing this huge talent.

While Luton were losing 2-0 at Man Utd, I was at Easter Road watching Rangers beat Hibs 1-0.

Luton lost the next game 3-1 at home to Tottenham. Despite Steve Foster giving us an interval lead, Spurs came back to convincingly beat us.

We then lost again at Aston Villa five days later, 2-1.

Our run of form leading up to Wembley was extremely poor. Seven defeats and a draw from the last eight meant we were now facing a relegation battle.

On Sunday April 9th we were back at Wembley Stadium defending the League Cup. The opposition was Nottm Forest, managed by the unique Brian Clough. Because of my escapades at SWMC on the night of the Millwall match, I was suspended from the club, awaiting the committee meeting. This meant I was forbidden to run a coach again from there to Wembley. The simple solution to that was to run it from nearby 'The Sportsman'.

In a repeat of 1988 I again booked the Somerset Tavern for a meal afterwards, to enable the ladies not attending the match to join us once more.

Wembley had now added seats to the upper terrace sections behind both goals. I had a seat at the upper end opposite the tunnel where the Luton fans were gathered (same end as previously). Sat next to me was Steve Toyer and his Dad. This was the first time in over 22 years Steve's Dad had been to a Luton game with us and sadly it was his last, for he died not long after.

We started well and Ashley Grimes went close with a sizzling effort.

Luton were the better side in the first half and proved it when Mick Harford headed us into the lead on 35 minutes. After very nearly adding a second, the game then turned on 53 mins. Les Sealey came rushing out and needlessly brought down Forest's Hodge for a penalty. Clough scored from the spot. You could see, hear, the relief and belief this had brought to the Forest fans and players.

The bizarre thing was, that Les had done the EXACT same action in the league game at Luton only three weeks prior. When Webb added a second then Clough another, it was 3-1 and all over. I'm sorry but it is my belief, that had Les not been so rash Forest never looked like getting into the match, such was the level of our play. Frankly, he cost us the Cup and sadly never played for Luton again, after 259 appearances. But apart from that major howler, everyone loved Les. He went on to have further success with Man Utd, winning FA Cup and European Cup Winners Cup medals, before tragically dying in 2001, at the young age of 43. RIP Les.

We still enjoyed the meal at the Somerset though.

The following game was on a date no true football fan will ever forget: April 15th 1989.

Alec Chamberlain made his debut in goal as Sealey's replacement at home to Coventry. We drew 2-2 after twice taking the lead through John Dreyer and Danny Wilson. What we saw on the TV screen in the Bobbers Club after this match had paled the result into complete and total insignificance.

Liverpool were playing our Wembley victors Nottm Forest in the FA Cup Semi - Final at Hillsborough, Sheffield, a repeat fixture from the year previous at the same venue. But this year was very different.

Because of numerous road works on the M62, the Liverpool fans journey was taking much longer than in 1988. Partly as a result of this, there were huge queues at the Leppings Lane (Liverpool end) turnstiles and some fans were getting a bit irate as kick off time approached. It was starting to become a danger, with lots of people beginning to get in a crush situation.

Despite being seen clearly on CCTV cameras from the police control room, the chief commanding police officer mistook this for rowdy fans misbehaviour. He then made a catastrophic error, by putting out the order to open the main gates and let the Liverpool crowds flow in. But instead of ordering police/stewards to direct/filter them into two side penned areas (with plenty of spaces), they were all heading into the central pen, which was already full to capacity. With the pressure of all these fans gathering pace a situation arose where some fans literally, could not breath and were being suffocated. When a crash barrier on the terrace buckled under this extreme pressure/chaos, more fatalities started to occur. These horrific scenes were actually being shown on CCTV to the match Commander. But he froze – AND DID NOTHING!

The police at the front of the fenced off terrace had no idea of what was actually occurring and were actually STOPPING people from trying to escape.

They refused to open the front gates. It was only after the Referee had stopped play after 6 minutes, that everyone began to realise the sheer horror, escalating in front of all.

Tragically, 95 Liverpool fans died that afternoon + another 2 at later dates. The real tragedy, apart from the obvious severe loss of life, is that the whole thing could have been avoided quite easily.

If the Officer in charge, Duckenfield, had experience of controlling high profile football matches (this was his first in charge), he would have seen what was happening and made the simple decision to get the ref to delay the kick off. The fans wouldn't have been so eager to get in the ground and this disaster would NOT have occurred - simple as that!

What poured oil onto the fire and made the situation a thousand times worse, were some of the events afterwards.

Families of the deceased were not allowed to touch them in the makeshift morgue and every victim's family was asked how much alcohol did the deceased drink – even though some of them were CHILDREN! It appeared, as though the authorities were trying to blame the fans themselves.

But worse was to follow.

Without finding out if this was genuine, The Sun newspaper printed a Front Page headline - 'Hillsborough The Truth!' Some low life scum had told the paper that the Liverpool fans had robbed and urinated on their dead, this rag went and printed the lies - without seeking any evidence whatsoever! Whoever was responsible for this shit piece of journalism (legally, I cannot reveal his name), should have been sacked on the spot and forced to make a FULL apology at Anfield. Merseyside ever since and to this day, refuses to sell this newspaper and I am in complete solidarity with them. When I was on holiday in Salou in 2006, I had a drink in the Liverpool Supporters' bar there called Shankly's. Adorning the walls amongst all the natural Liverpool paraphernalia was a notice, The Sun will not be tolerated in this establishment. I congratulated the owner on his stance and agreed 100% with him.

In the full Justice Taylor Enquiry, the Liverpool fans were absolved of any blame whatsoever, but astonishingly, gave an open verdict. It was stated at the enquiry that a cut off point of 3.15pm was when all the victims were already dead. This was UNTRUE and the campaign for justice continues. This also means that NOT ONE person has ever been made accountable for this horrific disaster. Liverpool fans have been campaigning ever since through 'The Justice For The 96' (now 97) Campaign, of which I am a proud member, and they will never give up, until that justice finally prevails. We, as all football fans, should back this campaign until the REAL truth comes out and that the victims' families get the compensation, or at the very least, full apology and TRUTH of what REALLY occurred, that is surely owed to them. The families of the deceased can then, start to move on and have closure - an apology from Duckenfield would be a start!

Pic of yours truly taken by Frank Abbott on that great 1988 Wembley day.

RIP *and justice for the 97*

Since I originally wrote the above and am currently updating this book, there has been good and bad news on the brave fight for truth and justice for the 97.

In September 2012, after months of graphic dealings of evidence by an independent panel, it was announced to the world, that the Liverpool fans were COMPLETELY blameless for this appalling tragedy. It was proven that many police officers had tampered with and actually changed their notes on the day, to cover up their failings. The second coroners' inquests were held from April 1st-26th in 2016. They concluded that the Liverpool supporters were UNLAWFULLY KILLED due to GROSS NEGLIGENCE and failures by the police and ambulance services to fulfil their duty of care. So the good news (which a majority knew all along) was that this was no accident, but nearly 100 fellow football fans lost their lives that tragic day - UNLAWFULLY. ...However, there is bad news. Since then at various court cases - Duckenfield and the police officers charged were all found NOT guilty due to lack of evidence.

FFS! In effect, they have all allegedly gotten away with Manslaughter. British justice still stinks, but at least the Hillsborough families can hold their heads high, knowing it was THEY with their years of refusing to accept our legal system's original verdicts - who finally got the TRUTH out there in the public & had the original verdict of Accidental Deaths correctly changed to UNLAWFULLY KILLED. So while those families got the truth of what really happened out there, they never received proper justice for the 97 and most important of all - ANY ACCOUNTABILITY. My heart goes out to them. RIP the 97.

The TRUTH has finally been declared to the world.

Lessons today have STILL not been learnt properly from Hillsborough though, as there are still nightmare situations occurring at various football ground entrances and turnstiles… as I write this just two days after attending QPR v Luton on Nov 19th 2021, it was a miracle there were no serious injuries or fatalities when ONE turnstile was open for the Upper Stand at Loftus Road to over 1,000 Hatters fans. A crush situation occurred because the legions of police had filtered a tiny flow system with barriers… only last month in Denmark, Rangers fans had suffered similar treatment, only this time getting battered by local police at the turnstiles as well for their troubles!

The week after Hillsborough, we played Newcastle away.

This naturally meant a Hartlepool weekender. Stopsley lads travelled on the Friday, but because of work commitments I drove up early Sat morning. We had all booked the Douglas Hotel again.

At St James' Park, a sombre minute's silence for the Liverpool fans was impeccably observed by every single one of the 18,493 there. We drew 0-0.

The following weekend was a vital game for Luton, at home to Derby. Due to the fact that we had secured only three victories in 1989, the last being 11 matches prior, we were now in 18th place and in a relegation spot.

At this very important match, we came flying out of the traps really meaning business and David Preece won us a penalty in the 2nd minute. Danny Wilson slotted it home. We kept up this tempo throughout the match and further goals from Mick Harford & Kingsley Black secured a 3-0 victory, even affording the luxury of a Danny Wilson penalty miss late on.

The next day, Deb and I flew to Ibiza to stay at my cousin Ken's apartment in Cala Llonga. Naturally, when I booked this I checked the fixture list to make sure there was no clash with a home game and knowing I would miss West Ham away. At the time of booking I did not take into account two things:

1) We would be in a relegation scrap and, 2) I certainly - did not envisage us making a Wembley Cup Final again!

So, on the weekend Luton lost at Wembley to Forest, we should have been playing at home to Charlton. This match was later rescheduled and you've guessed it - for when we would be in Ibiza!

This was in pre-EasyJet days, where today you could just reschedule flights on the Internet etc. Believe me, I looked into all sorts of ways to see if I could change it or even fly back to watch the match, but all to no avail. This resulted in my proud record of not missing a single home league or cup match since returning home from Australia over 15 years ago, ending. In fact, if you count my time of actually living in England, it was truly 19 years then.

I managed to ring the Bobbers Club at half-time for the Charlton update, to see how we were faring. To be told, "Alan stay away - we are 4-0 up!"

Obviously, my avid support was not required on this occasion although Charlton did win the 2nd half, resulting in a final score of Luton 5 Charlton 2.

Whilst still in Ibiza, we were brought down to earth losing 1-0 at West Ham.

The final game of 1988-89 was at home to Norwich. Knowing that a win would secure safety, a very tense crowd of 10,862 attended with fingernails ready to be bitten. Our nerves were settled when Luton won an early penalty but when Danny Wilson put it wide, it was tension time again. In the 62nd minute Mick Harford won us another spot kick. You have to admire Danny Wilson's bottle, as he immediately took full responsibility and lined up to take it again.

This time thankfully, he blasted it past the Canaries keeper. 1-0 was the final score and Luton were safe. It transpired, that had we drawn the Norwich game, we still would have escaped relegation on goal difference. Had we lost, Middlesbrough would have stayed up instead of us.

There would be 2 more matches I would attend in 1988-89.

The first was a baptism of fire, my very first Old Firm Celtic v Rangers match in the Scottish Cup Final at Hampden Park. We lost 1-0. Their late goal came from a throw in (right in front of where we stood) - which was RANGERS's but wrongly given to Celtic. They scored as a result of it - Gers were CHEATED!

My final game was at Wembley, to watch England convincingly beat Poland 3-0 in a World Cup Qualifier. I celebrated in style back in Luton at the Mad Hatters club.

RIP Justice AND Accountability for the Liverpool 96 – now 97! While of course never forgetting the 1971 Ibrox Tragedy when 66 Gers fans perished, including an 8 year old boy.

Staying Up – I'm a Dad!

In the summer of 1989, Deb and I went on holiday to Butlins in Minehead with her sister Liz, Geoff and their daughter Lauren.

On the Monday prior I had received my new company car, a Vauxhall Astra. I had it for a whole two nights - before it was stolen outside our house in Turners Road North! The police recovered it the next night in London, it was found with no damage and curiously, a crowbar on the back seat.

I'm afraid Butlins was a disaster, the girls hated it and I must admit that I probably didn't help things by getting pissed every night.

Before the season started we had said goodbye to some various Luton major players. Les Sealey, Steve Foster and Ricky Hill, were the three biggest departures. Fozzie in my opinion was our greatest captain in my time. He scored 14 goals in 212 LTFC appearances.

Mick Kennedy was our only summer signing.

We had a pre-season friendly at home on a Friday night against Hartlepool and our friends Les and co from the North East, spent the weekend in Luton after watching their team get hammered 6-1.

Luton's first match was away to Tottenham. Due to building renovations at White Hart Lane the match was to have a limited all ticket capacity, with no tickets for Luton fans.

Due to our existing away fan ban - we could hardly complain!

However, this did not stop yours truly from attending. During the week leading up to the game I purchased tickets for Keith McEvoy, Shaggy and I from the Tottenham box office.

On a beautiful August sunny day we watched us lose 2-1 from our seats in the Park Lane stand. A brilliant solo goal from Roy Wegerle was not enough. When he scored - I didn't see or hear too many Luton fans cheering!

The first home match of 1989-90 was against Sheff Wed, which we won 2-0. Luton then splashed out our record transfer fee (at that time, until 2019) of £850,000 for Danish striker Lars Elstrup.

He came on as a late Sub in the next match, a 0-0 draw at home to Liverpool. Before this game we had met a crowd of Liverpool fans in the Bobbers Club. We got on really well with them and they were obviously trying to see if anyone could help get them tickets. As previously written, I and all of my friends hated the away ban that our Chairman had introduced and with this in mind, we made sure that every single one of the Scouse lads not only got a ticket for the game, but came back into the Bobbers Club post-match too.

It was something for which they were extremely grateful to us for. One of them said, "We won't forget this, whenever you are in Merseyside we will guarantee you will all be OK."

It didn't take a genius to work out that these lads from Prescot were not angels shall we say, but they were true to their word, behaving themselves in the ground and we kept up friendships with them for years after.

Luton had a fantastic away all vivid bright orange strip and wore it at a 0-0 draw v QPR.

I missed this match as Deb and I were at Ken's Ibiza apartment again.

On return, I was treated to my very first experience of Corporate Hospitality, watching Luton from an executive box.

One of CBC's paper suppliers was a Charlton fan, his company hired a box for the Luton v Charlton match and I was invited as a guest. I have to admit, with all the meal and drinks that day, it was an experience I quite enjoyed and gave me food for thought about involving my employer CBC Print on to the corporate side of things, but that would be for a later time.

A Danny Wilson penalty was enough for Luton to earn three points.

I drove up to Highfield Road to see the usual defeat at Coventry, this time 1-0. In the League Cup, we had drawn Mansfield Town. I missed the first leg due to having Flu. In a high scoring game we won 4-3, Lars Elstrup scored his first two LTFC goals.

We then drew 1-1 at home to Wimbledon.

Luton were then away in the North West meaning only one thing, a trip to Blackpool. Deb needed no persuading anymore and it was off to see those famous lights once more. We had a brilliant time as usual and while Deb shopped, I drove to Maine Road for the match at Man City.

Being alone and my first visit there since that famous great escape six years earlier, I wanted to get out of Manchester after the game asap. Therefore I wore my Rangers shirt, meaning I didn't have to go in the Luton end and be kept in after the game for ages. I went in the City Supporters Club pre match and in there, met the white haired lady who famously chimed that bell at City for many years. Helen has since passed away. RIP. Sitting in the Stand opposite the Luton fans, I watched ex-Hatter David Oldfield give City the lead, they were on a high especially after thrashing rivals United 5-1 the week previous. Kingsley Black equalised and I had to restrain myself from celebrating too much, so it was just polite applause. Ian Bishop (remember him, Plymouth v Bournemouth) gave City the lead again. We lost 3-1 and Roy Wegerle had a penalty saved.

In the 2nd leg at home to Mansfield, Luton ran riot hammering the Stags 7-2, a score line I have never seen repeated since. Lars Elstrup scored a hat trick.

Due to Internationals, we had no game the next week so I took Deb and her Nan to Southend for the day. While they did what women do, I ticked off another ground and watched the Shrimpers beat Scarborough 1-0.

We then lost at home to Aston Villa 1-0 and manager Ray Harford was starting to get a bit of stick. He had a bit of a funny/weird kind of relationship with Luton fans.

There is no doubt, that he was one of the most successful managers we had and yet, he was also the least loved at that time. He came over as a bit dour and sometimes his tactics left a little to be desired, but compared to some future Luton managers - the man was a genius!

The very next week he sent out a team that played brilliant.

Against Norwich we won 4-1 at home. Kingsley Black, John Dreyer, Danny Wilson and Steve Williams all scored before the Canaries hit a consolation. Straight after this match I travelled to Glasgow with Richie Harding. We were up for the next day's Scottish League Cup Final at Hampden Park, Aberdeen v Rangers. In front of 61,190 we watched us lose 2-1 to the Dons, AET.

Two nights later, I drove Dave and Gary from work for the English version of the Cup, up at Everton. We held the league leaders to 0-0 at h-t with David Preece also hitting the Everton bar. But in the 2nd half it was single traffic, Everton won 3-0. This defeat was our first (apart from the final in 89 at Wembley) in the League Cup, since Norwich four years earlier.

We then obtained a very well earned point at Millwall, drawing 1-1. Lars Elstrup struck his first Luton league goal.

Rather than having a session with the Millwall boys I had my sensible hat on and travelled on the Bobbers coach.

Iain Dowie then scored the only goal in a narrow 1-0 victory at home to Derby. The following Saturday, while Deb was with her family at the Lord Mayor's Show in London, I wasn't far away at Selhurst Park, with my Vauxhall client Roy Whitworth. When I asked him to be my guest at the C. Palace match he was thrilled, but didn't want anything flash. He was quite happy to go on the train and be just like normal fans by having a day out drinking + the football. We went into the Palace Crystals Club for a few before the match and then watched a 1-1 draw.

We then had a home game against Man Utd. The crowd of 11,141 was proof that gradually away fans were finding ways of beating the ban, as when Utd won 3-1 there was a considerable amount of noise and celebration from the Manc fans at the Red Devils goals.

During the next week was the wonderful news I had been waiting on for a while. Deb was expecting our first child. To say I was excited - was the understatement of the century! I was absolutely thrilled.

I drove Micky Dolan down to Southampton but recent injuries were now having a major effect on the team selections, we had three centre halves out. At 47 mins and having battled to come from behind twice, Saints then ran riot by scoring another four goals. Lars Elstrup scored a consolation to make it a touch more respectable final score of Southampton 6 Luton 3.

Despite those injuries (Marvin Johnson was our fourth defender to be stretchered off) this was the first time I heard chants of 'Harford Out' by a sizable number of Luton fans.

In front of 12,620 our biggest home crowd that season we drew 0-0 with Spurs.

This was Roy Wegerles 59th and final appearance in a Luton shirt. He became the first Hatters player to be sold for £1,000,000 in a transfer to QPR.

I thought Wegerle was a wonderfully gifted player and he went on to score one of the best goals ever, for QPR at Leeds. But a million pounds was a huge amount of money. LTFC just could not afford to turn the offer down.

I drove alone up to Hillsborough for the Sheff Wed game and sat with the Luton fans in the Leppings Lane Stand. Before the match started I went down to the front of the stand to look at the closed terrace where such devastation had occurred just eight months ago, for a moment's silence and respect.

I couldn't help feeling that having stood in that very spot once in 1970 and remembering a lot of previous experiences of packed terraces - there but for the grace of God go I!

We drew 1-1 with the Owls and our young full back Julian James was involved in a bizarre incident for their goal. He hammered out a clearance from his own area, only for it to smack our own John Dreyer full on the face and ricochet like a bullet past Alec Chamberlain into the net. To his credit, James didn't let it affect his game and later headed in our equaliser.

Due to the chronic injury situation, old hero Mal Donaghy returned from Man Utd on a month's loan. He went straight into the team at Highbury but couldn't stop an Arsenal victory for the Champions. We gave the Gunners a real good game too, but lost 3-2. Lars Elstrup scored both our goals.

On Boxing Day, legend Mick Harford was on the subs bench against Nottm Forest at home. Big Mick had been out injured all season and when he came on to replace injured Lars Elstrup, he received nearly the biggest cheer of all season.

He was clearly unfit, but his sheer presence gave everyone a lift and it enabled Richard Cooke to get Luton's equaliser in a 1-1 draw. It was his only goal in 19 LTFC apps.

Another Xmas visit by cousin Bill Roberts from New York saw us lose 3-0 at home to Chelsea in the final match of the 1980s. In 13 clashes - this is the only time I have ever seen Chelsea beat us at Kenilworth Road!

On New Year's Day I missed the 2-1 loss at Everton, this was the straw that broke the camel's back as far as the LTFC board were concerned and they sacked Ray Harford. Sadly, Ray Harford died of Lung Cancer in August 2003 aged only 58. He had a successful career after Luton, managing Wimbledon and coach to Kenny Dalglish at Blackburn when they won the Premiership in 1995. RIP Ray and thanks for THAT April 1988 Wembley day. Terry Mancini was brought in as caretaker boss.

At this moment in time Deb was having serious problems with the pregnancy, as she suffered a threatened miscarriage. It was an extremely stressful time for the both of us, but obviously more so for her. The Doctor at one point said, "All she can do is rest severely, otherwise nature might have to take its natural course." Frantic with worry, I felt helpless and my state of mind was also affecting Deb. It reached the stage where my worrying was upsetting Deb so much, her parents ordered me to go away. They insisted for me to go and watch Luton at Brighton to give Deb space and also to take my mind off events (as if I could). I agreed to their request and drove to the Goldstone Ground for the FA Cup 3rd round tie.

This was the sole match that Terry Mancini took charge and we were promptly dumped out of the Cup, losing 4-1.

There was quite a bit of trouble involving both sets of fans at Hove station that day, but both that and the game itself, were frankly not in my thoughts much. Mercifully, Deb had the necessary rest and was OK after that (apart from constant morning sickness).

Our new manager was announced as Jimmy Ryan, an ex-Luton player from the 1970s who was currently a coach at the Club. This was a popular choice and went along with the recent appointments of promoting within (apart from Harford). Jimmy Ryan became the seventh boss of Luton in my 23 years and a bit, of support for the club. He had a nice easy start to his managerial career – the leaders Liverpool away!

The Reds had put eight goals past Swansea in the FA Cup in mid-week leading up to this first match in charge for Ryan.

I drove two mates from the Sportsman up to Anfield, both of them Luton/Celtic fans Micky Dolan and Shaggy (Steve Shadlow). We had an enjoyable time in the Liverpool Supporters Club pre-match, with the Scousers giving us gentle ribbing about how they were going to put ten past us. After paying our respects at the Hillsborough memorial we took our seats in the Anfield Road stand in the very front row, to get ready for the expected deluge. Barnes gave Liverpool the lead with a trademark free kick and we held them at bay until 70 mins. Then incredibly, Luton equalised through Kingsley Black in front of the Kop. Making his Luton debut that day was a youngster called Kurt Nogan. He made a dream debut because just after Black's goal, the boy gave us the lead to silence the Koppites & send us Hatters fans into dreamland.

It was one of the most celebrated Luton goals in all my life. This was a situation in which nobody would have thought possible, as it had been a full thirteen months since our last away win in the league.

But Nicol spoilt our party, by heading in a bullet equaliser for the Reds.

We just about held on to the 2-2 draw, of which any Luton supporter would have gladly taken before the match. This was still a fantastic result.

The attendance of 35,312 was the highest that watched Luton in 1989-90. The match at Anfield was Mal Donaghy's 488th and last competitive appearance in a Luton shirt. He did play one more game on the following Tuesday night, in his testimonial against Ricky Hill's Le Havre. Only 4,040 attended and just like for Brian Stein's benefit match, I thought that was a very poor turnout for such a Luton stalwart. He deserved far better.

After such a fine result against Liverpool, Luton then unbelievably sold Mick Harford to Derby. I know he was still recovering from a bad injury and had been out for most of the season and I know £480,000 was a lot of money for a 31-year-old, but this just proved once & for all, that Luton were, always have been and always will be - a selling club!

In the first post-Harford game, at home to QPR we drew 1-1.

Then we gained that elusive away league win, at Wimbledon. I wasn't alone in missing this game, as only 3,618 turned up for this top-flight fixture. We won 2-1. Jimmy Ryan had got off to a fair start, with an away win, a draw at Liverpool and a home draw to QPR.

When Luton had a free weekend due to Internationals, Richie Harding and I went to Ibrox to see Rangers draw 0-0 with Hearts.

The poor away from returned when I saw us lose 2-0 against Charlton at Selhurst Park. We then drew 1-1 at home to Southampton.

I drove up to Old Trafford expecting nothing but a defeat, this was indeed the case and we lost heavily. The only consolation was that at last, I had finally seen us score there in the 4-1 defeat, through Kingsley Black.

The lowest home crowd of all season 8,244 watched a cracking game against Coventry. Kingsley Black had given us a first half lead before the Sky Blues did their usual. The Sky Blues were 2-1 up with only 11 mins left. Everyone including myself thought that it was all over considering our bad record against them but an amazing finale occurred when this time, we came back. First, a young lad called Paul Gray equalised with his only Luton goal in 2 full appearances and then Iain Dowie scored a dramatic 3-2 winner, this being only our second victory of the new decade.

We travelled up to Villa Park with Mick Knight and lost 2-0 to the leaders. They eventually finished 2nd behind champions Liverpool.

Another welcome was given to 1988 Wembley hero Andy Dibble when we played Man City at home. He even tried to help us, by bringing down one of our players for a penalty. Danny Wilson converted, but then City levelled to end it 1-1.

A vital three points were secured when we beat Millwall 2-1 at home.

I then drove to Carrow Road to watch what I thought was our worst performance of all season, certainly under new boss Jimmy Ryan. We were truly awful and the 2-0 Norwich score flattered us.

The following week I went to Stamford Bridge and as on the previous occasion I stood alone on the Chelsea Shed terrace, hoping it would bring the same result. Alas, we lost 1-0 and as yet, I have never returned there. That day, there was a crowd of 15,221, changed days to playing in front of 40,000+ presently.

The next game was at home to high-flying Everton and what a game of ups and downs this was. We got off to a great start when Iain Dowie headed us into a quick lead. When he added another just before the break we cheered off the Hatters at half time in rousing acclaim. In the second period we gave away two daft goals, the final whistle blew at 2-2 and everyone, myself included, thought that was it we are down.

Specifically, for that reason I missed the away trip to Nottm Forest on Easter Monday. The Easter curse struck again, Forest won easily 3-0 and it was now just a matter of time before relegation was confirmed.

Our eight-season stay as a top-flight team, looked as though it was about to come to an end and the ONLY chance of safety was to win all our three remaining games. Considering we had won just seven games all season, this was a tall order and even if we did win them all, other results could still doom us.

When we played next at home to Arsenal, it was as if we had nothing to lose, such was the style and quality of Luton's play. Nothing short of brilliant could describe Luton's performance against the Gunners that day, definitely the best showing of 1989-90. We won 2-0 with goals from Iain Dowie & Kingsley Black - but surely it was too late!

The final home game was against Crystal Palace, who had recently succeeded in reaching the FA Cup Final. We tried valiantly all through the match but just could not break down their organised defence. It was still 0-0 with the match going into injury time and with thirty seconds left - we were relegated! THEN, little Jason Rees ran down the wing beating a couple of Palace defenders, he put a cross in and Iain Dowie met it with perfection to put the ball in the net up the Kenilworth Road end. I honestly do not think I have heard a louder cheer from the Luton fans - as I did that day! Another cheer almost as loud occurred, when news came through that Charlton had beaten Sheff Wed and we STILL had a mathematical chance of survival.

The last game was away to Derby and the task was simple. We HAD to win and Sheff Wed, who were to play Nottm Forest at Hillsborough - HAD to lose!

I had decided to make it a final swansong by going to the Baseball Ground in Fancy Dress.

This was a fad that was becoming popular with fans nationwide at final away games. Originally I had ordered a King Kong gorilla costume but as the weekend was nearing, the abnormal extreme hot weather made my choice absurd and I changed the outfit to something a bit cooler. My choice was now a mad Scotsman, tartan kilt, tam-o-shanter the works. Us Stopsley lads had decided to go by train and we met at an early time on Luton station to make sure we would arrive in Derby for opening time. The station was absolutely packed and it was obvious there was going to be a huge Luton support that day, aka Man City 1983. We set off in great spirits and the train's bar was in full focus for our most important league game since that Maine Road day seven years earlier. We arrived in Derby in great voice and headed to the designated pubs the awaiting police had given us. Without any trouble or problems whatsoever, we headed to the match in our thousands in the glorious sunshine. When we entered the Baseball Ground, the amount of Hatters fans had to be witnessed it was just like the City game, with over 5,000 of us there. We were all gathered behind the goal, in terraces at the front and seats behind. I had a front row seat in the middle stand next to Rasher Bacon.

Luton got off to a blistering start when Tim Breaker scored a 30 yard screamer past keeper Shilton after only two mins. We erupted, but when news filtered through that Forest had scored, the screams were even louder.

It became manic when Kingsley Black scored again to put us two up and when we heard that Forest had scored another after nearly half an hour, the miracle was truly happening - but I'm afraid being a Luton fan is never that simple!

When Wright pulled one back for Derby, the nerves had started to set in. Then calamity, just before the break the Rams had hammered in an equaliser.

At half-time it was 2-2 and although Nottm Forest were doing their bit by leading 2-0, at this stage we were relegated.

I will be honest and write that I thought we had blown it.

Luton came out for the second half with only one thought, Attack! Attack! Attack! Attack! Attack! But try as we might, it just was not happening until after 74 minutes, Kingsley Black hit a fierce shot into the Derby penalty area. It was blocked by a couple of Derby defenders before rebounding back to him, he hit it again, this time not so strongly and with his weaker right foot. It seemed to take an age but it hit the outside of the post and then went into the net.

Yeeeeeeeeeeeeeeeeeeeeeeeeeeees!

The scenes from the Luton end are impossible to describe, unless you were there. I was going mental aka Wembley 1988, this time dancing with Rasher Bacon. We just had to hang on for 15 mins or so. There was no chance of Sheff Wed winning, as they were still losing 2-0. A nerve shattering last couple of minutes were suffered before the ref blew for time up - WE HAD DONE IT!

Forest had added a third just to make it even sweeter. The celebrations by players and fans alike after the game were fantastic and I even saw myself on the end of season video. We stayed up by the skin of our teeth.

We carried on celebrating by getting off the train at Leicester for a night out. Things nearly turned a bit tasty later on though, as local Leicester hooligans thought we were Sheff Utd fans who they had played that day and decided they wanted to have a go at us. Thankfully, one decent Leicester lad among them convinced them that we weren't BBC Sheff Utd thugs, just normal Luton fans celebrating our escape from relegation. I noticed as the night wore on there were more and more Leicester Baby Squad arriving and when the decent lad quietly suggested it might be wise to carry the celebrations on in our own town, we took the hint and left for Luton.

What a night we had in the Mad Hatters club. It seemed as though half of Luton were crammed in as we celebrated until the VERY early hours.

The 1980s had ended and we were still a top-flight team as we were about to enter the Nineties.

CHAPTER FOUR

THE NINETIES

1990-91

Deb and I had no summer holiday in 1990 due to the forthcoming birth of our first child. Before that though on a very hot July night, we celebrated my Grandma Roberts' 80th birthday. She had a party at the Luton Naval Club with friends and family joining up for a terrific evening. Uncle Malcolm organised a fantastic band. We enjoyed a great night, including a heavily pregnant Deb.

9th August 1990 was the best day of my life. On that Thursday, Deb gave birth to our beautiful first child, Georgina. She was born a week premature and I was proudly there to witness this wonderful occasion. In fact not only was I present, but I as good as helped the midwife deliver her. As she came into this world, the midwife said to me, "Come on, Father don't just sit there, baby needs a touch of oxygen, so do the honours and get into action." So, with mask in hand I obeyed. My emotional feelings felt that day, could only be described by men who have achieved fatherhood. It is Simply The Best.

Georgina was born on the same date as Deb's mum Julie.

After leaving Deb and baby Georgina to rest for the night, I went out to celebrate and wet the baby's head with Larry and mates up at the Sportsman. But first I had some important other business to attend. Before actually registering Georgina's birth, I went to the club's office at LTFC to register Georgina as a Junior Hatter. At 7 hours old, she officially held the record as the youngest ever Junior Hatter to be enrolled at that time.

My Sales Career was now going extremely well, I was substantially increasing my turnover and in the summer was promoted to Sales Manager. One of the first things I did in my new role was to persuade Dave Kitching to have Corporate Hospitality at LTFC, in the form of an Executive Box. It was a pretty steep cost for the 5 Seat box but I convinced him as a football fan too, that it would be good for business by treating existing and potential clients. Especially, with Luton still applying the away fan ban scheme.

After negotiating with LTFC to print and help produce a new handbook, CBC agreed to my request. The package included a three Course meal with complimentary drinks before and after the game. The cost if I remember correctly, was £8,000 + VAT. I thought it was worth it for there is no doubt, we benefited as a company enormously.

LTFC was now under new ownership after David Evans had decided to sell his shares. It has been pointed out on a few occasions that Mr Evans had profited a great deal when he sold the ground to the Council and many people never forgave him for this. My personal opinion of the man has two elements.

I didn't like the way he used LTFC for political purposes e.g. The Away Ban and also selling Kenilworth Road to the Council.

On the other hand, if he did not make the money available to invest in the playing squad as he did in the Winter of 1984, we would never had gone on to achieve the glory of reaching two consecutive League Cup Finals.

The new owners were two Property Developers by the names of David Kohler and Peter Nelkin. One of the first things Mr Kohler did was to arrange a 'get to know you' meeting by treating all new and existing corporate members to a lunch. Which of course, now included us. As the CBC Representative, I attended and was sat next to Mr Kohler himself. He was a little Jewish man with a slight Northern accent and it didn't take long before we were chatting about all things football. I asked him what were his main reasons for the recent takeover. He replied that he was actually a Man Utd fan and originated from St Annes, near Blackpool. It was always an ambition of his to own a football club and while the likes of his boyhood favourites was out of his range, when this opportunity arose he jumped at it. He also honestly stated that as he was a property developer, his key aim was to relocate and find LTFC a new home. He told me that while staying at Kenilworth Road with its limited capacity, Luton would find it impossible to actually make a profit and therefore until a new site was achieved, we would have to get used to the economic reality that Luton would always have to sell to survive. Something I was unsurprised to hear.

I have to write, that I actually got on well with him and he genuinely warmed to me, he was also impressed with my knowledge of LTFC. Mr Kohler would go on to become extremely unpopular with the Luton support but I honestly write, that while he was chiefly interested in the new stadium issue, he did genuinely want good things for the club. I got to know him well and there is a true story about our relationship, which I will reveal in the 1995-96 season.

Peter Nelkin would only last a season and I never personally met him.

The only major change to the playing squad was Wembley hero Danny Wilson had left for Sheffield Wed. He appeared for the Hatters 142 times and scored 30 goals, including that famous equaliser against Arsenal.

At this point, no additions to the squad were made.

The first game of the season was a rather tepid 1-1 draw at home to C. Palace. I invited an Eagles supporting client from a London Design Agency, who went on to give us an enormous amount of print that year.

Four nights later, I took the train to see the customary defeat to Arsenal at Highbury. When Lars Elstrup gave Luton the lead with a deft header I actually began to wonder if this was finally the time for my first ever Luton win there. Alas, after they equalised and then added a second, the wait would have to last for at least another year. We lost 2-1.

But I didn't have to wait long for the first victory of the season.

At Southampton, Lars Elstrup netted both Luton goals in a fine 2-1 win. A pattern was beginning to take shape, in terms of our Executive Box.

I was beginning to get many requests by clients who themselves had clients, that were not officially allowed to attend and wanted to see their team play at Luton. This was indeed the case for the next match at home to Man Utd. It was also beginning to prove a very good ploy of winning Print work.

We lost 1-0 against United in a close fought game.

In the next match at home to newly promoted Leeds, I took a Leeds supporting client from a company in Luton that was giving us a large amount of business. This was only the second time I had ever seen Leeds play at Luton. After Kingsley Black headed us into an early lead, the truth is, we were hardly in the game after that but managed to hold on to 1-0 thanks to an outstanding goalkeeping display from Alec Chamberlain. This would not be the last brilliant game he had for us that season either. There were very few of Leeds notorious (at the time) fans present.

If I were to write that losing 6-1 and yet still play well was true, would you believe me? Well that was exactly the case when I went to see us at QPR. Apart from when ex-Hatter Roy Wegerle gave the hoops an early lead we were all over them. Even at 2-0 down I was still not concerned. When our young Welsh lad Ceri Hughes scored after it was 3-0 - Luton were seriously the better team! We still continued to dominate even at 3-1 down, however QPR then scored another THREE times with breakaway goals. I would love to know the match statistics that day, in terms of possession and shots at goal. It was really weird having left Loftus Road and despite losing 6-1, we did play well.

This was Luton's heaviest defeat since Ian Rush had put five past us in the 6-0 loss at Anfield nearly seven years earlier. A pleasing note was the response for the next game at home to Coventry.

Although we had the Box I also kept my season ticket in the Oak Road, because it was only fair that I did not have the monopoly for Corporate Entertainment. For this reason, one of our reps took his clients to the Sky Blues game. An early goal from Iain Dowie was enough to see off my bogey team.

In the League Cup 1st round 1st Leg, Bradford City were our visitors. The third division side battled hard to secure a 1-1 draw. In between the return leg I missed my first game of 1990-91 at Norwich. – And what a match I missed!

Norwich led 1-0 at half time from a very early goal. In the 2nd half Luton completely turned the game on its head thanks to an inspired performance by Steve Williams. He had been recalled to the team for his first appearance of 1990. He laid two goals on a plate from identical situations for Lars Elstrup within eight mins after the break. The Dane secured his hat trick as we romped home.

This 3-1 victory put us in 6th place in the top flight. LTFC have yet to reach that pinnacle spot since. I wonder if we ever will again?

For the return leg at Bradford City's Valley Parade, it was a new ground for me and so I drove Mick Dolan up for it. Just before the match, Luton announced the sale of full back Tim Breaker to West Ham for £600,000. It was the usual, 'We have to sell a player a season response from the LTFC board.' One of the Wembley heroes Tim, will always be remembered by me for his screamer of a goal at Derby in the relegation survival game just five months prior. Tim scored 3 goals in his 262 LTFC apps, none as vital as that 1990 one at the Baseball Ground.

At Bradford, Julian James (Breaker's young replacement) scored a spectacular OG, which flew into the net. Evidently there was some trouble pre-match at Bradford when their Ointment 'firm' gained some revenge on Luton fans for the slashings they had received in town at the 1988 League Cup QF.

Both Mick and I couldn't see Luton coming back until Kingsley Black equalised. It stayed at 1-1 AET and for the very first occasion, I was to witness LTFC in a penalty shoot out. I'm sorry to write, we lost 5-4 on pens. Iain Dowie was the man, whose miss knocked us out.

Which meant a very long late journey home. We then had an away trip to Roker Park, Sunderland and this naturally meant a weekender in Hartlepool. We had a full minibus from Stopsley and once more had booked into the Douglas Hotel. What a fantastic weekend it was too (apart from the result).

After another brilliant goalkeeping display by Alec Chamberlain, it was not enough and we lost 2-0. He really was in the best form of his Luton career, even the Hartlepool lads who joined us raved at his showing. We played well but could just not finish.

On return to the Douglas we all showered before meeting in the hotel restaurant for what was now the customary meal, including bottles of Champagne. We were all in top form that night and when we headed to the 42nd Street Night Club one of the lads pulled a 20-year-old, called Amanda. She rather amusingly said on meeting us, "What, are ya's all a bunch of fucking miners?" This was due to the fact that every one of us had a white shirt on (inadvertently) which shone brilliantly in the violet fluorescent lights. This unnamed lad actually saw Amanda for a while after this trip, as she lived and worked in London but was home in Hartlepool for that weekend.

When I returned back to work on the Monday I had my new company car waiting. It was a white Vauxhall (naturally) Vectra 2.0 Litre.

Lars Elstup scored his seventh goal in ten league games in a 1-1 home draw against Everton. After a stop-start first campaign, Luton's record transfer signing was now showing his worth.

We then had two away games, both losses, at Derby and Liverpool. I missed a 2-1 loss to Derby, but drove up to Anfield, for a 4-0 tanking by the Reds.

We played Man City at home next.

City led 2-0 at half-time, much to the delight of one of my Vauxhall guests. But a spirited fight back by Luton earned us a point. Iain Dowie scored and then in the final minute, John Dreyer levelled from the spot.

Tumble, as he was affectionately known, to us Luton fans had an unusual way of taking penalties. He had a very short run up before striking the ball - taking less than three steps!

An excellent home performance against Aston Villa followed. We won 2-0 courtesy of goals from Kingsley Black & Lars Elstrup.

I travelled with Magnet, Freddie Dann and a few others to Nottingham on the train, where we were staying the night after the match against Forest.

Meeting one of the lads on the train for this trip was Amanda from Hartlepool.

A brilliant display from Lars Elstrup earned us a 2-2 draw, scoring both goals on my 24th anniversary of being a Hatters fan.

Not that I remember everything vividly that day such was the alcohol intake, but I do clearly recall Lars outsprinting England's Des Walker which was no mean feat, for one goal.

Amanda was a total bitch to our mate all through the day and night. Their relationship ended after that weekend.

12,506 watched a 1-1 home draw against Arsenal. It was one of John Dreyer's odd pens that gave us the equaliser. The following Sunday, I travelled to see us play C. Palace who were having a good season and in third place. We did not play well at all, losing 1-0.

We then played a home Zenith Cup (old Simod) tie against West Ham. Only 5,759 were there but they missed a treat - as we hammered the Hammers 5-1!

The final game before Xmas was at Tottenham. The night before this we had our works Xmas party and I came home well pissed (shock/horror - coming home pissed from a Xmas party!) Deb took exception to this and we had a furious row. Now don't get me wrong, if someone is violent through drink, then in my opinion they should knock it on the head. If like me, sometimes you were sick or peed in the wrong place, it's hardly committing a murder. The drinking (or Debs dislike of it) was to be a constant thorn throughout my marriage and often, I took the easy way out by driving and therefore stayed teetotal, because that was the sensible thing to do. But I have Scottish blood in me, and Scots - like a drink! One reason I used to go away with Luton and Rangers a lot, apart from the actual enjoyment, was so that I could have a good drink without getting verbal about it. If you like, it was a form of escapism.

Well I wasn't actually going to go to Spurs that day but after the row I changed my mind, rang Mick Dolan and we went on the train. My cousin Bill Roberts from New York was over for the festive season again and I then arranged for him and his dad Uncle Bill, to meet us pre-match in the pub right next to White Hart Lane.

Due to the night before, it did not take me long to be in a merry mood again and Micky Dolan being half Irish, certainly needed no encouragement for the session. The four of us watched the match sitting in the Park Lane Luton end and saw a really good Hatters performance. We were a touch unlucky to lose 2-1.

After the match we all headed to the West End and had a terrific night. A couple of amusing memories from that night were as follows. 1) In the pub was a Geordie barman friend of Bill's and every time we ordered a round of drinks, he would take whatever note we handed over to him then reimburse us with the equal amount in change. 2) I ended up staying at Mick's parents' house and when I arose in the morning, I remember saying to Mick over breakfast, "Everywhere I looked when I woke up, I felt the Fucking Pope was staring at me." – His mum had pictures of him everywhere!

Deb had thankfully calmed down by Xmas Day and we had a nice festive day, our first as parents.

On Boxing Day, another Rep at CBC had the box and I sat in the Oak Road to watch us play Sheff Utd. We had a nightmare, losing 1-0 to the bottom of the table Blades and to make things worse Ceri Hughes was stretchered off with a serious leg injury, for which he would miss the rest of the campaign.

It was back to the Box for the final game in 1990 against Chelsea. We won our first game in six, beating the Blues 2-0.

On New Year's Day I travelled to Wimbledon now managed by our ex-boss Ray Harford. He sure got his revenge for us sacking him, by beating a very poor Luton side 2-0. I stood on the freezing cold open terrace and the attendance was a measly 4,521. If you took away the amount of Hatters there it would have been nearer 3,000. This was my 4th and final visit to Plough Lane.

For a top-flight club, they did not deserve 1st Division football and ironically in later years, they had nearly the same support as a reformed non-league side.

In the FA Cup 3rd round, we had been drawn to play Sheff Utd at Brammall Lane. Magnet & I arranged to travel on the train. En route to the station I slipped and fell over on a slippery path in High Town Road. My ankle immediatcly swelled up and was throbbing wildly. By the time we arrived at the pub opposite Sheffield station (The Howard if I recall) it was the size of a balloon. Even with the bottles of Becks going down nicely, it was hurting too much to walk the fair distance to the ground so we hailed a cab. As I could hardly walk, we sat in the seats behind the goal at the Luton end. At the goalless half-time stage Magnet persuaded me to seek medical help from the St John Ambulance people. They wrapped me up in a bandage, said it was not broken and I hobbled back up to the seats for the 2nd half. I didn't feel much pain after that, as Luton ripped Sheff Utd to shreds beating them 3-1 with another couple of goals from Lars Elstrup.

A seven goals feast at home to Southampton followed, unfortunately it was the Saints who won it 4-3.

For our next game at Leeds I took a young teenage lad from SWMC/Brickmakers Arms called Lee Adams with us. He was the son of a Domino team colleague. I am writing this because although he liked Luton he was actually a Leeds fan then. I write - he WAS! We converted him to a Hatter that day, and he remains a staunch Luton fan still, having turned his back on Leeds for good, they beat us 2-1.

In the FA Cup 4th round, we drew West Ham at home. Obviously, because it was a Cup game they were allowed 2,000 fans entry. This boosted the attendance to 12,087 one of the best that season. In a one sided game (Luton) the Hammers survived to draw 1-1 and earn a replay at Upton Park. For this replayed match, I took Deb & Georgina to her Nan's in nearby Wanstead, staying the night.

Parris (who also scored at Luton) gave West Ham the lead just before h/t, in what was an even opening half. But I'm afraid they pulverised us in the second period. The Hammers went on to thrash us 5-0. This was only the fourth time I had seen Luton lose on a total of 12 visits to Upton Park.

There was a book written by a West Ham fan out at around this time called "An Irrational Hatred Of Luton". Ironically, I had actually bought two copies from the West Ham Club Shop that very week, they were for a Hammers supporting work colleague Damon & myself. The title stems from the fact that every time the author had watched West Ham play us - they NEVER won!

I suppose I could rename this book "An Irrational Hatred Of Coventry". We played QPR at home next and three points is what was really needed.

Unfortunately, for the first time in 16 visits to Kenilworth Road, it was the Rs who succeeded and therefore did the double over us.

The next match was at home to Liverpool. Three nights before this game the Reds were involved in an epic FA Cup match at Everton. In a pulsating match, they drew 4-4 watched by a thrilled TV audience. The morning after, Kenny Dalglish stunned the football world by announcing his resignation and there was to be no going back on it either – Never, say Never! He returned to the job 20 years later.

He resigned citing pressures of the job was taking its toll on his health. I have to write, that joking aside, his whining at our plastic pitch/the wasted pies and Celtic past, that anyone who went through what he witnessed (TWICE) would have suffered the strains of it all. The dignity he showed after the Hillsborough horrors will always leave me with nothing but admiration for him.

Ronnie Moran, one of the famous Liverpool boot room staff, was installed as Caretaker Manager and he picked the team to play at Luton.

It seemed as though it would be Status Quo, as Molby gave the Reds an interval lead. In the 2nd Half however, things changed dramatically. Kingsley Black equalised and then soon after Iain Dowie incredibly gave us the lead. When he added another, the roof nearly caved in, such was the noise. A fantastic display of brilliant football from Luton had totally turned the game on its head and we won 3-1.

We had qualified for the Semi Final of the ZDS Cup (Simod replacement) at Crystal Palace. But my no win show against the Eagles at Selhurst continued, as we rather timidly lost 3-1.

Against Nottm Forest at home for the next match I was entering the Executive Box Bar area which was in the old Bobbers Club, when a couple of passing Forest fans pleaded with me to help them. They had travelled down knowing that they were not officially allowed entry. But as I have stated a few times I disagreed with this, especially as I loved going away with Luton myself. I only had two clients with me that day, so when I said to the Forest fans, "Not only will I get you both a ticket, but you can join me with my guests in the Executive Box too, if you want," they were astonished and very grateful. Even when Iain Dowie headed in the only goal near the end, they still had a brilliant day - all on CBC!

We didn't know it at the time, but that was Iain Dowie's 19th & final LTFC goal. I drove Mick Dolan up to Maine Road for the mid-week game at Man City.

We sat behind the goal in the old Platt Lane stand with the faithful 200 or so other Hatters. City overran us in the first half to lead 3-0. In what proved to be my 4th and final visit to the famous old ground, this was the full time result.

When I drove Mick to Villa Park (along with Tricky, naturally) four days later, it was to see a vastly improved Luton performance. We responded to the poor display at Man City magnificently, with a terrific first half showing. A bizarre headed own goal from Villa's Mountfield (a slight make up for the 1985 Semi) and a blinding volley from young Welsh lad Mark Pembridge just before h-t, was as good an away showing as any Luton side had given in years. Despite Villa pulling one back and then Alec Chamberlain saving a penalty, we saw out the 2-1 win. To date, this is our last top flight away victory- over 30 years ago!

The third away game in a row was at Coventry four nights later. When Graham Rodger had scored against his old side to give us a 1-0 lead at the interval, I was thinking, 'Is this it? - At LAST!' But alas, of course "I Should Have Known Better" as my musical heroes The Beatles, once sang in 1964. The Sky Blues came back to win 2-1.

We followed this up with a home 1-0 loss against Norwich, even though completely dominating the game.

On this season of 1990-91, Div 1 was being restructured and only two clubs were to be relegated.

After the loss to Norwich, Luton were now five places above safety. Our next game was a nice cosy one at Man Utd and before that match just to make it easier - we sold one of our strikers Iain Dowie to West Ham for £480,000! 'Rocket' man made 78 LTFC apps.

I drove Gary Hopkins from work and an Uncle of his partner Jane, by the name of Frankie Lemmon. Frank was an avid Man U fan and one of the nicest, most genuine blokes you could ever wish to meet. He drank in The Compasses a pub at the bottom of Farley Hill, ran by Jane's Uncle John (a Celtic mate of mine).

As always, we lost at Old Trafford, heavily 4 1. But I must tell you about the Luton goal. After United had taken an early lead, David Preece equalised with a truly bizarre freak goal.

He shot from outside the penalty area towards the famous Stretford End. It hit a divot in the area and the ball actually bounced and - FLEW over ex-Luton hero Les Sealey's head! The crowd of 41,752, the highest to watch Luton in 1990-91, then watched United dominate.

I missed a defeat at Sheff Utd. Despite Luton leading at half time, the Blades came back to win 2-1, climb above us and complete a double.

We were now one place above safety.

Next, Tottenham were fortunate to get away with a 0-0 draw at the Kenny. Particularly when John Dreyer missed a penalty for us.

I had a change of scenery on the social side at this time, in that I was now drinking in a pub in Stopsley called The Brickmakers Arms. There was a great crowd of lads drinking in there at that time, with all the boys who went on the Hartlepool trips including The Farm, Andy Lightfoot, Phil Odell, Magnet, Rasher, Freddy Dann to name but a few.

All of these lads went on a minibus to Chelsea for our next game and for the life of me I cannot recall why I was absent from that Stamford Bridge trip - I missed some game!

Luton were incredibly 3-0 ahead after just 22 minutes. Le Saux reduced the deficit for Chelsea, before being sent off for an elbow offence. But it was the ten men Blues who responded in the 2nd half, pulling back 2 goals to draw 3-3.

Hard to believe today - but the crowd at Chelsea that day was only 9,416!

In front of our lowest attendance 8,219 of 1990-91, we lost 1-0 to Wimbledon and by best memory of that game, was me shouting out a Dutch expletive to the Netherlands Wimbledon goalkeeper Hans Segers from our executive box. The look on his face and wry smile was priceless. This defeat left Luton one place above safety, with three games remaining. 2 of the matches were at home to the clubs below us and sandwiched in between, was a trip to Everton.

The next game v Sunderland was a day to remember apart from the result.

One of the Brickmakers Arms lads was a Sunderland fan appropriately known to all as Sunderland Bob.

He had organised through the landlord and Sunderland fanzine 'A Love Supreme' a coach load of Wearsiders to travel down with the assurance that they would ALL gain entry to the match. The landlord Chris laid on breakfast for them. We arranged for every one of the Makems, temporary membership for the Bobbers Club and all of us Stopsley boys managed to get them tickets, sitting near us in the Oak Road. The crowd of 11,157 had easily by far, the largest away support in the league since the ban was brought in nearly five years earlier.

They were all impeccably behaved and went home even happier, thanks to winning 2-1. I have to write, some of the local support was not best pleased at our helping Sunderland fans with getting tickets, but as far as we were concerned it was the correct thing to do. In fact, after the game, some of the local Luton thug element tried to stir things up but thankfully the Sunderland lads appreciated what we did for them and no trouble occurred.

In all my years of following Luton and personal experiences I have had the best camaraderie generally, with Hartlepool, Liverpool and Sunderland fans.

Two days later on Easter Monday, we all went to watch Peterborough v Hartlepool. Because of the link we had with the Poolie boys, we met them pre-match in a Peterborough pub amongst the many hundreds who had travelled the long distance south that day. The reason that so many had come was because Hartlepool were on the verge of being promoted for the first time in 23 years and for only the second time ever in their history. They drew 1-1.

I have always had a soft spot for Hartlepool going back years, even before the 1988 link. It started in the summer of 1971 when as schoolboys, Chris McEvoy and I had this zany idea that we would both pick a team from each league to support, apart from Luton (then in Div 2). Chris's big team was Chelsea and I chose West Ham. In Div 3 it was Scunthorpe & York respectively and our Div 4 teams Colchester & Hartlepool.

I have already written that I gave up West Ham after our FA Cup defeat in 1972, along with York soon after. Not Hartlepool though. I have looked out for their results ever since.

The next weekend all of us Brickie's lads were off to stay in Liverpool on a weekender, to see Everton v Luton. We booked the Shaftsbury Hotel in Mount Pleasant, not far from Lime Street Station. I discovered that weekend it was the hotel where scenes from the film, 'Letter To Brezhnev' were screened.

True to their word, the Liverpool fans we previously gained entry into Luton for, met us and took us to pubs/clubs, where it was obvious that they were known faces.

On match day, it being the final away game of the season I naturally had to attend Goodison Park in fancy dress. Now I hadn't told anyone about this, just putting my hired costume in the luggage before coming down dressed in it for breakfast to laughter from all, including the guests.

I knew I had made a good choice by the reaction - for I was in the full regalia of CHEWBACCA from Star Wars!

One fond memory was as we arrived by taxis to a pub near Goodison Park, a young boy looked in astonishment and said to his father at the bus stop in his finest Scouse accent, "Daddy, what's Chewbacca doing 'ere?"

The Prescot lads did not come to the match, only the pub beforehand for the session, citing, "No Way are we paying Everton money, we'll see you all tonight." We then watched Luton go down in a rather tame manner, losing 1-0. Although it was a blow, there was no way it was going to ruin our weekend. A fantastic night shared with the Prescot boys was had by all. The band playing live in the Hotel, kindly let me sing a Beatles number and an old Bob Rumble and I favourite 'The Boxer' by Simon & Garfunkel.

But there are always arse holes that want to spoil everyone's fun and try to put a mocker on events. Some local twats started getting a bit lippy with me. Now I usually never get involved in any trouble or anything like that, as I feel it is always best to just ignore that sort of behaviour, but on this occasion I was not going to have these pricks ruining a great weekend, so I gave one of them a slap. Unfortunately, the Prescot boys saw what was going on and true to their word, got involved and it turned into a bit of a riot. The Police were called.

Andy Lightfoot amusingly said to me, "Christ Adair - I go for a piss and come back to fucking World War Three! What happened?"

It was not really that mad, but the Prescot lads repeated, "We told you Luton boys that if ever you came to Liverpool we would make sure you are OK and a few divvies tried the big I am with you, so we decided to teach them a lesson."

In a similar scenario to the previous season, Luton had to win the last match and once again it was against Derby, this time though at home.

Sunderland needed a point more than us at Man City to be safe.

Already relegated Derby, arrived at Kenilworth Road and the best crowd of the season 12,889, were there to see if history repeated itself.

I declined the Executive Box wanting to be with the lads, in what I knew was going to be an emotional day and a hopefully, great atmospheric crowd. To be completely honest, I was not as confident as the previous year. We had won only 3 times in 1991 and had not won at home for nearly three months. The odds were hardly in our favour. We started out the match in the only feasible way, full out attack. But despite playing against a poor team, it seemed as though no breakthrough was forthcoming. Then, just before h-t we won a free kick. Young Jason Rees fired it into the Derby penalty box at the Kenilworth Road End it hit ex-Luton Legend Mick Harford on the head, before flying into the net.

Anybody who was not there would have said aye aye. Yeah, Mick Harford scores an o-g for Luton, but it was not intentional - or so I thought at the time!

It is only as I am writing this book, that big Mick announced recently – the header WAS intentional!

When Lars Elstrup headed another, the old stadium erupted in scenes of pure joy. Then we heard that Sunderland were losing at Man City and the party really did begin to commence. The final whistle blew and we had won 2-0. Sunderland had lost by the same score at Maine Road. Luton were safe AGAIN for the third year running, as thousands invaded the pitch in sheer elation.

A series of events occurred that day, some unbeknown to us:

1) It was the very last time I had seen a game from the famous Oak Road End. (Or so I thought then!)

2) It was the final match played on an artificial surface at Kenilworth Road.

3) It was the last time of no away fans officially disallowed entry in the ground.

4) It was Lars Elstrup's 27th and last goal + final 70th appearance for LTFC.

Finally, most shockingly: 5) It was the last game in charge for Luton boss Jimmy Ryan. More of which, I will explain in a later passage.

In the Bobbers Club post-match I was the happiest man alive.

Luton had escaped relegation, Rangers had won the League again and Hartlepool had gained promotion.

I actually celebrated a bit too much that night, going home extremely drunk and waking up Georgina, even disgracefully throwing up in her pram (I hasten to add, she was not in it).

Although I have never been a violent drunk I was slowly beginning to realise that this was not nice and how a father should behave. There is no doubt that every single problem in my life has been through alcohol and it sometimes had a strain on our marriage. For reasons I have already stated, it was just easier to drink out of Deb's sight and if you like, it was my kind of escape of life's pressures. I'm not saying it was the right thing to do, just the simpler option. Deb & I therefore came to an agreement that I would only drink when away from the home and so I began to lead a bit of a double life.

In the summer of 1991 we went to the New Forest for our holiday. Along with Deb's relations, we stayed in a caravan at a lovely site called Sandy Balls, in Fordingbridge. I was teetotal for most of that summer.

The Great Escape part 2. Baseball Ground 1990. To stay in the top flight after 8 years, Luton not only HAD to beat the Rams and we did 3-2, but Sheff Wed also HAD to lose at home to Nottm Forest and they did too – 0-3!

Relegation

A few major changes happened by the time the new 1991-92 season started at Luton Town. Our top goal scorer and record signing Lars Elstrup had returned to Odense in Denmark. For once, this was not Luton's decision to sell just Elstrup's, citing contract renegotiating breakdown as his reason.

We also started with a new manager.

Jimmy Ryan had kept us in the top flight for two seasons, despite having to sell Mick Harford, Iain Dowie & Tim Breaker with little, or no money to replace them. His reward for this - was to be disgracefully sacked!

My personal view of this was one of disgust and there are some Luton fans because of this action, turned their backs on the Club and NEVER returned. Every Luton fan I knew disagreed with the decision and it was only because David Pleat had been announced as the returning boss, that Luton fans were not in total revolt.

There is a famous saying that 'You should Never Go Back' especially, if successful the initial time. There are very few players or managers I can think of where this has not been the case. And speaking of coming back, we also saw the return of Brian Stein. He would - exactly prove my point in 1991-92!

The first game of the new season I attended was a pre-season friendly at Lincoln. In the Brickies, the landlord Chris was a Lincoln fan of Polish descent. When this mid-week friendly was announced, he immediately organised a coach to take us. What the local Imps fans must have thought at the sight of a full coach of lads arriving in Lincoln at 6pm for a FRIENDLY - I do not know!

It was a new ground for me. For the record, we drew 2-2 and 870 spectators watched. It would be over 20 years before I returned to Sincil Bank again.

I missed the first league game, a 0-0 draw at promoted West Ham as the Adairs were at Deb's relations' in Devon for the weekend.

While in Kingsbridge, I took the opportunity to conquer another ground and went to see Hartlepool play Torquay at Plainmoor. The Gulls won 3-1.

Three days after Devon, I drove up to see us play at Coventry hoping to finally break my jinx. NO CHANCE - Luton were thrashed 5-0! This was the sixth and final time I saw Luton play at Highfield Road - we had lost EVERY game there! CBC Print had agreed once again to hire out the Executive Box for 1991-92.

I would again renew my season ticket for matches when not in the box.

The Football League had by now banned artificial surfaces and Luton also permitted away fans back into Kenilworth Road. They were to be housed in the Oak Road end having 2,100 seats. Unfortunately, because the Bobbers Club was underneath that stand, the Police insisted that the Bobbers had to close on Match Days, otherwise LTFC would fail to get the licence to hold matches.

In compliance with the Hillsborough Report, seats were installed at the lower tier of the Kenilworth Road end.

A brand new covered stand, holding 750 seats was built on the site of the open terraced triangle. This resulted in the only remaining standing area being the middle and top sections of the Kenilworth Road end and even they would have to be seated within three years. All of this reconstruction work had left Kenilworth Road with a capacity of just over 13,500 (less than half the 1959 record attendance of 30,069).

The first home match was against Liverpool and making his debut that day, was £275,000 signing from Spurs, Ulsterman Phil Gray. He was the intended replacement for Lars Elstrup.

In a pretty even game we drew 0-0 with the Reds.

I took a Gunner supporting client from Hitchin to Highbury three nights later and there was no surprise at the result, Luton lost 2-0 to Arsenal. It was the 11th & last time I saw Town play there – NIL Luton wins, two draws and NINE defeats! I thought after the game that night this could be a long old season as after four matches we had yet to score a goal. When Luton accepted a record bid of £1.5 million from Nottm Forest for Kingsley Black - I KNEW it would be!

I missed a 4-1 loss at Chelsea for a valid reason.

Jane Glancy & Gary Hopkins were both work colleagues and also very good friends. They decided to get married on August 31st 1991 and I was privileged for the second time in my life to be Best Man. Jane was and still is, a lovely girl who I have a lot of time for and respect a great deal. To me, she is like a sister. Gary is originally from London and supports Chelsea. He is a very dry character with an articulate appearance. His writing and the way he exists can only be described as perfect such is his attention to detail. He is a top bloke and one of my best friends. This was Gary's second marriage (he has a daughter Zoe) and they married at Luton Register Office. The reception was at the Luton Labour Club.

Everything at the Reception was going great and according to plan, the drink was flowing. I recited my favourite Best Man speech, which I first heard at Liam O'Connell's wedding in the late 1970s and which I used at Larry's too.

"Would you all raise your glasses please, as I would like to propose a toast to Jane and Gary. I sincerely hope, that their wedding night goes as well as my Xmas dinner, a bit of leg, a bit of breast - and plenty of stuffing!"

Deb left not long after with Georgina, as I could tell she was not happy because the drink was flowing full throttle. In fact - I recall her even throwing one of the wedding presents at me! I naturally stayed until the end and when I staggered home late, what I did not account for was to be locked out of my own house.

After unsuccessfully trying to gain entry I resigned myself to going around the back alley and sleep in the garage.

Unfortunately, in my drunken stupor I tripped up on the kerb and knocked my two front teeth out. (They were capped from the kicking I had received on the tube by Arsenal thugs 8 years earlier.) On seeing the state of my face in the mirror the next day, I immediately took the decision that I needed to start to grow up and therefore cut down on the drink.

After VERY expensive dental treatment this was indeed what I started to do, but I'm afraid it was something I could not do on a permanent basis, if that's what some people might describe as Alcoholism - then so be it! I personally, believe I am a binge drinker. I can go for weeks and weeks without alcohol & it doesn't bother me one iota. But if someone was to say to me, you can NEVER drink again - I think I would find that a near impossible task!

On the Wednesday evening after the wedding I used my season ticket (I could hardly take clients, looking like Denis the Menace) to see Luton v Southampton. When Le Tissier gave the Saints the lead from the penalty spot I began to wonder if I would EVER see Luton score again - let alone win! But no worries, just 120 seconds later Phil Gray added to his Chelsea goal by levelling matters with a cracking volley. Then just before the interval Richard Harvey scored an even better goal. The 2-1 win gave us our 1st victory of 1991-92.

When I went to see Luton play Wimbledon in their shared stadium with C. Palace at Selhurst Park I did something I had never done before, left the ground early in disgust. Wimbledon had left their ramshackle Plough Lane ground.

Faced with huge costs to meet the Taylor report, it was felt by their chairman Sam Hamman that the Dons had no choice but to either rebuild Plough Lane or ground share. He took the cheaper option and this was the beginning of the end, literally, for them. In front of a pitiful crowd of just 3,231, indeed, the second lowest attendance in top-flight history, Luton put in a shambolic performance.

After 77 minutes and the score at 3-0 to Wimbledon I, along with most of the other Hatters fans, had enough and left. So bad were we that day - we had never even won a corner!

David Pleat had quickly realised the team were not good enough and said to the board if we do not strengthen now, we might be relegated by Xmas. Thankfully, Mr Kohler (Nelkin had left by now) listened and loosened the purse strings to bring back Mick Harford from Derby for £325,000, in time for the next game at home to promoted Oldham.

Now I know I always say never go back, well on this occasion I was delighted that we did. An increase of nearly 1,000 on the previous home crowd had pushed the attendance over 9,000. But with only five mins remaining and 1-0 down, it seemed as though - even legends couldn't save us! But all of a sudden our hero dramatically changed things, first he tapped in an equaliser that even I today, could score and then in the last minute he brought the house down.

Somehow he volleyed in the ball with his right foot over his LEFT shoulder. There has rarely been a goal met with such accolade. This 2-1 win alone, lifted us out of the bottom three from last place.

In between the shambles of Wimbledon and the rebirth of our hero I watched England lose 1-0 at Wembley in a friendly against Germany.

A crowd fifteen short of 10,000 turned up for the next match at home to QPR hoping to see more amazement. No repeat sadly, we lost 1-0.

I drove a full car up to Old Trafford and watched us fight quite hard in the first half. We went in only 1-0 down at the break. Once Bruce added a second for Man United, the floodgates opened. United ran out 5-0 winners in front of 46,491 and this, is the largest league attendance I have ever seen Luton play in. On the return journey, with scarves still flying defiantly I was pulled over by the police on the M6. The officer told me, "We clocked you travelling at 94mph. So where have you lot all been to today then?"

"Man Utd and we lost 5-0," I replied.

"Well look on the bright side son, you have got three more points than your team did today," along with a £40 fine – we had to laugh, a copper with a sense of humour! This heavy defeat had left us second from bottom after 10 games.

In the League Cup 1st leg I watched us draw 2-2 in an entertaining game against Birmingham from our Executive Box.

Promoted Notts County came to town and brought a pathetic following with them, one reason why only 7,629 attended. Phil Gray had given us a 1-0 lead & just as we thought a vital win had occurred, the Magpies scored a late penalty.

I took Tricky up to Villa Park and he was the happier, as we were crushed 4-0. It was back up to the second city three nights later, for the return leg against Birmingham. When 3rd division Blues went 2-0 up after an hour, a mate of mine sitting next to me called Shaun Tyler, upped and left. He must have felt a little foolish, as within three mins it was 2-2 thanks to Phil Gray's double. There was now only one team in it and it was not Birmingham. However, completely against the run of play, Blues snatched a last-minute winner.

A full Oak Road End of Sheff Wed fans then watched a 2-2 draw in which the Owls should have been dead and buried. Kurt Nogan scored his fourth and final LTFC goal to give us a 2-1 lead. No wonder it was his last for us, he should have had FIVE that day - three of them absolute sitters! We were punished for his poor finishing when Wednesday equalised in the final minute.

Full back Matt Jackson was then sold to Everton for £600,000 after only 12 appearances.

I drove to Norwich and but for goalkeeper Alec Chamberlain, we would have been thrashed, such was the onslaught. It ended 1-0 to the Canaries.

The same result then occurred at home to Everton.

In the next match at Tottenham, was a game of two halves. In the first period Luton played their best football all season. When Mick Harford gave us the lead just before the interval, it was fully deserved. The start of the 2nd half was no different and then the floodlights failed after an hour. When the teams returned after the delay you could not believe it was the same Spurs side. They changed the formation, bringing on two subs and then wiped the floor with us, scoring 4 goals.

I had a Man City supporting guest from Vauxhall in the box next game and we watched an excellent 2-2 draw, to prevent four losses in a row.

When Paul Telfer scored his first Luton goal at Brammall Lane with 11 minutes remaining I really thought that first elusive away win was ours.

But Luton being Luton just could not hold on. Sheff Utd equalised on 88 mins. League leaders Leeds, were the next visitors. The highest crowd at that point of 11,550 watched an even contest in the first half. But two Leeds goals in a minute finished us off. We were now in a desperate situation.

Bottom placed and without a single away victory and no win at all in 12 games. Only 7,533 turned up for a pre- Xmas Friday night game at home to Coventry.

There was just the one goal scored but thankfully, it was by big Mick Harford. Beating the jinx team and coming on the night of our works Xmas party, this turned out to be a fine end to the week.

I had also managed to win a contract with Vauxhall for at least three years, which secured everyone's jobs at CBC.

On Boxing Day, there was an early kick off at home to Arsenal. With the great news about Vauxhall I treated their graphic designers in the Box to a Champagne Breakfast.

A good crowd of 12,665 also shared my joy as we managed to beat the Gunners. Mick Harford once again scored the only goal with a cracking volley and suddenly we started to believe once more.

Two days later and again from the Executive Box, we entertained Chelsea. I took a Blues supporting client Mick James. Chelsea fan, Prime Minister John Major was also in attendance - though I hasten to add, not with us!

A stunning goal from Richard Harvey and a penalty from John Dreyer were enough to see out a brilliant 2-0 win. We even had the luxury of another penalty, but this time missed by big Mick.

The final three matches of 1991 had produced more victories than in the previous NINETEEN. It was akin to 1974-75 & had lifted us out of the relegation zone and gave everyone a huge lift for the forthcoming New Year fight. We just had to correct our wretched away results.

On New Year's Day I drove Deb and Georgina up to her Aunt Gill's on my way to Nottm Forest, a match I was eagerly awaiting.

After just 33 SECONDS Luton had taken the lead thanks to a pile driver from Mark Pembridge. We played excellent that day but just could not get that extra goal to finish them off. The Reds were eventually gaining more possession in the later stages and began to heap the pressure on. The fantastic Luton following among the 23,809 crowd was frantically screaming for the ref to blow for the final whistle. Then disaster, Forest equalised. Des Walker, of all people scored it - his one and ONLY goal in the whole of his fucking career!

In the FA Cup 3rd round for the second consecutive year, we were drawn to play at Sheff Utd. There was to be no repeat Luton victory this time, as we lost heavily 4-0. I must write though, we did not deserve such a thrashing.

Alec Chamberlain, for so long a brilliant performer in goal for the Hatters had a rare off day. Perhaps it was because he had a touch of nerves, playing instead of recent loan keeper Steve Sutton who was Cup Tied.

Sutton was installed back in goal for the daunting trip to Anfield, Liverpool.

When Tanner scored an own goal against the run of play to give us the lead, I just began to wonder. Despite incessant Liverpool pressure, we were somehow still leading with only five mins remaining. But I'm afraid to write, and this would not be for the last time this season, Luton capitulated by losing two goals. That 2-1 Liverpool win was (at this point in time) my 9th & last trip to Anfield.

Unsurprisingly, I have yet to see a Luton victory there in eight visits. After West Ham beat us 1-0 at the Kenny, we returned to bottom place.

I missed the game at Hillsborough, in which recent signing from Leicester Scott Oakes opened his Luton account to give us a 2-1 half time lead. Ditto the Luton collapse, this time conceding two goals in the last 12 mins.

There was a shocking first half display by Luton at home to Norwich that followed. But at least it was goalless. The vastly improved second period from the Hatters ended with a hugely needed 2-0 victory.

In the game at Man City, which I missed, according to the reports Luton played the better football and yet lost 4-0?

After 20 appearances on his return to Luton, Brian Stein finally scored with an early goal at home to Sheff Utd. The Blades levelled but we regained the lead with a Mick Harford header and despite John Dreyer missing a penalty, we held on to win 2-1.

In a mid-week game at Crystal Palace I headed straight from our London office with the Eagles supporting client. We earned a deserved 1-1 draw.

Two days later I received a sad phone call at work from cousin Ken Adair. Grandma Adair had a massive heart attack and was rushed to Hospital. I left for the L&D immediately. When I arrived it was pitiful, Grandma just looked asleep. I had never envisaged this day coming. Both Deb & I always said Isa would live to be over 100.

We stayed with her for a long time and I don't mind admitting to weeping many tears. She died the next day, aged 83. RIP ISA.

When Mick Dolan married, I missed a 2-0 loss at Leeds to attend his big day. Before C. Palace at home, we attended Grandma's funeral.

I adored Isa and know she was a good age, but she had been so good to me. Naturally, she worshipped all five of her grandchildren but please do not read this the wrong way, I always felt that I was the closest to her. Uncle Willie Adair came down from Scotland to pay his respects, but sadly Michelle could not be there as she was visiting Ann in New Zealand on holiday.

Once again I was with the Palace supporting client in the Executive Box against the Eagles and I'm pleased to write it was he, who went home unhappy. There was a stunning volleyed winning goal from Scott Oakes, right near our box to give us the winning goal in a 2-1 victory. It pleased me further, for he came over to shake my hand in the celebrations that followed the strike.

Then, another London client and I watched a dull 0-0 draw at home to Spurs.

I missed Brian Stein's second goal of the season on Merseyside, in a 1-1 draw at Everton because Deb & I were visiting her relations in Devon.

We had also sold our house in Turners Road North at this time and had managed to agree a deal to buy a 4-Bed detached house in Putteridge Road, just five doors away from the Adair family home of 1968-72.

A sign of the changing property market was the price we paid, £82,000. In 1968 my Dad had paid - just £5,000!

While staying at Deb's Granddad's, I ticked off another ground and watched Exeter beat Leyton Orient 2-0 at the other St James' Park, in front of only 3,070. The next weekend I was down south again, at Southampton. Mark Pembridge fired us into the lead at the Dell in the very first minute with a scorching free kick. But as was so often the case in 1991-92, we could not hold on to the lead. 2nd half goals from Alan Shearer and ex-Hatter Iain Dowie gave the Saints a 2-1 victory in front of a big travelling Luton support.

We then beat Wimbledon 2-1 at home to keep the escape dream still alive. Loan signing Imre Varadi scored his one and only LTFC goal.

I drove alone to Oldham for the vital game at Boundary Park. For once, it was a nice sunny day there and certainly the biggest crowd, 13,210 that I had been in at the Lancashire club. Mick Harford had equalised Sharp's goal, but a minute later the ex-Everton Scot added a second for Oldham. With ten mins left there was no change to the score, but then Sharp hit two more and the Latics finished winning 5-1. On the long journey home I felt we were doomed.

I then caught flu and it MUST have been bad, because I missed my first home game in three years and only the second in 18, against Nottm Forest.

Perhaps it was an omen, because although ex-Hatter Kingsley Black gave Forest an early lead, for a nice change it was us who came back to win 2-1.

Man Utd were in town next and a never to be beaten crowd of 13,410 turned up to watch the league leaders. United were trying to win their first title since the halcyon days of Law, Best and Charlton in 1967. Sharpe gave the Red Devils an interval lead but Mick Harford headed a deserved equaliser, in a final result of 1-1. Two huge points dropped for Utd, which would eventually prove very costly for them as Leeds eventually beat them to the title.

This was our legend Mick Harford's 92nd and final goal for LTFC. He was one of the greatest ever strikers to wear the Hatters shirt, certainly in my era and was the last Luton player to represent England as a full international. Having met the big man personally, many times – LEGEND, I SALUTE YOU – I didn't go to QPR on Easter Monday, as we had to get everything ready for our house move that week. But that didn't stop me from listening to the game on the radio. Incredibly, once again Luton caved in after taking the lead, through a Mark Pembridge penalty. The noisy cheering Luton thousands were silenced by 2 goals from QPR in the final ten minutes.

For the two remaining 1991-92 games, just as in the previous three seasons, we had to win both and rely on other results too. Anything less and we were down. I was kindly invited to join David Kohler in the Boardroom for lunch and sit in the Directors balcony at the final home match against Aston Villa.

At lunch I was sitting next to Villa Chairman Doug Ellis and we had a good chat. He was impressed with my football knowledge and seemed pleased to hear of my attendance at Villa's famous European Cup win in Rotterdam ten years earlier.

Luton were really up for this match and fully deserved our 2-0 win. At least if we were to go down, we were going to go with a fight. Mark Pembridge and Brian Stein scored – proving to be both their final LTFC goals.

Stein had an amazing Luton career as I have already written, but just 3 goals in 41 appearances (inc 8 as sub) in his comeback - is perhaps best forgotten!

Incredibly, due to other results that day we still had a chance of staying up going into the final game at Notts County. The scenario was simple Luton HAD to win at Meadow Lane (despite failing to win away all season) and Coventry (who had been in the top flight for 25 years) HAD to lose at Aston Villa.

I left our recently moved in house in Putteridge Road to meet the lads at the train station, having told Deb we would stay the night in Nottingham. This being the final away game meant I naturally, was in fancy dress and was dressed as a Teddy Bear. Having booked a B&B Guest House near Trent Bridge, we headed to nearby bar, the Aviary for opening time.

Of course there was an army of Luton fans in Nottingham that day and that pub like all the others near the ground, was soon mobbed.

We got on well with a group of Geordies who were down for their own relegation battle at nearby Leicester, in the division below us.

In fine voice, we headed for the match. Notts County should have already started demolition work on revamping their ground that week, to comply with the Taylor report.

Because of the importance of the fixture and the fact Luton were bringing over 5,000 fans with them, it made sense for them to delay the start, for another week. County had already been relegated but this decision boosted the crowd to 11,380 and almost half of the attendance, were Hatters fans. I took my seat to many admirers, it was only when I lifted off my mask for a fag that Yvette Brown recognised me and told me some good news.

I had won £100 on the daily LTFC Lottery the day prior. I prayed this would not be the last good news of the day. After just five minutes, there was a huge roar as news came in that Villa were beating Coventry 1-0. When Julian James gave us the lead 13 mins later, everyone was saying - it's happening AGAIN! The news got even better as Villa went 2-0 up before half time. But when Matthews equalised for County you could hear the sighs. Never mind, all we had to do in the second half was score more than them. When we really needed to push on in the second period I'm sorry to write, we froze and failed to grasp the situation. Nearly 20 mins from the end Matthews (who would sign for Luton later in his career) added a killer second goal to seal our fate. Everyone just KNEW that was it. Phil Gray missed a sitter near the end, but it was too late by then anyway.

After an incredible 10 years as a top-flight club, our reign was over and we were relegated, along with Notts County and West Ham.

For a club the size of Luton, to last that long in the top tier - it will NEVER, EVER happen again! The real pity about our relegation was a number of facts: 1) Just a single away victory would have saved us 2) We had let slip a lead to draw or lose, therefore costing us points, TWELVE times and worse, 8 of those were with less than ten minutes remaining 3) And for me this is the most galling, our Chairman was part of a committee to vote for major change in the way football was run from the top.

The Division 1 clubs decided to break away from the Football League and join forces with the FA to start a new Premier League heavily backed by satellite TV company SKY. This deal would change football forever and the Premier League became and still is today, the richest league competition in world football.

Earning staggering amounts of money for every partaking club in this elite league - we were ONE win away, from joining them!

Coming out of Meadow Lane that day I saw Maine Road hero Raddy Antic in the street looking equally glum, as I proudly shook his hand. What a difference from nine years prior. We went to a pub on our way back to the City centre, a pub in which I had frequented on numerous occasions on my visits to either Forest or County, to drown our sorrows. Unfortunately, the events of the day and emotions sadly resulted in a mass bar room brawl. Glasses, bottles and ashtrays amongst other items were flying in all directions, as lads viciously laid into each other.

What made it even worse, was these were LUTON fans fighting amongst themselves, with not a local in sight. The last thing I needed was to get involved in any way, so I just stood back and left the battle zone for a fag outside, before heading away with a couple of other lads. When the police arrived, apparently someone had said that a bloke dressed as a Teddy Bear was in the pub. As I walked innocently on the police asked me then to accompany them to the station. On being questioned, I politely told them that there was no way I was involved in any violence. "Just ask the landlord?" I pleaded. About an hour later, the officers came in and said I was free to go. They had indeed gone back and asked him. After this nightmare of a day I returned to the guesthouse, changed out of my outfit and had a quiet night in the hotel bar before leaving the next morning.

1992-93

Our summer holiday in 1992 was just for a week in Amsterdam. We flew from Stansted airport for the first time and this was Georgina's first flight. We stayed in a lovely hotel near Amsterdam Central Station. While there, I tried to track down Leo my ex-brother-in-law from days gone by, finding him proved fruitless though.

At work, things were going very well and I had negotiated a new company car, which was the new Vauxhall Calibra. It was flame red with a 2.0 Litre engine.

I took Deb & Georgina down to Devon in it for a weekend where we stayed in Plymouth. Luton were playing Argyle in a testimonial for one of their old players. My first Hatters visit to Home Park resulted in a 2-2 draw.

Now that we had been relegated from the top flight CBC could not justify the expense of an Executive Box anymore. However, I did manage to persuade them to still have some corporate hospitality and they invested in three season passes for the Kenilworth Suite, which consisted of a meal, car park space, programmes, all drinks pre- & post-match + seats in the Directors Balcony, all inclusive.

The first match of the new season at the lower level was at Leicester.

It was a weird set up Luton were now in. Due to the newly formed Premiership, the previous Div 2 had become League 1 – so we had been relegated from Div 1 to Div 1! A new rule had also been introduced, where the goalkeeper was no longer allowed to pick up the ball from an intentional back pass.

I took my place in the side stand at Filbert Street and including half of a terrace behind the goal in their Kop, a staggering 5,000 Hatters fans were present.

Players that had departed from our squad were:

David Beaumont, legend Mick Harford had left the Hatters for a final time as a player to sign for Chelsea, Darren McDonough, Kurt Nogan, Graham Rodger & Brian Stein. The biggest fee received was for Mark Pembridge who signed for Derby at £1,250,000.

Our only signing was Steve Claridge from Cambridge for £160,000.

Young Jamie Campbell scored his first (& only) LTFC goal to give us the lead as Luton were playing fast flowing football against the Foxes. But just as so many times the previous season, we could not hold on and Leicester won 2-1. It wasn't a great personal day as Rangers also lost, 4-3 at Dundee. But that would be the Gers' last defeat for an incredible 48 games - including being unbeaten in the Champions League! Rangers also went on to win a domestic treble and their 5th of nine titles in a row.

The night prior to our first home match against Bristol City, I drove to a nearby ground to tick off the list and saw Barnet overcome Colchester 3-1.

Against Bristol City, I took along Roy Whitworth from Vauxhall as a thank you for the continuing business. We arrived early (free bar) and I recall being amazed at how few people were not doing the same thing.

It was only after lunch that substantial numbers began to arrive. Most of the people in that area of the club were not drinkers like myself and I found that the few numbers present were similar at future games. Still, I thoroughly enjoyed the Kenilworth Suite, actually preferring it to the Box.

The main reason for this preference was the amount of famous football faces I would get to see and meet in this area over the years.

If I had any thoughts that the lower league was going to be easy, they quickly vanished against Bristol City. Andy Cole tore us apart in a 3-0 away win. The attendance of 7,926 had only been lower twice the previous season.

We travelled on the train to Upton Park to see Luton play Charlton there. The Addicks had left their ground share at Selhurst Park and were temporarily sharing with West Ham, until their prodigal return to the Valley. Against the early league leaders, we fought hard to obtain a 0-0 draw.

Four nights later I drove Keith McEvoy on the long trek up to Newcastle. It didn't take as long as I thought it would, thanks to my new Calibra.

The Geordies were on a mission to get back to being a big Club ASAP after giving Kevin Keegan his first managerial role. In front of a passionate 27,054 crowd, Luton more than held our own initially but two goals by the Magpies before half time killed us. 2-0 was the final result and Newcastle would go on to win the title by 12 points.

Our lowest crowd for over four years turned up at home to Tranmere. 6,801 watched a thrilling game. This was the first time I had seen Rovers for over 22 years. Steve Claridge opened the scoring with his first Luton goal and each team would take turns to lead, with Tranmere going in at the break 3-2 up. Only one goal in the second period, that was from Scott Oakes to end it 3-3.

The following Sunday I drove to see Luton at Griffin Park for the first time against newly promoted Brentford. It did not stop raining all day as I sat and watched a first Luton victory by 2-1. Julian James & Phil Gray scored the goals. An old competition from the 1970s was brought back called the Anglo Italian Cup. In our English group, to see who would qualify to meet Italian opponents was Bristol City & Watford. It was off to Vicarage Road, our first visit in 5 years. Although a Micky Mouse Cup, 5,197 watched as we fought out a 0-0 draw.

Around about this time at the SWMC, I had recently heard from Steve Toyer about this new thing they had started called 'Open The Box'. Basically, it was a raffle drawn to members all throughout the week leading up to the Sat night. Space dictates, so I will tell you that on my very first attempt I scooped the winning ticket and won £840. This allowed me to have the opportunity to open the box, which only had 3 keys left from the previous 10 weeks. If I successfully opened the box, I would win the accrued amount of another £2,200! – I DID!

This OTB raffle carried on for many years, but the Lottery eventually killed it off and SWMC ceased it - I was its biggest ever winner!

We were at home to Birmingham that day and despite Blues being near the top and us nearer the bottom, they certainly knew they were in a game. Steve Claridge scored a late penalty to give us a deserved point in the 1-1 draw.

In the League Cup, we had been drawn against Div 2 (old 3) Plymouth and the first leg at Luton produced a 2-2 draw, Claridge netting both Luton goals.

I missed my first game of the season at Notts County because we were in Blackpool for the illuminations weekend and I had treated Michelle and her daughter Kirsty to come with us, from my recent windfall. While staying at Blackpool I took the opportunity to go and see

Hartlepool win 2-0 at Preston. The result of the Town match I missed at Meadow Lane was 0-0.

In mid-week we were knocked out of the Anglo Italian Cup when Bristol City came and drew 1-1.

At home again a few days later, came an embarrassing 4-1 thrashing at the hands of Portsmouth. How the game was ever allowed to start I'll never know. The pitch was waterlogged but no excuses, we took a mighty beating.

In the 2nd leg of the League Cup at Plymouth we were knocked out. A brave fight back after going 3-0 behind was not quite enough. Steve Claridge scored his final LTFC goal in his very brief Luton career with another from David Preece, saw us exit 6-5 on aggregate. Claridge had scored five goals in 18 appearances for Luton. He was sold back to Cambridge for £195,000 and at least we had made a profit of £35,000.

We drove up to stay a night with Deb's friends Cherine & Gary in Wincobank, Sheffield for Luton's game at nearby Barnsley. This was my first visit to Oakwell. We lost 3-0 but I have to write we had no luck at all, hitting the woodwork THREE times in the 2nd half. After this result Luton were one place off the bottom.

Mark Pembridge returned to Luton with Derby and the Rams took the lead just before the interval. Marvin Johnson levelled with his first Luton goal. In front of a full Derby contingent in the Oak Road, Derby went on to win 3-1.

I went to see Luton at Peterborough for the first time. Two goals from Phil Gray and one from Paul Telfer gave us a deserved 3-1 half time lead in a fantastic Luton display. Posh pulled one back but we held on for only our second 1992-93 victory.

Next was a game at home to Southend, the honours shared at 2-2. We had now hit a run of eight home games without a victory.

Two nights before bonfire night had fireworks of its own, as I drove the short journey to Cambridge. In what was easily the best first half showing by Luton at that point in time, we cruised to a 2-0 interval lead thanks to Scott Oakes & Phil Gray. When Gray added another soon into the 2nd half, Ole's started to ring out from the big Luton away following. Cambridge had their first shot on target after 74 mins and scored what we all thought was a mere consolation. But thanks to a capitulation from the Luton defence and in particular goalkeeper Andy Petterson, Cambridge incredibly came back to draw 3-3. Petterson never played for the Hatters again.

The next night I cheered on Rangers as they beat Leeds 2-1 at Elland Road in the Champs League qualifier to go through to the group stages 4-2 on aggregate.

This was in the new Champions League qualifying round. Police had ordered both clubs not to allow away fans into both games for fear of crowd violence. Thanks to a Leeds supporting client of mine, he secured me a ticket at Elland Road for the second leg. When Mark Hately scored an early screamer, the overall score at 3-1, meant the tie was as good as over. My problem was, that I instantaneously jumped up to celebrate Hately's goal and was nearly lynched by Leeds fans.

When McCoist added Rangers second, I just sat there with arms folded and a Leeds fan next to me said, "Wise move, pal." Fortunately, I left with no further hassle.

Three days later, in front of just 6,928, I watched Luton thrashed 4-1 at home to Grimsby. It became even worse the next week when we were soaked to the skin at the

Manor Ground, Oxford as we embarrassingly, capitulated 4-0. The U's John Durnin scored all four goals.

Luton desperately needed a win and a performance in the next game at home to Millwall. We did not get the win, but sure got the performance.

Making his debut for Luton was Ian Benjamin a £50,000 signing from Southend, as a replacement for Claridge. He had a decent game but the best player by a mile in the 1-1 draw, was a young Scot, Darren Salton. He had come through the youth system and had played in every game. Phil Gray headed us in front against the Lions, but we could not quite hold on.

On the following Sunday was the game we had been eagerly awaiting Luton v Watford, the first local derby in over four years. But I'm afraid it was a very sombre and silent Kenilworth Suite and stadium before the game.

Darren Salton, whom I had lavishly praised in the previous match, was lying in Addenbrookes Hospital, Cambridge in a critical condition. He and his great friend and teammate Paul Telfer, had been involved in a fatal car crash in Paul's car near Beadlow Manor. It collided on a bend with another car and tragically, a pensioner in the other vehicle was killed. Paul escaped with minor injuries but sadly Darren was in a really bad way, it was touch & go at the time whether he could survive. He had severe brain injuries and was in a coma.

That day football rivalries, even Luton v Watford, didn't quite mean so much. However, when we scored two goals via Ian Benjamin & Scott Oakes, the especially loud cheers still meant a lot. This first home win at the end of November was for Darren Salton. He recovered very slowly, but was left slightly brain damaged and never added to his 19 LTFC appearances. It is my firm belief that this lad could and would, have gone on to play for Scotland. I had the privilege to meet and chat with him socially a few years ago, a nicer bloke you could not wish to meet.

The next week I drove to Bath. Bristol Rovers had been evicted from their Eastville stadium six years earlier and now shared Twerton Park with Bath City. Rovers eventually moved back to Bristol four years later.

We lost 2-0 and were now back in the bottom three.

I then went to Wolves and stood on the famous colossal South Bank terrace.

This was to be my final occasion standing there, an old terrace that once held over 25,000. Molineux, like the rest of country's stadia, was in the middle of being completely rebuilt to comply with the Taylor report. Wolves as a club had almost gone into liquidation a few years prior and this wonderful old ground had at one stage, just one stand open in their dark days of 4th Division football. Thanks to a rich Wolves fan called Jack Hayward, he saved them from oblivion and Molineux now stands as a cracking ground, with a capacity of over 30,000. Despite Wolves taking the lead, Luton came back to win 2-1 with a fine performance and both goals scored by Phil Gray. I had now seen Luton win on my last three visits there.

In the final game pre-Xmas, we drew 0-0 at home to Sunderland.

Two days after Boxing Day, we got the train to Upton Park for the match at West Ham. Football fans in general, were now behaving in a much better way than in the bad old days. A classic example of this was when we went for a pre-match drink in the Supporters Club behind the South Bank with our Luton colours on. This would have been simply unthinkable in the 1970s/80s. The fact that there were no problems for us on the tube, in the Supporters Club or in the ground and after the match, proved that things were becoming much more civil. Of course I am not saying Hooliganism had completely vanished, it NEVER will. It's just more organised now and most of the time is nowhere near the grounds and only with likeminded individuals. Naturally, there are rare exceptions. I prefer it like this, as there was a time when the hooligans actually very nearly killed football.

At the match, it was stalemate in the first half. When the Hammers including ex-Hatter Tim Breaker, went on to a 2-0 lead, we came storming back to earn a deserved point through Ceri Hughes & John (Tumble) Dreyer.

The first game of 1993 was at St Andrews, Birmingham. We lost 2-1. It would be 26 years before I returned there!

Against Notts County at home Phil Gray hit the post twice early on, this was the nearest to breaking the deadlock.

For a fair while at that point I had been suffering with a haemorrhoid (piles) problem. In fact, I recall that when I went to Plymouth for the pre-season friendly I had to drive sitting on a rubber ring, such was the discomfort. The time had now come to try and sort the problem out once and for all. I was admitted to L&D Hospital to have an operation to remedy it. Whilst in there, the FA Cup tie at home to Bristol City had been postponed because of the bad weather. I came out the day before the rearranged Cup Tie and perhaps rather foolishly attended. Because of the op I chose to stand on the Kenilworth Road terrace, rather than the Corporate Hospitality facility. We gained revenge for the August rout, by winning 2-0.

Four days later, we were at home again in the 4th round to Derby. The Rams battered us 5-1 with Mark Pembridge netting a hat-trick in front of a best at that point, crowd of 9,170. The FA Cup still meant a lot to clubs then.

This attendance was bettered at the next game as we, the bottom club held Newcastle the top team, to a 0-0 draw in front of 10,237.

Recuperating from my operation I missed a 0-0 draw at Bristol City. We followed this up with a fine 2-0 win at home against Leicester.

Three nights later I took my Mum's brother Uncle Malcolm to the home match v Brentford in the Kenilworth Suite. It was another 0-0 boring draw.

On the Friday my Scots pal Billy Smith, joined me on the train as we went away for the weekend to stay at the Shaftsbury Hotel once more in Liverpool for the Tranmere v Luton game. We had a fantastic weekend.

After checking in at the Shaftsbury we had a good afternoon drinking session in the famous nearby Adelphi Hotel, before having a singsong in a local Liverpool pub. I have written before, Liverpool folk are the same as Glaswegians, warm, friendly, good kind of people. If you are good to them, they most certainly will be good to you in return.

We travelled 'cross the Mersey' to Birkenhead and carried on drinking in the pub next to the ground. Billy was having such a good time, he didn't even bother going to the match. I would meet him back there after the game. He missed out though, as Luton put on a brilliant show winning 2-0 with goals from Marvin Johnson & Phil Gray. This was Tranmere's first home defeat that season.

We arrived back at the Shaftsbury and met up with the Prescot lads, having another great night with them and thankfully this time, peaceful too.

On returning home the Monday evening I found out the harrowing news about James Bulger.

He was a little boy absconded by two 10-years-old evil boys in the nearby Bootle Shopping Centre on the Friday afternoon. They led him away while his mother was in a Butcher shop, took him on a two mile trail of terror, battering him senseless with iron bars, stones and paint, sexually assaulting him and killing him, before laying him down on a railway track buried by rubble. Then, a train ran over him and he was found sliced in half on the Monday. Please forgive me for writing the horrific details but in case anyone reading, does not know the full horror that this poor boy was subjected to - they need to!

To think, that this unbelievable nightmare happened in a city when I was actually THERE. All the people in that pub, including Billy and I were having such a brilliant time and completely oblivious to what poor Jamie was being subjected to, it still sends a shiver down my spine. When I found out the full details I cried my eyes out and it still upsets me now. Heaven only knows what the poor mite's family must have and will always go through. The evil little bastards have got away with it for me. Yes, they served a few years behind bars but were released with all the luxuries of a new secret life, with hidden identities to start those new lives, as though it DID NOT happen. It makes my blood boil and one of the bastards is now back in jail again a SECOND time for possessing child porn on his computer. When you are born evil, you are always evil, until you die.

As far as I am concerned they should throw away the key and let the C**T die of starvation. The other shitebag - should be outed too!

Poor Jamie's family, are the ones serving the life sentence and my heart goes out to them. RIP James Bulger.

In our next game at home to Charlton, Luton had a new loan signing from Southampton in their line up, ex-Chelsea legend and Luton born Kerry Dixon. Phil Gray scored the only goal in this important victory.

In the week leading up to the next game at home to Barnsley the world of football was in mourning following the death of England legend Bobby Moore. He died of cancer at the early age of 51 and was the first player of that historic 1966 World Cup winning squad to perish. There was a minute's silence at every league ground, which naturally, was impeccably observed. RIP Bobby.

Just before that silence from my seat in the Directors Balcony, I spotted an old friend sitting in the Enclosure (where I currently sit today). It was Mick Tearle and I had not seen him for quite a while. I went down and had a chat pre-match, as we reminisced the good old days.

We drew 2-2 and Kerry Dixon netted his first goal for his boyhood heroes.

It was off to Portsmouth next for my first visit to Fratton Park. Despite Phil Gray giving Luton the lead, Pompey came back to win 2-1.

The lowest home crowd of the season 6,687 watched a convincing 3-1 win for the Hatters against Oxford.

After taking nine games to achieve our first home victory, we had now secured 3 out of the last 5.

Phil Gray was on a good scoring streak and this was his fifth goal in a row. I watched him make it six up at Grimsby but this was only a consolation, in a poor 3-1 defeat - I also got fined for speeding on the return journey!

Swindon came to Kenilworth Road and secured a point in a tedious 0-0 draw. Against Bristol Rovers at home, another dreary 0-0 draw also occurred.

I missed Luton's final appearance at the notorious Den, as Millwall won 1-0. For the next game at home to Cambridge I took one of my favourite clients at the time, Penny Miles and her husband Tony. As her company was called Cambridge Public Relations, I felt that this match was apt for her to attend. The match itself was nothing special except for two things. 1) We achieved a needy 2-0 win. 2) Both goals were contenders for goal of the season. Kerry Dixon's volleyed effort, followed by a cracking Scott Oakes header.

On the day of the aborted Grand National, I sat at Watford. I remember not feeling too good that day, but of course didn't want to miss the old enemy match. In what was possibly the worst derby ever, 0-0 was the score. I did not have any idea at all that day, but this was to be my final match of 1992-93.

When I arrived home I went to bed feeling terrible. So bad was I, that I failed to attend work all week and I MUST have been ill – because I missed my first home match and only my third in nearly 20 years v Wolves! It was a 1-1 draw.

Instead of attending that match I lay down on the sofa and watched Rangers in Marseille on TV. If Rangers were to win in France, they would qualify for the European Cup Final. Unfortunately for the Bears, it finished 1-1.

Having been off work all week, there was no way I would make the game at Swindon (even if I wanted to) where we lost 1-0. When I missed Luton v West Ham three nights later - even Deb thought something is wrong here! This had now been ten days of feeling absolute shit. I thought it was flu, but after my 2nd visit to the Doctor he said it was a virus.

Luton had an excellent 2-0 win over the Hammers in my absence, in front of the largest crowd of the season 10,959. A Phil Gray penalty was his 20th and final goal of 92-93 and he became the first Luton player since Mick Harford seven years earlier, to achieve this feat. Young Martin Williams scored our second.

By now I was starting to worry about the illness, there was no way I could go on the Hartlepool weekender for the next match at Sunderland. We drew 2-2.

Still off work, for what was over a fortnight I had now come out in a deep red/purple rash. After the 3rd visit to the quack's (once again he said it's a virus) CBC quite rightly wanted my return and decided to try and sort me out once and for all. The Chairman sent me to the company's private doctor in Harley Street.

My cousin Ken kindly took me in his Cab (he was now a London cabbie).

Deb couldn't as she was at Butlins in Skegness with Georgina, Cherine and kids. The Harley Street doctor took one look at me and gave me a thorough examination. He said, "Young Man, you are going to hospital NOW." He arranged with Ken to take me to St Thomas Hospital by the River Thames.

On admittance, they were doing all sorts of tests on me and by now I was beginning to feel VERY ill. Not only had I this funny colour everywhere, and full of spots and rashes - my face was actually expanding! I will remember this night of St George's Day (it was the first time I had failed to wear a rose since I was a kid) forever. As the night wore on I can remember being taken down to Intensive Care and looking in the mirror, I was horrified. My face was like the Elephant Man such was the distortion. I was taken to the Operating theatre, as they wanted to explore my piles operation from January. The next day I remember waking up and seeing Deb in the room. I asked where Georgina was and apparently because of my face, it was agreed by the medics that it would be too distressing for Georgina to see me. Deb was really frightened, but I must have started to feel a little better - as I asked her to find out how we had got on at Derby! (We drew 1-1)

I was in St Thomas for three weeks, as they did EVERY test under the sun to try and find out exactly what the illness was. When Ena my boss at CBC, came to visit on the Sunday her face went white with shock on seeing me and she had to leave the room in tears. Eventually, they diagnosed three things wrong. I had a Blood Disorder, a skin disease called Urticarial Vasculitis - evidently they had only ever come across three cases of this in St Thomas's history!

On top of all this I had Glandular Fever – Adair doesn't do illnesses in small ways! Apparently it was touch and go in those first couple of days and on that first night, had I not been admitted - the Doctors said I would have died! Such was my soaring temperature.

I was put on 60mgs of Steroids a day to assist my recovery. I also remember being humbled at the amount of visitors. I had clients, domino teammates, as well as footy friends of course, with family too. To my pleasant surprise my mum came to visit me EVERY day in hospital. Mick Knight taped every Beatles album track for me. The Fab Four really helped my therapy, as I lay in my solitary ward listening to the masters of music.

I did a lot of deep thinking in hospital and told Deb that if I ever get back to normal and make a full recovery, we were going to see Ann in New Zealand - no matter what the cost!

With two games remaining, there was still a possibility that Luton could suffer a second successive relegation. The final home match was a 0-0 draw against Peterborough, watched by a crowd of 10,011.

The last match was at Southend. While I was eagerly awaiting score updates on the radio, Chris McEvoy and all the lads were having a beano at the seaside. We lost 2-1 but thanks to other results, we survived by finishing two points and two places above safety. With only four away victories, LTFC did not complete a double over any team in 1992-93.

I finally returned to work after a very long two months.

After a few weeks back at work, we then spent a nice fortnight's holiday in Son Bou Menorca, as a final stint of convalescence and I returned back to CBC fit and raring to go. After the shock and trauma from my illness, I kept my word to Deb and one lovely Sunday in the summer we drove down to Hampshire to discuss booking our holiday to New Zealand with specialist travel agent Travel Bag. I explained the Budget we had and wanted flights to Auckland and then if it was viable because of the distance we were traveling, I asked if it was possible to include a trip to my old stomping ground of Adelaide, Lord knows if I were ever to get the chance to return there again. The lady came up with a fantastic package to suit all three of us. For only £2,500 including hotel costs, this is what we booked: Heathrow – Los Angeles – Auckland – 4 weeks with my sister Ann – fly Auckland to Adelaide – six nights in Adelaide – fly Adelaide to Sydney – 2 nights in Sydney – fly to Los Angeles – two nights in L.A. – fly home.

After discussing with Ann and booking this dream adventure I then managed to track down my old Ulster mate in Adelaide, John Foy. We chatted away for ages and I explained I was coming to Adelaide for a week, in early January.

I told him it would be great to catch up with him and the Wakefield Wanderers crowd again. "That's a fucking long way to come for a week Al," he roared. After explaining that we were staying at Ann's first, he gave me his address and asked me to write down as many names as I could remember and he would arrange some kind of reunion. I did just that.

One of the gates Millwall fans smashed down on that notorious, never to be forgotten 1985 night. Just for the record, most of them WERE Millwall fans too.

Wembley – I'm a Dad Again

Before the new season started there was disappointment as two major players left LTFC. Top scorer Phil Gray was sold to Sunderland for £775,000 and joining him there was keeper Alec Chamberlain. Alec left under the freedom of contract ruling.

Jurgen Sommer replaced Chamberlain after waiting patiently for a couple of seasons and we also signed a winger from Tottenham, Scott Houghton.

Larry Kinloch joined me to watch us draw 1-1 at home in a pre-season friendly with his Ipswich Town.

The opening game of the new campaign began at home to arch rivals Watford. We beat them 2-1 including a stunning strike from Kerry Dixon as I watched from my new season ticket seat in the New Stand. Watford had 2 players sent off and if I'm being truthful, we might not have beaten them had it been 11v11.

CBC renewed the Kenilworth Suite Membership but I also wanted to watch some games with the lads and obtained a Season Ticket too.

In the League Cup 1st round I drove to Cambridge for the 1st leg. I just knew that Steve Claridge would score against us and he did, netting the only goal.

I then drove to Fratton Park, Portsmouth to see Luton lose by the same score.

Claridge repeated his sole goal for Cambridge in the 2nd leg and we were out of the League Cup. This was the third successive Town 1-0 defeat.

In the next match at home to Nottm Forest a young Welsh striker who came through the youth system by the name of John Hartson, made his debut. He got off to a dream start when he headed us into the lead. But ex-Hatter Kingsley Black soon levelled. The full Oak Road end of Forest fans went home happy when they snatched it late on to win 2-1.

Luton were in the Anglo Italian Cup group with Southend and as the previous year, with Watford too. I drove to Watford as the Hornets took delight in beating us 2-1. Against Southend at home, just 1,823 watched a 1-1 draw and just like 1992-93 we had been knocked out - without playing any Italians!

When we lost our third home match out of four losing 2-0 to Bolton, it already looked like we were in for a season of struggle.

Because of an impending trip to Hartlepool I missed the mid-week game at Tranmere. Ian Benjamin scored his 2nd and last goal for Luton in a 4-1 defeat. Making his debut that night was midfielder Alan Harper, signed from Everton. We had another brilliant weekender in Hartlepool, which was boosted by our first point in five games at Middlesbrough where thanks to an outstanding display by keeper Jurgen Sommer, we drew 0-0.

I missed us gaining another point at Birmingham in a 1-1 draw.

The next game was both a fantastic day and evening. Barnsley were the visitors, I had yet to see Luton ever beat them.

On a lovely sunny early October day and after just three minutes, Barnsley were down to 10 men following a shocking challenge by Taggart on Julian James. Two goals by Scott Oakes and one each from John Hartson & Scott Houghton followed by a terrific solo goal from Julian James, gave Luton an emphatic 5-0 win, our first victory since the opening day and our biggest win since Southampton nearly five years earlier. That night my sister Michelle, Deb & I travelled to Earls Court in London to see Paul McCartney. As usual he was superb, this was the third time I had seen him perform live and it rounded off a perfect day.

Three nights later, we were at home again to Bristol City. I was hoping after the resounding win over Barnsley that our season might now Kick Start. How wrong could I be? Just as we were so good against Barnsley - against Bristol City, we were SO bad! We lost 2-0 and how the same side could contrast so much I'll never know. On top of that, the crowd of just 5,956 was our lowest home league attendance since the Three Day week in 1974.

All us Stopsley boys travelled to Derby on the train and apart from losing 2-1 we had a brilliant day and night before catching the last train home. This was my 5th & final visit to the Baseball Ground as three years later they were to announce that they would be leaving for a new stadium called Pride Park, which opened in 1997.

As a result of losing to Derby, we were 2nd from bottom, with just two wins out of 10 games. Maybe for this reason, we signed a striker on loan from Arsenal called Paul Dickov. He was a tiny Scot but leapt up to head home the only goal in the match v Notts County on his debut. It was his solitary LTFC goal.

There was no way I was going to travel mid-week to Sunderland, where we lost 2-0 - At least Phil Gray didn't score against us!

We secured our first 1993-94 away win at Oxford 1-0.

Highflying Leicester then beat us at home 2-0 in front of a full Oak Road End. At Crystal Palace we had a new debutant, Canadian Geoff Aunger. I listened on the radio as we lost 3-2.

We were then live on ITV the following Sunday at home to Charlton. A great header from Paul Telfer was enough to give us victory - just!

Before I drove to see Luton for the first time at Roots Hall Southend, we received fantastic news that Deb was expecting our second child and that there would be no problem about her travelling on the forthcoming Xmas New Zealand trip.

Mitchell Thomas had re-signed for us from West Ham and he made his second debut against the Shrimpers. We lost 2-1, despite an absolutely stunning equaliser from Kerry Dixon.

He scored many spectacular goals for us. After an initial loan period, we signed Dixon on a permanent deal and on a free transfer too. This was a brilliant bit of business when you consider that Southampton had paid Chelsea £575,000 not long before he joined us on loan.

In my last game before our wonder trip, Kerry Dixon was on fire against Stoke at home. It didn't start that way though as early on the Potters had a 2-0 lead.

But we incredibly turned it round, in the 1st Half too. Just after Stoke's 2nd goal, Kerry Dixon scored yet another unbelievable bullet of a goal. When Ceri Hughes and then Scott Oakes had given us a 3-2 h-t lead the cheers from the Hatters fans as Luton came off the pitch, were rapturous. In the second half it improved even more. Kerry went on to complete his only LTFC hat trick and John Hartson finished off Stoke to make it 6-2. We scored more goals that day - than in our previous SIX matches!

I didn't want to risk going to Charlton the following week, as we were due to fly early Monday morning. I didn't miss too much either the Addicks won 1-0. I was now set to miss the next six games.

Mum and her gentleman friend a lovely old boy called Cyrille, took us to Heathrow to see us off early on Monday December 6th. We actually saw Richard Branson as we checked in for our 11 hours Virgin flight to Los Angeles. I was OK on the flight although I have to write, the legroom was not brilliant for my long pins. Georgina at nearly 3 and a half was watching the films and playing with her Virgin flight pack & loving it. Deb however, was having a nightmare journey. She was bad enough carrying Georgina, but with this pregnancy - it was morning, noon AND night sickness! When we eventually arrived at LA she was feeling very ill. I actually tried to see if we could stay the night and catch a connecting flight the next day. Unfortunately, the next connection to Auckland was three days away and so she had to persevere. We waited 5 hours for our next flight to Auckland with Air New Zealand. When we boarded the Air NZ flight it was like chalk & cheese compared to Virgin. Ample leg room and much more comfortable. The 13 hours flight that she had been dreading was actually fine and Deb felt better.

We arrived in Auckland and were met by older sister Ann. When we arrived at Ann & Terry's house in Browns Bay on Auckland's North Shore, after initially meeting my niece Rachel and nephew Peter, we were so shattered we just went to bed.

I'm afraid Deb was ill with the pregnancy for virtually the whole time in NZ. Thankfully they had Tele-text so I was able to keep tracks of all the scores back home. The first game while I was away, we lost 1-0 at home to Tranmere.

We had a great time at Ann's. They kindly lent us a car for the duration and we travelled to many places with them.

Ann & Terry ran a Delicatessen. They left the Deli with one of their staff when we travelled up to the north of the North Island. The staff member, turned out to be a relation of ex-Hatter, Gary Parker.

Before we went away with Ann's family, the Adairs drove down to Rotorua in the Bay Of Plenty region for a weekend by ourselves.

Ann & Terry took us to some lovely places in the North, including Ninety Mile Beach, Whangarei, The Bay Of Islands and Taipa. We celebrated New Year's Eve at a nice hotel and the kids loved jumping on the outside trampoline there.

I did like New Zealand especially the scenery it is very similar to Scotland's beautiful mountains etc. The one thing I did not particularly like was the weather. I had always imagined New Zealand to have the same climate as Australia such is the proximity. Although it was never cold there - by God, does it rain! I think in the four weeks we spent in NZ, about four days in total were rain free. In fairness, the rain does come and go but they sure get plenty of it.

Whilst in New Zealand, Luton had decided to go on an unbeaten run in my absence. After losing to Tranmere, we earned a point at Watford recovering from 2-0 down at h-t to draw 2-2.

We earned another point at Peterborough drawing 0-0, beat Grimsby 2-1 at home and drew once again at WBA 1-1. In the FA Cup 3rd Round we had been drawn at home to play Southend and I was pleased when I heard it had been postponed due to snow.

It was really lovely to see Ann again but after four weeks both Deb & I were ready to leave for Adelaide. As we arrived at Adelaide Airport the first thing that struck me was the weather - it was peeing down with rain! I was really shocked at this because it was their summer. In the two summers when I lived there in the early 1970s I can barely remember it raining at all.

John Foy met us and took us to pick up our hire car before dropping us off at our city centre hotel that we had booked for a night. We would meet up with him later to try and find a hotel nearer the Morphett Vale area. We found an absolutely stunning place at a winery in Reynella, only about a 10 minutes' drive away. When the sun came out the next day it was just like old times. I had agreed to meet John in the evening at the soccer club and he had also arranged a reunion barbeque at his place for the following day. I drove Deb & Georgina around to show them all my old haunts. It felt really emotional going to all the places where I had such good times as an adolescent youth. I asked Deb to video them while I drove, getting out every now and then. First we drove to Brodie Road, which was where we stayed while our new house was being built and then we drove to that house in Timothy Road. I have to write, I was rather sad at seeing this. When we lived there it was a lovely bungalow (90% of houses are in Oz), but our house now was unrecognisable.

It had a storey added above and was painted a horrible brown colour whereas ours was pristine white. The most shocking thing though was the garden, instead of the nice hilly green lawn there now stood huge trees which had darkened the whole house and garden area - it was like a fucking jungle!

I knocked on the door to ask for permission to film on the video camcorder explaining, that my family were the original occupants from near 20 years prior. He didn't mind. It was really strange and rather sad too, that everywhere I went and filmed seemed to be in decline. My school Christies Beach High, looked positively run down. Christies Beach itself looked dirty and graffiti strewn, even the area I had lived in now looked tacky.

The Big Y shopping centre in Morphett Vale used to be a lovely indoor shopping Mall it was now a scruffy looking renovated supermarket.

I guess that anywhere you haven't seen for 20 years is bound not to be as nice as it once was. It was weird these mixed feelings of both nostalgia and sadness, in equal measures.

In the evening John took me to the new Noarlunga United Soccer Club Social Bar. I had already been to the old site in Acre Avenue when it was Wakefield Wanderers and once again, it was emotional looking at this flat barren piece of land, with not a hint of Sky Blue history in sight.

John had explained to me on the way to the new club that because all of the people he had contacted were coming to the barbeque, he said it was unlikely that I would know anybody in there tonight. "No worries," I replied.

Upon entering the club, someone instantly came up and asked in a surprised tone, "Alan Adair?"

"My god, Mick Racher," I replied.

John, looking puzzled, told me that he had only been in Australia about 3 or 4 years. Mick Racher had attended my school Stopsley High in Luton and - was in Ann's class! Mick then beckoned over to two other people, saying, "Colin come here." He asked them if they knew Alan Adair.

One of them replied, "No, but are you any relation to Ken?"

When I told Colin that I was Ken's cousin, he explained that he was in Ken's class at school and his father, who was beside him visiting on holiday, told me that he lived opposite Ken's mum, my Aunt Mary in Stopsley. This would not be the last time I met Colin

McPherson.

John Foy by now - was on the floor! "Fucking Hell Alan, you know more people in here - than I do!" I counted that there were thirteen people in the club at the time, including John & I. Four of those were from Stopsley, Luton - over 10,000 miles away! What a small world, what would the odds be on that occurring?

The next day at the barbeque at John's house was amazing. When I asked him the previous night how many people did he get in contact with he just said, "A few mate - but 20 years is a long time fella!" When we entered his house I was astounded. There must have been near 30 folk there. Joe Foley, Gary Jones, Harry Brown, Keith Dalglish, Glyn Davies to name but a few.

I was truly humbled, because at the end of the day I had yet reached 16 when I left Adelaide and it was a very long time ago. It was a brilliant special day, as we all reminisced the Wakefield Wanderers days, singing together the old Wakefield song, which they themselves hadn't sung in over ten years. I have it all on video as a permanent memory.

Keith Dalglish, a Geordie lad (who was seconds on the day I lost my virginity to Wendy White) as a result of this reunion, came and stayed with us when they returned to Newcastle for a holiday the next year. They spent their last night in England with us, before flying back to Oz.

One slight sour note was the letdown I felt over Harry Brown. Harry was a Scot and a Celtic fan, he was a man whom I really aspired and looked up to when I lived there. He was brilliant to me, as well as all the other teenagers on the Wakefield scene.

If you like, we kind of idolised him because he used to accept us as if we were genuine mates, not spotty faced teenagers.

When I saw his key ring had IRA on it I was stunned. I questioned him and asked him how could he support a terrorist organisation that had killed so many innocent people like in the Birmingham Pub Bombings. He replied very matter-of-fact, "Alan, don't believe everything the British media report - it was the British Government that killed those people!"

Seeing the reaction on my face, Deb quickly pulled me away and told me to remember where we were and why we were there. I was upset that a man, whom I had really looked up to as a lad, had been blinded by pish and I had lost respect for him that day, but was civil enough not to cause a scene. If you ever get to read this Harry, let's just say I'll remember you for the good times.

John and I had a little snigger to him though at the result from Parkhead on the day of the barbeque - the score was Celtic 2 Rangers 4.

The next night John, Joe, Keith, Glynn & I left our hotel to watch Adelaide draw 2-2 with South Melbourne at Hindmarsh Stadium, the arena I had spent so many Friday nights at when I was a lad.

The day before we left Adelaide we spent a wonderful afternoon at John's parents' house in McLaren Vale with both mine, and John's family. Moira & Geordie were brilliant to me when I lived there and they still had their staunch Belfast accents. She told me privately that day I was always her favourite of John's friends. We spent the afternoon relaxing by their garden pool and Georgina & John's kids got on like a house on fire.

The Foys are wonderful people and I will never forget them. We left Adelaide and headed for Sydney. One of my friends from the earlier Wakefield days was an Aussie called

Greg Simon.

At that time in 1973/74, it was quite rare for an actual Australian to play Soccer. He was one, and a good player he was too. He had moved to Sydney and was still in touch with John Foy. When John told him I was coming over and then to Sydney, he arranged for Greg to meet us. We did just that and spent a nice day with him, as he took us to the famous Bondi Beach. The other two days there, we went to all the tourist bits. Deb loved Sydney and said that was her best part of the whole trip. It's so ironic that over 17 years later - she would actually move to Sydney!

The area we stayed in was The Rocks, an area I would describe as Bohemian. During our stay some of the worst forest fires in history were raging and had even reached suburban Sydney. Fortunately, we were OK and allowed to fly out of Sydney on the last leg of our epic adventure to Los Angeles.

We thoroughly enjoyed our California experience too and had already decided that for the last two days would go to Disneyland for one and on the last, just relax and lay by the pool at the hotel in Anaheim.

We spent a brilliant day at Disneyland and obviously with Deb being pregnant (though not so ill now) she didn't go on many rides. I certainly did and I'm not sure who was the biggest kid myself, or Georgina. To see the joy and pleasure in Georgina's face was worth every penny spent on this holiday of a lifetime. We left on 16th Jan.

It was a good job it was on this day and not the next.

The very day after we had left LA, the city was struck by a huge earth quake killing 60 people, injuring over 7,000 and destroying over 5,000 buildings. Lord knows what would have happened had we stayed another night. One thing is for certain, the airport was closed and flights were grounded - for at least a week!

After the trail of destruction that the Adair family had left in their wake, we arrived back at Heathrow on Monday 17th January (my dad would have been 62 that day) and were collected by Deb's dad Alan, along with little niece Lauren. As soon as we sat in the car, 6 years old Lauren, in her innocence, told us - that the burglars had been in our house!

It transpired on that very weekend, burglars had indeed been in our house after removing a pane of glass from the kitchen window. They had gone through the house and yet - took NOTHING! Deb was convinced that the criminals must have known me, as why take zero items, not even the TV or video. Why take nothing? It was either what Deb thought - or perhaps we just had poor taste!

I had no idea of Luton's result at Notts County on the Saturday, so was delighted when Alan told me that the Town had won 2-1.

My first game back was the rearranged FA Cup tie at home to Southend on the next night.

Because of the postponement, both teams knew their reward for victory was a trip to premiership Newcastle. In front of a full Oak Road, we won 1-0 with a cracker by Paul Telfer. In truth, Southend should have buried us. They were all over Luton and should have scored at least 3 times in the first half alone.

Before the league game at home to Derby on the Saturday, there was a minute's silence in respect for Sir Matt Busby following his recent passing.

RIP Sir Matt.

This match against the Rams, saw the best goal scored at Kenilworth Road by a Luton player since the Graham French legendary goal in 1968.

Paul Telfer had opened the scoring just before the break. The Rams equalised, before the wonder goal by Scott Oakes. He collected the ball in his own half then beat SEVEN Derby players on a marauding run (not quite as many as Frenchie, or as far), before unleashing an unstoppable shot from outside the penalty box past the Derby keeper, to lift the roof off for the winning goal. Without doubt, it was the best Luton goal of the modern era and for some of the younger fans, of all time. It can be seen today on YouTube.

But I'm sorry maybe for nostalgic reasons or the fact that I was only 10 years old, Graham French's will always be the no 1 goal for me.

I remember in a fans survey conducted by LTFC historian Roger Wash in 2004, the four best goals ever voted for were: 1) Brian Stein's Wembley winner in 1988 2) Graham French 3) Matthew Spring v Watford in 2002 and 4) this one by Oakes.

For the forthcoming FA Cup tie at Newcastle, due to rebuilding work at St James' Park the Geordies had given LTFC two options for tickets: A) 700 tickets in a small corner or B) the whole terrace allocation of 4,000 but Luton would have to pay for all of those tickets, including any unsold. LTFC in my opinion bottled it and took the lower option, even though I personally think we would have sold them all. Both David Kohler and Secretary Cherry Newbery disagreed with me. In fairness, Luton did decide to pay for the match to be screened live in all corporate area bars (and charge accordingly).

Through being a corporate member, we had first priority on the Newcastle tickets and I purchased two. I took Larry Kinloch and drove up the A1 in eager anticipation.

A young midfielder was making his Luton debut that day called Tony Thorpe. When he scored with a scorcher of a shot it was no more than we deserved. In fact, until Beardsley dived for a penalty we were the better side. He scored from the spot and despite some pressure from the Magpies, we held on for a richly deserved replay.

Before that replay we comprehensively beat Oxford 3-0 at home. The first goal by Scott Oakes was another wonder strike and he was certainly in form. For the Newcastle replay CBC decided to jointly sponsor the match.

Gary Hopkins & I took along a few clients, for what turned out to be a memorable night. The Sky TV Cameras were present for the first time at LTFC and the live audience would not be disappointed in viewing a thrilling game. Young John Hartson put us in front when he pounced on an opportunity and we held on to this lead deservedly at half time. When the Hatters doubled the score with only 11 minutes left, everyone knew we were through. The goal was right in front of the full Oak Road Toon army and finished off by Scott Oakes after a sweeping move, along with Des Linton. Despite my guests, I celebrated this second goal wildly, as if I was with the fans and not in the corporate area. After the game in the Sponsors Lounge, the Newcastle boss Kevin Keegan rose to great heights in my estimation. His speech was full of praise for Luton, saying that we thoroughly deserved to go through and that we played football the way it was supposed to be played. He also went on to say that he honestly hoped that Luton would go on and win the FA Cup.

I actually had a brief chat with him and asked him how he felt about us stopping Andy Cole (the top scorer in the Premiership) from any goal scoring chances. "Simple, the Luton defence did not give him a sniff all night, which many bigger teams have been unable to do all season." Mr Keegan – RESPECT!

What pleased me even more was that the nation saw our performance too.

The next day at work I had a brilliant fax from Sunderland fan Mark, at Lloyd's of London, reading, 'Brilliant performance and result last night by Luton Alan, Paula & I were cheering you on - as if we were full blooded Hatters!'

We now faced Cardiff in South Wales in the 5th round. Before that, Bill McKinlay drove Steve Toyer, Rash & I to Leicester for the next league game. We had a drink pre-match in a social club next door to Filbert Street. I remember a load of the Leicester hooligan firm 'The Baby Squad' coming in looking for their MIG counterparts. It was only our shirts and beer monster fans in there, so they left. An absolute screamer of a goal gave Leicester an early lead. When they added a second that finished us. Despite a cracking goal from Julian James, we could not come back and lost for the first time in 1994 and also in 10 matches.

I drove alone, for what would turn out to be my 4th and final visit to Ninian Park. Despite an extortionate £16 to stand on an open terrace, we still sold our full allocation of 4,000 tickets. That day at Cardiff was like going back in time to the bad old days of mayhem, such was the behaviour of the anti-English hordes. It wasn't just the fans that were wild too ask anyone who was there, about the Cardiff stewards. It was THEY who sprayed CS Gas into the faces of Hatters fans at the front of the terrace. Ninian Park was then one of the few grounds left in the country, which still had fences post-Hillsborough. Anyone there that day will know why.

Scott Oakes (again) had given us an interval lead. When Cardiff equalised the atmosphere was now electric, when David Preece (mini) scored for Luton, that's when the Welsh fans erupted. He scored a perfectly legitimate goal, but it seemed as though the Bluebirds fans didn't understand the recent change in the offside law. If a player (Ceri Hughes) is coming back from an offside position and makes no attempt to be involved in the play - then play carries on! This is exactly what happened and Mini ran through to roll the ball into the net at the Luton supporters end. He jumped up onto the fence and celebrated wildly, just as all us Hatters fans were equally doing too.

It was at this moment, the CS Gas from the stewards occurred. I was standing at the back of the terrace so was unaffected, but some of the Cardiff fans from the Bob Bank (Soul crew hooligans) left the ground and came running round into the street behind us throwing coins, bricks, bottles, basically anything they could get their hands on into our end over the wall.

The match ended with Luton winning 2-1 and us through to the Quarter Finals. Despite being kept behind for an eternity, there were still plenty of Luton fans attacked and ambushed in the car park, as well as a large number of coaches & cars that had their windows smashed. I personally was OK, but I don't mind admitting I was pretty glad to get out of both Cardiff and Wales.

Mid-week, on a blanket of snow, we thrashed Portsmouth at home. With an orange ball used because of the snow, Scott Oakes scored his 5th goal in seven matches. With only 51 minutes gone and Luton already 4-0 up, I began to wonder how many? But the only other goal was from Pompey.

Mark Whitfield and his partner Paula from Lloyd's of London Insurers, joined me as guests for the Luton v Sunderland game. Mark wasn't so happy about a Luton win this time though, as we beat the Makems 2-1. Scott Oakes scored yet again and this victory lifted us to our highest position all season in 14th place. I missed Luton's 2-0 defeat at Nottm Forest due to attending cousin Malcolm Roberts junior's wedding, in nearby Derbyshire.

Three nights later, we drew 1-1 at home to Middlesbrough. Apart from a late equalising penalty by John Dreyer (his 12th & final goal for LTFC) my main memory from that night was heading the ball from the new stand. Taking the applause from the Kenny End I then stuck out my beer belly after lifting my Rangers top, to a chorus of 'you fat bastard' and 'who are ya?'

In the FA Cup Quarter-Final, we had been drawn away to West Ham. I took a West Ham supporting work colleague and fellow rep Damon, to this. After parking up we went for a pre-match pint in The Boleyn pub near the ground. This is the pub that used to house the notorious ICF West Ham hooligan firm, but times had changed and there was plenty of Luton fans with colours on in there, with not a hint of any animosity. We held out resiliently for a 0-0 draw. A young central defender called David Greene had an exceptional game in defence and played a blinder. I sat in the new Bobby Moore stand (old South Bank). This was my 18th & last visit to Upton Park.

Before the replay, we drew 1-1 at home to Birmingham.

Damon joined in with us Luton fans at the replay, in the new stand. I declined the corporate for this match, as I wanted to be with my mates. Once again Sky TV were present showing the game live.

This was the last season of terracing at Kenilworth Road and the crowd that night of 13,166 has never been bettered. The match itself has to go down as one of the greatest nights in the modern era.

Allen sent Damon into raptures when he gave West Ham the lead against the run of play. When Scott Oakes equalised in front of the Oak Road, it was our turn to go wild. He added another just after the break, to send us into heaven. But soon after, Ian Bishop (remember him?) levelled in this to and fro thriller. With 16 minutes remaining Scott Oakes grabbed his hat-trick with aplomb.

West Ham's Potts (father of current Hatter Dan) fell on the ball on the halfway line Oakes robbed him and went on a mazy run aka Derby, before hitting the ball with such force that the West Ham keeper had NO chance of stopping it. It was easily the best goal of the night and the winning one for Luton this was Scott Oakes finest LTFC moment. Indeed I had told him personally that he gave me one of my greatest nights as a Luton fan that night, when meeting him once.

Luton were heading for Wembley again - for the 5th time in six years!

The FA had decided recently to play the semi-finals at the famous arena. A decision that I personally disagreed with - but was certainly not going to decline! The clamour for the semi-final tickets against Chelsea began.

But thanks to Sky showing it live at the daft time of 5pm on a Saturday night, every Hatters fan that applied for a ticket was successful. In fact, thanks to Cherry Newbery CBC would buy a grand total of no less than 72 tickets to satisfy all my clients' requests.

After the West Ham match we played at Barnsley. Talk about after The Lord Mayor's Show. The Luton showing that day compared to three nights earlier was chalk and cheese. We lost 1-0 and our performance can only be described as complete rubbish.

Four nights later I drove to see my Millwall mates at The Anchor in Lewisham, before Luton's first visit to the New Den. In an entertaining match we drew 2-2. We then had a welcome 2-0 home victory against Peterborough, with Kerry Dixon scoring both of the goals. His second was a typical volley of his and it was the last time he netted for Luton in

1993-94. Before the semi-final at Wembley, we travelled to Grimsby and suffered a 2-0 loss.

For the Semi-Final, I felt that it did not warrant organising a coach and meal etc, like I had done on the two previous occasions at Wembley, as I have already stated the game should not have really been at the Mecca. If we won, now that would be a different matter for the final.

Don't get me wrong it was still an exceptionally important game, but on this occasion I just chose to make a day out of it with the lads and so it was at The Railway Tavern pub in West Hampstead for opening time (SIX hours before kick off), that we arrived in excitement. The pub was full of exclusively Luton fans and we were all in great voice and spirits. After the mammoth drinking session it was time to take the tube to Wembley Park. We excitedly made our way up Wembley Way and apart from a skirmish involving Chris McEvoy and a Chelsea fan the banter was flying. The actual game itself was I'm afraid to write, a total letdown. Apart from the first five minutes or so, Luton completely froze and did not turn up on the day. I don't know if the occasion just got to them, but frankly - they let us down! Kerry Dixon seemed to be more interested in lapping up the praise from his adoring Chelsea fans. Two Peacock goals were enough to give Chelsea a 2-0 win. This was so easy for the Blues it was embarrassing. We headed back to The Railway Tavern full of gloom to drown our sorrows. While we were in the pub, completely unbeknown to us, there was a major tear up going on up the road at the railway station between the Luton MIGS (Men In Gear, the Luton hooligan firm) and Chelsea Head Hunters. I found out at a later date from a reliable source that it had all been organised. The famous Head Hunters didn't take the offer too seriously, but thought they would turn up anyway to teach the MIGS a lesson. It is true to write that every known Luton face was at Wembley that day and they were all at the station too, in anticipation. This is no word of a lie, but Chelsea's top firm came very much second best on this rare occasion. Even my Millwall mates got to hear about this from their reliable hooligan grapevine network.

I truly felt low that night, almost as much as I had done in the 1985 Semi.

Three nights later, I took a couple of graphic design clients who were not even into football to see Luton v Wolves. We lost 2-0 and again, it was one sided.

Two 1-0 defeats followed at home to leaders C. Palace and away to Bristol City. On the night of my 36th birthday Luton played Millwall at home. We arranged for our London mates to have a drink with us before the game in the old Hatters Club, now called The Eric Morecambe Lounge. David Preece scored our first goal in six matches to give us the lead. Millwall equalised to gain a rather fortunate point. I missed the next game, another 1-1 home draw against Southend.

The reason for this was that I was watching my first Ibrox Park Rangers v Celtic Old Firm match. It was also a 1-1 draw.

The final home match of the season against WBA was an absolute belter. Our best League attendance and the only post-ten thousand crowd, 10,053 watched a thriller. Before the match began David Pleat had ordered the groundsman to heavily water the pitch, as he always liked to do. It was a miracle that the ref allowed it to start, for there were PUDDLES on the surface. I will just go through the goal sequence initially, before adding other factors. David Preece gave Luton the lead. Albion then equalised. Julian James put us 2-1 up and then John Hartson fired in Luton's third. WBA made the score 3-2 and that completed the goal scoring. Apart from these five goals, both goalkeepers had been taken off injured to then be replaced by their counterparts and on top of all that Luton's Mitchell Thomas and Albion's Strodder were sent off for boxing with each other. Two nights later, Luton played their first match on a Thursday night since my very first game against Exeter back in 1966. It was at Burnden Park Bolton. Once again Luton had a player sent off, this time John Hartson for an elbow offence.

We lost 2-1. John Dreyer made his 250th and final LTFC appearance.

The final match of 1993-94 was on the Sunday at Stoke City. Making his debut in goal for the Hatters that day was youngster Kelvin Davis. It was one of the most impressive debut's I have ever witnessed and even the Stoke fans warmly applauded him off the field. We drew 2-2 but if it were not for Kelvin, the Potters would have scored more than the 6 we put past them back in the December.

Alan Harper played his 48th and last LTFC game.

1993-94 had been another roller coaster of a season for LTFC. The high was undoubtedly the FA Cup run and the lows were the early season shows and that dreadful performance at Wembley. What was annoying for us Hatters fans was that had we beaten Chelsea in the Semi-Final, Luton would have qualified for the European Cup Winners Cup in 94-95. Chelsea's opponents in the FA Cup Final were Man Utd and the Red Devils winning the Premiership, would play in the Champions League.

On Monday morning at 9.25am on June 27th 1994, our beautiful second daughter was born. About time too - as she was two weeks overdue!

We named her Mollie Annie. I wanted it spelt the English way aka Mollie Sugden, as both Deb and I did not want it spelt with a y like Molly Malone.

And because Deb, Georgina nor myself had a middle name, we decided to give Mollie one and named her Annie after Grandma Roberts.

I rushed to LTFC and managed to register Mollie as an official Junior Hatter just as Georgina was, but this time, to a new record of just FORTY-FIVE MINUTES old. This record still stands today, for a girl.

Proud Dad in 1994 with my two daughters Georgina aged 4 and baby Mollie. Both were naturally registered Junior Hatters at birth – Mollie is still the youngest ever female at just 45 mins old!

1994-95

Following the departure of John Dreyer, which I have already mentioned, another player left Luton. Alan Harper wanted to return north and after a steady contribution in 1993-94 he left us for Burnley.

The only major signing was Dwight Marshall for £150,000. He was a striker who was top goal scorer at lower league Plymouth. Apparently the Argyle fans were very upset at him being allowed to leave.

At the Kenny, the last remaining terraces were no more. The middle section of the Kenny end had now been seated and the upper terrace was closed off, with seats having to wait another 11 years before being finally installed there too.

This now left LTFC with a capacity just shy of 10,000 in a ground which had a record attendance of 30,069 over 35 years earlier.

A relatively good crowd of 3,476 turned up for a pre-season friendly home match against Premiership team Southampton, in which we lost 2-1.

The first league game was at home to WBA interestingly, the last of 1993-94. I took a Baggies supporting client from Vauxhall and he was happy when Albion took an early lead. It wasn't until the 2nd half that Luton came out of holiday mode and it ended 1-1 after Scott Oakes had headed a leveller.

In the League Cup 1st round 1st leg he scored again, against Fulham. They levelled in the last minute to leave the tie balanced for the return away leg. I had made a conscious decision before the season started that it would be unfair on Deb to leave her every Saturday now that we had 2 children. Therefore, would cut back on some of the away games. For that reason I then missed two matches. They were a 0-0 at Derby and the return leg at Fulham. At Craven Cottage it was 1-1 AET. Fulham then won 4-3 on penalties.

We then drew again 2-2 at home to Southend. My best memories of this match were the quality of the first and last goals. The opener by John Hartson was a beauty, after he superbly turned the defender. The Shrimpers equalised, before Ceri Hughes gave us the lead. But the goal of the game came from Southend's Otto. It was a stunning volley that you could not help but applaud - as most of the Luton crowd did!

Three nights later on Merseyside, Tranmere beat us 4-2.

The Adair family now of course consisting of 4 went up to Blackpool for our traditional Illuminations weekend, once again staying in the Claremont Hotel. Now I know Burslem upon Trent is not exactly in Lancashire but hey, Vale Park was a ground I had not attended yet and so when the fixtures came about I decided that this would be our Blackpool weekend.

So after breakfast and a stroll down the prom, I left to drive down and see Luton take on the recently promoted Port Vale.

It was worth it for Dwight Marshall scored the only goal in front of us Luton fans.

As happy as I was to see us win at the Vale, I was equally unhappy losing the next week at home to Burnley. Especially as the only goal, was down to a clanger by Luton keeper Jurgen Sommer.

We then lost heavily at home three nights later 3-0 to Burnley's Lancashire rivals Bolton. In front of only 5,764, this was our lowest league crowd for 20 yrs since the Three Day week power crisis in 1974.

But the next game's result and performance was what mattered most, as we paid a visit to Watford. This match turned out to be the best and most convincing Luton display in all my time of watching the Hatters at the home of the enemy.

The police had decided to make it an early kick off on the Saturday morning. Vicarage Road was being refurbished and the old Rookery End had now been demolished, with just a boarded fence behind the goal. For the past 15 years or so the Rookery was where the Luton fans had been allocated. This is something I never got to grips with, because it meant the away fans had the covered terrace. Not only was it more acoustic, but the Watford singing fans opposite - also got wet when it rained! This resulted on that day with us Hatters fans housed in the side Rous stand opposite their old stand and the Watford singing element were now in the new all seated covered Vicarage Road stand. A crowd of only 8,880 (including plenty from Luton) watched a Luton master show from the three-sided stadium.

I drove a young work colleague Pete Morris there. Pete worked in the Accounts dept and a smashing lad, who became a good friend for years to come. When Watford went 1-0 up we thought, 'Here we go,' but then a mesmerising turnaround occurred. Two absolute screamers, the first from Scott Oakes and the second by Kerry Dixon had given Luton a 2-1 lead. When Paul Telfer added another, all of us Luton fans were going off our heads in wild celebrations. Even when Watford pulled one back before the break I knew that we would be OK, such was the style we had shown. Paul Telfer increased our lead in the 2nd half and it finished Watford 2 Luton 4. This remains my highest away win seen at the foe.

The truth is, we thrashed them and the score did not do our superiority justice. I went with Pete again the next week by train to Millwall. Naturally, we visited The Anchor again before the match but remembering my new added responsibility, came home straight afterwards. The result was a 0-0 draw and in truth Luton should have won, Millwall were hopeless that day.

The winless home streak continued, losing the next game 1-0 to Bristol City. After only two wins out of 10 Luton were just one place above relegation.

I missed the next match at Stoke because it was live on ITV.

We played exceptionally well that day to beat the Potters 2-1. David Preece scored the winning goal at the end where all the Luton fans were congregated and I clearly saw Magnet & Richie Harding celebrating on the television. This goal by Preecy made up for an earlier penalty miss, which was as a result of comical defending by ex-Hatter John Dreyer. To add even more woe for Tumble, he was also sent off that day against his old colleagues.

When highflying Middlesbrough came to town managed by former England captain Bryan Robson, we thought that this would be our sternest test so far. It was absolutely pelting down with rain and I have to admit I was more than concerned pre-match. How wrong could I be? Luton secured the first home victory of 1994-95 in swashbuckling fashion. When Boro's Wilkinson headed into his own net in front of their fans at the Oak Road end that was just for starters. Dwight Marshall and David Preece made it 3-0 before h-t. Marshall added another and then John Hartson fired home the best goal of them all. Luton were rampant 5-0 up and still with 27 minutes to play. Alas, the only other goal scored was a Middlesbrough consolation. This excellent Luton showing just proved that on our day, we could live with ANY team. It was the best LTFC performance in years.

Deb's sister Liz's marriage had unfortunately not worked out with Geoff and they had divorced a couple of years prior. She had met an American from Texas called Thom, who worked for the forces in a secret role to counteract terrorism. He lived in Ampthill and Liz met him while he was working at the nearby American base, Chicksands. When Thom had to move up north to be based in Harrogate a few months prior, Liz decided to join him and rent a house in Ripon, naturally taking her daughter Lauren too.

Luton's next game was at Sheff Utd and so this was the perfect opportunity for us to visit them. Thom was a good sort, with a dry sense of humour and I got on extremely well with him, as did all of Deb's family. I left Deb, Liz and the girls to do whatever they wanted to do (SHOP) while I drove down to Sheffield. Like so many grounds at around this time, Bramall Lane was being refurbished and their big Shoreham Street Kop terrace had been demolished with just a fence boarding behind this goal. We fell behind quite early and for the first half hour the Blades were all over us, until Gale somehow managed to head in his own net to level matters. A much better second half Hatters performance resulted in goals by Julian James & Kerry Dixon as we ran out comfortable winners by 3-1. Just when I thought we had got our season back on track at last after two very impressive victories, we then lost 1-0 at home to Barnsley in a pathetic display. This was followed by an even worse defeat three nights later when we lost to Grimsby, again at home.

Scott Oakes had managed to equalise (undeservedly) with a great goal late on, only for the Mariners to hit the winner in the last minute.

Typical of the inconsistency that Luton were showing in 1994 was the next game at leaders Wolves. Because we had two successive away games and remembering my pre-season vow, I thought I would miss Molineux and go to Oldham the following week, as we were bound to have a better chance of winning at Boundary Park. Pete Morris went to Wolves and came into work on the Monday raving about the Luton performance, saying that we played brilliantly. We beat them 3-2.

I took Pete to Oldham in eager anticipation following his drooling about this.

Boundary Park always seemed to me like the coldest, windiest ground in England on that hill and even though they now had an all seated covered stand at the Luton end - it was still freezing! We drew 0-0.

A week later, we had a fine 2-0 home victory over Portsmouth thanks to an early Kerry Dixon headed goal and a tap in from David Preece. We had no idea at that time, but this was to be David's 27th and final LTFC goal in his wonderful career at Kenilworth Road.

Once again, I drove Pete Morris, to Swindon. This was my first visit to the County Ground since 1970. It had naturally changed since then with two new side stands and seats installed in both ends behind the goals (our end being one of the few open stands in the country, at risk to the elements). A huge Luton following saw us come from behind to beat Swindon 2-1, with goals from Scott Oakes & Kerry Dixon. This victory had lifted Luton to 5th place, our highest so far.

During that week I received a phone call from an old school friend in Adelaide, who was in the UK visiting relatives. My memory is usually pretty good but I'm sorry I have forgotten his name, even though he and his family came to stay the weekend with us. I took him to the next match at home to Sheff Utd. What a game it was too. Just five or so weeks after we comfortably beat them away, it was now time for the return. Unfortunately, with Sheff Utd already 2-0 up at the break, the Blades added a third just after h-t. John Hartson scored to give a bit of respectability, but soon it was 4-1 and there were still 20 mins left. Within minutes we had pulled it back to 4-3 and Kerry Dixon very nearly made it even. But a further two goals from the Blades finished us off. The 6-3 defeat was a home score line defeat I had not witnessed either before, or since.

We were at home again the following Sunday to the live TV audience against Derby. TV perhaps thought it might be another goal feast - it was 0-0!

I drove up to the Hawthorns to see us lose 1-0 at WBA in a very poor showing. On Boxing Day I missed the third consecutive blank, drawing 0-0 at Reading. The next day, it was time for Mark from Lloyd's of London and his partner Paula to join me in the Kenilworth Suite for the Sunderland match.

Like numerous occasions around that time, David Pleat had ordered the groundsman to water the pitch (in the RAIN I might add) and the sight of puddles on the pitch had left us all in amazement that the ref allowed play to start. As we had done a few weeks prior to Sunderland's neighbours Middlesbrough, we pulverised the Makems that day. A fine 3-0 win with 2 from Scott Oakes and one from John Hartson, in what turned out to be John's 11th & last league goal for LTFC, sent me home happy - but not my guests!

The final game of 1994 was at Notts County and I once again drove Pete Morris there. A cracking goal from Paul Telfer was enough to beat the Magpies and see out the New Year on a high.

On a freezing cold night and a bone hard Kenilworth Road pitch I watched us lose 1-0 to Charlton in the first match of 1995.

In the FA Cup 3rd round, we had been drawn to play Bristol Rovers at home and the Pirates fans filled the Oak Road End. The Gas held us to a 1-1 draw with John Hartson equalising in his final game in a Luton shirt.

I was actually in David Kohler's office when the John Hartson transfer deal was being negotiated on the telephone to the Arsenal Chairman on loud speak. While visiting Mr Kohler on printing business, he gestured to me to sit down and listen. The conversation at this stage was something along the lines of this:

Mr Kohler said, "I don't care what you say - Hartson is not for sale - even if you offer over £2 million!"

His response, "You drive a hard bargain. £2.5 million is my final offer, take it or leave it?"

Mr Kohler with his thumb up to me replied, "DEAL."

We had received our record transfer fee (at the time) for a teenager who had played 63 LTFC games. I have always hated it when we have consistently sold our best players, but I am realistic enough to know that a club our size with a low ground capacity to generate big money, will always have to sell to survive and this time the Arsenal offer simply HAD to be taken. The thing was, Mr Kohler would have been happy with - £1.5 million!

Another trip to Deb's friend Cherine in Sheffield was on the agenda when we played at Barnsley.

After a goalless first half Kerry Dixon gave us the lead with another wonder goal of his. He scored more than his fair share of brilliant goals at Luton and this one was no exception, a beautiful delicately lobbed effort from fully 30 yards. I cheered this on from the Barnsley Directors Box, as I was a guest of Mr Kohler's that day. The old 1960s era Man Utd goalkeeper Alex Stepney was sitting next to me, as he warmly applauded Dixon's goal.

I'm afraid that was as good as it got though, the Colliers, or Tykes as modern fans call them, came storming back to win 3-1.

I drove down to Bath for the mid-week FA Cup replay against Bristol Rovers and was relieved when a lone Dwight Marshall headed goal was enough to see us through to round 4 at home to Premiership club Southampton.

In that Saints game, a late equaliser from recent loan signing Wayne Biggins, made it 1-1 in front of our biggest home crowd of 1994-95 a sell out 9,938, to take us to a replay at the Dell.

Dwight Marshall added two more goals in the next game at home to Oldham. The first after just 30 seconds & the 2nd was the winning goal in a 2-1 victory. I missed the next game at Grimsby thankfully - as we were tanked 5-0!

The replay at the Dell was my 8th & final visit to this quaint old ground. After the Taylor report, the Dell was left with a capacity of just over 15,000 nowhere near big enough for a Premiership club to survive long term and so the Saints became one of many clubs to relocate, as there was just no room for expansion. The night of the replay should have been called the Matthew Le Tissier show. The talented winger dictated the whole game and scored twice as Southampton thrashed us 6-0. I can never recall two such successive heavy defeats suffered by the Town - 5-0 and 6-0!

We made up for it slightly, the next week at home to Swindon. Two more goals from Dwight Marshall and an own goal was enough to see us win 3-0.

I missed a mid-week game at Fratton Park where we fell to Portsmouth 3-2. I did see two brilliant goals by Scott Oakes at Bristol City to give us a 2-0 lead alas, we could not hold on and City came back to draw 2-2. Ashton Gate continues to be one of those stadiums I have never seen LTFC win at.

Millwall came to town, which meant that we naturally met up with our Lions mates pre-match. Dwight Marshall gave us the lead, 1-1 was the final result. Three nights later, at home again to Port Vale Luton took the lead for the fifth successive match via Paul Telfer. Kerry Dixon hit the Hatters second and despite Vale netting a late goal we hung on to win 2-1. This was Kerry Dixon's 20th and final LTFC goal.

We had a family day out at the seaside, but a very poor Luton showing at Southend resulted in a 3-0 defeat.

Typical of Luton, we then took on league leaders Tranmere at home and played superb, winning 2-0. Wayne Biggins scored his only league goal in his loan spell. For the seventh time in the last eight games Luton took the lead, at Burnley and for the 4th time out of those 8, we failed to capitalise. We lost 2-1.

Luton v Watford on the Sunday was chosen for live TV. Paul Telfer scored early on (that's 8 out of 9 Luton openers now) but once again, failed to win. The Hornets came back to draw 1-1 but it could have been worse had it not been for Kelvin Davis saving a penalty.

Our highest league gate of the season 9,651 watched a thriller against high-flying Wolves. Naturally, Luton took an early lead (9 out of 10) through Paul Telfer and he added another soon after. There were no more goals in the first half but Wolves were back in the game when Kelly scored. Recent £200,000 signing John Taylor scored his first Luton goal, but with still over an hour left Wolves came storming back. Kelly scored his and Wolves 2nd, before they equalised with only a minute left and it ended 3-3.

Paul Telfer was in the best form of his Luton career. He scored Luton's first AGAIN (10 out of 11) in the next game at home to Notts County and Scott Oakes finished the Magpies off to end it 2-0. These two goals were both of the players final goals of 1994-95 and for Telfer, it was his 22nd & final LTFC one.

I missed a mid-week 0-0 at Bolton.

A full minibus left Stopsley on the Friday for a Hartlepool weekender, in preparation for the Sunderland game at Roker Park.

Taylor gave us the lead, but a header by ex-Hatter Phil Gray shared the points in a 1-1 draw. I arrived home on the Sunday night after another brilliant weekend in Hartlepool, only to hear some dreadful news from Deb.

My great friend from Kilsyth Jim Moffat had been trying to contact me at the weekend. Mobile phones were not ten a penny then and Deb could only tell him I was away in Hartlepool. His eldest son David had been involved in an accident at work, falling off a forklift truck, and tragically died.

He was only 27 and married with two young daughters. I was stunned into silence, obviously I knew David, although not quite as well as his younger brother Sandy. I was devastated for my dear friends, but heaven only knows how they must have felt. They arrange funerals very quickly in Scotland but it was too soon after I had returned to work for me to attend. RIP David.

Taylor scored again on Easter Monday, unfortunately it was in his own net against play-off challengers Reading and that was the only goal.

I couldn't be bothered to travel to Charlton where we lost 1-0.

The final away game was at leaders Middlesbrough on the Sunday and this was to be an historic occasion, it being the last ever game played at Ayresome Park. Middlesbrough, like so many other clubs, were about to move into a new all seated arena called the Riverside Stadium, with an initial capacity of 33,000. I drove alone and for the one and only time in my visits there I had no crowd problems at all, due to the carnival atmosphere. I even managed to have a drink in a pub pre-match with Luton colours on, something that would have been impossible on any previous visit to Teesside. A sell-out crowd of 23,903 including about 500 Luton fans saw Hendrie give Boro the lead just before h-t. John Taylor quietened them when he equalised, but Hendrie had them bouncing again when he scored a second and the final Ayresome Park goal.

I saw Phil Gray in the Luton end that day, cheering on his ex-teammates.

A week later, was the last game of the season at home to Stoke. A stunning Richard Harvey goal opened the scoring for Luton just before the break at the full Oak Road End, with plenty of Stoke fans in fancy dress. In the 2nd half, an outstanding Stoke performance saw the Potters come back to lead 2-1 before Gary Waddock levelled with his sole Luton goal of 1994-95. But back came Stoke again and they finished winning 3-2.

Although this was a cracking spectacle, it ended Luton's season on a slightly sour note. We had lost more games at home, than we had won (9-8) and from being a top ten side nearly all season, just one victory from the last 10 games resulted in Luton finishing in 16th place, five places & six points above safety.

Kerry Dixon, David Preece and Paul Telfer were all to move on. Luton did not want to sell Telfer but when he stated he wanted to leave we sold him to Coventry for £1.5 million.

Dixon left for Millwall but was in the twilight of his career, so it was no loss to see him move on - however he lost a bit of Luton's fans respect by then leaving Millwall for Watford!

But the saddest exit for me was David Preece. Signed from Walsall over ten years prior he was genuinely a Luton great. He played nearly 400 times in Luton colours and played at England B International level. Many people including myself thought he deserved higher England honours. He left the Hatters for Derby in the summer but played one final game for Luton, his very well earned testimonial match. A near full house of 9,800 came to honour Preecy against a young Man Utd team, thanks to some influence from Jimmy Ryan who was now on the United Coaching staff.

In the Red Devils team that night, were youngsters by the names of Neville, Scholes and - a certain David Beckham! At one stage, we had led 3-0 before United came back to draw 3-3.

Boundary Park, Oldham v Luton 1977
Me, Baggy and Chris McEvoy. Baggy sadly committed suicide in 1988.

Best Man at Larry Kinloch's wedding 1982.

Myself and Ricky 'GOD' Hill at his 2019 Book promotion dinner. My 2nd all time favourite Hatters player – only Malcolm Macdonald (just) comes above him!

Myself and Legend Brian Stein. He scored 154 goals for Luton, only Andy Rennie (162) and Gordon Turner (276) have scored more Hatters goals in our entire history.

On honeymoon in Gozo 1986.

At Ken Adair's apartment in Cala Longa, Ibiza 1989.

Me and Uncle Malcolm Roberts 1990 (No, it's not a Celtic top) - Malc was tragically
killed by a drunk driver, while cycling in 2005.

Rochdale's Tony Ford shaking my hand at Luton v Rochdale in 2001 after I had
told him it was lovely to see someone nearly as old as me still playing.
I didn't know the LTFC photographer captured this moment until it was in the next
programme.

Blackpool v Luton 2004. Good friend Barz is standing to my right.
Another photo taken by Gareth that I was unaware of.

Myself and LTFC Legend Sir Mick of Harford.

Luton v Preston 2006. I sponsored the match along with my friends,
to celebrate 40 years of watching my first Hatters game.

The awesome sight of 42,000 Luton fans at the JPT Final when we beat Scunthorpe 3-2 in 2009. Had the F.L. not been so pigheaded by refusing to sell us any more tickets (despite nearly 35,000 empty seats), we would have sold many more.

Lowering the tone of the neighbourhood, my house before the heartbreaking Play Off Final defeat to Wimbledon 2011.

Luton v Newport 2017. A memorable reunion day of ex Hatters players to celebrate friend Peter Anderson's first return to Kenilworth Road since saving us from going bust, by signing for Belgian club Royal Antwerp in 1975. L-R David Court, Myself, Alan Garner RIP, Peter Anderson, Club Historian Roger Wash & Ken Goodeve.

The flag great pal Stuart Fisher-Mack had specially made for one of my Adair Travel Group Blackpool trips.

Some of the first Adair Travel group/bash in Blackpool
for the Southport v Luton game 2013.

The lovely Janet Betts in Santa gear to my left and Rangers/Luton pal Rab to my right.
Adair Travel Blackpool Group trip no 4 Morecambe v Luton in 2014. We were
stuffed 3-0, one of only two defeats in the 11 trips from 2013, to date. (8 wins & a
draw)

Relegation

That summer we returned to Sandy Balls in the New Forest for our holiday, only this time staying in a beautiful log cabin, rather than a caravan. The weather was perfect, glorious sunshine every day. We drove down in my new company car. It was another Calibra, only this was a special edition. Metallic Blue (Rangers), with cream heated leather seats. It was my favourite car ever.

A few days after we returned, I found out that Luton were to play three games in Devon on a pre-season tour. Swinging into action, I suggested to Deb that as the weather forecast was still lovely sunshine, why didn't we take off another week and go down to Torquay? In fact, why don't we invite all of your family? She thought it was a great idea and said go for it. I booked a nice hotel on the seafront for her Mum & Dad, sister Liz & Lauren and her Nan too. I had booked a guesthouse for us 4 with an outdoor pool, which just happened to be down the road from Plainmoor (Torquay's ground). The German owner was a nice old gentleman, it turned out he was a fellow WW2 POW & best friend with the famous German goalkeeper Bert Trautmann.

There were already a major number of changes at LTFC for 1995-96, which had taken place during the summer. Manager David Pleat had once again uprooted and left us, this time for Sheffield Wednesday and youth team coach Terry Westley had been promoted from within to take Pleat's place. I have already mentioned the departures of Dixon, Preece & Telfer. We had three signings, paying Scunthorpe £100,000 for defender Graham Alexander, from Ipswich we had signed Bulgarian World Cup International forward Bontcho Guentchev on a free. We also paid Leicester £150,000 to bring back ex-Hatter David Oldfield.

When we arrived in Torquay Deb immediately smelt a rat when about half a dozen people said hello to me walking down the street within hours of arrival. I came clean but she didn't care a jot and she loved the place we were staying at, especially the secluded outdoor pool.

I drove to Tiverton Town for the first match and although they were only a non- league side, we looked really good and won 5-1. Guentchev especially impressed me, he scored a hat-trick. I came back to Luton after the trip raving about him to the lads saying, "We have a superstar on our hands."

My father-in-law Alan, joined myself and 677 others as we walked to Plainmoor for the 2nd friendly against Torquay where Guentchev was once again magnificent, scoring twice in a 4-1 Luton win.

On the sixth night of our mini holiday I drove to Exeter for the match at St James' Park where we won 2-0. It was obvious that in the 1,100+ crowd, there were more than a few Hatters fans, who had done exactly as I had and made a holiday out of it. We returned home having had our tans topped up thanks to the glorious sunshine in three out of the previous four weeks.

There was one further friendly match at home to Tottenham and a healthy crowd of 5,712 turned out to see us lose 2-0.

The first league game was at home to Norwich and was on a Sunday, having been chosen for live TV. In truth, we were given a football lesson.

The Canaries were 2-0 up before Guentchev pulled one back via a penalty, but Norwich added another and went home 3-1 winners.

Terry Westley paid £750,000 to Burnley for centre half Steve Davis. This was a staggering amount of money for LTFC in fact, only £100,000 short of our record fee paid for Lars Elstrup. Although I have to write, he was worth every penny going on to be an inspiring captain in what was a poor team. Stevo made his debut in the League Cup at home to Bournemouth, in which we drew 1-1 and he was instrumental in Dwight Marshall's equaliser.

I took Deb and the girls along with her Nan, to Southend for the day on another scorcher. We secured our first points of 1995-96 when Tony Thorpe opened his account with the only goal.

Bournemouth knocked us out of the League Cup, winning 2-1 AET.

Old SWMC friend Billy Smith was down on holiday from Scotland and he joined me to watch Luton v Leicester. Ceri Hughes opened the scoring but ex-Hatter Garry Parker levelled. Goalkeeper Jurgen Sommer played his 101st and last game for Luton that day, before being sold to QPR for £600,000. This was one transfer I didn't object to as I felt young Kelvin Davis was the better keeper anyway.

I missed a mid-week 0-0 draw at Grimsby watched by only 4,289, the lowest crowd to watch Luton all of that season.

Dwight Marshall scored his first league goal at home to Derby, then the player I was raving about, Bontcho Guentchev, missed an OPEN goal before the Rams came back and punished us to win 2-1.

In this year's Anglo Italian Cup, we were actually going to play Italian opposition. In the first group game we were tanked 4-1 at home by Perugia.

I attended my first Rangers match of the season to see a 4-0 win over Raith Rovers. While I was at Ibrox Park, Luton were playing at Elm Park, Reading for the final time and went down 3-1. Surprisingly, Kelvin Davis was made a scapegoat that day and Ian Feuer was drafted in, initially on loan from West Ham. It would be a full 2 years before Davis played for Luton again.

Feuer made his debut at Millwall alongside another signing Danish midfielder Johnny Vilstrup, who we had paid £205,000 for. I'm afraid he was a dud, playing only six times for Luton. I missed the game at the New Den where we lost 1-0.

CBC had decided to alter the Corporate Entertainment. Rather than pay £1,000 per Kenilworth Suite membership, we decided to just book on an individual basis, as and when. The first occasion was at home to Sunderland.

I was joined as usual by Mark & Paula. They were very happy to see Sunderland win 2-0.

The pressure even at this early stage was already mounting on the manager who sadly, appeared to be out of his depth.

Whilst the Adair family were having our traditional Blackpool Illuminations break, Luton were grinding out a 0-0 draw at Wolves to earn only our sixth point out of 27. In Blackpool, I watched the local team beat Crewe 2-1.

At the next match at home to Portsmouth, we made a right day of it in the Kenilworth Suite. Not only did I invite a fellow CBC rep Mark Lees with his clients (FIVE women, including a couple of loud and beautiful stunners) but I had wangled a couple of SWMC mates in too, Sunderland Bob & Terry McCann. What a belter of a day we had, the wine was flowing merrily and Terry still talks today about the great time we had then.

It helped that we won our first home match of 95-96 and only our second in 10 games, to ease the pressure (for now) on Terry Westley. Dwight Marshall opened the scoring before Steve Davis scored his first for Luton, then ex-Hatter Paul Walsh pulled one back for Pompey. Guentchev sealed it with a penalty to make it 3-1 and top off a fine day.

On the Monday morning I received a letter from the taxman - with a £250 demand for undeclared income! The previous summer I had decided to help raise funds for LTFC by selling scratch cards. I certainly wasn't doing it for the money, but obviously did not turn down the commission received.

I immediately went to pay the chairman David Kohler a visit. Upon arrival he said, "Hello Alan Adair, what can I do for you?"

I threw the letter at him and said, "What's all this about David?"

He responded rather smugly, "Looks like a tax demand to me, Alan."

"I FUCKING KNOW THAT." (It's OK, we often swore at each other.) "I try to help out the club raise some money and this is the thanks I get."

After telling me to calm down, he explained that the club have to declare any money paid out to the Inland Revenue. He then told me that he would promise he would sort me out, but could not do it through the books or anything official, but WOULD sort me out. I just thought, "Aye right," and left.

I then missed a 1-0 away defeat at Tranmere.

On the Thursday, Mr Kohler rang me up and summoned me back to his office. "I told you that I can't do anything official, but how about this as a compromise? A travel agent is organising to take fans to Genoa for the Anglo Italian Cup match, if you were to go as an unpaid unofficial steward on the plane, I will pay the travel agent myself." This included a return flight from Gatwick and a night in a Genoa Hotel. We shook hands and I said - DEAL! I wonder how many current chairmen of football clubs would do that today?

David Kohler received an enormous amount of grief from many Luton fans, as indeed did I a little for sticking up for him, without of course revealing why.

I guess now this is out in the open - maybe he can be cut just a wee bit of slack! Pete Morris from work joined me along with Roy Sebbage. We had a brilliant trip without any hassle from Italian fans whatsoever. We flew out on the morning of the game and after checking in at the fabulous hotel, all of us (flags, scarves & all) went on a pub bender all the way to the ground. The locals could not have been friendlier and dispelled my belief of Italians at the time (certainly in Genoa anyway).

I lost count of the bars we visited and after a delicious meal in one of them, we headed for the Luigi Ferraris Stadium, which Genoa share with Sampdoria. In a bar directly behind where Luton fans were to be housed, there must have been 250 or so who made it via planes, trains and automobiles. Yes, there were only 3,759 and yes, we were thrashed 4-0 and yes, it was a Micky Mouse Cup, BUT this was a memorable occasion and I'm glad I was there.

This is one of just two times I have seen the Hatters play abroad.

The next day, before going to the airport, one of the Luton fans at our hotel had his wallet stolen while out having a stroll. I organised a whip round from the Hatters in the hotel and he was chuffed. I still see him at games today.

The players and officials flew home with us, we actually felt sorry for Westley. It was blatantly evident he had lost the dressing room and it was only to be a matter of time before he was to be put out of his misery.

Upon our return, the next game was at home to high-flying WBA and saw Richard Harvey open the scoring with his 5th and final LTFC goal. Two late Baggies goals were enough to keep us rock bottom. The attendance of 8,042 was our best home crowd at that point.

Eight days later on live ITV we somehow managed to secure all three points at Ipswich thanks to a goal from David Oldfield, his first since returning.

I'm afraid it was back to normal though, when we lost 1-0 at home to Charlton. Making his debut as sub, was Norwegian Vidar Riseth another signing by Westley for £110,000. Nobody could accuse him of having no money to spend on strengthening the squad. In just three months, Westley had spent an incredible £1,315,000 on players. He was to sign yet another, Darren Patterson from Crystal Palace for £150,000. That's nearly £1.5 million spent on players, simply unheard of in LTFC history.

The situation worsened the next week. Luton's final appearance at the Victoria Ground, Stoke, saw us walloped 5-0 and thankfully I missed it.

During mid-week I decided to conquer a new ground for the short journey to Northampton's Sixfields stadium v Preston, in which the Cobblers lost 2-1.

Two more players made their debuts in the following game at home to Oldham. Stuart Douglas, a 17-year-old from the youth system, scored a brilliant debutant goal made by fellow debutant Darren Patterson, to give us a 1-0 lead. We couldn't hold on to it though and Oldham levelled 1-1.

We then managed a home 0-0 draw against promotion seeking Birmingham. Three nights later, it was local derby time at Vicarage Road. I will admit to travelling to Watford with a huge travelling army of Hatters, in trepidation. Steve Davis sent us into raptures by heading the opening goal. Ian Feuer then managed to save a Watford penalty and with the clock ticking down, it looked like a rare enjoyable victory was heading our way. Alas, the enemy equalised undeservedly late on and it ended 1-1.

If Luton were to show this level of passion and commitment again for Terry Westley, we could still be OK.

With renewed hope and optimism after the display v the Hornets, it was off to Barnsley via Sheffield, to Deb's best friend Cherine & Gary's.

We should have buried the Tykes. Dwight Marshall hit the post when it would have been easier to score and there is no doubt 3-0 to Luton at h-t would be fair, however 0-0 it was. Barnsley then punished us by scoring the only goal.

I then witnessed a fantastic game and a quite brilliant, heartening LTFC display in the next game at home to Tranmere. Despite falling behind, Dwight Marshall equalised soon after. Tranmere again took the lead against the run of play. I wondered if Luton had the resilience to come back because at that point, we were the better side. Marshall scored a brilliant second to level, before Paul McLaren netted his first LTFC goal, in what turned out to be the winner.

3-2 to Luton was a vital win, however we remained 2nd bottom.

Eight days later in front of the TV cameras, Wolves came to town. Surprisingly, Wolves had been struggling also and were only two places above us. At half time it looked all over for us, as Wolves were ahead 3-1. We tried hard to come back and when Dwight Marshall made it 3-2 it was game on. Despite a frantic Hatters effort Wolves hung on and we returned to bottom place.

I took my work colleague Ena's husband Gavin, to the next match Luton v Ancona as he was a big fan of Italian football. They must have been a pretty poor Italian team because we thrashed them 5-0.

The next game at Portsmouth I missed, due to taking Georgina to the SWMC kids Xmas party. We were hammered 4-0. This was Terry Westley's bridge too far, the following day he was fired. As mentioned earlier, he was out of his depth and rather annoyingly had spent more money in three months than any Luton manager had in ALL my time of following the Hatters. He simply had to go.

After 22 games, one short of the halfway mark, we had won just four games and were bottom of the table.

Our next boss was Lennie Lawrence, who had done a sterling job in keeping Charlton a top-flight club for years before moving to Middlesbrough. His appointment was met with genuine popularity by most Luton fans and his first match in charge was at home to Huddersfield. As is so often the case with a managerial change, the team rallied and raised their game.

Dwight Marshall had given us a deserved lead but the Terriers came back to lead 2-1. It looked like same old same old, but when David Oldfield headed in a brilliant equaliser the roar was the loudest heard that season. It finished 2-2 but was a very spirited Luton performance. This was the first time I had ever seen Huddersfield at Kenilworth Road in league action, because the only other time they played here in my era was in 1972, when I was living in Adelaide.

Due to the inclement weather it was to be a full 14 days later when we played the next game at Grimsby in the FA Cup.

I drove John Farmer, Bill McKinlay & Rasher Bacon to Cleethorpes for the eagerly awaited Cup Tie, with plenty of Hatters fans joining us too - it turned into a horror story!

The Mariners were 3-0 up and despite Dwight Marshall pulling one back it was 4-1 at the break. Some Luton fans had left at h-t. I refused to and even at 5-1 stayed but when Grimsby made it 6-1, it was time to say goodbye. We headed for the famous Grimsby Haddock & Chips and heard the roar when it became seven. It finished 7-1. This is the only time in my 55+ years to date, that I've seen Luton ship SEVEN goals in a match (mercifully I missed Brentford 7 Luton 0 in 2019) - the Haddock was lovely though!

The following week at home to Southend, the players knew they owed us fans a performance and we got one, winning 3-1. Bontcho Guentchev (remember him) scored his first goal since Sept to put Luton ahead. Two more goals from Scott Oakes including one sublime rocket effort finished the Shrimpers off, even though they hit a late consolation goal. We certainly did not know at that time, but Oake's 33rd and 34th LTFC goals were to be his final ones. He played exactly 200 times for Luton and left after 95-96 to join up with David Pleat at Sheff Wed. To be fair to Scott, he possibly stayed a season or two too long at Luton. If he had left at the end of 93-94 the world was his oyster, he chose to remain and stay loyal & for that, he should be admired. He will always be in Luton fans hearts for his heroics in the epic FA Cup run that took us to Wembley in 1994.

We gained another fabulous 1-0 win in a game I missed at Norwich. This was repeated with another penalty, the only goal again in a vital win at home to bottom club Sheff Utd, this lifted us out of the relegation zone and our league record under Lennie Lawrence, was three wins & a draw.

The good form continued at Leicester when I watched another impressive Luton display in a 1-1 draw at Filbert Street for Luton's final visit there. Tony Thorpe scored our goal.

That night we had a party at SWMC for my mum. She was about to move to New Zealand to live near my sister Ann, this was a leaving and joint 60th Birthday Party. Well at least that's what it was intended to be, because on the night she told us that she was actually born in 1935 - not 1936!

Mum had been to visit Ann on numerous occasions through the years and finally decided to move there.

There was no doubt that the change of manager had a positive effect and the FA Cup thrashing at Grimsby was avenged in the next fixture. Grimsby came to Kenilworth Road and Graham Alexander scored his first Luton goal. Despite then falling 2-1 behind, we rallied back. Bontcho Guentchev scored his fourth in 5 and then Dwight Marshall hit a superb winning goal, to result in a 3-2 win.

Then a very tight game at home to Millwall occurred and we just managed to squeeze a win against the Lions when Tony Thorpe scored a late penalty.

I missed a mid-week draw at Derby and a sign of how far we had come under Lawrence, was when we held the league leaders to 1-1.

A convoy of cars left on Friday heading to Hartlepool, in preparation for the Sunderland match on our weekender. After checking in at the Douglas Hotel, it was SSS time before we headed to the Newmarket pub to meet the Hartlepool lads for a Karaoke fest. There must have been twenty-odd Stopsley boys in that pub, when in walked PC Palmer the Luton police liaison officer, in plain clothes. He obviously knew somehow that we would be in Hartlepool but Lord knows how he found us in the Newmarket, as that was the first time I had ever been in there. PC Palmer asked if we would have any objections to him joining us and I told him providing he got a round in for all the lads, I would have no complaints personally. He knew we were no problem and just beer monsters not hooligans, but I would find out to my cost six years later - that he was no friend! We had an amazing night and I got a standing ovation for my Beatles effort 'When I Saw Her Standing There' – full dance routine too!

The next day we needed a 32-seat minibus to take us to Roker Park, including the Pool lads. Naturally, we went in my favourite Sunderland pub The New Derby near the ground and the banter between us, and the Makems was top class. We stood on the open Roker End terrace in eager anticipation as Luton came into this game on an unbeaten run of eight matches and yet to taste a league defeat in 1996. It was a pretty even first half, despite Julian James heading into his own net just before the interval but with 25 mins left disaster struck. Dwight Marshall fell and lay down screaming in agony it looked serious & it was, he was stretchered off to sympathetic applause by both sets of fans.

You could tell it was bad immediately and it transpired later that he had a broken ankle and would miss the rest of the season.

We tried in vain to score but it remained 1-0 and the question all Luton fans asked was who would score the goals now to keep us safe?

This was mine, and Luton's last ever visit to Roker Park. I went to this famous old ground six times and & never saw us win there. Sunderland would move to a new stadium on the site of the old Mine Colliery in the city a year or so later.

A great night at 42nd Street in Hartlepool topped off the fantastic weekend (apart from the result and Dwight). The next day before preparing to drive home I won on the new lottery having picked 4 numbers and won £85.

After returning home we hosted Reading in mid-week. Without Marshall the onus was now on Guentchev and he got us off to a flyer, slotting home an early penalty. But the Royals equalised just before h-t. They scored a winning goal and this 2-1 loss had now left us just two places above safety and back in a relegation fight again.

I drove to another new ground for the visit to Huddersfield Town. They moved the short distance from their old Leeds Road ground in 1994. The new McAlpine Stadium was a nice modern arena which when built, had three stands and 18,000 seats, on completion a few years later this rose to 24,500. After meeting Bill McKinlay, who was staying with his Huddersfield-born wife Janet for the weekend, we had a drink in a local pub and set off for the match.

A good Luton following in the 11,950 crowd watched Guentchev have one of those days where he would not score in a brothel. We lost 1-0 to a single Terriers goal. Magnet got pulled for speeding on the way home.

On Wed 13th March 1996 I remember hearing some shocking news coming from Scotland. A lunatic lone gunman had walked into Dunblane Primary School and he randomly started shooting at a class of FIVE- & SIX-year-old children, killing 15 kids and their teacher, who was trying to protect them. Another child died on the way to hospital before the asshole evil bastard, turned the gun on himself fatally. I gave my two girls an extra special hug and kiss that night, for this upset me immensely. Georgina was the same age as many of those poor mites. RIP The Dunblane victims.

The very next weekend I was actually in a sombre Scotland for the Rangers 1 Celtic 1 match and even accounting for the hatred that match involves, there was still an immaculate moving minute's silence for the shooting victims.

I didn't attend the Palace match at Selhurst Park. Luton lost again 2-0.

That result had left us in a relegation place. I also missed the next match, a 1-0 defeat at Sheff Wed and it seemed that without Marshall's goals, we were doomed. I took Larry and a CBC Director's husband to the Kenilworth Suite for the Ipswich match, as they both supported The Tractor Boys.

Lennie Lawrence had brought in two new strikers from his previous clubs, to make their debuts that day. He paid Charlton £250,000 for Kim Grant and Paul Wilkinson was signed on loan from Middlesbrough. Ipswich took an early lead and then Grant hit a fine debut equaliser. But we soon gifted Ipswich a second and it ended 2-1. A vital three points were then secured at The Hawthorns, WBA when we beat the Baggies 2-0.

I met a Charlton-supporting client Ray Thomas, for a pre-match pint before heading to the Valley. This was my first visit to The Valley since Charlton returned to their spiritual home. I sat with Ray in the Charlton main stand and cringed as fighting broke out when Luton fans charged Charlton rivals to our right. This was the first time I had seen actual trouble inside a ground since Luton v Bristol Rovers in 1986.

Tony Thorpe gave Luton the lead with a rather fortunate cross/shot. Had Kim Grant not missed an absolute sitter, we would have won the game comfortably. Unfortunately, a hotly disputed penalty for Charlton saw them equalise and it finished 1-1. Even Ray thought the penalty was dubious.

Against Stoke at home four nights later, this game was tagged as a MUST win. When Kim Grant scrambled home a goal the omens were looking good. But very late on Stoke scored twice to win 2-1. This result could be described as fatal. I must admit I thought we were down after this, especially the cruel way it ended. This was beyond doubt at the next game away to Birmingham, where we were thrashed 4-0. I'm glad I missed it.

Yet still, the biggest home crowd 9,454, of 1995-96, attended the derby v Watford. In drawing 0-0, at least it looked like we would take Watford down with us too. Graham Alexander was sent off in the 90th minute, proof that HE still cared.

To sum up how our luck was at that time, we signed a player on loan from Man Utd called Graham Tomlinson and while making his full debut at Port Vale in mid-week he was stretchered off with a broken leg, which obviously ended his loan spell with us. We lost 1-0.

The inevitable finally happened at home to Barnsley. A pathetic first half Luton performance led to them being booed off as Barnsley led 2-0. I have or never will, boo Luton Town but on this occasion even I was close to doing so.

Mathematically, we had still not been relegated before the game so one would have thought that the players would at least TRY. Tony Thorpe did score after the break, but that was it as far as Luton were concerned, Barnsley added a third & that was enough for a lot of Luton fans, as they streamed for the exits.

After 26 years in the top two tiers, LTFC were now officially relegated.

The day after my 38th birthday, my lowest league crowd at Kenilworth Road since April 1967, just 5,443, watched the final home game against Port Vale. It was time to blood in some youngsters, Ben Chenery & Sean Evers made their debuts. When Vale scored early, we just wanted some respect. The players answered as Thorpe scored twice and Guentchev made it 3-1, then Vale scored, to end with a 3-2 Luton win. It was our first at home since February.

I drove up to the last game at Oldham on the Sunday. Fancy Dress just did not seem appropriate, nor joining the lads for an end of season beano in Blackpool. The campaign was summed up when Scott Oakes hit the bar and then Oldham scored the only goal on 84 minutes.

We finished bottom, seven points off safety but at least had the consolation of Watford joining us, along with Millwall.

I maintain to this day, that if Dwight Marshall had not broken his ankle when we were on an unbeaten run of 8 games, we would have DEFINITELY survived.

My football attending had not finished for 1995-96 yet, as we had the little matter of Euro 96 being held in England for the first time.

Cherry Newbery the LTFC Secretary, managed to secure FIVE tickets for me at England v Scotland. A crowd of my friends from Kilsyth flew down and stayed in Luton for another memorable weekend. England won 2-0. Paul Gascoigne scored one of the best ever goals scored at Wembley. The majority of the crowd went berserk and even my Kilsyth mates were standing applauding (well Gazza was a GER). We headed back to Luton and then on to SWMC for a brilliant night. The Scots naturally wanted to carry on after the Club closed and we headed into Town. We headed for the Rumours Club, which was ran by my good black friend John Ashton and after a quick word with the doorman, we received complimentary admission. It was hilarious seeing all my Scots mates faces and reactions when we entered the dance floor area and bar.

Now there are not too many Black faces in Kilsyth, even today. We were the - ONLY white people there! We had a ball. We had no problems, as I knew we wouldn't and the memory of all of us dancing to the hit of the time 'Killing Me Softly' by the Fugees, will live with me forever.

John, when you read this mate - they had a BLINDING night!

Cherry Newbery had once again came up trumps and managed to secure two tickets for the Spain match. I took Damon from work. We were at the lower tunnel section in the 75,440 crowd. If I'm truthful, England were rather fortunate to end the game 0-0 AET, the match went into a penalty shoot out (at our end). England won 4-2 on pens.

We all know England lost to Germany & they beat the Czechs in the Final.

The LTFC boss John Still (who finally ended our 5-year non-league hell) and I
at Cambridge United v Luton 2013

1996-97

As we prepared for our first season in the third tier since 1969-70, Scott Oakes had left and joined David Pleat at Sheff Wed. Terry Westley's flops Riseth & Vilstrup had departed and John Taylor too, who had returned to Camb Utd.

After relegation there was no chance of CBC buying Corporate again, apart from the odd game when I could buy individual tickets.

There were two home pre-season friendly matches I watched, against West Ham and Norwich. We defeated both teams 4-2 and 2-0 respectively. One lad who caught my eye in those games was Andrew Fotiatis, a youth team product.

I had now become good mates with a bloke called Gus Watson and had known him for years to say hello to when he used to drink in the old Bobbers Club, although he drank in the bottom bar with his friends, playing cards.

After the police closed the Bobbers Club in Oak Road on match days and in between when the away ban was lifted, I got to know Gus more in the Eric Morecambe Lounge. He became a good mate and eventually one of my best friends. We decided to buy our season ticket for 96-97 in the Enclosure singing section next to the Oak Road away fans. Sean, Gus & I had seats on the back row. It was in this section that the best atmosphere in the ground came across.

Our first game from the new position was against Burnley and the Clarets fans filled the Oak Road, something that would be a rare occasion in 1996-97.

Anyone who thought that this level would be a stroll got an instant reminder that it would not be, as Burnley raced into a 2-0 lead. Although Tony Thorpe would reply soon after Burnley's second, it ended 2-1 and Bontcho Guentchev also missed a penalty.

We had drawn Bristol Rovers in the League Cup with the 1st leg at home. Luton cruised the game winning 3-0 courtesy of Grant, Thorpe and Oldfield.

Evidence that Cup games were not as popular anymore, was shown by a gate of just 2,463.

We travelled to the away game at Brentford and despite us twice taking a lead via Tony Thorpe & Ceri Hughes, the Bees came back to sting us and won 3-2. We had a drink pre-match in one of the four pubs that adorn each corner of Griffin Park.

Three nights later at Bristol City, any talk of a quick return to Div 1 rapidly vanished. Luton were thrashed FIVE nil and thankfully I did not travel.

Making his debut that night was recent midfield signing from Bradford City for £50,000, Paul Showler.

An absolutely awful game followed at home to Rotherham. At least we secured our first victory though, beating the Millers 1-0 with a goal from Mitchell Thomas.

A young centre half came on as a Sub that day by the name of Matthew Upson, to make his debut.

It was his sole League appearance for LTFC and near the end of the season we were to receive an incredible £1 million from Arsenal, with add-ons of another £1 million too. Upson, would eventually play for England and score in a World Cup Finals game against

Germany, but this was a deal we simply HAD to take.

I didn't bother travelling to Bristol Rovers for the 2nd leg at their new home the Memorial Ground A) because it was mid-week and B) because I thought it was a dead rubber. We lost 2-1 on the night and went through 4-2 overall.

The next game, I drove to a new ground to see Luton play Wycombe Wanderers for the first time. A big Luton following on a nice day saw David Oldfield hit the only goal of the game. He made it three in a row, along with Bontcho Guentchev to beat Gillingham 2-1 at home four nights later. This was to be the Bulgarian's only goal of 96-97 and his 12th and final LTFC one.

The pitiful 4,604 there, was the first sub 5,000 attendance I had ever been in at a league match at Kenilworth Road.

The style, tactics and quality at this level were blatantly obvious in the next match at home to Chesterfield. The Spireites played with 11 men behind the ball and came for a point. When they had the bonus of a penalty and scored it, everyone knew it would kill the game and it remained 1-0. It was an appalling spectacle.

Three nights later, saw a much better game at home to Premiership Derby in the League Cup 1st Leg. Luton put on their best showing yet and beat the Rams 1-0, actually deserving more than the sole Julian James goal.

It was time for a Blackpool Illuminations trip, as we were playing at nearby Bury. All of Deb's family joined us and we once again stayed at the Claremont.

After I parked up near Gigg Lane I went for a pre-match pint in the Bury Supporters Club under the Main Stand, us Luton fans were made welcome and I met the Bury Commercial Director, Neville, the father of Man Utd brothers Phil & Gary. It was a drab 0-0, but another ground to tick off my list.

At the match my left leg had swollen up a bit and I was walking with a bit of a limp. The next day while spending the morning in the Blackpool Pleasure Beach Fairground, I went for a ride on the Pepsi Max Big One. Having been the only one in our party with the balls to go on the fastest, quickest and steepest rollercoaster in the world (at that time), I enjoyed it so much I rode it again. By now I was really struggling with my leg so we agreed it was time to leave and returned to Luton.

I struggled on at work and having just had a big pay rise to keep me at CBC after a rival had tried to poach me, I felt I had to stay loyal and persisted that week, even though my leg was getting worse.

As I was due to fly to Glasgow on Friday, I missed the 2nd Leg at Derby. It was on this night that Derby announced that they would be leaving the Baseball Ground for a new stadium, which would be built and opened the next year. We drew 2-2 on the night and the Hatters went through 3-2 on aggregate.

Although I was resting my leg at night, the swelling hadn't appeared to go down much and so I decided to play safe and visited the quack. I wanted assurance that I was OK to fly to Glasgow the next day and showed him the swelling, asking him if it needed any fluid draining off. He assured me it was fine and there would be no need for any draining. Doc knows best, so I flew up to Glasgow for the Old Firm game at Ibrox on the Saturday and was in Kilsyth Friday afternoon. The next day Rangers beat Celtic 2-0. It was a great day all round as I found out that Luton had beaten Blackpool 1-0 at home.

The next morning in the Kilsyth Golf Club, my friends noticed that I was now limping quite badly. I rolled up my trouser leg and my left leg was huge. I flew home that night and immediately visited the Doctor first thing Mon-Am. I asked him if he thought my leg had swollen enough to be drained NOW (it was TWICE the size of my right leg), he arranged for me to go straight to the L&D Hospital - after informing me that I had a Blood Clot!

After being admitted, I explained to the hospital doctor that I had checked on Thursday and asked if it was OK to fly to Glasgow. On learning that I had rode the Pepsi Max the week before flying to Scotland and back he said, "Young man, you are lucky you are still with us, the clot could easily have travelled to your lung or brain and frankly - could have been fatal!"

I immediately thought of my St Thomas Hospital drama three years earlier and said, "Jesus, when I'm ill - I don't do things in half measures!" I was kept in for two weeks and treated with Warfarin to thin the blood to rid the clot, until my leg had reached its normal size again.

As was the case at my previous hospital stay, I was visited by lots of family and friends. Naturally there were no visits from Mum this time, although she did regularly telephone from New Zealand. I was absolutely thrilled and gobsmacked when LTFC arranged a visit from three players. Graham Alexander, Ceri Hughes and Steve Davis came to visit me and gave me a fully signed away top from that season, the yellow one with blue sleeves. I was touched, as it was a nice gesture by the club.

I then listened on the radio the next day as Luton beat Walsall 3-1 at home.

An amusing side to the hospital stay was when one of the CBC Directors Penny, came to visit and said, "That was lucky we sorted out your nice pay rise when we did," and gave me a wink. I was discharged on Sat 12th October and Gus picked me up. I remained on Warfarin for a while with regular check ups, until all was ok. That day I obviously didn't travel to Shrewsbury as we won 3-0.

I also missed a 1-1 draw at Stockport. Had it not been for the recent hospital stay I would have gone to this mid-week game, as Edgeley Park was a ground I had yet to visit.

My first game back in a month was at home to Peterborough. A fine 3-0 win against the Posh after goals from Showler (2) & Steve Davis.

In the League Cup 3rd round we were drawn at Wimbledon. I missed this, but almost a third of the 5,043 crowd at Selhurst Park were Luton fans.

We gained a good 1-1 result against the Premiership team.

Tony Thorpe was enjoying his new striker role and he bagged another two goals against Bournemouth at home when we beat the Cherries 2-0.

Three nights later a huge Luton following went to Watford for the derby. We sat in the new Rookery stand and I would say that out of the 14,109 crowd at least a third were Hatters fans. When Luton hit the woodwork THREE times I began to wonder. We were all over the Hornets, yet still level and then Paul Showler scored a peach of a goal and we went delirious. Watford equalised in the bloody 92nd minute - with their only shot on target all night! I would have been happy with 1-1 before the game, but this actually felt like a defeat.

I didn't travel to Plymouth, but it looked like I missed a treat in the pouring rain. Despite Tony Thorpe netting a hat-trick we could only draw 3-3.

Luton then made it ten games undefeated when Tony Thorpe & Ceri Hughes both scored to beat Notts County 2-0 at home and lift us up to 5th position.

In the League Cup replay against Wimbledon, a crowd of 8,076 attended, easily the highest attendance so far. We had led 1-0 from a Wombles o g until the last minute, before the Dons cruelly equalised to send the tie into ET. When they added a second in that period it was all over. LTFC exited with their heads held high to the team who were 3rd in the Premiership.

After that game Sean Tyler drove me down to Torquay for another Cup Tie, in the FA Cup 1st round. Several hundred Hatters fans there were rewarded when Ceri Hughes scored the only goal.

Three nights later, Luton had to travel to Preston and lost 3-2. I wasn't there but perhaps the travelling of over 1,000 miles in such a short space of time was a key factor to us losing our first league game in 11.

Dwight Marshall made a welcome return from his broken ankle for his first game of 96-97 at home to Bristol Rovers. He gave us the lead to rapturous applause. When Rovers equalised late on it looked like two points dropped until a Pirates defender handled in his own area in the final minute to gift us a penalty. Tony Thorpe scored it, we won 2-1 and had rose to 4th place.

It was on this day I heard some sad news from my old mate Mick Tearle. His closest friend and a mate of mine too, Nigel Doggett, had passed away. Nige was an old drinking buddy from the Sportsman in Stopsley.

He had suffered with Cystic Fibrosis for years yet never complained, he defied Doctors' orders telling him not to drink many years before and died aged only 42 years old. My best memory was of him diving into the river on a works trip to Bologne, France in 1981 - despite the fact he could not swim! RIP Nigel.

I drove down to Bournemouth a few days after attending his funeral for my first visit to Dean Court since 1969. The game was topsy-turvy we went 1-0 down, before a blockbuster of a goal from Julian James levelled matters and then another superb goal from Dwight Marshall's head, sent us into the lead. Alas, Bournemouth came back into the game and their pressure paid off to win 3-2.

Four nights later I used the Kenilworth Suite for the first time in 1996-97 to take a client from Sports Aid Foundation in London, called Kate Hampsall. She was a York City fan, so it was natural I would take her to this match. She loved the evening (apart from the result), Luton won 2-0 with goals from Tony Thorpe & Dwight Marshall. A real disappointment was the attendance of just 4,401, the lowest home crowd of 96-97 and my lowest ever (at that time) for a league match at Kenilworth Road.

Many years later I was watching the TV Quiz show 'The Weakest Link', when who should be one of the contestants - but Kate!

We then welcomed Borehamwood for the FA Cup 2nd round. This was the first time I had seen non-league opposition play Luton since Oxford City in 1967.

When the Hertfordshire side took the lead, just as Oxford City had done 29 years earlier, I began to fret. But thanks to two goals from Dwight Marshall (his 5th in 4 games since returning), the rather fortunate 2-1 Luton victory was exactly the same result and similar performance as in 1967.

Three nights later, another Cup Tie at home was in the Auto Windscreens Shield against

Leyton Orient. Joining me for this were work colleagues Gary Hopkins and Orient fan Kevin Wyebrow. A whopping crowd of 1,594 watched us win 2-1 on an absolutely freezing cold night.

My cousin Bill Roberts was home for Xmas from New York and I took him to the Luton v Crewe match. Because there were no spare seats available in my season ticket area, I sat with him in the Main Wing Stand directly behind my usual seat. It brought back memories of going with Dad in the 1960s and I had not sat in this area since I took Sharon back in 1982. It would be a while before I returned too, as the legroom there is appalling. Bill and I watched the best performance of 1996-97. Graham Alexander opened the scoring early and this was soon followed by two goals, including a penalty, from Tony Thorpe. The Crewe defender was dismissed for the foul that led to the pen against Dwight Marshall. In the 2nd half we moved seats to be nearer the Kenilworth Road end and Thorpe claimed his hat-trick on the hour.

Paul Showler made it 5-0 and then Crewe were down to nine men, before David Oldfield finished them off to make it 6-0.

Bill was extremely impressed and I remember him saying that in all the years he had watched Luton on the odd occasion, this was the best he had EVER seen us play - some praise! This fantastic win had lifted us up to 3rd.

Four nights later regretfully, I missed the game at Millwall as Ceri Hughes only goal late in the game was enough to send Luton top of a league - for the first time since 1982!

I drove to Gillingham on Boxing Day in what would turn out to be the final game of 1996 and the last for over three weeks due to the inclement winter weather. We won 2-1 at Priestfield Stadium thanks to another pair from the prolific Tony Thorpe. He had now scored 18 goals before the year had ended. Ian Feuer also saved a last minute penalty for us.

When Luton finally played at home to Wrexham it was the Welsh team who looked like they were top, not us. We just could not get going and it ended 0-0. On arrival home that night I received a call from cousin Ken Adair, asking me if I would like to join him as a guest in the Corporate Box at Highbury the next day. It was for the Arsenal v Everton match. Naturally, I accepted. Arsenal won 3-1 and this was my 23rd & final visit to Highbury. Nearly ten years later they moved just down the road to a new 60,000 plus all seated plush arena after selling the famous old ground for flats. It makes me angry that Arsenal can move in central London with no planning or permission problems - yet Luton have been trying for over 60 years!

Two nights later in the FA Cup 3rd round I watched Luton take on Div 1 leaders Bolton at home. We drew 1-1 thanks to a last minute equaliser from Marvin Johnson. I drove up alone to Burnden Park on the Saturday for the replay knowing that this would be Luton's final appearance there. Bolton would be ANOTHER club to seek pastures new and would move to the Reebok Stadium in Horwich on the outskirts of Bolton, in September that year.

We went behind early on but came storming back to lead 2-1 thanks to goals from Tony Thorpe & Dwight Marshall. I'm afraid the gulf in a higher league showed and the Trotters went on to score a further five goals to send us back south with a heavy 6-2 defeat ringing in our ears.

A local derby at home to Watford was next and the best league crowd at that stage of 7,428 watched. In a rather dull showing in front of the live TV cameras, it was to be the second home 0-0 in a row.

I drove Pete Morris up to Meadow Lane for the match against 2nd bottom side Notts County. We were 1-0 down to the Magpies and frankly, struggling.

Thankfully, Ceri Hughes pulled us level (his 20th and last Luton goal) and then a late winner from Graham Alexander secured us the three points and out of jail.

I then joined a full Luton contingent for the Auto Windscreens tie at nearby Northampton. The fact that Luton had a quarter of the 4,201 fans did not make a difference to the result as we tamely lost 1-0.

Two days after this I went into the clinic for the man's operation (snip/snip). It actually wasn't that painful, as when I asked when it would be over I was told, "It is." I thought that was easy, I'll make the home game against Plymouth tomorrow no bother – WRONG! Let's just write that the next day SEVERE swelling made me change my mind, so I listened on the radio to a 2-2 draw.

The Memorial Ground, Bristol was my next port of call to see Luton play Bristol Rovers at their rightful base, back in Bristol. Driving past their old stadium on the way to their shared Rugby ground brought back old memories. Eastville was also used for Speedway and Greyhound Racing and it is now demolished. An IKEA store is now on the site.

From leading 1-0 via an early Tony Thorpe penalty, daft defending then led the Pirates to lead 3-1. Despite a very good goal from Gary Waddock, we could not break them down and did not help ourselves when Guentchev got himself red carded. Rovers won 3-2.

The next week was Luton's best performance in 1997 by far.

At home to Preston, we thrashed them 5-1. David Oldfield scored a perfect first half hat-trick and along with what turned out to be Gary Waddock's third and final Luton goal, we went in at H/T 4-0 up to rapturous applause. Mitchell Thomas scored the lone Luton goal in the second period.

Another ground to conquer followed the next week, at York. This meant that a family trip to Ripon to stay at Liz & Thom's was in order. Steve Davis headed us into a lead but York levelled and 1-1 was how it remained.

I then drove Mick Dolan up to Saltergate, Chesterfield mid-week for yet another venue to tick off my list and see Luton at. I write see, well that was not quite true, as the extreme fog made viewing almost impossible. I swear that when Luton received a penalty and Tony Thorpe despatched it, I could not see a thing - as it was up the other end! The match finished 1-1, but I was oblivious.

Then in front of a full to capacity Oak Road End of Millwall nutters, a best crowd at that point of 8,585 watched an unbelievable game. The Lions won 2-0 with two late goals, but until then Luton were all over them and had hit the woodwork FOUR times, despite being down to 10 men for over an hour after Julian James was sent off. Straight after this game I immediately went up the road to the CBC car park to meet Deb and the CBC staff. It was for a coach trip to take us on an organised works outing to Walthamstow Greyhound Track.

After chatting with Pete Morris about how on earth we just lost that game, we had a fantastic evening in the paddock grill bar area - I even won a few bob!

I had yet to miss an away game in 1997 but decided not to travel to the mid- week trip for the Wrexham match. We lost 2-1.

My seventh new ground that I had visited in 96-97 was at Gresty Road, Crewe. Apart from a David Oldfield lob, which hit the bar, it was a drab 0-0 draw.

I had a couple of days off sick at the end of the next week and so thought it was only correct not to attend the Luton v Brentford match. Luckily, it was being televised live on Sky TV on the Friday night and as I did not have the satellite dish I went round to a neighbours to watch it. Another 8,000 + crowd turned up for the top of the table clash and when Tony Thorpe scored with a sweet low drive into the net, both Geoff and I jumped up to celebrate. It was the only goal of the game and Luton were back on top - if only for one night!

When Luton played at Turf Moor, Burnley the next week two players were to make their Luton debuts, loan players Gavin McGowan & Andy Kiwomya.

I persuaded Deb that it was time to stay at Liz's again and I drove across the M62 after dropping the family off in Ripon. I had a very enjoyable couple of pints in the Burnley Cricket club behind Turf Moor, in which I teamed up with a couple of Clarets fans in a pre-match football quiz. They were quite impressed with my football knowledge and we actually won it. A terrific crowd of 15,490 created a great atmosphere. We silenced them when Tony Thorpe hit two first half goals. Despite Burnley pressure in the 2nd half, we held on to the 2-0 for a fabulous three points.

We then played Bristol City at home in mid-week and as was often the case against the Robins, we struggled. After going behind 2-0 Steve Davis pulled one back before Tony Thorpe earned us a point in the 2-2 draw.

On the day the Grand National was cancelled because of a bomb threat by the IRA, the Adairs drove up to Cherine & Gary's to visit them at their new house in Rotherham. Naturally, we were playing the Millers and I went to Millmoor to see Luton play in front of just 2,609 (inc a fair few Luton fans). After a pre-match pint in the Tivoli nightclub I watched Luton tear the struggling Millers apart. We won 3-0 thanks to a Tony Thorpe hat-trick and one very humorous moment I recall was when I started a song about Mitchell Thomas. His hair had grown all 'afro' like and 'One Jimi Hendrix' was soon caught on by the Luton faithful.

Interestingly - in the next match he had shaved it all off!

Against Wycombe three nights later at home, we came up against a brick wall of a defence. Managed by John Gregory (who I always hated as a player, after a spat with Mick Harford) the Chairboys had no interest, or intention, of playing any football they just wanted a 0-0 draw and Gregory was absolutely delighted when they achieved what he came for. I was so incensed by his smirking face as he was strutting across the field to a chorus of boos, I ran to the tunnel and shouted, "I bet you must be proud of that football exhibition eh Gregory!"

He just smirked even more and I know my little rant meant nothing to him - but by God I felt better for shouting it! These two dropped vital points had left us out of the automatic promotion places for the first time since December.

I drove Pete Morris to the Bescot Stadium, Walsall (another new one for me) and we enjoyed a couple of pre-match pints in their excellent Supporters' Club by the ground. A packed Luton contingent saw Walsall lead 1-0 at h-t. When Kiwomya levelled and then Steve Davis headed us into a 2-1 lead, us Hatters fans erupted with joy. But two Walsall goals in the final half hour beat us 3-2 and left us feeling deflated. The car journey home was very quiet and both Pete and I felt that we had blown our chance of automatic promotion.

Yet three nights later I refused to surrender and the two of us were defiantly on our way up north to Blackpool. After parking up in the Central Car Park we went for a stroll on the deserted promenade, had a pre-match pint then stood on the decrepit old open Kop terrace with a few hundred other Luton fans. Bloomfield Road had obviously seen better days and it looked positively dilapidated. The once huge Spion Kop covered end, had now lost its roof and was half closed off and even the floodlights, had been reduced by half. We battled hard, but 0-0 was the only likely outcome and that's how it ended.

Our first victory in 4 followed, by beating Shrewsbury at home 2-0. Tony Thorpe scored his 31st and final goal of the season. He became the first Luton player since Malcolm Macdonald in 1971 to top 30 goals.

Dwight Marshall added the second, his seventh since his return from injury. Against the leaders Bury at home, saw a game identical to the recent Wycombe match and the Shakers were also happy with a 0-0 draw.

On my 39th Birthday, Gus drove Pete Morris, Sean Tyler and I to the final league away game at Peterborough. As I hadn't dressed up since 1992, I felt it was time to don the fancy dress again and I went as a chicken. After a mammoth drinking session pre-match, we joined the 5,000 plus Luton fans to see us beat Posh 1-0 thanks to an Andrew Fotiatis goal.

The final game was at home to already promoted Stockport and was an all ticket Sell Out weeks before, as this was thought to be a battle for the title. It became a Mad Hatters party due to Stockport sharing our nickname, something of which I had only recently discovered at that stage, but in my eyes there's only ONE Hatters - that's US!

Bob Rumble had joined me to watch the 1-1 draw in which Fotiatis scored again. As I write, this is the only match in 8 that I have failed to see Luton beat County. Straight after the match we headed to Luton Airport with our hand luggage to catch a flight to Glasgow. We once again stayed at Jim's in Kilsyth, preparing for the Holiday Monday Rangers 0 v Motherwell 2 clash. This result stopped Rangers equalling Celtic's nine Scottish titles in a row.

But just a few nights later, it did occur when we won at Dundee United.

The following Sunday I drove up to Crewe for the 1st leg of the Play-Off Semi- Final. I was fortunate to get one of the limited few hundred Luton tickets. Sitting next to me in the Luton end was old mate Russell Kenneford, from Runfold. I had not seen him since the Oak Road days in the mid-70s. The match began and when David Oldfield gave us an early lead, cue bedlam in our end. Unfortunately Crewe came back to win 2-1, but I must write that Crewe's big forward Adebola blatantly controlled the ball with his hand leading to the Crewe equaliser. Three nights later, it was the return leg and 8,168 were there, including surprisingly few from Cheshire. After some early Crewe pressure, David Oldfield then raised the roof by shooting Luton into a 1-0 lead. When he added another to give us a 3-2 aggregate lead, the noise was the loudest I had heard at Kenilworth Road in a long time. But just two minutes after our euphoria, Crewe hit back to score and level the overall score. It should not have, but there is no doubt in my mind this goal flattened Luton. The Railwaymen equalised and held on to go through to Wembley to meet Brentford. In truth - they deserved it! What was so annoying was that five months to the day, we thrashed them 6-0 in our best display of the season, if only we had saved a couple of those goals for this night? - If is such a big word!

Crewe beat Brentford and were promoted with Stockport and Champs Bury. The final game I attended in 1996-97 saw a little history being made. I had managed to secure a ticket for the FA Cup final between Chelsea and Middlesbrough.

The history made was because Roberto De Matteo scored the quickest ever goal (until

2009) in an FA Cup Final after just 42 seconds. The Blues added a second to lift their first major trophy since beating Real Madrid in the 1971 ECWC Replay. I remember seeing a Crawley Green Sports Club mate there.

He was Chelsea fan Tony Talbot and was part of a Vauxhall syndicate that had recently won a Lottery jackpot. I shouted out to him, "Didn't expect to see you in these cheap seats Tony," he just smiled, but knowing Tony as I did and still do, he would be much more at home with the Shed boys.

Although 1996-97 ended in heartache for us Hatters, there were plus points. For the first season in ages we had won over 20 games and had topped the league on a few occasions. In Tony Thorpe we had a proven goal scorer at last. I went to 20 away games my most in 8 seasons and visited 7 new grounds.

Work was still going great and we had our summer holiday in Disneyworld, Florida for the first time. We stayed in a Disney hotel called All Star Resorts Music and with the great complimentary bus travel that took us everywhere in the resort, we stayed in Disneyworld for the whole two weeks. The joy in the faces of the girls made it worthwhile and we would return there twice again.

Steve 'Sumo' McNulty and myself. When I saw him make his debut at Barrow in 2013, my first reaction was 'OMG what are we doing signing pub players' he looked SO big and unfit. Proved myself and every other doubter TOTALLY wrong. Cult hero and a great player in our Conference 2013-14 title winning side.

1997-98

By the start of 97-98 Luton had bid farewell to Kim Grant who had already left for Millwall earlier in the year and Bontcho Guentchev was released on a free transfer. Ceri Hughes was sold to Premiership Wimbledon.

The only signing was Simon Davies, a midfielder from Man Utd for £150,000.

A fair sized crowd of 4,685 turned up for a pre-season friendly at home against Premiership side Southampton and the Saints won easily 3-0.

I missed the first league game at a baking hot Blackpool, where the Tangerines won 1-0.

However, I did drive mid-week to Layer Road Colchester, for the League Cup 1st leg. This was my first visit there since they beat us in the Watney Cup in 1971. It was our turn to win 1-0 this time and Tony Thorpe scored.

The first home match was moved to a Monday night for live TV coverage against Southend. Goalkeeper Ian Feuer suffered a bad injury, but Stuart Douglas won the match for us by scoring the only goal.

The following Saturday we spent an enjoyable day out in the sun at London for the Fulham game at Craven Cottage. We battled hard to earn a 0-0 draw and suffered another injury when Graham Alexander had to go off early.

In the return leg at home to Colchester we drew 1-1 to knock them out 2-1 on aggregate.

The next night I took some stick from Gus big time after Rangers had lost 3-0 at IFK Gothenberg in the Champs League 1st leg qualifier. Now although Gus came from a Protestant family (his mum Scots and dad Ulster), he chose to rebel and decided at a young age to support Celtic. He managed to see the light eventually after meeting all my Kilsyth friends and actually changed sides - to become a staunch bluenose and still is to this day!

I missed the next game at home to Oldham because I was in Kilsyth preparing for my first visit to Parkhead for the Old Firm match at Celtic on the Sunday. Luton drew 1-1. Rather worryingly, we had only scored 4 goals in six matches. After the usual great night in the Kilsyth 39 Masonic club, Jim Moffat woke me up on Sunday morning with some startling news. "I'm afraid we won't be going today Alan, as there has been some shocking news and the match will be off." He went on to inform me that Princess Diana had been involved in a car crash overnight in Paris and had sadly died. The shock that moment and all through the day and night, was stunning. I flew home Monday am on a silent plane.

Diana was only 36 and being the royalist that I am, I was not alone in the nation to be overwhelmed by this tragedy. RIP Diana.

The next night, Luton were at home to Millwall & even the notorious Lions fans impeccably observed the minutes silence in her honour. We lost 2-0 and our injury problems were mounting with both Julian James & Mitchell Thomas now being struck down. The season was yet to reach a full month and we had already lost four key players to injury.

When we played at Northampton (near to where Diana was laid to rest) on the Tuesday night, another minute's silence was correctly observed by the capacity attendance. We got off to a nightmare start when the Cobblers scored in less than 30 seconds. It was not helped when McGowan was sent off and it ended 1-0.

I missed a 1-1 draw at Bournemouth and my next game was at home to WBA in the League Cup 2nd round 1st leg. I decided to treat some clients in the Kenilworth Suite and took Ray (Charlton fan) and his boss (a Baggies fan) from Corinthian Insurance. We played really well and it was no surprise when Stuart Douglas gave us the lead. Albion levelled soon after and it finished 1-1. Both clients felt that Luton deserved to win.

At the next game v Wrexham at home we had two old LTFC faces in our lineup. Wembley 1988 hero Andy Dibble was brought in on loan and Phil Gray had re-signed permanently from Dutch club Fortuna Sittard. Unfortunately, Dibble had a nightmare in goal. Wrexham raced 2-0 ahead before Steve Davis headed one back. After the break, Phil Gray equalised. That was as good as it got though, Wrexham added another three goals to win 5-2 and such was our injury-plagued defence, Trevor Peake the reserve team coach had to put his boots on and became the oldest outfield player in LTFC history - at 40 years 222 days!

Lennie Lawrence was now beginning to get some stick from Luton fans, rather unfairly I thought considering our injury woes.

I drove Pete Morris and an old mate Tony Bojko up to WBA for the 2nd leg. Steve Davis blasted us into the lead with a rocket of a free kick. Alas, Albion equalised soon after. The Baggies added a further two goals, before Tony Thorpe made it 3-2.

Future Luton player Peschisolido added his second and Albion's 4th, to see them win 5-3 overall.

The injury situation at Luton was now critical. I drove down for the Bristol City match with Pete Morris and when I saw the starting lineup at Ashton Gate, there were FOUR Luton players making their debuts. Three of them - I had never heard of!

We paid Lawrence's old club Middlesbrough £40,000 for centre half Alan White and three youngsters also played a part, Liam George, Matthew Spring and Rob Kean (his sole Luton appearance). We lost 3-0.

Next, was my most humiliating experience of supporting LTFC - EVER!

I had seen Watford play at Luton on 21 occasions and the Hornets had won just twice, but on this day it was a disaster. 9,041 had turned out, easily our biggest attendance of 1997-98. With 30 minutes not yet on the clock, I'm ashamed to write - that Watford were FOUR nil ahead! The atmosphere had turned to sheer poisonous hatred. I was told at a later date by a reliable source, that at half-time the Referee visited the Watford dressing room and suggested to the Watford team and officials, "Look, you have won the game, you are 4-0 up and if it gets any worse we could have a serious situation on our hands here." All I'll write is - the match ended 4-0!

That was a day I'm sorry to write, that for some of us (me included) it was just too much to take, on this rare occasion I could quite easily have become a post-match hooligan. We left the ground totally ready for any gloating Hornets.

Fortunately, the police had sussed the severe tension and managed to block most attempts of seething Luton fans from attacking their rivals. This sorry episode had left us second from bottom, with just one victory in ten.

We NEEDED a performance at home to Plymouth after that shambles and just 4,931 hurting fans attended. Us loyal fans were rewarded when Luton beat Argyle 3-0, two Tony Thorpe goals and one from Simon Davies (his sole Luton strike) cheered us up a touch. Young Matthew Spring on his full debut, was sent off and despite sporting pleas for leniency from the Plymouth boss Paul Sturrock, he was down the tunnel.

I missed the next two games, away to Wigan and Carlisle.

We drew 1-1 at Wigan and then Luton won 1-0 in a mid-week victory at Carlisle. My mate Gus drove alone to the Carlisle match - cap doffed!

We then beat Brentford 2-0 at home thanks to goals from Alexander & Thorpe, which meant that we had won three and drew one since the Watford debacle. I drove the short journey to Wycombe and saw us come from behind twice to draw 2-2, through David Oldfield & Tony Thorpe. The recent mini run came to an end at home to Burnley. Once again, we had come back from being 1-0 down to lead 2-1 via two Graham Alexander efforts, but two Clarets goals, led to us losing 3-2 and the return of 'Lawrence Out' chants.

Four nights later Burnley's Lancashire rivals Preston came to town and also went home victorious having won 3-1.

We had hoped for some success in the FA Cup 1st round when we hosted bottom of the entire Football League, Torquay. An appalling Luton performance saw the Gulls deservedly knock us out by winning 1-0 via a penalty. I had never seen Luton lose three home games in a row in my life - it became FOUR the next week! Walsall defeated us 1-0 and the knives were sharply out from a growing Luton faction for Lennie Lawrence to go.

The next weekend was away to York and that naturally meant a visit to Ripon for the Adairs to see Liz & Thom.

We had a loan signing making his debut at Bootham Crescent that day, Chris Allen a left sided midfielder. A MUCH needed and deserved 2-1 victory over York occurred, thanks to Graham Alexander & Tony Thorpe.

Three nights later Thorpe scored again along with Steve Davies, to earn a point in a 2-2 draw at home to Gillingham.

On a bitterly cold freezing December day, I stood on the open terrace at Chesterfield to watch a shocking game that was always going to end 0-0.

An old friend of mine, Phil Francis and I dropped off our daughters at the SWMC kids Xmas party, before we made our way to the Luton v Bristol Rovers match. Chris Allen scored his only Luton goal to give us an early lead and in a topsy-turvy 1st half, Rovers came back to lead 2-1, before David Oldfield levelled.

The Pirates once again took the lead then made it 4-2 and all this before the interval. It stayed 4-2 at full-time and Luton's situation was grim.

A healthy Northampton following came to Kenilworth Road for the first time since 1968 and boosted the crowd to 8,035. The high-flying Cobblers raced into a 2-0 lead after just 12 minutes and we were thinking, 'Please, not Watford again!' Thankfully, a spirited fight back resulted in goals from Oldfield and Thorpe to rescue a point in the 2-2 draw.

At this halfway stage of the season we lay in 3rd from bottom place.

The final match of 1997 took place at the New Den, Millwall. Pete Morris and I travelled to New Cross on the train, naturally visiting the Anchor in Lewisham en route to see the Millwall mates. The match was fizzling out goalless, when suddenly Steve Davies headed in a goal with just a minute left. The large Luton support went bonkers and it became even better when Tony Thorpe made it 2-0 in injury time. The locals were NOT happy at all and the police kept us in the ground for an eternity - obviously for our own safety!

After seeing the New Year in, I drove to Southend for our match at Roots Hall. Once again, another big Luton following watched a second successive away victory when Graham Alexander scored both Luton goals in a 2-1 win. The away results were actually very good and this was the seventh unbeaten game on our travels, we had not suffered defeat away since Bristol City in Sept.

A fantastic 3-0 home victory against Blackpool then occurred and that man Thorpe, netted a hat-trick.

He scored again in the home Auto Windscreen Shields tie against Brentford, along with David Oldfield in a 2-1 win.

Regretfully, the away run ended at Oldham. I drove up to a freezing cold (as always) Boundary Park to see the 2-1 loss. Goalkeeper Ian Feuer was at fault for both goals, failing to deal with corners. Graham Alexander's goal was futile.

The visit of high-flying Fulham attracted 8,366 but we took a 4-1 thumping. Tony Thorpe's goal turned out to be his last in the league for the Hatters in 97-98.

Three nights later, against the same opposition but at Craven Cottage for the Auto Windscreens Quarter-Final I watched Thorpe score again, along with Dwight Marshall to beat Fulham 2-1 and send us into the Semis.

A truly bizarre memory of that night standing on the Putney End open terrace, was of a crackpot Luton fan continually singing towards the famous Cottage in the corner 'Where's your Dodi gone?' Dodi was the boyfriend of Princess Diana, killed in the car crash along with the Royal (this rant was presumably at owner Mohammed Al Fayed, Dodi's father). Very strange, in the end he persisted so much that he was ejected.

Another poor home defeat followed against Bournemouth. This was our NINTH home defeat out of 16, it was not that long ago when I remember teams used to hate coming to Kenilworth Road, it was such an intimidating fortress.

I missed a 2-1 defeat at Wrexham in front of a paltry 3,527 because I had been invited to Coventry v Sheff Wed as a guest of SWMC. One of their Brewers, Courage, had a Box at Highfield Road and when I was invited to join by the committee I jumped at it. We had a nice jolly, with a meal and all drinks were complimentary. When the lady came along to take bets on the match I told everyone to bet on the Sky Blues - for I had been to Highfield Road six times - and Coventry had won all 6! Needless to write, they won this too 1-0.

This was my final visit there, as they were to move to a new 32,000 all-seated stadium in 2005.

On Valentine's Day it was the local derby match at Vicarage Road. After the horror show earlier in the season at home, Luton owed us fans a committed performance. The police had insisted on an early lunchtime kick off and one thing I vividly recall was the abnormal February temperature that day and night. It was still winter yet around 20 degrees astonishing for that time of the year and so we waited for the match to start, in short sleeved shirts.

Before it did, there was a slight skirmish in the Rous stand. A small group of Luton fans were fighting with their Watford counterparts but it was almost over as soon as it began when the police immediately stepped in. It was a pretty even 1st half, with both sides at H/T goalless. When Watford scored the Hornets fans began to gloat again, reminding us of October. But we responded magnificently and from that moment onwards, there was only one team in it - and they certainly didn't play in Yellow & Black! Unfortunately, we could just not break through, until late on our faith was rewarded when a deflected effort from marvellous Marvin Johnson crossed the line for the thoroughly deserved Luton equaliser.

When Marv scored, the noise and celebration was immense.

It finished 1-1 but we were delighted with the Hatters showing and commitment, at least we put the 4-0 to bed. Watford also more importantly - did not complete the double over us!

I took Deb up to the West End of London in the balmy winter sunshine that night for Valentine's night and we enjoyed a lovely evening.

The match at Watford turned out to be the last in Luton colours for Tony Thorpe in 1997-98. He was transferred during the next week to Fulham for £800,000. In four years, Thorpe had played 105 times for the Hatters and had scored 57 goals, a fine return for a player who began life as a midfielder.

The first game post Tony Thorpe was at home to Bristol City. The question on all Luton's fans lips was where would the goals come from now? - The result was 0-0! It would have been worse, if not for Kelvin Davis. Young Kelvin was brought back in goal, following the dramatic loss of form by Ian Feuer.

The lowest crowd of the season of just 4,403 turned up for the next match at home to Wigan. Perhaps it was a protest vote at the continuing policy of selling our best players. David Oldfield equalised in a 1-1 draw.

We then had a lovely weekend in Devon, visiting Deb's Aunt Jean (Deb's Granddad George, had by now sadly passed away). We were in Devon because Luton were playing at Home Park, Plymouth. Goals from Andrew Fotiatis & Sean Evers secured a great 2-0 victory and a vital three points too.

I missed our 1-0 mid-week defeat at Preston.

A home 0-0 draw to Wycombe followed and this result had again pushed us back into the relegation zone.

One of CBC Print's paper suppliers, very kindly invited me in joining their Warrington branch, for Corporate Hospitality at the Burnley v Luton game in which Modo were sponsoring the match at Turf Moor. Not only this, but I was asked if I wanted to bring a few friends along to join them at the Hotel on the Friday, but if asked, were told that they worked for CBC. "Is the Pope A Tim?" was my response to Tony Gray the Modo Rep, a great bloke and lifelong Hatter. He was an ardent Luton fan from Sandy.

I invited along my SWMC mates Bob Rumble, Paul Keating, Bob Crawley and also Pete Morris from work too. Naturally, the Stopsley lads had been primed of their jobs as - Guillotine Operators, Fork Lift Drivers etc! What a weekend we had in store for us. We drove up after work on the Friday to meet Tony and the Modo folks at the Sparrow Hawk Hotel in Burnley. After all the checking in details etc, it was straight out on the lash.

Not far from the hotel and Burnley ground was The Burnley Miners Club.

Bob Rumble was SWMC Secretary and we were all CIU Affiliated members so we were welcomed in the Miners as guests for the weekend, what great hosts they were too. We mixed with them playing Dominoes and I remember meeting an old Burnley player called Billy Ingham, he was impressed when I reminded him that he scored the only goal against Luton on my very first visit to Turf Moor in 1975 – 23 years earlier!

An interesting fact we learnt about the Miners' Club was that it was in this very establishment, that the liqueur Benedictine founded by French Benedictine Monks is the world's largest single consumer of the drink after Lancashire Army regiments acquired a taste for it during WWI. This is a true fact and the locals insisted we sample the drink - well of course it would be rude not to!

The older SWMC lads went back to the Hotel with Tony and his northern counterparts, while Pete and I went nightclubbing. On our return, the Club lads were still at it in the hotel bar with the Modo crowd. Bob Rumble had privately told me that when he went to buy a round, the Modo Warrington Director told him to put his money in his pocket as the CBC Luton lads had a tab set up. After a late night, we all arose promptly for breakfast before walking to Turf Moor for the Hospitality. Naturally, all suited and booted I was proudly wearing my Orange and Blue LTFC tie.

We had a wonderful lunch, along with the wine flowing and some people sat with us was an extra bonus, because ex-Burnley and Luton player Alan West along with his lovely wife Cathy, joined in sharing some great memories. They were smashing company. Alan had found God to become a church minister and future LTFC chaplain. The match was no classic, it ended 1-1 but at least we didn't lose. Mitchell Thomas headed in the late equaliser.

We went straight back to the Miners Club for a swift couple, before heading back to the hotel for a SSS in preparation for the evening meal there. Joining us in the Miners' Club was good mate Tony Bojko and some of his Northern ex-Paratrooper colleagues from the Falklands War - cap doffed to them all!

The SWMC guys were enjoying the company with Modo so much that they stayed at the Hotel bar all night with their new friends. I must add, that my mates insisted on buying rounds for the Modo crowd, as they did not want to give the impression that Luton folk were freeloaders. Pete and I once again headed into town then later into a nightclub. Incredibly, we met some of the Luton players there. David Oldfield & Paul McLaren had stayed overnight at their teammate Steve Davis's house and I was quite pleased when Steve walked over to us. After he recognised my Luton tie, he then recalled visiting me in hospital and they were all very civil. We appreciated, that THEY were also on a night out and gave them their space accordingly.

A fantastic weekend was had by all so much so, that the Modo Warrington director promised us that if both teams were playing in the same league next season, they would repeat the sponsorship and ask us as guests again.

All of us Stopsley lads were extremely appreciative to Tony and the Modo guys. It was really worthwhile for Modo too, as after that weekend I exclusively sold only Modo paper to all my clients - that's how business works!

The next week it was back to fighting relegation when we faced Grimsby at home. The Mariners were chasing promotion and when they led 2-0 it was looking ominous. However, a stirring fight back occurred when first Sean Evers, then Steve Davis scored to earn us a good point.

We then drove up to Walsall and had a pre-match pint in the Walsall Supporters' Club. Joining Pete and myself was a great LTFC fan Terry Toone and his young son. The boy has learning difficulties and is a wonderful lad. Pete & I made a fuss of him.

Luton had a new loan signing from Tottenham playing that day. He was Rory Allen and what a signing he turned out to be. On his debut, he made the first goal for David Oldfield to open the scoring and then scored himself to give us a 2-1 lead after the Saddlers had levelled. He was also involved when Dwight Marshall made it 3-1, which sent us Hatters fans loopy. Despite Walsall pulling a goal back, we held on to win 3-2 and earn three vital points.

The next day Gary Hopkins and I went to Wembley to see his Chelsea beat

Middlesbrough 2-0 in the League Cup Final. I purchased the tickets via LTFC. Luton climbed out of the relegation zone the next week after a fine 3-0 win at home to York.

A Graham Alexander penalty (amazingly our 1st of the season) and strikes from David Oldfield and Phil Gray gave us this important victory.

Three nights later I drove Pete Morris & Tom up to Grimsby for a mid-week match at Blundell Park. In a frantic game you would not know which team was fighting for survival or promotion. The very impressive Rory Allen scored the only goal tapping the ball in off David Oldfield's shot, which had hit the post. Each and every Luton player had played their part that night none more so than Kelvin Davis in goal, who was magnificent.

I missed our 2-1 loss at Gillingham.

The final home game I attended in 97-98 was against Chesterfield. A comfortable 3-0 victory for Luton occurred, including another inspirational performance by Rory Allen. He made a goal for David Oldfield, scored one himself (his fourth in 5 games) and following an own goal, this completed the scoring. This win almost ensured safety.

My 40th Birthday was creeping up and I had long since booked a party at the Riverside Suite, in the new Vauxhall Recreation Club. Thanks to my working relationship with Vauxhall, excellent rates were given for the hiring of this beautiful new function hall. I wanted somewhere big enough to hold 250 people or more, comfortably.

I invited many family, friends and clients and was thrilled that Mum had come home from New Zealand for a month's holiday for the event.

I had also invited all my friends from Kilsyth and was pleased when they all accepted and booked flights. They stayed at the Shamrock Hotel in Luton. Seven couples were to come down, Sandra & Jim Moffat, Liz & Duncan Angus, Margaret & Bobby Young, Linda & Neil Mitchell, Rab Keir & partner Elaine, Gordon Duff & partner Elsa and Jerome & Michelle.

It was because we went shopping at the Hatfield Galeria for my party attire, that I missed the away game at Bristol Rovers. We lost 2-1, but worse news was to follow. Our full back Julian James was stretchered off. Post-match reports discovered that Julian had broken his leg badly.

My 40th party was on Saturday 25th April, a day prior to the actual birthday. Luton were playing at Brentford and for the short trip to West London I hired a minibus to take us all from the SWMC including the Scots lads, who had arrived in Luton on the Friday. To continue with my occasional tradition for the last away match I hired a fancy dress outfit - this time as a Canadian Mountie! We didn't have time for pre-match drinks in Brentford thanks to leaving SWMC later than planned and heavy traffic en route. The match itself was a bit of a blur and I don't remember too much of it, apart from Dwight Marshall & Rory Allen twice giving us the lead and twice being pegged back by the already relegated Bees, to end the game 2-2. We left immediately after the game to get home in preparation for the party. I was sorry to hear later that there had been problems involving Luton fans causing trouble, by fighting with Brentford fans and smashing up a pub. It was evidently because Bees fans had racially abused our black lads in the pub.

The minibus dropped us all off and I prepared for my big night. I made sure Deb, the girls and I arrived early and that I was suitably dressed for the occasion.

Along with my massive 40th birthday badge I wanted to make sure I represented both Luton & Rangers, so I wore a beautiful silk Royal Blue shirt and - the brightest pair of ORANGE jeans you could ever see!

The Scots crowd, were naturally one of the first arrivals and I was pleased to see that Jerome (the only non-Scot, he was Canadian) had his Rangers Kilt on.

My party was a brilliant night and I know that everyone loved it we really did have a ball. It was wonderful to see so many friends, some of them I had not seen in a while like the Windsor Castle lads. My best memory of the event was when I was on stage about to recreate The Full Monty. Only Georgina & Mollie were begging me not to. How could I do that to them? So, I just stripped to my pants – the HALF Monty if you like!

The next day on my actual 40th we carried on and I joined all the Scots at the SWMC for another great night too.

As my Mum had made the special effort to come all the way from NZ, I decided that we would treat her to a few things. The first was to take her to the restaurant where CBC took important clients. It was The Kings Head, in Ivanhoe. I had been there on numerous occasions when we treated the likes of Vauxhall and this really was a special place. Although VERY expensive and exclusive, it is worth every penny and indeed, we took Deb's parents Julie & Alan there for their Ruby Wedding Anniversary. It is still open I believe, although I have not been for a while now. If anyone gets the opportunity to dine there I thoroughly recommend the special, Aylesbury Duckling – but take plenty of money!

The following weekend we treated her to a weekend at a Butlins Hotel in Cliftonville, Margate, followed by a couple of days in Yarmouth.

While at the hotel on the Saturday, I was eagerly watching the football score updates. Although I was naturally pleased to see that Luton had beaten Carlisle 3-2 in the final match of 97-98, I was distraught to see the news coming in from Ibrox Park. Rangers had lost 1-0 at home to Kilmarnock and had almost certainly aborted the chance of creating history by winning 10 SPL Titles in a row.

The night after we had returned from Margate I watched Marvin Johnson's testimonial match at home to Sheff Wed. We lost 2-0, which didn't matter at all, but what did matter was the attendance of only 2,504 - a poor turnout for Marv! 1997-98 ended well for LTFC and largely thanks to Rory Allen, we ended in 17th place our highest position since September. IMHO Rory is our best ever loan signing in my era. Without him I believe we'd have definitely been relegated in 97-98. We finished seven points above safety in a season of few highs but plenty of lows, the worst undoubtedly being the 4-0 hammering by W**ford. What made that even worse, was that the Hornets won promotion by winning the title.

Mum flew back to New Zealand and I prepared for one final match of 1997-98 to watch – in FRANCE!

General Motors were one of the chief official sponsors of the 1998 World Cup and thanks to a dear long-time friend of mine, Liz Jeffries (nee Harrison), she managed to secure me two tickets for England's opening group game against Tunisia in Marseilles. Three of us flew to France, Gary Hopkins, Roy Sebbage from the Eric Morecambe Lounge and myself. As I only had two tickets, it was always going to be Gary that had the spare. Roy would just have to chance his luck out there. He did not take too kindly to that and he was never the same with me after the World Cup. Gary was a much closer friend and also work colleague, plus of course the fact that I was Best Man at Gary & Jane's wedding - meant it was a no-brainer!

The Kilsyth lads had been to Marseilles with Rangers in 1993 and had warned me not to stay there citing it as a hellhole, with the large Arab population in particular, hating the British. I heeded Duncan's advice and thanks to EasyJet and CBC's French speaking telephonist Nicole, we booked flights from Luton to Nice. £40 return each, plus a nice hotel in Nice for only £28 per person per night. We left Luton Airport early morning two days before the match and at the Airport, was Luton's police liaison officer Pete Palmer. He was checking for banned hooligans trying to travel. After sharing some banter with him he quite rightly passed us through.

I was delighted at choosing Nice for our stay, what a beautiful city. The weather was glorious and there were plenty of England fans in Nice that shared our thoughts and opinions about staying in Marseilles. In the 3 nights/4 days in Nice, there was not a hint of any trouble whatsoever. All the English mixed with the locals and fellow World Cup citizens brilliantly. We got on exceptionally well with the Chile fans, but the best was this crazy Mexico fan that latched on to us. Remembering the song as an 8-year-old from the 1966 World Cup, I borrowed this bloke's huge sombrero and started the chorus of 'Mechico, Mechico, Ra Ra Ra'. He absolutely loved it and joined in with us England fans singing it as we were doing the conga much to the amusement of the locals and tourists, who were taking photographs frantically. The next day after a glorious hearty breakfast on a seafront café, Gary absolutely pissed himself laughing at my attempts to speak French when asking for the waiter. In my best French I said, "Billet s'il vous plait," obviously asking for the bill. Gary was creased up - evidently I had asked for the ticket!

When the three of us strolled down the seafront in scorching hot sunshine, I saw some lads Paragliding. After initial enquiries I simply HAD to have a go. It was a breathtaking experience, as I flew with not a care in the world for about 20 minutes, the enjoyment was immense. By the evening, the news was full of TV pictures showing rioting involving England fans in Marseilles. I knew that this would happen, but on this occasion it was the local Arabs who initiated it with all sorts of provocation and with the English fighting back, the problems just escalated. Both Gary & Roy were glad I took the Kilsyth boys advice and booked Nice as our base. Also staying in Nice and joining in with our fun was England regular, mate Dave Hare & his crowd. I happened to meet them on my last England trip abroad too in 1988 - Stuttgart, West Germany.

On the morning of the match and because of the previous night's rioting, Gary was in two minds whether to actually travel to Marseilles saying that he was quite happy to stay in Nice and watch it in a bar. I eventually persuaded him to come and we headed off by train.

On arrival at Marseille station, we were met by the French Riot police, searched and put on a fleet of escorted buses to take us to the match at the beach area.

There were approximately 40,000 England fans in Marseilles and for those like Roy without match tickets, were led to an area with a huge big screen for the game. We arranged a meeting point to get Roy after the game, before Gary and I headed for the 'Stade Velodrome'. Of the 54,587 in the stadium I would estimate that over two-thirds of them were English. We had no problems before or during the match and watched with baking hot sun burning down on us from the open side stand. It was actually so hot, that I had to eventually use my huge St George Flag occasionally - to protect us from getting sunstroke! Alan Shearer headed us into the lead & Paul Scholes finished off Tunisia with a goal in the final minute.

Upon arrival on meeting Roy at the beach area - it resembled a war zone! There had been a mass riot and Roy explained that it had started when England scored the 1st goal. Until that moment, he said that everything was good natured and calm with no problems. When Shearer scored, the Tunisia fans backed by the local Algerian, Moroccan and other Arabs bombarded the England fans with missiles. England fans, being England fans, retaliated with such force that the big screen was switched off, as the innocents on both sides ran for cover. After meeting Roy we were then informed, that EVERY England fan had to make their own way back to Marseilles central. The only problem with that was - that ALL trains, buses, coaches and taxis had been cancelled! We had no option, but to walk the SEVEN MILES which by the way - included going through the infamous Arab sector!

On the long walk back I met an old mate of Baggy's from the Strawplaiters called Eamon Kane (he was similar to my mate Liam O'Connell, Irish by name but VERY English by nature). After a couple of miles, we were fortunate to locate a taxi and a nice-natured cabbie took us back to safety. Some of our other compatriots however, were not so lucky. Many took severe beatings and knifings in the Arab sector, as they were carefully ambushed en route back to the Centre. At the train station I witnessed one local Arab provoking the English by shouting, "Princess Diana, fuckie fuckie by Muslim," laughing his head off. He knew that with armed police by his side he was untouchable - but if looks could kill!

We could not wait to get back to civilisation and flew back to Luton the next day. I have yet to see England play abroad since.

Myself and Matt Tees RIP at Grimsby v Luton in 2018. Ex Hatter from the late 60's/early 70's, but a Grimsby Legend. At the time of this pic he was sadly suffering from Dementia but came alive when I started chatting with him about his Luton days with Malcolm Macdonald. Has sadly died of his illness since.

Administration – Part One

The Adair summer holiday in 1998 was back to Son Bou in Menorca, only this time we stayed at the Sol Pinguinos Hotel rather than the apartments as previous. We came back nice and tanned and I eagerly waited for the new season to start.

I also had a new company car at this point. Vauxhall had ceased producing the Calibra much to my disappointment. I therefore chose the new Omega 2.5v.

On the LTFC playing front goalkeeper Ian Feuer had returned to the USA having made 115 LTFC apps. Richard Harvey left for local side Aylesbury. He served LTFC well having played for over 12 seasons but had his bad share of injuries, hence playing only 192 times. On the subject of injuries, Julian James was forced to quit following his bad leg break. He played a very respectful 335 games for his only club. David Oldfield said goodbye for the second and final time and Darren Patterson left for Dundee Utd. Gary Waddock retired.

We had two new signings, Ray McKinnon, a midfielder from Dundee Utd and Frenchman Herve Bacque. He was originally on loan from Monaco but had impressed so much in two pre-season matches, that he was signed on a permanent deal. In those friendly home games I missed a 1-1 home draw with Arsenal because I was still in Menorca, but had returned to watch us beat Coventry 2-1. He did play really well in the game I saw and scored a near post header (rare in those days). Bacque gave me a similar feeling as I had with Guentchev three years earlier but I'm sorry to write he also failed to shine, in fact he only played 10 times - seven of those as sub!

The first league game was played in sweltering heat at nearby Wycombe Wanderers. Tom, from the Eric Morecambe Lounge, drove us the short distance and we went home happy after a stunning free kick goal by Steve Davis was enough to give us victory. We stopped at a country pub on the way home for much needed thirst quenchers, as the temps reached 30 odd degrees.

In the League Cup 1st round 1st leg Luton played Oxford Utd at home. Just 3,165 turned up for the game, less than the friendly v Coventry proving that this competition was not as popular as it once was.

We were 2-0 down at h-t, but two Graham Alexander goals brought us right back in the game. However, Oxford won it 3-2 with a very late goal.

Dwight Marshall scored his final Luton goal, the equaliser in a 1-1 draw at home to Preston. He played only four more games before returning to Plymouth. I liked Dwight, he scored 38 goals in 155 LTFC apps and I maintain, had he not broken his ankle at Sunderland in 1996 - we would NOT have been relegated! I drove alone to Oxford for the 2nd tie League Cup leg and was quite surprised at the larger than expected Luton following at the Manor Ground.

When Oxford opened the scoring, despite Luton playing the better football, we all thought game over as Oxford were now 4-2 ahead overall.

But a fantastic Luton performance including an inspired showing from young Sean Evers, saw us come right back into the Cup Tie. Just before h-t Phil Gray levelled on the night and then Evers put us 2-1 ahead, 4-4 on aggregate. With Luton now well in the ascendancy, Paul McLaren then gave us an overall lead. He hardly ever scored for Luton but this was his best goal as he smashed the ball into the net to send us through to round 2.

I drove home very happy that night and was pleased that I had decided to attend.

The following Saturday I drove Gus, Sean & Pete to Reading for the opening match at their new Madejski Stadium. Very impressive it was too. Apart from the natural teething problems of the road networks entering the ground, I was actually jealous. This ground, with an all-seated capacity of 24,500, is EXACTLY what Luton need. A large Luton following boosted the attendance to 18,108 (Reading's biggest league crowd since our visit to Elm Park in 1970).

Unfortunately for us, the Royals won easily 3-0.

A comfortable 2-0 home win against Colchester followed, with goals from Stuart Douglas & Steve Davis.

On August Bank Holiday Monday I drove up to Wigan's Springfield Park for the last time. An excellent 3-1 Luton victory occurred and Phil Gray in particular, played a blinder. He scored his 1st league goal of 98-99 along with Steve Davis & Sean Evers but the game was slightly tarnished when Liam George was stretchered off with a broken foot following a nasty foul.

A sole Stuart Douglas goal was enough to see off Burnley at home and place us 2nd. Attendances were slowly rising, although still poor. That day it was 5,554. I drove up to Wrexham mid-week for my first visit to the Racecourse Ground since 1981 and was accompanied by Freddie Dann & Magnet. Ray McKinnon scored his 1st Luton goal, but the Dragon's equalised soon after. It finished 1-1 the attendance was a pitiful 2,951 - despite both teams being in the top six!

Our highest crowd (by FOUR) turned up next to see us beat Bristol Rovers 2-0. Both goals came early on by Steve Davis and Graham Alexander.

My old mate Larry Kinloch, drove his son Michael (my god son) and I to Ipswich for the League Cup 2nd Round. He went home the happier, having seen Ipswich narrowly win 2-1. Stuart Douglas's goal gave us hope for the 2nd leg.

I missed my first game of 98-99 at Blackpool where we lost 1-0 in Dwight Marshall's final LTFC appearance.

For the 2nd leg tie against Ipswich, Larry & I went Corporate in the Kenilworth Suite and it turned out to be one of those famous LTFC nights.

The biggest crowd (at that point) of 5,655 saw Ipswich open the scoring to extend their overall lead to 3-1. Andrew Fotiatis then levelled on the night and then with only six mins left, Stuart Douglas scored to level the overall tie and send it into extra time. It was all Luton possession at this stage, Steve Davis soon made it 3-1 (4-3 aggregate). But incredibly, he then scored a spectacular own goal - just two minutes from time!

We went straight up their end from the kick off and marvellous Marvin Johnson, somehow scored his 9th goal in eleven years, to send all of us Luton fans into orbit and into the Third Round. The noise at this goal and on the final whistle was one of the loudest and most celebrated of the Nineties. Just as in Round One we had come back from the dead, only this time in much more spectacular fashion.

After the Ipswich drama you would think that for the next game at home to Walsall and with us in the top six, a decent crowd would attend. But no, just 5,530 could be bothered - LESS than the previous match! I was appalled and I don't know if it had a bearing on the Luton players, but we lost 1-0 to the Saddlers and also had a man sent off in frustration.

I missed the best Hatters league performance of the season at Fulham because we had chosen that weekend for the annual family Blackpool Illuminations trip. Fulham, backed by their billionaire owner Mohammed Al Fayed, were on a mission and had installed Kevin Keegan as manager along with players like Peter Beardsley. We earned a magnificent 3-1 victory and not for the first time, Kevin Keegan was full of praise for a Luton team stating that we were by far the best team to play at Craven Cottage in his reign as manager. Pete Morris told me this was the best he had EVER seen Luton play away in his near 15 years as a Hatters fan.

We were away again the following weekend and I took the girls to stay at Liz's in Ripon, while Thom joined me for the match in York.

I had booked the Abbots Mews Hotel in this fantastic City and we met up with the Stopsley crew. Rasher Bacon, John Farmer, Tony Price, Bill McKinlay and Phil Odell joined Thom & I on the Friday afternoon. After a great night out, we all met up for breakfast before heading to the Bootham Tavern pub for opening time. We had more than a few in there, before heading to the Social Club opposite York's ground. There was a great spirit in there with the many Luton fans and York supporters getting on fine together. I remember seeing John Bates there. He was a Stopsley lad who had moved up to Newton Aycliffe in the North East many years before. He had his two boys with him, all decked out in Luton colours and despite their strong Geordie accents (even John sounded like one a bit now) they were still avid Luton fans and watched the Hatters as many times as they could whenever we played up North.

When the match started, some of the lads were really tempted to return to that club, as York had taken a 2-0 lead after just ten minutes. But after I persuaded them to stay (or at least unless York scored a third) I was rewarded when Stuart Douglas and then Sean Evers, evened things up by half time. When Phil Gray scored to make it 3-2 we thought we had completed a brilliant comeback. Alas, York scored again and thanks to keeper Kelvin Davis, it ended 3-3. We headed straight back to the hotel for a SSS after a quick post-match pint in the Social Club.

Before heading out in the City for the night, we had our traditional Champagne Dinner in the Hotel Restaurant and everyone was in top form, especially the Farm, as always. He is a comical genius. Thom was made to feel welcome by the lads as they all took to him, enjoying his dry American wit. They called him Texas Thom all weekend and he loved them all. One rather sad moment occurred later that night at a Club when I bumped into an old friend. Clive McEvoy is Chris & Keith's elder brother who was quite a face in the original Skinhead Oak Road days and also known as Mac. He had moved to Bognor Regis years ago and had a family there, but still occasionally came back to see his beloved Hatters. He had hit hard times when his marriage had broken up and also had a bit of a drink problem. Clive had recently been drinking more and more, at the end of that night I saw him slumped at a nightclub entrance. I tried to help and get him sorted out but he didn't even know whom I was. It was sad, he refused any help, even turning a bit funny which of course did not bother me. I have a lot of time for Clive and I really like him, he was a true Luton fanatic.

A week later, we were back in the top four after beating Oldham 2-0 at home. Phil Gray headed in his third successive goal, followed by a late debut goal from tiny substitute Andre Scarlett. This was the youngster's only Luton goal.

Three nights later, we beat Northampton 1-0 at home in a one-sided affair with Graham Alexander netting before our highest crowd at that point of 6,087. This win, had lifted us into 3rd and would be the apex of our league placing for 1998-99.

I then took Georgina & Mollie to their very first Luton game, at Gillingham. Gus and his daughter Kristy joined us on the Junior Hatters coach. My girls loved it on the coach but had no interest in Luton or the game unfortunately, unlike Kristy who went to nearly every match with Gus. When we left it was pouring with rain and didn't stop all day, on arrival we could only stand on an open terrace. Poor little Mollie who was only 4 and Georgina 8, were getting soaked and wringing wet.

I went over to a steward and pleaded with him for us to enter the covered seating area, explaining that she was only 4 and at her very first match. The jobsworth wanker was having none of it and I was beginning to lose the plot.

Fortunately, a senior steward had seen the situation and after I had rationally explained my dilemma, common sense prevailed and he let us all in, where at least the girls would now be dryer. We ended up losing 1-0 and while my girls enjoyed the coach part, I knew that I would have a hard task to convince them to see Luton again.

Three nights later, it was the League Cup 3rd Round at home to my jinx team Coventry. At that time I had seen us play The Sky Blues on 20 occasions.

We had lost on all six visits to Highfield Road, in the 14 home games it was 6 wins 1 draw and 7 defeats, although I have to write the pattern was slightly shifting, as we had beaten them in the last 4 games at Kenilworth Road. It became five, as thanks to Phil Gray & Steve Davis, we knocked out the Premier side in front of 9,051, the best crowd so far and proceeded into the last 16.

I then drove Gus, Kristy & Tom up to Stoke to see us play at their new Britannia Stadium. We lost 3-1 in a bad-tempered match. At h-t I had the pleasure to meet and chat with future LTFC Chairman, Nick Owen. What a nice chap he was too. Luton were drawn at home again in the League Cup, this time against Div 1 side Barnsley. A healthy crowd of 8,435 watched a very tight game. It looked as though it was heading for 0-0 until Phil Gray scored the winning goal on 81 mins. As a result, we were in the Quarter-Finals for the first time in 9 years.

The following Sunday I travelled by train for another Cup Tie at nearby Elstree in the FA Cup 1st round against Borehamwood. I went with Tony Bojko and he informed me of the sad news that our good mate Mick Dolan's father had died. We managed to find a pub that was open and admit Luton fans, as the town was swarming with Police. There had been a tip off, that nearby Watford fans were going to Elstree to teach the MIGS a lesson. (Aye Right.) I never saw a Hornet all day and we watched Luton win 3-2.

The next week's 2-2 draw at Lincoln I missed, as I was at Sandra & Jim's in Kilsyth. This was my second attempt to attend a Celtic v Rangers match at Parkhead having missed the previous year due to Princess Diana's tragedy. I'm sorry to write that my first visit there turned into a nightmare - we were hammered 5-1!

The next Saturday, saw Luton playing Man City at home. Whoever would have thought that a club that size with their history of winning Leagues, FA Cups, League Cups and European trophies, would be playing in the third tier.

It was bad enough for the City fans when we relegated them in 1983, but this was a new low for them.

In front of a full Oak Road End and the highest league attendance of the season 9,070, we watched as City took in a 1-0 lead at the interval. Young Gary Doherty followed up with his second goal in a week after he had scored at Lincoln, to earn us a point. The 1-1 draw had left us in 7th place and City 8th. I heard there was a lot of trouble post-match in town at the Sports Bar and that Luton didn't come 2nd.

In the League Cup Quarter-Final we had been drawn away to Div 1 leaders Sunderland. I would have attended this mid-week game even if Sunderland were still playing at Roker Park but now they had moved to a new ground wild horses would not stop me. So 32 years to the day after my first LTFC match I took the long drive up north, driving Gus, Pete Morris from work and a Sunderland fan Ian Collier, a client of mine.

I think The Stadium Of Light is up with the best of all the newer stadiums I have visited, along with The Emirates and City Of Manchester Stadium. At the time it was built it had a capacity of 42,000, which was later increased to 48,000.

For the first 35 minutes Luton more than matched their opponents in every department before the referee Mr Lomas sent off Mitchell Thomas for only he knew what for? The Luton & Sunderland players and fans alike were equally mystified. This was a major turning point in the game and just five minutes later Marvin Johnson deflected a shot into his own net. Luton went in 1-0 down at half time, clearly deflated. Without ever looking like we could get back in the match, Sunderland cruelly finished us off with two further goals in the final two mins for a flattering 3-0 victory. Even Ian, on the long journey home, said that we did not deserve that. If Thomas had not been sent off and we went in at h-t 0-0, it is my belief that the natives would have started to become restless and then who knows? – The famous IF word!

Four days later it was Cup time again, this time the FA Cup 2nd round at home to Hull City, who had the unenviable position of being rock bottom of the Football League. This did not stop the Tigers fans quite rightly, going mental when they knocked us out by winning 2-1. Just 11 years later - Hull would be playing in the Premier League!

The day after the CBC Xmas party, I wearily drove Pete Morris, Tom, Gus & Shaun Tyler up to Macclesfield. Pete was dying with a hangover and would feel much worse later on, watching Luton's performance. Despite us making an excellent start when Stuart Douglas scored early on - we went on to play CRAP! The Silk men turned it round to lead 2-1 and it was only thanks to a late equaliser from Phil Gray, that the Luton team did not leave to a chorus of boos.

The following week Millwall and their lovely fans, celebrated wildly when they won 2-1 at Kenilworth Road, their third successive win at Luton.

Due to the Festive period, I decided that family came first and missed our 1-0 defeat at Bournemouth.

This was our ninth winless game and I also missed the tenth in a 2-2 draw at Colchester.

In between these 2 games, Luton did the usual and sold our captain and best player Steve Davis, back to Burnley for £800,000. I suppose the directors looked upon it as sound business, we had a brilliant inspiring leader and top class player for over three years and made a profit of £50,000 too.

I for one - was GUTTED!

It became 11 games without a win when we lost 3-0 at home to Walsall in a pathetic display in The AWS. My self and just 1,869 others suffered it.

The next game was at home to Wycombe and I was invited by the SWMC as a guest by the committee. The invite was from their Brewers Courage, in the Executive Box. The

Courage rep was a Wycombe fan, hence that match. After the meal, we had a splendid day and the rot was finally stopped as Luton won 3-1 with goals from Matt Spring, Sean Evers (his 7th & last) and Stuart Douglas.

Wycombe scored a penalty, to make our host feel slightly better.

I then drove alone to high-flying Preston. Andrew Fotiatis opened the scoring at Deepdale and it stayed that way until North End equalised.

At the death and happy with a well-earned point, Preston scored in the SIXTH minute of injury time to cruelly deny us.

The next game at home to Wigan was simply embarrassing. Not only were we thrashed 4-0 but goalkeeper Kelvin Davis was red carded too.

At home the following week, the team owed us a performance v Bournemouth. It was a much better showing as we drew 2-2 the only pity, was that we had let slip a 2-0 lead. The first from Ray McKinnon proved to be only his 2nd and last for the Hatters, Gary Doherty scored our second.

After the fantastic weekend at Burnley the previous year, there was no way I was going to turn down the offer of a repeat by Modo this season. Once again I drove up to the Sparrow Hawk Hotel on the Friday with the same SWMC crowd. We enjoyed the Miners' Club again on the Friday night and set off Saturday to the Corporate Hospitality area at Turf Moor.

On this year's occasion, a group of lads from Blackpool were with us, on behalf of the Modo Warrington branch. What a fantastic bunch of guys they were too, it was blatantly obvious that these were a set of lads who could look after themselves, without being hooligans in any way. We all got on fine together. Once the meal was finished we joined the Blackpool lads in the bar area, where they wanted to stay and watch the match on the TV Screens. Some of the SWMC lads stayed with them but Pete, Damon, Bob, & I left to sit in the balcony seats outside. When we sat down, immediately in front of us were a bunch of Burnley yobs. They greeted us with abuse and taunted us as soon as we had sat down.

I said to our group, "Ignore them and don't bite, remember who we are with and don't rise to them." They carried on with the verbal and when Burnley opened the scoring, this massive bloke leapt up screaming at me, "What's the score you Cockney Basstard?" Now I had a good drink pre-match and after topping up from the previous night's session, let's just write I was quite merry. But remembering what I had told the lads, I sat there and didn't react the way the Burnley louts wanted me to. When Andrew Fotiatis equalised soon after, we all jumped up in celebration and cheered wildly. This was too much for our Clarets friends and they reacted by trying to attack us (me in particular). Bob could see I was right up for them and thankfully, dragged me away and led me to the bar area, where we joined the Blackpool boys. Half-time came I had decided it was best if I stayed at the bar for the 2nd half with them. The drink continued to flow and although neutral, the Blackpool lads were all cheering for Luton. What happened next was actually a bit embarrassing on my part, but here goes.

Just 3 minutes from the end, Gary Doherty scored an incredible goal with a blockbuster of a shot. We all leapt up as one in the bar, celebrating wildly and regrettably my emotions took over. Remembering the abuse I had received earlier I ran through the bar area with a bottle of Bud in hand, headed to the balcony area, opened the door to scream at Burnley Big Bollocks, "What's the score now then, you Northern C**t's?" – Cue mayhem!

I was dragged out by the stewards, had the bottle taken out of my hands immediately and brought back inside while outside, half of Burnley were trying to climb over to attack me. After deep profound apologies to my hosts and the Burnley stewards and Corporate staff, the situation calmed back to normal and we all settled down to celebrate our fine 2-1 win. All the Blackpool boys thought it was hilarious.

After the bar shut about an hour post-match, we all left and headed for the nearby Miners Club. Last season there were no problems in there at all, but I sensed that this year was different. We were in there for about ten minutes when one of the locals said, "You've got your 3 points, now why don't you all fook off out of our club?" I knew that with us lot and the Blackpool crowd, there would have been NO chance of us coming off the worst, but I saw the look on Tony Gray's face and it was his kind hospitality that was the reason we were all here. I decided it was time for us to make a quiet exit and if they did start, then that would be a different matter. Thankfully, it passed off without a rumpus and we headed back to the Sparrow Hawk. It was agreed that it would be best to just stay in the hotel bar and enjoy the Modo friendship, rather than venture into town to risk any more aggro.

On the Sunday drive homeward bound, I got pulled up and fined for speeding on the M62, but it was still a brilliant weekend.

Just as we were so good in the 2nd half at Turf Moor, we were so poor in the first at home to Wrexham. We did take the lead through Gary Doherty again, but Wrexham came back to win 2-1, before only 4,759.

During the next week, Chairman David Kohler resigned after his elaborate plans to build us a new stadium called the Kohler dome next to the Junction 10 slip road on the M1, were turned down by John Prescot. This resignation pleased a lot of Luton fans but for reasons written earlier, I was not one of those fans.

I missed the next game, a 1-0 defeat at Bristol Rovers.

Three nights after that match, we played Notts County at home. The attendance of 4,021 is the lowest I have ever seen Luton play in at Kenilworth Road for a league match. It still is, at the time of writing this book. Even in all our 5 Conference seasons we only had one non-league crowd of less than 5,000 (4,847 v Hyde). We lost 1-0.

A needed 1-0 win occurred at home to Blackpool courtesy of Stuart Douglas. We then lost 1-0 at Walsall, another game I missed.

Runaway leaders Fulham then came to town. The difference between Luton's result and performance from 5 months earlier was like night and day. A full Oak Road Fulham contingent helped boost the crowd to 7,424. Once Alan White had been sent off after 30 mins, there was only going to be one winner. Fulham went on to torment us 4-0.

We were now plummeting down the table and when Stoke led 2-0 at Kenilworth Road after 10 minutes, I feared another humiliation.

But Graham Alexander scored a penalty to give us hope it was his 17th and final LTFC goal. The score though remained 2-1 to Stoke.

I drove alone to Chesterfield and witnessed an appalling LTFC showing. Phil Gray's 12th goal of the season was a mere consolation in the 3-1 loss.

The next game at home to Reading, was preceded with news that Luton were in dire straits financially and I decided to do my little bit, by paying for Corporate Hospitality in the Kenilworth Suite. It was in there, pre-match - that the news came filtering through that LTFC had entered Administration!

The news actually seemed to galvanise the players and crowd.

When Matthew Spring opened the scoring the roar that greeted the goal was the loudest of 1999. We nearly won, but the Royals equalised late on.

Because of the severe financial problems, two players were forced to depart. Sean Evers was sold to Reading for £500,000 and everyone at the time thought that they had got a bargain. But sadly for Sean, he never made it at Reading due to constant chronic injury problems. However, the £50,000 received from Preston for Graham Alexander - was a disgraceful insult!

In nearly 4 seasons with LTFC he played 183 times, further proof that this fee was derisory was that he was playing Premiership football in 2010.

We were permitted to sign two players on loan in time for our next game at home to Gillingham. Sean Dyche, a centre half from Bristol City (and future W**ford boss), along with Tony Thorpe, signed from the same club. Tony Thorpe needed no introduction and he received a huge welcome home, as the crowd rallied up to 6,705. Dyche scored the only goal in the welcome win. It was his only Town one.

I missed the game at Oldham because we moved house the day before.

There are certain things in life, which I said I would never do. Cruising, skiing and moving away from Stopsley, were three such examples. These were all things that I eventually did, proving that the old saying of never say never - is certainly true!

A few weeks prior, Deb had privately visited a new housing estate being developed at Barton-le-Clay. This is a village halfway between Luton and Bedford, off the A6. She persuaded me one day to just go and have a look. After entering the sales showroom and Deb innocently asking if there was anything still available, the Sales lady told us that all of the developments had been purchased except for one that had just fallen through, on the point of completion. Deb immediately asked if we could at least just go and look at it.

Reluctantly I agreed, we viewed this stunning 4 Bed Detached brand new house and there was no doubt that this really was a dream house, even I loved it, but when we sat down in the sales room I tried to delicately explain to Deb that this was way out of our league.

The rep countered, by saying, "I think you might be pleasantly surprised at the actual cost." She was doing a good sales pitch by telling us that all the carpets had already been fitted and were included in the price, along with the front & back lawns, oven and hob, dishwasher & all the curtains, which we could choose from their range. She then came up with a key clincher, the Builders could buy our current house in part exchange and we wouldn't have the hassle of selling. The only sticking point was that for these things to happen, we would have to move in by April or it could not occur. Deb could do all the legal work herself and would save costs. We worked out our budget and concluded with a selling price for our house in Putteridge Road. Any less offered by the builder would mean no deal.

Without going into too much personal details, we both worked out what the mortgage payment would be on the new house (HUGE) but there was no doubt we could afford it and both agreed, that we might never get this opportunity again. The builders actually offered £3,000 over our budget and so the dream was on.

We excitedly moved into our brand new home on Friday 1st April 1999. Barton is a lovely village and although I'll always be a Stopsley boy, I do love living here.

In the game I missed at Oldham, Phil Gray scored his 13th and final goal of 1998-99.

The Latics came back to draw 1-1.

I took York supporting client Kate Hampsall from SAF again, to the mid-week home game and she was happy when they led 1-0, but two goals from Matthew Spring and a last minute winner from Stuart Douglas, his 11th and final goal of 98-99 - sent me home the happier!

When I travelled to nearby Sixfields for the Northampton match I wished I had not bothered, we were abysmal and lost 1-0.

Because of the distance and our recent house move, I missed the mid-week game at Man City. This was Luton's final visit to Maine Road. We lost 2-0.

Luton then lost at home to Lincoln 1-0. Emerson Boyce made his debut.

Pete Morris, Sean Tyler & I went to Notts County and had a fine day & night. We beat the Magpies 2-1. Tony Thorpe scored them both. This win assured us of safety and we celebrated well into the night at old Brannigans nightclub.

Thorpe scored the only goal of the game in the next match at home to Chesterfield and in the final home match we entertained Macclesfield.

At half time the surviving players of Luton's only FA Cup Final team from 1959, were presented to the cheering Hatters fans and warmly greeted. It was a pity the 1999 team were not so good, we lost 2-1 to the bottom side.

I was once again kindly invited by Courage/SWMC to a corporate night out at the Leicester v Derby match. This was my 10th & final visit to Filbert Street, as they were to move to the nearby Walkers Stadium 3 years later. Derby won 2-1.

The final match of 98-99 was at Millwall. Pete, Sean & I travelled by train.

Tony Thorpe scored the only goal and the large Luton support went home happy. Some things will never change though, on stopping off for a drink at London Bridge homeward bound, this Millwall nutcase was looking for trouble with Luton fans. I am not exaggerating - he was SIXTY odd years of age!

I returned to London for one final match of 98-99 to see England 0 v Sweden 0. At about that time, we had a surprise visit from my sister Ann with her children Rachel & Peter. She told no one she was coming home from New Zealand for a holiday. Things hadn't worked out with Terry and they had split up. Ann had met a new man in her life called David, a Kiwi and they were expecting a new child when Ann decided she needed some time to assess the situation, so she came back to England for the 1st time in over ten years to clear her head. I'm pleased to write that she went back with her head straightened and they had a girl called Katrina. Ann and David are still happy together today in Auckland.

LTFC finished 1998-99 exactly halfway in 12th place.

1999-2000

It was back to the magical Disneyworld Florida for the Adairs' summer holiday and once again we stayed in a Disney Hotel, this time upgrading to the Port Orleans and being a touch more adventurous, we hired a car this year. We also ventured out to Universal Studios, the two Universal Theme Parks, Wet & Wild Water Park and SeaWorld. I was probably at the happiest stage of my life around then, a wonderful family with two beautiful children and a wife that I genuinely loved (apart from her not liking me drinking) on a holiday from paradise, things going as well as possible at work and in a brand new dream home. Yes, life was at a peak for me then.

In preparation for the final season of the millennium I watched Luton in a couple of home friendly matches against London opponents. We drew 2-2 with Crystal Palace and beat QPR 3-1 as I watched from a new vantage position in the ground. During the summer Cherry Newbery had informed Gus, Kristy, Tom, Shaun, Pete and myself, that our seats in the back row of the Enclosure were being dismantled for safety exit reasons. Cherry added that we could choose any seat available in the ground for no extra charge for 1999-2000 only, or alternatively if we all wanted to sit together again, we would have first refusal on a new row of seats being created. These seats were to be installed where the old dugouts were, which was in the front row at the halfway line in the Enclosure D Block. New dugouts were to be installed opposite by the Executive Boxes and so we jumped at the chance of having these prime view seats and still watching altogether. From our new position I would have great fun on many occasions and would have some excellent banter with players of both teams, and the officials.

This was not the only change at LTFC, it was decided to bring back Orange as the home shirt with blue shorts, there was certainly to be no complaints from myself on that front. It lasted one season, before we returned to White & Black. I know that White & Black are our true colours but we have had spells in the Orange top previously and would revert back again in 2009.

On the playing front Goalkeeper Kelvin Davis was transferred to Premier club Wimbledon for £600,000 and Mitchell Thomas had left Luton for the second and final time to join Burnley. Both players had given LTFC good service.

Davis playing 107 times and Thomas in particular, played 341 times in his two spells with us making him the 12th highest serving player in LTFC History.

The only signing was Julian Watts, a defender from Bristol City.

We were still officially in Administration and there were genuine concerns about whether we would be allowed to start the new campaign at Notts County.

Gus, Shaun & I travelled to Nottingham by train on the Friday afternoon anyway, in the hope that things would be resolved and we could start at Meadow Lane.

We booked the hotel next to the station at Nottingham, where I had stayed previously in 1983 when we played County. I swear, it had not changed one iota but it had a bed, a bar and breakfast included and was cheap.

We went out that night to meet old mate Freddie Dann, who was living in Nottingham at the time. He took us to a venue where I personally, had one of the greatest nights of my life. For my taste in music it was NUMBER UNO. The venue was called the Old Vic I think and the music was sensational. Upstairs I was dancing to Beatles, Tamla Motown, Sixties reggae like Desmond Dekker and all the Bluebeat/Ska stuff along with Northern Soul, while downstairs was the 1970s music, as well as the Glam stuff like The Sweet & David Bowie. I was in my element and kept switching every hour or so. That particular night was right up there in terms of personal musical enjoyment with the John Lennon tribute night at Sands in 1980.

We returned to the Hotel in the wee small hours - still not knowing if we had a match to attend! When we arose for breakfast the news had filtered through that the Football League had given the OK for Luton to go ahead and play. We were determined to celebrate big time, there was a huge Luton support that morning in Nottingham clearly wanting to do likewise. We had a couple in the bar opposite the station at opening time before heading to where all the Luton fans were gathering at a bar called Hooters. For those who have never heard of Hooters, it is a chain of bars/restaurants where the Staff, are female babes dressed with an Orange theme and with the tightest skimpiest shorts imaginable to the eye. The place was FULL of Luton fans celebrating before a ball had been kicked, just thankful for still having a team to watch.

Two players made their Luton debuts that day, Matthew Taylor, a young full back from the youth system and Julian Watts. The match itself was a 0-0 draw but with so many Hatters fans there, they frankly did not care about the result. I have to write, that some of them slightly over-celebrated and the Notts Police Force took exception to this. Quite a number of Hatters were arrested for fighting with them and I knew at least two of them personally.

I don't know exactly how many were arrested but one nameless mate ended up getting banned from home games for over a year, along with a heavy fine.

In the League Cup, we had drawn Bristol Rovers for the third time in my era. The first leg at Kenilworth Road saw the Gas win easily 2-0.

Our first home league match was v Blackpool. From our new viewpoint we watched a thrilling match. Liam George opened the scoring and it stayed that way until he added his 2nd, it looked like being a comfortable home win but the Tangerines came back into the game thanks to goalkeeper Nathan Abbey. He was at fault for two Blackpool goals. Fortunately, Matthew Spring scored in between those to give a final result of Luton 3 Blackpool 2.

I drove Gus, Shaun & Pete Morris to the Madjeski Stadium to play Reading in the August sunshine. Last season the Royals easily beat us 3-0 but this time, it was Luton's turn to outplay them. Andrew Fotiatis scored at the Hatters fans end, but Reading quickly equalised. Liam George scored the winning goal near the end to give Luton a fully deserved 2-1 victory.

I didn't go to Bristol Rovers for the return leg Cup Tie and we put out a reserve side anyhow. It was a 2-2 draw and we exited 4-2 on aggregate.

The next match was at home to promoted team Cardiff City. On the Friday, I was having lunch in The Bedfordshire Yeoman pub when I overheard this 50+-year-old Welshman telling all and sundry that the Luton fans had better be on alert tomorrow, as 5,000 Soul Crew (Cardiff's Hooligan Firm) were coming to teach Luton a lesson. I politely explained to Bobby Bullshit that they might have a bit of a problem - as the away stand has only 2,000 seats! "I know that," he replied. "They have tickets in the Luton end too." Well, he missed a 0 off - as there were 500 Cardiff fans in the Oak Road TOPS!

The tension did increase however, when a Town fan in the Main Stand near the Oak Road - decided to burn a Welsh Flag, which sent the Sheep Shaggers mental! I found out at a later date the culprit and know him personally. For obvious reasons, he shall stay anonymous.

By now I had begun to strike up a repertoire from my new seat with Phil Gray. I had met him on a number of occasions in the Eric Morecambe Lounge and the Ulsterman was a big Rangers fan, like myself. I began to always get the thumbs up from him when I shouted out, "NO SURRENDER PHIL!" - in my best Ian Paisley voice! That day against Cardiff, he scored the only goal and guess where he came running over to in celebration?

I took Deb and the girls to Bournemouth for the weekend when we played at Dean Court. We lost our first league match, rather unluckily 1-0.

In the next game at home to Bury, the CBC telephonist Julie, was up in the Directors Balcony with her daughters watching and supporting The Shakers. The reason, her husband was 1st team Coach, his name - Kevin Blackwell!

The lowest league crowd of 1999-2000, just 4,633, watched a 1-1 draw. Andrew Fotiatis blasted us into the lead before Julie rose from her seat in celebration at the Bury equaliser. 1-1 was a fair result.

We were at home again the next week to Wrexham. Luton won 3-1. The best goal was Matthew Taylor's first for LTFC. Matthew Spring's and Liam George's were quality efforts too.

Gus, Shaun, Pete & I travelled by train for a day/night out in the smoke for the Brentford trip. The Bees defeated us 2-0 in what was a tame Luton showing.

We certainly made up for it in the next game at home to Oxford. The first 6,000 + crowd of 1999-00 watched a brilliant Luton display. Liam George had his best game in a Luton shirt, scoring twice along with young Stuart Fraser (his only Luton goal) to give us a commanding 3-0 H/T lead. But in the 2nd half we gifted Oxford two goals and the nerves were beginning to set in. Recent signing Adam Locke ended those nerves when he scored from fully FORTY yards out, to see us home 4-2. This great performance had left us in 3rd place.

I had to miss the next game at Wigan even though it was a new ground for me at the JJB Stadium. The reason being, it was my Scots mate Duncan Angus's 40th Birthday Party in Kilsyth.

The Scots had all made the effort to attend mine, so it was common courtesy to replicate this. The party was on the Saturday night so naturally we saw Rangers play at Dens Park, to beat Dundee 3-2.

I had a mobile phone now and Gus was keeping me abreast with the score at Wigan, we lost 1-0.

The next weekend Luton were away to Oldham and that naturally, meant we had to book our Blackpool Illuminations trip for the game in Lancashire, once again staying at our favourite Claremont Hotel. On the Saturday I caught the train from Blackpool to Oldham and sitting next to me in Boundary Park, was Danny Clubb. He was an Executive Luton fan and an old Stopsley boy from Tin Town. He had moved to Blackpool a while ago and ran a hostel/hotel for people in need. He kindly offered me a lift back to my Hotel after the game, along with his accompaniment the ex-Luton player and manager Allan Brown, who also resided in Blackpool.

The match itself was an Oldham attacking blitz. We held out until the Latics scored, but against the odds we equalised soon after through recent loan signing from Ipswich, Neil Midgley. Just as I began to think we had stolen a point, Oldham scored a deserved winner in injury time. This was my ninth visit to Boundary Park with Luton, as of yet I have not returned. Of those nine visits, the amount of Hatters wins - NIL! The car journey conversation back to Blackpool was very enjoyable. Although not quite so young anymore, I found Allan Brown to be a true Scots gentleman and clearly, still held a love for all things Luton Town. We reminisced and I was delighted that he remembered initially signing my cousin Ken Adair back in 1968 on schoolboy terms. He told me that when Ken signed he had untold ability but like many boys at that age, just did not have the ruthless dedication to be a full Professional. Talent of course is vital, but without the willingness to drop the girls and the drink, you will NOT succeed.

Allan, a member of the 1959 FA Cup Final team, scored 58 goals in 175 LTFC appearances and won 3 caps for Scotland. He sadly died in 2011, aged 84. It was my pleasure to meet this lovely man and the Manager of LTFC - when I first started supporting The Hatters! RIP Allan.

Deb's cousin Laura had a new boyfriend (later married to him, with two lovely girls) called Cliff. He is from Brighton and a keen B&HA fan. I got on and still do, brilliantly with Cliff because like me he is a football fanatic. He is a top quality man without a bad bone in his body. All of the Loughborough relations were down visiting Deb's kin and he joined me for the Luton v Gillingham match. He sat alongside us in the Enclosure. It was a bit of a bonus celebration that day also, for we had officially come out of Administration. Cliff was extremely impressed with Luton that afternoon and the best crowd at that point of 6,394 created a great atmosphere. Despite losing 1-0 at h-t, we stormed back to win 3-1. Liam George scored twice and was in great form, having scored 8 League goals in 10 games. Stuart Douglas scored the other.

Three nights later I was a proud Dad as my 9-year-old daughter Georgina had been chosen by The Junior Hatters to lead out the team at home to Wycombe as a mascot. Deb & Mollie joined me in our complimentary seats in the Main Wing Stand. It was almost in the exact spot that Dad & I used to sit back in the 1960s. Mollie was only 5 and so Deb left with the girls soon after Georgina had returned with her complimentary kit. Within minutes of them leaving Wycombe had opened the scoring. I went down to take my usual seat and saw a magnificent Stuart Douglas headed equaliser. It finished 1-1.

I drove the short journey to Oxford to watch Luton at The Manor Ground for the final time as they were due to move to a new ground, but it was 2001 before they finally did, due to funding shortages.

An early Liam George goal was the only one, enough to secure us three points. Next up was the FA Cup and we had drawn non-league Kingstonian at home in the 1st Round. They really gave us a fright that day. After Phil Gray had put us 1-0 ahead they levelled and then in an attack by ex-Hatter Dwight Marshall, they took the lead. Thankfully, Liam George, Matthew Spring & Matt Taylor fired in the goals to see us out 4-2 winners. Spring's goal that day was one of the best I had seen in years, a 30-yard blockbuster.

Luton then played Millwall at The New Den but I missed a 1-0 defeat as I was abroad sampling a European adventure with Rangers at Bayern Munich, in which the Gers also lost 1-0 but were extremely unlucky, as they played fantastic. I thoroughly enjoyed my maiden European trip with the Gers.

Luton's next home game v Burnley attracted the biggest home league crowd of 1999-00. 7,205 watched as we welcomed back former hero Steve Davis (and warmly greeted) with his high-flying Clarets. Two goals by Neil Midgeley were enough to see off Burnley 2-1 and we had now moved up to 8th.

I drove the short distance to Cambridge and after having a pleasant pre-match drink in their Supporters Club with Liam George's mum, there wasn't much to cheer for us.

A third of the 6,211 there were Hatters fans and we all watched an inept display, losing 3-1. Liam George's late goal really didn't matter.

In the FA Cup 2nd round we could only draw 2-2 at home to Lincoln, thanks to a pair from Gary Doherty.

We then lost our unbeaten home league record by tamely surrendering a 2-0 defeat to Preston. Because of that abject performance I didn't travel to Bristol Rovers - we lost 3-0!

In the live televised FA Cup replay at Lincoln, Gus & I watched it in the Vine pub. Stuart Douglas scored the only goal to send us into Round 3.

Tony Thorpe made another loan return and was in the team to play Notts County at home. He was back to normal when he scored after making Gary Doherty's opener. But from 2-0 up, the Magpies came back to draw 2-2.

I missed the FA Cup tie at Fulham, where we earned a fantastic 2-2 draw. We then lost 3-0 at Colchester and had now reached five win-less games. I had flu and had to miss the Fulham FA Cup replay.

I listened on the Radio as the largest 1999-2000 home crowd of 8,170, watched Luton hold out until three Fulham goals in six second half mins, took its toll.

On Boxing Day, Chesterfield came to town and despite Adam Locke giving us the lead with an exquisite curled effort, the Spireites came back to draw 1-1.

I then missed a 0-0 encounter at Bristol City.

In between Xmas and New Year we flew up to Aberdeen with Deb's parents for her cousin Steve's wedding in the Granite City.

On New Year's Eve, the very last night of the 1990s, we went to a party that Deb's friend Wendy had organised. It was held in the Scout Hall in Applecroft Road Stopsley, a mere stone's throw from my Grandma & Granddad Adair's old house. It was the first time I had been down that road in over 15 years and it certainly brought back nostalgic personal memories as we entered the car park. Before we went to the party we visited Grandma Roberts who at 89 years, was now not in the greatest of health this was sadly her last Xmas.

The first game of the Noughties saw the seven games winless run come to an end. Scunthorpe were the visitors and this was the very first time I had seen them play, as they were one of the very few teams in the 92 club league yet to play Luton in my 33 years LTFC supporting era. It was a cracker of a game and Luton went 3-0 up, all of the goals coming just before half time via Stuart Douglas, Phil Gray & Matthew Spring (another screamer). The Iron pulled one back before Spring netted another beauty, to finish it 4-1 to Luton.

The following Saturday I drove Pete Morris to Stoke. This was a crazy match in which the Referee Mr Foy was determined to rule the roost. He awarded the Potters a penalty that NO ONE in the ground saw, even the Stoke players looked bewildered having just played on.

Then after sending off Matt Taylor for a mere tackle, he was consistent with his baffling decisions by awarding us a penalty - for Lord knows what? Spring duly obliged the gift to make it 1-1 and then just when I thought we had earned a hard fought point, Nathan Abbey made one of his notorious cock ups to gift Stoke the winning goal.

I drove alone the following week to Blackpool. From the kick off, we attacked and should have been at least 3-0 up, before they scored. Adam Locke equalised. When Blackpool added a further two goals in the first eleven mins of the 2nd half, it was too much for some Hatters fans. A barrage of 'Lawrence Out' cried out and more than a few Luton fans left the ground, with pockets of more and more doing the same as the game progressed. I stayed, but have to admit that had I not been driving or if I was staying in Blackpool, I possibly would have joined some of them going to the promenade pubs. When Phil Gray scored that stopped the exodus and in the final seconds Matthew Taylor hit a shot from fully 30 yards that somehow managed to creep in. The resulting goal produced great cheers from us remaining Hatters on the crumbling old Kop open terrace. In the end I was delighted to get a 3-3 draw.

I have already written about Bloomfield Road being positively run down.

Yet today, all 4 sides have new stands (one temporary) and now seats over 16,000. It just goes to show how a clubs fortunes can sometimes change for the better.

We then played Reading at home and the Royals were near the foot of the table. Luton had to take advantage of this and we did. Julian Watts scored his 1st Luton goal. Reading equalised, before Liam George finished them off by scoring his 13th and 14th goals of the season, to complete a 3-1 Luton victory.

The following Sunday, I listened on the radio to the game at Ninian Park, Cardiff. It was our first game there since the FA Cup notorious CS Gas attack by stewards on our fans in 1994. We bettered the last time's score by one goal, winning 3-1. This was our 1st away success in the league for three months.

After two fine wins and 9 goals in three games, it was back to disappointment when Bournemouth visited. Emerson Boyce opened his account with Luton, but the Cherries were 2-0 ahead at the time and they left Luton with 3 points.

Just as the Luton performance was so poor against Bournemouth, it was so good at home to Stoke. I decided to take some clients to the Kenilworth Suite. Despite being 1-0 behind at h-t, we were playing very well. Two goals from my Ulster mate Phil Gray turned things right round and we beat the Potters 2-1.

After that great showing I drove up to Bury. We narrowly lost 1-0 but were denied a BLATANT penalty when a Bury player handled the ball in his area.

In the next game at home to high-flying Bristol Rovers, Luton came out of the blocks like a team possessed and for the first 25 minutes we were unplayable. Phil Gray gave us a fully deserved lead.

I'm sorry to write that our calamitous goalkeeper Nathan Abbey made two more desperate howlers to gift the Pirates a 2-1 lead. This clearly deflated his teammates as well as the crowd, Rovers added a further two, we lost 4-1 and Abbey had played his last game of 1999-2000.

Ben Roberts was brought in on loan from Middlesbrough as his replacement for the next game at home to Brentford. It was almost déjà vu though.

Gray had once again given us the lead but Roberts messed up TWICE with goalkeeping gaffes, to gift the Bees a 2-1 victory. I'm afraid he was at fault for the only goal of the game at Wrexham the following week too. I missed that game, as the Adair family were going on a holiday, of which I had previously said I would never attempt to try as I thought it was for snobs.

Deb and the girls had persuaded me to go on a skiing holiday and we left Luton for Salzburg, Austria on the day Luton were playing in Wales.

We had booked a Crystal Holiday skiing package on pure costs alone and chose Kranjska Gora in Slovenia, one of the countries that made up old Yugoslavia. The deal that we had booked was absolutely fantastic, a week's full board (Breakfast, Lunch & Dinner) in the Hotel Alpina, which was located right on the ski slope along with the use of the indoor swimming pool and sauna. All of Deb, Georgina's & Mollie's Ski Hire & lessons + lift passes & flights, including my hotel/flight - for just £1,100 in total!

All three of the girls had previously practiced on the dry slopes at Hemel Hempstead, but my two daughters had never attempted skiing on real snow. It is inspirational to see how quickly children adapt to such challenges. Within hours, they were gliding along with no fear or problems at all. Initially, I had no interest in skiing myself and was quite happy to just watch the enjoyment on their faces. Mollie especially, was only 5 and took to it like a duck to water. The evening social side was terrific fun also and we made many friends. After a couple of days I was beginning to get a bit bored though, as the rest were having such fun. They eventually got me to pluck up the courage to hire some boots and skis to have a try. I have to write, I thoroughly enjoyed it and before the end of the week I had paid for a few private lessons and even started getting adventurous by going up the drag slopes. The feeling coming down the mountain was sensational, although I sometimes struggled to stop & fell over many times. By the end of the week I had regretted not joining the girls earlier.

As they had loved the holiday so much, I definitely agreed that we should repeat it and come back the next year, but this time with myself fully indulging.

While in Slovenia I checked on two important results.

LTFC gained a very impressive 2-0 victory at Turf Moor, Burnley - I wonder if the thugs from the last year were there - waiting on my presence! Then the night after was a vital Celtic v Rangers match. We won 1-0.

We flew home from Salzburg and arrived at Luton Airport. I knew before the holiday that it would be a pretty tight schedule, so I had prepared and took my season ticket book with me. Because the time was so tight, we booked a black cab and by the time we reached Kenilworth Road (not even 3 miles) the meter read an astonishing £9. When the girls reached Barton it had passed TWENTY QUID – Christ, at that time I could fly to Glasgow return for that price!

I shouldn't have bothered with the rushing, Luton were awful and we lost 2-0. This was Millwall's fourth win on the trot at Kenilworth Road.

The following weekend I missed our 1-0 defeat at Preston because I was in Scotland, seeing Rangers beat Motherwell 6-2. Due to the flight arriving back in Luton on the Monday night and after a wild weekend in Scotland, I decided to give the Cambridge home match the next night a pass. We drew 2-2.

All the Kilsyth folk were coming to Luton for the first weekend in April and for that reason, I gave the Chesterfield match at Saltergate a miss too. I wished I had gone though - Luton won 3-1!

My friends flew into Luton the following Friday pm. They had all booked into the Shamrock Hotel again. On the Saturday, while the ladies went shopping, us lads headed to the Luton v Colchester match. We sat in the Enclosure D Block, amid baffling looks from some locals (we were all in Rangers tops).

Julian Watts gave us a lead and frankly, that was as good as it got in the 1st half. When Colchester hit us with two goals after the break, I was giving my pals stick telling them that they were jinxing my team. But the Hatters came storming back to win 3-2 with goals from Gary Doherty & Matt Taylor.

Our little party certainly added to the atmosphere in the 5,125 present.

Gus, Shaun and our season ticket friends, including the two Pete's and Bean, joined us up the SWMC for an excellent evening entertainment with the Scots. After initially meeting my Scots friends at my 40th, Gus & Shaun also became buddies to the Kilsyth crowd. Gus in particular, would visit Kilsyth on many occasions during the next four years.

The following weekend, Luton were playing at Scunthorpe. We decided to make this a CBC weekender for two reasons. 1) I had never been to Scunthorpe's Glanford Park (or their Old Showground for that matter) and 2) One of our IT Guys at CBC, Mike Pearmaine, was born there. He booked the hotel and a fleet of cars from both work and Stopsley headed north on the Friday. My old mate Steve Toyer was now not in the best of health and was struggling to walk and had a walking stick, the kind that folded up. The hotel Mike booked was cheap and cheerful it was near the centre and also had an in house nightclub. What he didn't tell us - was that it was also the local drug dealer's den! Most of my friends were and never have been, into drugs, so it didn't bother us.

We have always been too fond of the alcohol, rather than that drug crap. Rather amusingly, the local police in a town centre pub on match day thought Steve's cane might be deemed as an offensive weapon and tried to confiscate it. After we explained Steve's plight the Old Bill saw the funny side & returned it.

It was another great trip and still remains my only visit to the Lincolnshire club. The match was pretty good too, goals from Phil Gray & Gary Doherty, gave us a 2-1 victory.

After initially letting us in to the Supporters Club post-match, they then changed their minds and asked us to leave as there was simply too many of us. Rather than cause a commotion, we just left and headed to The Brewers Fayre opposite to meet Gus in there, who was just up for the match.

This third successive victory had lifted us up to 10th position with 5 games left. The following game was at home to Bristol City. The Robins like Millwall, had become a bit of a bogey side to us at Kenilworth Road. It was back in 1981 (Steve White) when we last beat them in the League and this bad run continued, as we lost 2-1. Gary Doherty scored our goal and it turned out to be his 15th and final LTFC goal, before being sold to Tottenham for £1 million.

Gus & Shaun decided to make a weekend of the next game at Gillingham. That place did not appeal to me - AT ALL! I missed a 2-0 defeat.

The season was drawing to a close as promotion- seeking Wigan came to Town. Even though Luton were by far the better side, somehow Wigan led 1-0. In the 2nd half the roles were reversed with the Latics showing their class, but Phil Gray headed in an equaliser and overall the 1-1 result was fair.

I drove to the final away game at Wycombe and we had a pleasant pre-match drink in the

Supporters Club at the ground. The full Luton end was delighted when Matt Taylor netted the only goal late on.

In the final match of 1999-00 at home to Oldham, Phil Gray headed in his 12th goal of the campaign to give us an early lead. It stayed that way until the last minute when Alan White handled in his area. Oldham scored the penalty and it ended 1-1. That Latics goal cost us 2 points and three places in the final league table. As a result, we finished 13th.

The last season of the 90s had produced its usual level of pluses and minuses. The positives were, that it was great to just have a team that started the season and to come out of administration. The early season form was also particularly good. The emergence of talented youngsters, like Liam George, Matt Taylor & Matthew Spring was great, along with Phil Gray proving some of his critics wrong. On the negative side, it was a shame to sell YET another player in Gary Doherty.

I attended 2 more matches after the Oldham game. Both were friendly Internationals, which were England 1 Brazil 1 and my final Wembley visit before demolition, England 2 Ukraine 0.

This was my 65th game I had seen at the world famous home of football.

Just a side note, on the day of the League Cup Final Paul Keating and I were playing for the SWMC in the Semi-Finals of the National Dominoes Pairs 5&3s in Chatteris, Cambs. We won and I'm proud to write, that we then beat a pair from Dagenham, in the Final at Brentwood, Essex to become the Champions for the South Of England Region National Title 2000.

Work wise, things could hardly be better and there was no doubt I was at the peak of my career earning fantastic money. So what did I do? Well on my 41st birthday I made one of the biggest mistakes of my life (I would go on - to make many more!) and looked for another job.

I felt that I was beginning to get a bit stale at CBC and was thinking that after 18+ years, it might be time for a change and challenge my skills elsewhere. I rang the company that CBC shared the Vauxhall Contract with and asked the M.D. if he would be interested in my joining them. His response was one of excitement and we agreed a meeting at their plant in Wembley.

To this day - I bitterly regret that phone call!

After numerous meetings and discussions I eventually plucked up the courage to go for it. It took me a full three months to take the plunge, knowing what the consequences would be for CBC. The crazy thing about all of this was that I was to leave and start with the London Company for a - LESSER package! Nearly £4k down on my basic wage I thought that I would just be able to earn more in commission, because of their capacity to print more than CBC due to the larger size of their presses.

I knew and both Westway and CBC knew, that my decision would mean the end of the road at some point for CBC. It was with this in mind, that I was promised a bumper bonus on completion of this case in kind. When CBC eventually ceased to exist (within a year) the Vauxhall Contract became exclusively Westway's.

I repeat I made a huge error that I would regret for many years.

CHAPTER FIVE

THE NOUGHTIES

2000-01

In the summer of 2000 there were to be major changes in both my personal life and at LTFC. We did not have a holiday because I had taken the plunge to leave CBC Print, to work for Westway in Wembley. I began there in August.

Grandma Roberts had reached the grand old age of 90 on July 13th but was now in hospital and very poorly. She sadly passed away on August 31st. It was the end of an era as she was the major link where all the Roberts clan would meet up and sadly in time, these meet ups would gradually diminish.

My mum came home twice that summer to see her, in hospital for her 90th and again in September for her funeral. I was honoured to be one of the Coffin Bearers. I dearly loved old Annie, as of course Isa equally. 90 is a ripe age but it was still my Gran and I miss her. RIP ANNIE.

I started my new job and almost immediately regretted my decision and the situation was not helped because the country was in a fuel crisis. Within a month of starting due to blockade protests because of rising fuel costs, petrol was severely limited and difficult to purchase anywhere, this had a major impact on my job. I was not able to service my clients to maximum ability and even getting to the office in London every day, restricted my mileage use.

As the saying went, I had made my bed - I had to lie in it! Things did gradually begin to improve and work started to flow in again thanks to my loyal clients, for whom the majority moved with me. I had opened an account with a design agency in Luton that worked with Vauxhall called BMB Design. The fact that their print buyer Jo Clennett, was a keen Luton fan and the wife of a mutual friend of Gus & I helped and within weeks they would become a major client.

At LTFC it was all change too. The new owner Mike Watson-Challis and the Board decided to relieve manager Lennie Lawrence of his duties and sack him. The announcement of his successor had everyone stunned. It was a major shock when Luton legend (and friend) Ricky Hill, was given the job after a short time coaching the Youth team at Sheffield Wednesday. Despite his minimal managerial experience it was an extremely popular choice with the fans, myself included. He appointed Chris Ramsey as his assistant and was given good financial backing to purchase new players.

Luton reverted back to White and Black as the home kit in this new era. There were some exits from the playing staff, with my Ulster mate Phil Gray among the departures. In his two spells with the Hatters, Phil scored 53 goals in 161 appearances.

Alan White was transferred to Colchester and goalkeeper Ben Roberts returned to

Middlesbrough. In his place was Mark Ovendale, signed from Bournemouth for a staggering (by LTFC standards) £465,000. Ricky also brought back ex-Hatter Mark Stein on a free, 12 years after leaving Luton.

Hill signed Dean Brennan & Peter Holmes from Sheff Wed, players he knew from his employment with the Owls.

The first game of the season was at home to Notts County and a hugely enthusiastic crowd of 7,059 (nearly 2,000 more than the corresponding fixture in 99-00) turned out to give Ricky Hill a rapturous welcome home.

Unfortunately - the party fell flat! Luton were hopeless, the Magpies won 1-0 with ease and we hoped this was just a blip, due to the players being nervous.

I drove up for my first visit to the JJB Stadium, Wigan's new ground. A crowd of 6,518 looked very sparse in the 25,000 all-seated arena. Wigan took an early lead, then Julian Watts headed in Luton's first goal of 2000-01 to equalise. But a great goal gave Wigan a 2-1 victory.

Three nights later, we drew 0-0 at home to Peterborough in the League Cup 1st Rd. We actually played well and dominated, but just could not score.

Our first victory came against Bournemouth at home, thanks to Mark Stein earning a penalty against his former mates, in which Matthew Spring scored. I drove the short distance to Wycombe the Chairboys were rather fortunate to lead 1-0 at h-t. Tresor Kandol equalised and it finished 1-1.

I had to miss the return leg at Peterborough mid-week because working in Wembley, now resulted in most away mid-week games being not possible for me to attend. However, Luton did not miss me. We drew 2-2 and advanced to the next round on the away goal rule.

The Adair family paid Cherine & Gary a visit at their Rotherham home, while I saw Luton play at Millmoor for the 4th and last time. Andrew Fotiatis opened the scoring with a fine goal but Rotherham levelled and it finished 1-1, a fair result.

At the next match home to Northampton, we were never in the game and lost 2-0 to the Cobblers, their second goal was scored by a certain Steve Howard.

The new Ricky Hill era was brought down to earth in the next game at home to Walsall. Just 4,362 (the lowest for 00-01) watched a terrible game. We had a new striker making his debut in Peter Thomson, who we paid £100,000 to NEC Breda, in Holland. He made no impact in a drab 0-0.

Due to the ongoing fuel shortages, there was no way I could travel to Swansea and I'm glad I didn't. Luton's poor start continued and after the Swans thrashed us 4-0, alarm bells were beginning to ring.

In the League Cup 2nd Round we had drawn Premiership club Sunderland with the 1st leg at the Stadium Of Light. We managed to hold them to 0-0 at h-t but three Sunderland goals finished us off.

Mark Stein scored his first goal in his 2nd spell, to open the scoring at home to Swindon. Swindon bounced back to lead 2-1, before Liam George opened his 00-01 account to level. Alas, Swindon scored again to win 3-2.

In the meaningless return leg v Sunderland, a big away following boosted the crowd to 5,262. We fell behind to 2 goals before a late goal by Tresor Kandol gave us a speck of respectability, as we exited 5-1 overall.

I missed the next three matches. At Cambridge we lost 2-1. This result meant that Luton had officially made our worst start in history, just one win from the opening 12 games - so much for the new beginning!

It was blatantly obvious that Ricky Hill was struggling, but such was the esteem in which he was held, everyone was desperately hoping he could turn things around. We battled to earn a point in a 0-0 draw at Oxford.

On the Saturday home match v Brentford I was enjoying a pre-match pint with Gus and the usual crowd in the Eric Morecambe lounge - when I received a phone call to return home urgently! Before I left for the match, Deb had gone shopping. I was at home while the girls were playing upstairs. They were jumping around on their beds having fun, when Mollie fell off and hurt her wrist. After she had stopped crying I gave her some Paracetamols and she appeared to be OK. I left for the game but when Deb had returned, Mollie's hand was throbbing. Deb took her to the L&D Hospital and rang me to inform that she had broken her wrist. Naturally, I immediately left to return home. As she was resting I listened to the Brentford game on the radio and typically - I missed the best Luton performance so far this season! Stuart Douglas made his first start after a pre-season injury and he tore the Bees apart with his pace. He scored twice and Matthew Spring added a 3rd. Gus rang me at h-t to say - STAY AWAY! It ended 3-1.

Chris Ramsey, Ricky Hill's assistant, had just been fired before the game. This result had me feeling much better and positive as I prepared for my second adventure in Europe with Rangers, in Austria against Sturm Graz.

After watching Rangers lose 2-0, I returned home & the next day Luton were at home to Wrexham. Mark Stein opened the scoring then Julian Watts added a second. I felt at h-t that 2-0 flattered us a bit but who cared? We needed some luck in our position. When Liam George made it 3-0, I felt more secure and looked forward to seeing us gain a needy 3 points. Wrexham pulled one back on the hour and when they scored a 2nd soon after I suddenly felt very uneasy. To the point that I said to Gus, "We are going to blow this." I was not wrong, the Dragons equalised and when they scored the inevitable winner, I did something I had NEVER done in my 34 years of attending Luton matches at Kenilworth Road before. I threw my season ticket book on the floor in disgust - and stormed out in the huff! Fortunately, Shaun picked it up and returned it back to me before the next match.

I quickly came back to reason and drove to Gigg Lane, Bury the next week.

In a last throw of the dice Ricky Hill signed three players, adding them to the squad for this match. Foreigners Kent Karlsen a Danish fullback and Finn International midfielder Petri Helin started, plus striker Rocky Baptiste a non-league signing, was on the bench. The lowest attendance for a Luton game in 00-01 of only 2,861 (including a fair few from Luton) watched an inspired Luton performance. After a goalless 1st half we fell behind. Helin then scored on his debut and Baptiste came close to winning it for us late on, we drew 1-1.

None of those signings had much influence at LTFC. Baptiste made two more appearances (both as sub), Karlsen, a further five games (2 as sub) and this was Helin's only goal in 27 matches.

The following week at home to Bristol City, sadly ended Ricky Hill's short reign. It pains me to write this, but it had to happen. We lost 3-0 to City and five days later, with just two wins in 21 games Ricky was sacked. I must write that even after this unfortunate episode, he will always be a Luton legend and I KNOW that he would receive a fine warm welcome from us fans anytime.

Lil Fuccillo, another ex-Luton player, was installed as our new manager. His first game in charge was in the FA Cup 1 at home to non-league Rushden & Diamonds. It was chosen for live TV coverage by Sky on the Friday night, they obviously sensed a shock. The Northants fans filled the Oak Road and I used some of my entertainments budget to take a R&D supporting client, for Corporate. We won 1-0 rather fortunately with Liam George scoring the goal.

I missed Fuccillo's first league match at Port Vale and evidently it was Luton's poorest showing of 2000-01 so far, losing 3-0.

The next week, Gus & I chose to take our girls to Stoke on the Junior Hatters Coach. I was thrilled when Mollie's name was pulled out of the hat en route to be the Luton mascot that day. (Even if she was oblivious.) She would receive a complimentary full kit and photos at kick off and face painted, along with the others. I was as proud as punch when we walked out of the tunnel. Mollie, with her Stoke counterpart, led the teams out onto the pitch. Even she enjoyed that moment. Although Mollie couldn't care two pence about LTFC or football, both her and Georgina did enjoy the day. Things got even better for me, as Paul McLaren hammered in a 30-yard goal into the net we were sitting behind at the Luton end to give us the lead. Stoke equalised and the teams went off level.

Luton were playing well and I had good vibes, further evidence of this was when the much maligned Peter Thomson scored his 1st and 2nd (& only) goals for Luton, we ended up winning 3-1 to round off a perfect day.

I drove alone for the long trek north to Darlington in the FA Cup 2nd round. This was my one and only visit to the Feetham's Ground as they were to move to a new 25,000 seated arena in 2003 - which would lead to later dire consequences! I sat next to Scottish Stuart Fraser's dad and brother as we saw Peter Thomson miss an open goal in a 0-0 draw.

The next game at home to Colchester was incredible. We lost 3-0 but truthfully - Luton were the better team!

Gus, Shaun, Pete Morris & I decided to have a pre-Xmas booze up for the game at Reading travelling by train, via Paddington. We should have stayed in the Walkabout pub in town instead of going to the match.

Although Luton started off the better team and should have led by 2 or 3 before Reading scored, in the end it was embarrassing as the Royals thrashed us 4-1. Recent signing Lee Nogan scored our goal.

On Boxing Day the best home crowd yet of 7,374, watched Luton win just our fourth league game of the season at this halfway point against Peterborough. Matthew Spring gave us the lead with a beauty and then Peter Holmes hit his first Luton goal.

Just before the interval, ex-Hatter Sean Farrell pulled one back for the Posh. Emerson Boyce made it 3-1 before Peterborough reduced it via a penalty, to set up a tense finale. Thankfully we held on to win 3-2 but were still second bottom. The final game of 2000 was at home to 3rd placed Wigan. The Latics had two shots on goal and scored from both of them, to win 2-0.

We were about to enter the year 2001 - a year that would see my personal life change dramatically!

I missed the game at Bournemouth on New Year's Day in which we lost 3-2. In the FA Cup 3rd Round, QPR were our visitors and their fans filled the Oak Road in a crowd of 8,677, which was the highest home gate of 2000-01. The 1st half display by Luton was fantastic as Andrew Fotiatis & Liam George gave us a 2-0 lead against the higher league side. Unfortunately, the Hoops came storming back and two goals from beanpole striker Crouch, levelled matters. When Stuart Douglas restored our lead, we were looking forward to a home tie with Arsenal, until injury time struck. Disastrously, Lee Nogan handled in the area to give QPR a penalty for reasons only he will know, they scored from the spot to end it 3-3 and a replay at Loftus Road.

The following Friday night Adam Locke gave us the lead at home to Wycombe with his 5th and final LTFC goal. Unfortunately, Wycombe came back to beat us 2-1, this was the first time that I had seen them beat us in 9 attempts.

The day after, we flew out to Salzburg again for a repeat skiing holiday in Slovenia. We stayed at the Hotel Alpina once more, only this time I skied from day 1. We had a brilliant time once again and I was now a committed ski fan. This trip had some comical moments.

One day I was screaming at everyone to get out of the way as I was coming down the slopes at full speed and struggling to stop (they all called my style of skiing, kamikaze) when suddenly - a dog came from nowhere and began to chase me! I was now screaming to all and sundry to clear my path, only coming to a halt when I reached the bottom of the piste - and had run out of snow! My skis stopped instantly and I flew out of them to land in front of a startled crowd at the bar area, who were by now in hysterics. To everyone's (inc all my family) glee, I just remarked – "I'll have a Beer please!"

I gradually began to learn more of the skiing technique and although no expert, by the end of the week was certainly adequate and no longer known as Kamikaze. We loved skiing so much now, that we would definitely repeat it.

Whilst in Slovenia, I (well, Georgina) managed to access the Internet and find the result of the QPR replay. Sadly, we lost 2-1 AET.

We returned from Slovenia on the Saturday but had no match because of the FA Cup. Incidentally, Arsenal won at QPR - 6-0!

There was no chance of me attending a mid-week 2-0 loss at Oldham.

Shortly afterwards news filtered through that had us Hatters fans in disbelief, not at the news that Lil Fuccillo was to step down from Manager to Coach, but at the announcement that Luton's fourth manager in less than a year was – Joe Kinnear! He was a high profile Premiership manager at Premiership Wimbledon, before suffering a Heart Attack - and he chose to join Luton!

His first match in charge was at Northampton and I was unable to get a ticket such was the demand. His reign got off to a good start as we won 1-0.

Gus was there with his daughter Kristy. I was shocked when he told me that night, his marriage to Sara was over and he had moved out of their house.

I won't go into details, as they are personal, suffice to write that I had no idea of this coming. This was the beginning of a long road ahead for one of my best mates. I really wanted to help him as much as I could but Gus, being Gus, was a stubborn/proud man and would refuse any assistance. One thing was certain, he was devoted to his daughter and she would ALWAYS be his number one concern and priority. Unfortunately for my pal, his marriage break up was the start of many problems for him.

After Northampton, Luton were away again in mid-week at Notts County, there was no chance of me making that in time from London so I listened on the radio to a great 3-1

Hatters win over the Magpies.

Nearly 2,500 more than the previous home game, turned up for Joe Kinnear's 1st home match in charge against Swansea to boost the attendance to 7,085. Lee Mansell & Stuart Douglas had sent us Hatters manic by racing to a 2-0 lead. The Swans made it 2-1, but Lee Mansell had us singing again with his 2nd goal.

Even when Swansea reduced it to 3-2 I was not concerned, such was the movement of Luton's style. The team were playing with a new swagger and soon after, recent signing Keith Rowland made it 4-2 before Swansea scored again in this highly entertaining match. The goal scoring was completed at 5-3 when Liam George rounded off a great day.

In his first 3 matches Joe Kinnear had achieved as many victories - as poor old Ricky had managed in 21! This win had lifted us above Swansea. Just a matter of weeks prior it looked hopeless, but safety now seemed achievable.

We were brought down to earth at Walsall when they beat us 3-1 in mid-week. Gus & I then took our girls once again on the Junior Hatters Coach, to Swindon. We had another brilliant day and Luton played superb at the County Ground. The large Hatters following in the 7,160 crowd watched Swindon undeservedly take the lead. Fear not, Keith Rowland headed an equaliser. Emerson Boyce then scored and Lee Mansell made it 3-1 in injury time. The support from Luton fans that day was tremendous.

Unfortunately, I could not convince my girls to become regulars, even though their two matches they witnessed in 2000-01 were both 3-1 Luton victories - they have never seen us play since!

The highest 00-01 league home attendance of 7,405 watched Luton v Bristol Rovers. The Pirates, or The Gas to more modern fans, were just a place above us in this 6 pointer. Alas, it finished 0-0 as neither team gained much ground.

Three nights later, we played Cambridge at home and everyone knew that with 13 games remaining, we had to win the majority of them to have any chance of avoiding the drop into the basement league.

In the Kinnear reign we had won 4, drawn 1 and lost 1. This was the form needed for the remainder of the campaign. 6,370 turned up to watch a keenly fought battle and with only 4 mins remaining, it was still 0-0. Mark Stein then valiantly chased a ball in which the Cambridge keeper raced off his line to clear the ball from Stein to launch it up field. From a full - FORTY yards out! Matt Taylor returned the ball into the empty net, to win the match and send us Hatters mental. 16 points from 21 is PROMOTION form we were bound to survive, said everyone exiting Kenilworth Road.

Well over 1,000 Hatters travelled to the New Den to face league leaders Millwall. I doubt if any clubs fans brought more in 2000-01 than we did that day.

Although they had an excellent recent record at Kenilworth Road our record there, was more than decent. Despite the Lion's league position, we took the game to them but we just could not finish. Millwall scored late on, our keeper Nathan Abbey had little else to do all game but we lost 1-0.

We didn't have a match for over a fortnight and I had to miss the next one at Peterborough, as it was mid-week.

Joe Kinnear had signed a striker from Northampton called Steve Howard paying £50,000 for him - what a signing he would turn out to be! The match at London Road ended 1-1.

The problem was, draws were no good to us now - it was WINS that were required!

I drove Gus & Shaun across to Colchester. The match (and our survival hopes) were over by H/T, as Colchester led 3-0. Steve Howard opened his Luton account via the penalty spot to give us some scant respect and it finished 3-1. This was my third and final visit to Layer Road. Colchester would move to a new stadium seven years later.

We played Reading at home next, the first of 4 home matches, knowing only a win would suffice. It finished 1-1. Next up was Stoke. After Lee Mansell gave us an early lead Stoke fluked an equaliser. Kavanagh doubled his scoring soon after although it has to be written, this was a brilliant volleyed effort. Stoke won 2-1 and we were as good as doomed.

Then we played already relegated Oxford. Julian Watts opened the scoring but Oxford equalised near the end. The 6,010 loyal Luton crowd knew it was just a matter of time. This 1-1 draw turned out to be goalkeeper Nathan Abbey's 68th and final LTFC appearance.

On Easter Saturday, it was clear why Luton were about to be relegated when we could only draw 0-0 with Oldham, yet the goal scoring chances nearly ran into double figures.

Two days later, we played at Wrexham and I just did not have the heart for it even though Gus did, taking Kristy. His loyalty wasn't rewarded as the Welsh club won 3-1.

I took Jo and Johnny Clennett for Corporate Hospitality to the Luton v Bury match. The Loyal Luton Supporters' Club sponsored the match and it turned into an 'All Our Yesterdays' booze up - which was far more entertaining than the match! Liam George stumbled the ball into the net to open the scoring, only for Bury to equalise soon after. The Shakers summed up our season when they scored a winner in the last minute.

Three nights later, just 4,854 turned up for the match against Rotherham, yet considering the Millers were on the verge of promotion their following could only be described as pitiful. On the night, we fought like tigers (unlike the previous relegation five years prior against Barnsley) but alas, lost 1-0. Luton were officially relegated to Div 3 (old Div 4) - back to where I had started my wonderful adventures of following LTFC over 34 years prior!

All the lads decided to make a day/night out for the next game at Bristol City. Bob Rumble, Gus, Shaun, Pete Morris, Bean, Pete Newington and I travelled by rail in fine spirits determined to enjoy ourselves, even if we had gone down. We set off early for London and travelled to Bristol with a HUGE carry out.

After finding an excellent pub on the quayside in Bristol where they made us very welcome, we headed for Ashton Gate. I remember as we sat in the away stand we spotted Lee Mansell with his dad and naturally the Lee Mansell chorus went up by seven VERY merry chaps, but we were no hassle to the watching eye of PP the Luton police liaison officer. He knew us all from long ago and as I have previously written we were just beer monsters, never a firm. The match itself was a bit of a blur and we lost 3-1. Liam George's goal turned out to be his 25th and last in a LTFC shirt. On the train back to Paddington we had a ball with the other passengers genuinely enjoying our banter, as we sang merrily along to many old classic Luton tunes. The party carried on in London's West End and I recall meeting Gordon Taylor (PFA boss), before catching the last train back to Luton. My strongest memory of a great day (result apart) was the fact that our kitty had reached - a staggering £1,000!

After that brilliant weekend, I decided not to travel to Brentford on the following Thursday, playing dominoes for SWMC at St Josephs Club instead. I missed a cracker, for this was no end of season stroll. Goalkeeper Mark Ovendale was sent off in the SECOND minute for bringing down a Brentford player in the area.

Teenager Scott Ward came on for his only LTFC appearance and - saved the penalty! Steve Howard opened the scoring from FIFTY yards and Paul McLaren made it 2-0 with his sixth and final goal on his 200th LTFC appearance, before the Bees came back to draw 2-2.

The season ended when Luton drew 1-1 at home to Port Vale.

2000-01 was a disaster, 3 managers during the campaign, our worst points tally since 1963 (if you count 3 pts for a win). NO wins in our final 13 matches (after five in Kinnear's first seven) and not a single team had we had beaten twice, the 1st time in my supporting lifetime. It was so sad, what had started as an exciting new adventure led by a Luton legend, ended in relegation to the bottom league.

Banned

When we travelled up to Kilsyth for Duncan Angus's 40th party in Oct 1999, Bob Rumble proposed to Kath that weekend. She accepted and I was given the honour of being Best Man at their wedding (my 3rd time in this role) and just like the Beatles sang about John & Yoko - they married in Gibraltar, near Spain! They rented out a lovely Villa for a couple of weeks in Fuengirola, near Marbella with all of their families and I joined up with them for a few days around the wedding date of May 30th. (The day before my own 15th wedding anniversary.) I flew out alone, as Deb had a Hen party to attend herself and could not join us. The truth is, she probably wouldn't have come anyway knowing that severe drinking would be involved and there is no doubt, that signs were beginning to show of a strain in our marriage at that time. Deb was spending a lot of her free time at the gym and the continuing fact that I had to either stay out or travel away, whenever I wanted to have a good drink was beginning to take its toll.

Don't get me wrong I loved my family life and adored the girls, yet inside this feeling persisted of thinking I could not be the personality that Deb appeared to want me to be. I AM a football fanatic and I DO like a drink and have always been that person since I was 15, yet for all the wealthy lifestyle we shared I secretly knew that I was not making Deb completely happy. Things would come to a head on our summer break.

In July, the Adairs headed off to Euro Disney in Paris. Trouble struck near the end of the week when having a day off from the park, we decided to take a stroll seeing the sights near our hotel. It was a baking hot day and after a few hours I was getting bored of the walking, shopping, sightseeing and really felt like a beer. Knowing the fuss this would cause I pretended I was not feeling too good and told the girls I was returning to the hotel for a lie down. In truth, I was fine but just fancied a few beers in the sun & went to an Irish Bar near the hotel, where I sat outside chatting to some Irish tourists. Just as I was getting into the swing of things, Deb appeared raging and confronted me in front of everyone, screaming her head off and totally humiliating me. We had a massive row and the holiday was ruined. Looking back - I genuinely believe that this was the straw that had broken the camel's back! I was fed up of living this false life, my home situation would get worse on our return.

In that summer, my work situation would change also as Westway relocated from Wembley to Luton which logistically at least, was handy.

The night before the 2001-02 fixtures were announced I was playing dominoes at the TUC club for SWMC. Gus & Shaun had recently joined our club and now accompanied us on our Thursday domino nights.

We discussed whom we wanted first game and all agreed that Carlisle away would be the perfect choice as we could make it into a Kilsyth weekender. The plan would be to fly to Glasgow, stay in Kilsyth and travel to Brunton Park from there.

When the news came through the next day that it WAS indeed, Carlisle away - Adair Travel flew into action. I booked flights for Gus, Shaun, Pete Morris and myself.

Before that first match, we would attend 3 home pre-season friendly games. There were major changes to the LTFC squad that summer as Joe Kinnear publicly declared, "Only Promotion will suffice, anything else - will be failure!" The exodus included Nathan Abbey, Rocky Baptiste, Stuart Fraser, Petri Helin, Tresor Kandol, Kent Karlsen, Paul McLaren (to Sheff Wed after 8 years and 201 LTFC apps), Lee Nogan, Andre Scarlett, Keith Rowland,

Mark Stein, Peter Thomson, Julian Watts and Adrian Whitbread. All 14 of these players had played a part in 2000-01 but would not be in Kinnear's plans.

He drafted in seven newcomers, Carl Emberson, Adrian Forbes, a £60,000 signing from Norwich, Carl Griffiths, Ian Hillier, Paul Hughes, Russ Perret and his last signing turned out to be the best of all, midfielder Kevin Nicholls, who would turn out to be one of the most popular captain/players in the modern era.

Another addition of extreme importance was legend Mick Harford, as Coach. The friendly results were Luton 1 QPR 0, Luton 1 Norwich 3 and Luton 1 Tottenham 1 (watched by an amazing crowd of 9,175).

The day before flying to Scotland for the Carlisle match I took a day off work to celebrate Georgina's 11th birthday. Although tensions with Deb & I were increasingly growing we tried to make sure it was not in front of the children and we spent a lovely day skiing at the Escape complex in Milton Keynes.

Gus, Shaun, Pete & I flew to Glasgow the next night for a weekend that would lead to a dramatic change in my personal life - beyond belief!

After booking in at Annie's Guest House (too many of us to stay at Jim and Sandra's), we spent the evening in the 39 Masonic Club and met up early next morning there. There was a minibus organised to take us 4 Luton lads and 12 Kilsyth boys to the Carlisle v Luton match, naturally with a big carry out included. We arrived in great spirits, Gus & I were proud that these 12 Rangers fans had made the effort and had come to support the Hatters. Unfortunately, not all of the Luton fans took kindly to our pals being there. It became evident early on that some of the 1,000 plus Hatters had taken exception to Rangers fans being in our section, the fact that they were there with us and SUPPORTING LUTON - flew above their heads! I think word was spreading that these Ger's were there for trouble with Luton fans and some factions of Hatters (those with an affinity to Celtic) were ready to pounce at half time. Obviously, those that knew me knew the score and the fact is these lads were my friends. What pissed Gus & I off the most was that here were lads, coming to support Luton - and getting hassle! Some serious words were spoken at H/T and thankfully, things calmed down a touch. I'm pleased to write that under the watchful eye of PC PP all was OK in the 2nd half. It certainly helped matters when Paul Hughes & Carl Griffiths opened their Luton accounts in our new life in Div 3 (old 4)… and we won 2-0.

Humorously, we had to be a touch aware from BOTH sets of fans after the game, but thankfully got back to the minibus with no further actions needed. While most of the traffic headed out of Carlisle to venture south, we headed north for the town of Lockerbie to watch the live TV Dunfermline v Rangers match. We watched & cheered on Rangers to a 4-1 win.

The next night, events occurred - which would change my life!

In short I met someone in Kilsyth - who I was to have an affair with for over a year!

Space and tact dictates that I cannot go into the full extent of how we met and all the explicit details. I'm afraid you will have to read my first two books for any sordid personal details RE: the affair. In this 3rd book I am going to be more respectful to Deb and my daughters, as much water has flown under the bridge in these last 20 years since it happened.

Obviously, she must remain anonymous and will be coded C for any reference.

Now that Luton had been relegated to the basement division the Police had given permission for the Bobbers Club to re-open on match days for the first time since 1991. We were all delighted to return there, it has always been my favourite pre-match venue and still is today.

We beat Cheltenham 2-1 in the first home game.

The League Cup was now just one-legged and we were drawn away to Reading. I drove to see us thrashed 4-0 by the Div 2 Royals.

On the Saturday the lads headed off to Bristol on the train for a repeat of our great day in April with the same set of boys, this time against Bristol Rovers.

We had another terrific day/night just as before, only there was a little hassle with some Rovers fans after the match. Walking back from the game there was a crowd of them (a lot more of them, than us) clearly looking for trouble but we did not bite. We lost 3-2, with Matt Taylor & Lee Mansell scoring our goals. After another blinding night in London, we missed the last train home & ended up sleeping at St Pancras - with all the tramps! This still raises a laugh today.

Then we beat Southend 2-0 at home thanks to Carl Griffiths & Andrew Fotiatis. The next weekend was brilliant, one to remember forever.

I drove Gus & Shaun down to Exeter early Sat morning for our match at St James' Park. Gus had recently been working down there and had arranged the B&B and pub for us. This was on the day that England were playing in Munich against Germany at the vital World Cup Qualifier. Luton's match would have an early kick-off, to give people a chance to watch the International. After a hearty breakfast we headed to Gus's favourite pub, where they had a stock of 72 bottles of Bud in just for us, as people rarely drank that in this particular pub. Before the end of the night – the 3 of us had drunk the lot!

The match ended 2-2 with Matthew Taylor netting both Luton goals. The night was a dream to behold. Despite me constantly on the phone and text to C, we did have a brilliant night. Exeter and Luton fans united to watch England and we all know the final score was GERMANY 1 ENGLAND 5, the atmosphere in Exeter was electric. We celebrated wildly in the city centre, even with our Luton Town St George's Flag the locals were great.

The week after, our best crowd of 6,736 at that point watched us draw 1-1 with Oxford. Kevin Nicholls scored his first Luton goal.

Three days later, events occurred - which shook and changed the world! 9/11. RIP all the victims.

Luton were playing at York next.

Gus, Shaun & I had bought rail tickets on a special offer price at just £9.50 each, day return. We left Luton station at 6.30am with the carry out and embarked on a trip that became unbelievably memorable. We met some young Barton Luton fans on the train and had a fun trip, teaching them the old 60s/70s favourite Oak Road songs. We arrived at York to head for the Minster pub, just in time for opening.

By the time we had reached the ground after a visit to the Social Club opposite, the 3 of us lads were steaming.

What happened at the match was sheer and utter lunacy - in many more ways than one!

York took the lead and now read this folks. York had made it 2-0 but in our drunken stupor, none of us lads had realised - it had been ruled out for offside! Carl Griffiths scored just before H/T to equalise (but it was 2-1 to York in our eyes remember).

Don't forget it was 2-1 to York as far as we knew. Luton won a penalty and Skelton was going to take it only for Steve Howard to pull rank and take the ball from him. He took it and the keeper saved, but the Ref ordered it to be retaken as the keeper had moved first. Howard stubbornly DEMANDED to take it again and no one argued with the big man, he struck - the keeper saved it AGAIN!

Kinnear was absolutely fuming and he immediately replaced Howard with Ian Hillier. The drama had not stopped. Hillier scored a late peach of a goal to make it 2-2 (remember). When the final whistle blew the Luton fans were going barmy. It was a bit OTT for a draw I thought, but I was OK with a point. When Pete Morris rang to ask how we had played in the win. I said, "What win? – We drew 2-2!" To howls of laughter, us drunkards would not believe we had actually won 2-1! Don't ask - but that night we ended up in Kilsyth, Scotland.

Duncan would kindly let us stay at his place after Babylon's. He wasn't one for nightclubs, so just the three of us went to Kirky and I met C inside the club. We all got a cab back to Kilsyth. C desperately wanted me to be with her for the night but of course we both knew that was impossible. Our next meet up would have to wait a wee while.

We flew home amid the post-9/11 chaos from Glasgow on the Sunday and the queues were horrendous, amid the turmoil of thorough searches etc.

When I finally arrived home late that night Deb had told me that my Dad's cousin Elaine, had been frantically trying to call me to no avail. Her brother Bill Gibson, who my Dad was close to, had sadly died that weekend aged only 60. He was a diabetic and not in the best of health generally, but I was still saddened to hear the news. Like Dad, I was fond of Bill too and I have some good memories of him. RIP BILL.

Two nights later Luton drew 1-1 at home with Lincoln in front of the lowest crowd of 2001-02, just 5,066. Aeron Skelton opened the scoring but recent signing and Australian defender Chris Coyne scored an OG.

LTFC had another signing making his debut against Torquay and what a player he was, possibly the most dramatic debut I have EVER seen from a Hatter.

He was a Frenchman by the name of Jean Lois Valois, a left footed winger signed from Lille and he certainly made an input. No one had heard of him, but we all knew him by the end of this game against the Gulls he absolutely ran the show with a level of skill not seen at Kenilworth Road for years. Steve Howard opened his account for 2001-02 and appeared to be forgiven for the York penalties fiasco. Carl Griffiths made it 2-0 before Kevin Nicholls scored an o g. Griffiths went on to score his hat-trick but despite this, Valois stole the show with a goal of such quality, it was like watching Bruce Rioch all over again. He picked the ball up out on the left, ran past a couple of Torquay players like they were not there and - hit an unstoppable shot from fully-35 yards into the roof of the net!

The place was in meltdown and was easily the best goal of the game in fact I would say the best goal since Scott Oakes against Derby in 1994. We won 5-1 and even taking into account Griffiths treble, the French wonder was the main talking point.

I missed the next 2 games at Leyton Orient and Plymouth.

Gus kept me updated of the proceedings at Orient, explaining another Valois pile driver in a great 3-1 Luton victory. In this match, striker Carl Griffiths, who had started the season in terrific form with 7 goals in ten games, suffered a bad stress fracture to his leg and would miss the remainder of the season.

Joe Kinnear signed a replacement on loan for Griffiths in Dean Crowe, he gave Luton the lead at Home Park alas, Argyle went on to win 2-1.

Around this time my sister Michelle had announced that she was going to migrate to New Zealand early the next year, to join Ann and Mum there.

On the Friday night that week Luton played Darlington at home and I recall seeing cousin Ken Adair in the Bobbers Club pre-match, he had come to see Jean Louis Valois who everyone was raving about. It was 1-1 at h-t Matthew Spring scored our goal. Darlo again took the lead but Luton stormed back in front of 7,219. Steve Howard, Dean Crowe and a Kevin Nicholls penalty had made it 4-2, before another screamer from Jean Louis Valois finished off The Quakers. Ken had now seen for himself this special talent.

I missed the game at Scunthorpe as we were having our annual family Blackpool Lights weekend. This trip was different though.

We could not stay at our usual Claremont Hotel, as it was fully booked. We stayed at a dump called the Doric Hotel and with both Debs sister & parents there too, the tension was unbearable. I selfishly wanted to be elsewhere and I could not wait to return home. On the return journey we stopped off in Loughborough to see Deb's Nanny Helen, who was now in a home near Deb's Aunty Gill. Helen was 90 on that day bless her, but her mind was diminishing and she sadly died on March 1st 2002. I loved old Helen but my selfish personal life was more important to me at that time and I now regret my actions then - at least she was oblivious to what I did! RIP HELEN.

Luton won 2-0 at Scunthorpe while we were in Blackpool and we led the table for the first time.

The next match was a top-of-the-table clash at home to Rochdale and a best so far crowd of 7,696 attended. Rochdale won 1-0, but my abiding memory of that day was shaking hands with the Rochdale player Tony Ford.

From my front row seat I said to him as he came over to collect the ball while play had stopped, "Christ Tony, I HAVE to shake hands with a player - who is older than ME!" Totally unbeknown to myself, the LTFC official photographer Gareth Owen caught the moment and snapped a picture of us shaking hands, which appeared in a future programme.

After this result, Rochdale leap-frogged positions and replaced us at the top. Our next match was three nights later, at The Shay Halifax. I never attended the FA Cup match in 1977, so this would be my first visit (and to date only one). C & I came up with a plan to spend the night together, but deviously I involved Gus. I'm afraid that's all I'm revealing about the plan.

We entered the covered away terracing with a fair number of Hatters fans in the sparse 2,140 crowd. Lowly Halifax took a shock early lead then Dean Crowe struck twice to see us 2-1 up at h-t. We were making very hard work of it and it was no shock when the Shay men equalised. Fortunately, late goals from Kevin Nicholls & Adrian Forbes saved our bacon as we won 4-2.

After the Halifax victory we thrashed Swansea 3-0 at home with goals from Crowe, Perrett and Forbes.

Deb had by now found out about C and I decided to keep a low profile that week and not attend the next match at Mansfield. It was a good job too, as we were thrashed 4-1 by the Stags. Of the 5,973, nearly half were from Luton and Gus told me there were crowd problems that day. The Nottinghamshire Police were out in force (possibly after the problems with Hatters fans at Notts County two years earlier) and restricted Luton fans movements in Mansfield confining lots of them to a pub and escorting them straight out of Town post-match.

Due to England v Sweden, Luton played Shrewsbury at home on the eve of it. In a really tight affair it appeared to be heading for stalemate until Matthew Spring smashed home the only goal.

All of the lads had a prearranged trip to Kilsyth the next weekend to see Rangers v Dunfermline, while Luton lost 3-2 at Southend in the FA Cup. Bean, Gus, Shaun, Pete Morris, Pete Newington and I travelled. Rangers won 4-0.

During that week Luton played Hull at home.

The Tigers were up there with us challenging for promotion and they won 1-0. Because of my personal turmoil and strife and with a Rangers European trip looming I decided to miss the Macclesfield away game and I'm glad I did. The lowly Silk men heavily beat us 4-1.

The following weekend was blank because of our FA Cup exit.

A couple of days before that on 29th November, I heard very sad news on the radio, of the death of George Harrison from Cancer aged only 58. He was the youngest member of The Beatles and now 2 of my 4 musical heroes had passed away at an early age. RIP GEORGE.

I was preparing for my third trip abroad with Rangers to Paris. We flew out on Wed for the Thursday game and would return late Friday.

I went to stay at Gus's house in Maulden and Bob Rumble picked us up in the early hours to drive us to Stansted Airport. After the 3 days (in which Rangers had beaten PSG on pens) our Scots friends flew back from Paris to Glasgow and us to Stansted.

I watched Dean Crowe score the only goal at home to Rushden & D and this was followed by another home match versus Hartlepool.

Steve Howard scored, Hartlepool hit back to lead 2-1 before Marvin Johnson came on as sub and earned a point to draw 2-2. This was marvellous Marv's 10th and final goal for LTFC in a brilliant career. He would appear 11 more times before retiring in 2002 with a fantastic 439 outings for Luton - only six players have appeared more times in LTFC history!

At this halfway stage Luton were in 2nd place.

On Xmas Eve, Gus and his daughter joined us for the family Xmas Disco at the Bull Pub in Barton.

On Boxing Day morning, Shaun drove Gus & I to see Luton at Oxford's new Kassam Stadium.

We won 2-1 at Oxford with a huge Hatters following of over 2,000 in the 11,121 there. After falling behind we responded with goals from Dean Crowe and Matthew Spring.

I wanted to go to Southend for the last game of 2001 and felt it best to take Deb & the girls for a day at the seaside. They shopped after we visited the funfair and I watched Luton win 2-1. Once again we came from behind with goals this time from Crowe and Matt Taylor.

I drove Gus up to Kidderminster (new ground for me) for a mid-week game. The game sprang into life when we fell 1-0 behind. Soon after, Matthew Taylor equalised at the end where all of us Hatters were congregated. Of the 4,147 I would say over a quarter there were Luton fans. It was 2-1 when Matthew Spring pounced following a howler from the Kiddy keeper, two further goals from Steve Howard & Matt Spring again, made it 4-1 and game over.

Four days later I took Deb and the girls to Cheltenham to try and forget our problems, at least for a day. We drew 1-1 with Steve Howard netting, following a stunning Cheltenham goal. Totally unbeknown then - this would be the last time I watched Luton away for over 2 years!

The following Saturday we drew 1-1 again at home to Carlisle, this time Russ Perrett heading our leveller. I missed our 3-2 defeat at Darlington.

The following Friday night was my sister Michelle's leaving party in Brighton where she had lived for 20+ years. We all turned out in force and a lot of my mates joined the Adairs at a B&B on the seafront. Other relations also there, were 2nd cousin Elaine and husband Max, along with my Auntie Joan, Mick and their three youngsters. Gus, Shaun, Bean, Pete Morris and Pete Newington all stayed as well and we had a fabulous evening to see Michelle off in style, before leaving for New Zealand in the March.

After breakfast we headed back to Luton and then watched the eagerly awaited top-of-the-table clash at home to Plymouth.

Argyle, were top and we were 2nd and the match was a sell out. Before the game there was a lot of trouble in the town centre between the two rival hooligan gangs. Evidently, it was the most arrests and problems since 1985.

The crowd of 9,585 was the highest in the league since Wolves in 1995.

It was obvious from the start that the Pilgrims had come for a draw and they continued to frustrate us all until the 80th minute, when suddenly Matthew Taylor was brought down for a penalty. Kevin Nicholls scored it, to huge Luton roars and when Steve Howard headed a second, we erupted with joy.

Another new ground was to be ticked off my list the next week at Rochdale - or so I thought!

On the early morning of the Rochdale match Gus, Shaun, Pete Newington & I had booked a day return by train from Milton Keynes to Manchester. Duncan from Kilsyth would meet us, having been working near Rochdale all week. We left MK at about 6.30am with a huge carry out, which we had drank by the time he met us. Duncan drove us to Rochdale and after dropping off his car at the hotel he was staying at we headed for the Church pub near Rochdale's ground. The 4 of us were scheduled to get the last train back to MK that night.

All of us were in top form, singing and in great spirits as had been the case at many away games that season, we all had a very good drink in us.

Pete Newington & I headed for the ground with the others following behind shortly after. When we arrived at the turnstiles a police officer said, "You are not going in, you've had too much to drink."

I replied, "What? Are you having a laugh? I have not done anything wrong."

He then explained, "I am arresting you for being drunk, trying to enter a Sports ground." - I never knew such a law even existed and Pete was also arrested on the same charge!

Now I am not going to write here and now that I was sober BUT all I had done wrong, was what thousands of I and other football fans throughout England, had been doing - for DONKEYS' YEARS!

Duncan, having seen what was occurring suggested to a police officer, "If you were to arrest someone in Scotland for having a good drink before the game - you would have to charge most of the population!" Gus immediately realised that Duncan might be joining us & quickly removed him out of the way before events became worse.

On arrival at the police station I tried to explain that if they could just please have a word with the Luton Police liaison officer PP.

He would realise the situation was a misunderstanding and assist us with our release, then just escort us either back to the pub or train station, without attending the game – NO CHANCE!

Because of the problems caused at the Plymouth match the week previous and the fact that Luton were bringing at least 1,000 fans (a big away turn out for Rochdale) the GMP flooded the area with officers from all around the region.

When it was obvious that there would be no trouble, they needed arrests to justify the amount of resources spent. Not for the first OR last time in my life - it would be a case of wrong time, wrong place!

We were both charged and they asked us what time our train home was.

I replied 9pm - they let us out of our cells at 9.05! Knowing we would be stuck. We had to return for trial at Rochdale Magistrates Court during the week.

Duncan let us crash out in his hotel room and when I tried to explain to Deb, she frankly refused to believe me and said that I was with C. It was only when Duncan & Pete spoke to her telling the truth, that she began to believe.

Duncan told me in no uncertain terms, to sort myself out - or else I would end up losing EVERYTHING in my life!

The train journey back next day (at more expense) was a long one and when Deb collected us, the car journey home was in silence. Oh - Luton lost 1-0!

On the Monday morning I rang PP for advice and asked him why he did not check to see if there were any arrests from Luton (HIS JOB). He told us to put a suit on in court, say we were extremely sorry and as an Executive LTFC Member with 2 daughters who are Junior Hatters, to say this was completely out of character and plead Guilty. "You will probably get a fine and a warning," he added.

I did exactly what he advised in court and nearly collapsed when the Magistrate gave his verdict – "You have pleaded Guilty and will now receive a Banning Order for THREE YEARS!"

It was explained that this meant I would be banned from attending any professional football match in England and Wales. Also, when England played abroad I would have to surrender my passport until they had returned home. – FUCKING HELL I was distraught! I would have preferred a £5,000 or £10,000 fine. Pete received exactly the same punishment and there was no appeal, until at least two thirds of the sentence. We were both flabbergasted to say the least, but also extremely angry. We would have both been better off being charged with Drunk & Disorderly, but because it was football related the punishment was draconian.

Even Deb felt sorry for me when I arrived back, she knew how much this would devastate me.

The first game after the ban was at home to Scunthorpe, we lost 3-2 and there was actually a tiny part of me that was glad at this result, such was the injustice.

When I spoke to Pete Newington next he felt exactly the same.

There was one saving grace for me personally regarding the Banning Order, the rule only applied to England & Wales plus travelling abroad to see England or English Clubs, after consultation with PP (and also thanking him for all his support to try and get me out of this nightmare NOT), the ban did not apply to Scotland. I was free to attend Rangers matches.

Without that, I honestly think I might have gone under.

This resulted in me spending the next few years devoting my time and support to Rangers, but of course I still wanted the Town to win and get promotion.

After the Scunthorpe defeat we thrashed Bristol Rovers 3-0 at home.

Naturally, my ban meant I spent a lot more time at home and despite knowing I wanted out and the house was sold, Deb was making a real effort to try and save our marriage. My drinking was suddenly not an issue at all anymore and I was allowed back into the bedroom, where our sex life had dramatically improved.

She also insisted on joining my next couple of Rangers trips (without attending matches of course, some things were TOO much to ask for).

In the UEFA Cup, Rangers had been drawn against Dutch side Feyenoord with the 1st leg at Ibrox. I booked flights and hotel for the 2nd leg preferring to base ourselves in Amsterdam, rather than Rotterdam.

Two days later, Luton came from 1-0 down to beat York 2-1 at home. On the night before the Holland trip Luton won 1-0 at Lincoln.

A whole crowd of us travelled to Amsterdam, including Deb. Rangers lost 3-2 (4-3 on aggregate). Despite us getting back very late on the Friday night, Gus drove all the way to Torquay early the next morning to see Luton win 1-0.

Three nights later against Orient at Kenilworth Road, we won 3-0. This victory was our 5th in a row and it became 6 four days later when we beat R&D 2-1 at Nene Park. Exeter were then dispatched 3-0 at home.

The following weekend I had booked a trip to Glasgow for Deb & I at the exclusive 5-Star Hilton Hotel. We were in Glasgow for the League Cup Final on the Sunday between Ayr and Rangers.

Unbeknown to ANYONE else I was still in daily contact with C and she told me that her husband had heard through the Kilsyth grapevine, that I was coming up to Scotland for the first time (or so he thought) since all hell let loose.

She told me he was threatening all sorts of things, like meeting me at the airport on arrival and had already put the word out to my circle of friends - that I was unofficially banned from entering Kilsyth! Evidently, when he found out I was coming up with my wife and staying in Glasgow, he decided to leave alone out of respect for Deb. C was kept virtual prisoner in the house ALL weekend - watching her every movement!

Gus & Shaun flew up after Luton had beaten Kidderminster 1-0 at home on the Saturday night and stayed in Kilsyth. Rangers won the League Cup easily 4-0. The day after we returned home Deb's Nanny Helen died, naturally I was sad at her passing anyway but the hurt in Deb's eyes and the extra grief I was putting her through - haunted me!

The next weekend I spent the day in the Bobbers Club as Luton played bottom side

Halifax. I have to write it was pretty tough when the lads and other fans left for the game, you could see in their faces that they were feeling for me. We hammered the Shaymen 5-0 to equal the LTFC record of 9 successive league victories. When the lads returned to the Bobbers post-match I took some more stick - they all agreed that this fantastic run was all down to my ban!

I felt bad enough that day but was even worse the next week, as Luton gained promotion at Swansea. The Hatters travelled to Vetch Field with an army of fans, knowing that a victory would secure promotion. Gus kept me informed with events but equally knew how gutted I was feeling at missing out, as we created history by winning 10 games in a row in the 3-1 win.

On Easter Monday, the Adair family went to London on the train for the day and took in the new London Eye attraction.

Once again Gus was updating me at the Luton v Mansfield game and what a cracker of a match it sounded. We fell behind to an early goal, before Jean Lois Valois levelled which sadly turned out to be his 6th and final Hatters goal. The result was Luton 5 Mansfield 3.

When we arrived back at Luton station I asked Deb if she would mind if I went to the White House to join Gus & Shaun and share in the celebrations. Naturally, she agreed and when I arrived many folk were delighted to see me. There was a bit of tension inside because a Mansfield firm were up the road being held back by police, trying to attack their rival fans at the pub entrance. If they had seen the sheer numbers and who was actually inside the White House - I think they would have dramatically thought twice!

The next week at Hull, we convincingly made it 12 in a row by thrashing the Tigers 4-0 to finally put Luton top of the table, although Plymouth had a game in hand. Obviously I would have been there had I been allowed and because Hull moved to a new ground the next year, I never once went to Boothferry Park.

The magnificent run surprisingly came to an end in our penultimate game at home to Macclesfield when we could only draw 0-0.

Plymouth won the league two nights later.

In the final match, over 2,000 Hatters travelled to Gay Meadow, Shrewsbury.

Gus & Shaun made it a weekender and were rewarded with a 2-0 Luton win. Steve Howard scored and had struck a brilliant 24 times for LTFC in 2001-02. It had been an incredible and emotional season for both Luton and myself.

All sorts of records were achieved in 2001-02 for LTFC. Highest League wins: 30 - Highest Away wins: 15 - Highest Away goals: 46 - Highest Points: 97 and of course the highest sequence of successive wins: 12.

Despite all of these brilliant achievements, we still could not be Champions and finished 2nd trailing Plymouth by 5 points. For this, credit must be given to Argyle - any other season we would have romped home with the title!

Mansfield joined us automatically, along with Cheltenham via the Play-Offs. Unbeknown to anyone in Scotland I flew up to Glasgow for the Old Firm Scots Cup Final, but by not telling anyone I was travelling meant I had NO chance of securing a ticket. I watched a fantastic 3-2 Rangers victory, with a last minute Gers winner at Memories Bar in Partick.

We had booked our summer holiday to Disneyworld in Florida again the previous summer, before my dramatic life change. It was a really weird situation, in that we would travel in June and on our return I would move into my new house and Deb would move into hers, as the house move would complete. I had purchased a new townhouse on the old British Gas site, off Dallow Road in Luton. It was a nice house, although not in one of the town's best locations. Deb had purchased a house in Stopsley almost opposite her sister Liz, whose marriage to Thom had sadly failed with him returning to USA. Prior to the World Cup I had to gain special written permission to travel to Florida, proving that I was on a family holiday and not going to the World Cup in Japan & Korea, in line with the Banning Order criteria. We left for Florida and bearing in mind we knew that on our return Deb & I would be parting, we were both determined to make the holiday as civil as possible for the sake of the girls. We did just that and once again stayed in Disney, this time at Dixie Landings Hotel Resort. We still had a nice time and after flying home I was about to begin a new chapter in my life - or so I thought!

Town great Kirk 'Basher' Stephens and I. He only scored two Hatters goals in 248 LTFC apps. I saw them both. One at Bolton last game of 1980-81 when we won 3-0 and of course the late only goal Boxing Day 1979 winner at Watford. He might have mentioned it on the odd occasion since lol. He brought my 2nd book in 2013.

2002-03

It was all change in the life of Alan Adair in the summer. I moved into my new house in Dunraven Avenue immediately after returning from Florida in early July and Deb moved into hers. One severe heavy price I had to suffer for the family break up was Georgina's relationship with myself. She was coming up to 12 years old and took the split badly, to the point that when I moved out she point blank refused to have anything to do with me, refusing to take my calls or visit. I had broken her little heart and she decided that she would stay fiercely loyal to Deb. It broke my heart too. Mollie on the other hand, had recently turned 8 and absolutely loved coming to stay at mine every fortnight.

She loved my new house and the fuss I made of her and thankfully, showed no signs of upset whatsoever.

On the football front, my first game was a friendly in Belfast between Linfield and Rangers. Linfield are the Belfast equivalent of the Gers. 99.9% of their support comes from the Loyalist Protestant community. This was my first visit to Ulster and Rangers won 2-0.

Obviously, being banned from watching Luton meant that I travelled many times in 2002-03 to see Rangers play. My first league game was at home to Dundee. Rangers won 3-0.

On the LTFC front there were a number of comings and goings. The saddest exit was when Jean Lois Valois had a bust up with Joe Kinnear and left us to sign for Hearts. He scored 6 goals in 34 LTFC appearances but what an impact he made on Hatters fans in his short stay. Marvin Johnson also said farewell as a player after hanging up his boots. Marvellous Marv was a credit to the club.

Premiership club Portsmouth signed highly rated Matthew Taylor. He scored 17 goals in 146 games.

We signed three players. One of them, Robbie Winters, played just 45 minutes.

Alan Kimble played in only 13 games but one very successful signing was Ulsterman Steve Robinson, a midfielder signed from Preston who would play for LTFC for over six years. One of Joe Kinnear's best signings was when he brought Sol Davis, a defender from Swindon. Sol would go on to achieve cult status with us fans.

While I was at Ibrox watching Rangers beat Dundee, Luton kicked off with a disappointing 3-2 home loss against Peterborough, our first since February.

On the Tuesday night Duncan from Kilsyth met Gus in Blackpool for the match at Bloomfield Road. We were heavily beaten 5-2.

After Blackpool another long trip, involved Luton travelling to Plymouth and left there pointless following a 2-1 loss. The poor start continued with a 3-2 home defeat at the hands of Barnsley, the league table looked dire - played 4 and lost 4! That day I watched Rangers beat Aberdeen 2-0.

I arrived home on the Bank Holiday Monday and that day Luton secured the first point of the season by drawing 0-0 at Cardiff.

The following week saw Luton's first win when we beat Chesterfield 3-0 at home.

I came to a conclusion, was Deb and my marriage THAT bad? No it wasn't and then plucked up the courage to ring Deb and ask for forgiveness. I know it was selfish, but why should I lose EVERYTHING? I pleaded with Deb for another chance to see if we could try again. Fortunately, Deb was receptive to the idea and said, "I was wondering how long this would take and hoping for this moment for the last 6 months." We both agreed not to rush things, to take things steady by dating each other again, like a courting couple. It was not as though I hated being with Deb, the truth is, had Deb been like she was in 2002 rather than prior to then - I would never had strayed anyway!

The next weekend Luton drew 0-0 at Brentford and then three nights later I watched Sky Sports News in disbelief.

In the League Cup 1st round Luton had been drawn to play at hated rivals Watford. This was the first derby clash in over 4 years. The TV screens showed live pictures of Luton fans battling with their Watford counterparts - ON THE PITCH! This was indeed a rare occurrence and I had not seen scenes like this since the 70s and 80s. On top of that, there had been major trouble in a Watford town centre pub where Luton MIGS had ambushed their rivals in a pub.

As a result of all the fighting 29 Fans were prosecuted (4 from Watford) and most were given jail sentences and seven year Banning Orders, with the Luton fans receiving life bans at Kenilworth Road too. There is no doubt it caught the eye of the nation and on my next trip to Glasgow I was inundated with questions about the Luton v Watford rivalry.

On the pitch, it finally got underway after 15 mins' delay and the 5,000 Hatters fans were in ecstasy when we beat the Horns 2-1. The bragging rights were ours. This result really helped in some way to make up for the calamity in 1997 - it's just a travesty that I was not allowed to be there to witness it!

Following the Watford riots, we had to battle back from 2-0 down in the home match with Notts County to earn a point.

My next match was for the UEFA Cup in Prague. Rangers had drawn a team I had never even heard of called Viktoria Zizkov and we lost 2-0 in this 1st Leg as well as missing a penalty, before winning 3-1 in the 2nd but went out on the away goals rule. The night we were in Prague, Luton lost 3-2 at home to Mansfield.

I then flew up on the Saturday morning to see Rangers beat Partick 3-0 with Pete Fowler, a Bobbers Club mate. I had recently spent a lot more time in the Bobbers Club due to where I was now living and the Fowler family in there had become really good friends. I had known Graham for years and was now also friends with his brother Pete & Graham's girlfriend Alyson, along with son Pete and father Harry. Graham's brother Pete is a Liverpool fan but also likes Rangers and he jumped at the chance when I invited him up to see Rangers play the Jags.

When Rangers were beating the Jags, Luton had a good 1-0 win at Huddersfield. This first Luton win at the McAlpine Stadium had lifted us out of the relegation zone for the first time.

The next weekend it was a 3-0 home victory over Swindon.

Then, over 5,000 Hatters fans travelled to Villa Park for the League Cup tie with the Brummies.

The class of opposition showed, as Aston Villa easily beat us 3-0 in a game I was obviously banned from attending.

On the Saturday Luton won the 3rd successive league game 3-2 at Stockport. It became 4 in a row by coming from behind at home to beat Cheltenham 2-1.

Against Oldham at Boundary Park the following week we won 2-1. This win was the first in the league there since 1977.

That day I watched Rangers beat Motherwell 3-0 at Ibrox. Great though that result was, the highlight of my day occurred earlier at the Hilton Hotel.

I took Deb and the girls altogether for the first time, both Georgina & Mollie loved this exclusive place equally. In the morning after Breakfast before setting off to join Duncan and the Kilsyth lads, I happened to stroll past the lobby in my Rangers colours when a loud voice commented, "Oh, I see the fancy dress is in toon."

Completely unbeknown to who said this, I turned round and replied in a mocking sarcastic tone, "What, are you some sort of fucking Comedian?" before I realised it was the legend BILLY CONNELLY – Purple Goatee beard too! He actually found my comment amusing and said that he loved my witty reply, before beckoning me over for a chat. Not only did we chat away about all things football (after the normal 'What's an Englishman doing supporting Rangers?' question) - he then brought us both the biggest ever cigar I had seen in my life! It lasted me all day, as I proudly told all concerned where it had come from.

It was while watching a Video with the Stopsley lads one Sunday afternoon in my bachelor flat back in 1984 that I became a massive Billy Connelly fan. The tape was called 'Billy Bites Yer Bum' - him on tour in the early 80s. I had to keep pausing the remote control as we ALL howled with pain - splitting laughter. I remain a big fan today but regrettably, have yet to see him perform.

The following week, leaders Wigan came to Kenilworth Road and drew 1-1. Three days later at Crewe we won 1-0.

Luton were then thumped 3-0 at Northampton, our first away defeat in 8.

The following week Luton drew 0-0 at home to Port Vale and then played non- league Guisley in the FA Cup 1st round, once again at Kenilworth Road. We saw off the Yorkshire/Humbersider's 4-0.

In the third successive home match, against QPR, we did well to hold them to 0-0 despite having both Steve Howard & Kevin Nicholls sent off in front of the largest home crowd of 2002-03, a near sell-out - 9,477.

In Merseyside Luton then had a great 3-1 victory at Tranmere.

Gus & I flew up to Glasgow mid-week for the league game at home to Livingston, in which Rangers won 4-3 after being 4-0 ahead. I went straight to work on the Thursday and incredibly - was back in Glasgow the NEXT night!

I had already pre-booked lots of flights ages before and this time, was up for the first Old Firm game at Ibrox that season in which Rangers won 3-2.

Alone this time, as Gus had travelled to the JJB Stadium for Luton's 2nd Round FA Cup exit at Wigan, where we lost 3-0.

Luton's next game was a 2-1 loss to Colchester in front of 5,890 the lowest home attendance of 2002-03. Andrew Fotiatis scored his 19th & final LTFC goal. He would only appear twice more in Luton colours. Despite playing his first Hatters game over six years earlier, injury curtailed his career. He made 146 LTFC appearances before trying his luck at Peterborough, to no avail. I liked Fotti and thought he had tremendous skill, but was out injured too often.

Four days before Xmas we drew 1-1 at Bristol City.

I was getting on fine now with Deb again and our relationship was back on track. I spent Xmas at her house with my family as one again and it was wonderful.

After Xmas, Deb would sell her house and they all would move into mine. On Boxing Day Luton beat high-flying Cardiff 2-0 at home.

At this halfway point we were in 6th place, the apex we would achieve in 02-03. Good - when you consider we lost the first four games! We ended 2002 by winning 2-1 at Wycombe.

Deb's parents Julie & Alan, kindly agreed to have our girls while Deb and I flew to Glasgow on New Year's Day. We tried to book The Hilton but it was full, so we booked the Grosvenor Hilton in the West End of Glasgow. Although not quite so plush, it was never the less still lovely. Staying there at that time was Highland League side Deveronvale, who were scheduled to play at Greenock Morton in the Scots Cup while we were up for the Rangers v Dundee match. Deb actually joined me for this match, along with Gus & Shaun who were both in Kilsyth for Hogmanay. Rangers won 3-1. The Deveronvale Cup match was called off due to a frozen pitch. Both Deb and I really enjoyed their company as we socialised freely with the players, directors and officials alike. I still look out for their results today. Our stay was enjoyable and a great start to 2003.

Whilst in Glasgow, Luton had lost 2-1 at Chesterfield.

Because of the turmoil involving C, we didn't having a skiing holiday in 2002. Now that things were OK with Deb and I again, we booked our winter holiday and travelled to Borovets, in Bulgaria. The hotel was called Rila and was sited right at the foot of one of the many ski slopes, in an ideal location. I could honestly write that at this point in time, my skiing ability was reasonable - but by the end of the holiday I was skiing down Black runs! (the most difficult).

Our holiday was interesting, to write the least.

The Hotel was large, comfortable and had an indoor swimming pool. I liked it - but the local mafia used it as a brothel for their prostitutes! In fact, the Brit teenagers had sussed what was occurring - and were counting on how long the hookers were taking upstairs with their clients! We had an eventful week too. On the 2nd day, Georgina whilst learning to Snowboard, fell and had to see the local doctor at the hotel. He and Deb drove her to the hospital, where she was diagnosed with a broken wrist. Incredibly, after a day or so she was allowed to ski but not to snowboard.

While Deb was getting Georgina checked out with the doctor to see if he would allow her to return to the slopes, he said to Deb, "I have to leave, as someone has called me to an incident outside." – THAT INCIDENT WAS MOLLIE!

I was taking Mollie to the slopes carrying all our skis etc., when I slipped on the ice and fell right on top of her. The doctor came out and carried her back to his office, with Deb by now - nearly having a cardiac arrest! Thankfully, I didn't break any of Mollie's bones, she just had a sore back but unfortunately her skiing was over for the duration. She had a wheelchair and absolutely gloated in all the fuss and attention she was receiving from everybody - almost to the point that I think she was actually glad that I fell on her! Despite everything, we still had a fantastic time.

The locals were all British football fans and I managed to hear Luton had won 3-2 at Barnsley. We enjoyed Bulgaria so much (accidents apart) and would return the following year. On our return home, Luton beat Wycombe 1-0 and then drew 1-1 at Peterborough.

Gus & I flew up once again to Glasgow in a repeat of the mid-week EasyJet sales like in December, this time electing a League Cup Semi Final at Hampden Park, for the Hearts v Rangers match. Rangers won 1-0.

Luton had a good 2-1 win at Port Vale, before losing 3-1 at home to Blackpool. Graham Fowler from the Bobbers Club and his girlfriend Alyson, along with his brother Pete, then flew up with Deb & I for the weekend in Glasgow to watch the Hearts league match at Ibrox, in which Rangers beat them 1-0 again. While we were in Glasgow Luton beat Northampton at home 3-2.

The following week, visitors Brentford left with all 3 points having won 1-0. Three nights later at the same venue it was 1-0 again against Plymouth, only this time in our favour.

Now that Deb and the girls had moved back in with me, I would curtail on some of the Rangers trips - well at least alone anyway!

At Meadow Lane, Notts County the Magpies won 2-1. Then at nearby Field Mill, Mansfield, Luton lost again by 3-2.

On home turf, Luton then easily beat Huddersfield 3-0. We then gained a very good point in a 1-1 draw at runaway leaders Wigan.

The Adair family stayed at the Hilton once again that weekend, as we were up in Glasgow for the Old Firm League Cup Final. I'm delighted to write, Rangers lifted the Cup by winning 2-1. I also ticked off a new ground the day before at Firhill, attending Partick 0 Hibs 1.

The night after we returned, Luton drew 0-0 at home to Oldham.

We then suffered a home tanking at the hands of Crewe. Any remote hopes of reaching the play offs ended after this game - Crewe won 4-0!

They were most definitely over after the next match, a 0-0 home draw with Tranmere.

Three nights later, another draw occurred at Cheltenham 2-2.

In front of the largest league attendance of the season - 15,786, the Town then went down 2-0 at QPR.

It was Easter the next weekend and we were all back at the Hilton once again for another Hampden Park occasion, this time the Scots Cup Semi Final Motherwell v Rangers. The Gers won 4-3.

Gus was staying in Kilsyth for Easter and he was now coming up to Scotland almost as much as myself. That weekend in the Hilton I met a Geordie character in the bar by the name of Pete Bramer and his wife Sarah. I got on brilliant with him.

We flew home on Easter Monday and that day Luton were playing at Colchester. Gus was still in Kilsyth and told me to update him while he was on a session in the 39 Masonic Club. I rang him at H/T to tell him the score – Colchester 0 Luton 4! Carl Griffiths, after a long lay off, scored his 8th and final LTFC goal in his short injury-ravished career with us. There was one more goal in the 2nd half when Steve Howard completed his hat-trick. This 5-0 away win was the best LTFC away win in the league since 1967 when we won by the same score at Exeter.

The following weekend Gus & I were back AGAIN, for the home Old Firm match. He was in Kilsyth and I in the Travelodge in Glasgow.

Usually, I would get tickets for any Rangers game but Old Firm briefs were harder to locate, this time I had to watch our 2-1 loss on TV in a Glasgow pub. In the final home game of Luton's season, we drew 1-1 with Stockport. The 46th and final match was at Swindon, where we lost 2-1.

Luton finished in 9th position. Considering that we had lost the first four matches, it was a satisfactory season after our promotion. One interesting fact was that we had won more away games in the league than home. The ratio was 9 to 8. This occurrence had only happened once previously in my support of Luton, when back in 1972-73, the ratio was 9 to 6. Very bizarrely, these two seasons in question had happened when I had not seen a single game.

In 1972-73 I was living in Australia and in 2002-03 - I was banned!

The Scottish season was now reaching a thrilling climax. With one match each remaining for both Celtic and Rangers, the two teams were level on 94 points, level on goal difference - but we had scored ONE more goal than them 95-94! This meant that the title would be decided on the last day, for the first time in 12 years. The final matches were Rangers v Dunfermline and Kilmarnock v Celtic.

Hell on Earth would not stop me from attending this last encounter and so the Adair family booked the Hilton once again for the weekend.

To cut a long story short, Celtic won 4-0 (missing a penalty) at Kilmarnock and we beat Dunfermline 6-1 to win the SPL by just 2 goals. The atmosphere at Ibrox Park that day was simply the best – an experience I have yet to equal!

It was a joy to behold and I was there, to witness probably the most exiting climax in Scottish football history. The season had still not finished quite yet and I was back in Glasgow the next weekend with Graham and Alyson. We were up for the Scottish Cup Final - Rangers v Dundee, in which Rangers won 1-0 to complete a fantastic treble. This finished a brilliant campaign in Rangers long illustrious history. I attended 16 of those games (17, including the Celtic match I failed to get a ticket for).

Administration – Part Two

Throughout the summer of 2003 various issues occurred which would have a big bearing on my personal life, where I was living, working and indeed, LTFC. Georgina and Mollie were nearing the end of their relevant schools in Barton. In Georgina's case she was due to finish at Arnold Middle School, to begin at Harlington Upper School in September. Mollie was ending her time at Ramsey Manor Lower and was due to start at Georgina's old school. We had been informed that if the girls both wanted to join their new schools, they would have to live in the catchment area by Sept 1st, or permission would be refused.

Clearly, Dunraven Avenue in Luton was not in that catchment. It therefore became imperative that we had to move back to Barton-le-Clay, as a matter of urgency. Both schools were excellent and there was no way in hell I would send my girls to the nearby Luton ones (Mollie's equivalent was 94% Asian attended). I am not a racist, but sorry - that was not on!

We sold my house to a man that would lease it out and although we had to drop more than I would have liked, we still yielded a small profit (as did Deb from her house sale). In August we moved to Smithcombe Close, on the same Grange Road Estate as our previous house in Barton. This more modest 3 - Bed Semi was nowhere near as elaborate as the old house but such is life, we were just relieved to return for the girls' new schools.

Deb & I were fine again now and this was a chance for a new beginning.

Work had become a problem in 2003 though. I always regretted leaving CBC but it was impossible to return there, as they had closed down within a year of my exit. The first year at Westway was OK while they were at Wembley and they then relocated to a huge plant in Luton in 2001. Logistically, this was good news for myself but when they moved they brought in a new guy to oversee all aspects of the business. Sales, Production, Marketing, the Factory, was now under his domain and it was blatantly obvious from day one, that he was utterly ruthless. Things would be done his way and his way ONLY. He didn't like the way I worked, which was and always will be, to give my clients the best possible personal service. This included picking up jobs, delivering Proofs to them personally and delivering their file copies on completion of the job. His philosophy was that I was wasting fuel, time and therefore money by working in this way, he wanted Sales people to stay in the office citing that computers etc proved there was no need for going out to visit clients, everything in his mind was achievable by not leaving the office. I totally disagreed and told him that my personal attention to detail of SEEING AND TALKING IN PERSON with clients, had not done me any harm in the past and my track record in Sales over the past 13 years had proved this to be correct. We clashed over this and in time, he made things very difficult for me. It became personal, when he made me take a 3k a year basic pay cut at the beginning of 2003 citing that I was under target (only just).

But the final straw happened when he took my biggest client away and turned it into a house account. This decision had left me with no choice, he KNEW that I would have difficulty replacing a top client like BMB and a few months down the line, would have grounds to sack me for under – achieving. I wouldn't give him that satisfaction and began seeking a new job and found one almost immediately, called GPR Printing in Hitchin.

GPR in comparison was like chalk and cheese in terms of size etc. There were only a total of 12 people employed there, compared to ten times that number at Westway.

It was with a great deal of pleasure and I might add, dignity and professionalism that I gave in my notice. Upon leaving, I told him that every firm I had worked for in the past - had ceased trading after I had left! He replied there was no chance of that occurring. 'Never say Never' was my smiling response – within 4 years I had been proven correct and they closed down!

At the interview with Geoff at GPR, I had to tell one small white lie. He asked if I was a football fan and I explained that I was a Luton Town fanatic and being half Scottish, also followed Rangers. He explained, there were three members of staff including himself that were LTFC Season Ticket Holders and asked where I sat. It would not have gone down too well had I told him that actually - I am currently a third of the way into a 3-year Banning Order. I told him the D Block Enclosure and came clean later.

There was also unbelievable drama at Kenilworth Road in the summer of 2003. Within weeks of the old season ending, farcical scenes occurred. In May, LTFC owner Mike Watson-Challis who had been in charge for four years, announced he was selling up to an unnamed consortium. He wasn't getting any younger and had invested very heavily to help save the club and had decided it was time to step down. There was concern that the new owners had not revealed themselves and then utter despair and equal rage, when it was announced that Joe Kinnear and assistant Mick Harford - had been SACKED!

Totally understandably, this resulted in fury from the fans and they angrily protested outside the gates (I would have joined them, had I been allowed to). The two interim spokesmen for the unnamed new owners soon realised the severity of the protest - and rapidly quit! It was announced that the front man was John Gurney. I had never heard of him but it quickly became knowledge that he was a man with a past of sports ownership that lets allegedly write, was not the best.

Among his absurd announcements, were changing our name to London-Luton, building a SEVENTY THOUSAND seated new stadium, which included a Grand Prix Racing Circuit and this, with an underground Car Park to hold TWENTY THOUSAND vehicles. It became even worse when he said that we would be as big as Man Utd and Real Madrid & have various sports clubs like Gridiron, Baseball and Ice Hockey. We rapidly became the laughing stock of the football world.

There was an underground movement set up within days of his ramblings, when over 3,000 fans pledged their support to the newly formed TIL, Trust In Luton.

The first aim was to starve the club (him) of any money and refuse to renew season tickets.

His next crazy plan was to announce that fans would VOTE for the next manager. Of course no one voted and he announced that the man he wanted in charge, was our new manager ex-Luton player, Mike Newell.

It was quickly decided, that there was only one single way to get rid of Gurney. TIL helped secure a deal that would put LTFC in Administration for the 2nd time in four years only this time of course, it was intentional - TO SAVE THE CLUB!

Within days of Receivership, Gurney was gone.

Announcements were made by the Administrator that severe cuts would have to be made, including scrapping the reserve team and a complete transfer embargo on player signings. LTFC was literally fighting for its life - there is never a dull moment at this club I love! Some good news did arise. Mick Harford was back to assist Mike Newell. Mr Newell had a job on his hands, he was the Manager no one wanted and could not sign any players.

Most players to their credit stayed loyal and Tony Thorpe in particular - begged everyone to rally round!

I actually attended a pre-season friendly 0-0 draw at Hitchin, as I found out that my ban did not apply to non-league friendly matches.

On the day that Luton kicked off the league campaign at home to Rushden & Diamonds, we spent the day in London celebrating Georgina's 13th Birthday. On a scorching hot day Gus kept me informed with events as Luton came back from 1-0 behind to win 3-1.

LTFC welcomed league newcomers Yeovil Town in League Cup 1. The Somerset team were knocked out 4-1.

Tony Thorpe, who had recently called for unity and everyone to pull through this crisis together, would play just one more time before deserting the sinking ship by moving to QPR. The Hatters fans were in uproar with him and started a bad song about his mother, which is still sung today. It must be noted though, that in his four spells at Luton, he played 192 times and scored an impressive 84 goals (only 8 less than the legend Mick Harford).

This record makes him the 10th highest goal scorer in LTFC history. His final LTFC game was a 2-1 win at Stockport.

My first game of 2003-04 was Rangers v Hibs at Ibrox. We won 5-2.

While we were in Scotland, Luton lost twice, 2-1 at home to Notts County and on the Holiday Monday, 2-0 at Brighton. We flew home that day and then Gus and Bob Rumble joined Deb & I the next day, to fly to Copenhagen for Rangers Champ's League 2nd Leg qualifier against FC Copenhagen. We met our Kilsyth friends and all stayed in the same hotel I had booked for us. We had a wonderful trip. Deb loved the beautiful Danish city. Rangers won 2-1 to go through 3-2 on aggregate and qualify for the Group stages.

After our return from Denmark, Luton beat Hartlepool 3-2 at home. Steve Howard scored twice against his hometown club and Thorpe's replacement, loan signing from Coventry Gary McSheffrey, netted his first Luton goal.

The following week we drew 1-1 at Notts County.

Trialist Enoch Showunmi, made his Luton debut at Plymouth. The Pilgrims came back to win 2-1. Luton then beat Port Vale 2-0 at home.

On the Saturday, QPR came to Town and Tony Thorpe was given a warm welcome back – NOT! The crowd of 8,339 was the highest at that point of the season and they saw a 1-1 draw. Three nights later, Luton were at the Valley to play Charlton in the League Cup.

A work colleague Nick Dear (the chap who had not, at that point, missed a home LTFC league game since Aug 1969 v Barrow), remarked the next day that this epic of a match was a classic and he finally arrived home - at near 1am! The large Hatters support that travelled, watched as the match went into ET after a 3-3 draw and then a penalty shoot out at 4-4. Incredibly - we lost 8-7 on penalties!

Three days later I watched Rangers beat Dundee 3-1 at Ibrox. That day, Luton lost 3-0 at Oldham and lay 14th after 10 games. We then drew 2-2 at Swindon. The lowest home crowd of the season 5,002 watched Luton beat Tranmere 3-1. A home 3-1 victory followed against Wycombe, this time recovering from 1-0 down. We then had two high scoring away defeats in a row.

Brentford won 4-2, before we travelled to Bournemouth mid-week. Gus went to Dean

Court and updated me by text, resulting in a 6-3 win for the Cherries.

Luton then drew 1-1 at home to Peterborough.

While Luton were drawing 1-1 again, away to Bristol City, I watched Rangers beat Partick 3-1 at Ibrox.

Bob & Gary Rumble and Gus & I were all members of the Rangers Travel Club and when we applied for tickets for Man Utd v Rangers in the Champ's League, we were all successful. I drove Gus up to Old Trafford and met the Kilsyth crew there. The police had set Manchester up like a war zone as the city was completely dry, with no pubs allowed to open. The Gers performance was frankly embarrassing, but the non-stop singing and support from the Gers fans was a credit to them. The difference in quality was men against boys, as United won 3-0.

That same night Luton had won 2-0 at R&D's in the LDV Vans Trophy. Southend would eliminate us in Round 3 by winning 3-0 at Roots Hall.

After Old Trafford, Gus drove to watch Luton in the FA Cup 1st Round at non-league Thurrock. I actually saw this 1-1 draw on live Sky TV.

The next game at home to Wrexham I remember winning money, by predicting we would win 3-2. What made it even sweeter, we were 2-0 down and this result won me £56.

In the FA Cup replay an Adrian Forbes hat-trick saw off Thurrock as we won 3-1. Luton then drew 0-0 at Sheff Wed as we prepared for my next Rangers European adventure in Stuttgart, Germany, in which Deb and her sister Liz, joined us all.

Rangers lost 1-0. The girls had an absolute whale of a time with the Scots.

A lone goal was enough to beat Chesterfield 1-0 at home to put Luton into 10th position. The following Saturday was the FA Cup 2nd round.

Of all the teams we could have drawn - it was ROCHDALE away! How ironic. I was inundated with calls about this and was delighted to hear we won 2-0 - to give me some payback for the ban! On that day, the Adairs were in Glasgow staying at the Hilton again. I watched Rangers beat Dundee United 2-1.

The next Saturday, 1-0 was enough to see off Blackpool at Kenilworth Road. Unfortunately, the next match again at home, was a 1-0 defeat to Barnsley.

On Boxing Day, Lee Mansell scored his 10th and final LTFC goal in a 1-1 draw at Colchester.

With the season at the halfway stage Luton were in 9th place and the final game of 2003 saw Luton win 2-0 at home to Notts County.

In the FA Cup 3rd Round, Luton were drawn at Bradford City. We had never won at Valley Parade before but did so that day, to win 2-1 and create history.

In the next match at R&D's we led twice, but could only draw 2-2.

While Luton were repeating that 2-2 result at home to Stockport, I watched Rangers beat Motherwell 1-0 at Ibrox.

After returning from Glasgow we travelled to Bulgaria again for our winter skiing holiday break. Once again, we stayed at the Rila Hotel in Borovets and I'm pleased to report that there were no accidents involving any of my family this time. We had a fabulous time and my skiing ability came on a treat, by the end of the week I could justify in writing I was a proper skier.

Just before we returned Luton had exited the FA Cup 4th Round by losing 1-0 at home to Tranmere. The crowd of 8,767 was the largest in 2003-04.

Two weeks later, Enoch Showumni netted his first LTFC goal in the 1-0 home victory against Colchester. Luton doubled that three nights later, when we secured a 2-0 home win over Brighton. I remember my boss Geoff raving at the quality of that Hatters performance.

A player by the name of Keith Keane made his debut in the next game at Wycombe, where we drew 0-0.

Two years into my banning order had now been reached and under the terms this was two-thirds into the sentence, which entitled us to appeal if we wished. Pete and I did just that and drove up to Rochdale Magistrates Court and listened intently to the case described to the Magistrate. After just 5 minutes, the female judge gave her verdict ending the Ban and we were allowed to watch our beloved Hatters again. I have to write, that the expression on her face when the case was read out in its entirety was one of, 'Why were these two individuals arrested in the first place? They shouldn't be here at all!' The two of us excitedly exited court after thanking her and punched the air in delight. We rang all and sundry to tell them the good news & Pete rang Bean, to get him a ticket for the Brentford home game.

Unfortunately, I would not be able to attend that match as I had pre-booked Rangers v Hibs which the Gers won 3-0.

Pete's return to Kenilworth Road was a winning one, as Luton romped home to beat Brentford 4-1, to lift us into 6th place. Enoch Showunmi scored his only LTFC hat-trick that day.

Despite being allowed to, I could not make the next two games, both away. The first was a 3-2 mid-week defeat at Grimsby & then a 2-1 win at Peterborough. The moment I had eagerly been awaiting came on a Tuesday night at home to Bournemouth. There was great banter in the Bobbers club pre-match and then we took our seats in the Enclosure, where I had my old seat back. With great excitement I looked forward to kick off - only for the Referee to call it off before it had even started, when he deemed some parts of the pitch frozen and therefore unplayable! Everyone saw the funny side of it - I STILL hadn't seen the Town play since Feb 2002!

That moment finally arrived when I drove up to Barnsley on the Saturday. In the away end at Oakwell many fellow Hatters fans greeted me and I was welcomed back like a lost brethren. The teams lined up and of the eleven Luton players, there were only six I had previously seen. Despite having most of the possession for nearly all the match we could only muster a 0-0 draw.

Next day Gus & I were at Parkhead for the Scots Cup Quarter-Final tie. Rangers lost 1-0 in a drab game. I will never set foot in that place again.

The next game I watched was a hugely entertaining affair between Luton and Blackpool at the Kenny. After an Emerson Boyce goal, the game burst into life after the break. Peter Holmes made it 2-0, before Blackpool pulled one back via a penalty. The goal of the game came when Enoch Showunmi fantastically curled a free kick in, to increase the lead to 3-1. The Sea-siders refused to quit and they made it 3-2. Fortunately, we held on to win, it felt brilliant to be back.

I missed the mid-week 1-0 away defeat to Port Vale and also a big match at home to Plymouth. The reason for missing the Argyle match was a longstanding booking with the

Bobbers Club Domino team.

Although I played Dom's for SWMC, when the Bobbers invited me to play for them in the 5s & 3s National tournament in Bridlington, Yorkshire, I jumped at the chance. Deb & I drove up for the weekend and joined all the Fowler family, plus the rest of the Bobbers team with their families and friends including a lovely old boy called Jack Odell. We had a thoroughly enjoyable time with them, even managing to reach the last 16.

While in Bridlington, Gus was keeping me informed of the Plymouth match. In a 1-1 draw, the Pilgrims cruelly equalised - in the 93rd minute! The gate of 8,499 was the highest home league crowd of 2003-04.

The following week, a load of us lads travelled to QPR on the train for a day and night out in London. We travelled to Loftus Road in great spirits, although I was very aware of not having TOO much to drink after my past experience, as this was my first social away day since returning from the ban. A huge Luton following filled the away end in the near capacity QPR crowd of 17,695. There was a new signing in the Luton side making his debut that day, midfielder Paul Underwood signed from R&D's. Unfortunately, this talented player would go on to have a history of injuries and illness in his LTFC career.

Indeed, he went off injured in this very match. In his four years at Luton he would only play 72 times. QPR took the lead but we came back to draw 1-1 through Enoch Showunmi, to give us a deserved point.

I missed a 1-1 home draw with Oldham as I was watching Rangers lose the Old Firm derby by 2-1 at Ibrox. This loss was my last Rangers game of 2003-04.

In mid-week at Hartlepool I missed a high scoring affair where we lost 4-3. The Play-Offs were definitely out of our reach following another two defeats, 1-0 away at Tranmere and a 3-0 thumping at home to Swindon.

Next, we led Bristol City at home 2-0 thanks to Steve Howard & Emerson Boyce. City came back to level with just a minute to go. It looked like another jinx team had one over us again, as it was 23 years since we beat them at Kenilworth Road. However Keith Keane scored a late fabulous long-shot goal with venom, to win 3-2. Bogey over. The rearranged Bournemouth home match followed and we drew 1-1. Steve Howard scored but future Hatter (and friend) Warren Feeney scored the equaliser. I missed a 2-1 defeat at Wrexham.

The final home game of 2003-04 was against Sheffield Wednesday and what a cracker it was too. Owls fans filled the Oak Road and contributed to a fine atmosphere. They were also very happy at h-t, as they led 2-0.

In the 2nd half we witnessed a great comeback by the Town, ending with a superb 3-2 victory. Steve Howard had got us back into the game, before Steve O'Leary levelled with his first Luton goal. Howard brought the house down when he scored his second, which was his 16th and final 2003-04 goal for the winner in the dying seconds. This was the first time I had heard Luton fans sing, "2-0 and you fucked it up."

The curtain came down at Saltergate, Chesterfield.

I hadn't adorned fancy dress since my 40th against Brentford six years prior, it was time I made up for it and visited the Fancy Dress Shop on the eve of travel. A whole host of us booked the early Saturday morning North bound train and hundreds more Hatters had shared our travel plans. After a full breakfast at my favourite café in Barbers Lane, off Guildford Street I received huge cheers at Luton station when I arrived - dressed as a 1970s Pimp!

The Purple flared Velvet Suit, Huge Gold Medallion, Afro Wig & Silver Crocodile Skin Platform Boots looked amazing. It brought howls of laughter from everyone on board the train, football fans or not and my philosophy is that if you make people laugh, who cares? Even if it is you - they are laughing at!

We had a great day out, no hassle, plenty of drink (not TOO much, of course). Chesterfield had a serious issue to the match, anything but a Spireites victory would end in their relegation. On 88 mins in a rather dull game, the home fans wishes came true when Chesterfield scored the only goal to achieve safety and their fans went into raptures.

We shared their happiness after the match in the local pubs, where we were made welcome and the atmosphere was of a carnival nature, although had they had been relegated - it might have been a touch different!

On the journey back, it was equally joyous when we joined the train full of celebrating QPR fans who had won promotion at Sheffield Wednesday that day. So the domestic season had ended and I was thrilled to be a part of it again.

On the weekend of the Man Utd v Millwall FA Cup Final, Deb and I had joined Gus, with Liz & Duncan from Kilsyth for a Liverpudlian, Rangers friend of ours called Brian, whose wedding we attended that day. A mutual Gers friend was also at the wedding, the famous Liverpudlian/Luton fan, Keith Brooksbank.

When I was banned from watching ALL football involving English/Welsh clubs in the UK and abroad from 2002-04, my 2nd love Rangers saved me from Lord knows what! I attended 27 Rangers games in that time, plus two Old Firm fixtures I couldn't get tickets for. Rangers saved my sanity in this period.

2004-05 Champions

With our daughters now both settled in at their respective schools, there was no way we would be allowed to take them out of school for the Summer holidays.

Therefore, when we returned to Son Bou in Menorca that Summer, I had to miss Luton's first two league matches. We returned to the Hotel Pinguinos and had a wonderful time again.

The week before our holiday I attended two pre-season friendly games.

LTFC had somehow managed to arrange a home match with the famous Dutch club Ajax Amsterdam. I think I am correct in writing that a female member of the office staff (Keith McEvoy's then girlfriend), faxed Holland to request if Ajax would be interested in playing at Luton seeing as they had arranged a match at QPR already. If true - cap doffed!

Ajax brought the full 1st team squad as well as a few of their notorious F Side Hooligan fans, a good crowd of 7,500 attended. The class of this elite team showed as they cruised to a 4-0 victory and we all thought that night we might be in for a long season. The next day Gus & I travelled to see Rangers win 2-1 at Fulham. Of the 14,000+ attendance, nearly 10,000 were Gers fans.

Luton started 2004-05 with various changes to the squad.

After 212 appearances and 9 goals, full back Emerson Boyce moved to Crystal Palace. Adrian Forbes left for Swansea and Matthew Spring had already joined Leeds earlier in the year. Goalkeeper Marlon Beresford had signed a permanent deal and striker Rowan Vine was on a season-long loan from Portsmouth.

I watched Soccer Saturday on Sky in a Son Bou bar for updates of our opening game at home to Oldham. The Latics led 1-0 at h-t before we turned it round to win 2-1. Then in mid-week Luton were playing at Swindon and we beat them 3-2 to give us 6 points out of 6.

When we returned from our summer break I turned my mobile phone on to see untold missed calls from work. Space dictates telling the full story suffice to write, that before my holiday I had bought a raffle ticket for £1 for Breast Cancer awareness – I only scooped first prize of £3,000! Naturally, I was chuffed and this was the 2nd time I had won a large amount of money after the SWMC Open The Box experience years earlier. I decided to put it towards next year's summer holiday, a P&O Cruise.

I didn't travel to Barnsley the next day but wished I had done. At one stage we were leading 4-1 at Oakwell, the Tykes did come back late on to make it 3-4. This win had meant we had won our opening three League games for the first time since the victorious 1982 Div 2 Championship year. My first League game of 2004-05 was at home to Torquay and I really hoped I wasn't about to jinx us.

Fear not, Steve Howard scored the only goal to make it 4 wins in a row and eclipse that great David Pleat led side's start.

I drove up to Boston for a League Cup tie only to find that after parking up, the match had been postponed because of a waterlogged pitch - in AUGUST!

In all my years of following Luton this was only the 2nd ever time I had travelled away and actually reached a ground before finding out the match was off, the other being Bolton in 1976.

The Adairs travelled to Blackpool for our away match there on August Bank Holiday weekend. Joining us, were my old good friend Barz and his family. They had booked a Guest House for all of us and although we would have preferred to stay at The Claremont Hotel as usual, we went along with their more economic choice. While all the females went shopping on the day of the game, Barz, his son Ben & I headed for Bloomfield Road, via the then Rangers Supporters Club in Central Drive.

Gus had booked to fly up from Stansted to Blackpool with his daughter Kristy and had arranged to meet us in the Rangers Club. The fact that he failed to appear at all and his phone was switched off, gave me cause for concern.

Looking back, it was the beginnings of his acute personal problems. He had not renewed his season ticket after telling everybody he had and apart from the Ajax friendly, we rarely saw him at Kenilworth Road again for years.

We had a fabulous time with Barz and his family. Luton won 3-1 courtesy of Steve Howard (who had scored in all 5 games) and 2 Ahmet Brkovic goals. Not only was it 15 points out of 15, the bonus was that Barz had bet on the Town to win 3-1 at 25/1. We celebrated in style at a Chinese restaurant.

The day after returning from Blackpool we played Bournemouth at home. A crowd of 7,404 attended to see if we could make it 6 on the spin. We did just that winning 1-0. Howard failed to score this time, leaving it to Kevin Nicholls.

I drove up to Hillsborough and Sheff Wed halted our excellent 100% start by drawing 0-0, still - this was the best Luton start to a league season since 1913!

I drove to Boston for the 2nd attempt, but unfortunately our league form did not transfer to the League Cup. We lost an entertaining match 4-3. Enoch Showunmi opened his 2004-05 account and even though we came back from 3-1 down to 3-3 - Boston clinched it and went through with a late winner in the last minute. Paul Gascoigne had a very short spell as coach at Boston then.

Rowan Vine returned us back to winning ways when he scored the only goal in the home win against Chesterfield. The home crowds were steadily increasing, 7,532 watched this match.

Two days later I drove to Edgely Park for the first time to see Luton play at Stockport, taking Barz and his son Ben. The League leaders strolled to a 3-1 victory. I actually cheered when Stockport scored as I had backed Luton to win 3-1 and Luton were winning 3-0 when the other Hatters scored.

Thank you Steve Robinson, Rowan Vine & Ahmet Brkovic - for £50+!

Vine scored his third successive league goal, along with Paul Underwood when we narrowly beat Peterborough 2-1 at home.

9 wins and 1 draw from the first 10 games was outstanding form in anyone's eyes. Luton then lost 2-0 at Swansea in the LDV and I did not care an iota.

I had long booked the Rangers v Kilmarnock match for my first Ibrox trip of 2004-05 and Rangers won 2-0. The day before that game while watching Sky Sports in a Glasgow pub, I saw that Luton had drawn 1-1 at Tranmere.

One of the friends I had met on previous stays at the Hilton was Geordie Pete. He and his wife Sarah live in East Kilbride. I called him Geordie Pete as he originated from Tyneside and although having lived in Scotland for over 35 years, he still had a wee Geordie twang.

Pete had gone on for ages about how he would love to see Luton play, so I booked an EasyJet flight for him and arranged for his stay at our house when Luton played Hartlepool at home the next Friday night. Deb was away at Cherine's for the weekend so it would be a perfect time for him to visit. Gus met him at Luton Airport on the Friday afternoon. We took him to the Bobbers Club pre- and post-match and we had a terrific time that night.

There were a few Pool fans in the Bobbers and one of their lads that we were chatting with was their famous mascot 'Angus The Monkey' although I hasten to add, he was in civilian attire.

Everyone was delighted to see Gus, for this was his first showing at a Luton home game and the Bobbers Club in 2004-05.

We took our seats in the front row of D Block in the Enclosure. Luton played superb in front of the 7,865 crowd and we were rewarded with a 3-0 victory. Gary McSheffrey was enjoying his 2nd loan spell with us and I know he would have joined us in a minute on a permanent basis. Alas, we just could not afford the fee Coventry wanted. He scored that night, his 10th and final LTFC goal in 24 games. Steve Howard & Ahmet Brkovic netted the other two goals in an excellent display. Ten wins and two draws from 12 games, is officially the best ever start in LTFC history and I don't think it will ever be beaten.

After the game in the Bobbers Geordie Pete was drooling, he thought that everything about Luton was top class. The quality of the team, the supporters, but especially, our old dilapidated ground with its closeness to the pitch and atmosphere it generated, he told us THAT was our asset and was priceless, we must NEVER move to a new stadium as we would lose that uniqueness, he added. I actually disagreed with him. We need a new stadium if we are to ever return to the top flight, although it was nice to hear him rave about our beloved club. They both stayed at my house as we took a carry out home and boozed all through the night. Pete thought Gus was a brilliant bloke.

The Hartlepool lads that night, told us some startling things about our manager their ex-boss, Mike Newell. They told us of his alleged fondness of a drink, before adding that one day his nature would make him implode and that everything around him at LTFC would come tumbling down. – We all laughed off their ridiculous remarks! Ironically, there would be an element of truth in those comments in latter years.

The following week Huddersfield visited Kenilworth Road. With the start that we had made, a biggest home attendance at that point of 8,192 gathered to see us play the Terriers. We were in shock when they led 2-0. Paul Underwood pulled a goal back but it was not enough, we suffered our first defeat of 04-05. Three nights later, it became two at Walsall. I missed the 2-0 loss.

I then drove Barz and Ben to Hull. This was my 1st visit to the new KC Communications Stadium, indeed - it was my first trip to the city of Hull!

I had never been to Boothferry Park before. We passed that old ground on the bus when we travelled on the park & ride scheme from the outskirts of Hull. A big crowd of 18,575 turned up to see the Tigers take on the league leaders. They left delighted, having seen them turn us over 3-0 and for the first time, questions were being asked after the third defeat on the spin. On leaving the ground to catch our bus, there was a bit of trouble outside as a local Hull firm attacked some our fans. From our viewing point the Luton lads certainly gave as good as they got. As I write, I have yet to return to HCFC.

The questions being asked about those 3 defeats were answered in the best possible fashion in the next match at home to Bradford City. This was the Bantams first league visit to our home since 1969 when they were thrashed 5-0, including a Malcolm Macdonald hat trick. It was only one less this time, when we emphatically silenced the critics with a 4-0 win, 2 goals from Brkovic (inc a spectacular overhead kick) Howard & Underwood.

The following week's display was even better, as we put the show right back on the road.

Wrexham visited from North Wales and wished they hadn't.

We beat them 5-1 and had five different goal scorers, namely Robinson, Davis (his first LTFC strike in 2 years at the club), O'Leary, Howard and Brkovic.

It was FA Cup Round 1 time and we had been drawn to play Southend at Roots Hall for the second time in 3 years. The match was covered by Sky for live transmission and was screened on the Friday night. I decided not to travel and watched it at SWMC as we put in a master class display winning 3-0 at ease. The watching packed club audience that night were hugely impressed by a super LTFC performance.

At the next match, some Luton fans refused to attend at the Hockey Stadium in Milton Keynes. This was in protest at the decision to relocate Wimbledon FC 50 miles north and rename them as MK Dons. In their view and like many fans around the country, they believed Milton Keynes had stolen a football club. I have to agree with them on that point.

However, each to their own and it did not stop me from attending to see Luton play them, although I do understand and respect those that chose not to. I'm glad I did attend and along with the sell-out Luton allocation, we witnessed another brilliant Hatters performance.

Vine scored early with a fantastic long distance goal before Steve Howard went on to claim a hat-trick as the Town went on to win 4-1. It completed a fantastic personal day, as Rangers had beaten Celtic 2-0 earlier.

I had to miss our 1-1 home draw against Doncaster as the Adairs were attending the wedding of Deb's best friend Cherine to Kals in Litchfield, Staffs.

Gus then surprisingly travelled to Amsterdam with us, (I later found out he had borrowed money off a local in the Bedfordshire Yeoman) for Rangers UEFA Cup game against AZ 67 Alkmaar. We stayed in Amsterdam because the AZ ground only held 8,000 and Rangers allocation was just 800, with over 5,000 Bears fans travelling and most staying in Amsterdam like us.

None of us managed to secure a ticket for the 2-0 Rangers defeat.

After returning from Holland I missed an FA Cup 2nd round tie at Wycombe, where the same 3-0 Luton score applied as the 1st round.

I also missed a mid-week game at Brentford where Steve Howard was sent off. The Bees inflicted our fourth loss in 20 games, winning 2-0 at Griffin Park.

We returned to winning ways by beating Port Vale 1-0 at home with Brkovic scoring the only goal, another spectacular overhead one. Only 213 Vale fans attended, the lowest away support of all season.

The next week I saw Rangers beat Kilmarnock 1-0 at Rugby Park. Whilst I was in Scotland, Luton beat Bristol City at Ashton Gate 2-1 - to give us our first win there for 31 years!

I travelled to Saltergate, Chesterfield for the final time on Boxing Day. On a bone hard surface Enoch Showunmi scored the only goal to beat the Spireites. In the final game of

2004 Luton entertained Colchester. A crowd of 8,806 watched as Rowan Vine scored twice, but it was only enough to earn a point.

The opening game of 2005 was watched by our first sell-out crowd of the season, 9,500, against Sheffield Wednesday. Steve Howard carried on his scoring feats by netting his 16th goal of 2004-05 in the 1-1 draw with the Owls. Two days later I drove to Peterborough. Kevin Nicholls opened the scoring but Posh rallied to come back and lead before Howard saved the day to earn us a point in a 2-2 draw. Of the 7,662 there that day - 3,590 were Hatters fans!

In the FA Cup 3rd round, a surprisingly poor home performance against Brentford resulted in them winning 2-0 and knocking us out. Brentford fans filled the Oak Road and went home delighted having beaten us twice in 2004-05, without conceding a goal. Their manager Martin Allen was an arrogant twat - he walked off the pitch strutting like a peacock!

The lowest league crowd of the season 6,603, saw Luton beat a poor Stockport side 3-0.

The other Hatters were bottom of the league and it showed.

Goals from Coyne, Howard and a Kevin Nicholls penalty gave us 3 points after three League 1 draws in a row.

I missed the 0-0 draw at Colchester, as we were on our annual skiing holiday. We chose a different country for 2005 and went to Kop in Serbia, former Yugoslavia. This was a very bizarre, yet thoroughly enjoyable trip. Unlike our previous 4 ski trips where there had been plenty of fellow Brits, this resort had hardly any at all. We arrived at our large hotel which was beautiful, to find that NO-ONE spoke any English. In fact throughout our whole week there, we only met two other Brits. Fortunately, our instructor spoke English and the six of us had exclusive lessons, which resulted in expert tuition. The snow and ski conditions we had were the best of all the ski holidays we had experienced. We returned for me to watch Luton v Tranmere. Rovers were also highly placed & challenging for promotion. A Kevin Nicholls penalty shared the points in a 1-1 draw.

The same result occurred again the following week when I went to the McAlpine Stadium, to see us draw at Huddersfield. Brkovic scored our goal. There was no doubt we were suffering a slight blip, having won only once in the last seven including 6 draws. Other teams were slowly creeping up.

When 2nd placed Hull City visited Kenilworth Road it was obviously a sell-out crowd of 9,500, the Tigers fans along with Sheff Wed, were the only team's supporters to fill the Oak Road in 2004-05. Such was the demand for this game, it was later reported that this match could have sold three times the amount. As expected, this was a tight game and despite our numerous efforts it looked like we were heading for our seventh draw in 8 as the board showed we were into time added on.

Suddenly in that time, the old ground erupted with joy when Ahmet Brkovic majestically rose to head in near post at the Kenilworth Road end net. The roar that greeted that goal was even louder than when we beat Plymouth in the promotion season 3 years earlier. It was definitely the loudest noise of the decade so far and sweet revenge for the 3-0 loss at Hull.

This 1-0 victory now gave us the impetus to go on to a promotion push.

I missed the long mid-week trip to Mike Newell's ex-club Hartlepool. We won 3-2 to secure our first away win of 2005, the 357 Luton fans there was the lowest away turnout of all season.

I drove up to Valley Parade to see us beat Bradford City 1-0. The ground had been completely rebuilt on all four sides since the tragic fire of 20 years prior with two magnificent stands in particular. The attendance of 8,702 looked positively sparse in the all-seated 25,000 arena. Rowan Vine scored the only goal with a fine shot.

The same score was repeated at home to Walsall thanks to Kevin Nicholls.

I missed our first defeat of 2005, a 3-1 loss at Port Vale. Kevin Foley scored and although he would have another two full seasons at LTFC, this was Kevin's 5th and final Town goal. This was only our 5th defeat in 35 games.

The following week at home to Bristol City was possibly the finest Luton performance of 2004-05. We simply wiped the floor with the Robins and thrashed them 5-0, easily our best score against them in my time. What was now a regular spectacular goal from Brkovic, along with a 2nd for him, plus a penalty from Nicholls, a rare Sol Davis goal. Peter Holmes completed the rout and double against a so called bogey team.

The same players (Davis apart) repeated the scoring feats at home to another team from the West Country when we beat Swindon 3-1.

I missed our 2-2 draw at Oldham. The reason I was not at Boundary Park was because I was in Glasgow that weekend for the Scots League Cup Final at Hampden Park, in which Rangers hammered Motherwell 5-1. This was named the 'Davie Cooper Final' in his honour on the 10th anniversary of his tragic death, having played for both clubs.

Six days later, Luton had a rare bad day at the office. Barnsley completed our 6th and final defeat of 2004-05 by easily beating us 3-1 at Kenilworth Road.

I couldn't travel to Torquay on Easter Monday unfortunately, but listened intently on the radio. When Torquay scored early on I was a touch concerned after the poor Barnsley showing but fear not, the mighty Hatters came storming back to beat the Gulls 4-1. Promotion was now within our grasp.

The following week a single Steve Howard goal was enough to see off Blackpool at home and we played another seaside club Bournemouth away, after that. I couldn't join the throngs of Hatters fans at Dean Court because I had a longstanding agreement with my Kilsyth friends, who had booked flights and hotel for a weekend in Luton at that time.

On the Saturday, Gus made a rare appearance in the SWMC to join us all, as a packed audience watched the Scotland v England rugby match. Gus & I were only interested in the football updates though. When it was announced that Enoch Showunmi had given Luton the lead late on, a huge cheer went up in the club. We all started dancing. Luton won 1-0 and promotion was almost assured, though not quite mathematically. That would have to wait just a few more days and it did occur, when Tranmere failed to win at Brentford.

After nine long years, LTFC were back in the 2nd flight of English football, in my honest opinion, I think this is where we belong.

Against Milton Keynes, a sell out 9,500 crowd would have occurred but the franchise failed to sell 500 of their allocation for the short distance trip. We won 1-0 courtesy of an own goal.

The following Saturday was St George's Day and we were playing Wrexham away in North Wales. Good friends John Ashton & Freddie Dann had been running regular coaches all season from one of John's pubs. No one wanted to miss this trip and so from his Sugar Loaf pub in Leagrave, 5 coach loads of lads left early in fine spirits. I naturally had my England shirt and rose on, to celebrate St George. In the bar pre-trip EVERYONE was there (bar Gus, sadly). John had booked a pub on the outskirts of Wrexham and we stopped off for a few jars pre-match.

The sing song in that pub was memorable, as I decided to bring back some of the 60s & 70s classic Oak Road Songs like Tiptoe Through The Oak Road and You've Got Your European & You've got Your FA Cup.

The atmosphere in the Racecourse Ground was a party one, thanks to the 2,151 Hatters following. A Luton win would seal the championship, but it was Wrexham that opened the scoring. When Curtis Davies scored his first LTFC goal to equalise, the party began to get started. It was in full flow with the Conga too when Coyne scored the winning goal. Us Hatters went wild in celebration as We Are The Champions bellowed out. It was moments like these that you cherish being a Luton fan and life at that time was fantastic.

The final home match was against Brentford who had beaten us twice already in 2004-05. The fact that Martin Allen was their manager, made it essential in my view that we HAD to win this one. The Bees though stung us badly when they led 2-1 and the near sell-out crowd (Brentford were 287 short of their allocation) were slightly in shock. I did not want our final home match to end in defeat. At this time Brentford had put 6 past us without reply in 04-05.

Fear not, we were not champions for nothing and the rip roaring mighty Hatters came fighting back. A Nicholls penalty, Showunmi and finally Robinson, all scored as we blitzed our way back to win 4-2. The after match celebrations began in full with a friendly pitch invasion.

Recent signing from Bournemouth, Warren Feeney, made his debut that day and he would go on to become a friend of mine. The celebrations continued well into the night and carried on the next night too at the end of season Supporters' Club presentation awards night, at the Vauxhall Recreation Club, Riverside Suite. We had booked a table of 10 and the designated player on our table was Russ Perret. It really was a crying shame that there was no sign of Gus, what a pity that in our finest season for YEARS, one of Luton's staunchest fans felt unable to be there.

Manager Mike Newell had everyone laughing at his opening speech when his first words were, "Well - you voted for me!"

One of my boyhood Luton idols Bruce Rioch, was a speaker and he gave some wonderful praising comments about LTFC. Bean, on our table, even won 1st prize in the raffle - a pair of season tickets for 2005-06! I met Warren Feeney that night and finding out he was a staunch Rangers fan, we hit it off immediately. After that night he would always make a point of coming over to me at some stage of every home game.

There was one final game at Doncaster and a win would give us a magical 100 points. I booked 4 Rail return tickets for three of the Fowlers and myself. It being the last away game I HAD to go in fancy dress like tradition dictated, although there were plenty of other Hatters joining me this time. My choice of attire was Sgt Pepper from the Beatles. We had a day to remember of pure celebration and joy.

This game, along with the vast majority of Luton fans, was my first visit to Belle Vue with Luton as it was 1969 when we last played there. It would also be our final visit too. Doncaster would move to a new venue two years later.

To enable as many Luton fans to attend as possible, Doncaster wisely gave us nearly half of the ground and 3,535 Hatters made the journey to South Yorkshire. We were still queued to get in when Doncaster scored - on 43 seconds! Early on it was all Rovers, you could see why they had only lost twice at home (like us). On the half hour mark it was 1-1 when Russ Perret (who was steaming drunk on our table 6 days prior), guided his header into the net. Steve Howard then sent the barmy Hatters Army into raptures when he tapped in his 22nd and final goal of 2004-05. Luton were on course to make history by reaching 100 points. But just after the break it was 2-2, following a bizarre own goal. From our Slovenian goalkeeper Seremit's kick, the strong wind blew it right back and from a Doncaster fierce cross - it flew in off Steve Robinson's head into our net! The wind was playing havoc and then Luton led again.

In what was truthfully Luton's first attack of the 2nd half, Kevin Nicholls hit a screamer from 25 yards, which went into the roof of the net opposite us like a rocket. It really was one of the goals of the season, but just a minute later it was 3-3. Warren Feeney came close to scoring his 1st Luton goal near the end but the Donny keeper prevented it. The final whistle blew and the 3-3 draw had left us finished on 98 points.

This total had broken the League 1 record from 3 years prior and stood until 2012 when Charlton claimed it.

It was a fantastic achievement, as we had finished 12 points clear of Hull. Sheffield Wed joined us after defeating Hartlepool in the Play-Off final.

Not one team had achieved the double over us although we failed to beat five teams, namely Sheff Wed, Tranmere, Huddersfield, Doncaster and Colchester. My 2004-05 season had one more game left to attend.

I travelled up for the Bank Holiday weekend in May, to see Rangers beat Motherwell 4-1 at Ibrox Park.

It was also an incredible ending to the season for the Gers.

On the last day Celtic only had to win at Motherwell to win the SPL, no matter what Rangers result was.

Rangers were playing at Hibs and naturally, all my Kilsyth pals were there. Although Nacho Novo had scored for Rangers at Easter Road, Celtic were also 1-0 ahead at Fir Park. With 5 minutes remaining at both games, the title was heading to Parkhead. Then suddenly, Scott Macdonald (an Aussie, from a Celtic supporting Scots family) scored for Motherwell. This equaliser meant if the scores remained unchanged at both games, it was our title. The Helicopter was on its way to Motherwell - when it suddenly had to change direction for Edinburgh! Macdonald scored a winner for Motherwell and this fantastic achievement will forever be known as Helicopter Sunday. No doubt, on a personal level with my Luton and Rangers passion, 2004-05 was perfection.

The Championship

In June 2005 we sold our house in Smithcombe Close and moved up the road to Brookend Drive. This was our third house on the Grange Road Estate, it is still known today as the new estate in Barton - even though it is over 22 years old! I still live here as I write this book.

Before our Summer Cruise I attended a couple of pre-season friendly matches. The first was at Portman Road, Ipswich to see Rangers win 2-0 there. I also watched Luton draw 2-2 at home to Serbian side, OFK Belgrade.

Following our promotion, LTFC had added a further 760 seats to the rear of the Kenilworth Road Stand to push up the capacity to 10,260. This was the smallest capacity in the 2nd tier - further proof of needing a new stadium!

The new LTFC strip was brilliant, just the plain white shirts and socks with black shorts, just like the old days of the late 1960s and early 1970s.

There were three new Luton signings for 2005-06.

Dean Morgan a striker from Reading plus two international players. Centre Back Markus Heikkinen a Finn, was signed from Aberdeen and midfielder/winger Carlos Edwards, from Wrexham. He was a Trinidad and Tobago cap and would go on to play in the 2006 World Cup, the first Luton player to do so since Mal Donaghy in Mexico 86. A Wrexham/Rangers friend had told me that we had signed their best player.

Rowan Vine had been on loan from Pompey and had now signed a 3 years deal. The only departure of note was Lee Mansell, who went to Oxford after scoring 10 goals in 62 LTFC games.

Steve Howard continued where he had left off from 2004-05 by heading both our goals in the friendly draw with the Serbs.

Two days later, we sailed off from Southampton on board the P&O liner Oceania for our Mediterranean Cruise holiday. We had an absolutely fabulous time, travelling 4,602 nautical miles and visiting 8 destinations. It was not cheap, but worth every penny, for the cuisine alone. Whilst on the Cruise I managed to listen to updates of our first league game. There was no doubt Luton had been given a baptism of fire to face in the first three games at this higher level. Our opening game was at Selhurst Park against relegated Crystal Palace, followed by another demoted side Southampton, at the Kenny and the day after my return - at home again to Leeds!

I listened intently for any Palace updates as Luton gave a brilliant display at one of the promotion favourites. We even had the luxury of a Kevin Nicholls penalty being saved, before the Hatters achieved a fantastic 2-1 victory over the Eagles. I discovered later, there were nearly 2,500 Hatters fans at Palace.

3 nights later I was on the Internet to check the Luton v Southampton score. We won 3-2 to give us the perfect start - 6 points out of 6 and against 2 teams who were in the Premiership the previous season.

We returned home from the fantastic voyage and I watched my first league game of 2005-06 the next day at home to Leeds. The highest home attendance for over 11 years of 10,102, were present to watch a tight battle in a 0-0 draw.

I missed the Stoke away match. 1,114 Luton fans travelled and witnessed Luton dominate the opening play after taking an early lead. Steve Howard was then controversially sent off. We held on for an hour before Stoke came back to win 2-1. Stoke's Manager had said in his post-match interview that the better team had lost.

I drove to see Luton play at Leyton Orient in the League Cup 1st Round. It was my first visit to Brisbane Road since 1984 and only 2,383 were there, 577 of them Hatters fans. We knocked them out comfortably 3-1 with goals from Coyne, Feeney (his 1st for Luton) and an own goal.

The Adairs travelled to Loughborough to see Deb's Aunt Gill, as I took in the Leicester v Luton game. This was my first (and so far, only) visit to The Walkers Stadium, they had moved from just down the road in Filbert Street in 2002 and flats now adorned the old site. 2,161 Luton fans watched yet another stunning acrobatic overhead goal from Ahmet Brkovic to give us the lead. Kevin Nicholls added a 2nd Half penalty in a superb 2-0 away victory.

Incredibly, it would be four long years - before I personally saw Luton win an away 'league' match again!

On the August Holiday Monday Luton beat Millwall 2-1 at home. Warren Feeney scored early on, before the Lions levelled following a gift from Dean Morgan. We had not played particularly well that day, but didn't care when Curtis Davies scored the winner. It turned out to be his 2nd and final LTFC goal in 62 games.

This exceptionally talented player was sold to WBA two days later for a club record £3 million. Curtis is still playing at this 2nd tier level today, for Derby.

The next game at home to Wolves saw the Centenary celebration of Kenilworth Road. Lots of old LTFC legends were paraded around the ground, all of them wearing Black & White bar scarves and Straw Boaters. It was a nice heart warming sight in the rain. We drew 1-1 in front of 10,248 and Nicholls scored our equaliser. One memory of that day was seeing the Wolves players at the end, all lying on the ground looking completely knackered - they certainly knew they had to battle hard for their point!

Three nights later I travelled on John Ashton's coach to QPR. We narrowly lost 1-0 at Loftus Road somehow. Luton should have scored at least three in the 1st half alone.

I then went to Glasgow for my first Rangers league game of 05-06 against Kilmarnock, which we won 3-0.

The Hull v Luton match was being screened live on SKY TV for the lunchtime transmission and an old Luton mate Tony Bojko, watched it with me in a Rangers pub before the Kilmarnock game. We watched intently as the Town played great and were by far the better team. With just minutes remaining it looked like Hull would gain an undeserved point.

But when big Steve Howard leapt up to head in the winner, Tony and I let out a huge roar and went mental with delight in the packed Grapes Bar - amid some bewildering looks from the local punters!

I missed our League Cup 2nd Round Exit at Reading, where we lost 1-0.

We were live on Sky for the 2nd week running when we played Sheff Wed at home on the Friday night. The viewers saw an entertaining 2-2 draw. Howard opened the scoring with a header, only for the Owls to draw level with a header of their own. Wednesday took the lead before Howard headed his 2nd goal to share the points. After ten games we lay in 3rd place with 5 wins, 3 draws and 2 defeats, a very satisfactory start.

The next day Sept 24th, is etched in my memory - as a day I will never forget! I went to the office as we had no game, to catch up on some paperwork and returned home to relax in front of the TV to watch the football updates. That night at around 7.30 I received a phone call - which shook me to the bones!

Richard Hines, my cousin, was on the line and sounded terribly distressed to the point where he could hardly get his words out. I immediately knew it was serious and asked him what was wrong. Deb watched in horror as I visibly wilted when he told me that our Uncle Malcolm (my Mum's brother) - was dead! I was reeling at the news and had to sit down as Richard tried his best to explain what had happened.

Malcolm was a keen cyclist and one of his favourite routes was on the A505 Luton to Hitchin road. He was returning home that morning from Hitchin and had just past the Lilley turn, when he was hit by a 4x4 and killed.

It transpired later, that the driver was over the drink driving limit and had rammed into him, claiming he did not see him and sent Malc flying through the air - killing him instantly!

After I had visited his wife my Aunt Carole, to offer my condolences and sympathy, I had to ring my Mum in New Zealand that night to inform her that her younger brother had died. It was a night when every family member had a sleepless one. Malcolm was just 63, not only was he my Uncle but a brilliant bloke and friend too. He thought the world of my Dad and I can definitely write, that the feeling was very much mutual. Malcolm had worked for Dad at one time as a Painter and told me that my Dad was more like a brother to him.

After having his leg amputated as a young boy due to gangrene setting in, Malcolm never let his disability get the better of him or hold back in his life which like Dad, he lived to the full. Amongst his many achievements was doing a parachute jump - even suffering a back injury doing that! He was a respected and very popular man and known by many, especially in his role as a freemason. Malcolm left behind a devoted wife Carole and 3 grown up children in Malcolm, Vickie & Sarah, along with several Grandchildren. I remember attending Carole & Malcolm's wedding in 1968, Carole was only 16 and he is the only man she had ever been with.

Malcolm's funeral was organised by his Masonic Lodge at the Church where they, and nearly all of the Roberts/Adairs had married, St Thomas's in Stopsley. It is no exaggeration to write, that this was by far the largest gathering at a funeral I had witnessed. There were HUNDREDS of folk, all wanting to pay their respects to this great man. More people were outside the Church than were in such was the esteem in which he was held. The celebration of his life followed the service and cremation at SWMC.

Because of the huge numbers of mourners present it was packed to capacity.

In court, the driver pleaded guilty to causing death by Reckless Driving and was jailed for 18 months, with a three-year driving ban. He had admitted to drinking 8 pints of Stella the night before in a local Lilley pub and was on his way to a cash point that fateful morning when he claimed that he just did not see Malcolm, even with the bright luminous cycling outfit Malc was wearing. An expert for the Prosecution made a back calculation, which was not consistent to the amount of drink he had admitted. The prosecutor said he must have drunk more than that, or had some alcohol prior to driving. He was out of prison in less than the 8 months. The driver, from Lilley, is not going to be named by me, he has to live and sleep at night with the knowledge that he killed an extremely popular family man. I believe that is a life sentence in itself.

I have wonderful treasured memories of my Uncle and still deeply miss him. RIP Malcolm.

Four nights after the Sheff Wed draw we were at home to Preston.

The Hatters' performance that night can only be described as sublime. We led early through Feeney when he used his pace for a brilliant diagonal shot across goal and soon it was 2-0 thanks to a Brkovic header. When Howard made it 3-0 following a lovely lay off from Feeney, I wondered how many we could actually achieve. Despite the continued excellent quality of football from Luton it finished with no further goals.

I missed both the next two matches away to Cardiff and Crewe.

At Ninian Park, Cardiff there was another terrific Luton showing. Despite falling behind to an early Bluebirds goal, the Hatters rallied to win 2-1.

Against Crewe, we took the lead this time but the Railwaymen came back to win 3-1 for the Alex's first win since the opening day.

This blip was rectified in style when Norwich came to town. A sell-out crowd watched a scintillating 1st half Luton performance. There was a mixture of poor Norwich finishing, a wee bit of luck and sheer brilliant Town attacking football. The score at half time was - Luton 4 Norwich 0! There were 4 different goal scorers in Feeney, Edwards (luckily, with the Canaries keeper Green slipping) Holmes and Howard. Norwich did score twice to win the 2nd half and end it 4-2. Against Plymouth at home, Feeney opened the scoring but this was not one of the better Luton displays.

Argyle, had ex-Rangers loan Djordjic in their side and mins after I had shouted out, "Ibrox reject," to him (which he clearly heard) he scored the equaliser and made a point of running directly to me with a 'right up you' look on his face. It ended 1-1.

An astonishing 3,928 Luton fans travelled to the new Ricoh Arena for our match at Coventry. I had really hoped that the new ground would bring us better fortune than Highfield Road - in which we had lost in all my six visits there! I'm afraid it was to become 7 out of seven defeats in Coventry. We lost 1-0. Although there was an attendance of over 22,000, the new stadium lacked any atmosphere, like many of these new arenas and was very quiet.

I missed the game at Brammall Lane and I was glad I did. Leaders Sheff Utd thrashed us 4-0 in a rare bad performance.

On fireworks day I watched Luton v Burnley, in which we suffered our first home defeat in 8 months. Akinbiyi was brilliant that day for the Clarets and he had scored 2 good goals in the 1st half. But we were given a lifeline when the Burnley keeper was sent off for handling outside the area. With no substitute goalie on the bench and within minutes Steve Howard had scored in his 200th LTFC game. In the 2nd half, Akinbiyi completed his hat-trick from a penalty and although Feeney pulled one back, it finished 3-2 to Burnley.

I travelled to Norwich on John Ashton's minibus with Freddie Dann and Magnet for my 10th visit to Carrow Road. Of those ten matches, the attendance of 25,383 (inc 2,300 Hatters) that day was the largest of them all. – Since beaten in 2013. The blip continued as Luton lost 2-0 for our fourth successive defeat.

I missed the mid-week game at home to Crewe, as on that morning we were flying out to Porto for my next European adventure with Rangers. The Gers drew 1-1. Gus & I had slept in and missed the flight home.

I paid £500 for us both to return to Gatwick as Gus had no money.

While in Porto, Luton halted the bad run by beating Crewe 4-1. The attendance of 7,474 was the lowest of 2005-06 with just 204 Alex fans present.

Three days later, it was a sell-out at Kenilworth Road when Crystal Palace came to town. Markus Heikkinen scored his 1st Luton goal and Vine the other in the fine 2-0 win, to give us a double over the South Londoners.

I missed the next two games at Reading and Southampton. Reading were on an amazing unbeaten run and after beating us, led the table. Though according to reports, the 3-0 defeat to the Royals was very harsh.

I genuinely can't remember why I did not go to Southampton, especially as it was at their new St Marys stadium, a ground I have still yet to visit.

Maybe it was because it was live on TV and I took the lazy option. The match was dreary and Luton were poor. We lost 1-0.

At this halfway stage we were in a respectful 6th Play Off position, having won 10 - drew 4 - and lost 9 with a 34 points total.

Luton's next game was at home to Stoke. Brkovic gave us the lead and we were in total control at that stage. However, Stoke levelled just before h-t in a rare attack. The 2nd half started with Luton once again dominating, but failing to take their chances. The Potters grabbed an undeserved lead near the end, before a Nicholls penalty made it 2-2. In the dying moments Chris Coyne put through his own net to give Stoke a 3-2 victory and double over us.

On Boxing Day I drove up to Derby for my first visit to their new stadium, Pride Park. The crowd of 26,807 including 1,574 Hatters was the largest I had been in (at that time) for a Derby v Luton game, even when they had won the top league back in 1975. It was also the biggest crowd to watch a Luton match of 2005-06.

The 1st goal was a brilliant strike from a Derby free kick. We looked as if we were heading for our 7th away defeat on the spin, until Brkovic pounced to earn us a point and stop the rot in a 1-1 draw.

Deb's cousin Laura and husband Cliff came to visit us with their daughters Ruby & Scarlet. They came to see us because it was near Xmas, but of course the real reason was because it was Luton v Brighton and Cliff being a Seagulls fan, this was his chance to see an away game. Cliff and I went to the match and in the Bobbers Club for pre-match liquids. He had bought a seat in the Oak Road to be with his brethren.

That night Luton had returned to the early season form and simply demolished Brighton 3-0. Howard bundled in his 1st goal in seven and then Feeney made it 2-0 on the stroke of h-t. Steve Robinson completed the scoring and if truth were told - 6-0 would have been a fairer result!

Cliff told me after the game that the Brighton fans were saying this Luton side was easily the best they had faced all season and he also said that personally, Luton were the best team he had seen in the last 5 years - high praise indeed!

I missed the final match of 2005 at Ipswich, where we lost 1-0. The referee that day was Andy D'Urso and he has a history with LTFC. He had sent off Steve Howard twice previously and when he disallowed a perfectly good goal from Howard tempers frayed, it was never going to be our day.

The first 2 matches of 2006 were at home and both eagerly awaiting.

Local rivals Watford was first, our 1st league derby since 1998 and then in the FA Cup 3rd Round - European Champions Liverpool were to come to town!

Against Watford the worst thing that could happen occurred when they scored an early goal. We all knew that they would try to kill the game and they did just that. But it got worse when they made it 2-0. The teams went off at h-t and I feared another 1997 drubbing. Just into the 2nd half though, it was 2-1 when Carlos Edwards scored – game on! Or so I thought. We could only splutter and even when they went down to 10 men, the Hornets clung on for the win.

Their time-wasting antics were criminal but it was they who were laughing at the end. This was Watford's second win at Kenilworth Road in a row, only the 4th in the 23 derby matches I have seen at the Shrine.

The next game was one of my greatest - EVER seen at Kenilworth Road! BBC Match Of The Day Cameras were showing the Luton v Liverpool FA Cup 3rd Round tie to a live audience with a 5.30pm Saturday kick off, which gave us all day in the Bobbers Club to get in good voice for the match and we did, along with the Liverpool fans there in friendship and good natured banter. When Gerrard opened the scoring with a goal of such high quality I simply couldn't fail but to applaud it - something I rarely did for an opposing goal! Steve Howard was then put through with a lovely pass from Brkovic, he rounded the keeper and slotted it into the empty net to make it 1-1. With the break approaching and Luton playing exceptionally well, the old ground erupted as Steve Robinson gave us a 2-1 lead after turning Carragher over with a sublime piece of skill. The H/T score was fully deserved. At the start of the 2nd Half Liverpool were harshly awarded a penalty, but Marlon Beresford saved Cisse's effort superbly. Within minutes - Kenilworth Road exploded when we had a penalty of our own!

Nicholls showed no sign of nerves and dispatched it easily, to find us unbelievably 3-1 ahead. During all this fantastic excitement yours truly then got involved and managed to get commented on Match Of The Day by John Motson and co. Let me explain.

From my Enclosure front row seat in D Block, the ball came over the wall and landed at my feet for a Liverpool throw in.

Stevie Gerrard came over to take it, but before handing him the ball I stuck my hand out in friendship and returned him the ball after he replicated my action. This was mentioned in the live commentary along the lines of 'And there is a Luton fan showing the true meaning of getting into the spirit of the game, by shaking Steven Gerrard's hand'. It brought a smile to all the fans near me and to be honest made me feel good. I also happen to think he was an exceptional footballer. – They even ended their transmission with my action frozen on the credits!

Liverpool were the reigning Champions League holders for a reason though and they came back at a tiring Town with a vengeance. When Pongolle came on as a Liverpool substitute he immediately outpaced a tired Luton defence and scored to make it 3-2. The Mersey men attacked relentlessly and Alonso then equalised with a dipping volley. Pongolle scored his 2nd and as we tried valiantly to get a 4th to earn a replay at Anfield with our keeper joining in the attack in stoppage time, the ball broke out and found Alonso where he astonishingly hit a shot from inside his own half to score a spectacular goal to end the match - Luton 3 Liverpool 5! Both sets of fans gave the two teams a deserved standing ovation off the pitch and the BBC pundits were drooling. Alan Hansen described it as the best game he had seen ALL season - by a country mile!

He said it had everything and Luton must get full credit for giving Liverpool one heck of a game, they just ran out of steam.

Mr Hansen, you were not wrong.

I missed the next two games at Wolves and at home to QPR, as it was our annual skiing holiday.

We fancied somewhere new this time and chose Passo Tonale, in Italy. The week was fantastic as always. There was no way I knew at that time but sadly, this would be my sixth and final skiing adventure - more of which I will explain why, in passages to follow!

Whilst in Italy, we lost 2-1 at Wolves. This defeat had stretched our winless away run to 10 games. We won our 1st game of 2006 by beating QPR 2-0.

I also missed the mid-week match at Sheffield Wed. We won 2-0 to give us our first away victory since Cardiff nearly 4 months prior. This win had left us still in a creditable 8th place, with a third of the season left.

Keith Keane started his 1st game of 2005-06 and headed us into an early lead in the home match v Hull. The Tigers equalised soon after. After a Hull player had blatantly handballed in his own area, the Referee waved play on and then Hull scored a 2nd & 3rd goal. Chris Coyne pulled one back, but it came too late to stop the 3-2 Hull victory.

Thankfully I missed the Preston game at Deepdale, because they murdered us 5-1 and even our goal was an own goal.

On Valentine's Night I watched another thrilling match when Cardiff visited us. Vine opened the scoring and then added another just 40 seconds later. In the 2nd half Cardiff made it 2-1, it soon became 3-1 following a Bluebirds own goal. We appeared to take our foot of the gas and it came as no surprise when it became 3-2, then 3-3. It might have been even worse, for Cardiff had a valid claim for a penalty right at the death.

I watched another high-scoring match when we played Reading at home. Vine scored twice and Dean Morgan scored his 6th and final goal of 2005-06 against his old club. We won 3-2 against the runaway leaders. The Royals only suffered ONE other defeat in the whole of the 2005-06 season.

As I was soon to travel to Spain with Rangers, I missed our next games at Leeds and Millwall. Nearly 2,000 Hatters travelled to Elland Road and witnessed an historic moment for a LTFC player. Steve Howard scored his 100th goal for us in our 2-1 defeat. This milestone was a fantastic achievement, as only 5 other Luton players in history have ever managed this feat. These were, Herbert Moody, Andy Rennie, Ernie Simms, Brian Stein and record goal scorer with an amazing 276 goals, Gordon Turner.

Steve can be rightly proud of joining those special talents. At the New Den lowly Millwall beat us 2-1.

I went to see Rangers play in Villarreal in the Last 16 of the Champ's League. The Gers were the first Scottish club to achieve this. It was also the 1st (and at present, only) time Rangers had qualified. It was a 1-1 draw but we sadly exited on away goals, as it was 2-2 at Ibrox.

A few days after returning from Spain I watched Luton v Leicester. In a poor 1st half Luton performance we fell behind to a Foxes goal. However, in the 2nd half we upped the tempo and Howard headed in the equaliser. It remained 1-1 until late, then Leicester scored to win it 2-1. This was our 3rd loss on the trot.

Steve Howard then stopped the mini rot with the only goal of the game against Derby at home. Just as the final whistle blew, the ball landed in my lap - I took it home as a souvenir!

I drove down to Deb's cousin Laura in Burgess Hill for the Brighton match, which I would attend with Cliff and his brother. This was my first visit to the Withdean Stadium, they had been playing there since 1999 although at long last, Brighton were finally given permission to build a new stadium outside town in Falmer and moved into a 22,000 seated arena in 2011. Later expanded to 30,000+ capacity.

We had a few pints in the friendly bar at the ground, before I joined my fellow Hatters in the open temporary stand behind the goal. The rain that day had to be seen to be believed - it pissed down ALL DAY! We fell behind but Luton battled back in the driving rain to earn a point via a Brighton own goal.

I had never wanted a match to end so quickly and on return to Laura & Cliff's - I had to have a bath and borrow some of his clothes!

Ipswich were next to visit Luton and this match was hardly a classic. Steve Howard netted the only goal of the game late on. It was his 15th and final goal of 2005-06 but what we didn't know at that time, was that it turned out to be his 103rd and final official LTFC goal.

The local derby at Vicarage Road was next and after the Luton fans previous antics on the last occasion nearly 4 years prior, the police operation was bordering - on a scale of a military invasion! We were restricted to just 2,316 tickets. The Luton supporters coaches including ours from John Ashton's Bedfordshire Yeoman pub, had a police escort from Luton to Watford - AND BACK! Everyone was dropped off immediately outside the ground and frog marched to the away turnstiles, with no access ANYWHERE else. It was like 1984 and Big Brother.

Watford were in a Play-Off position and their fans were hoping to achieve the double over us, something that had only ever occurred once in my life-time (1986-87). They all thought it was going to happen when King opened the scoring but to our relief and joy Ahmet Brkovic scored his 1st goal of 2006 to send us Hatters into raptures. Watford had thought they had won it twice in the final minutes. First Mackay had a goal ruled out for clear offside and then Marlon Beresford made a brilliant save from King very late on. It ended 1-1, we were happy - and so were the police!

Coventry travelled to Kenilworth Road for the penultimate home game and brought back with them their jinx status again. They beat us 2-1.

I then missed a Luton comeback at Plymouth. Argyle took the lead, before we recovered to win 2-1.

The final home match was against runners-up Sheffield Utd and it ended 1-1 with Brkovic scoring his 7th and last goal of 2005-06. Our final game was at Turf Moor, Burnley where we drew 1-1 again. I was at Rugby Park that day watching Rangers win at Kilmarnock 3-1.

All in all, 2005-06 had been a more than satisfactory one for Luton Town. We finished in a very creditable 10th place, the highest of the promoted sides. But I couldn't help feeling disappointed with our record in 2006, just 6 wins out of 19. Reading were Champions by a streak and had only lost twice all season, their sole away defeat was at Luton. Sheffield United joined them and I'm sorry to write, Watford went up via the Play-Offs after thrashing Leeds 3-0.

The football world lost George Best in 2005. He died aged 59 after years of Alcohol problems. I would like to add, that he was THE best player I had ever seen play in my life time and as a young 16-year-old, I shook his hand after running onto the pitch at full time when he played for Dunstable in 1974.

A colossal 200,000 plus Rangers fans congregated to Manchester for the 2008 UEFA Cup Final v Russians St Petersburg. I was one of the lucky 40,000 who purchased a ticket (face value £50 via being an original and ongoing Rangers Travel Club Member) for the final at City's Ethihad Stadium. Sadly the Gers team froze and we were well beaten 2-0.

2006-07

My eldest daughter Georgina, left school in the summer of 2006 and had enrolled at Hitchin College, studying Travel and Tourism.

We decided to have a change for our annual summer holiday and chose to just have a normal 2-week break in Salou, Spain. Deb's sister Liz would be joining us with her new boyfriend Deryck - a Liverpudlian Arsenal fan!

Forced to holiday in the school closure, I would miss Luton's first two league matches of 2006-07, at home to Leicester and away at Sheffield Wednesday. Before we headed to Salou I watched a few friendlies.

I took the train to nearby St Albans to see us hammer them 6-0. Steve Howard opened the scoring. It was to be his final goal in a Luton shirt for shortly after this, Luton accepted a bid of £1 million from Derby. For a 30 year old that was not a bad bit of business - but 103 goals in 228 appearances would take some replacing!

Three days later we beat Stevenage 2-1 at Broadhall Way, my first visit to the somewhat local ground. The last friendly was at home to Premiership Fulham. 3,432 attended and Fulham won 2-1. Kevin Nicholls came on as a substitute but just days later, he had departed to Leeds for £700,000. I'm sorry, but selling your captain AND top scorer even though it was for good money, proved that Luton had gone back to the old days of being a selling club again. Equally true to write, that while we are at the limited capacity Kenilworth Road - we ALWAYS will be! There were two new signings against Fulham. Midfielder Richard Langley from QPR and full back Lewis Emanuel from Bradford City.

The 1st league game of the new season at home to Leicester had a lunchtime kick off and was shown live on Sky, meaning that I could watch it in a bar in Salou. I feared for us, having sold such quality players and said to Deryck this could be a difficult season.

We had spent £500,000 on a player at Mike Newell's old club Hartlepool. Adam Boyd was bought in as Howard's replacement.

Leon Barnett got us off to a fine early start with a firmly placed header, his first LTFC goal. In truth, Leicester looked a poor old side and we never really looked in any danger. The only surprise was, that it took until 79 minutes for us to score again, through Carlos Edwards. The Salou punters congratulated me and said Luton have nothing to worry about on that showing. 3 nights later, I was delighted to hear us win 1-0 at Hillsborough, Sheff Wed.

I arrived back from Spain too late to travel to Norwich so had to settle for Soccer Saturday. When I saw that we had a 2-0 lead on 52 mins, I was thinking Steve Who? Kevin Who? – We were top of the league!

But then Norwich woke up. They fought back to win 3-2.

My 1st league match of 2006-07 was at home to Stoke and it was a great game. Stoke took the lead early on. In the 2nd half we were rejuvenated. Coyne had hit the bar, before Leon Barnett equalised.

On the hour, we led 2-1 thanks to Richard Langley's 1st goal via a penalty (It transpired to be his only LTFC goal).

Following a rare Marlon Beresford howler, the Potters levelled and then hit the woodwork late on. On reflection, 2-2 was a fair result.

I drove down to the Memorial Ground at Bristol Rovers for a mid-week League Cup tie and took Shaun Tyler & Gary from Hemel, who later became The Duke Of Clarence pub landlord in town. 272 other Luton stalwarts joined us to watch what would turn into - a VERY long night!

Adam Boyd opened his Luton account to give us a dream start. Mid-way through the 2nd half Rovers equalised. It ended 1-1 and went into ET, with the deadlock still not broken at the end of that. The penalty shoot out was at the other end of the ground in front of the Gas fans. This was only the 2nd time I had witnessed a Luton match enter penalties, the last being at Bradford City 16 years earlier, in which we lost.

We went first and Brkovic dispatched it cleanly into the net. After Vine and Foley had both succeeded it was 3-2 in our favour. Beresford then saved and Morgan made it 4-2. If Rovers were to miss the next kick, we were through but they made it 4-3. Up stepped Sol Davis, who to my knowledge had never taken a penalty for us. He scored, we won and were through to Round 2 - I finally arrived home at near 2am!

On the day before I travelled on John Ashton's coach to Wolves, we had paid Ipswich £340,000 for striker Sam Parkin. This was a considerable amount of money for Luton, as was the fee paid for Boyd. There is no doubt that when Parkin was at Swindon his goal scoring record was very good, but he had suffered a lot of injuries at Ipswich and I felt this was a high risk. I take no pleasure in writing that my judgement proved correct. In three injury-laden seasons with us, he played 56 times and netted 10 goals - hardly prolific!

We lost 1-0 at Molinuex, this was the 1st time in 2006 that we had failed to score and never looked like doing so. Ex-Hatter Curtis Davies, then a player at Wolves rivals WBA, had no game that day and came into the Luton end to cheer his ex-teammates on.

We returned to winning ways by beating C. Palace 2-1 at Kenilworth Road. The first Oak Road sell-out of 2006-07 saw Carlos Edwards give us the lead after 65 SECONDS. Vine made it 2-0 and although the Eagles scored, it was in the 94th minute and far too late for them.

Our next match at home to Colchester three nights later finished 1-1, but Lord knows how we did not win this.

Sam Parkin had scored his first LTFC goal before Colchester levelled soon after. The 2nd half had to be witnessed, to be believed, such was our domination.

Langley had hit the bar from a penalty and the Colchester goalkeeper Davidson had what MUST have been - the best game of his career! His saves from Vine, Edwards and Emanuel were from another planet.

Carlos Edwards destroyed the U's on the wing that night, but we just could not get past their supreme number one.

I missed Luton's final appearance at Ninian Park, Cardiff, where we were soundly beaten 4-1. Three years later they moved to a new ground holding 27,000 just yards away from the old arena.

I drove Pete Morris and Shaun Tyler to Brentford for the 2nd Round League Cup tie. Thanks to 598 Luton fans attending, it pushed the gate up to over 3,000 - by five! Morgan & Feeney both scored and Vine secured the result in an easy 3-0 victory. This turned out to be my 6th and last Griffin Park visit. They moved to a new ground in 2019-20, just down the road near the A4.

The following Saturday, saw the largest home crowd so far of 9,332 at the Luton v WBA game. Rowan Vine gave us the lead with a superb goal. It was 1-1 soon after. He then restored the lead. The Baggies once again, came back to level. For the 2nd successive home game of Luton dominance, we failed to win and it ended 2-2.

I missed the Barnsley away match because it was my first Glasgow trip of 2006-07 for the Rangers v Aberdeen game, in which Rangers won 1-0. Whilst watching Soccer Saturday in a Glasgow pub the day before I was delighted at the Hatters 2-1 victory at Oakwell. This win had left us 11th after 10 games.

Birmingham were the next visitors and a five goals thriller occurred. Blues took the lead after an even start, then the in-form Rowan Vine equalised with his 7th of the season and just a minute later, he gave us a 2-1 lead. The 2nd half excitement continued with both sides attacking at will. It became 2-2. Then four mins later, summer signing David Bell from R&D's, came on as sub for his LTFC league debut and the winger scored the 3-2 Hatters winner. Birmingham hit the post in the dying seconds, but we hung on to secure three points.

I missed a 0-0 draw at Hull in mid-week.

The next two Luton matches had proved how far our club had come, by the calibre of the opposition at the time. First, Leeds United visited and then three nights later, it was off to Goodison Park for the League Cup 3 tie at Everton.

The weekend of the Leeds match was a fantastic one.

Our first sell-out in 2006-07 of 10,260 watched a sublime 2nd half Luton performance. We took the lead when Edwards waltzed around the keeper after being put through by a fine pass from Feeney, only for Leeds to equalise soon after. As the teams left level at h-t, no one could predict what was about to happen.

Rowan Vine made it 2-1 with a Feeney assist again and a minute later, Bell shot home for 3-1. It became 4-1 when Marcus Heikkenen scored his 1st (and last) goal of the season. When Edwards finished off Leeds in injury time, this magnificent 5-1 victory had lifted us into 5th place.

My younger sister Michelle had decided to come home from New Zealand for a holiday on her own around that time. It was her first time back in the UK for over 4 years.

After visiting us and seeing the relations, she went back to Brighton where we would meet her for a night out with all her friends straight after the Leeds match. The Adairs stayed in pub accommodation for the night and our girls cousin Lauren, joined us. I was buzzing after the 5-1 Leeds win and that night in Brighton was fantastic, one of the best nights out I can remember. My Aunt Joan and her children, cousins Richard, Tim & Anna Hines also came, we all went out and partied until the wee small hours. Michelle took us to a club, which played 60s/70s music all night. I was in my element and danced non-stop. Even the teenage Georgina, Lauren and young Mollie loved the music - proving that oldies music will always be the best!

Michelle is a wild one just like myself (unlike our older sister Ann & Mum) and loves having a good time. There is no doubt both Michelle and I take after our Dad's personality, rather than Mum's.

Three days later I joined old mate Barz on John Ashton's coach for the trip to Everton. We left early enough, but the traffic was an absolute nightmare and we only just arrived in time for kick off. It was my first visit to Goodison Park for 16 years. 2,334 Hatters fans helped make up the 27,159 attendance and while the Luton support was brilliant, the team performance was not, we were taught a football lesson. Everton were rampant and easily won 4-0. This was my 8th and probably last visit to Goodison, as they are another club who are going to move to a new arena soon.

On the following Sunday an event would happen which would become a catalyst in our season. Indeed, the events of that day was a turning point in LTFC's fortunes, in which our season would nosedive & we would eventually find ourselves in a situation which took over seven YEARS - to fully recover from!

I didn't travel to Ipswich for the game because of the £27 ticket cost (as against £20 for the Everton match). I refused to pay that rip off price, especially as the game was live on TV. So I watched it at a packed SWMC.

Luton were annihilated 5-0 at Portman Road and we shook our heads at how a team that could beat Leeds 5-1 just a week earlier, could perform so abysmally. It was announced after the match, that our popular player Sol Davis had suffered a stroke on the team coach en route to Ipswich the previous day.

The announcement was intentionally made post-match, for reasons that are understandable. However, how anyone can play a game of football - with a teammate fighting for his life is just beyond me! Some things are more important than football and the game should never have taken place. Mercifully, I'm pleased to write that Sol would go on to make an astonishing full recovery and would be playing again - just two months later!

Two nights after Ipswich, we lost our unbeaten home record against Burnley. The Clarets won 2-0. No excuses, but we were short of six unavailable players.

I missed a 3-0 defeat at Preston. Not only was this our 3rd defeat in a row, but also the third blank.

Luton v QPR was next and this game was a thriller. Despite complete total Luton dominance in the first half hour, it was QPR who opened the scoring with their first shot of the match.

Adam Boyd ended a 300 odd minutes goal drought by equalising and seconds later it was 2-1 to Luton, via Brkovic. But within ten mins of the restart it was 3-2 to the R's. This is how it ended. We had lost four in a row and were sliding down the table. The goal by Adam Boyd that day was his only league one in 18 appearances (13 of those as sub) – he turned out to be a VERY expensive £500,000 flop!

Our win-less streak continued when Steve Howard's Derby County came to town. The Rams won 2-0 and he went home happy as he scored one of the goals too. His dignified response to his goal in which he refused to celebrate, was a touch of class by the ex-Hatter and proved his worth as a man.

Next up was my latest European adventure with Rangers, in France, for the UEFA Cup group game against Auxerre. It was a 2-2 draw. A brilliant Adair Travel trip in Paris.

I missed the Southampton v Luton match at St Marys, where we lost 2-1 with Russell Perrett scoring his 9th and final LTFC goal.

It became defeat number 7 in a row when we lost at Plymouth 1-0. This nightmare run had seen us slide down the table from 5th to 20th and just three points above a relegation place.

The next game though, was one of my most memorable days at Kenilworth Road. I had been planning to celebrate my forthcoming 40 years as a Luton supporter for a few weeks leading up to the Preston home match and decided the best way to celebrate this moment was to actually sponsor the match, which was just a day past the actual 40th anniversary.

Knowing the Commercial Department well I struck a deal with Peter Davies, head of Corporate Hospitality. For £1,800 18 of us including myself, would pay £100 each. This would entail a pre-match tour of the stadium, with official club photographer (& friend) Gareth Owen, taking photos in the dugouts and on the pitch, a 4-course meal including wine (officially 3 bottles per table, but for us - unlimited!), followed by post-match photos with some players.

John Farmer, Pete Morris, Bob & Gary Rumble, Mick Tearle, Pete Newington (my Rochdale partner in crime), John Vivash, Mick Knight, Andy Lightfoot, Richard Green (Bean), Eddie Kelly, Shaun Tyler, Pete & young Pete Fowler, plus a friend of theirs, Martyn Bacon and a Polish friend of Eddie Kelly's, all joined myself.

I will admit that seven successive losses (8 if you include Everton in the League Cup) and the fact that Preston were top, had me concerned that this could turn into a bad day. In fact - the complete opposite occurred!

After just 70 SECONDS, Rowan Vine scored following Robinson's pinpoint cross. The first 20 minutes went completely against recent form, we dominated and now led 2-0 after Edwards netted. PNE were stung and had no choice but to attack and push men forward, however we were rarely troubled.

Luton went in at h-t 2-0 ahead, to a standing ovation. Some of the lads who had not seen us for a while, indeed for 2 of them it was their first Luton game, said, "How on earth are Luton struggling? It looks like Luton who are the top of the table team, not Preston." I had no reply - if I did, I would be a rich man!

The 2nd half continued in the same vein but North End were definitely growing stronger as time passed. Our recent loan goalkeeper signing Dean Keily was having an inspired afternoon and went on to make 3 great saves. We ended the terrible run by winning 2-0 and celebrated in fine style. The drink flowed in the Eric Morecambe Lounge and although we were boisterous and loud, everyone was just too happy to worry about us. We left there for the Bobbers Club before finally ending a fantastic day in the White House in town.

My Kilsyth mate Duncan Angus, had been invited for Corporate Hospitality by his firm to any Sunderland match of his choice, he chose the Luton game for his Stadium Of Light jolly. After just 5 mins he rang me to say that he had jumped up to cheer the 1st goal by Luton's Dean Morgan - amid some displeasing looks by Makem fans! But soon after, Sunderland equalised although Duncan had said that Murphy blatantly handled it into his path before scoring. Luton were the better team on the day Duncan had informed me, but Sunderland won 2-1. The crowd that day of 30,445 was easily the largest to watch Luton in 2006-07.

We then drew 0-0 at home with Southend but in truth were grateful for a point because in the dying seconds the Shrimpers Eastwood had rounded Dean Keily and with an open goal gaping - somehow managed to hit the post!

My bogey side Coventry visited for the final home game of 2006. A boring first half ended happily when Brkovic scored in the dying seconds. He scored again just on the hour - unfortunately it was in his own net! Luton played much better in the 2nd half and went on to deservedly win 3-1, with goals from Vine and a free kick by Morgan to give us a vital three points.

On Boxing Day, Luton played at Layer Road, Colchester for the final time. The U's would move to a new 10,000-seated ground in 2008. Just 12 games and two months after his dreadful stroke, Sol Davis was named as a Substitute that day. Colchester easily beat us 4-1.

Three nights later I watched the live TV match of Birmingham v Luton, it was the final game of 2006 and against the leaders. In a thrilling match Luton played great and I was actually upset in the end at only getting a point. Before the game I would have grabbed a 2-2 result with pleasure, but the fact that Blues equalised in the dying seconds was gut wrenching. I felt that after this Hatters performance, we still had enough quality in the team to avoid relegation. We then drew 0-0 at home to Cardiff, before the news was announced - that would almost guarantee relegation!

Before 2006-07 had started we had sold our top goal scorer and captain, now we were being informed that Luton had considered accepting fees totalling over £4.6 million to sell current top scorer Rowan Vine to Birmingham and best player Carlos Edwards to Sunderland - I was sickened! Yes, it was for big money but LTFC took years to recover from this!

We had now entered 2007 not only would this be a bad year for LTFC, but also on a personal level it was my annus horribilis - a year in which I would suffer all sorts of life changing events!

The next match I attended was for Rangers Scottish Cup tie at Dunfermline.

I actually drove up for this match and took friend Dean Rutter, but it was in sad circumstances the reason for being there.

One of my many good friends from Kilsyth was Bobby Young and he had sadly lost his wife Margaret to Cancer. There was no way I was not going to pay my respects and I wanted to attend her funeral. It was too late to book flights, so I drove Dean up in the early hours of the Sunday morning to stay with Jim & Sandra Moffatt. The funeral was on Monday morning, the day after the Dunfermline Cup Tie and of course, both Dean & I went to the match with Duncan and co. Rangers were having a nightmare season and it went from bad to worse. Already out of the SPL race and out of the League Cup, we were then out of the Scots Cup too, losing 3-2 to the Pars.

The night before Margaret's funeral I was back in Kilsyth, the first time for over four years. The last thing I wanted was any trouble regarding C's husband, but Duncan assured me there would be no problem. If there was I would just leave immediately, taking whatever would come my way. Duncan was right though because in the Games room in the 39 Masonic Club, C's husband appeared. He knew I was there - but more importantly, he also knew WHY I was up! In fact, he let things drop and even accepted my offer of a drink. It took sad circumstances, but I was now officially allowed back into Kilsyth.

Margaret was a lovely lady and I have fond memories of her and her trips to Luton. RIP Margaret.

C was at the funeral and I briefly saw her outside the Church. It had been nearly four years since I had actually seen her in person - I have never seen her since!

Around that time there was a new addition to the Adair family. We bought a West Highland Terrier puppy and called him Clyde - a boy Adair at last!

In the FA Cup 3rd Round Luton had been drawn to play at QPR. I had to miss the game as we were celebrating Deb's parents Julie & Alan's Golden Wedding on a weekend P&O Cruise to Belgium, on the liner Oriana.

I discovered on board that we had drawn 2-2 at Loftus Road. Rowan Vine in his final Luton game had equalised the R's 1st goal. It was his 33rd goal in 111 LTFC appearances.

Warren Feeney scored our 2nd.

I then watched Luton live on Sky the following Friday night at WBA. The Luton performance at the Hawthorns was a credit to them and yet football can be such a cruel game. When Albion undeservedly went ahead in the dying seconds of the 1st half (admittedly, with a great goal), I thought, 'Here we go again.' Keith Keane then scored a fabulous equaliser after an amazing run when he beat player after player. Ten mins later it was 2-1 courtesy of Warren Feeney, which had me punching the air in delight. On 88 mins we still led and while David Bell lay on the floor injured, Luton wanted the play to stop for him to receive treatment. But the Ref allowed play to continue and Phillips, made it 2-2.

The ex-Hornet then sickened us by heading in a winning 3-2 goal in stoppage time. I would have been gutted at only getting a point such was our performance - but to get none!

Barnsley were our next visitors and before the game they were 5 points below us, making this match vital. They had not won away from home since August. We lost 2-0, leaving us only two points clear of relegation.

There was a welcome break from the poor league form (2 wins in the last 16) when QPR came to town for the FA Cup 3rd round replay. Joining me for this match was my mate Ian Adams from Kilsyth, who had been working down in Portsmouth and had decided to drive up to cheer us on. It was a poor game and in truth the R's created more chances. QPR's Bailey was sent off for a horrific tackle on Ahmet Brkovic, which saw our Croatian stretchered off the pitch - Berko only played 3 more times for Luton after this! The only goal of the game was scored by QPR. Fortunately for us, it was an own goal.

In the next round 4 days later, we were at home again to Premiership club Blackburn and it would be covered live on BBC 1 with a 12.30 kick off.

You would think that the folk who ran LTFC - would know a little about how our club was run! So with an early kick off, on live terrestrial TV and knowing that the FA Cup was not as popular as it once was, it was decided in their wisdom to make the game ALL TICKET - AND charge full prices!

Even with 723 Blackburn fans in the Oak Road, the attendance was a pitiful 5,887, easily the lowest home crowd of 2006-07. I sometimes wonder what planet these people are on.

Naturally, I still went and was hoping the omens would be on our side, for in the eight times I had seen Blackburn play at Luton our record was Won 6 - Drawn 2. I'm afraid it meant nothing that day - we were thrashed 4-0!

I refused to travel to the Ricoh Arena knowing my record at Coventry - but it made no difference we still lost 1-0!

In my personal life, I was a little disillusioned and down after being informed by older sister Ann that Mum had developed Breast Cancer.

I missed the next games at Leicester and Stoke. We drew both 1-1 and 0-0. Dean Morgan's goal at the Walkers Stadium turned out to be his 12th and final LTFC one. What an enigma this player was. I felt he had talent in abundance, but his attitude sucked and he never would go on to fulfil his potential.

In the January transfer window I have already written about the sales of Rowan Vine and Carlos Edwards, coming in were three signings.

Matthew Spring returned and we paid Sheffield Wed £250,000 for striker Drew Talbot, as well as signing Bjorn Runstrom on loan from Fulham.

Spring was not a popular choice for some Hatters fans, because we had signed him from foes Watford. Personally, this never bothered me. I always rated Springy his vision at times I felt was beyond some of his teammates.

The mid-week game at home to Sheffield Wednesday was simply crucial.

Both sides had yet to win a league match in 2007 and when the Owls went in front it was looking ominous. But soon after, Runstrom opened his LTFC account to level and it was 1-1 at h-t. It became 2-1 to Luton following a Sheff Wed own goal, only for Wed to equalise with a spectacular goal. Drew Talbot had the final say against his old side when he scored the winning 3-2 goal to give us some breathing space in the relegation fight by lifting us 4 points above safety.

I travelled to Selhurst Park on the train with Chris & Keith McEvoy and 858 other Hatters, seeking my first Hatters victory there. (Apart from when Charlton were at S.P.) In a poor 1st half, we fell behind on the stroke of h-t and were then gifted an equaliser with a Palace OG. When Richard Langley was sent off for a bad challenge, the writing was on the wall. The Eagles scored what proved to be the 2-1 winner. This Palace victory left us just a point above safety.

That night Deb & I attended my good friend Jane Hopkins's brother Jim's 50th Birthday party, at St Margaret's Club in Farley Hill. I had no idea then - but that turned out to be the last time Deb & I socialised as a married couple together! After Jim Tennyson's party, Luton entertained Norwich in a thriller.

I went in the Kenilworth Suite that night as a guest of Alan Corkhill. He ran Regal Litho, the printers of Luton's programmes then, and invited me with a view to offering me a job there. I actually accepted it, but when I gave my notice in to GPR they begged me to stay citing that if I left, the company would close down.

They matched the package on offer. I decided to stay loyal and remain at GPR. Ironically, I eventually joined Alan in Dec 2011 and they printed my first two books. Bjorn Rulstrom gave us the lead following great work from Bell. Future Hatter loan player, Chris Martin made it 1-1. Talbot headed us back in front, only for the Canaries to once again level. There was then a dramatic finale. First, Spring was denied by an acrobatic save from the Norwich keeper. Then, in the 3rd minute of injury time Norwich scored the 3-2 winner with a wonder strike.

That exact score line occurred in the next match in front of a sell-out Oak Road at home to Wolves. From falling behind, we recovered to lead 2-1 with goals from Emanuel and Barnett. It was the first time since August that they had both scored. Alas, Wolves came back after the break with 2 goals to give the Old Gold men a 3-2 win.

Around about this time I had a recurrence of my arthritic knee problems. My left knee had swollen up with fluid again, this was only the second time in roughly 20 years or so and I don't know if it was stress related or not. The personal issues in my life were certainly not helping.

It didn't stop me from going on John Ashton's coach to the vital match at Leeds though. A few days prior to that game, ex-Hatter and Leeds captain Kevin Nicholls had announced that he wanted to leave Leeds and return to Luton. The Yorkshire club took exception to that and promptly stripped him of the captaincy and also dropped him from the side, as well as placing him on the transfer list. They refused to sell him to us and he would leave Leeds in the summer for Preston.

His action had added to the tension in the crowd of 27,138, including 1,404 Hatters.

After hitting the bar three times in the 1st Half, Leeds deservedly took the lead. The

Whites had further chances to finish us off but failed to do so. Then on 87 mins, we were gifted a chance of a point when Leon Barnett was fouled in the area for a penalty. Dean Morgan stepped up, he looked extremely nervous and I'm afraid I was not confident. Unfortunately, my feeling was proved correct when his pathetic tame shot was saved to almighty roars from the Leeds hordes. This 1-0 defeat had now left us 3rd from bottom and in a relegation place. I've yet to add to my 6 Elland Road visits.

We played Hull at home three nights later and after losing 2-1 to the Tigers it was the final straw for the Luton board. Mike Newell was sacked the next day after a run of 3 wins in 24 games. Although what he was meant to do after selling our four best players - was beyond me!

I had actually heard of his sacking in Pamplona, Spain while there for Osasuna v Rangers, in which we lost 1-0 and were knocked out of the UEFA Cup. The Spanish police brutally dished out to innocent men and women Rangers fans - defied belief!

When I returned from Spain I remember that Deb was acting in a strange way at that time. She explained that she thought she was suffering a bit of a crisis in our marriage and needed some time on her own.

She therefore went away for a break - to AUSTRALIA! Deb told me that she would be meeting up with some of Liz's friends who were touring there and needed time to think things through - about whether she wished to remain married to me anymore!

I can honestly write that I did not see this coming and it had caught me totally by surprise. It would be a full nine months later, before I discovered the REAL truth behind all this, the bit about meeting up with Liz's friends was bullshit.

I agreed to let Deb 'Find Herself' and genuinely believed our marriage was still good. After my affair with C, I thought that we had left this behind us and there were no signs of anything being wrong, certainly not in the bedroom dept.

Although I must equally write - I had ALWAYS believed Deb would one day gain revenge for my past affair!

Brian Stein had been installed as Caretaker Manager for the next Luton game at home to Ipswich. We had a new loan signing from Liverpool making his debut that day, Austrian striker Besian Idrizaj. We lost 2-0 to the Tractor Boys.

This defeat had left us in equal bottom place with Leeds on goal difference and the situation was now critical. With seven games remaining and 4 points behind safety, there was still all to play for though.

Our new manager was announced as Kevin Blackwell, the ex-Leeds boss. He was a local lad who had played in goal for Barton Rovers and was in their team that lost at Wembley in the 1978 FA Vase Final, their most famous 90 minutes.

On his appointment, he announced his love of LTFC by saying he remembered listening to the roars from the crowd at Kenilworth Road from his house. My immediate reaction to that was a strange one and I thought – 'Well, why were you not there SUPPORTING us!'

His first game in charge was at Burnley. A 0-0 draw did not really help us, but at least we ended a six game losing run and the clean sheet was our 1st in 8.

We were now bottom, but still only 4 points behind safety with six games left. Mr Blackwell's first home game was against Southampton, who had a youngster in their side by the name of Gareth Bale. The Saints were comfortably the better team in the 1st half.

Saints fans, who had filled the Oak Road end, were delighted as they led 2-0 at h-t. Blackwell changed the formation in the 2nd half and we improved considerably, in fact we were unlucky to lose after Brkovic had hit the post and Talbot had 2 goals disallowed for offside.

On Easter Monday we lost 3-2 at QPR. 880 loyal Hatters travelled to Loftus Road. I'm afraid I was not one of them, not only had I given up the ghost by then but had more important personal issues to sort out. Luton lost 3-2.

This result had left us all but doomed, 7 points adrift and with only 12 now available. When we then lost 2-1 at home to Plymouth, we were as good as relegated. Steven O'Leary scored his 3rd LTFC goal that day and although he would play another 16 times for us, this was his final one.

At promotion-chasing Derby, we were screened for live Sky TV coverage on the following Friday night. 288 brave Hatters attended to see the official last rites. Although we put in a hearty display, we never looked like scoring and the Rams won 1-0. It was a warm moment by Steve Howard to see him genuinely console his relegated ex-teammates after the match.

I do regret not travelling to the seaside for the final away game at Southend. Not just because we won. I really should have shown stronger loyalty but having mentioned previously, I was also battling to save my marriage too.

We managed to secure Kevin Blackwell's 1st victory at Roots Hall. The 3-1 Luton win was our first away win since September. This result also relegated the Shrimpers.

In between the Plymouth and Sunderland home games, we also had a new Chairman taking over by the name of David Pinkney.

At the final match of 2006-07 we were at home to promoted Sunderland and the LTFC officials decided to sell tickets to Sunderland fans in all areas of the ground, as well as the Oak Road. Obviously this ensured a sell-out crowd of 10,260 (which has yet to be equalled), but some Hatters fans were not at all happy. They were perturbed at having Sunderland fans with colours on, sitting next to them. Personally, it did not bother me in the slightest but there were pockets of trouble in some areas and the directors issued a statement after the game regretting their decision and would not repeat their actions again.

Before the match I drank in John Ashton's Bedfordshire Yeoman pub. Freddy Dann had introduced me to a Mackem supporting (one of many in there) friend of his and it turned out he was a bit of a celebrity. He had starred in a TV programme about clashing with his Newcastle supporting mother-in-law.

This lad from Blyth was a smashing guy and we got on fine with the Sunderland fans in the pub, as I reminisced with them about the great times in the past I had with the late Harry and co.

The less written about the match - the better! They annihilated us 5-0.

2006-07 had finished, with us winning only 10 matches out of 46. Only three of those came in the last 33 matches - a ratio of just one win in 11! We finished 2nd from bottom and went down with Southend & Leeds. The famous Leeds club had gone into administration and finished bottom, following a 10 points deduction.

I attended one more game in 2006-07 when Rangers lost 1-0 to Kilmarnock at Ibrox Park. While it was great to be back in Kilsyth without any hassle regarding the C situation, I was really showing signs of the stress in my home life. With the Deb scenario (she was in Australia at that point) and the fact my Arthritis was back in a bad way, I remember breaking down in tears in front of Duncan & Liz. After I returned from Scotland, Deb had rang from Oz to say that she had thought things through a great deal and had decided she had missed the Girls & I too much and was coming home, to sort things out and wanted to remain married to me. I was both relieved and ecstatic to hear that news. She came home on the following Saturday evening. I met her at the Heathrow Hilton Hotel, where we stayed the night. I had no idea, but that night was the final time we were intimate.

After breakfast the next morning I innocently asked what time we would be heading home, as Rangers were playing at Aberdeen in the afternoon and the match was on Sky. Many months later I found out (amongst quite a few other things) from her, that my asking this simple question - was to end our marriage of 21 years! She explained, that when I asked that question she thought that after all the time of her being away in Australia, all I cared about was how soon I could get home to watch Rangers. For that reason, she immediately changed her mind about wanting to stay married and announced that night, that she was going to leave me. She moved into the spare room and told me that she was going to move out at the end of June to stay at her sister Liz's vacant house in Stopsley. I pleaded with her many times over those next few weeks not to leave and I simply couldn't comprehend why she had changed her mind.

It would be a full 6/7 months before I learned of the true reasons why Deb had left.

Administration - Part Three

It goes without writing - there was no Summer Holiday in 2007!

There was no doubt these were testing times for myself but I was absolutely determined to do the right things and be a better father for my daughters.

Nobody could deny I was a good one anyway, but my circumstances made me fiercely resolute and mentally tough. Naturally I was missing Deb, as of course were the girls but they were coping fine, much better than I had ever imagined possible. It was almost as if they were equally determined to stay loyal to me. I was and always will be, very proud of them. I equally made sure they did not turn on Deb and she could come and see them whenever she wished. My way of coping with the split was to hope that Deb would come to her senses and return home. I was oblivious to the real reasons for her leaving, at that time.

In the summer of 2007 LTFC had lost one of its favourite sons and a legend.

On July 20th David Preece died, aged just 44 years. At that time he had been in remission for over a year following surgery for throat cancer, but died following a short illness. Preecy/Mini played 395 times for Luton and scored 27 goals. He gained 3 England B Caps in 1989 and was a member of the victorious League Cup winning side of 1988. Legend is a word often overused, but this fine player truly was a LTFC legend, the Family Stand built in 1991 was later renamed The David Preece Stand in his memory, a fitting and proper tribute. There were also a couple of personal sides to David involving myself too. He helped out as a Painter and Decorator for my cousin Elaine's son Nick Shane, as well as being a brother in law to my future boss Mark Filmer. He was one of the greatest players of the modern era and I was privileged to witness the vast majority of his games for LTFC from 1984 – 1995.

RIP David.

As expected, there were many changes following relegation from the Championship with 7 players exiting and 8 newcomers signing.

The majority of those new players signed by Kevin Blackwell were experienced to say the least. Five of them were over 30, including Chris Perry 34, Don Hutchison 36, Paul Peschisolido 36, Paul Furlong 38 and Darren Currie 32. The under 30s were full backs Richard Jackson & Alan Goodall, along with Welsh Under 21 cap Dave Edwards. Of these signings, Edwards was by far the best. The rest I'm afraid were average to crap.

Leaving for pastures new were Leon Barnett to WBA for £2.5 million, Peter Holmes, Michael Leary, Danny Stevens, Russ Perrett, my Ulster pal Warren Feeney and expensive flop Adam Boyd.

We played 4 pre-season friendlies, drawing at Dagenham, 0-0 at R&D's, which I attended (new ground) and winning 2-1 at both Oxford and Stevenage.

The opening game of 2007-08 was at home to Hartlepool and a healthy crowd of 8,013 watched, including 608 Pool fans that made the long trek south. In an entertaining match 2 of the new lads scored in our 2-1 victory. Darren Currie and full back Alan Goodall.

I drove to another new ground for a League Cup tie at League newcomers Dagenham & Redbridge. As I sat down I noticed ex-Town striker Carl Griffiths was near us, here to cheer on his ex-team. Just before the break Matthew Spring scored from a penalty. Drew Talbot doubled the lead and although the Daggers pulled one back, it was not enough as we proceeded to Round 2. Luton played at Swindon and then at home to Gillingham.

Over 1,000 Luton fans watched as we suffered our first defeat at Swindon, 2-1. We had another signing when midfielder Paul McVeigh joined from Norwich.

I watched a dire Gillingham side come to Luton and they returned home with a 3-1 defeat, which in truth should have been much greater. David Bell scored with a cracker. The Gills somehow levelled, before Paul Furlong restored our lead. The last goal was from a Matthew Spring penalty.

I then travelled to Belgrade for 4 days to see Rangers draw 0-0 v Red Star and qualify for the Champs League Group stages. This was THE most intimidating atmosphere I've ever experienced inside a football ground.

While at the game I had received a text with good news. Luton had beaten premiership Sunderland 3-0 at home in the League Cup 2nd Round. It was not their reserves either and this was sweet revenge for the 5-0 drubbing just months earlier. I later found out in disbelief that the crowd was only 4,401 including nearly 800 from Sunderland.

I was too knackered to travel to Leeds, where we lost 1-0 and didn't care about missing a JPT home game against Northampton, in which we won 2-0. Paul Peschisolido scored that night - his only senior LTFC goal!

There was a lunchtime kick off at home to Bristol Rovers on the Saturday due to Internationals. I watched a bizarre game. Rovers Ricky Lambert hit an unstoppable 30-yard goal and then afterwards came farce. After Furlong was brought down for a penalty Matthew Spring scored it, only for the Ref to rule it out, for some Luton players encroachment in the penalty area. Spring scored again but incredibly, the Ref repeated his actions for exactly the same reason - to the Hatters fans and team bench outrage! One has to admire Spring's bottle as he stepped up for a third time to score. I'm convinced had the Ref disallowed this one - there would have been a riot! The score remained 1-1 on 80 mins and in fairness it was only our goalkeeper Forde that kept it level. Lambert then scored again, this 2-1 defeat was Luton's 1st at home in 2007-08.

I missed the long trek to Tranmere on a Friday night, where we lost 2-1.

Luton v Port Vale was next and we secured a needy three points by beating the Potteries side 2-1.

Paul Furlong might have been 38, but he showed no sign of his age when he swept the ball home from a David Bell corner. Even though Vale were down to 10 men in the 1st half, it was not until the 86th minute before we could relax when Bell hit a glorious 25-yard shot to make it 2-0. Vale scored but it was too late for them.

Three nights later, I watched Charlton come to town for a League Cup 3rd round tie.

I saw them play us in the same competition 40 years earlier in front of 9,001 when we were a bottom tier side at the time. On this night, there were 4,534 - how times had changed! We witnessed a thrilling encounter as Charlton took an early lead, before we came battling back with a force. Steve Robinson scored a fantastic equalising goal, his 1st for 18 months and his 12th & final LTFC one. It remained 1-1 on 90 minutes and went into ET. Just before the break in that 1st period, Spring powered us into the lead with a bullet header then Drew Talbot scored his only goal of 2007-08, his 5th and final LTFC goal, to end it 3-1 and knock out the Championship side.

I drove alone to Huddersfield to watch a dire Luton performance. We lost 2-0 to the

Terriers. After two 1st half goals, the moment Furlong was sent off went any chance of salvaging anything. This defeat was our 4th out of 4 on the road and it was a long journey home for the 543 suffering Hatters.

I missed our mid-week trip to Yeovil and I would have normally attended as it was a new ground to visit, but I was in France watching Rangers incredibly win 3-0 at Lyon in the Champions League. It was Rangers best result in Europe in the modern era.

We secured our first away point by drawing 0-0 in Somerset.

Luton were up against Doncaster at home. After falling behind, five days after his 39th Birthday, Paul Furlong headed an equaliser in a 1-1 draw.

After 10 games we were in 16th place, only 2 points above the relegation zone. I genuinely hadn't expected this poor position.

The following weekend I had booked a week away in Tenerife for Georgina, Mollie and myself, staying at my Aunt Joan's apartment in Los Cristianos. Before we left for Tenerife Luton had inexplicably lost at Gillingham in the JPT. Luton were leading 3-1 then we somehow contrived to exit - losing 4-3!

Fortunately for me, our game at home to Northampton had been moved to the Monday night and was screened live on Sky TV. I sat in the Rangers Bluebell Bar proudly wearing my LTFC top to watch the game. Darren Currie scored his first goal since the opening day of the season. It was a fantastic curling long-range shot, which had me out of my seat cheering and earning praise from Rangers fans at the quality of the strike. The Cobblers then equalised with a goal of equal aplomb. A Spring penalty made it 2-1, before Furlong made it 3-1. It became 4-1 to the Hatters a minute from time by another Spring penalty. This victory was not only our best performance of 2007-08, but our largest win. Later on that week I discovered that Luton had lost 2-0 at Crewe.

Prior to the next LTFC match at home to Nottm Forest, the supporters' group TIL (Trust In Luton) handed out leaflets to supporters seeking answers from the new owners to seven questions, in which the Board would reply in the next programme. The 7 questions were:

1) Why have LTFC losses continued to increase?

2) Have running costs increased?

3) Why do we continue to sell our best players?

4) Why has the planning application for a new stadium been delayed?

5) Why have those projected stadium costs risen to £55 million?

6) Why have you stated that we own the new training ground - when we don't!

7) Why have you never clarified exactly how much you paid to take ownership of LTFC?

All of the above were given explanations four days later. I will not reveal those answers suffice to write that within a month of the replies, our new owner had put us into our THIRD Administration - in eight years!

On the day of the Forest match there had been disorder in High Town Road before the match, which led to a number of Luton fans receiving Banning Orders. The 8,524 attendance was the highest so far, with the Oak Road selling out. Chris Perry scored his one and only LTFC goal and Bell added a 2nd. Forest scored in the last minute and the 2-1

Luton victory was very satisfactory.

Everton came to town four nights later in the League Cup 4th round, the second successive season that we had played the Toffees in this Cup. Boy, did we give them a fright this time. In front of 8,944, we more than matched our Premiership opponents. It was 0-0 at the end of 90 minutes with both teams having great chances to win it. Sadly, it was Everton who took the lead in ET. Spring then had a shot cleared off the line but Everton went through 1-0.

I went to visit Deb's cousin Laura & Cliff in Burgess Hill, for the Brighton v Luton match. We were appalling that day losing 3-1. One amusing pre-match memory in the bar was the comment from Cliff to his friends. After learning I was to attend Barcelona v Rangers in the Champs League a few days later, he remarked, "From the Withdean to the Nou Camp - what a difference in class!" Sadly this was the last time I saw the couple, as they too would part in later years.

I had booked three days in Barcelona and had decided not to attend Luton v Carlisle on the Tues night, as I was scheduled to meet Bob & Gary Rumble at 4am the next day.

Luton had dominated the game but could just not score and it ended 0-0. The trip to Spain I was about to embark on - resulted in one of those life-changing moments that I have experienced in this old life of mine.

No one can ever accuse me of leading a dull or boring life, events in Catalonia - still affect my quality of life today!

I cannot write the full details due to space limitation, but basically what occurred at the 2-0 Barcelona win, was that Spanish Police had thrown me down a flight of 20-odd concrete steps in the Nou Camp (in the Rangers section) and this resulted in my left leg being broken. I was merely trying to find my seat and although drunk, I hand on heart & swear - that I was not causing ANY problems! At the hospital, they asked me if I was insured (thankfully I was) and after what seemed an age, a doctor came to examine me. They did X Rays and he later explained that I had broken my left leg - in THREE places! He set my leg in plaster but added, that on my return to the UK I would need an operation.

I had managed to contact Bob Rumble back at the Hotel to explain my nightmare. Him and Gary waited until I had returned to the Hotel by Ambulance and helped me on the stretcher to bed in the early hours of Thursday morning.

The next day, all kinds of horror were going through my mind. First, I had to arrange and explain everything to the insurance company who I have to write, were fantastic. Then the moment I dreaded, having to tell Deb to inform the girls with the news (and prepare for the Deb backlash) and then also to inform work. On the Thursday, a local doctor came to examine me and explained that if EasyJet were OK with me flying I could still return home on the Friday night. The Insurers had re-booked my flight with 3 seats (to allow for my leg in plaster) and mercifully, I was allowed to fly home, as more than 24 hours had passed after the incident. Evidently, it is airline procedure that you are not allowed to fly within 24 hours, if in plaster.

It hit home when Duncan said, "That's you Fucked now Al, I don't know how you are going to get round this one." – Cheers mate! As if I didn't know already!

Upon arrival at Luton Airport, a waiting Ambulance took me to Bedford Hospital (my choice). This was in the early Saturday hours and after waiting for an age there, I was informed that I would have to return on the Monday because it was a weekend. On the

Monday, a South African surgeon by the name of Dr Gill examined me and informed me that the 3 fractures were in the femur, kneecap and somewhere else on the leg. He added it was one of the worst breaks he had ever seen and asked me how it had occurred - my answer mortified him! The operation took over four hours and I was in hospital for a week. Deb actually came to visit me the night after the operation and seeing how distraught I was - even she felt sorry for me! That week was an extremely low time for me, but I have some good friends.

They visited me in hospital and those friends know who they are. I will always remember them for their loyalty when I was extremely down.

To my relations that rallied around, I will always be grateful for their support. Dad's cousin Elaine Shane was exceptional and helped me a great deal. Joan & Mick Hines visited me in hospital too and my late Uncle Malcolm's wife Carole was a godsend, as she helped me out financially. Without her help - Lord knows what might have occurred!

Finance was now a major problem. When I told work I would be off work for four months, the situation was this: November was OK, as I received full sick pay. I took my full 2008 Holiday allowance for December, but in January and February would only receive SS Pay, a pathetic amount. Carole came to my rescue by lending me the money to pay those two months' mortgages.

Deb came round every morning and night to take Georgina to Hitchin College and back. Georgina was also learning to drive at the time.

I was at my lowest ebb in those dark winter months and did a lot of deep thinking lying in my bed and soul searching. I wondered how I would ever get back to some form of normal life. I'm afraid that I was to face further daunting challenges in the coming months.

My life was in crisis and I know that more than a few people, were genuinely concerned about my state of mind at the time.

However, I would refuse to go under. I had two daughters to think of and they would be my inspiration to begin the fight back.

While I was in hospital it had been announced that LTFC had entered Administration AGAIN for a THIRD time in nine years and had immediately been deducted 10 points, which plummeted us back down to bottom of League 1 and 4 points adrift of safety.

It goes without writing that it would be a while before I could watch LTFC again. Luton's first game after my return from Barcelona was at Walsall, where we drew 0-0. This was followed by another draw, this time 1-1 at home to Brentford in the FA Cup. We followed this with a 1-0 win at home to Southend.

In the FA Cup replay at Griffin Park we beat Brentford 2-0. Chris Coyne completed the win with the 2nd goal. This turned out to be the 16th and final LTFC goal for our Australian skipper. The Administrators would sell him in January to Colchester for £350,000. He would not be the last player to leave Kenilworth Road in these harsh times.

After a 1-1 draw at Oldham, Nottingham Forest visited for a 2nd time in 2007-08. This was in the FA Cup 2nd round and they once again left us with a defeat, this time 1-0.

As a result of this, we received a glamour tie and would play Liverpool at home in the 3rd round for the 2nd time in two years.

Before that match though, there were five other games to face.

Luton lost for the first time since entering Administration, 1-0 at Cheltenham. We beat Tranmere 1-0 at home, before a remarkable resilient Luton performance at the Memorial Ground, Bristol.

Dave Edwards scored his 4th and ultimately, last LTFC goal in a 1-1 draw v Bristol Rovers. He would only play another 3 times before becoming another player forced to leave, to Wolves. What made this game remarkable was that Luton gained a point after having - THREE players sent off!

Chelsea loan player Anthony Grant (his sole full LTFC game) Chris Coyne and Steve Robinson all saw red and each had an early bath.

On Xmas Day I attended Xmas dinner with Deb's family at a Restaurant in Loughborough. My girls had refused to leave me on my own and at their insistence, I was invited too. Deb drove us up in Georgina's new car to join her Aunt Gill & John, along with her parents. It was a pleasant day with no bitterness, as Deb & I sat at opposite ends of the table.

The final match of a torturous 2007 for both LTFC and myself saw us gain our first away league victory of the season, 2-1 at Port Vale. Jaroslaw Fojut, on loan, scored in his penultimate game before having to return to Bolton. I wish we could have kept this exceptionally talented defender, but of course with Luton's perilous financial position there was no chance of that happening. This was only the second away league victory in all of 2007.

The year was over thankfully. Apart from my Arthritis returning, discovering my Mum had Cancer, Deb leaving me, breaking my leg in 3 places - it could have been worse!

When Luton scored an only goal to beat Yeovil at home on New Year's Day it actually lifted us out of the relegation zone at this halfway stage. There is no doubt that we were fighting for our lives and this was the 7th undefeated game in 8 since receivership, in fact our 11th in 12 overall.

The big Cup Tie had arrived and not only was it nearly sold out, but it was shown live on SKY TV meaning I could watch the game.

The two above facts would bring in acutely needed finances to the club. I sat down with (ex) father-in-law Alan, to watch an inspiring Hatters show.

Luton played truly fantastic that day and were severely unlucky to find themselves 1-0 down. Fortunately, it was to only last three mins, before we deservedly equalised. The tireless efforts of Drew Talbot were rewarded when he produced a cross that saw Rise put through his own Liverpool goal for 1-1. It ended that way to the delight of the Administrators and earn Luton a replay.

The Anfield replay would earn LTFC even more vital revenue, especially when it was chosen for live TV again on Sky.

The Liverpool home game turned out to be Dave Edward's 26th and final LTFC appearance. This talented player and easily Kevin Blackwell's best signing was sold to Wolves shortly after for £675,000.

There were further shocks in the Town camp when before the home match with table toppers Swansea, Kevin Blackwell gave a month's notice, that he and his coaching staff were quitting. – Solidarity eh, you're having a laugh!

He stated that when he joined LTFC he was promised all sorts of commitments and having had to sell £3 million worth of players and suffer Administration, it was too much to take. He added that he had ended up with a squad of players not knowing if they were going to be paid or have a future with the club, therefore he was quitting. I now understood why as a youngster he listened to the roar of the Kenilworth Road crowd from his house, instead of attending - he was never a Luton SUPPORTER! In other words when the going got tough – he fucked off!

Swansea became the 2nd away victors at the time with a resounding 3-1 win. In the replay at Anfield, an astounding show of support for Luton was shown when a staggering 5,716 Hatters travelled to Merseyside. This was the highest away support in our history, apart from Semi/Cup or Play Off Finals. Since broken in 2018 at Newcastle.

Luton had little choice but to defend and try to contain the Reds and for the first 44 mins we did just that, before Liverpool scored. In the 2nd half the floodgates opened & it was the Steven Gerrard show, he hit 3 & they won 5-0.

The score was harsh on Luton. It has to be noted that the amazing Luton fans never stopped singing throughout.

The following day, Kevin Blackwell and his staff were sacked.

Luton legend Mick Harford was appointed as new manager and the Administrators also announced that a new consortium led by celebrity fan Nick Owen by the name of LTFC 2020, would be the preferred bidder to take charge of the club. After proving they had sufficient funds to see out the season, 2020 would eventually become the new owners of LTFC - but would have to face further draconian obstacles in 2008!

Mick Harford's first game in charge was at Leyton Orient. We were back in the relegation zone and a point off safety. Over 1,000 Luton fans travelled to Brisbane Road and it was sods law that ex-Luton flop Adam Boyd, should open the scoring for Orient. It became 2-0 when he set up another. Keith Keane scored his only 2007-08 goal but no breakthrough occurred and we lost 2-1.

Three nights later at Bournemouth saw a Luton result that I thought would almost certainly condemn us to relegation.

The Cherries raced into a quick lead and then doubled it. Spring scored a penalty on the stroke of h-t and then Dean Morgan equalised with his 12th and final LTFC goal. When Paul Furlong made it 3-2 I thought that we had completed a fantastic comeback and would be right up for the relegation fight. But oh no - this is Luton we are talking about here! With just a minute left on the clock it was still 3-2 - only for Bournemouth to strike TWICE and win 4-3!

Leeds were in town next and naturally filled the Oak Road to give us easily our best home crowd of 2007-08, 9,756.

Had Leeds not been deducted 15 points at the beginning of the season for not exiting administration, they would have been top. Instead, they were 5th but still in a Play-Off position. We drew 1-1.

Forgotten man Sam Parkin came off the Luton bench for his first game since the opening day, having spent the previous 5 months injured. (As always)

It was a good comeback, for he rose to head in the equaliser in the dying seconds. The point gained had left us 2nd from bottom, yet still only three points from safety with 19 matches still to play.

Against one of Parkin's former clubs Swindon we lost 1-0 at home before the long trek to Hartlepool, where we were thrashed 4-0.

When Bournemouth also put 4 past us for the second time in a matter of weeks, the writing was on the wall. Leyton Orient made it four defeats in a row and 7 out of the last 8 by beating us 1-0.

I have a fantastic record against the O's. In the 17 times I have seen them play at Kenilworth Road, we have won 14 and drawn 3. So of course, that is the reason we lost this one – I WAS NOT THERE!

This result made Orient one of 6 teams to achieve a double over us in 2007-08. Luton battled bravely at leaders Swansea, only to lose 1-0. Naturally, had I not broken my leg I would have been at this game due to Swansea playing at the Liberty Stadium, their recent new ground.

It was around this time that I had discovered the true reason why Deb had left.

Having spent many hours lying on my back after the leg break I did a lot of deep thinking and soul searching on reflexion. She had a male 'friend' called James, who was allegedly helping her out with jobs at Liz's house. It took me THREE MONTHS to suss out and for it to click, that her ex-boyfriend before me in the 80s was called James and he had migrated to Australia after their split. I put two and two together and knew it MUST have been him that she visited for her 'time out trip' to Oz earlier that year. The next time I saw her I challenged Deb by stating, "It must be lovely to finally be with your true love James, after all this time." Deb went Scarlet Red and I just knew. I pleaded that she just be honest and tell me how it had occurred. I always knew that one day I would get paid back for my affair with C and this is how it happened.

Earlier in 2007, she had been out in town one night with friends when she bumped into him in Charlie Browns nightclub. She told me she honestly had no idea he was back in Luton on a holiday, visiting his mum. They did arrange for her to travel to stay with him in Australia and this would be her test on her feelings still for him. Deb told me that she had honestly made up her mind out there to return home to me, draw a line under everything and just say that she had gained her revenge and move on - calling it 1-1 if you like! However, me innocently asking her at the Heathrow Hilton about watching Aberdeen v Rangers - was the catalyst to her changing her mind there and then! She also expressed that I never once pleaded for her to return, to which my answer was I just wanted to give her the space I thought she needed.

Their plan was to return to Australia when Mollie had left school and take her with them.

So there you have it – it's Rangers' fault my marriage had ended! Georgina had by now passed her driving test and was the owner of a new Peugeot 107, which I purchased for her in my name, but she made the monthly payments.

At this point I was almost ready to finally return to work after four long months' absence. I was due back on March 1st, but before then Luton had stopped the losing streak by drawing 1-1 at home to Millwall, with Paul Furlong scoring his 12th and final LTFC goal.

My leg had sufficiently healed enough for me to return to work, but I had now been left (and still am) riddled with Rheumatoid Arthritis. Not just in my knees, but other joints like my hands, feet, arms and shoulders. After seeing a specialist I remain on daily medication taking the likes of Steroids, Methotrexate and Folic Acid amongst others, to try and counter the inflammation and pain. I still have the condition today and it is something I have to live with for the rest of my life. I just have to get on with it, though sometimes it is extremely uncomfortable - thanks Spanish Coppers!

I returned to GPR Printing and was rather excited.

All of the time that I was off work, my clients stayed loyal and gave GPR print work, enabling me to at least earn some small commission.

When I arrived all chirpy I was summoned up to the Owners' office. They told me that they were very sorry - but I was being MADE REDUNDANT!

They could hardly look me in the eye and I was in complete shock. I had prided myself on the fact that in 34 years of employment I had never once been laid off, something not many folk can equal. When I asked them why the hell did they wait so long until the day I actually returned, it was explained that it is actually illegal to make someone redundant while off sick.

The manner in which they quickly removed me from the premises and took me home was a disgrace. I pointed out to them that when my customers find out the news, the clients would immediately stay loyal to myself and totally finish using GPR for ANY business. I finished by saying a couple of things, "1) You will lose all of my clients and 2) Each company I have left (Four Printers) has closed down following my leaving. I will give you a couple of months at the most."

Their response was, "We'll see."

One WEEK later, after all my clients were horrified at their actions and told them they would refuse to use GPR – they went into liquidation and closed!

On my return home I was distraught, but knew I had to act immediately. I remembered an old Roydon Printers colleague Mark Filmer, who had his own small Printing Company in Ampthill. He once told me that if ever I was stuck to come and see him. I did exactly that, on that very afternoon. After explaining my predicament, he said that he would willingly take me on as a Rep but could appoint me on a Commission only basis. I was extremely grateful to Mark and although not ideal, I knew I had to act urgently if I wanted to retain all my current clients. I started with Mark the very next day.

The Print industry has changed beyond belief now and the days of earning fantastic money have long gone. I like to think that I was good for Mark and he was good for me. I left him on good parting terms in Dec 2011. Mark got me out of a hole and I will always be grateful to him for that.

Eventually in the summer of 2008 I received the minimum Government Redundancy package, not a fortune, but it helped me to pay back Carole for my Mortgage payments in January and February.

Luton were at home to Walsall the night I was scheduled to return to work and understandably, I postponed attending. We lost 1-0.

My return was at Roots Hall, Southend. The SWMC Committee kindly invited me as one of their Brewers had a box and entertained us to Corporate Hospitality. I naturally took things steady on the alcohol front, having just a few glasses of Red Wine. It was my first drink since Barcelona over 4 months prior. Luton lost 2-0 and frankly, it was men against boys - I don't think we had a shot on goal!

There was no chance of me travelling to Carlisle mid-week. David Bell scored his 9th and final LTFC goal in our 2-1 defeat.

My first game back at Kenilworth Road was against Oldham and it was our first victory under Mick Harford. The 3-0 win ended an appalling run of 15 win-less games. 18-year-old

Ryan Charles on his full debut opened the scoring. It was followed by a Matthew Spring penalty and a Lewis Emanuel goal. The home attendance that day of 5,417 was the lowest in 2007-08.

We were now eight points adrift of safety with 9 games remaining.

A week later, Sam Parkin headed us in front at home to Cheltenham. Despite dominating the game, Cheltenham hit back to draw 1-1. Drew Talbot was stretchered off to end his season.

Luton travelled to Millwall to gain a point in a 0-0 draw, but draws were of no use anymore, only victories would suffice. This would be the case when we beat Crewe at home next 2-1, thanks to a brace from Matthew Spring. Not only was this our last win in a miserable season, but also his final Luton goals.

In his two spells at Luton he played an impressive 357 games, making him 12th in the all time list of LTFC appearances and he scored 43 goals.

Three successive 2-1 defeats saw the final confirmation of our relegation. Losing at Gillingham and Northampton, before the fatal one at home to Brighton. Luton lost the penultimate away game 1-0 at Nottingham Forest and following that was the final away match at Doncaster's new Keepmoat Stadium, in which we lost 2-0. Normally I would have attended this as it was a new ground, but it was the day of my 50th Birthday and although I had long ago decided to cancel the 50th party, I did still plan to have a celebration with close friends at the SWMC. It was a thanks to those who helped me at my lowest point and we had a great night as I ended up getting pissed for the first time in 6 months.

Before that I watched Town's final game at home to Huddersfield and we lost 1-0. Of the 23 games Luton played in 2008 we had won just 13 points out of the 69 available, truly awful. In this horrific season we ended bottom of the league 17 points off safety, we couldn't even say that the ten point deduction had caused the demotion. What cost us, was an appalling away record, just ONE win and 5 draws - a miserable 8 points out of 69!

On the morning of May 14th 2008 I drove up to meet Duncan and the Kilsyth clan in Oldham. After my nightmare in Barcelona, Rangers went on to be eliminated from the Champions League group. They qualified for the UEFA Cup and went on a magnificent run knocking out Panathinaikos, Werder Bremen, Sporting Lisbon and Fiorentina to proceed to the final against Zenit St Petersburg at the City of Manchester Stadium. Duncan and my pals had been to every game and pre-booked an Oldham Hotel after the Semi victory in Italy. As a Rangers Travel Club Member, I automatically qualified for a Final ticket at £50 if I wanted one. (Is the Pope a Catholic?) It transpired that on that day of the final over 200,000 Rangers fans had descended on Manchester - 160,000 of them with no chance of attending the match! It was a sight to behold and will never be repeated by a British club in my lifetime. Alas, Rangers lost 2-0.

After a traumatic year, I wanted to move on and look forward to better times.

2008-09

After the Administrator had chosen 2020 as the preferred bidder to be the new owners of LTFC on the day of the Liverpool FA Cup replay in January, they (2020) loaned money to the club to keep them surviving.

On 26th February 2008, 2020 had their takeover bid conditionally accepted and were official custodians of the club until the end of season 2007-08. The Football League would then negotiate terms with 2020 to return the golden share to them for the 2008-09 campaign.

Life is far from easy as far as Luton Town is concerned and in June, an FA probe into past transfer irregularities was complete and we were found guilty on FIFTEEN charges. LTFC was then handed a ten-point deduction for 2008-09 and also a £50,000 fine by the Football Association. This was just the beginning, for we still had to face charges by the Football League on other financial matters. According to Football League rules, LTFC had violated them by leaving Administration without having made a CVA (Company Voluntary Arrangement) with its creditors. The Football League would only allow 2020 the return of the Golden Share (allowance to play/compete in the Football League) on the condition that we start with a FURTHER TWENTY-POINT DEDUCTION for entering Administration a third time – with NO appeal! Basically, we were fucked and had to accept the 20-point penalty or be thrown out of the League.

We appealed against the FA deduction, but that was thrown out and therefore Luton were effectively relegated to the Conference before a ball had been kicked in 2008-09, by having to start on - minus 30 points!

I totally understand that Clubs have to live within their means and I actually agree with point deductions for this reason, but all the offences were by the previous owners and it was THEY, who escaped without - ANY punishment! While us fans, and the people trying to save LTFC (2020) - were shafted!

On top of that nightmare scenario, Mick Harford had to practically rebuild the playing squad from scratch. From the previous season, a mammoth total of 23 players including loans had either left or returned to their clubs.

Players I have not already mentioned include Calvin Andrew, who understandably jumped at the chance of joining Crystal Palace for £80,000, Marlon Beresford after 132 games, Ahmet Brkovic had joined Millwall, following 38 goals in 223 appearances, David Bell to Norwich for £600,000 (there is a story to that, which legally I am not allowed to reveal), Darren Currie, Paul Furlong, Alan Goodall, Don Hutchison, Richard Jackson, Richard Langley, Dean Morgan, Steve O'Leary, Chris Perry, Paul Peschisolido & Steve Robinson (12 goals in 211 appearances), all left Kenilworth Road.

It must be noted that Don Hutchison not only refused his final pay packet, but also sponsored two youth team players for 2008-09 - cap doffed to him!

We had 4 pre-season home friendlies v Leicester, Northampton, Colchester and Brighton, with the few players remaining and a host of Trainee/Trialists.

I was amongst 1,290 loyal Hatters in a 0-0 draw with Northampton.

On the opening day of the 2008-09 Season, Luton were at home to Port Vale. New faces that appeared in the slim LTFC squad included Claude Gnapka, Asa Hall and George

Pilkington, signed from opponents Vale.

There were also a couple of season-long loan players from Norwich, Chris Martin & Michael Spillane. But the best and most welcome signing of them all, was the prodigal return of warrior Kevin Nicholls. He had taken a substantial pay cut to join our battle from Preston and it was an enormous lift to see him in a Town kit once again. He was immediately reinstated as captain and a great crowd of 7,149 were there to see it. The atmosphere pre-match was electric as we prepared to chase down the mammoth 30 points deficit.

Despite a terrific 1st half Luton performance, we lost 3-1 with Parkin scoring. Night matches were still too difficult for me to attend due to my knee problems and I took the decision to miss them for the foreseeable future, hence not renewing my season ticket and instead, buying the new open Five - match packages.

After the Vale defeat we secured our first victory, at home in the League Cup by beating Plymouth 2-0.

At Priestfield Stadium, we gained our first 3 points by beating Gillingham 1-0. Georgina became the first Adair to enrol for University and her choice to study Travel and Tourism was hardly a surprise, given our family background for travelling. The fact that she chose to study the four-year degree at Caledonian University in Glasgow also thrilled me personally (Rangers).

With Georgina in Scotland I decided to take Mollie away for a deserved holiday and chose an All Inclusive break for the first time. We went to Cancun in Mexico staying at a fabulous 4-Star Crown Paradise Club Hotel. The Hotel was luxurious, right on top of the beach and the quality & range of food was magnificent. We had a fabulous time and it remains Mollie's favourite holiday.

While in Mexico I discovered that Luton had drawn 1-1 at home to Notts County, were thrashed 5-1 at Reading in the League Cup and beat Exeter 1-0 in Devon.

After returning home I drove Pete Morris up to Macclesfield for my first away game. We were joined by an impressive 731 Hatters fans in a crowd of only 2,349 - nearly a third of the attendance were away fans! It was a poor Luton display and we lost 2-1. Ryan Charles scored our goal. My first 2008-09 Luton victory was at home to Aldershot, this was the first time we had played the Shots since 1968 and the result was the same as then, 3-1 to Luton.

Michael Spillane scored, before they equalised. A minute from time Asa Hall gave us the lead, it became 3-1 in when Chris Martin swept home.

I drove up north for the away match at Rotherham. The Millers like us, were a club that had suffered acute financial problems and along with Bournemouth and Luton, had been deducted points for entering Administration.

They, as well as Bournemouth, had suffered a 17-point deduction for entering a second period, rather than our third. On top of all that, Rotherham had been forced to leave their Millmoor home. Following disputes with their landlords and along with an unfinished new stand, the Millers had to leave after playing there for over 100 years. Rotherham moved to nearby Sheffield's Don Valley Athletics Stadium, with the Football League demanding a £750,000 bond for the team to play outside the town's boundaries for a maximum of four years. If they did not return to Rotherham in that time, they faced eviction from the Football League. They did return in 2012, to a new stadium just down the road from Millmoor.

650 Luton fans travelled to the Don Valley in a 4,095 crowd. We lost 1-0 when a Rotherham cross, deceived goalkeeper Dean Brill and fluked into the net.

In the next game at home to Chester the LTFC Match Programme printed a tribute to someone I knew personally. Paul Vann had died of Meningitis in June 2008 at the age of 48. I had known Paul for years, as he was a Stopsley lad who lived at Corncrake Close. 2020 did a magnificent gesture by retiring his seat for 2008-09. My friend Anthony Brown, a 2020 director at the time, stated in the match programme, that even if we drew Manchester United in the Cup this season there would be one spare seat in the ground, with Paul's name on it. RIP Paul.

The Chester game was a drab 1-1 draw.

I missed another 1-1 draw at Valley Parade, Bradford City in front of 13,083, easily the largest league attendance (thanks to a £100 Season Ticket Offer), to watch Luton in 2008-09.

We then drew 2-2 at home to Brentford in the JPT. With no ET in this competition, it was straight to penalties and we secured victory 4-3. I missed the Darlington home match, which we lost 2-1.

After 10 matches it was already gloomy, needing promotion form to have any realistic chance of staying in the League, we were on - 18 points, instead of an ideal Zero.

My next match was Luton v Accrington Stanley.

If I had felt depressed about Luton playing this calibre of opposition at the time - I was crestfallen after they beat us 2-1! It was possibly my lowest moment of supporting the Town at the time and I'm afraid there would be worse to follow. Asa Hall scored our goal.

In the 5,492 attendance - EIGHTY away fans were in the 2,100 seated Oak Road End, the lowest away following of 2008-09. The one bright spot, was the debut of £80,000 signing from Middlesbrough, Centre Forward Tom Craddock.

He opened his LTFC account three nights later, when he scored both Luton goals in a 2-2 draw at Grimsby, then managed by ex-Hatters boss Mike Newell. History was made at Blundell Park that night when Jordan Patrick came on as Substitute for Luton to become the youngest ever Hatter at 16 years 16 days old. Since been broken by Conor Tomlinson at 15 years 199 days in 2016.

We then gained a morale boosting 2-1 victory at Gigg Lane, Bury.

Around this time, the death was announced of controversial former Chairman David Evans. He was on the Board at LTFC for 14 years, five of those in the Chair. He made many enemies by introducing the away fan ban, the artificial pitch and selling the ground to the Council. While I disagreed with those decisions, I have already written about his 1984-85 funding which certainly saved us from relegation and built the foundations for our only major trophy and 2 Wembley Cup Finals. For that reason, I am grateful to him. RIP Mr Evans.

I drove up to Shrewsbury's new Polestar Stadium with 804 other Hatters fans in the 6,185 crowd. I'm afraid we were poor against the Shrews and lost 3-0.

In the JPT a late winner at Walsall secured a 1-0 Luton victory.

At around this time I was in a relationship with a friend of Jane Hopkins, called Elaine. I took Elaine to a match at home to Dagenham & Redbridge. She was a good omen, as we won 2-1 with Sol Davis scoring a rare goal and Paul McVeigh the other. This game took place after a 0-0 draw with non-league Altrincham in the FA Cup. At the replay in Cheshire, Luton went through after winning 4-2 on penalties, following another 0-0 draw (AET).

Memories came flooding back when I finally achieved seeing Luton play at Rochdale. I drove Pete Morris up and took plenty of stick that day, following the Banning Order over six years earlier. After falling behind to an early Rochdale goal, we were never in the game and went on to lose 2-0.

Three nights later I missed a 1-0 home defeat to Brentford, as well as the FA Cup 2nd Round 3-1 loss at Southend. I would have gone to the Cup game but was in Scotland watching Rangers lose 2-1 to Hearts in Edinburgh.

My relationship with Elaine didn't last long and had just finished, so I decided to fly up to visit Georgina and the Kilsyth lads.

I missed a seesaw 3-3 mid-week home game with fellow point deduction sufferers Bournemouth, who were a place above us. That point had wiped out Bournemouth's deficit, while we were still on minus 10.

In the next game at home to Barnet, I remember being impressed by a huge Barnet/Rangers flag in the Oak Road. This was Barnet's first visit to Luton. We sent them home, beaten 3-1.

The largest 2008-09 league Luton away following of 1,118, travelled to Wycombe to see us earn a good 0-0 point at the League Leaders.

In the JPT area Semi-Final Luton beat Colchester 1-0 at home.

Although relegation was a near certainty, a trip to Wembley would be nice and in the area Final we had drawn Brighton over two legs, with the 1st leg to be played in the New Year at the Withdean Stadium.

Four days later, Luton drew 1-1 at home to Morecambe with Spillane netting our goal. The match was dedicated to the late Eric Morecambe due to our famous ex- director's links with both clubs, Morecambe being his birthplace.

I took Georgina & Mollie away for Xmas and we had a lovely relaxing time in the Dominican Republic. We stayed at the All-Inclusive, Four Star Grand Oasis Marien Hotel in the Costa Dorada resort.

Luton's two games in my absence were a 2-2 draw at Chesterfield's Saltergate (for the final time) and a 3-2 home victory against Lincoln. At this halfway stage of the season we had minus 1 point, 15 points adrift off safety.

I was now in a new relationship with a lady called Judy, from Hockwell Ring. We had been introduced to each other, at a family party by my Dad's cousin Elaine. After our first date at the SWMC New Year's Eve Party, I went out with Judy for four months.

The first game of 2009 was at Chester in mid-week where we blew a 2-0 lead to draw 2-2. Lewis Emanuel scored his 5th and final LTFC goal that night.

It had taken 25 games for us to finally shrug off the -30 points deduction and with 21 games remaining we were a full 17 points off safety, behind Mike Newell's Grimsby.

I drove alone on the long journey north for my (and Luton's) first visit to Darlington's new ground. If ever there was a case of over ambition, this was it. When it opened as the Reynolds Arena in 2003 it had a 25,000 seated capacity, there is no doubt it is a nice stadium. Due to lack of finances it had been cut to a 10,000 limit when I attended the game and as I write this book - they had been liquidated and no longer play there! The crowd that day was 3,319 including 494 Hatters fans and needless to say the atmosphere was positively dead. Prior to the match I parked up at the Stadium Car Park before bumping into Tom Craddock and his Dad, who are from Darlo and then had a couple of pre-match pints in the impressive Supporters Club there. That was about as good as the day was, because we were thrashed 5-1.

I missed the next four games, in part due to my next bit of misfortune. It might have been a New Year and a new start but on one Saturday January morning I woke up to discover that my Astra had been stolen from the front drive.

Somehow, thieves had got in through the back entering in the kitchen door, before taking the keys out of the front door and driving off with my motor.

I borrowed cousin Ken Adair's car while they were at their Ibiza apartment, before buying a 2003 Vectra. I never saw the Astra again, but fortunately had Gap Insurance cover, which pays out if you are still paying off the finance.

In the 1st leg JPT final at Brighton we drew 0-0 and the next game against Bradford City at home we drew 3-3, but the match ended in controversy. Referee Mr Kettle awarded the Bantams a penalty in the dying seconds and everyone I know - swore blind it was never a pen in a month of Sundays!

After a Bournemouth own goal at Dean Court, we once again failed to hold on to a lead. They equalised to end it 1-1.

Four days later I watched Asa Hall give Luton the lead against Bury at home, in what was an impressive 1st Half Luton showing. The second period can only be described as abysmal, it was no surprise to see the Shakers come back to win 2-1. This was when - I KNEW we were doomed to a 3rd successive relegation!

I didn't have the heart to travel to Dagenham and the fact that 733 Hatters fans did out of a crowd of 2,310, speaks volumes of their loyalty. We lost 2-1.

The next match was the return JPT leg at home to Brighton. Adair Travel had already swung into action by provisionally booking two 49-Seat Coaches for the final at the new Wembley Stadium to leave from SWMC before this particular Brighton match, as I knew that Coach Companies would be inundated with requests should we beat the Seagulls. I intentionally did not attend the game for two reasons: 1) I felt that as I had not attended any games in this tournament run, I might jinx the team and 2) I genuinely felt I didn't deserve to go and be a glory hunter. So I watched it on SKY TV at SWMC.

The biggest home crowd of 2008-09 of 8,711 was boosted by easily the largest away following of the season 1,546. When Tom Craddock pounced on a terrible mix up between the Brighton keeper and defender to score in only the 2nd minute, the SWMC erupted. We were playing well against the higher league team until Brighton equalised. The Seagulls steadily became more threatening until they had a player sent off for a bad foul on Michael Spillane. It ended 1-1 and with no ET in the JPT, it had to be decided on penalties, which took place at the Kenilworth Road End. This is how it panned out: Brighton took the 1st with their goal scorer Forster - 0-1, Martin 1-1, Virgo 1-2 Brighton, Craddock 2-2, Elphick for Brighton 2-3, Hall 3-3, Jarrett of Brighton had his penalty saved by Lewis Price (who only played twice on loan for LTFC) on to the post, still 3-3, Charles 4-3 Luton - Birchall stepped up and when Price saved again to send Luton to Wembley, everyone in the SWMC and the ground (bar the Oak Road) went barmy! We were through to play Scunthorpe at Wembley in 46 days' time. The Luton fans swarmed onto the pitch and we were all dancing in the Club. After two years of sheer hell, at last - we Hatters fans finally had something to cheer about!

A question I was immediately asked was, how many Luton fans would attend at Wembley? I replied that night, over 30,000 easily and was laughed at. The person laughing suggested we would do well to take 20-25,000 absolute tops. Even I, did not think we would actually take 42,000 fans and if the F.L. had not been so pigheaded and allowed us more tickets - we would have sold over 50,000! Yes, I know some people were jumping on the new Wembley bandwagon, but I would much prefer that scenario, rather than the likes of Wimbledon in 1988 - when they couldn't sell their allocation in their FA Cup Final against Liverpool!

The incredible support that would travel to Wembley for what was in essence a Mickey Mouse Cup Final, proved beyond doubt that LTFC has the fan base within the town and surrounding areas to justify a bigger new home stadium.

On top of the two coaches I hired, I had booked us all into a Wembley pub called the Green Man and an unnamed friend of mine asked me to assist him in the selling of Wembley souvenir Polo Shirts and Jackets.

But just two days later on February 19th, 2009, my emotions turned from elation to despair - when I heard news that my Mum had died!

I received a phone call in the middle of the night from a sobbing older sister Ann in New Zealand, to inform me that Mum had died that morning. My initial thought was - I am now an orphan! But I was in total shock, for although I knew Mum had Breast Cancer, because of other personal issues which I won't reveal, Ann had never really let on to Michelle and I just how seriously ill Mum truly was (at Mum's command/wish, I hasten to add). RIP MUM.

Michelle had moved from Auckland a few years prior and had been living in the Gold Coast, Australia for a while at this point and it is true to write that Mum and her sadly, never really got on. In fact they clashed big time, but when I told Michelle the bad news I was surprised at how she took it. It is no exaggeration to write - that she wailed in desperation. I think if you were to ask her today, even she would be startled at her reaction. There was sympathy of course from my friends and family. I know that Georgina and Mollie were now very worried for myself. I privately joked with them, it's OK you can tell God he can leave me alone now. I've taken my punishment for the crime/sins I committed. I mean apart from my arthritis returning, my wife leaving me, being thrown down stairs by Spanish Police and breaking my leg in 3 places, losing my job on return to work after having no wages for 2 months, being left riddled with Arthritis, having my car stolen and my Mum dying – I was Fine!

Seriously now, people WERE concerned, about how much more I could take after what I had been through in the previous two years. I was going to fight back and turn my life into a positive one.

I am utterly convinced you get what your mind thinks about most of the time, if you think negatively all the time, negative things WILL happen in your life.

After Mum died I decided to start thinking more positively about life in general, just as I once used to. The glass became half full from the moment she died - not half empty!

On the back of the fantastic feel-good football factor, we entertained Shrewsbury at home four days after the victorious Brighton victory. Tom Craddock once again opened the scoring, only for the Shrews to equalise soon after. After Sam Parkin scored his first goal since August, there only looked like one team would win. Unfortunately, this was Parkin's 10th and final LTFC goal. He played 56 times in three injured blighted seasons, before heading to Perth in Scotland, for St Johnstone the following summer. Asa Hall went on to score a third and this 3-1 victory was the first league win of 2009.

With two thirds of the season gone, we were a massive 18 points behind Barnet in a safety position – Mission Impossible! But the spirit had now returned and we were to go on a semi decent run in the build up to Wembley. A mid-week 0-0 draw at Accrington Stanley was followed by a great 3-1 win at Port Vale.

I missed a home mid-week 0-0 draw with Gillingham, but attended the next game at home to Exeter. The Grecians will always have a small place in my heart, being the first opponents at my very first LTFC match nearly 43 years earlier.

Exeter took an early lead and we then fell 2-0 behind, before Craddock pulled a goal back. Alas, Exeter held on to win 2-1.

After waiting four months for an away win, we then had two in 2 weeks when we beat Notts County 2-0 at Meadow Lane. The safety gap was now 14 points, with 11 games remaining.

I travelled to Aldershot on Gary's (the landlord of the Duke of Clarence pub) coach for my first visit to the Recreation Ground. I wasn't going to miss this game as apart from it being a new ground to tick off my list, it was the only ground that my cousin Ken Adair played for the Luton 1st team on, back in 1969 in a pre-season friendly.

I'm afraid it was a poor Luton performance and although Craddock levelled, the Shots went on to win 2-1.

Three nights later, Mike Newell was back at Kenilworth Road with Grimsby. He received a mixed reception, the majority giving him almighty stick and some like myself, applauding him. Personally, I chose to remember the good times he had given us and it was his team that had given us some great joy, most notably promotion to the 2nd tier in 2005 as Champs.

We fell behind to the Mariners but Mark Bower then scored his only LTFC goal. Substitute Asa Hall had replaced Bower and it was a good decision by Harford, for Hall fired in the winning 2-1 goal late on.

This victory was followed by another one at home to Macclesfield when Tom Craddock scored the only goal, a penalty. In the next game at Morecambe after falling behind, we recovered to win 2-1. This was the 3rd successive victory and winning six out of the previous 10 had cut the deficit down to 11 points, the closest we had been to safety all season, with seven games left to play.

Five nights before Wembley, we took on fellow points sufferers Rotherham at home. If the Millers had not been deducted 17 points they would have been in a play-off position - form in which we had needed to produce! This difference showed as they raced into a 2-0 lead. Martin made it 2-1 but Rotherham restored the two goal advantage. It became 3-2 thanks to Asa Hall, but the Millers ended winning 4-2.

We had all known for some time that we were doomed in the league and so on Sunday April 5 2009, all Hatters fans were determined to enjoy the day at Wembley. I had the Wembley flag and scarf proudly hanging from the house, before setting off to Stopsley Working Men's Club.

98 of us had congregated and set off with Luton colours and straw boaters proudly being worn by everyone on the two coaches and we were all in great spirits. Upon arrival at the Green Man pub in Wembley just before 10.30, I was staggered at the amount of Hatters fans

there already. I knew that the pub would be exclusive to us beforehand, but there were HUNDREDS there early, determined to have a great day out. I saw faces at the pub that I had not seen for years, an old mate called Mick Williams being one of them - I had not seen Mick since the mid-1970s!

It was a carnival atmosphere and among the many there, was cousins Tim, Richard and Anna Hines. After a great session we left in plenty of time for the kick off. I wanted to savour as much of the occasion as possible. My first impressions of the new Wembley were very good, it was a magnificent structure and so it should be - given the cost of the thing! It is easily the best of all the new stadia erected.

My Dad's cousin Elaine Shane has a son called Nick, who is married to Helen and she worked with the girlfriend of Luton player Rossi Jarvis, he secured prime view seats for our party of six. The sight when we took our seats was awesome. The left half of Wembley as we looked out was totally full of Luton supporters. Of the 55,378 there that day, over 42,000 were Hatters fans. Why the F.L. refused us any more tickets is simply beyond comprehension. It's not as though they did not need the money following the astronomical costs of this wonderful new site. Still - logic and the authorities do not go hand in hand!

As the teams were being presented to the despised Football League Secretary Mr Mahwinney, I formed my own little protest at what he and others had done to my beloved club, by turning my back on him and booed him relentlessly.

I know he couldn't give two damns about the protest or LTFC, but it was the principle.

The match kicked off in a wall of noise, in truth, for the first 15 minutes before Hooper scored for Scunthorpe - the Iron were murdering us! It was no surprise that they were so dominant, after all they were challenging for promotion to the Championship. However, Luton began to settle more comfortably and when Tom Craddock crossed superbly to Chris Martin, he chest the ball down and banged in a great equaliser into the far corner of the net to send us into raptures, the Luton roar was deafening. The teams went in at half-time level at 1-1. During the interval I saw old mate Mick Dolan in the loo and I spotted ex-1980s Hatter Darren McDonough there too, he was one of many ex-Town players at Wembley to cheer on their old team.

In the 2nd Half Luton were the better team and when Craddock scored with a half volley in the 70th minute, 42,000 Hatters danced with joy. With just two mins remaining we were all getting ready to rejoice when McCann hit a stunning goal for Scunthorpe, it ended 2-2 and the match went into Extra-Time. I must be truthful, at that time I thought that our chance had gone. Tom Craddock had run himself into the ground and was replaced with Claude Gnapka in an inspired substitution by big Mick. He played in an unusual forward role and 5 mins into ET Claude ran onto a ball from Keith Keane and carried the ball high over the Scunny keeper's head into the net, to send us all bonkers again. This time, there was no comeback from the Iron and we lifted the JPT winning 3-2 AET, while also sticking two fingers up to the authorities.

After two extremely long years of nothing but heartache, it was a joy to watch big Mick do the Eric Morecambe jig during the Town's lap of honour. My Man of the Match that day was Captain Marvel, Kevin Nicholls - he was simply immense!

The Lincolnshire side would not have long to get over their disappointment and were back at Wembley soon after, to beat Millwall in the Play-Off final and gain promotion.

We arrived back to the SWMC to a sight I'll always remember. The Club was still heaving with fans all decked out in Hatters colours, many of them youngsters, which gave me great hope for the future of LTFC. It was proof that Luton Town will NEVER die, the support is there and further evidence of this was when I went into town that night to continue celebrating. The whole of the Town Centre was buzzing into the wee small hours. Quite simply, this was a special day - one of the best in my life of following the mighty Hatters!

The following weekend I missed a 0-0 draw at Lincoln (which almost assured relegation) because I was in Scotland for the Rangers 3 v Motherwell 1 match. Just two days later and only 8 days after the Wembley euphoria, Luton were officially relegated following the home 0-0 draw with Chesterfield. The hurt was plain to see in all the 6,000-plus Hatters fans' faces.

Who would have predicted just 36 months earlier when Luton had finished as a top 10 Championship side - that we would soon be playing Conference football in such a short time span!

1,058 other Hatters fans and myself travelled the short distance to Barnet the next week. The away support was more than a third of the total 2,808 crowd, something that would occur on a regular basis in the near future. Rossi Jarvis scored his only goal of 2008-09 in a 1-1 draw. This was the only time I ever saw Luton play at Barnet's old ground Underhill.

It was around this time that we heard sad news of ex-LTFC skipper Mike Keen's passing. He was our leader from 1969-1972 and made 160 appearances scoring 11 goals, my favourite being the one at Vicarage Road in the 1-0 win at Watford in 1970. He became one of the rare players to join the Hornets from us, becoming their player manager - but I'll forgive him for that now! Although I had never met him, he was a friend of my cousin Bill Roberts from his Wycombe days. Mike Keen died aged 69. RIP Mike.

Wycombe happened to be our next opponents three nights later. They were challenging for promotion and brought 1,116 fans (TWO less than we took to them) this was easily the largest away league following in 2008-09.

They beat us 1-0 and ended the season promoted.

Our last home match in the Football League (At That Time Of Writing) was against Rochdale and we drew 1-1. Tom Craddock scored from a penalty and proof of our fantastic loyal support was an attendance of 7,025.

We ended the 2008-09 campaign losing 2-0 at the Champions Brentford.

At the end of this brutal season which in reality was over before it had started, we finished bottom 15 points adrift of safety behind Newell's Grimsby.

Without the criminal points deduction, we would have finished in 15th place. Chester City joined us into the Conference.

I then heard some sad news at the passing of a friend. He was Frank Lemmon, who died aged 62.

Frank was my good friend Jane Hopkins' uncle and was a regular in the Compasses pub in Luton. I had known Frank for many years and spent hours of pleasure in his company, along with his wife Helen. Jane & Gary thought the world of Frank, as did anyone who knew him. I remember taking him and Gary to Old Trafford a couple of times when Luton played the Red Devils. He was a very popular man and this was evident by the numbers attended at his funeral. Along with my Uncle Malcolm, it was the largest gathering at a funeral I have ever witnessed and it is no exaggeration when I write, over 400 mourners were present. At his life celebration in the Compasses after the funeral, we all cheered on Man

Utd playing Arsenal in the Champs League Semi-Final, for Frank. He had class taste in music too for like myself, Frank was a Beatles fanatic and it was in his memory to have the Fab Four's music played all of that day in the Compasses. RIP Frank.

And so 2008-09 had finished, joy at Luton's Wembley win and Rangers achieving a double and despair at being relegated - and now supporting a non-league Conference team!

After the season had ended, my younger sister Michelle came home from Australia to stay with us for a holiday and brought her youngest daughter Chloe with her. They were home for our cousin Richard Hines wedding to Ann-Marie. Everyone had a fabulous day and night at the wedding in St Albans. It was great to see relations from all over, including cousin Bill Roberts from New York and my Aunt Ann from Toronto, Canada. Just before Michelle returned to Australia I took her and cousin Anna Hines on the Bobbers Club annual seaside day trip. This year it was Brighton and as she lived there for many years, she arranged for all her friends to meet up with us. The day/night we spent in Napiers bar at the end of Brighton pier was memorable. So good was it, that the three of us decided not to return on the Bobbers coach back and stayed, getting the last train home in the early hours of Sunday.

The next month I received my share of Mum's Will. There are issues regarding the Will that are too personal to reveal, so I shall just leave it at that. The first thing I did on receiving my money, was to immediately pay a small sum off my mortgage and to create my own Will - with EVERYTHING split 50/50 to my two daughters (a tiny clue there to some of the Will issues). I also used some of Mum's money to book the three of us to fly to Michelle's for the forthcoming Xmas/New Year in Australia. When I told Ann of my plans, she was pleased and wanted to join us out there. I replied, that the only way this could happen was for us all to thrash the Will issues out conclusively in Oz, once and for all and agree to change Mum's wishes. Thankfully, she agreed to do this and as a result, Michelle would buy a house back in Auckland in 2010. I try to remember the good times with Mum and there were in the old days when we were young, but it is difficult at times to shed the legacy she has left behind.

I'm afraid to this very day, that legacy is still creating problems in Michelle's family, sadly.

Conference Non-League Football

Before the new season was to start I had booked tickets to take Georgina, Mollie and myself to see a concert in London. This was to see Michael Jackson in his eagerly awaited comeback and final 'This Is It' tour. Of course, everyone knows he sadly died shortly before his shows were to commence. RIP Michael.

As LTFC prepared for life as a non-league club, we said farewell to a number of players. Wembley goalkeeper Dean Brill had left for Oldham and the very popular Sol Davis left after 7 years and 229 LTFC appearances.

Chris Martin & Michael Spillane returned from their loan spells to Norwich, while Paul McVeigh was released. Injury prone Sam Parkin moved to SPL club St Johnstone, Ian Roper to Kettering and Drew Talbot to Chesterfield.

Coming to Kenilworth Road were Shane Beckett a defender and local lad, Andy Burgess, a midfielder (and Hatters fan), Liam Hatch, a striker was signed on a season-long loan from Peterborough, Adam Newton a winger, ex-Hatter Alan White returned from Darlington and initially on loan, was Irish full back Freddy Murray. The best signing of them all though was Dean Brill's replacement in goal from Peterborough, Mark Tyler. His quality was to shine through all season and all I can write - is that Posh must have had some quality in goal to release him.

Luton played in a pre-season tournament in Devon and won it by beating Belgian team Montegnee 3-1 in the final.

After losing 1-0 at home to Swindon in a friendly, we were then meant to play Leyton Orient at home too, only for them to drop out and cancel at late notice having had a better offer to play Newcastle at Brisbane Road. Not very professional of the O's, but Peterborough stepped in at late notice and sent a side to play us, with all money raised on the day to be the transfer fee for Shane Blackett. 1,598 watched us beat Posh reserves 3-0.

Three nights later, we entertained a Manchester United youth team, such is the pulling power of the Red Devils a staggering attendance of 7,480 watched, with not a 1st team United player in sight. We lost 2-1.

Our new Sponsors were announced that night and not before time in my opinion, EasyJet were the famous backers. We would revert to Orange as the home strip in alliance with them.

The weekend before the BSP campaign began I attended the Emirates Cup pre-season tournament in which Rangers had been invited to participate. This was my first visit to Arsenal's new stadium and lovely it is too. We watched Rangers beat PSG 1-0 on the Saturday and then lose 3-0 to the Gunners the next day. My Kilsyth mates were down and stayed at The Red Lion Hotel in town.

One young lad who really shone brightly that day for Arsenal was Jack Wilshire, who started out on Luton's books as a schoolboy player.

The new era began for LTFC and the support stayed very loyal with over 4,000 Season Tickets being sold. The first game in the BSP was at AFC Wimbledon.

As a result of my leg break, I suffered (and still do) from chronic Rheumatoid Arthritis in all my joints, but especially the knees. Therefore, there is no way I could stand for 90 minutes, this would curtail my attending many away games that had no seating arrangements available for visiting fans.

I would love to have been able to attend the Wimbledon game, but could not for the above reason.

The revival of Wimbledon is a nice story for true football fans. When a franchise stole their club and relocated them 50 miles north to Milton Keynes, it was nothing short of criminal in my eyes. In 2002, supporters formed AFC Wimbledon and they started out life in the Combined Counties League sharing grounds with Kingstonian. In their first season they averaged over 3,000 fans & by 2009 had achieved 4 promotions, to join us for the first game of 2009-10. As I write, the Wombles have done brilliantly to not only climb back up to the 3rd tier of the Football League, but also in 2019-20, moved into a near 10,000 all seat capacity new ground on the site of the old Greyhound/Speedway stadium in Plough Lane, yards away from their old home.

A penalty for each side resulted in a 1-1 draw.

Three nights later, a fantastic crowd of 7,295 turned up for the first home game against Mansfield. The football played by Luton that night was a joy to witness. Even after falling behind, we rallied and came back to convincingly win 4-1.

George Pilkington scored twice. It was 3-1 late on following a Stags own goal and Tom Craddock wrapped it up with an injury time penalty.

That night was as good a Luton showing as I had seen in the last few sad years. Unfortunately - it would be a while before I witnessed anything similar!

If someone had told me a few years prior that Luton would be playing Gateshead in a league match, I would have laughed (or cried). Well we were and we all knew the reasons why, but we had to get used to these occasions.

The Oak Road End originally had 2,100 seats for visiting fans, although the police restricted it to 1,800 in 2009. For this match against Gateshead there were FORTY EIGHT! from Tyneside and this pitiful away support would not be a rarity - or the worst! After the brilliant showing against Mansfield an expectant 6,829 were looking forward to a Luton goal feast. This was to become my first reality check of 2009-10. Not only did the North East side take an early lead but in the 1st half, were by far the better team. It was blatantly obvious that a lot of teams would arrive at Kenilworth Road and seeing what for some of them, was the biggest crowd they ever played in, raise their game as if it were their Cup Final. Thankfully, two goals in a minute from Hall and Gallen gave us a narrow 2-1 win, but this was a wake up call.

Three nights later, Luton played at Forest Green Rovers. I didn't even know where they played but discovered it's in leafy Nailsworth in the Cotswolds, near Stroud in Glos.

In another inept performance we won 1-0. 869 Luton fans travelled, this was nearly half of the overall attendance figure of 1,805. On seven occasions in 2009-10 - we would have more than half the total gate!

Chester came to Luton with all sorts of acute financial problems and in Administration. They had been docked 25 points and like us a year earlier, their task looked hopeless. They went bust before the season ended and were evicted from the BSP.

The 0-0 result and Luton performance was a poor one.

I went on the train for my first away game of the season to Kettering and the police operation that day for our visit was incredible - totally OTT! Helicopters, Horses, Dogs the works. I don't know what they were expecting but judging by the numbers of police present, perhaps they had thought we were coming to rape and pillage the local population. From the railway station, we were frog marched up to a town centre pub via the outskirts and were told to stay there until they were ready to escort us to the game. Anyone who disagreed with this - was sent back to Luton! Nearly 2,000 Hatters watched an appalling game, which ended in stalemate.

I genuinely believed after watching the recent Mansfield match that this league would be a stroll, but dramatically changed my view following the two previous games. However, I restored a bit of faith when we beat Crawley 3-0 at home.

Pilkington scored twice, along with Craddock.

We had two away matches coming up. I chose not to travel to Salisbury, where we drew 1-1 preferring the eagerly awaited Oxford clash instead. I drove alone to the mid-week match at the Kassam Stadium. Knowing that parking was at a premium, I left early and arrived in plenty of time to have a bite to eat and a pint in a nearby pub. When I was waiting for the away turnstiles to open I was sitting on a bank and noticed an Oxford hooligan firm had gathered, I said to the bloke next to me, "Watch this, any minute now this will kick off," and as soon as the Duke Of Clarence Coach arrived - that's exactly what happened! They attacked the Luton fans violently and there would be more clashes inside the ground. An amazing 10,613 were there that night, including 2,331 Hatters fans - I wonder how many 5th tier league clubs anywhere in the World could attract those sort of numbers! The match had got off to a frantic start and early on Oxford were awarded a disputed penalty. It was never a pen, such was the dive and justice was done when we roared in delight after Mark Tyler saved it. But seconds later, Constable gave them the lead in what was now a pulsating atmosphere. It became 2-0 soon after and although Luton actually played well on the night, no further goals were added and we lost our 1st game of 2009-10.

Barrow were our next visitors.

Although they had played at Luton twice in the late 1960s before losing their league place in 1972, this was actually my first time I had seen them play us. We narrowly won 1-0, with Adam Newton scoring his first LTFC goal.

I then flew up to Scotland on the Tuesday night to stay at Duncan's in Kilsyth. This was in preparation for my first Euro trip with Rangers since THAT night in Barcelona almost two years earlier. We travelled to see Rangers draw 1-1 at Stuttgart in the Champ's League, thankfully with no problems this time.

I missed the next two Luton matches at Wrexham and Cambridge United. We were thrashed 3-0 at Wrexham and my mate Freddy Dann who attends most games, said that was the worst he had ever seen Luton play.

Following that result and performance, the very first signs of unrest from Luton fans about legend Mick Harford's capabilities as a manager, were just beginning to show. Things would soon get worse, but not before an enthralling game at the Abbey Stadium. At Cambridge I watched the updates on Sky's Soccer Saturday. We found ourselves 2-0 down and worse still, Liam Hatch had been sent off. But Luton came out firing for the 2nd half and we turned it round to eventually win 4-3.

Three nights later, came a match I never thought I would see in my lifetime on a league basis - Luton v Stevenage! For years, I had looked upon Stevenage in the same way as I did the likes of Dunstable, Hitchin and Barton Rovers. Looking out for their results and as a local side, hoping they would win but never in a month of Sundays expecting to play them in a league match. But this is where we had fallen to. Not only were they in the same league, but also 4 points clear and more alarming, five places above us in 3rd place. This in a league - where only one team automatically would gain promotion! The leaders Oxford were already THIRTEEN points above us & this vital game was already a MUST win.

The largest away following at that stage, unsurprisingly came from Stevenage, but I was shocked that only 793 contributed to a total attendance of 8,223.

This match overtook the Accrington Stanley home defeat the previous season - as my lowest point of being a Luton fan! (I'm afraid there would be many more.) They beat us 1-0 playing Watford style hoof ball with a late goal. Not only did this end our unbeaten home record, but the chants by a large number of Luton fans shouting 'HARFORD OUT' was heartbreaking for me. Just like Ricky Hill, Mick Harford is a Luton God in my eyes and equally like Ricky, big Mick was sacked, the following day. As much as it hurts to write this - it was the correct decision!

Alan Neilson was put in temporary charge as Caretaker Manager until Mick's successor was named.

I would miss the next game at home to Tamworth, because I had long ago booked a flight to visit Georgina in Glasgow and of course take in Rangers v Celtic while up there. Luton beat Tamworth 2-1 and the next day I was delighted as I watched Rangers beat Celtic by the same score at Ibrox Park.

It became two 2-1 victories on the spin when we won the next week at Kidderminster.

The following week I missed the game at Altrincham because I was at Stadium MK. Now before anyone starts ranting, I was on a Corporate jolly at the Milton Keynes v Gillingham game. It cost me nothing. The Printers, Regal Litho, used to print our programmes and were one of the creditors that the previous LTFC crooked owners had shafted (twice). I took them up on their offer of a free day out including meal and drink to watch the Stealers beat Gillingham 2-0.

I took a bit of stick from friends in the Bobbers Club namely Michael Capp and Alan Putman, but my conscience was clear having spent NOTHING towards helping the Franchisers. The crowd of 11,764 (lots of free tickets for kids) - sounded like 1,176!

I was delighted at seeing Luton's result at Altrincham and let out a big 'YES - COME ON YOU HATTERS!' at seeing our 1-0 victory on the TV Screen in the Corporate Lounge. This third win in a row under Neilson had lifted us to 5th place (a play-off position).

The winning streak ended when I watched us only draw 1-1 at home to York. Asa Hall scored a brilliant equaliser. This was the 7th time I had seen York at Kenilworth Road and that night was the first time I had seen York fail to lose. It was then FA Cup time and for the first time in my life Luton had to play a Qualifying round, at home to fellow BSP team Grays Athletic. I missed the 3-0 Hatters win, as I was watching Rangers draw 1-1 at home to Hibs.

LTFC had then announced our new Manager. He was ex-full back from the early 1980s, Richard Money. He had managed Walsall previously, before going on to become Newcastle Youth team coach. It was too late for him to take charge at home to R&D's and Alan Neilson picked the team. His unbeaten run was ended in a 2-0 defeat.

Then I visited Rumania for the first time, to see Rangers draw 1-1 with Unirea in Bucharest (and what a shit hole that place was).

Richard Money's first game in charge was the FA Cup 1st round home tie with League 2 high flyers Rochdale. Striker Steve Basham had not started a Luton game since August and he was brought in as Money rotated the team a touch. It certainly appeared to have worked - for after 29 minutes we were 3-0 ahead!

Basham had scored twice (they would be his only LTFC goals), along with Newton. I had taken a Rochdale supporting client Carol Harrison and her husband for a couple of pre-match drinks in the Bobbers Club.

They later told me that the discussions with their fans in the Oak Road were, how on earth is Luton Town a non-league side? Rochdale did come out all guns blazing in the 2nd half as expected, but it was still 3-0 with 33 mins remaining. They scored what looked like a consolation goal, only to then notch a second. I'm afraid I just KNEW they would score again and a minute into stoppage time they did just that, to earn a replay. Usually replays are played ten days later on police orders, but the game was scheduled for live TV coverage on ITV 4 and played four nights later. An extremely loyal 129 Hatters fans travelled to Spotland easily the lowest away LTFC support all season, but were rewarded for their devotion, when Luton secured a fantastic 2-0 victory thanks to two Kevin Gallen goals.

Three days later, I drove to Essex for the match at Grays Athletic. Of the attendance of 1,668 there that day - over 1,000 were Hatters fans! In extremely windy and heavy conditions, we strolled to a 2-0 win against the struggling side. Craddock and Gallen netted our goals.

Incredibly, this was the 1st time I had seen Luton win an away 'league' game - spanning over 4 YEARS, since beating Leicester 2-0 in 2005! At last, my jinx was over.

The next game at home to Cambridge was a lively affair. Backed by 7,458, it was pretty tight in the 1st half and remained goalless at h-t. Claude Gnapka then scored his first goal of 2009-10 with a fine volley. It became 2-0 with an even better goal from Craddock. He let fly from fully 25 Yards and it screamed into the net to send us Hatters into raptures. But we all know that Luton do not do things the easy way, just a minute later future Hatter Danny Crow made it 2-1 and 120 seconds after that, a penalty was awarded to the visitors following Freddy Murray's harsh foul. When it was saved we all rose as one and sung 'Who Are Ya?' at the Oak Road end. In a frantic final minute - another Cambridge penalty was awarded! Crow scored it this time and it ended 2-2.

I vividly remember coming out of the ground that night muttering to someone, "Sometimes I HATE being a Luton fan - this club is fucking cursed!"

In the FA Cup 2nd round we had been drawn away to Rotherham. I would have gone to the Don Valley Stadium but my Dad's cousin Elaine's daughter Gemma Shane, was getting married that day and remembering how good Elaine was after breaking my leg, family came first.

Mollie and I had a wonderful day/night with what was left of my Dad's side of the family. Singing in the band that night, was my cousin and godson Tim Hines. At the afternoon reception Gemma's Dad Max and cousins Nick & Robert (all Hatters fans) and I were eager to find out how Town were faring in South Yorkshire. We credibly drew 2-2 against the League 2 side, to earn a replay.

Four nights later, Kettering became the first team to beat us under Richard Money, when a lone goal settled it at Kenilworth Road.

We played at bottom club Chester following that. The Seals at this halfway stage were still on minus 4 points and 24 adrift of safety. Of more importance, they were fighting for their very existence, due to severe finance problems. We could only muster a 0-0 draw (the same as at home). This turned out to be full back Lewis Emanuel's 88th and final LTFC appearance in four injury, hampered seasons. He would later serve time in prison - for armed robbery!

Unfortunately for Chester, they only completed a further 9 fixtures (without gaining another point), before the Football Conference expelled them with all of their results expunged. The Cheshire clubs demise actually benefited Luton because we only lost 2 points, where as some teams like Stevenage, had lost 6. Their fans soon did a Wimbledon though and started again at the bottom pyramid 8th tier. 2010-11 was to be their first season and they won the title.

Chester then won the next league in 2011-12 and had just won the BSN title, to return back to the Conference for 2013-14. Well done to the Seals.

The new phoenix club managed to stay at the Deva Stadium by leasing the ground from the local council.

This proves that along with Wimbledon and Aldershot, as long as passionate fans rally round with their true loyalty and backing, there will always be hope.

In the FA Cup Replay I watched us tear Rotherham apart. The 3-0 victory was easily the best performance under Richard Money so far. Newton scored an early goal and was followed by another from Alan White. This was White's only goal on his return and he would only play once more. Claude Gnapka rounded off the win to send us into Round 3, to play at Southampton.

I was gutted to be missing out on a trip to St Marys, because I was not due back from my forthcoming holiday to Australia until the day after the game. I have still yet to visit there.

Georgina, Mollie and I flew off from Heathrow Airport on the day we played at Cambridge in the FA Trophy. I found out when we arrived in Singapore en route to Oz, we had lost 3-1 - I did not care a jot! Promotion was the sole aim.

Due to my Arthritis, there was no way I could take a long-haul flight to Australia without a stopover and when I booked the holiday, Singapore was our chosen destination. We booked 2 nights in the Park Royal Hotel and the 3 of us absolutely loved Singapore. It was a spotlessly clean country, with very friendly locals and the food was delicious. The Clarke Quay area was spectacular at night & we dined there both nights, enjoying a fantastic Oriental meal by the Singapore River. Naturally, we had to visit the famous Raffles Hotel for a Singapore Sling - at £13 a glass FFS! Georgina howled with laughter at my remark when we drank them. I commented, "You would think that for an exclusive Hotel - they would sweep the floor from these monkey nut shells!" Now I might be a seasoned World Traveller and have visited 5 Continents and nearly 40 countries - but I had never heard about the tradition of throwing your shells on the floor at Raffles!

When we arrived at Brisbane Airport, Michelle and her youngest daughter Chloe greeted us. We caught the bus to Robina in the Gold Coast where she lived. She was renting a house in a nice private complex, with a swimming pool for residents and family guests only. Michelle's eldest daughter Kirsty and boyfriend Elliot had also flown over from Auckland, as Kirsty was at Uni there.

Older sister Ann and partner David, along with my nephew and niece Peter & Katrina were due to arrive a couple of days later from New Zealand too. They were staying in an apartment in nearby Broadbeach.

I had never met Ann's partner David, or youngest daughter Katrina and the last time I had seen Ann & Peter was in 1999 when they came home for a holiday.

Ann's eldest daughter Rachael had not been invited by her for reasons I did not know - or ask why!

When Ann arrived at Michelle's and saw me it was quite emotional, there were tears in her eyes. I don't know if it was because she could clearly see I was struggling with the Arthritis, or that it was over ten years since we last met - maybe a bit of both! One thing is for certain, it was a full 21 years plus since Ann, Michelle & I were last together in the same place. I quickly arranged for a private meeting where the three of us thrashed it out over Mum's Will issues.

Michelle had reluctantly decided Australia was too expensive to live in and would move back to NZ in 2010.

I could not believe how everything in the Gold Coast was so dear. Apart from Fuel and Public Transport – EVERYTHING else is incredibly expensive! Australia used to have a very low cost of living – clearly no more!

On Xmas Day we spent a wonderful day at a Hotel, where the 11 of us had a traditional Xmas Feast. We all got on fine throughout the holiday. We spent some great times in Surfers Paradise and Broadbeach, which was my favourite place. Robina was nice where Michelle lived and when I went to the local 'RQ's' pub I was in heaven. It was adorned with British Football Memorabilia, Scarves & Shirts etc. and full of ex-Pats. I frequented it many times and got to know lots of the punters in there. One was ex-Rangers player Kirk Broadfoot's cousin and I also met a lady who was ex-Liverpool player Phil Thompson's sister - she was married to a staunch Evertonian! There were also friends of Michelle, a Luton Couple called Des & Denise Gallagher. He used to play in goal for Stevenage and his brother Alan runs a pub in Luton.

The local football team was called Gold Coast United (sadly now gone bust) and played a mile or so away, sharing the Rugby Ground called Skilled Park. RQ's ran buses from the pub to matches and I was invited along for 2 games played there while I was on holiday. The first match (naturally, in my Luton Top) was against Perth Glory. Ex-Luton captain Chris Coyne was playing for Perth. GCU won 2-0. The standard was better than I was expecting but the 4,310 crowd in a 27,000 seated arena left the atmosphere a little subdued, although they did have a singing section behind the goal - all of whom drank in RQ's! The match on Boxing Day was a livelier occasion with a 10,024 attendance, creating a much better atmosphere. It was a local derby against Brisbane Roar and GCU hammered their rivals 5-1. Georgina, Mollie, Kirsty, Elliot & Peter came along too and had a great day meeting my new friends. We returned to the pub after the game and when the youngsters left, I stayed for the Karaoke night and was brilliant as Ian Drury - singing Hit Me With Your Rhythm Stick! I was the last to leave the pub that night.

We also had a fantastic night on New Year's Eve at the Casino. On our last night the following evening Michelle and I attended the Dracula's theme Show in Broadbeach. The youngsters in our families had attended it earlier in the holiday and dressed for the occasion in Black Gothic gear, with the full make up etc. They told me that I would be in my element at the finale of the show. We sat back to enjoy the entertainment with a meal, even though I had a hangover from New Year's Eve. They were right about the finale. A 20-minute Beatles tribute was performed by the cast, it rounded off a perfect holiday. I was delighted that contrary to Mum's wishes, we were all a family as one again. We flew back on Jan 2nd, again staying at the Park Royal Hotel in Singapore.

In all the time I was away, due to the adverse weather in England I had only missed two Luton games.

We beat Eastbourne at home 4-1 in the final match of 2009 and narrowly lost 1-0 at Southampton in the FA Cup. 3,017 Hatters fans in the 18,786 crowd evidently saw Adam Newton miss an open goal for Town.

Due to the harsh winter weather, Luton did not play again until the 23rd January at Gateshead. 569 Loyal Hatters fans (nearly half the 1,218 attendance) took the long journey north and were rewarded with a 1-0 victory.

Luton had a new signing in the January transfer window when Hungarian Centre Half Janos Kavacs was signed from Lincoln. He started well in the game at Histon and scored on his debut in a 2-0 Luton win.

My first game of 2010 was at home to Ebbsfleet. We lost 3-2!

The next week at Holker Street, Barrow it was 1-0 to Luton in our first visit there since 1970. Then, came the match that everyone had been eagerly waiting for - Luton v Oxford!

It was no surprise that the highest home attendance at that point of 8,860 were there to see it, including a sell-out police limit of 1,500 Oxford fans. Oxford were still top, but the early season runaway leaders had been caught up by Stevenage who were now level with them. We trailed both teams by 11 points, although with two games in hand. Needless to write, that if we had any hopes of automatic promotion - this was a MUST win game for us!

After a bright Luton start, Oxford began to gain the upper hand. Just before the break Craddock came close to scoring twice. In the 2nd half for the first 20 mins it was all Luton. Sensing this, the Oxford manager changed tactics and within minutes of Green coming on, he scored for them. We continued to press but to no avail, at 90 minutes it was still 0-1. A few Luton folk had given up the ghost and had left, but when the board came up showing a minimum of 5 mins left to play, I leapt off my seat and roared into action. Now I swear this is true, I screamed out, "Come On Luton, we can still WIN this!" Some Hatters around me looked in - a kind of pitiful look! In the 3rd minute of stoppage time George Pilkington somehow managed to stoop down low and head the ball through a sea of bodies at the Kenilworth Road End into the net for the equaliser, as all around went mental in celebration. The drama was not over yet however, in the 96th minute Luton won a corner, everyone knew it was the last chance. Keith Keane took it and the ball somehow found itself, to DIRECTLY hit the back of the net - cue absolute pandemonium!

That goal and 2-1 win was one of the loudest cheers I have ever heard in recent times at the old ground and all around me folks were coming up saying, "You said it mate - you said we could win!" I went home elated and convinced we would gain promotion.

One shameful statistic from that night though, was from some so-called Luton fans.

We all knew that there could be trouble due to the Oxford fans behaviour earlier in the season, but who could have predicted that our OWN fans would damage 140 seats and vandalise toilets, causing thousands of pounds damage to our own club. – Words sometimes fail me!

There were two away trips that followed which I had to miss. Hall scored the only goal at Eastbourne, it turned out to be his 16th and final LTFC one. This was followed by a 0-0 draw at York City.

AFC Wimbledon came to Kenilworth Road next and were one of only three teams all season to bring a decent following with them (1,012 to be precise). I'm afraid that after all the good work done by defeating Oxford, we went on to lose our 5th home game of the season when the Wombles beat us 2-1.

The following Saturday I travelled to Crawley Town by train with a number of friends for a day and night out. I joined Bobbers club friends Phil Bateman and Greg Lansbury and they introduced me to Father and Son, Vinnie & Liam Brandom, as we met at Flitwick Train Station.

We left early and had a drink in London by Victoria Station, before boarding the Sussex bound train to Crawley. After hailing cabs to a pub near the ground, we settled in there for a fantastic pre-match session and I was on top form belting out the 60s/70s Oak Road classics, in which the younger element of the many Hatters fans in the pub were loving it. - It's just a pity that the match was not as good as our morning!

With over 1,000 Luton fans in the 2,119 crowd, we watched a poor Luton showing as we lost 2-1 for the second week running. This dampener did not last long and we were soon on the piss again in the same bar as earlier, before heading back to London. We had a great night in a pub near London Bridge Station, before getting a late train home.

It was actually on this day, that when I was reminiscing about the good old days of following Luton, Liam suggested I write a book about my LTFC experiences and it was he, who gave me the inspiration to write this, having often thought about doing such a thing in the past.

One fact we certainly did not know at the time was that this was Kevin Nicholls very last appearance in a Luton shirt at Crawley. Injuries were to take their toll and he quit in the forthcoming summer. Nicho scored 33 goals in 238 apps during his two Hatters spells. A fine skipper.

I missed the next two matches, a 0-0 draw at Mansfield and a 3-2 victory at Hayes & Yeading. Evidently there was a big QPR firm at the game trying to cause trouble with Luton.

I watched a dramatic finale in the home game against Forest Green Rovers. Craddock scored a penalty and it stayed that way until Rovers equalised with their own and it looked like another 2 points were about to be dropped, before Craddock fired in his second to seal an important 2-1 victory. This win had left us in 3rd place, with 11 games remaining. Oxford had now been overtaken by Stevenage at the top.

The win over FGR was the start of the best run of results for us in 2009-10.

Next was another narrow victory at home to Wrexham when Tom Craddock scored the only goal. A third win on the bounce followed at home to Kidderminster. Jake Howells scored with a brilliant volley, before Gallen made it 2-0. However, Harriers were soon back in the game and scored. Gallen added his second after Luton had dominated, to end it 3-1.

It became 15 points in a row the next week at Ebbsfleet in a game I would have attended, but was in Glasgow for the Rangers v St Mirren Scottish League Cup Final that weekend.

I spent the Saturday with Georgina and after visiting her flat we had a meal in a nearby bar while I had my phone on the table to keep tabs on the Ebbsfleet v Luton score. After falling behind to a Kovacs own goal it remained 1-0 at h-t.

Georgina was embarrassed when I next looked and leapt up to punch the air in delight and shouted – "YES! We are 2-1 up!"

There were bemusing looks from our fellow diners. By the time we had finished our meal and I had reached Queen St Station to board my train en route to Kilsyth - we had added another FOUR goals! Claude Gnapka claimed a hat-trick, the first Luton player to do so in the league since Steve Howard at Milton Keynes in 2004. Craddock and Barnes-Homer had completed a 6-1 rout. This was our best away league victory for 7 years since Colchester in 2003.

It was the first time LTFC had scored 6 away from home in a 'league' game in my time, in fact we have to go back to 1964 when we won 6-2 at Brentford for the previous occasion. This brilliant win had pushed us up to equal 2nd with Oxford and 5 points behind leaders Stevenage, but with both of those teams having a game in hand on us.

The next day I watched Rangers bravely win the Scots League Cup by beating St Mirren 1-0 - despite us having 2 players sent off!

Six days later I witnessed personal history being made at Kenilworth Road, when Luton played Hayes & Yeading. For the first time in my life - I saw Luton score EIGHT goals!

Gallen, Gnapka and Craddock each scored a pair, along with a goal each by Keane and Howells. What made this 8-0 score line even more remarkable was that at half time we had led - SEVEN NIL! When Tom Craddock had made it 8 there were still 34 mins left and everyone was convinced we could reach double figures. But how can you be disappointed at an 8-0 win?

This was the first time since 1955 that Luton had scored eight goals, when we beat Sunderland 8-2 in the top flight. It was our first 8-0 win in 79 years after Thames FC were thrashed.

Along with the six 2nd half goals at Ebbsfleet the game before, it was the first time that LTFC had scored 13 times in 90 minutes, beating the record 12-0 victory (kind of) at home to Bristol Rovers in 1936 when Joe Payne hit 10.

Three nights later it was 'only' 4-0, beating Salisbury at home. Gnapka, Craddock, Howells and recent loan signing from Barnsley, Simon Heslop, were the Town goal scorers in our seventh successive win.

Yet we still trailed Stevenage by 5 points and they had a game in hand. Credit had to be given to our neighbours. The next match was away to them and I drove the short distance to Hertfordshire. We all knew we simply HAD to win to stand any chance of catching them and this would be no mean feat, for they were unbeaten at Broadhall Way all season. The Police were worried about crowd trouble and had insisted on it being a 12-noon kick off, with it being an all ticket match too. Luton naturally sold all our 2,785 allocation, this contributed to easily Stevenage's biggest attendance of 2009-10 at 7,024. The match was as tough as anyone predicted and was even, we had to thank Mark Tyler for keeping it goalless at h-t.

When Craddock was replaced with Barnes-Homer he had an immediate impact, for just a minute later he had given us the lead. From a long Murray throw in, Stevenage failed to deal with it and from a defenders miss kick, it fell to Barnes- Homer who turned and hit a terrific goal. It was at the end where all us Hatters were congregated. It was backs to the wall after that but despite some anxious moments, we held on to 1-0 and the 3 points.

On Easter Monday we walloped Grays Athletic 6-0.

After waiting over 5 years for a Luton hat trick - Kevin Gallen became the second Luton player to score one in a couple of weeks! Craddock (2) and Hatch (his 4th and final LTFC goal), were the other scorers. The crowd of 7,860 that day - included a pathetic TWENTY fans from Grays!

Even after 9 successive wins and 27 points, we STILL trailed Stevenage by 2 points and had played a game more. The fantastic run in which we had scored 34 goals (inc two 1-0 wins), had come to an end at Tamworth the following week along with our automatic promotion hopes, it ended 1-1.

We were back to scoring for fun three nights later, in a very entertaining home game against Histon. Craddock became the 3rd Hatter in 23 days to score a hat trick. It ended Luton 6 Histon 3. That night was another embarrassing away following. Histon is hardly a great distance - yet they brought just 44 fans!

Our Play-Off place had long been secured and the final regular home league game was against Altrincham. A 0-0 draw was drab to say the least. The final game before the Play-Off Semi Finals was at Rushden & Diamonds. We were all hoping that the game at Nene Park was going to be a promotion party and we had sold our two stands allocation ages ago. These numbered 2,797, our biggest league away following of the season. This contributed to R&D's biggest gate of 2009-10 of 4,820. I decided to go to this match on the Bletchley Hatters Coach, which was organised by a Bobbers Club regular George Clark, a Luton/Celtic good friend of mine.

It was a boozy day in the sunshine and the 1-1 draw hardly mattered. Tom Craddock scored with his 24th and final goal of 2009-10. This was my 2nd and last Nene Park visit. In later years just like Kettering, they went bust & both grounds are now sadly demolished.

The Play-Off Semi Final 1st Leg against York at Bootham Crescent was on the following Thursday night. I drove up taking Father and Son, Alan & Phil Putman, friends from the Bobbers Club.

I have to write, I was quietly confident, for not only were we undefeated in 14 games, but in the 11 times I had seen Luton play York - we had yet to lose, having won 8 and drawn 3! In the noisy 6,204 crowd the Luton fans numbered 1,240, most of them stood on the open terrace - where it rained all night!

Naturally I was sitting, in the side stand and sat beside me was long time mate Dave Lee and his wife Jackie.

The LTFC display that night was as good as any I had seen away from home all season.

The only problem was that despite numerous chances, we just could not score. When Gnapka struck the post just before HT, it appeared to be one of those nights. The match seemed to be heading for a 0-0 draw (which I would have gladly took) when Blackett's misplaced header allowed Brodie to run in and score for York in the 89th minute. Apart from that one mistake, Blackett's performance that night was flawless. Yes, I was gutted at losing to such a late goal, but we definitely did not deserve to lose and said to the lads, "If we play like that in the 2nd leg - we WILL definitely win!"

A sell-out crowd of 9,781 (inc a police restricted 1,500 from York) turned up for this crucial match on the Bank Holiday Monday afternoon.

It is heart wrenching to write this - but LTFC just did not turn up and perform! I don't know if it was nerves or what, but we were nowhere near the quality of play that we showed at York. Not only did we lose 1-0 and exit 2-0 on aggregate but crowd problems at the end of the match, were screened live to the nation on Sky. Following a pitch invasion (at first good natured) at f-t, York City players had quite rightly been celebrating with their own fans, before being escorted to the changing room by the police. It was via the back of the Oak

Road Stand under a hail of missiles, with the live TV pictures being screened nationwide.

The scenes were embarrassing and clearly, throwing coins at players is totally wrong, but it certainly was not a major riot as portrayed by the media. Anyone who was at the Millwall match 25 years earlier, will agree that this was NOTHING compared to then. I am not condoning the minority of idiots responsible, but sometimes we have to draw a line at a complete OTT reaction. In 2009-10 we had ended in 2nd place, but that is failure if you do not gain promotion - and so we knew we would have to play in this shit league for at least another year! York went on and lost to Oxford 3-1 at Wembley in the Play-Off Final. Oxford joined champions Stevenage into the Football League.

I had travelled up to Glasgow for the Rangers SPL title party a couple of weeks later against Motherwell, but disgracefully missed going to the game. Opting instead to stay with Duncan and the Kilsyth lads in the Grapes Bar to watch a 3-3 draw on TV. I cannot believe that I had travelled 400-odd miles to watch the game in a PUB. That's the demon drink for you I'm afraid.

I had also booked to attend a SWMC mate Vinnie Whelan's stag party in Madrid. Vinnie is a great friend and a Dubliner. His brother Greg organised everything and we flew out on EasyJet on the Friday for three days.

After checking in and dumping the bags at a cheap hostel he had booked us, we hit the first bar next door. I met a married Irish lady outside this bar who lived in Portugal and was in Madrid for the weekend like us, but to see a friend in a band on that night of the England v Algeria World Cup game.

Therefore, she would not be joining us to watch it. However - within twenty MINUTES of meeting her - I had pulled!

Later, she left to go to the gig and left her night bag there, explaining she would see me either later - or in the morning! Naturally, when I returned to the bar next door the banter was merciless.

We lads left to watch the England game in an Irish Bar. What a load of shit it was too. 0-0 and England NEVER looked like scoring. I still had a fantastic evening though and ended up clubbing with half a dozen lovely young American lasses. When I got back to near the hostel in the early hours, I somehow managed to get mugged by a local prick. As he took the wallet out of my trousers I chased him up the road (even with my dodgy knees) he at least dropped it on the floor, to just nick the cash and save me the hassle of cancelling credit cards etc. It turned out that one of the other Stag lads had been robbed that night in the same area (probably by the same bloke). The Irish lass Maria, did return in the morning and after discovering what had happened, took pity on me. We returned to the bar next door and had a liquid breakfast (Bottle of White Wine - EACH!). She stayed with me all weekend and after her generosity - I could hardly decline her friendship could I?

The pre-planned itinerary on Saturday was to all dress in Orange (Luton shirt was sorted) and watch Holland play Japan in a pub, cheering on the Dutch.

Supporting Holland was never going to be a problem for me, as I have a long history of liking Nederlanders. Holland won 1-0.

On the last day, we dressed Vinnie up as a Spanish Bullfighter/Matador and he looked brilliant. He must have REALLY looked good, as the locals in Madrid were queuing to take photos with him. I had a fantastic weekend with Vinnie and the lads and would see them all again at his wedding that summer.

Vinnie is a top man.

Some losses to football in 2009-10 were Sir Bobby Robson, ex-England manager, ex-Luton Captain from the 1974 promotion team Bobby Thomson, Tony Parry ex-Hartlepool player and the first black player I had seen play live, plus ex-Hatter George Cummins and ex-Luton loan youngster Besian Idrizah - aged only 22!

RIP to them all.

The Adair family united as one on the night of eldest daughter Georgina's 21st birthday party. A fab time had by all as Cali R DJ Sid Hudson spun the discs to the Fancy dress G themed guests. Here we are, me as a Glaswegian, Mollie home from Australia for the party as a G.I girl and Deb as the lass in Grease, along with Georgina as a Greek Goddess. One of the best nights of my life.

2010-11

I was dropped a bombshell concerning Mollie by Deb. It was always her intention to take Mollie to Australia with her bloke (an Australian Citizen) once she was past 16 and as her father I had to sign an official document giving my consent. While on the one hand I really would miss her and did not want her to leave - on the other, it would have been selfish of me to deny her the opportunity of living in a great country, like I had at a similar age!

After I signed the agreement they would go through a Visa application process and once confirmed, would sell their house and move to Sydney. With the housing market at its lowest point for years, this could take time for it to happen. The original plan was for them to move around August. I think they had until March 2011 before the application ran out. They would have to reapply again if the move had not occurred by then. The house eventually did sell and they moved in January 2011, so at least I did get to have Mollie with me for an extra 5 months bonus.

In the LTFC world they were about to embark on the 125th Anniversary. Following the huge disappointment of failing to return to the Football League, a number of players departed Kenilworth Road as well as new faces coming in.

By the time of the opening game at home to Altrincham there were 8 signings and 7 exits. Bidding farewell, were Steve Basham, Ryan Charles, Asa Hall, who left for Oxford after 16 goals in 89 appearances and Simon Heslop also preferred Oxford to us. Liam Hatch returned from his year loan and Rossi Jarvis went to Barnet. Lewis Emanuel was finally released - after failing to turn up for pre-season! Asa Hall is still playing at the 5th tier Conference level today for Torquay.

We signed two Cambridge players in full back Dan Gleeson and striker Danny Crow, along with ex-loan goalkeeper Kevin Pilkington from Notts County. Andy Drury, a very talented midfielder, was surprisingly signed from Champions Stevenage and would really prove his value. Adam Murray also joined from Oxford.

Various friendly matches were arranged at non-league local teams before ending playing at Marlow, who were LTFC'S very first opponents back in 1885. The 3-1 Town win was commemorated by Luton wearing the kit colours of that bygone era. A replica shirt of the Pink & Blue Halved Shirt was also soon available for public sale. These colours would appear on the team shirts for a selected number of matches in 2010.

There were 3 home friendly matches arranged, against Liverpool, Newcastle (both reserve/fringe squads) and Kilmarnock. I'm sorry to write, that the 2020 Board made a rare howler by charging full admission prices for the elite opposition, despite not a single 1st team Premiership player in sight.

The Kilmarnock charge of £12 was slightly better, but £18 each to watch reserve/youth team players was absurd.

This decision backfired big time and the attendances of 2,769 v Liverpool and 2,036 v Newcastle, proved that fans voted with their feet in absence. The year previous, they charged reasonable prices against Man Utd Youths and were rewarded with an attendance of 7,480. I hasten to add, that I attended all three games but I, along with many fellow Hatters, contacted 2020 with complaints on this matter. It is to 2020's great credit that I received a personal reply by email, stating that they had realised their error and would take the fans concerns on board by rectifying the matter in future. 2020 indeed, took those views on board the next year. Caps doffed to them - the best custodians of LTFC in my time as a Hatter!

Although there were few fans I was quite impressed with the Luton performances. We won all 3 matches, beating Liverpool 3-0, Kilmarnock 1-0 and Newcastle 4-1. Three trial players were signed following these games - Dan Walker a lad from Bedford and 2 Czechs in Besta and centre half Kroca.

Of these three, Besta never really made it and was soon released, Walker became a squad player and Kroca was a success. Big Kroca scored the only goal against Kilmarnock, he must have made an impression on them - they signed him a year later! He also opened the scoring against Altrincham in the first BSP match as we wore our Pink & Blue colours that day.

Matthew Barnes-Homer crashed in a goal for the 2-1 winner. I remember commenting after the game - we would not have won that match last season! After the 4 matches witnessed I was confident for the season that lay ahead. When I drove up to Kettering and watched Luton put in a great performance - I was even more so! We beat the Poppies 3-1 and Barnes-Homer secured a hat trick. The victory had left us in top spot and 1,664 Hatters fans out of a crowd of 2,906 went home very happy.

Our good start continued the following Saturday when we travelled to newly promoted Fleetwood Town. As I mistakenly thought there were no seats for visiting fans (a familiar case in this league) I had to miss out on this game. Luton ran out convincing 3-0 winners.

Nine points out of 9 and eight goals scored, was a perfect start.

It was good to see a fairly decent away following for a change when newly promoted Newport County visited Kenilworth Road for the first time since 1967-68. 423 Welsh fans came in good voice to this night match and helped create a lively atmosphere. There had been some minor crowd problems pre- match by the Bedfordshire Yeoman, but none in the ground I'm pleased to write. Future Hatter Charlie Henry gave Newport the lead, but big Kroca poked home an equaliser. It ended 1-1.

The 100% record had ended although we should have won it 2-1, only for Barnes-Homer to ruin his great start by having a penalty saved.

On the day prior to Tamworth away, two players had left us. Alan White was released but it was the departure of Kevin Nicholls that was the saddest news.

This extremely popular player had decided that injuries had taken their toll and had volunteered to be released from his contract. The fact that he stated he did want to drain LTFC'S finances any further, while not contributing to the cause - spoke volumes of the man! His value as an LTFC player cannot be underestimated and in his 2 spells played 238 games and scored 33 goals. He was and remains, one of Hatters fans favourite players of the modern era.

I travelled to Tamworth with the Bletchley Hatters, by train. It turned out to be a bad day for LTFC in more ways than one. Not only did we lose in a poor display, but Richard Money disgraced himself and for a lot of Hatters fans - he would never be forgiven!

After a good pre-match drink in a local Wetherspoons where I met up with old chums and brothers Chris & Keith McEvoy, we headed off to the match keen to continue our good start. In the 1,694 crowd, there were 976 Hatters fans. We fell behind to an early goal, only for Tom Craddock to equalise. Unfortunately this turned out to be Craddock's final LTFC goal, for on the last day of the August transfer window, he chose to move to Oxford after 38 goals in 86 LTFC appearances. I was sorry to see him leave. Tamworth regained the lead and following this, saw some disturbing scenes involving Richard Money. In front of the Luton dug out after a substitution had been made, a fan behind had shouted to Money, "Too fucking late to make changes now Money." Money's reaction defied belief, as he tried to attack the Luton fan aka Cantona style - and had to be held back by assistant Gary Brabin! I'm afraid the situation became even worse. Tamworth finished us off to win 3-1 and as the teams left the field to a chorus of some Luton fans booing, he totally lost the plot again - by gesturing to the Hatters fans with 2 fingers and wanker signs! This clearly enraged many and although he was forced to apologise by the 2020 board, for some folk there was no going back. We also lost our top spot that day.

Two days later, we entertained Hayes & Yeading. In the programme notes was an obituary for a friend of mine by the name of Michael Capp. Mick had played Dominoes with us before every home game in the Bobbers Club for a few years. He was a Century Club member and always very smartly dressed, to leave us after Dominoes for his pre-match lunch with fellow Executive members. He was also a considerable financial backer to LTFC and his favourite role at the club was to sponsor many Youth Team Players over lots of years, hence the programme obituary. He died on August 2nd 2010 aged 68 and his loss was felt by many. I miss his wit. RIP Mick.

That day of the Hayes game was another bad day at the office. In front of just 80 away fans, the team that we had beaten 8-0 a mere five months prior, managed to gain a point in a 1-1 draw. Andy Drury scored his first LTFC goal, only to get himself sent off late on - to sum up the day!

All of a sudden, the excellent start to the season was slowly faltering.

I missed the next game at Grimsby because Georgina and I were in Cyprus.

Earlier that year I'd been invited as a guest by Regal Litho, to a Luton Town Legends Dinner at Crawley Green Sports & Social Club for their fundraising event. I took along a SWMC mate Keith Shotton. Speaking that night were ex-Luton greats Kingsley Black & Kirk (Basher) Stephens and also attending, but not speaking was ex-hero Ricky Hill. I have already written about my friendship with Ricky, but I had not seen him for nearly 10 years and after telling my hosts all about that I was a touch anxious that he would not remember me. Fear not, I walked in and was greeted by a warm handshake and, "Al, you haven't changed a bit." I was chuffed and we had a brilliant night reminiscing, as all the memories came flooding back from the great LTFC days.

The point I am trying to make about Cyprus is that pre-dinner, we had been requested to put a £5 note in an envelope and sign it. At the end of the night a draw would be made, the envelope pulled out first would win 1st prize. I had a weird feeling that I was going to win this - and even told Keith so! Well I did indeed win and the prize was a Monarch Airlines flight for two, to any chartered destination that they flew to from Luton Airport. There were a few stipulations: I couldn't travel in school or public holidays and for that reason, ruled out Mollie. I wanted to choose a country I had yet to visit and out of all Monarch routes from Luton, there were only 2 such countries - Cyprus and Turkey! I didn't fancy Turkey (after 2 Leeds fans were murdered in 2000) and so Cyprus was my choice. Georgina jumped at the chance of a free week therefore I booked an All-Inclusive week at the 4-Star Princess Louis Hotel in Larnaca. We had a fabulous relaxing week in the sun. As always, we met some lovely folk, in particular a Dutch couple Linda & Renee. While in Cyprus, Luton lost 2-0 at Grimsby. At the Airport for the homecoming flight I was staggered to meet old mate Dave Lee with his wife Jackie, they had been to a mutual friend's wedding over there at the same time - it's a small world!

I returned in time for the Luton v Cambridge match and after 4 winless games, this was already being billed as important. We returned to winning ways with a 2-0 victory, with goals by Drury and Pilkington.

Three nights later I attended my 1st Rangers match of the season at Old Trafford. Rangers gained a thoroughly deserved point in a 0-0 draw with Man Utd in the first Champ's League Group game. It was the only time United failed to score at Old Trafford in all of 2010-11.

I watched Luton v AFC Wimbledon, which was being shown live on the new Premier TV station. The Town performance that night was one of the best all season. Pilkington headed us in front, before Kroca made it 2-0. When Barnes- Homer scored his 6th goal in 9 games, it was all over. The 3-0 win was in front of 7,283 (a larger attendance than the M Keynes crowd that same night).

There was no chance of me attending a mid-week game at Darlington, where we drew 2-2. We then lost 1-0 at Gateshead, in front of only 1,075.

Our next game at home to Mansfield saw something occur that night that I had never seen in my near 44 years of support - Luton missed THREE Penalties!

Just before h-t Gnapka had missed, but the Referee ordered a retake after an infringement. When Crow had his effort saved, this sparked a 19-man brawl in which both the Mansfield captain and manager were sent off. 13 seconds into the 2nd half, it was penalty no 3 after Gnapka was sent sprawling. Up stepped Barnes-Homer - only to blaze his shot over the bar! The Hatters fans in the 6,024 crowd were now howling for blood in this unbelievable situation. However, Danny Crow finally relieved the tension by scoring his first LTFC goal, the relief was immense. Making his debut that night was Amari Morgan-Smith. He had arrived on a free transfer from defunct Ikkleston Town. When he scored Luton's second, we could relax a little and it finished 2-0.

Luton played at Barrow next and we beat them 1-0.

League leaders Crawley were the next visitors to our shrine. They were loaded with big financial backing and there is no doubt the moneybags owner had invested well in signing the 2 top scorers from 2009-10, in Tubbs from Salisbury and a player all Luton fans loved to hate from York after his play off shenanigans, Richard Brodie - but their support remained shit!

I also, did not like their Manager Steve Evans, who allegedly had been up to lots of financial irregularities at his previous club Boston - and he supports Celtic! We trailed Crawley by 5 points so this match therefore was important - certainly one not to lose anyway! I'm afraid it became eight points following a late turnaround by the Gatwick men when they won 2-1.

Andy Drury was excellent that night and his performances were beginning to attract interest from several Football League Clubs.

The away following in the 6,895 crowd that night - was a pathetic 153!

There were goals a plenty at the next match when over 1,000 Luton fans travelled to the Seaside to see us beat Eastbourne 4-2. Once again, I thought with no seats available (mistakenly) for Hatters fans, I was unable to attend. When Forest Green visited us three nights later, the number of fans they brought with them in the Oak Road Stand numbered

EIGHTEEN – I counted them! Scots club Kilmarnock, brought more than that - for a Friday night pre-season FRIENDLY FFS!

FGR were 3-0 down on 34 mins following goals from Drury, Morgan-Smith & Crow, before reducing the deficit. Further goals from Crow (again) Barnes-Homer & Dan Walker demolished the men in Green 6-1. A hilarious moment occurred near the end. Young Dan Walker, who had signed for Luton after impressing in a pre-season friendly for Bedford against us, came on as a late substitute. This was the first time I had seen him play.

He spurned a great chance after being put through one on one with the goalkeeper and I muttered, "He's fucking useless - this lad hasn't got it!" Well in stoppage time, he ran with the ball and blasted home an unstoppable shot from way out - for what was easily the best home Town goal of 2010-11!

Everyone around me cheered wildly and gave me lots of friendly stick, quite right too - What do I know about football?

It was FA Cup time for Luton and in the 4th Qualifying Round we had been drawn at home to near neighbours St Albans City. They brought a healthy 537 fans and only Wimbledon and Cambridge had larger away followings at that point. Despite a valiant showing from the Saints, an Amari Morgan-Smith hat trick and one from Crow saw us win 4-0 to qualify for the 1st Round.

On the day prior to the actual LTFC 125th Anniversary, we entertained Bath City and to celebrate, Town wore the Pink & Blue strip. It was also the 75th Anniversary of the Bobbers Club and there would be a party post-match too.

We secured our 6th victory in 7 with a fantastic 3-1 win. This win had left us in 3rd place, two points behind leaders AFC Wimbledon.

It was time for my next European adventure with Rangers, in Valencia Spain. Rangers lost 3-0, but that result was a touch harsh as we hit the post twice. In the FA Cup 1st Round Luton almost got knocked out by Corby Town again.

They had knocked us out after a replay in 1965-66 and came close to repeating the feat in 2010. We drew 1-1 and equalised late on to earn us a replay at home, as in 1965.

Luton had a new signing in midfielder Alex Lawless from York City and he made his debut the following Thursday night at Wrexham. It was live on Premier TV so I decided to watch it in the Eric Morecambe Bar at the ground. Our winning streak came to an end at a windswept Racecourse Ground. 200 Loyal Hatters fans travelled (our lowest league away support all season). A howler from Freddie Murray got us off to the worst possible start as Wrexham scored.

Despite Town dominating and creating many chances, it was the only goal of the night.

Just two days later, 559 Hatters fans travelled to Altrincham and were rewarded when new boy Lawless scored the only goal. In another milestone, that match was LTFC'S 5,000th competitive one!

Prior to our FA Cup replay against Corby, a new signing was paraded on the pitch. He was Jason Walker, top scorer at fellow BSP team Barrow.

Corby had brought 412 fans with them and they were a noisy boisterous bunch. They created a good atmosphere in the 3,050 attendance. It was a stroll for the Town as Barnes-Homer, Atieno (2) and Gnapka all scored to give us a 4-0 lead, before the Northants side scored with two late goals. This result had paired us at League 1 side

Charlton in the 2nd round.

Jason Walker opened his LTFC account against struggling Histon. He scored along with Gnapka, Drury, Howells & Atieno, as we beat the village side 5-1 at home. This result left us in 2nd place, two points behind leaders Wimbledon. The FA Cup match v Charlton was next at the Valley and I decided to travel on Gary's coach from his Duke Of Clarence pub in Town. An amazing 2,870 Hatters fans made up almost a third of the 8,682 attendance and watched a brilliant Luton performance. LTFC did us and the BSP proud that day.

Any neutral would have struggled to see that we were two tiers behind the Addicks. Andy Drury put on a master class show in particular, by scoring 2 great goals. His second especially, was a brilliant far range effort late on to earn us a 2-2 draw and replay back at the Kenny. This was played a week on the following Thursday night - the first home game played on a Thursday since 1967!

Both teams were given a huge financial incentive to win, as the victors would play Tottenham at White Hart Lane in Round 3.

Before the replay I attended the LTFC 125th Anniversary Dinner at the Auction House. Although priced at £60 a head and not cheap, I am so glad I went. I shared a table with Freddie Dann and his wife Deb, along with old mate Martyn (Rasher) Bacon & Val. Also on our table was one of the founder members of the Norwegian Hatters, called Lars. What a nice guy too, along with Jim a Bobbers Club mate, who lives in Kent. The evening was memorable as many ex-LTFC players were there and gave nostalgic memories when speaking. The compere, ITV commentator Peter Dury was lavish in his praise of LTFC citing that we had been slaughtered by the authorities, and the rest of the football world could not wait to have us back where we belong - in the Football League! It was a brilliant evening although I'm afraid the unlimited wine took its toll - I had to be nearly carried into the taxi by Val & Rash!

It was travel time again with Rangers and although I once said I would never travel to Turkey, well just as I had also once said I would never go skiing, or cruising - NEVER, SAY NEVER! I travelled to see Rangers draw 1-1 with Bursaspor, the Turkish Champions.

Because I was shattered (hung-over) from my Turkey exploits, I decided to watch the Luton v Charlton replay that night on live TV. Charlton fans had obviously agreed with my choice, as only 409 of them travelled in a near 6,000 attendance. The LTFC performance in the 1st half was the best I had seen us play in ages. Any viewer watching would think it was us the League 1 side and not Charlton. We dominated and after Danny Crow had smashed the crossbar, Croka then gave us a thoroughly deserved lead. But just a minute before the break and completely against the run of play, Charlton were level. We continued to be the better side and overall on both games for the first 150 minutes, Luton were far superior. However after Charlton changed tactics following a substitution, the game suddenly took on a new dimension. When Anyinsah touched home to give Charlton the lead, it meant we had no choice but to go all out attack and were caught on the break for a third. The 3-1 victory flattered Charlton, but we more than matched our higher ranked opponents over the course of the 2 games. It was such a shame to get knocked out, as I felt we would have took many thousands to Spurs.

The following Sunday Luton drew 0-0 v Welling at home in the FA Trophy. Richard Money played the kids. He brought in a few experienced players for the replay and we won 2-0 in Kent.

The winter weather was causing disruption and the next three matches were called off.

The first at home to York was abandoned at 0-0 on 56 mins because of a snow blizzard, the 10 mile journey home that day - took me 3 hours!

After a terrific New Year's Eve night at SWMC I attended the Luton v R&D's game, before preparing to fly up to Glasgow for the Old Firm game at Ibrox the next day. Our first league match for nearly six weeks saw us easily beat Rushden 3-0. Only 279 R&D fans were present out of a near 7,000 crowd, rather humiliating I thought.

I carried on the New Year celebrations straight after the match by visiting friends Jane & Gary Hopkins at a packed Compasses pub. Although I had a brilliant night, I should never had gone there knowing I had to be at Luton Airport early the next morning. I was meant to be on the first Glasgow flight and had booked it ages before, as it was a special Old Firm game. This was the 40th Anniversary of the tragic Ibrox Disaster when 66 Rangers fans sadly perished. I remember vividly the night it happened as a 12 year old back in 1971 when we arrived home from the Nottm Forest v Luton FA Cup tie.

I had been planning to pay my respects all season.

When I carried on drinking at the Compasses after what was basically 2 days on the piss I was in such a drunken state leaving there in the taxi - that I lost my I- phone! Georgina was home for the festive season & it was she who took a call from the taxi company, to inform her that I had left my mobile in the Cab.

It was very decent of the Cabbie to do this, as that phone was basically my work, with all contacts and email details etc. Georgina however, decided (quite correctly) to teach me a lesson and refused to wake me up on the Sunday - therefore I missed the flight! When I woke up I was as usual, full of regret at A) losing my phone and B) Missing the flight & game. The demon drink had once again caused me grief. I know I have already written this elsewhere, but it is true to say that EVERY bit of trouble I have had in my life - has been down to the booze!

After the relief of finding out that the phone was okay, I then had to inform Duncan that I had missed the flight, although I was reassured to know he would have no problem in selling my ticket. Apart from being gutted at missing the match, I was more annoyed at missing the tribute to the 66 victims. The only consolation about missing the game was that Celtic won 2-0.

The following Tuesday night Luton beat Hayes & Yeading 1-0 away. These were followed by two goalless draws at Bath City and AFC Wimbledon.

On the day of Bath game I was feeling sad because this was the day my youngest daughter Mollie, left for Sydney Australia with Deb and her bloke. Although there were tears, I had to keep saying to myself that it was in her best interests. The house was extremely quiet after she had left and my family now just consisted of myself and - Clyde the dog!

I missed her dreadfully, but at least in this modern techno world of Skype and the Internet etc., it is much easier to keep in touch.

Now I knew how my Grandparents must have felt when we left for Australia back in 1972. It was much harder for them of course because the only way of communication in those days, was by Airmail letter.

The game at Wimbledon was very important and the draw left us still trailing them by 3 points as we lay in 3rd place. Crawley were 2nd only a point behind the Wombles at this half way stage but had 3 games in hand on them.

In the FA Trophy 2nd Round, we thrashed Uxbridge 4-0 at home.

The rearranged home game with York was particularly enjoyable and especially the result - after last season's Play-Offs fiasco!

Following those games there was now a bit of friction between the two clubs, in particular from a female member of the York City Board of Directors. So it was immensely satisfactory when we walloped them 5-0 at Kenilworth Road, although in fairness they were down to ten men early on. When their goalkeeper was sent off and with no keeper on the bench, they were always going to be up against it.

Making his LTFC debut that night was Lloyd Owuso, a big experienced striker we had signed until the end of the season, following a spell in Australia. It was a scoring debut too.

He and 4 other players were on the list as Kroca, Gnapka, Drury & Atieno made it a cracking night by beating York - it was 4-0 at Half Time!

The sought after Andy Drury had scored 8 goals for Luton and triggered a clause in his contract, which allowed him to be released if a bid of £150,000 came in.

He signed for Championship side Ipswich after just one more game for us. Naturally, I could respect his wish to play at a higher level that his quality deserved but I was devastated to see him leave, he stood out a mile as our best player. I am certain that we should have negotiated a deal with Ipswich to lend him back to us for the rest of the season and then wish him all the best from then on. Atieno had scored a respectable 7 goals in 11 games (+ 9 as Sub) before being released and eventually signed for Torquay.

Gateshead made the long trek south and brought just 30 fans with them, only FG Rovers brought less all season. However, they must have been over the moon as the Geordies, or the Heed as they prefer to be known, swept into a quick 2-0 lead. Crow and Gnapka levelled, but this was a below par Town performance and it ended 2-2.

The Kenilworth Road pitch was now beginning to take its toll following a bad winter. The fact that this was the 3rd out of SEVEN successive home games, would have it in a dreadful state soon after.

In Andy Drury's 26th and final LTFC game (or so we thought), we secured another 3 points by beating Grimsby at home with a lone Gnapka goal.

We had a new signing in place of Drury when Robby Willmott, a speedy winger, was signed from Cambridge. He made his debut the following Tuesday night at home to Darlington.

We thrashed Darlo 4-0 with Gnapka, Lawless and Lloyd Owuso (2) netting the goals. Big Lloyd's celebrations, where both his hands were raised above his head in motion, were now being replicated by the Town faithful. Recent signing Luke Graham scored the only goal (his sole Luton one) in a FA Trophy victory against Gloucester.

Two days later, I DID fly up for an Old Firm match at Ibrox this time for a Scots Cup Tie, in which the score was 2-2.

The following Saturday Luton completed their seventh successive home match against Fleetwood. The pitch had taken a battering and was in a right old state following the unprecedented amount of games and harsh winter. Heaven knows what it would have been like, if 2020 had not decided to pay for a new drainage system in the previous summer. This would prove to be a godsend, as by the end of the season the pitch returned into an excellent condition.

When Owuso opened the scoring early on, we shared his unique above hands celebrations and I thought we were in for another treat, as recent results and performances had shown – BUT I WAS WRONG!

Fleetwood went on to give the best away performance of 2010-11 and they came back with a vengeance to beat us 3-1.

This was our first league defeat since Wrexham in November and only the 2nd home defeat all season. Fleetwood certainly gained revenge for our 3-0 win at their place.

I missed the next game on a Friday night at Newport, where we drew 1-1. Before Luton played at Guisley in the FA Trophy Quarter-Final, I was off to Lisbon for Rangers Europa Cup last 32, second leg against Sporting Lisbon. Rangers drew 2-2 and proceeded to the last 16 on away goals.

I listened to the radio commentary of the Guisley v Luton game and was pleased to hear us win 1-0, to send us into the Semis.

Similar to Rangers' European scenario, where the SPL title was all that mattered (of which, we had drawn PSV Eindhoven in the last 16), there were many Hatters fans that had no interest in the FA Trophy run, at the expense of promotion. I wanted BOTH and therefore provisionally, made plans for Wembley by booking the same coach firm and pub as in 2009, before the Semi legs against Mansfield.

Before my next game v Kidderminster, the Hatters travelled to Forest G Rovers and won 1-0.

With a third of the season remaining we still remained in 3rd place ten points behind leaders Wimbledon, but now with 5 games in hand. The frequently consistent Crawley Town were 2nd, trailing Wimbledon by four points, but with an incredible 6 games in hand - they had lost just 3 times in 30 games!

The Match Sponsors at the Kidderminster match were the Scandinavian LTFC Supporters Club. 48 of them had flown over from Norway, Iceland & Sweden and were celebrating their 20th Anniversary. I have already written about Lars one of the founder members when he shared my table at the 125th Dinner, well he was naturally there for this match and they hired a number of executive boxes.

I'm afraid it was not a classic match they chose.

It finished 1-1 with us dropping two more points. In this 31st league match, it was the 14th time (nearly half) we had conceded points and we all knew that was simply not good enough to win this league.

Three nights later, Tamworth were the visitors, after losing their goalkeeper to injury on just 10 mins and with no sub keeper on the bench, they were always going to be up against it. From that moment on Luton dominated and it ended 2-0 to the Town.

Two days later I flew to Eindhoven in Holland, for Rangers 1st leg last 16 Europa Tie against PSV. A very creditable 0-0 result was secured but alas, Rangers lost 1-0 in the 2nd Leg & were now out of Europe. That night post-match in a Dutch bar, I met a great Bears couple from Paisley, Claire & John and am still good friends with them today 10 years on. After my return from Holland, Luton played the 1st leg of the FA Trophy semi-final at Mansfield and we lost 1-0. This was followed by a 0-0 draw at Cambridge.

There was no doubt that our aim of finishing top was as good as over and although we had only lost one league game in 4 months, many points had been dropped by drawing too many games. With Crawley unstoppable as they just kept winning, we lay 11 points behind them with just 12 games left.

In the 2nd home leg of the FA Trophy against Mansfield, the Stags fans had easily the largest away following at that point, with 912 of them helping to create a terrific atmosphere. As already written, I had made provisional arrangements for Wembley and was ready to take coach bookings after the game - if we won of course!

Luton began the brightest and Owuso missed a great chance and when he then hit the bar, I was beginning to worry. But just 50 seconds into the 2nd half Lloyd Owuso had us all with our hands above our heads celebrating. He scored to level the tie overall. He really should have made it 2-0 on the day soon after when he rounded the keeper - only to somehow shoot the ball over the bar!

It looked as though both teams were settling for Extra-Time when suddenly late on, Gnapka was sent off. It became even worse in the last minute, when Lawless was shown a straight red and we would have to face ET - with only 9 men!

Mansfield attacked relentlessly in Extra-Time but we battled on and with 2 mins remaining it was still 1-0. Then the referee had no choice but to give Mansfield a penalty following an idiotic handball by Luke Graham. Briscoe smashed the penalty and for a split second we were rejoicing wildly as Kevin Pilkington saved it, only for the ball to cruelly spin back to Briscoe as he followed up to slot it into the net - to our utter despair!

For the second time in a year I had to cancel provisional Wembley bookings and coming out of Kenilworth Road that day I had one of those horrible sick feelings in my stomach, which you would think I would be used to by now but the hurting was as strong as ever.

Fortunately, I didn't have time to dwell, as the next morning I was at Luton Airport flying to Glasgow for the Celtic v Rangers League Cup Final at Hampden Park. I'm pleased to write, Rangers won by beating Celtic 2-1, AET.

Two nights later and with an impending Blackpool weekender coming up I missed a Luton 1-0 win at Rushden & Diamonds. The 1,227 Hatters fans made up nearly half of the total attendance. This would be the final fixture between these clubs. R&D sadly soon went into liquidation.

In the days leading up to the Southport away game Richard Money pleaded with Hatters fans to travel up and cheer the Town on in a final surge to make the Play-Offs. He suggested possibly making a weekend of it.

Now we had booked a weekend for this a long time ago anyway, with George Clark the Luton/Celtic fan from the Bobbers Club, to travel on his Bletchley Hatters coach choosing to stay in Blackpool, rather than Southport.

But I do wonder how many fans actually took up Mr Money's plea?

George had organised a coach to leave Bletchley WMC on the Friday afternoon and I went along with fellow Bobbers mate Greg and long time pal Barz. We had a brilliant time in Blackpool staying at the Brooklyn Hotel on the North Shore, where the owners made us all extremely welcome. Following a cracking Friday night and after breakfast on Sat, the coach took us to Cleveleys for opening time in the Wetherspoons, before meeting George's parents (who live in Clevelys) in the United Services Club. We left in good time for a pre-match drink or three in Southport town centre and I have to write, the Southport locals were not as friendly or welcoming as their Blackpool/Cleveleys counterparts. Not in a threatening way, just a touch on the snobby side.

It was agreed before the trip, that the majority would wear flip flops, shades and shorts etc. as a theme, it's just a pity that on this particular March windy day - it was absolutely fucking FREEZING! I had a seat for the game as usual (Arthritis) but when sat on my own and seeing all my compatriots on the open terrace behind the goal, with my alcohol fuelled intake I decided to join in with the fun and stood there too. This was most Luton fans and certainly mine, first visit to Haig Avenue. The last time we played there was a night match in 1969.

The LTFC performance in 2011 was - THE worst I had ever seen in my life! Truly, an atrocious effort and even though Barnes-Homer gave us the lead, the Sandgrounders deservedly came back to beat us 2-1 with late goals. They had a little Scouse player by the name of John-Paul Kissock who particularly shone - he reminded me of one of the Krankies, with his headband!

The fact that Richard Money had hauled off two Luton players (Graham and Gnapka) in the 1st half said it all. After pleading with fans to pay good money and travel up for this long journey, our reward was disgusting and the fact that Money did not even have the grace to acknowledge the support, choosing to head straight up the tunnel, finished me with him - personally!

I was not alone, although many Hatters had refused to forgive him for his Tamworth antics this act, was the last straw for the majority. 2020 obviously shared our views and action was needed, two days later he had left by 'mutual consent' - I love that description of being sacked!

It was the correct decision, he might have stated, that his record in charge was statistically and percentage wise, the most successful in terms of number of games managed by LTFC boss's. BUT, this was in this God Awful league - the FIFTH TIER! FFS.

His assistant Gary Brabin, was placed in charge for the rest of the campaign. The coach journey back to Blackpool was sombre but we soon shrugged off our woes and spent a fantastic evening drowning our sorrows in my old haunt the Claremont Hotel, which was just up the road from our base.

Two nights after returning from Blackpool we entertained Barrow in Gary Brabin's first match in charge. Perhaps reflecting the disastrous Southport performance, our lowest home attendance of 2010-11 turned up of 5,528, including 41 from Barrow. It was the lowest league crowd for two years.

Although we only drew 0-0, manager Gary Brabin immediately did something tactically to get the fans on side.

A tactic that Richard Money persisted with that used to drive us fans bonkers, was his insistence on bringing all 10 outfield players into our own penalty area for opposing corner or free kicks - even if we winning 8-0! This used to infuriate us fans and he KNEW it. I actually used to think he was doing it as a matter of spite. Looking back now as I write, Money was not alone in this tactic. Many managers share this idea (inc McCoist, the then boss at Rangers), with the common excuse being that while you have 10 men in the box, there is less likelihood in conceding - I can see that point but in my opinion, as soon as the ball is cleared, it invites immediate pressure back on to the defence.

In the early moments of the Barrow game Brabin had left not one, but TWO players at the half way line for the first Barrow corner. The ironic cheers by the Hatters faithful were comical - it was the loudest cheer all night!

Another Money decision (among more than a few) I could never fathom out, was why he had signed Jason Walker? He started him in just TWO league games since signing him in November - a full 4 months prior! Gary Brabin recalled him from the Kidderminster match onwards and with a decent run in the side, you could see the quality player that he was. That Kidderminster away match on the following Saturday was a six-goal thriller. Although we trailed to a penalty, we came back to draw 3-3.

Prior to the kick off at home to Kettering three nights later, there was a minute's applause in memory of the recently departed Ian Pearce.

Ian was a hugely popular local Radio presenter. His affection for LTFC was well documented. He had recently died suddenly aged only 56, the tributes paid to him by 2020 and the LTFC players & officials and local media were very moving. It was also sad that his final match he commentated on, was the Southport debacle. The applause pre-match was both warm and loud, although I have to write that I disagree with this recent mode of remembrance, a minute's silence is the traditional way to show your respect at a person's passing.

I just feel that clapping at someone's death sends out the wrong signal and does not feel correct. If it was his relatives' wishes for applause, then I apologise - but for me - silence is golden! RIP Pearcey.

We drew 2-2 with Kettering to deny Gary Brabin his first win, although he had not lost yet. He only had to wait a further four days and the wait was worth it - in style!

We gained revenge for that dire showing at Southport, by thrashing them 6-0. This made up for the Haig Avenue misery - slightly!

Three nights later, Luton visited champions Crawley Town. Their manager Steve Evans was annoyed with LTFC at not applauding his side onto the pitch and publicised this, accusing us of a lack of professionalism - well FUCK him!

I do not like this bloke, end of. He must have sniggered though when Brodie the player Luton fans loved to hate, opened the scoring for them after only 33 SECONDS. Thankfully, Alex Lawless equalised and it finished 1-1 to stop Crawley doing a double over us.

It became six matches undefeated for Mr Brabin when we travelled to Mansfield and drew 0-0. Mansfield is definitely a bogey ground for Luton.

I missed this particular game because I was in Tenerife for my cousin Tim Hines Stag Party.

Even though he wasn't getting married until August, he arranged this early. It was a brilliant trip as 32 of us travelled on the Thursday morning from Luton. We were all in great spirits and on the flight I was in top form. We managed to locate two separate hen parties on board one of those, was from Watford (so you can imagine the banter), the other from Bedford. I ended up sitting and chatting to ex-Town player Phil Gray's wife - what a lovely nice lass she is too!

Brabin's unbeaten record came to an end at York. Not only did we lose 1-0 but he was sent off as the 1st half ended for exchanging heated words with York's Assistant Manager and stewards, following a bad tackle on Keith Keane.

Eastbourne visited next and brought just 30 fans with them.

After the battering the pitch had taken earlier in 2011 it was now dramatically improving with the better weather and was nearly back to pristine condition. Against the Sussex team, it ended 3 0 to the Town - 10-0 would not have been an overstatement!

On Easter Monday and the day before my 53rd Birthday, I travelled to nearby Histon on the Bletchley Hatters Coach. They had kindly agreed to pick me up in Barton en route and we soon arrived at a pub next to the Histon ground for some pre-match liquid refreshments. The attendance that day was 1,159, even taking into consideration that Histon were bottom and already relegated, the number of home fans present was just - 320! It was a stroll in the park for Luton. Gary Brabin took advantage of the situation by resting a few players.

Goals by Morgan-Smith and Barnes-Homer gave us a 2-0 lead.

I had backed us to win 3-0 and was delighted when Gnapka made it that score, but as there were still 43 minutes left, I knew we were bound to add to that. On 90 minutes it was still 3-0 and my bet was looking good, until Barnes-Homer ruined it with a stunning goal in stoppage time.

I think this was possibly the most muted LTFC goal celebration - I had ever cheered at! This 4-0 away victory was amazingly my best witnessed on the road with Luton in the 'league' for over 26 years when we beat Stoke at the old Victoria Ground in 1985 by the same score.

The final regular game of the season was at home to Wrexham and coincidentally they would be our next opponents in the Play-Off Semi-Finals. Wrexham manager Dean Saunders rested almost his entire 1st team for the meaningless 46th league match and I have to write, that they were the better side on the day. It ended 1-1.

The BSP was completed. Crawley were promoted as runaway Champions with a remarkable - 105 points! They were a full 15 points clear of Runners-Up AFC Wimbledon and a staggering 21 points clear of us, in 3rd place.

Credit must be given where it's due, in 46 matches Crawley lost just - 3 times! Fleetwood finished 4th and completed the Play-Off Places, they would play Wimbledon at home the following Friday night, the night after our 1st leg at the Racecourse Ground v Wrexham.

Despite all the Play-Off games being shown live on Premier TV, there was no way I was going to miss the Wrexham match. I booked my seat on the Duke Of Clarence Coach for the long trip to North Wales. 829 Hatters fans boosted the attendance to 7,211, Wrexham's highest 2010-11 attendance - by a mile!

Although there were more than a few Luton fans tense pre-match, I was quietly confident of getting a draw at least. What occurred in the 1st half that night though was simply - MINDBLOWING! After a positive Luton start, on 16 minutes Alex Lawless created space and ran with the ball before unleashing an unstoppable shot from 25 yards, for an absolute screamer of an opening goal.

While we were going mental at the opposite end from the goal, Jake Howells had a shot, which smashed against the Crossbar from just inside the area. Ten mins or so later following a beautiful pass from Howells to Gnapka, the Frenchmen hit the ball with such force it nearly broke the net at the near post, to send us into dreamland with a 2-0 lead. It was truly a phenomenal strike.

It went from dreamland to fantasy, when on 33 mins Ed Asafu-Adjaye chose this moment to score his first ever (and only), LTFC goal from the edge of the area to make it an incredible 3-0. We Hatters fans were in such a state of ecstasy, that a small band of Wrexham lads in the corner stand next to our end had lost the plot and tried in vain to make a pathetic attempt at attacking us Hatters fans. Gnapka very nearly made it 4-0 before the interval and the Town players went off to a rapturous ovation from us Hatters. Wrexham fans were just shell shocked into stunned silence - some left at H/T! There was no let up in our attacking play in the 2nd half either.

Gnapka had a shot blocked off the line and Wilmott should really have scored soon after.

It was actually the 81st minute before Wrexham had their first shot on target and Kroca very nearly made it 4-0 a minute later, when he hit the post. We won 3-0 this was easily the best LTFC away performance I had seen in donkey's years. It was our best display in the BSP bar none.

Even though the Welsh police kept us behind for an eternity from the baying mob outside after our blood, nothing was going to stop us celebrating this momentous result - the long trek south was bliss!

The very next morning I was onto the Coach Company to book my transport for the Play-Off final. At first, the owner would not take my booking for an 82-seater coach on the grounds that it was only half time, in her words. She told me to come back the following Wednesday after we had been assured of qualification. I refused, stating that she would be inundated with calls then and so I insisted on paying a deposit there and then. She finally agreed, but told me it is a 20% deposit and if Wrexham won I would lose that money.

I replied, "If Wrexham win 4-0 or 5-1 at Luton - I will be the next POPE!"

The next day I flew to Glasgow for my final Rangers match of 2010-11 against Hearts at Ibrox the following day. We won 4-0 and went on to win the SPL in dramatic style for the third year in a row. Rangers knew that if they won the last game at Kilmarnock, the title was theirs, no matter what Celtic did vs Hearts.

After SEVEN minutes, it was 3-0 to Rangers and we went on to eventually win 5-0.

The amusing story went about that Rangers had scored at Killie - while Celtic were still doing their huddle!

The Wrexham supporters have to be commended for the number of fans they brought to Kenilworth Road for what was in effect a dead rubber - or WAS IT! They contributed to the highest 2010-11 home attendance of 9,078. When the match kicked off Wrexham had nothing to lose and went out all attack. They attacked more in the opening minutes than they did for the entire 1st leg and were rewarded by taking an early lead. I don't mind admitting it, but I started to slightly worry about my deposit - and becoming Pope Alan!

When Gleeson idiotically handballed, to gift Wrexham a penalty soon after - I was positively SHITTING MYSELF! as the Welsh fans went ballistic. Mercifully, Taylor's feeble penalty shot had been saved by Mark Tyler. Kenilworth Road AND I erupted and we all knew that Wrexham's chance had gone when Kroca headed in the equaliser before h-t. Jason Walker added a goal to win 2-1 on the night and 5-1 on aggregate.

Prior to the match in the Bobbers Club, I was a touch apprehensive having sold only 16 places for my 82-seater coach to Manchester. I needlessly worried, after the game that figure had risen to 53 - by the weekend I had sold them all! This was despite the obscene pricing structure and difficulty in buying tickets that the Football Conference was organising for the Play-Off Final.

In their wisdom, they had decided that the only way of securing tickets was via a ticket agency. You could not buy tickets from LTFC direct and we then found out you had to pay a booking fee PER PERSON - as well as the postage!

In summary, the cheapest available ticket was a mind-blowing £41 with no discounts allowed for pensioners at all. LTFC had been given an initial allocation of 22,500 seats, with more promised if we sold all those. We would easily have sold out that number, but considering it would cost a MINIMUM of over £60 per person to travel and attend the game, along with it also being screened live on Premier TV, it was hardly surprising that a huge boycott from both Luton and Wimbledon fans occurred.

I emailed the Football Conference asking them how they could justify charging more for the cheapest seats than the League 2, League 1 AND the Championship (at Wembley) Play-Off Finals. Their reply: It is only the cheapest levels that are more expensive, the higher level of pricing - were all more expensive than ours! These idiots just could not comprehend that had it cost even £25 a seat as the cheapest, we would have sold out our allocation AND more. As a result, many Hatters fans refused to travel and we only sold 12,000 plus. The Play-Off Final as well as Leagues 1 and 2's finals were not at Wembley this year, due to UEFA's insistence that no other matches could be played there just before their Champions League Cup Final.

We set off for Manchester's Eastlands Stadium in the Play-Off Final against AFC Wimbledon the following Saturday morning at 9 am sharp from SWMC and picked up Barz and his pals in Flitwick en route. In hindsight, we should have left at 8am, as due to horrendous traffic - we did not arrive in Manchester until nearly 1.30pm! I had booked a pub near the ground called Mary D's with a capacity for over 1,000 people. But this was full up with Hatters fans when we arrived and the police were not letting any more folk in. The owner Mike, came out to meet me and apologise and took us to a nearby pub ran by a mate of his, in which we secured entry no problem.

He was absolutely staggered at the amount of Luton fans waiting at the entrance before opening time - they were full up by NOON! He also told me that in the years since the Eastlands Stadium had opened, this was the highest amount of fans that had ever been in his pub.

My cousin Elaine's husband Max and son Nick & I, took our seats in the magnificent Stadium along with his neighbour John. Though £46 a ticket, the view and legroom was faultless along with the refreshments, with absolutely no queues at all.

There was little to choose between both teams in a frenetic start and both sides went close, before Wimbledon thought they had broken the deadlock.

Kedwell scored for them but thankfully, it was ruled out for offside. The Dons keeper then saved well with a reaction save from Walker, before acrobatically tipping over Gnakpa's header. It was Gnakpa again, who had the best chance so far when he headed over the bar from 10 yards out.

The 2nd Half was similar with both teams cancelling each other out. I never felt we were in any danger, but we needed to up the tempo. The final ten mins proved to be the most exciting of a tense match.

The Wombles failed to take three chances - then it was our turn! Jason Walker went through and was about to hit the target when he was BLATANTLY brought down for what everyone could see - was a stonewall penalty! The Referee incredibly waved play on to our disgust and allegedly said after the game, "I didn't give it because Luton had the advantage, but then failed to score from it." – UN FUCKING BELIEVABLE!

It became sheer cruelty when in the last minute, Walker rose to head the ball seemingly into the net only for it to hit the inside of the post and bounce into the grateful arms of the

Wimbledon goalkeeper. Right there and then - I worried that this might not be our day! Even after that excitement, there was a further opportunity for AFC when Kedwell had a chance to win it for them, but thankfully dallied on the ball too long and Asafu-Adaye tackled him to save the day. In the 1st period of ET Alex Lawless nearly scored with a 25-yard pile driver that just flew wide. It was the only chance for both sides in that period. On 107 minutes, it should have been 1-0 to the Wombles, but thankfully the shot was straight at Mark Tyler. After Walker had headed just wide, it was Wimbledon's turn to hit the post. The Wombles finished the strongest & very nearly won it when the unmarked Yakubo headed wide and it ended 0-0 AET. A penalty shoot out beckoned.

Alex Lawless had reached the Play-Off Final with York in the previous year and it was he, who stepped up to take the first spot kick. When Brown saved it, I had my head in my hands and physically felt sick. However, when Mark Tyler saved Mohammed's penalty at 2-2, we all screamed with joy and were back in it. But Jason Walker, who I had so admired, for some bizarre reason decided to think he was Lionel Messi - and tried to CHIP in his penalty! Of course Brown got a hand to it - I was back to utter despair! Yakubo, then our Jake Howells both scored and it was then Wombles top scorer Kedwell's turn. He knew that if he scored, Wimbledon were back in the Football League and not US. You all know he scored it and I, like the masses of Hatters fans, just sat there for several minutes staring into the sky with a blank state of mind. It is times like these on the very rare occasion, that I wished I did not like football. The hurt can sometimes destroy you and boy, have we been hurt and let down - so many times following LTFC! How much more could one take as a Hatter?

That feeling of utter despair was shown in the faces of all Luton fans leaving Eastlands for the long journey home. Instead of having a glorious night out back in Town celebrating, the silent Coach drove straight back home - I just went to bed utterly depressed!

To rub salt into us Hatters wounds, QPR had been charged by the Football League with seven charges of financial irregularities.

They were found guilty on 2 of them and their punishment - a fine of £875,000 (a pittance, considering their promotion to the vast financial resources of the Premier League) and with no points deducted!

Of course had their name been Luton Town, the Football League would have probably closed us down. Talk about one rule for one and another rule for another etc.

Sadly, three members from the LTFC Div 4 1967-68 Championship season died during 2010-11. Our captain Terry Branston was lost to us, as well as Ian Buxton, the only LTFC player to have played professional Cricket at the same time (in my time of following the Hatters). The manager of that side Allan Brown had also recently passed away. RIP to them all.

Play Off Heartache – AGAIN!

I embarked on 2011-12, my 45th of following the mighty Hatters and I had hoped and prayed this would be 3rd time lucky in our pursuit of regaining League status.

At the beginning of the season we had understandably lost some good players who chose to continue their careers at other clubs. The big Czech defender Zdenek Kroca must have impressed Kilmarnock in the 2010 pre-season friendly, because he signed a two-year deal with the Scots. He scored 6 goals in 53 official LTFC appearances.

The enigma that was Claude Gnapka signed for League 1 side Walsall and in 2012 he went on loan to Inverness CT. He was a popular player, but sometimes a touch on the lazy side when it came to defending. He will always be remembered for his JPT Wembley winning goal, as well as his thrusts down the right wing along with his fantastic heading ability. The Frenchman scored 27 goals in 124 LTFC appearances. His final goal at Wrexham in the 2011 Play-Off Semi-Final was the best of them all.

Jason Walker said that his family could not settle in Luton and moved back up north to York City. Once again a player I liked, although his last act for the Hatters was the dreadful penalty miss in the Play-Off Final. Adam Newton and Lloyd Owuso were released along with Matthew Barnes-Homer and Kevin Pilkington has retired. The incomers, were midfielder Aeron O'Connor from defunct R&D's, defender Dean Beckwith, Stuart Fleetwood a striker, James Dance and pleasing myself, the little dynamo midfielder who tormented us at Southport, John-Paul Kissock. During the course of 2011-12 we also added Greg Taylor, Craig McAllister, Andre Boucaud and re-signed Janos Kovacs.

I attended two pre-season friendly matches each for both Luton and Rangers. With the Bears I visited and stayed in Belfast for a weekend match against fellow Blues brothers Linfield. Rangers won 4-1. Two nights later I drove up to Blackpool for Rangers friendly at Bloomfield Road, in which Rangers won 2-0.

Luton played three friendly home matches against Gabala a side from Azerbaijan, managed by Tony Adams. We also played Serie A team Parma and Premiership QPR. We lost both games against the Foreigners, 3-2 and 2-0 respectively. I missed the QPR game as it was my cousin Tim Hines Wedding day but was pleased to find out at the Reception, that we had beaten them 3-1. (Their first team too.)

Mollie and Deb were home from Australia the week before the wedding. They had travelled back for Georgina's 21st Birthday and we had a party for her at SWMC, the night after the wedding. A fantastic night topped off a brilliant weekend following the wedding. I was chuffed that Duncan, Rab and their wives had flown down from Scotland for her 21st.

It was an extra special night with all the Adairs, Roberts, Gibsons and Gales in attendance.

It made a lovely change that we were all together for a happy occasion for once and the fact that I had managed to secure Sid Hudson the Cali Reunion DJ, made it the truly memorable night that it was.

It was great to see Mollie again and I was also pleased that Deb and I mixed amicably for Georgina's night. The fact that most of the guests were all dressed up in Fancy Dress simply added to the occasion. Georgina decided to make it a G theme, the sight of Greek Goddesses, Golfers, God, Lady Ga Ga, Geisha Girls, St George, Grease, Gardens, Gangsters, Gooners and myself as a Glaswegian, with full kilt regalia - just made it a wonderful night to never forget!

The world is still a mad place - proof of this was when Luton were not even allowed to kick off the season! Our first game at Telford was changed by the local police force to a noon kick-off. This was because the EDL (English Defence League) decided to have a march that same day in nearby Wellington. The Police then amended it to a 7.45 pm start and stated we could only pick up tickets at a Service Station on the M54 - before being escorted by coaches to Telford's ground!

On the night of Georgina's Party, rioting developed in Tottenham and this was followed by many other cities in England over the next 3-4 nights. It was worse than the 1981 Riots and the looting, robbery and vandalism reached new appalling heights, the Police had actually lost control of the streets in many parts of London, Manchester, Birmingham and Bristol, amongst others. Surprisingly (and I'm glad), Luton had not suffered the same fate many folk believed it would. It took 16 THOUSAND Police Officers to regain the streets of London alone. As a result of these riots, the West Mercia Police managed to get the Telford v Luton game postponed citing that the EDL march and our game would be too much for them to handle - UNBELIEVABLE! The match was called off on the Thursday then just a day later the EDL march was banned - which meant the game could have taken place all along! So 2011-12 commenced.

After ten games we were top, despite only drawing 1-1 at bottom club Bath. This would be the only time in 2011-12 we reached the pinnacle spot.

I had attended nine out of those matches including my first visit to Mansfield since 1970, where we drew 1-1 and first visits to Hayes & Yeading (sharing at Woking's ground, 2-2) Telford (2-0) and Bath City.

The first defeat occurred at York (3-0). I paid my first visits to Ebbsfleet (2-2 after being 2-0 ahead) and a late Danny Crow goal at Newport (1-0). We suffered three more losses, as our position at the halfway stage was 7th place, outside even a Play Off position. At this stage of 23 games I had attended 17.

I missed a 1-1 home draw with Telford because I was in Hamburg watching Rangers lose 2-1 in a friendly. For reasons to be explained later, this would be Rangers last game in Europe for a while - certainly a competitive one at least! One brilliant weekend occurred when we played Lincoln at home.

The night before was my Bletchley mate George Clark's 50th and he organised a 60s/70s fancy dress party. When I arrived in my Beatles suit and wig he was dressed identically, so he was George and I, John. After a terrific night we decided to attend the match in our outfits (and Beatles wigs) to much glee. Even Gary Sweet chuckled in the Directors Seats at us and a 1-0 Hatters victory topped off an ace weekend.

Before I took Georgina to Michelle's in Auckland (staying en route in the fabulous Dubai for two nights) for Xmas/New Year and would fly Mollie over from Sydney to join us in NZ, I watched the Hatters play at Sincil Bank, Lincoln for the first time since 1991. We drew 1-1.

Proving that life holds no grudges on my part - even Deb came to stay with us at Michelle's! It was great family time and we all had a ball. Michelle and Ann had fallen out again big time over trivial issues, but I'm glad to write they made up again – until the next time.

I stopped at Kuala Lumpur for three nights on the return journey to London, while Georgina flew and stayed with Deb in Sydney before returning to Glasgow. While I was away, LTFC had won all five games to reach 3rd place.

My first game back was watching an exciting 3-3 draw at Southport.

At the end of February with 13 games remaining we were still 3rd and also in the Semi Final of the FA Trophy.

After beating bottom club Bath 2-0 (later having a great night in the Bobbers Club with a load of Luton/Italian and Luton/Norwegian fans), we then went on a very poor run.

We again cruelly lost in the Semi - Finals of the FA Trophy. (This time to York.) I therefore had to cancel ADAIR Travel coaches to Wembley - for a THIRD time in two years!

Losing 5 out of 7 games, including an appalling 3-0 defeat that I saw at Forest Green Rovers, manager Gary Brabin was correctly fired as we languished in 7th place, outside the Play Off positions.

In his 1 year role as Manager, he never once played the same team twice and his habit of changing formations, along with playing players out of position was both frustrating and beyond belief. We played a total of 49 League games in his time as boss and his record was: Played 49 Won 21 D 19 L 9.

There lay the problem, we drew almost as many times as we had won. In this Conference - that is simply not good enough!

Rangers had at this time, enormous financial problems and unbelievably entered into Administration on Valentine's Day. It turned out, that the person who David Murray sold Rangers to in 2011 for a £1 (along with £18 million bank debts) was a blatant crook. He managed to dupe Murray and all at Ibrox by paying off the bank debt at an instant. What he failed to announce, was that he had raised the money by getting his hands on 3 years future Rangers fans season ticket money.

Not only that, but incredibly deducted all Rangers Players and employees tax from their earnings and KEPT THE CASH - refusing to pay HMRC any Income Tax or VAT, as well as refusing to pay ANY suppliers. The fact that he was allowed to run up such a mountain of debt in just nine months defies belief. As a result of his crookedness, Rangers old company would eventually be Liquidated and punished beyond any logical reason. But that is for later!

I flew up to Glasgow to do my tiny financial bit and joined an astonishing crowd of 47,521 to watch an old Rangers legends team beat AC Milan legends 1-0, with super Ally McCoist scoring. I wonder how many clubs in World football could attract such numbers - for a kick about?

The next day I watched the Gers beat Motherwell 2-1, my first visit to Fir Park since seeing the Aston Villa game there in 1970 with my Dad. I would attend Ibrox for the last home game of 2011-12 and many Bears were very scared that it might be the FINAL game played at the world famous Ibrox Park - thankfully a 0-0 draw v Motherwell was not the farewell! The Ibrox legions would rally round in huge numbers to help save Rangers from perishing. The awful cost though, would be to suffer appalling penalties as the rest of Scotland's SPL clubs - lost the plot and demoted Rangers to bottom tier Div 3!

Our 29th full time Manager appointed was Paul Buckle, who won Torquay promotion from the Conference, but was sacked by Bristol Rovers in his next job. Before his first game in charge, was ANOTHER extreme low in my life of following the Hatters.

My first visit to Braintree started off well enough, as we had a terrific pre-match session in the Orange Tree pub near the ground with George and all the Bletchley Hatters. The Luton performance that day was atrocious as we made a pub team like Braintree look like Barcelona as they deservedly beat us 3-1.

Buckle immediately then gained results with 4 wins and 2 draws. His first game in charge saw us beat Hayes & Yeading at home 4-2. Keith Keane scored his 8th and final LTFC goal that day. We finished 2011-12 in 5th place to qualify for our third successive Play Offs.

The final BSP game was at runaway champions Fleetwood. Luton easily won 2-0 (only Fleetwood's 5th defeat all season) this, on a memorable weekender in Blackpool again.

Travelling with George Clark and his Bletchley Hatters again, we repeated the previous year by staying in the Brooklyn Hotel. On the Friday I found this magnificent bar called Soul Suite and there were dozens of Luton fans in there. The music played there made me feel as if I was in heaven. All Cali R stuff - I was Northern Soul dancing big time! I managed to pull a Blackpool lass, called Marie and we met again the next night in the same venue. On the Saturday night there must have been 50-odd Hatters fans in there including a load of old school, football lads who I had not seen for a while. It was my best football weekend I had enjoyed in years.

We had once again drawn Wrexham in the Play Off Semis and the 1st leg was watched by our biggest crowd of the season 9,012. Luton won 2-0 with goals from top scorer Stuart Fleetwood (his 16th) & a top Brabin signing, Andre Gray. Despite finishing a mammoth 17 points behind 2nd placed Wrexham and losing the 2nd Leg 2-1, we qualified for the Wembley Play Off Final by knocking them out 3-2 on aggregate. George Pilkington scored his 12th and last LTFC goal.

The final had been returned to Wembley once again and we were to play our new nemesis York City.

I have an unusual record against them. The first 11 times I had seen us play York we were unbeaten, winning 8 and drawing 3 - but since 2009, Luton had played them 10 times and won just ONCE!

Despite the same ludicrously overpriced tickets as the previous year, £41 or £46, we still sold over 30,000 tickets against York's 9,000. Adair Travel ran a coach again and I booked the Green Man pub once more. Marie from Blackpool came down to stay the weekend at mine and joined us on the coach.

The match got off to the best possible start when Andre Gray fired us into a 2nd minute lead as we all erupted with joy. Were we finally going back to the Football League where we belong?

Alas, no! York came back to beat us 2-1 with two goals that should not have been allowed. My mate Duncan in Scotland text me that the 1st goal was not a free kick that led to it and the second - was at least a YARD offside!

Looking back, he was correct but equally, I felt our showing on the day did not merit winning the game.

So here we were again - having to accept yet another year in the Conference! Keith Keane and George Pilkington both played their final game in a Luton shirt at Wembley. Keane served us loyally making 285 LTFC appearances, before leaving for Preston and skipper Pilkington would move to Mansfield after 172 Hatters games.

2012-13

I made a vow at the beginning of 2012-13 to attend every 'league' game at home and away, a feat I had only achieved once previously. This was in 1982-83 when we famously stayed up in the top Division after beating Man City.

The fact that I was having books to sell helped me make this decision.

Various players came and went. I have already written about the departures of Keith Keane and George Pilkington. Pilks transfer to Mansfield was rather sad as after a mere handful of games for the Stags he was dropped, never to play for them again. A whole host of other players departed too.

Will Antwi and Curtis Osano left for AFC Wimbledon, Ed Asafu-Adjaye (1 goal, 82 apps) joined Forest Green. Matthew Barnes-Homer (23 goals, 81 Apps), Charlie Hendry, John-Paul Kissock and Amari Morgan-Smith would all end up at Macclesfield. Shane Blackett, Andre Boucard, Danny Crow, Aaron O'Connor and Robbie Willmott (all to Newport). Dan Gleeson, Jamie Hand, Freddie Murray and Godfrey Poko were also released.

Paul Buckle bought in wholesale changes and joining the Hatters throughout 2012-13 were: Simon Ainge, old LTFC keeper Dean Brill, ex-Stevenage Captain Ron Henry, Amaud Mendy, ex-Fleetwood skipper and fondly known as Sumo Steve McNulty, Scott Rendell, Jake Robinson, Lathaniel Rowe-Turner, Jonathon Smith and the biggest signing of them all, striker Jon Shaw from Gateshead, who had scored over 30 goals in 2011-12 for the Heed.

I watched three pre-season home friendlies against Football League opposition. We drew with Wycombe 0-0, beat Ipswich 2-0 and Leyton Orient 1-0. The result against the Os continued my remarkable home record against them of: Played 14 Won 13, Drew 1, Lost 0.

We kicked off at home to Shaw's old club Gateshead and with 76 Heed fans in the 6,743 attendance - we soon found ourselves 2-0 down! Fleetwood and Shaw scored to earn us a point in the sun.

The first three away games produced victories at Kidderminster (2-0), Hyde on a Fri night (2-1) and a good 3-1 victory at Ebbsfleet.

Joining me for all those matches was a character known to many as Curlz.

Back in the days of a BBC football internet forum called 606, I met this guy. He is originally from Middlesbrough, lived in Holland and is a fanatical Hatter (LTFC Orange clogs too). When the site closed down, a replacement was set up by the name of Sports 262 and from this site I would get to meet many new good Hatters friends such as LTFC Mick, Ironman, Lord Stevo, SW19, Hatter 57, Sussex, Madpig, I Knew Joe Payne and Melbourne Hatter, to name but a few.

Curlz would fly over frequently throughout 2012-13 and he would join me on numerous away trips around the BSP.

When he joined me with a Barton mate called H, who drove us to Alfreton for the 8th game, it was to be the first (of many) downers of the season.

We were thrashed 3-0! On the way home from there we stopped in a Harlington pub and I would meet the son of ex-Luton News Sports reporter Eric Norris.

After a 0-0 draw at home to Wrexham, George Clark drove me to Grimsby for a televised live game the next Friday night. Due to horrific traffic, we made kick off with about TWO minutes to spare and the Bobbers Club Coach - missed the 1st Half! They were the lucky ones for although we didn't play that bad, we heavily lost 4-1.

Four nights later I drove Curlz up to Tamworth and we made up for it by winning 2-1. After seeing off Southport 3-1 at home, I saw us win at Lincoln for the first time. We beat the Imps 2-1 and there was a bit of a fracas pre match in a Lincoln pub, involving several personal friends of mine.

Against Nuneaton Town at Kenilworth Road I was in the Eric Morecambe Sponsors Lounge. We were there as guests of Mick Donahue (LTFC Mick) and had a fabulous day. There also that day was Kirk (Basher) Stephens, as he is a Nuneaton lad.

The match was pretty poor but came to life in the final ten minutes with two excellent Alex Lawless goals – oh and Basher purchased my book too!

I missed our 2-0 win at Cambridge in the FA Cup Qualifying Round as I was up in Scotland for the real Glasgow derby at Ibrox Park. But instead of attending the Old Firm one as usual, this was for Rangers v Queens Park - in Div 3!

I've already written about the crook who almost managed to put this famous institution out of business. Well on this particular day, a colossal 49,463 attended the old Glasgow derby. It was a world record attendance for a 4th tier football match and Rangers won 2-0.

The punishment meted out to Rangers in the summer of 2012 was incredible. Apart from being relegated to Div 3, having the vast majority of their players walking out, with no transfer fees paid, an enforced transfer embargo and banned from Europe for at least 3 seasons AND with an ongoing case against HMRC for alleged misdemeanours involving Tax Loan Schemes (which they would eventually be proved of NO wrongdoing) AND an SPL charge of alleged Breaches of their Rules (which they would be eventually proved NOT GUILTY of rule breaking) to think that we at LTFC had been shafted by the authorities in 2008 - made our punishment actually look pretty lenient!

It does make one wonder what reasoning was truly behind this vindictiveness, to actually try and finish Rangers off once and for all. But they failed. Rangers would go on to romp home with Div 3, to begin the long road back to recovery.

Lord Stevo would drive us to Forest Green Rovers, where we won with a great 2-1 victory in front of over 1,000 Hatters fans. Stuart Fleetwood scored his 10th 2012-13 goal. We had NO idea at the time, but this would be his last BSP LTFC one.

At that time (end of Oct), we were in 2nd place having played 16, won 10 (inc 6 out of 8 away) Drew 2 and Lost 4.

I have to write, that all seemed fairly well under Paul Buckle then but looking back now I believe that this is where it started going wrong for him.

Incredibly - FGR was the very last away BSP win under his management!

I drove Curlz down to Hereford for Luton's (and my) first visit there since 1977. We met a couple of Hereford/Rangers mates of mine. We lost 1-0 with Hereford's only shot.

The next weekend I was on Greg Lansbury's Stag party at Butlins in Bognor Regis. It was my first visit there since I was 6! What a blinder of a time we had too with Vinny Brandom sharing my room, the fun the party of lads had there was immense for the 80s Soul themed celebrations.

There was a friend of mine called Nigel Martin, commonly known to many as Santa. He lived in Portsmouth and was a fanatical Hatter who drove up to every game. Santa very kindly picked up James Sellars and I up from Butlins to take us to the Luton v Dartford match, before dropping us back the same night.

I wished we hadn't bothered! Luton were awful and we lost 2-0. This was our third home defeat already and the names of opponents in those losses sum it all up - Telford, Braintree and fucking Dartford!

Driving Curlz up to Field Mill, Mansfield I thought we were going to see the Hatters win our first ever league victory there after leading 2-1 with minutes to go. Alas, the Stags grabbed a late equaliser. At the time we were in 6th place and Mansfield 10th I think this late goal, was a turning point for them and they would go on a brilliant run to eventually win the BSP.

In the FA Cup, we knocked out Nuneaton (saw Basher again, in the Bobbers Club post match) and Dorchester Town, both after replays and had a bit of a plum tie in the 3rd Round, at home to Championship club Wolves.

Before that game, George Clark drove me to Newport (another new ground, as they now share with Newport RFC). On what was one of the coldest nights I can ever remember, we were pathetic and were thrashed 5-2. Coming home that night in his car, the heating had failed and I thought I was going to freeze to death - sometimes you think, are LTFC worth it?

In the festive period we played Woking at home on Boxing Day. The biggest home 2012-13 BSP attendance of 6,744 watched us win 3-1.

Before the away fixture there on New Year's Day, Curlz and I attended Greg Lansbury's wedding reception to Elle at the Novotel in MK on NYE.

The next day (EARLY morning) we joined George Clark and Pip on the train journey to Woking for the 1pm kick off. Again, I wished we had not bothered. Luton were crap in a 3-1 defeat and the fourth winless away game run was beginning to have an effect on our promotion hopes - AGAIN! Incidentally, at HT that day I smoked my last Old Holburn baccy smoke and have never had a puff of any fag since - to this day over 9 years later!

In front of a sell out 9,638 crowd, it was a joy to see the Oak Road full with Wolves fans instead of the usual BSP dozens. Alex Lawless scored a cracker, the only goal and our win against opposition three tiers higher was thoroughly deserved. The cup run was exciting, even though it was covering up some lacklustre BSP performances.

We were drawn against Premiership Norwich at Carrow Road in Round 4 and the clamour for tickets began.

Before that I saw Towns best league performance of 2012-13. At home to Barrow, in front of only 5,165 (the lowest league crowd since we had been non-league) including only 31 away fans, we thrashed them 6-1 with Jon Shaw netting a hat trick.

I drove Curlz up midweek to bottom side Telford, where we could only draw 0-0. Pre match in the Telford Lounge I introduced Curlz to Gary Sweet, explaining his devotion to the Hatters cause by traveling over so many times from Holland to follow the Town. When I also explained that as LTFC had sold out our full 4,000 allocation of tickets for the Norwich Cup tie, arrangements were immediately made by Mr Sweet for Curlz to have one. Gary made a phone call for me to collect one of his allotted tickets the next day.

When the draw was made, Adair Travel immediately swung into action and I organised a 49 seated coach for the trip to Carrow Road from Stopsley Working Men's Club.

Curlz and I even managed to appear on Sky Sports news, as we were interviewed a couple of days before the match. We appeared on Friday and the morning of the game - even though my stardom lasted all of TEN SECONDS!

We left on a cold late January day, more in hope than expectancy.

The day and night turned into a memory to cherish and is right up there, in my all time top ten LTFC experiences.

Pre-match, we had a fabulous time in a pub near the coach park as Norwich fans and Hatters freely mixed in terrific camaraderie. The fact that Norwich had priced tickets at only £10 for Adults and £1 concessions meant that this game had sold out immediately. We had been given 4,000 seats of the 26,521 attendance, but they could have trebled our allocation and we would have still sold out.

With Luton more than holding their own against the Canaries, the minutes were ticking down and we were looking forward to bringing Norwich back to the Kenny. Paul Buckle had made his substitutions, bringing on the trio of Fleetwood, O'Donnell and Rendell. When those three combined in a run late on, you had to be there to experience it.

Stuart Fleetwood fed JJ O'Donnell down the left wing, he managed to cross the ball into the area and Scott Rendell came in on the blind side to sweep the ball home. The eruption of noise was unbelievable, as 4,000 Hatters went bonkers. I kissed a lady next to me that I had never met before and she turned out to be a fellow Sports 262er (2020 Phoenix). The final whistle blew and LTFC had created history, by becoming the first ever non-league side to knock out a Premiership club away in the FA Cup.

I have to write that the Norwich fans were great, many of them congratulating us, shaking hands and saying, "Well done, you thoroughly deserved to win."

That night we celebrated in fine style returning to SWMC, then Phil Fensome, Curlz and I continued at a packed Compasses pub, where I was in full Karaoke mode. I eventually arrived home at 5.45am - a full 19-hour session!

After the fantastic Norwich win we had been drawn at home to play Championship side Millwall in Round 5. Naturally, memories came flooding back of that appalling violent night in 1985. Millwall to their credit immediately announced that their 1,500 allocation would be for Season Ticket Holders only. Three nights after the Norwich win, we were eliminated at the Quarter Final stage of the FA Trophy by losing 3-0 at Grimsby and in truth, no one cared.

I made my first (and probably only) visit to Holker Street, Barrow next. Because it was such a long distance to travel I chose not to drive and took up a bargain £20 return price on Three Star Coaches. The journey was never ending and a 14 hour round trip occurred. Making his LTFC debut at Barrow, was Centre Half Steve McNulty. He was the ex-Fleetwood captain and seeing the size of him - sumo and Pie man came to mind! Although I had never seen such an unfit looking player in my life, he would go on to prove my doubts incorrect.

We fell behind to an early Barrow goal thanks to a defensive error by Greg Taylor and never recovered, losing 1-0 to a side near the bottom of the table. It was Barrows first win in ages and Paul Buckle lost a bit of support that day post-match, when he slaughtered Taylor publicly.

Any realistic hope of promotion vanished in my view, when we could only muster a 1-1 draw at home to Forest Green and then lost 1-0 at Dartford, to enable them to complete a double over us.

The Millwall FA Cup 5th Round tie was screened live on TV with an understandably police inspired 12.45 kick off time. Now I know the nation's eyes were on LTFC because of A) The 1985 Riot and B) A chance of Luton being the first non-league side ever, to reach a FA Cup Quarter Final. But the police operation that day - bordered on the RIDICULOUS! As I entered Oak Road for the Bobbers Club pre-match, not only was I amazed that the Police allowed it to be open but the TWO barricades in operation were a sight to see.

It honestly reminded me of Belfast at the height of its troubles. I had to literally walk in and out of both of them.

The worst possible start occurred when Janos Kovacs made a mistake to gift Millwall an early goal. It became 2-0 before Half Time and when the Lions added a third, we were out. The 9,768 attendance was the biggest for 3 years.

LTFC were out of the Cup but at least had made a very healthy financial profit as a result of our best FA Cup run since 1994.

Three nights later George Clark and his son Scott, drove Curlz, Pip and I to Macclesfield. When we had a bite to eat in McDonald's pre-match, we were astounded to hear the news that manager Paul Buckle - had QUIT, only hours before kickoff! There was a mixture of opinions at this shocking news. I personally, was glad to hear it. In my honest opinion I think that Paul Buckle was one of the worst Hatters managers in all my time.

Coincidentally, Buckle managed exactly the same amount of LTFC games as Gary Brabin (49) only he lost 14 games, as opposed to Brabin's 9.

When he first took over from Brabin he steadied the ship and did well to get us to Wembley for the Play Off Final and at the start of 2012-13, did more than ok by managing a team to win 6 out of its first 8 away games. Buckles problems started as soon as he began swapping and changing formations, tactics etc. He fell into exactly the same trap as Brabin, only worse. Because of his insistence at bringing in his own players (nearly all of whom were crap) and dropping Stuart Fleetwood (our top scorer at the time), the wheels began to fall off the bus. It was only the FA Cup run that was covering up his inefficiencies and in truth Buckle was totally out of his depth. MANY a Hatter I spoke to, agreed with my opinion that he had left us with the WORST LTFC squad in history.

We drew 1-1 at Macclesfield. After a great start where Andre Gray scored, we hit the post and then Macc were down to 10 men, we just seemed to stop playing and tried to hold on to that lead. Inevitably they levelled and in truth we were lucky to finally gain a point.

Luton then lost 3-2 at home to Mansfield and another massive low, when we lost 2-0 at Braintree (another side to complete a double over us).

Our 30th manager was announced as John Still, leaving Dagenham in League 2 for us. This is a man who HAS been a successful manager at this level having gained promotion twice with Dagenham and Maidstone.

He started with a 1-0 win at Stockport, only our second BSP victory in 2013 and the first away for over four months.

Jake Howells scored in a refreshing performance, even though Stuart Fleetwood missed a penalty (his confidence shattered by Buckle IMO).

This was a very enjoyable weekend as I was staying at my old haunt, the Claremont Hotel in Blackpool. We were there (a coach party) to celebrate the late Frankie Lemmon's daughter Deanna's 40th birthday. In a fabulous deal, we paid only £125 + coach fare (£28) for 2 nights Bed, Breakfast, Lunch, Evening meal AND all drinks included. Enjoying the company of great friends Jane & Gary Hopkins, along with a brilliant Compasses crowd.

I booked an identical package in September (49 of us) at the same hotel, for Luton's last game of the season at Southport on Apr 19-21, for what we hoped and prayed - would be a promotion party!

One tactic I did notice with John Still was his insistence at bringing all 10 out field players back in the area for opposition corners, aka Richard Money.

This is a modern tactic that most Premiership, Foreign Managers use. In their views, while 10 players are in the area you are less likely to concede. I personally hate it, but who am I to question?

Following two draws away to Nuneaton and at home to Hereford, came yet another all time low in my history of following the Town.

Until a year or so prior, I had never even heard of Hyde FC. Not only did they thoroughly deserve to win 2-1 at Kenilworth Road, but it was watched by only 4,847 (inc just 19 away fans) - our first & only sub BSB 5,000 crowd and our lowest for over 12 years!

Mr Still certainly had a job on his hands with this lot of Buckle duds.

After a good 0-0 draw at Wrexham, we completed our first double of 2012-13 by beating Stockport at home 1-0. Steve McNulty scored his first Hatters goal. I have a terrific unbeaten record v Stockport. In eight games against the other Hatters my record is - 7 wins and a draw!

Following a 0-0 at home to Tamworth, I enjoyed a nice Corporate Hospitality day at Cambridge Utd, via LTFC Mick's kind invitation. We drew 2-2 and I was pleased at shaking the hand of ex-Rangers player Robert Fleck pre-match and having my photo taken post-match with John Still.

We lost our SIXTH home BSP game 2-1, to promotion seeking Kidderminster before what is now officially - my DEFINITE all time low as a Hatter!

The only BSP ground I had yet to visit was the Gateshead International Stadium. Due to their pitch being unplayable since Xmas, they had been playing at various stadiums in the North including Hartlepool, York, Blyth, Boston and Middlesbrough. So when it came to a venue for the Luton game, Brunton Park in - CARLISLE was chosen FFS! It's nowhere near Gateshead?

Had I not been on this mission of attending every BSP game in 2012-13, I would never have gone. But I chose to board the Bobbers Travel Club coach and we set off at the ludicrously early time of 7.30am.

There were only 33 loyal/stupid supporters on it.

We arrived in lovely sunshine and I met fellow Sports 262ers SW19, Curlz and Mr & Mrs Ironman in the beer garden at the Beehive pub, for some much needed thirst quenchers. That was the climax of the day - what followed was appalling! Not only were we thrashed 5-1 (a record LTFC BSP loss and our heaviest defeat for 4 years) by a team who had forgotten what it was like to win, but the attendance of just 382 (inc 126 mad hatters) was officially the lowest attendance to watch a professional LTFC game. I PRAY that this was our nadir!

Three nights later we were at home to Lincoln and the players owed us a performance big time. We got one, as the Hatters beat a poor Imps side 3-0 to achieve another double.

Premier TV cameras were present for the next two games at home to Grimsby and Newport. We drew both (1-1 and 2-2) and there were signs that all was not lost yet, with some players looking like they did actually still want to be professional footballers.

The day after we beat Ebbsfleet 2-0 at home, we set off for the final game of the season at Southport on another Adair Travel beano.

This was a fabulous deal at my old haunt the Claremont Hotel in Blackpool. I had booked 49 of us, for an unbelievable package.

The coach (inc taking us to Southport on the Saturday) Bed, Breakfast, Lunch, Evening Meal AND Drinks for 2 nights was only £125 + £30 coach cost.

Including the Town winning 3-1 at Southport, this was one of the best trips ever. Each and every one of the 49 folk mixed brilliantly and we had a ball. After the cabaret had finished on both nights I naturally carried the fun on at Soul Suite in Blackpool, where I danced myself dizzy to the fabulous sounds of Northern Soul, Motown etc.

This had completed my 46 BSP games, along with George and Scott Clark. George had special tee shirts made in Blackpool for us reading, LTFC 46 GAMES PLAYED NOT ONE MISSED.

My final match of 2012-13 saw Rangers beat Berwick Rangers 1-0 at Ibrox in front of a staggering world record 4th tier attendance of – 50,048!

There were a few sad losses during the season. An ex-workmate and colleague of many years at both Roydon Printers and CBC, died of cancer. He was Barry Tebbut, who i bought my first car from back in 1976. A lovely gentle guy.

Two ex-Hatters also both passed away at a young age. Our ex-lodger and in my opinion, one of the top 3 LTFC goalkeepers in my time died in October 2012 in South Africa. Milijia Aleksic, known to many as Elastic, played 92 times for LTFC from 1976-78 and a loan spell in 1981.

At the end of this season, another ex-player who I knew personally, lost his battle to cancer at only 56 years of age. Tony (Paddy) Grealish was a fine midfielder who played for LTFC from 1979 to 81. In his 86 appearances I saw both of his goals at Charlton and Chelsea in 1980.

RIP friends.

And so we ended what was a dreadful 2012-13 (FA Cup run apart). John Still managed to steady the Buckle disaster ship a touch. In his 15-game reign, we lost three times and finally finished in 7th position.

Many of the previous Buckle players were released, including Ainge, Rendell, Brill, Rowe-Turner, as well as Dance, Fleetwood, Kovacs and Mendy.

I do wonder if I will EVER see LTFC play in the new stadium, we so desperately require. We have been waiting this long, over 50 years and while over a third of 92 League Clubs have moved into new homes - our wait continues!

NOT ONE GAME MISSED

George Clark and I at Southport v Luton. These shirts were made to celebrate completion of attending every LTFC home and away game in 2012-13.

CHAPTER SIX

BACK WHERE WE BELONG

So here we are in 2021 starting this third updated book. Clearly, a lot has happened in these past eight years.

In the Spring of 2013 I began a relationship with a lady I had known since I was 16 in 1974. Her name is Louise Winter, née Holmes. This all started when she heard about my book and contacted me on Facebook wishing to purchase it.

I didn't know at the time that she had sadly lost her husband Melvyn to Cancer a few years prior. I knew Melv back in the late 1970s and he was a lovely guy, mainly more of a mate with my much-missed pal Baggy, RIP.

Taking the book round to her house in Stopsley (Louise still lived in the house next door to St Thomas's Church where so many of my family including myself married) one thing led to another over a period of weeks and we started being a couple following a mutual friend's (Phil Francis) Silver Wedding Party at Stopsley Working Men's Club.

We always remained living separately in our own homes and staying together most weekends (mainly at hers). The relationship was in the main a good and happy one, but one thing I have learned since writing these books is to try and not be TOO personal with privacy matters.

Sadly, I ended our time together over five years later in the autumn of 2018 and will not publicly reveal the personal reasons as to why.

For now let me just say, our time together had run its course on my part, but she will always be a close dear friend and I certainly have absolutely no regrets that we were once an 'item'.

On the football front Luton Town FC were about to embark on our FIFTH season in the Non-League Conference, under John Still for his first full campaign.

Among the Hatters leaving for pastures new pre- and during 2013-14 were: Lathaniel Rowe-Turner, Greg Taylor, Dean Beckwith, Janos Kovacs, Norwich FA Cup hero Scott Rendell, Simon Ange, Adam Watkins, James Dance, keeper Dean Brill, Dan Walker and after 27 goals in 88 LTFC appearances - Stuart Fleetwood.

Players coming in pre- and during the season were: Paul Benson, Mark Cullen, Fraser Franks, Luke Guttridge (a fab signing), Cameron McGeehan, Andrew Parry, Luke Rooney, a certain Pelly-Ruddock M'Panzu and highly rated Shaun Whalley from Southport.

I attended several pre-season friendlies to see both my loves. These included watching Luton beat Football League side Dagenham 3-0, Aston Villa (mostly first team) 2–0 and Arsenal Youth Team which we won 7 (SEVEN) – 0!

Long-time Luton/Rangers mate Richie Harding and I had a great weekender in Bristol to see the Gers beat Bristol City 0–1 at Ashton Gate and then a few nights later I drove to stay in Sheffield for the night, joining 5,000 other Bears at Hillsborough, creating an unreal atmosphere in the Rangers' 1–0 defeat to the Owls. The Sheffield Wednesday fans were gobsmacked at not only how many Bears had attended for just a FRIENDLY, but were genuinely moved and the whole stadium applauded when several Gers fans paraded a Lee Rigby memorial flag around the pitch pre match.

Luton's first game of the season was at Southport and I went up on George Clark's Bletchley Hatters Minibus.

An expectant 839 travelling Hats out of the 2,210 crowd saw a disappointing start, losing 1–0 and to add to our woes recent signing Shaun Whalley missed a late penalty against his old club. NOT the start we envisaged.

In truth, after just two wins and a mere five goals from our opening eight games, it looked like same old, same old.

After losing meekly 2–0 at Wrexham – NOBODY had any idea that this would be our last Conference defeat – until MARCH 17th!

After Wrexham we saw off Dartford 3–0 at home and then the tenth game at home to Lincoln was IMHO, a turning point to our season.

When the Imps led 1–2 on 51 mins, a so called Luton 'supporter' had been giving the team stick from his Enclosure seat continuously throughout. Captain Ronnie Henry came over and had a frank 'discussion' with him telling him to get behind YOUR team and actually support the lads.

Well it worked, the fan shut up as supporters all around him raised their voice as one from that moment on. Luton came back to eventually win 3–2. I firmly believe it galvanised all at the club from that moment on. At full time, boss John Still began having a short team huddle and brought in a fan every time – starting with that heckler I believe?

We then went to Woking and won 0–4 and drew at Hereford 0–0 before facing Halifax at home. Similar to the previous Lincoln game, we were behind (this time 1–3 after 30 mins). But no moaning from the crowd just nonstop support and again it worked. We went on to beat the Shaymen 4–3, with a 25-yard screamer from Alex Wall settling it on 83 minutes. Utter scenes broke out all around Kenilworth Road.

Another high scoring game followed at my second and last (to date) visit to Aldershot midweek where we drew 3–3.

Then on game number 15 something special happened when we played Hyde at home. Such was their small support, LTFC decided to put their 30 (THIRTY) fans in a tiny corner section of the Kenny stand and give Luton supporters our whole old traditional Oak Road home end back.

I HAD to be there for my first time in the Oak since 1991. We witnessed a 4–1 victory with Andre Gray netting his first Luton hat-trick.

That day was the first time in 2013–14 I thought – is this IT? Is this going to be when we FINALLY do it and return to the Football League?

The result pushed us up to third place and we then went on to face six successive away games.

A 3–4 Town win at Tamworth (1–4 up) we then knocked out Woking 0–1 in the FA

Cup, both of which I missed, before a visit to Gateshead in the Northeast for my first time at their shared International Athletics Stadium.

I had pre-planned to stay with a Rangers pal Gary Shaw who lived in South Shields, along with meeting my old Windsor Castle dominoes partner Pete Taaffe who was working up there. What a day/night we had. The three of us had a good session in the excellent Gateshead bar at the ground where I met my favourite ever No 1 Luton player Malcolm Macdonald, who was working on the local Tyne radio station covering the game.

Gary stayed in the bar (he IS Scottish) and Pete and I took our seats to join the other 300 Hatters. We watched a dour 0–0, but the weather conditions had to be seen to be believed. Those there will know a fucking MONSOON like storm occurred during the game.

Didn't stop us all having a blinding night in South Shields mind and Pete bought one of my books.

The next week I went to see us play at Welling in the FA Cup First Round.

We would get knocked out, losing 2–1 and for the one and only time in my life I didn't actually care too much, as promotion WAS the *numero uno* priority for 2013–14.

Three nights later I drove to Essex where we won 1–2 at Braintree on a freezing cold night, at a ground where we had lost 3–1 and 2–0 (and played utter shite both times) on our previous matches there.

The sixth successive away game was completed at Chester. The Deva Stadium was another new ground for me to tick off, but I would be going there – from Blackpool!

After the hugely successful ADAIR Travel, Blackpool All Inclusive coach trip at the Claremont Hotel versus Southport in April, I booked trip number two for this fixture. Yes I KNOW Chester isn't actually near Lancashire, but because the hotel only did the All Inclusive deals from when the Illuminations finished in mid-November until July, this was the nearest ground to Blackpool on the dates available, so Chester it was.

Another blinding trip, we drew 1–1 with the Seals. Pre-match drinks in their excellent supporters bar at the ground, where they kindly let most of our coach party in.

As I write this 2021 updated book, to date I have now organised TEN of these group coach trips to the Claremont Hotel. This Chester match is the only draw we've seen, just two defeats and SEVEN Luton wins at the others.

By Christmas time Luton had won another four successive games including a fab 0–5 away win at Alfreton (where we were four up after only 17 mins!) which I missed (lightweight). Then a great personal experience.

My Mollie and her Oz boyfriend Lachlan, along with my niece Kirsty from Auckland, New Zealand were all coming to stay with me for the festive season. I was thrilled as I hadn't seen them for two long years.

On Boxing Day the company I worked with, Regal Litho, were sponsoring the Barnet versus Luton game as we printed their programmes. I was allowed to bring a couple of guests for Corporate Hospitality and as Louise didn't want to go, I invited Bletchley Hatter mate Gary Donovan and his brother. We watched a fine Town 1–2 win, but the match was marred on the stroke of half time when we were two up, by a horrific injury to our Jonathan Smith right in front of us.

Following a terrible 'tackle' on him by Barnet's player Nurse. The awful crack/snap could be heard all around the ground!

A deadly hush occurred as the medics rushed on to treat the stricken Smith. Incredibly the Ref only booked Nurse, until his linesman called him over to describe exactly what happened and the yellow card was correctly replaced by a red. The shocking challenge resulted in Jonathan being stretchered off with a badly broken leg and would miss the rest of the season.

Post-match in the sponsors lounge was definitely a muted occasion drinking our festive champers.

Two days later came the performance of the season IMO. Luton versus Kidderminster. We thrashed Kiddy 6–0 in an incredible display and went top for the first time in the season. That win was for 'Smudger' Smith.

It also turned out to be the last Luton game attended by an old early 1980s Sportsman pub mate of mine.

Tom Sweeney died of cancer not too long after this. He was in the same 1969–70 LTFC youth team as my cousin Ken Adair and my Uncle Mick's brother the late Vic Hines. RIP Tom and Vic.

Incredibly that day – ludicrously – some Luton fans were locked out of the ground in the attendance of 8,488! That was despite nearly 1,500 empty seats in the Oak Road because those seats were for away fans only (203 from Kiddy). This made LTFC have a rethink about allowing more Hatters fans in our traditional end by either sharing the Oak and creating a buffer zone (like we've now had since returning to the FL) or by moving any low numbers of away supporters, like we did against Hyde.

The next game on New Year's Day was the return versus Barnet where I took Lachlan to his first Luton match. Frankly, the game should never have started because of the constant torrential nonstop rain and the pitch had puddles all over it.

It only survived and began purely because it was live on TV.

When we led 2–0 the Barnet players were desperately trying to get the Ref to abandon it. Our skipper Ronnie Henry countered by stating to the Ref, you've started it and must end the game. The fact Barnet then scored to give them hope actually worked in our favour and the match was completed. We began 2014 in top spot.

On Jan 25th we beat Nuneaton 3–0 at the Kenny with Andre Gray scoring his second of three LTFC hat-tricks in 2013–14 and his 17th goal in 24 appearances – he didn't even start until the 11th game at Woking! Just like at Gateshead in the November, in the second half there were freak weather conditions. Such was the hail/lightning force – both teams had to be taken off the pitch for a ten minute spell!

The next game was midweek at Macclesfield. I drove up the M6 (making sure I had a business appointment in Solihull on route) in snowy conditions, not knowing if the game would even go ahead. Upon arrival it DID start and we won 1–2 with another Andre pair in front of 401 Hats at a Moss Rose ground where we had never previously won.

Driving home that night was the first time I began to believe – is this IT? Are we FINALLY going to end our horrid five-year non-league spell?

But we still had Cambridge breathing down our necks, so no room for complacency.

What I was about to witness was just sheer bliss. We slaughtered Hereford 7 (SEVEN) –

0 at KR, with Andre netting his third and last LTFC hat-trick. This was the seventh time I had seen Luton score seven goals (eight versus Hayes & Yeading) in a match. As I write this, there have been another four matches I've seen repeated since.

The Town juggernaut marched on.

On to Nuneaton by train for a pee up with George Clark and his Bletchley Hatters. We won 0–5 and this was now my biggest ever Luton away win (having missed Exeter in 1967 (too young) Colchester 2003 (banned) and Alfreton 2013 (lightweight).

When we followed it up with another 5–0 win at home to Wrexham we had now scored an incredible 30 goals – in just our last eight Conference games!

The excellent Luke Guttridge scored his 13th goal of the season in a 3–0 home win versus Alfreton, but was sadly stretchered off on 68 minutes and would miss the rest of the season. His popularity and quality were proven when voted by his teammates Players' Player of the Season.

Fourteen points clear at the top with 13 matches remaining including two away at Salisbury and the key one at Cambridge.

I went for my one and only visit to Salisbury. A 0–0 stalemate ended our six game winning run and there was no doubt we missed Guttridge's play and influence. Then Cambridge at the Abbey Stadium.

This was THE big one. Town had long prior sold our allocation of 2,286. In this massive game Cambridge came at us with everything but it was still goalless at half time.

To be honest it was all them for the first hour and then came a breakthrough on 62 mins when Elliott scored for the U's. Their fans were naturally joyous, ours still backing us to the hilt.

Incredibly, it was the first time we had been behind since at Tamworth – in October! We pushed for the all-important equaliser. 90 mins up, still 1–0 – then it HAPPENED!

A desperate long ball was sent in, Cameron headed on and Mark Cullen met it by incredibly volleying home on the turn – untold joyous SCENES In the away end! Possibly the most celebrated Luton goal in the last decade (Norwich FA Cup and Scunthorpe Wembley JPT apart).

At the end of season awards night manager John Still was asked when did he ACTUALLY begin to believe we were up? He typically answered, "Only when Kidderminster beat Cambridge." But then with a wry smile said, "When Cully equalised with that late goal at Cambridge, I secretly knew we were as good as up but would never publicly declare that then."

How ironic that we would lose our six-month 27-game unbeaten run in the very next game at home to Woking 0–1. The live TV jinx had struck again. Apart from the New Year's Day swimming pool win versus Barnet, I think we only won one other game in all our live TV games covered in the Conference.

I've lived in Barton since 1999 (bar a year in 2002–03 when Deb and I first parted) and despite living a mere few hundred yards away (since 2005) I had never seen Barton Rovers play. That was put to bed when I attended our Beds Senior Cup Semi Final at Sharpenhoe Road. Luton Youth went through to the Final 0–0 AET, winning 4–3 on penalties. I've sadly not returned there for a game since (yet).

The following Saturday I was back in the Oak Road to see us beat Chester 3–0. Then I stayed the night at Cleethorpes in the Blundell Park Hotel when we played Grimsby midweek. We beat the Mariners 1–2 coming from behind. I sold three of my books that night including two to Grimsby fans Phil Lambert and Graham Precious, who I've been pals with since.

I missed going to the Shay (lightweight) where Halifax comfortably beat us 2–0 before I saw us come from behind again at Dartford to win 1–2. Two late goals by Pelly and Andre in a game we seriously looked like losing. There was no doubt at all we were not in great form performances wise (yet still getting results). No coincidence these were without the influential Luke Guttridge.

Finally getting over the line nerves were effecting us a touch, but it was only a matter of time.

I missed the next game at home to Aldershot as was up in Kilsyth, Scotland. We narrowly beat the Shots 1–0.

It was to see Rangers play in the Ramsdens Cup Final (Scottish JPT) at Easter Road, Hibs against Raith Rovers. Embarrassingly RR beat Ally McCoist's Gers 1–0 AET.

This was the second season of Rangers 'journey' back from the wilderness of Scotland's fourth tier after being shafted there because of crooked RFC owners and charlatans. As expected the Gers cruised through League Three (fourth tier) and would win this 2013–14 in League Two (third tier) – remaining undefeated all season in fact! But no doubt, this Cup Final defeat was not good.

Back to the mighty Hatters.

We beat Tamworth at home 2–0 in front of an away attendance in a tiny corner of the Kenny – of just 13 (THIRTEEN) fans! The lowest away support ever officially counted at KR.

The day we had been waiting for what seemed an eternity, finally arrived on April 12th versus Braintree at home. A sold out 10,020 (including 96 from Essex) attended. The atmosphere pre-match was as expected, utterly bouncing in front of the live TV cameras (oh NO!!!)

But the live TV curse struck AGAIN on this day of all days.

16 mins 0–1 Braintree to stunned silence – five mins later 0–2!

Half time. COYH we can do this, remember Lincoln and Halifax?

When they made it 0–3 on 56 mins I wanted to cry. Isn't this SO fucking Luton Town!

After 62 minutes a penalty to Luton, 1–3. Then 65 mins 2–3 when Alex Wall scored.

On 72 minutes – FFS Mark Cullen hits the post! Full time, the five-year wait would have to continue for a few more days.

Post-match John Still famously said, "Never too high, never too low." – Well sorry Sir John of Still – I WAS low! So much so I drowned my sorrows in a session at the Bobbers, meeting Louise there in what SHOULD have been a night of massive celebration. We continued onto fans pub the Bricklayers Arms, only for me to end up getting barred from there (for life FFS!) because, I quote from the female manager/owner, "You're always pissed when you come in here." … I swear and Louise was there as my witness, along with several others, I hadn't done anything wrong – not loud, or out of order in any way, just pissed and feeling sorry for what should have been a great occasion!

Well DILLIGAF. The place was always too cliché – cliquey for my liking anyway and I much prefer/preferred the Wheelies.

The magic moment finally came on April 15th but sadly, we had no Luton game to celebrate promotion as Cambridge had lost 2–0 at Kidderminster. Some Hats went up to Aggborough to cheer Kiddy on including mate Curlz. I chose to stay at home in Barton.

When promotion finally arrived I was straight over the road to fellow staunch Hatter Tim Norman and we went to the Bull, where I ordered a bottle of Champers like many other Hats did that night and we drank to celebrate the Town's magnificent achievement.

We still had three games to play and at all of those, partying was the order of the day. At Welling where they kindly let us Hatters onto the pitch at full time after we won 1–2 to see our beloved players. 2,000 Hats were in Kent out of a 2,650 total attendance.

The final home game Luton will ever play in nonleague was versus Forest Green Rovers. Even though Forest Green went 0–1 ahead in front of their 114 fans we just KNEW this was not going to be another Braintree. On the stroke of half time Andre Gray equalised with a penalty, the first he took all season. Cameron McGeehan put us 2–1 up, then Andre scored his 30th goal of 2013–14. It was the 100th LTFC goal of this incredible campaign and Mark Cullen made it 101 in the last minute 4–1.

This turned out to be Andre Gray's 110th and penultimate LTFC career appearance. He scored 57 Town goals.

The finale of this non-league journey was on my 56th birthday at Hyde.

I had long since booked an Adair Travel All Inclusive Blackpool Weekender, my third such trip and while I can remember I must write this.

One of the coach passengers was a mate I had met in the Bobbers Club, a Yeovil Hatter who came up from Somerset fairly regularly, known to all by the name of Howie (Howard Fosse). On the Blackpool bound Friday coach journey, was another passenger by the name of Anita Smyth (just going with a female friend Elaine Beamon and not that big a football fan) well these two met for the first time on the coach and I'm delighted to write – are now a happily married couple! Adair Travel matchmaking at your service lol.

As expected, we had the time of our lives, most of us in fancy dress at Hyde, including *moi* on my birthday dressed as Fred Flintstone – with orange wig naturally! Hyde FC went out of their way to welcome us 2,253 Hats, letting a lot of lads/lasses I know even pay for Corporate Hospitality at the game.

Louise and I sat together and cheered with the rest of the Hats when Alex Wall scored the only goal on 68 mins.

But the loudest cheer of the day came when Jonathan Smith came on as a late sub for Andre Gray. A HUGE ovation for both players. Smudger, returning after his terrible leg break and Andre for his 30 goals and massive part in getting us promoted.

Some stats here from this season to remember, when at that time only 1981–82, 87–88 and 2004–05 beat it in terms of feel-good factor:

101 Points – a new club record.

23 Clean sheets – a new club record.

102 goals scored – the most in a season in my era attending from 1966.

27 games unbeaten from September to March – a club record (since beaten).

17 different goalscorers.

7,387 home average attendance – our highest since 2007 in the second tier.

1,086 average away attendance – a Conference record to this day.

Our Five Year Conference Seasons:

Played 228, Won 119, Drew 64, Lost 45 Goals scored 419, Conceded 215, Points 421.

93 clean sheets.

44 Different clubs played.

8 LTFC hat-tricks.

8-0 biggest win versus Hayes & Yeading, 2010.

199 most appearances – Mark Tyler.

The weekend of Tranmere 0 Luton 1 Easter 2015. Myself at the iconic Penny Lane in the city of my musical heroes. Liverpool is a fab place, with fab people.

2014–15

Things were developing very well with Louise and I. We saw each other most weekends, mainly me staying at hers in Stopsley, rather than she at mine. For Louise's personal reasons she chose it that way and in all our time together I can count on one hand the amount of times she stayed overnight at my house in Barton.

We were an 'item' for over five years before I ended the relationship in the autumn of 2018 mainly for personal issues which arose.

In the July of 2014 I attended the funeral of a lovely old boy and father of a friend called Ian. Wally Allsop was an old LTFC stalwart supporter and backed the club financially in corporate hospitality terms for many years RIP Wally.

We eagerly awaited our first season back in the Football League since 2008–09. This would be LTFC's 129th campaign.

2014-15 would have an indifferent start, partly disastrous finish, with some excellent parts in between.

Pre-season among those players departing were the fabulous Andre Gray. He was a major reason with his 30 goals in 2013–14 and total of 57 goals in 111 appearances why we were back where we belong in the FL.

With a year left on his contract he could have stayed with us, then in the January of 2015 sign a pre-contract with another club, leave in June and we would receive – ZILCH!

Instead he would leave for second tier Brentford with a far greater contract in terms of earnings than we could ever afford to offer with our budget. So thinking of him AND the club, we did a great undisclosed deal with the Bees. It is my belief the initial transfer fee was in the region of £600,000 but definitely with all sorts of add-ons that would eventually total a fee of around £2.5m. Andre left on good terms with all Hatters blessings and our thanks.

He would later move to Premiership Burnley, then become agent Andre by signing for and taking W**ford for around £65k a week. Then help relegate them from the Premiership in 2019–20.

Other notable departures were: Skipper Ron Henry back to Stevenage after no goals in 87 apps, J.J. O'Donnell 3/51 and Jon Shaw 10/51.

Arrivals pre and during 2014–15 were: Nathan Doyle, a second coming of Andy Drury for £100,000 from Crawley, full-back Michael Harriman on loan from QPR, Elliot Lee on loan from West Ham, Ricky Miller, Luke Wilkinson and another loan mid-season Jayden Stockley.

New contracts were offered and signed by Mark Cullen, Luke Rooney, Steve McNulty and long serving Jake Howells.

Before the season started LTFC decided to run a poll for all the supporters with a question once and for all: Do you want orange as our predominant home kit, or prefer to return to our old traditional white and black? Despite owner Gary Sweet and Director David Wilkinson voting White and Black, orange won the vote – which included mine.

I attended various preseason friendlies, including our regular Hitchin visit to Top Field, where we won 0–5, a 2–2 home draw versus Colchester, but before that a very special day against Belgian club Royal Antwerp.

Their fans were incredible, many of them making a weekend of it in Luton. Louise and I met a few of them at The Sportsman pub in Stopsley on the Friday night – I even sold a few of my books to a couple of the RA fans in the Bobbers Club post-match on Saturday.

The reason why it was so special was because without a word of exaggeration, they created THE best ever away fans atmosphere at Luton I've ever seen in all my 55-plus years of supporting the Town.

Despite us winning 4–0 they never stopped singing from the minute they arrived in Luton until they left. An absolute credit to football and Belgium. Absentees missed a treat.

Another friendly I saw was for my second love. I drove Bob and Gary Rumble up to Derby to meet pal Duncan Angus from Kilsyth at a local hotel for an overnight stay. This was for Rangers game at Pride Park. We were well beaten 2–0 by the Rams, but an incredible 9,000 Bears attended! The support was outstanding – just like Royal Antwerp – nonstop singing and support of their team!

One of those Bears was old pal fellow Luton Loyal Gus Watson, who we met pre- and post-match in a Wetherspoons. It was the first time I had seen him since THAT Porto trip in 2005. I've seen him several times since at both Luton and Rangers games. The £250 flight debt was never mentioned and I've basically written it off – though would naturally still like it back one day!

Our first game back in the FL was at Carlisle – and I chose to MISS IT!

Normally I'd have naturally been there, but it was my daughter Georgina's 24th birthday and she was down from Scotland for a family party (her Nan's same birth date) at my house for a lovely garden party in the sun. I took the correct decision that my kids come before football.

It didn't stop me constantly checking Sky's Soccer Saturday updates and screaming out 'YES' when Mark Cullen scored a 30th minute goal, which turned out to be the winner.

An incredible 1,088 Hats travelled to near Scotland to see Luton's first FL opening day victory since we beat Hartlepool 2–1 in 2007.

My first game of the season was a 1–2 home League Cup defeat versus Swindon. Taking advantage of my new 'Diamond' Season Ticket which for an extra £150, gave all sorts of fantastic extra benefits, including this free first home cup tie ticket. Other Diamond benefits were five Adult and five kids free tickets (subject to availability) to any home league games, £100 hospitality ticket, free LTFC shirt and priority for away ticket allocations.

The first league home game was against AFC Wimbledon (lost 0–1) and my first away game was a 2–2 draw at Accrington Stanley where I ticked off another new ground. (Been back five more times to date since.)

TBH our start had been indifferent to say the least.

After the first six league games we had not won since the opening day at Carlisle. I finally saw my first Luton league win versus Cheltenham 1–0 at home. It was my first in the FL since beating Macclesfield at home by the same score in 2009.

I then drove mate Steve O'Dell up to the beautiful city of York midweek.

Steve is a good mate and son of an old Stopsley WMC domino legend teammate Jack, who sadly passed away that year. Steve had recently moved up from his Welsh home of many years to live back in Luton permanently and sort out all the financial and legal issues with Jack's house etc.

We booked a lovely guest house in Bootham Crescent, same street as the ground and fabulous Social Club that I had been in several times before. Luton gallantly drew 0–0.

My first away win came at Cambridge United four days later when we beat the U's 0–1 with Mark Cullen scoring again as he had done on that special night six months prior. Astoundingly, this was the first time I had seen Luton win an away FL fixture since 2005!! when we beat Leicester 0–2 on my only (to date) visit to their new Walkers (or whatever it's called now) stadium.

We then beat Oxford 2–0 at home and had steadied the ship at 10 games played: with 4 wins, 3 draws and three defeats. We were 10th/24.

These last two wins against the famous university cities, were the start of a fantastic sequence of SEVEN successive victories. Luton truly were BACK.

On Oct 25th LTFC topped the fourth tier for the first time since April 2002.

Among the victories I then saw were 1–2 at Stevenage, where a fantastic Alex Wall late strike clinched it, another brilliant strike, this time by Alex Lawless helped to beat Southend 2–0 at home.

For this match I took long time Stopsley WMC friends Paul Keating and his partner Christine. We had a brilliant day and night in the Bobbers Club and sitting in the Oak Road.

Then the return of the famous Hartlepool weekenders, my first since 1996.

Many Hats joined us and I booked a few of us in the Travelodge hotel at the beautiful marina area. Hartlepool is a cracking modern town full of great folk as we know, having been there SO many times.

We beat Pools 1–2 then on the Saturday night in the Mill House pub saw a good live band. With us in the audience was old mate Paul Clark (Clarky loves Hartlepool too having relations live there). It was also the first time I met Sky TV's massive Hatter fan, the lovely Faye Carruthers in there.

Then against Northampton our first 10,000 full house of the season saw an utterly brilliant Luke Guttridge last minute strike against his old club to seal the three points. His celebrations in front of the Cobblers fans were exactly how three and a half parts of KR were feeling.

After this I had to miss Exeter at St James' Park (lightweight), where a 1–1 draw cost us top spot down to second.

In the FA Cup First Round versus Newport I took my Kiwi nephew Peter Bristow to see his first Luton match, we won 4–2.

Peter was now living with me for a little while having now had a two year UK employment visa and worked in the City of London. He would later move to Wapping as it made more sense to live in the smoke and he currently lives in Japan with his Oriental girlfriend.

I was back in the Oak Road to see us beat Tranmere (my very first league opponents back in 1966) 1–0. Pre-match I met up with a Facebook friend and Rovers fan Mick Cattrell.

This was the last time we topped the table in 2014–15.

Then another new ground ticked off the list at Burton Albion, where we were disappointing and lost 1–0 to the Brewers in front of a sold-out allocation of 1,998 travelling Hats – Luton had nearly half the gate!

When we beat Mansfield 3–0 at the Kenny, a couple of brilliant long-range efforts by Shaun Whalley deservedly gave us the win. I rated Shaun but some Hats didn't – proof in my belief is that he is still playing in the third tier of English football today at Shrewsbury Town.

The day after, I took Georgina and her boyfriend (then) to Heathrow Airport where they were flying to Sydney to see Mollie, as well having a period working there.

With a forthcoming Blackpool Adair Travel trip coming up (my fourth) I gave our FA Cup second round tie at Bury a miss, we drew 1–1.

This Blackpool trip was for our relatively local game at Morecambe – another new ground for me!

I'm sorry to write, but this was Luton's worst performance of the season to date, we were well beaten 3–0 by the Shrimps AND had skipper Steve 'Sumo' McNulty sent off. The result never stopped us having another sensational time at the Claremont. These trips were growing and growing in popularity, to the point that because I was getting full bookings so soon, I had to ask some folk to make their own way to Blackpool as I booked their hotel package only.

In the FA Cup replay we beat Bury 1–0 with Luke Rooney scoring the only goal. Amazingly in the 11 clashes I've seen us play against Bury from 1970 – 2015 – this is the ONLY time I've seen us beat the Shakers!

Tragically, they sadly no longer exist having been liquidated in 2019 by yet another crooked bent owner. As I write though, there are moves to try & buy out the owner with Bury Council's blessing. Gigg Lane is still there today intact. Good luck to them and all Shakers fans.

Next up was a great 3–0 home win versus Newport, a side that had gone nine matches unbeaten.

Luton then had a bit of an indifferent spell of four winless games around the festive period.

In the New Year around mid-January I was feeling a little strange. Louise came round and took one look at me insisting we book a doctor's appointment NOW. She told me I didn't look right at all and I must admit, I didn't feel great. The Barton GP examined me, did an ECG and told me my heartbeat was slow and irregular and asked Louise if she could get me to the hospital ASAP for them to check me out more thoroughly. To cut a long story short the GP was correct, I DID have an irregular heartbeat.

I was kept in – for nearly a fortnight, missing both Plymouth (we won 0–1) and Cheltenham (1–1) away!

I must admit it did give me a bit of a scare but thanks to the brilliant NHS staff I was soon on the mend and actually liked the hospital food lol. Best mate Larry Kinloch picked me up and took me home, only to discover upon entry my hall radiator had split open with fluid everywhere all over the hall floor. I rang a plumber friend who immediately came round to switch off that radiator so no more leakage could occur.

Fortunately, I had been a British Gas Homecare customer for years and they soon sorted me out with a brand-new replacement radiator.

I was also out of hospital in time to see us beat Cambridge Utd 3–2 in which a foreign pal I had met at the start of the season flew over for this game too, so I joined Dutch Fred in the Bobbers Club and Oak Road.

Louise and I went to Oxford versus Luton (1–1) on our own as guests of Regal Litho to have some corporate hospitality in an Executive Box. Oxford were one of several clubs who Regal printed programmes for. Two other guests were in the box who turned out to be the LTFC Finance Director and his wife. Very nice couple too. 2,264 Hatters plus us four were at the Kassam Stadium.

The indifferent spell continued with only two wins out of six in February, before calamity then struck in all of March and the first match in April – losing EVERY single game!

One of those February wins (2–0 versus Accrington Stanley) I was joined in the Bobbers by nephew Kiwi Hatter Pete, Aussie Hatter Mike Jakins and a Chelsea supporting neighbour Ian.

The rot started with a midweek 1–0 defeat at Bury where Steve Odell and I had an overnight midweek stay in a nice hotel near the ground called the Rostrevor. Pre-match we met a couple of brilliant Bury lads and Facebook pals Carl Mason and Phil Lyons. They looked after us a treat and we had a good drink with them both pre- and post-match.

Portsmouth away we lost 2–0 with a big Luton turnout of 2,680 including a large squad of MIGs.

Pre-match in the Good Companion pub was when I first met Pompey pal Phil Hibbert, as well as an old 1970s Oak Road lad who now lives in Cornwall by the name of Del Osbourne.

Walking back to the station post-match was a bit like the old days with both sets of fans on opposite sides of the road goading each other. Nothing too serious though and in time several of the 657 Pompey mob and our lads have a healthy respect for each other after the generosity they showed both financially and in terms of friendship when one of our young lads suddenly died in his sleep in 2016. RIP Brett.

Another overnighter was at Newport three nights later where we stayed at Steve's Welsh son Richard's, who lived near there and at that time was married to a Luton lass (whose mum used to live in Crowland Road, Stopsley, around the corner from my old house – small world! Richard met his Mrs (now ex) on holiday abroad. Luton lost 1–0.

We lost SEVEN successive games – FFS.

This disastrous run sent us tumbling out of the promotion/play-off places down to ninth. For the first time, some fans wanted John Still sacked – but how could you fire a bloke so soon after all he had done for us! Social media has a lot to answer for with some of our lot.

The awful run ended at Tranmere on Easter Monday with a late Cameron McGeehan goal settling it, when following up a penalty miss by Mark Cullen. The goal/win sent us 526 Hats nuts with unbridled joy.

I drove mate Mark Griffiths (first time I met him) up on Easter Sunday to Liverpool, where he was meeting some of his ex-army mates and girlfriend Perri, then going to Tranmere next day. I was also staying in Liverpool at the famous old Adelphi Hotel. Grand and nice enough that it is, sadly it was now showing its age. That Sunday I had a brilliant day going on the Magical Mystery Beatles Coach tour. I was in my element and two hours of bliss seeing some history of my musical idols. The cost was only £16 and included admission to the Cavern Club that evening, where as you can imagine I had the time of my life – especially with a crowd of West Bromwich girls on a hen night!

It was my first, but not last time I'd go in the Cavern – Apr 26th 2018 (my 60th birthday) watch this space!

On the Easter Monday I drove under the Mersey Tunnel to Birkenhead, where I had booked an overnight Travelodge for the Tranny game. Pre-match in lovely sunshine I sat with some nice Rovers folk in a pub beer garden.

I've only been to Prenton Park twice and both times we've won. This 0–1 and 0–2 in 1993.

We were still far from the team who were SO good in the autumn though. Any lingering play-off hopes were down to the penultimate game of the season at Southend, who were also chasing promotion.

We were in eighth place, one behind play off seventh and frankly – HAD to win in all reality! I had pre-booked another Adair Travel coach trip for this, but in hindsight it was a mistake.

The lovely Westcliff Hotel was nice enough, but unlike the Claremont in Blackpool (who, as far as I'm aware, is the only all-inclusive hotel in the UK) this was 'only' two nights Bed, Breakfast and Evening Meal – no drinks inclusive! For this reason (obviously the pricing reflected that) only 29 travelled on the 49-seat coach and I lost a fortune (£600) on the trip.

Louise, myself and all the others still had a fabulous stay there though.

The hotel staff were great, friendly and welcoming and the food was lovely (though it could never beat the Claremont) but a lesson was learnt – if there's no 'free' booze – forget it!

I made up for my loss by asking everyone for an extra tenner on the next AT Blackpool trip and everyone was absolutely fine with that explanation.

Two thousand two hundred and seventy-six Hatters travelled to the seaside for what, apart from the match and the immediate depression straight after the game, was a fun filled day/night everywhere with Hats taking over the seafront bars. We soon forgot our woes.

I'm afraid we lost any realistic chance of promotion by losing to the Shrimpers 1–0. The goal was a calamity too, when Timlin's speculative tame shot from 25 yards was not held by our keeper Elliot Justham – and the ball rolled under him into the net to break our hearts!

But we are Luton and despite the short-term heartache for an hour or so – drink intake soon had us partying again and drowning our sorrows!

Although the drink took its toll on me eventually sadly.

Louise and I were going to see the Real Thing band in Southend that night, but I ended up in the room Donald ducked and missed 'You to me are Everything' – LIGHTWEIGHT!

We finished 2014–15 by beating locals Stevenage Reserves 2–0 at home in front of a sold-out Kenny. The only chance we had of promotion was a nigh on impossible EIGHT goal swing over Plymouth. Argyle won at Shrewsbury and that was that.

We finished our first season back in the FL in 8th place. Just one place and three points behind a play-off position. But let's be honest here, if anybody had offered Luton that before a ball was kicked in August, most Hats would have gladly accepted that.

I attended two further games at the end of this season.

Although I have lived in Barton for over 21 years as I write, I had only seen local side Barton Rovers play once and that was supporting LTFC Youth team in a Beds Senior Cup Semi Final tie (0–0 AET we won on pens), this despite me living a mere few hundred yards from their Sharpenhoe Road ground since 2005. So I decided to go on and cheer the Rovers in their Southern League Division 1 Play Off Final at Bedworth Utd, near Coventry. I travelled on the official coach, with players, officials and fans. Sadly 'we' lost 2–0 in front of 919.

A few more than that would attend my last game of 2014–15.

It was at Ibrox Park for a Scottish Premier League Play Off Quarter Final 2nd leg versus Queen of the South. We had won the first leg in Dumfries 1–2.

Since the disgrace of basically having to start from scratch again in 2012 after being TOTALLY shafted by a crooked owner and Scottish football authorities, my second love were now on the verge of hopefully straight away (in the least timespan) returning to where the Gers should never have been taken away from and where we belong – in the top tier!

Although we only drew this 2nd leg 1–1 in front of 48,035, it was enough to send Rangers through to the Semi's. We would also win that beating Hibs 2–1 on aggregate.

What happened in the Play-Off Final against Premiership Motherwell was both shocking, but also a reality check. We lost 1–3 in the Ibrox 1st leg and were humiliated 3–0 at Fir Park.

The truth is Rangers were not ready on the park for the SPL – and still a basket case OFF it! With clowns who were 'allowed' but NEVER should have been – to take over from the Craig Shyte farce!

The Ibrox Boardroom was one full of clowns and jokers trying to control and run this institution, only we were not laughing.

The hated MA as a major stakeholder and powerbroker was in NO doubt, trying to FINISH Rangers off, take Ibrox Park, raze it to the ground and finally kill off the Gers. We Bears fans had already discovered that in 2012 Charles Green was sold the naming rights by MA – for a POUND!

I could write a book alone about how Rangers FC were fleeced left right and centre by faceless moneymen.

In the end for season 2014–15 the ONLY way Rangers fans could hit back at people destroying their beloved club was to try and force them out by starving them of finances.

Bears fans way of doing what WE Hatters fans had to do in 2003 – to oust that maniac Gurney!

Around 15,000 (over 1/3) refused to renew Season Tickets and boycotted. Some perhaps understandably simply couldn't face not watching the Gers – even if it was slowly destroying the club!

To cut a long (VERY) story short, the start of the fightback began in March 2015 when ex-Director (before Whyte had SOLE say in 2011–12) Dave King and his Three Bears Consortium, managed to convince others to sell and buy enough of their shares to oust the current regime. It was joy all round but it would still be four long years before FINALLY getting rid of MA and most of his ties to Rangers FC.

Who I must write, it was discovered by the new owners, he had been given SUCH a lucrative merchandise deal by CG, that for every £10 Rangers shirt sold, the club would 'earn' something like 90p TOPS! The rest going to the MA empire.

The two clubs I love have no doubt, both been shafted like no others from

a) BENT Owners allowed to purchase and run Luton and Rangers and;

b) by both countries football authorities.

But as I write this now we both HAVE recovered from the dead. Luton currently a mid-table second tier club in a league we have spent the most years of our history in – and Rangers finally back at the top of the table on the crest of a wave, winning our first SPL title since 2011 and a Scottish record 55th in all – ending Celtic's 9¾ bid 'Terry Munro' in a row!

Luton's return to the Football League attracted an average home attendance of 8,702 – 663 more than when we won the League Cup as a top flight club in 1987–88! – as well as an away league average following of 1,197.

Outstanding Support.

Myself next to the John Lennon statue outside the world famous Cavern Club. On the night of my actual 60th Birthday in 2018. An unbelievable day/night on the Magical Mystery Tour bus/Cavern Club and staying at the Hard Day's Night Hotel, as well as having dinner in 'Blakes' restaurant (the designer of Sgt Pepper album cover). All this with my elder sister Ann, who was home for my big party 5 nights earlier. She was in the UK for just the 2nd time since 1988.

Another 100 Per Cent Home and Away Season Attended

My first match attended of 2015–16 was in honour and memory of a Rangers pal who was tragically killed in a building site incident back in September 2014, Brighton Dave as he was known to so many Bears. I first met him in 2002 on one of Rangers European trips. We nearly always seemed to meet up together in some foreign city or ground where the Bears were playing, him and his partner Millwall Bev.

Dave fell 20 feet from scaffolding working on a stable block. He was rushed to hospital in a critical condition, then went into a coma and tragically died four weeks later in a Brighton hospital.

More than 900 attended his funeral (regretfully I had a business meeting I couldn't get out of that day). SO popular was Dave that even Rangers Manager and Legend Ally McCoist personally rang Bev to give her condolences on behalf of all Rangers fans – as well as allowing the team coach to be used for part the funeral cortege!

A match in his honour was arranged and set up for July 4th at Bognor Regis FC between a South Coast Legends team versus Rangers Legends including Mark Falco, Alex Rae, Andy Goram, Derek Ferguson and Michael Mols among many others.

An incredible 1,500 attended the match including Luton Loyal great pals Bob and Gary Rumble. Rangers Legends won 5–4.

We stayed the night in a Bognor hotel and also attended the benefit dinner in the evening at the football social club. Where we celebrated the life of Dave in style and had a great night, in particular with Derek Ferguson and the 'Goalie' Andy Goram.

A millionaire businessman and his working partner were later arrested, charged and eventually convicted, serving a jail sentence after being found guilty of manslaughter and gross negligence. RIP Brighton Dave.

I followed this up with the regular Hitchin friendly where we drew 0–0 and three home friendlies versus Coventry, Brentford and Walsall, resulting in a 1–1 draw, 2–1 win and 0–1 defeat in that order.

There was plenty of movement in and out of LTFC pre- and during the 2015–16. Players signed included a two-year undisclosed fee for Cameron McGeehan, as well as a free transfer for Brighton's Scottish International Craig Mackail-Smith.

Some other frees included, also from Brighton, Paddy McCourt, Josh McQuoid, Dan Potts from West Ham (son of ex-Hammer Steve) Danny Green from MK, Olly Lee from Birmingham, Jack Marriott from Ipswich, Scott Cuthbert, a rugged Scot from Leyton Orient, and another Scot from Partick Thistle, Stephen O'Donnell.

Leaving Kenilworth Road were: Ross Lafayette 0 goals 14 appearances, Andy Drury to Eastleigh 10/65, Fraser Franks to Stevenage 0/34, Alex Lacey to Yeovil 1/51 and Mark Cullen, top scorer from 2014–15 who turned down Luton's contract offer and was then sold to Blackpool for £180,000 after 23 goals including THAT one at Cambridge, in 82 LTFC apps. Mark will forever be remembered by Hats for that goal and also the first back in the FL. He has a lovely missus too, who was often in the Bobbers Club.

It was also revealed in the summer that LTFC had received £1.1m in sell on fees on top of the original £600,000 when Andre Gray was transferred from Brentford to Burnley. We would then receive a further £700,000 after Burnley were promoted to the Premiership, making a total of £2.4m to shut up those fans moaning on social media when we sold Andre (with only a year remaining on his contract).

I had already decided that 2015–16 was going to be only my third ever 100% attending Luton games home and away season – God willing! As I write this I cannot see me doing another, but never say never.

The first game of the season was away to Accrington Stanley and I drove mate Steve O'Dell up to stay the Saturday night in an absolutely glorious hotel in Accy. It is called the Mercure Dunkenhalgh Spa and was stunning with a frontage like a castle. We would return there often again.

An added bonus upon arrival was discovering the LTFC team and 2020 Officials were also based there since Friday, along with Wolves who were playing at nearby Blackburn.

Pre-match on a lovely sunny August day in the fabulous Crown pub back garden, was where we met now good friends and regular Adair Travel Blackpool stalwarts, Kevin Carroll, known to all as 'Jesus is a Hatter' and his partner Di for the first time.

We saw a 1–1 draw with Jonathan Smith rescuing a point after a late 92nd minute equaliser in front of 1,175 travelling Hats – nearly half the 2,359 total gate!

That evening we had a fantastic night in the Crown before several other Luton fans joined us for a curry in town. Dover Hatters Ian Moulson and Peter Buckthorpe among them.

When the owner of the Indian Restaurant found out we were Luton fans, he bought a round of beers on the house as his cousin ran the Baltisan Restaurant in Round Green, Luton. A very satisfying start for no 1/46 games (plus 5 cup ties).

Three nights later was one of those cup ties when we beat Championship (old Division 2) Bristol City 3–1 at the Kenny, for which I satisfyingly used my free Diamond cup voucher.

We unluckily exited the next round versus Premiership Stoke at home 1–1 AET losing 7–8 on penalties in front of the live Sky TV cameras.

Town got off to our notoriously slow start under John Still, by winning only one of our first six league games and that first win was at the sixth attempt, a fine 1–3 win at Cambridge Utd which included a marvellous Luke Guttridge lobbed opening goal. This run included my first ever visit to Yeovil where despite a contender for goal of the season already by CMS with a fantastic long range angled drive – we lost 3–2 in weather conditions that were unreal! Glorious sunshine at the beginning turned into a monsoon like freak rainstorm where most Hatters in the open end were drenched. I luckily was in the covered seated side stand.

The week after Cambridge we had a fantastic day in Nottingham by rail for the Notts County game. Despite a negative result (lost 3–2) it was a good game in which we came back from 2–0 down to level at 2-2 with Smith and McGeehan goals, only for Scott Cuthbert to get sent off on 91 mins and Notts to then cruelly snatch a 3–2 winner at the death on 93 mins. This in front of an impressive 1,689 Hats away support.

Next up was our first home league win 1–0 versus Mansfield scored by a CMS penalty. But the main talking point was the goal Craig scored that was NOT given. In the first half he scored what would have been one of THE best goals ever seen at KR. A magnificent spectacular overhead scissors kick, only for the joe hunt of a lino to be a killjoy by raising his flag for offside – because he felt CMS's toenail was off, FFS!!! After SUCH a quality strike the linesman should have just kept the flag down for a second or so and we'd have been celebrating an all-time classic strike.

After another home win 2–0 versus AFC Wimbledon, I drove long time Luton/Rangers pal Richie Harding up to Morecambe midweek where we stayed overnight in a local seafront hotel. We saw a brilliant 1–3 Town win with Paddy McCourt shining, then post-match I managed to find the only midweek karaoke bar open where the two of us celebrated our win long into the night and I sang the Beatles.

I drove home the next day then two days later was back 'oop north' again, this time for an eagerly awaited clash at Hartlepool. Another of our famous weekenders, this time the added bonus and capping off a terrific week with a wonderful Town 1–4 away win. Four wins in a row had now lifted us up from 20th/24 to 11th.

Then we hit a run of four winless games, including a very disappointing 2–1 defeat at Crawley where we led until the 67th minute.

On a cold November 1st Sunday I went by train to meet up with some Bletchley/Markyate Hatters for our game at Dagenham. Meeting Sharon Heyward, George Clark and co in a Euston bar, when in there I noticed old England/QPR star Stan Bowles with whom I discovered was his agent. Me being me went over for a chat (and selfie) with them. Sadly, Stan was now suffering early signs of dementia but he livened up when I mentioned about his penalty for R's at Luton in 1974 – it had to be retaken when an Oak Roader threw a ball over the goal at the same time as his spot kick was taken! It turned out they had been at the Friday night Brentford versus QPR game working with Sky covering it.

Luton beat the Daggers comfortably 0–2.

The next week it was back to Crawley for an FA Cup First round tie and this time WE won 1–2 with a pair of Josh McQuoid goals, the winner on 90 minutes.

We then beat Barnet 2–0 at the Kenny. Not ONE person in the crowd could imagine – this would be the very last time Sir John of Still took charge of a winning Luton Town team!

Because what followed was only one point taken from our next 12, culminating in a 3–4 home defeat versus Northampton after we had come back from 1–3 down to 3–3, only to lose.

John was sacked five days after the Cobblers defeat.

What for many was unthinkable at one time was now sadly true. Some modern social media fans wanted him gone at the end of last season after blowing the play off places by losing seven in a row in March. But most sensible Hatters KNEW he deserved far more respect than that option. However, John had now reached the stage where many believed he had taken us as far as he could after this run of just two wins in the last 10.

Most Hats were saddened at the news but it was the correct decision. However, nothing will take away Mr Still, our 30th Manager's legacy at LTFC.

He will always be loved by all Hatters as THE man who brought us back from non-league oblivion and paved the way for others to take us onwards in our revival. THANK YOU Sir John of Still.

Other sad news in December 2015 were the premature deaths of two long-time friends.

Old Sportsman/SWMC and West Ham pal from the early 1980s Graham Clay, died of a heart attack aged 56, then just two days later on Dec 10th Willie Hood succumbed to his cancer aged 59.

Willie a fellow Bobbers Club stalwart drove the likes of Jimmy Oates, Bill McKinlay, myself and others to many games in the early/mid 1980s, as well as him being a keen domino player like myself. RIP Graham and Willie.

The first game post John Still was at Exeter. I drove down alone to stay overnight in this excellent city and had a fab time all day and evening.

I met a Grecian fan in their cracking Supporters Club pre match by the name of Dave Green, then in non-stop rain, watched a belter of a game with a sensational ending.

Town took a HT 0–2 lead with a Cameron McGeehan penalty and well taken Danny Green goal. But Exeter came right back at us with two goals on 71 and 82 mins to equalise. Pre-match I'd have willingly taken a draw but was now gutted at blowing a two-goal lead and actually feared we'd go on to similar recent losses the way we did versus Carlisle and Northampton.

But fret not. For in the hundredth minute, Paul Benson somehow, scrambled in a close on the line 2–3 winner, which caused utter SCENES and wild celebrations amid us 416 travelling Hats.

What an evening I had in the rain too, going on a bit of a city pub crawl. It was in one of these pubs where I first met a fellow Hatter living in Exeter by the name of Hugh O'Rourke. Having lived around a bit in all parts of the UK as well as serving in the Royal Navy (with a mutual pal Bob Cowley) 'Rocky' has more clubs than Jack Nicklaus lol – Peterborough, Portsmouth, Exeter and his with his Irish Catholic background, C**tic. But after reading HIS excellent book titled *A Pair of Steaming Bats* about his life in the Navy, our beloved Hatters will always be his numero uno.

We disappointingly lost 0–2 at home to Wycombe on Boxing Day, a 0-0 at Portsmouth (the ONLY non-defeat in my five Fratton Park visits to date) and a hopeless Luton performance at Bristol Rovers, losing 2–0.

Then our new 31st manager was announced as Nathan Jones. A Welshman I'd never heard of to be honest and was shocked to discover he was actually a Hatters player in 1995–96 under Terry Westley, but without making a single first team appearance.

We had appointed him from Brighton where he was a coach. So this was his first job in management aged nearly 43.

His first match in charge was a dreary 0–0 at home to Cambridge Utd which left us 18th/24, just about hovering above the relegation zone with 20 games remaining.

The first win under Nathan came at Mansfield in an absolutely outstanding Hatters performance. THE best I had seen all season. We won 0–2 with Paddy McCourt scoring his only LTFC goal. Paddy was only with us for this 2015–16 season, making 26 appearances as he had to return to Londonderry in the summer to be with his sick wife.

His goal was followed by a stunning Pelly strike in the roof of the net. This fab win is our ONLY ever league victory at Field Mill in LTFC history.

Also making a debut that day on loan from Bradford City, was full-back Irishman Alan Sheehan. What a debut, what a class player (and man) and one that we would eventually sign in May on a two-year deal.

After a couple of winless home games, NJ's first KR defeat (0–2) versus Notts County and a stunning free kick first Alan Sheehan goal versus Yeovil (1–1) we then kept up our amazing run of having NEVER lost at Wycombe by beating the Chair boys 0–1 with a

Cameron McGeehan winner.

It was followed by my first visit to AFC Wimbledon's Kingsmeadow home (before they returned to Wimbledon in 2020) I have to write, it was possibly THE worst ground in the FL. We were sadly hammered 4–1.

I saw my Kiwi Hatter nephew Peter there with his new partner Roz.

After a welcome 2–1 home win versus Hartlepool, it was Adair Travel adventure time for my fifth Blackpool Coach group booking – versus York!

Now I KNOW York is nowhere near Blackpool, but when the fixtures came out I had no choice.

The hotel only did (then) the all-inclusive package from Nov – July after which the Blackpool lights had finished. Nearby Accrington was in August (summer holidays) and Morecambe was midweek. This was the ONLY fixture left 'oop north' – so Bootham Crescent, York it was!

It never stopped us having a blinding time still.

Although more than a few opted out of coming to the game with us, some staying in the hotel and a tiny few choosing to see the York sights, we still had plenty up for the craic and WHAT a craic we had – eh Janet Betts! (AKA DJ Janet.)

We had a real good session and sing song pre-match in the York Social Club opposite the ground, where I'd been to several times before.

Then watched an amazing 2–3 Luton win. Twice we led and twice were pegged back, before Olly Lee scored a fine individual 92nd minute winner.

Louise and I were still going strong but she had some health issues that sometimes I found difficult to deal with. This was one example when she cried off on the Friday morning before we left her house – obviously too late to get a replacement. I'm afraid this was not the only time it happened. It wasn't her fault though, bless her.

Four narrow 1–0 scores followed.

Against Morecambe at home (Jack Marriott goal) this turned out to be the great keeper Mark Tyler's 297th and final LTFC appearance before returning to Peterborough in a player/keeper coach role. He has only just retired as I write.

Without a doubt Mark was easily the best goalkeeper we had in the modern era. He was fabulous for us in nearly seven years.

In LTFC history only Bernard Streten (299) and Ron Baynham (434) have played more times in goal than Mark Tyler.

Jack Marriott scored the only goal again at Leyton Orient, before we lost 0–1 at the Kenny to Crawley and the long trip to Home Park, Plymouth for my fourth and last visit, kindly driven by mate Phil Pratt and his young son Ben (who sit near me in the Enclosure) to see Jack Marriott AGAIN score the 0–1 clincher with his 13th goal of the season.

Then three successive defeats occurred, at Barnet (2–1) where Steve O'Dell and I enjoyed Corporate Hospitality once more with Regal Litho, at home to Stevenage (0–1) then against an impressive Accrington Stanley (0–2).

The morning after our Accy defeat I flew up to Glasgow with Kent Hatter and fellow Bear Ian Moulson. We met up with my pal Dougie Craig (who I first met at Belfast 2011

Linfield versus Gers match in the Sandy Row Rangers Club) for pre-match swallies, then headed on a Rangers supporters bus to Hampden Park to see Rangers take on Peterhead in the Petrofac Cup Final (Scots version of our JPT)

As expected Rangers easily won (4–0) in front of 48,133 – of which over 43,000 were Bears fans! We flew home on the Monday.

After having lost four out of our last five, Luton then went on to win three in a row. A narrow 1–0 home win versus Dagenham, then a couple of fine away displays starting at Oxford.

I went on George Clark's Bletchley Hatters minibus, where we stopped off on route for liquid refreshments at a nice pub in Kidlington. Town then played very well and won 2–3.

Next was the longest drive of the season to Carlisle – midweek!

I took mate Phil Marlor, a fellow Hatter Beatles pal, and we prearranged an overnight hotel stay. (NO WAY was I going all the way to near Scotland and back same day/night just to watch a football match.)

We met up with another Hatter James Brittin and had a few pints in a bar in Carlisle's Main Stand before the match. There were only 235 stalwart Hatters at Brunton Park for my fifth and final visit there (to date). It HAD to be better than the last visit – my all-time low LTFC match losing 5–1 versus Gateshead in 2013 – a mere three years prior!

It most certainly was as we won 1–2 with loanee Joe Pigott opening the scoring, soon to be Hatter Jack Stacey equalising and Josh McQuoid netting our winner with his fifth and final LTFC goal.

We celebrated big time when a sizeable crowd of us including mates Mark Griffiths and Bob Rumble's Grandson James 'the MAJOR' Higgs, hit Carlisle town centre on a Tuesday night. All in all, a fine night.

The final three games which would complete my 100 per cent set were a 1–1 home draw versus Newport, losing 2–0 at Champions Northampton in front of a record (then) Sixfields attendance and a convincing 4–1 home win against Exeter, including a fab lobbed Joe Pigott effort.

Luton finished in a credible 11/24 position, seven places above where we were when Nathan Jones took on the job in January. Our average attendance dropped slightly to 8,225 and away average also slightly down to 986.

I had one last match to attend in 2015–16 in Glasgow for the Scots Cup Final Hibs versus Rangers.

In the main this campaign was a good one for the Gers, on and to a degree, off the pitch. Dave King and his consortium known as the Three Bears were slowly but surely ousting all the Ibrox dead wood at Boardroom level. But there was still one person they could not get rid of entirely – YET!

The stronghold he had over us in Merchandising terms, that was Mike Ashley. That I'm afraid was still going to take some time.

A new manager was appointed in the summer of 2015, Mark Warburton who was the manager that signed Andre Gray at Brentford from Luton in 2014. Warb's signed a three-year deal to take charge at Ibrox.

He got off to a great start in the Championship with 11 straight victories in all competitions, including a 2–6 thrashing of Hibs at Easter Road in the Scottish Challenge Cup, which as I wrote earlier Rangers went on to win.

That run came to an end when SPL club St Johnstone knocked the Gers out of the League Cup 1–3 at Ibrox. Most importantly though Warb's led us to the Scottish Championship title, losing only five out of 36 league games – but two of those were away at Scottish Cup Final opponents Hibs!

So after four long seasons Rangers were back where we belong – in the top flight!

In the Scottish Cup after thrashing Cowdenbeath, the Gers then knocked out three SPL clubs Kilmarnock after a replay, Dundee were thrashed 4–0 at Ibrox and then incredibly but SO delightfully – Rangers knocked out Old Firm rivals Celtic in a Hampden Park Semi Final 2–2 AET, then 5–4 on penalties! It was a joy to behold watching it live on TV, a result that would have seemed unfathomable ever since the 2012 Whyte fiasco/implosion.

So the first ever Scottish Cup Final involving two second tier clubs took place. I just HAD to be there.

I flew up for a weekend staying in my old favourite Kilsyth (past personal problems there long since over) staying in the Coachman Hotel and going on Duncan Angus's Parkfoot Masonic 39 club bus.

To cut a long story short the Final turned into a nightmare in more ways than one. Hibs had not won the Scots Cup for 114 years and after the Celtic Semi victory we were clear favourites.

It took them all of THREE minutes to take the lead. But one time ex-Hibee Kenny Miller equalised before HT and things were looking rosier. Then on 64 mins it was our turn to have scenes (and we WERE) when Andy Halliday put us 2–1 up with a great 20-yard strike.

With just 10 mins remaining we were preparing for party, party time – then calamity! First Stokes made it 2–2 and just when it looked like Extra Time was beckoning, the 92nd minute arrived with Gray heading in what the entire stadium knew was their winner.

Now as pig sick gutted as all us Bears were, a part of me could totally understand the Hibs fans wild celebrations.

If they'd have stayed in the seats/stands fine, BUT thousands invaded the pitch en masse (even that maybe could be understood) but when they then started ATTACKING Rangers players and then headed towards our side and end stands to goad AND assault Gers fans, that was it. Enough was enough for some Bears and they (quite rightly) leapt over the wall to defend their teams players and fellow fans. Typically though the MSM (mainstream Scottish media) wiped their hands and swept under the carpet the Hibs fans actions, excusing the violence as 'EXUBERANCE' at having had to wait so long to win the Cup again.

I'm actually proud of those Bears who fought back totally outnumbered. I'll write here and now had this occurred 30/40 years ago, the Hibees wouldn't have even reached the halfway line. Rangers old school lads would have kicked fuck out of anyone attacking our players.

Had I been 10/20 years younger or not had fucked arthritic knees – I'd have been on the pitch defending us TOO!

Then for a female *Daily Record* 'reporter' to invent and write an article on the Monday that blamed RANGERS fans then printed – and I 'quote' – 'Afterwards in the streets Rangers fans were even putting their children in front of police vans and ambulances in a bid to prevent them reaching Hampden' – sheer and utter disgusting vile LIES!

A sorry end to what should have been a glorious Rangers 2015–16 finale.

IMHO I truly believe Mark Warburton never fully recovered from this and he was gone by February 2017.

A personal sad family time in May 2016 when we lost my Aunt Mary to cancer aged 83. She was the wife of my dad's only sibling Tom and mother to cousins Ken and Bob. After Tom died in 1969 of MND aged only 40, Mary then met Barry and eventually remarried. A lovely lady and a character who I really liked. RIP Mary.

That's all of the Scottish Adair family of four who came to Luton pre-WW2 when my dad and Tom were schoolboys, and now their English wives they married, every one of the six are now sadly no longer with us.

In 2016 A young Hatter by the name of Brett Beasey-Webb tragically died in his sleep aged just 21. These two items were kindly sent to me by a Bradford City (hand oil painting) and Bristol Rovers fan (1980's handmade replica of Kenilworth Road.) The painting raised £1,000 and was kindly donated to Brett's father George. The ground model, takes pride of place in Brett's name at the LTFC Heritage centre in his memory.

2016–17

On June 9th 2016 it was lovely to welcome Mollie and Lachlan back. This time they were to stay in the UK for the immediate future and living with me in Barton. Lachlan had a two-year working visa and I almost immediately got him a job as a commercial plumbing engineer (his trade) working with a friend of mine Mick Donahue's CME Engineering. He would work with CME for a few months until work dried up a touch but then managed to get another contract working in Cambridge.

It was absolutely lovely having my wee girl back living with me.

In the July that year Louise's daughter got married at St Thomas's Church. This was the Church that most of the Adair/Roberts family married in and one that Louise (living literally next door for years) was heavily involved with, as were her parents.

Lou was an active and extremely popular member at ST's with the Luton supporting Vicar (he bought my book lol) as well as the parishioners. She was a regular church goer, though not every week.

Something happened around the wedding that deeply upset me at the time and to be honest was the catalyst for the very beginning to the end of our relationship – it just took me over two years before finally ending it! Out of respect to Louise I shall keep the main reasons private.

In essence, I wasn't invited to the church wedding service.

Yes, we all had a good time at the Reception where I stayed there with the bride's mother for the night, but it had happened. As far as I was concerned, things were never 'quite' the same with my feelings towards Louise from that moment on.

As for LTFC, our third season back in the FL was about to begin. The support was still strong with over 6,000 ST renewals, myself once again buying a 'Diamond' one.

Our average home gates in both seasons were over 8,000 and away average was around the 1,000 mark. Still excellent support that would gradually grow even larger in the next four years.

Player ins and outs pre/during 2016–17 saw some interesting signings and departures.

Notable incomers were Oxford United's top scorer Danny Hylton and their captain Johnny Mullins, who were both out of contract. Danny was a proven striker at this level.

We signed Alan Sheehan on a permanent deal after his successful loan spell from January. Other OOC signings were Jordan Cook, Isaac Vassell who Mick Harford had scouted at non-league Truro and Jake Gray.

Signed for undisclosed fees were: Glen Rea from Brighton, who Nathan Jones knew when a Brighton and Hove Albion coach, Jack Senior, Lawson D'Ath and Luke Gambin.

A total of 21 players were released from July 2016 – June 2017. Notable departures were Paul Benson 25 goals in 85 appearances, Scott Griffiths 3/115, long serving Jake Howells moved to Eastleigh after making exactly 333 Town appearances, scoring 31 goals in his nine loyal years as a Hatter.

Also leaving were keeper Elliot Justham, Paddy McCourt, Nathan Doyle and Alex Lawless left for Yeovil after 22 goals in 202 appearances.

My first game of the season saw a little personal history made when I saw us beat Bedford 0–9 (NINE) away in a friendly. It was the first and only (to date) time I've seen Luton score nine goals in a match.

A couple of home friendlies I attended were Brighton (2–1 win) and Walsall (0–1 defeat).

Our first league game was away at Plymouth, but I had to miss the trip to Home Park as I was hundreds of miles away in Glasgow on a long standing prior pre-booked weekender to see my second love.

I always vowed that whoever and wherever Rangers would be playing on their return to the Scottish top flight – I WOULD be there! and so I was. While Town were just after ('Gers was a live Sky TV lunchtime kick off) magnificently beating Plymouth 0–3, I was at Ibrox Park with 49,124 others versus Hamilton Accies to somewhat disappointingly see a 1–1 draw.

My arthritis was giving me particular gip at this time, certainly not helped by climbing Mt Everest to watch the game in the Main Stand Club Deck – never again will I watch a match from there!

I remember struggling so much on the walk back to the Kilsyth Rangers Supporters' bus, that by the time we reached the Masonic 39 Club, I'd had enough of the pain and instead of going in the club with all the others I went to my room in the Coachman Hotel opposite and watched the football updates to see how Luton were faring. Rather well in my absence it must be said, lol.

Four nights later I watched us play a League Cup tie at home versus Aston Villa as we superbly knocked them out 3–1 in front of the Sky TV live cameras. Making his LTFC debut that night was a young local Stopsley lad who came all the way through our academy since he was nine – by the name of James Justin! It was the first of his 114 Town appearances (6 goals) – watch this space!

There would be no repeat 100 per cent attending as in 2015–16 because I'd already missed Plymouth and then flatly refused to pay Stevenage's rip off prices for Luton fans (only versus US) where we lost 2–1. I was also fed up with going to Cambridge, where we had a fab 0–3 victory against the U's.

At the end of August we were second after five games with three wins, a draw and a loss.

Leeds knocked us out of the League Cup at the Kenny 0–1 in front of 7,498 including a sold out 1,510 Oak Road away contingent. Lachlan and I were kindly invited into Mick Donahue's CME company Exec Box to watch this.

I then missed a fab 4–1 home win versus Wycombe for a valid reason. Great friends (and also indirectly my biggest work client) Jane and Gary Hopkins, were celebrating their Silver Wedding that weekend as well as renewing their marriage vows (with my help as a Life Member), they also held a big party at Stopsley WMC.

As Best Man at their 1991 wedding, it was my duty to be there and although more than a few actually said in the Town Hall, "Blimey Al, you're missing a Luton home game – you must be a good friend to Jane and Gary." – Well I AM!

Sometimes Loyalty and friendship HAS to come before football – even Luton Town! It was a lovely ceremony, party and great day/night all round. Luton beat Wycombe 4–1, with Danny Hylton scoring his first LTFC hat trick.

At the end of September we drew 1–1 midweek at Hartlepool and NATURALLY this meant an overnight stay there with good friends.

Alan Sheehan scored our goal with a stunning trademark free kick.

We ended the month in second place after 10 games.

I drove alone to Cheltenham four days later for another 1–1 draw, then a third successive 1–1 draw at home versus Crewe occurred. For this game I took friends Paul Keating and Christine again. It turned into an eventful (VERY) evening!

Ever since I became a Diamond Season Ticket holder I regularly took them both to at least one Town home game a season, where we would have a great time pre-match in the Bobbers Club then watch the game in the Oak Road, before returning to the Bobbers immediately post-match and continue socialising elsewhere.

This particular night I had prearranged and purchased tickets for us all to see a John Lennon show at Luton Library Theatre on what would have been Lennon's 76th birthday. We enjoyed a fabulous performance and I remember seeing long time old friends Mr and Mrs Dave Cockfield there.

Already having had a good drink all day and then post-match and a few more in the theatre, we then left to walk the short distance to the nearby 'Wheelies' pub. This was now my favourite town centre pub because:

a)   it was a proper LTFC fans pub – FAR better than the clique Brickies,
b)   it had a late all-night licence (then) and,
c)   it had THE best Juke Box in town, where I always put on a string of at least 20 old school 1960s/70s reggae tunes – I digress!

Walking there I suddenly collapsed on the pavement as my legs just simply gave way on me (nothing to do with the drink guv) I fell flat on my face and was momentarily stunned. Paul and Chris sat me down in the Wheelies where my face and eyes were already starting to swell up.

Mate Mark Griffiths and his lovely lass Perri wiped me down tenderly in front of a shocked bar, then after much laughter we all carried on as though nothing happened, but next morning I woke up – and looked like I'd gone 10 rounds with Mike Tyson!

As a result of my 'incident' I gave the next couple of away games a miss in October, winning 1–2 at Leyton Orient and a 0–0 at Notts County in front of 2,033 travelling Hats that saw loanee Town keeper Christian Walton earn us the point by saving a late penalty.

My next trip was a long-distance overnighter for our FA Cup first round tie at Exeter. At the game sitting next to me was long time buddy Keith McEvoy with his partner Laura. Us three were among 310 Hats who saw a brilliant Town performance at SJP, winning 1–3.

I had an awesome night in Exeter city centre celebrating our cup win big time, eventually meeting up in a club with a lovely couple of young female locals. 58 years old and still clubbing it – outrageous!

This would be my last trip for a wee while before my latest Adair Travel trip to Blackpool in December, this time actually playing the Seasiders.

Before that we knocked out Conference side Solihull Moors in the FA Cup second round, winning 6–2 at the Kenny, but only coming back after they gave us a massive fright when leading 0–2.

By the time of my sixth Adair Travel All Inclusive trip (Louise was another last-minute no show) in mid-December, we had slipped down to fifth place after 20 games.

One of my regulars in Blackpool an absolute blinding bloke and right character Stuart Fisher-Mack, had just had a flag specially made for the trip. An Orange on white background St George Cross, with black lettering spelling out LTFC in each four corners and reading on the centre across was 'ADAIRS CREW.'

The pre match Saturday lunchtime session in a pub near the Tower called the Castle Bar on Central Drive, was a special, special, occasion I shall take with me to my grave. The atmosphere created by almost exclusively hundreds of Hatters at the lunchtime Disco, had to be seen to be believed. Those who were there KNOW what I'm talking about.

For a period even CEO Gary Sweet and members of the 2020 Board were there and they were stunned at the level of partying. The numerous times Hats sang our version of 'Hey Jude' will live with me forever.

The lovely Janet Betts (DJ Jan) and I had a chat with the pub DJ (a Crystal Palace fan). He told us that night after we returned post-match, he had never known an afternoon like the one he had that day. He had been doing this job in Blackpool for over four years and said – and I quote – "That was the best atmosphere I've had in this pub since I began. Not only that, but it was THE best I've ever experienced in all my DJing days. You Luton fans are a credit to football. Loud and Proud and without a hint of malice." – He was 100 per cent bang on correct.

To top off that wonderful morning/afternoon joy, we beat Blackpool 0–2 in front of 1,095 Hats (of which I estimate three-quarter of them were in Blackpool on the lash for either an overnight or weekend stay).

We went back to the Castle Bar for the start of round Two, before heading to the Claremont for Dinner, the All-Inclusive cabaret of singer/comedian/disco, then topping off a perfect day in the Soul Suite. After the Soul Suite finished at 3 a.m., Stuart Fisher-Mack and I then even continuing in a Tranny bar until gone 4.30 a.m..

The entire weekend went off to perfection and to date, right up there as one of my favourite of all the Adair Travel trips I've organised.

Roll on Adair Travel number seven, which I booked up immediately after Christmas for our game at Accrington Stanley end of April.

A disappointing (very) Boxing Day 0–1 home defeat versus Colchester followed, before beating Barnet 3–1 at the Kenny on New Year's Eve.

The first game of 2017 I saw our customary defeat (1–0) at Portsmouth. I went by train to this.

1,547 Hats at Fratton Park saw Cameron McGeehan stretchered off with a broken leg. Some Pompey fans didn't cover themselves too well by booing him and singing, 'You're going home in a fucking ambulance' a bit crass that. The Pompey fans I know are far better than that.

It turned out to be Cam's 106th and final LTFC appearance, in which he scored 31 Hatters goals, as he would leave for Barnsley after the season ended.

Five days later Steve O'Dell and I booked the wonderful Dunkenhalgh Hotel in Accrington again for our FA Cup third round tie. As always, the team and 2020 were also staying. However in deep fog we exited 2–1.

The following weekend was one I had long since pre booked. Two nights/three days staying in a Berlin hotel for Rangers first game in Europe since the Armageddon of 2012. It was a friendly arranged during the SPL winter break at Red Bull Leipzig.

Fellow Luton Loyal Bears Gary and Bob Rumble, flew to Berlin where we met Kilsyth pals Duncan Angus, Stewart Clark and Robert Frew (Pele). I had also pre booked for us all to travel on one of eight buses from Berlin to Leipzig return, organised by the Glaswegian Loyal.

Now I knew there would be a lot of Rangers fans up for this because it had been SO long since our last match abroad (another friendly in Hamburg which Duncan and I attended in 2011) but was astounded when EIGHT THOUSAND Gers travelled – for a fucking FRIENDLY! How many clubs in Europe could pull that kind of support? Yes we were stuck up in the God's freezing our nuts off in nonstop snow, yes we were outclassed and thrashed 4–0 by an excellent RB Leipzig team, but I'm still glad we went and it didn't stop us having an awesome stay in Berlin.

The first day/night in a Berlin German Beer Kellar, in which a pair of lovely Gers Lesbians were on our table and the second night after the game, in an excellent club (which I only found out after we left was a gay club, lol). All the staff had THE most brightest vivid orange fluorescent ties on that I'd ever seen. I just had to have one and after constant nonstop badgering, one of the barmen threw it at me to get rid, lol.

I was delighted to find out in Germany that Luton had won 1–2 at Crewe.

I missed two away 1–1 draws at Wycombe (bored of going there too) and Grimsby. Around those fixtures I saw four home wins and a poor home 2–3 defeat versus Cheltenham.

My next away day was by train from Stevenage to Doncaster. Louise was kind enough to take me to the station and collect me from there later that night (slaughtered).

This was my first visit to Donny's new Keepmoat Stadium, as the only other time we played there prior was in 2008 on the day of my 50th birthday and I wasn't in the right frame of mind at that time in my life to attend back then.

I met long-time pal and Blackpool AT regulars Bob and Christine Cowley in the Wetherspoons for Breakfast (liquid naturally, taking advantage of the Spoons three bottles of Sol for a fiver, as well as a fry up) and we had a right old session in there, then in a fabulous Supporters Bar at the ground. We returned there after the match and got on so well with a crowd of them, they then insisted on taking us to their pub before I caught the 9 p.m. train home. These lads were clearly an old school Doncaster firm but looked after us a treat in their pub, one of them even giving us a lift back to the station where Bob and Christine made sure I got on the train ok to meet Lou in Stevenage (by then I was well steaming, lol) before they carried on as they were staying the night in Doncaster.

Oh we drew 1–1 btw.

By the end of Feb after this 33rd/46 game we were still in a play-off fifth place.

I drove alone to see a convincing 0–4 Hatters win at Yeovil, meeting up with Bristol Hatter Jeff Stott-Everett pre-match, before seeing Bob and Chris again a couple of weeks later for a midweek game in Newport. (They live in South Wales.) I drove Steve and I, where we stayed in the town's Travelodge overnight. We drew 1–1, the first time in four Rodney Parade visits that Luton had avoided defeat there.

In between those games Oxford beat us 2–3 at the Kenny in the EFL Trophy Semi Final. We came back from 0–2 behind to level at 2–2, only for the Yellows to win it with five minutes remaining. The live TV curse had struck again.

Four days after Newport I drove to Colchester for mine and Luton's first ever visit to Colchester's new Community Homes Stadium. It is one of those typical bland, all look the same, out of town new builds. Ten thousand all seated capacity, but far better than their old ramshackle Layer Road, though their fans will probably tell you a much poorer atmosphere now.

We were desperately poor, losing 2–1 in front of a sold out away allocation of 1,775 Hats.

In April we were unbeaten with four out of six wins. I missed a 1–1 at Mansfield but before that saw Luton win 0–1 at Barnet with a well taken Olly Lee goal. Once again Regal Litho, as match programme Printers, sponsored the game and I was kindly invited, taking Steve along. I had now worked with Regal for over five years and things went well there generally. Sadly, that would not be the case for much longer.

We then had Adair Travel Blackpool trip number seven for Accrington Stanley versus Luton at the end of April, a couple of days after my 59th birthday.

These events were growing in popularity all the time where not only did the coach always sell out quickly, but many more were now either booking the hotel direct (including my Rangers friends from Kilsyth) or making their own way to Blackpool with me still booking the hotel in my group, so that we could all dine together in the restaurant. It had now got to a point – where over 80 of us were staying in the All-Inc hotel!

We were of course well known by now to the hotel staff everywhere. I must tell you that we also always got on well with the other guests too. Never TOO loud or lairy. In fact one northern couple I got to know on one of these weekends said to me, "Al, if we'd have known a football crowd were booking the same weekend as us, we'd have immediately cancelled – BUT, having met you all we have to say you Luton folk are a credit to football fans and your town."

Another example was two lovely northern couples we met that very weekend Kimberley Trantner and Joanne Bradwell with their husbands. They mixed so well with us, that they would purposely book another Blackpool trip the next year when we returned. They would not be the last folk we met in the Claremont who did the same.

Luton went into the game at Accy in fourth place knowing automatic promotion was out of reach, but the Play-offs guaranteed.

This penultimate regular league fixture saw many of us leave the Claremont after our Fish, Chips and Mushy peas lunch, in fancy dress. Yours truly as a Red Indian Chief – tomahawk too, which I surprisingly was allowed to take into the Accy Crown Ground!

Town easily won 1–4, including the first of his six LTFC goals for young local Luton star James Justin.

As always, a fab weekender with Stu and I once again going in that Tranny bar after Soul Suite, only for some bird (genuine female lol) – to bloody NICK me tomahawk!

After beating Morecambe 3–1 at home in the final regular league game, we knew that third placed Luton would face the team in sixth for the Play-off Semi Finals two legged games – BLACKPOOL!!! The following Sunday away leg first.

It was obviously too late to book the Claremont for another group booking (the hotel was sold out anyway) so a number of us booked into the nearby Cliffs Hotel. They were a sister hotel to the Claremont part of the Choice group, but the Cliffs didn't do an All-Inclusive option, only Bed, Full Breakfast and Evening Meal.

Among those booking two nights (Sat and Sun) were Steve and I, Janet Betts and her

Paul, Jesus and Di, Richard Harding and a couple of Hatters who lived in Spain. I have to write, the Cliffs was more than ok, nice food, rooms etc – but not a patch on our old favourite the Claremont!

Janet got in touch with the Castle Bar Palace fan DJ again, so another brilliant repeat of the classic December session occurred, this time with even MORE Hats attending.

A staggering 1,648 travelled to Bloomfield Road. Incredible support for a Sunday 6.30 p.m. ko, and live on Sky TV.

I'm afraid we lost this first leg 3–2 and that after us leading 1–2 at HT. Annoyingly – ex-Hatter Mark Cullen scored ALL three bloody Blackpool goals!

It didn't spoil our Sunday night at the Soul Suite, as we were still very much in this play-off and had the second leg at the Kenny four nights later to correct things.

An expectant partisan sell out Kenilworth Road crowd of 10,032 was at fever pitch when the teams came out roared on with such passion.

Trailing 3–2 from the first leg we were utterly devastated when on 22 mins Delfouneso scored for Blackpool and they now led 4–2 overall.

But after a couple of stunned hushed mins, we Hats had to still believe and the noise levels were soon raised again.

When their Mellor put through his own net for 1–1 on the night on 36 minutes it was lift off time again.

But on the stroke of HT when big Scotsman Scott Cuthbert brilliantly glanced a headed effort into the Kenny net – the old lady ERUPTED in a wall of elation. Half time 4–4 on aggregate – all to play for!

We all held our breath during the break, the game firmly in the balance but we believed once more.

12 minutes into the second half we Hats were in sheer Fantasy Island when a penalty was awarded for a foul on Danny Hylton. Yes, it looked dodgy and evidently TV replays suggested Hylts 'bought it' – but DILLIGAF!!!

He then chipped his penalty in off the bar – chaotic scenes in all parts of the ground bar half of the Oak Road! TBH if I was an opposing player or fan I would hate Danny Hylton for his petulance/arrogance. But this was his 27th goal of the season and us Hatters loved him.

Three one to Town on the night 5–4 overall with less than 15 mins now remaining, surely, surely our play-off history nightmare was about to come good? But WAIT!

From a Mark Cullen cross on 76 mins our loan keeper Stuart Moore came rushing off his line to try and punch Cullen's cross away, but he was way too late and Gnanduillet bravely headed in. 3–2 on the night 6–6 all square overall.

Were we going to have to do this the hard way in Extra Time, or God forbid – Penalties! The answer to that was no.

We had now reached the FIFTH minute of time added on and Luton were the team under pressure. TBH at that stage we screamed for the final whistle to regain our composure and go again.

Then the unthinkable occurred.

From their corner an opportunity arose for Blackpool and as Jordan Cook tried to clear Mellor's header off the line, it then hit the back of keeper Moore and crept over the line. Game and season over. Joyous incredible scenes in one corner of the Oak Road, stunned Luton players on the pitch lying flat out in pure despair. Us Hatters in the stands looking on in stunned silence. The Play Off curse had struck AGAIN!

Sometimes rarely, I hate football. Right at that time was one of those moments in question.

This was now our fifth Play-off attempt and FIFTH failure.

1996–97 Semi Final versus Crewe,

2009–10 Semi Final versus York,

2010–11 Final versus AFC Wimbledon,

2011–12 Final versus York,

and now this versus Blackpool.

I believe only Preston have a worse record than us – 0 wins in EIGHT playoff SF/F attempts!

Luton Town ended 2016–17 averaging 8,016 at home and 1,065 away. My season was now over after attending a total 47 games from July 16th – May 18th. A full 10 months – I needed a break!

Sheff Wed 0 Rangers 2 pre-season friendly 2017. 9,000 Gers fans travelled to Hillsborough to create a carnival atmosphere. This pic was snapped by a pro photographer and was unknown to myself until one of my Kilsyth pals Ian Adams saw in a BOOKIES. He immediately located who to get a copy from and at my 60th birthday party, him and all my Rangers pals presented it to me as a cherished gift. It now takes pride and play on a wall in my man cave.

Going Up, Going Up, Going Up

On June 10th 2017 I went to see an old friend to lend him a mutual pal Simon Greene's recently published book The Search for The Goose's Palm. I hadn't seen Steve Toyer for a while so the visit was long overdue. In fact the last time I went round his house to see him was when he was one of the first to purchase and who I took my original book to.

I knew Steve hadn't been in the best of health for a while and that he was now wheelchair bound, but I was still shocked at how frail and ill he looked. Of course no way would I show that and we soon got into reminiscing as well as putting the world to right. I was there a good couple of hours with Steve and I'm so glad I visited – because sadly that would be the last time I saw him alive. He suddenly tragically died just two months later. More of that to follow.

About a week or so later I had another grand old meet up with other great friends of old at the Bull pub in Barton.

Ex-Windsor Castle pals Eamon Taaffe, Dave Ventris (who I had worked with at Roydon Printers and again then at Regal) had arranged for us to see their old school colleague Andy Ormes, who had lived in Perth, Australia for years. I went on a summer holiday to Benidorm in 1978 with Andy and Dave Lee and also to see Wings with him at Wembley Arena in 1979. Andy, like Dave Ventris and I were all huge Beatles fans. His younger brother 'Daney' too, who also joined us at the Bull. A very pleasant evening was had by all it was great to catch up with them.

Louise and I joined Alyson and Graham Fowler among others as we all went on the Holy Ghost Club coaches to Ascot for Ladies Day and had a wonderful day, all dressed up in the hot sun. Plenty of food, drink and I even picked a few winners too.

On the football front there was the usual ins and outs of LTFC at various stages pre and during 2017–18.

Major Hatters signings were: Jack Stacey from Reading, then regular lower league goalscorer Crawley's James Collins, Harry Cornick from Bournemouth and Cambridge United's Luke Berry, all for undisclosed fees, as well as the experienced Brentford player Alan McCormack, keepers Marek Stech and James Shea and the return of Elliot Lee, all on free transfers.

Among those leaving KR after the old season finished and pre/during this new one were: Danny Green, Craig Mackail-Smith, Stephen O'Donnell who went back to Scotland to sign for Kilmarnock and is now a full Scottish International, the very popular Jonathan Smith left for Stevenage after 11 goals & 176 LTFC appearances. Jack Marriott was sold to Peterborough for an undisclosed fee rumoured to be £400,000 plus addons. I liked Jack and was sorry to see him go after his 28 goals in 91 apps for Luton. It was particularly galling when just two games into the season Isaac Vassell was sold to Birmingham for another undisclosed fee (as most modern exits are at Luton now). This time it was Luton who did not want him to leave, but Isaac electing (understandably) to earn FAR more than we could afford in wages. There was concern who would score the goals but we had to trust in Nathan Jones with Danny Hylton and of course the new forward James Collins.

One important season long loan signing from Birmingham was Scotsman Andrew Shinnie who began at Rangers as a youth. What a player he turned out to be for us.

Before the Hatters season began I had the little matter of Rangers playing in Europe competitively for the first time since 2011, in the Europa Cup. The Gers opponents in the first qualifying round were a team from Luxembourg I'd never even heard of Progres Niederkorn – I soon WOULD know them! I naturally had to be at the Ibrox first leg. So on Thursday June 29th I flew up to Glasgow and stayed overnight in a hotel near Ibrox to see us narrowly win 1–0 with Kenny Miller netting the only goal before flying home next day.

Before that game I had already booked the away leg in Luxembourg with Duncan Angus to stay two nights for the game on July 4th. The draw had also been made for the second qualifying round and the winners of our game would in all probability, face AEL Limassol of Cyprus.

I decided to take a chance and pre-booked a three night/four day stay in Paphos, Cyprus at an All-Inclusive hotel with Rab Kier, the game was hopefully scheduled for July 19th.

Disaster struck when Rangers experienced one of the all-time shocks in our long European history. We crashed out of Europe in Luxembourg by losing 2–0 on the night to the Progres minnows. It didn't matter that we hit the crossbar twice – we were out! In my honest opinion the clueless boss Pedro Caixinha should have been sacked on the spot when he was snapped by the press – arguing with Bears fans near trees in the street FFS!

He was out of his depth and was sacked in October, making his the shortest reign ever as an official RFC team manager.

Naturally Rab and I still went to Cyprus (along with many other Gers fans who had also pre-booked similar trips). An absolutely fab time in the sun with my great mate. Four days of sun, pool, food and drink – plenty of drink!

One minus was a lunatic female Geordie at the hotel I made the mistake of befriending. When it was evident I didn't want to know her obvious advances, she turned loopy and threatened to put a contract out on me when I got home from a male friend of hers – inside jail FFS! Lol.

A couple of days before we left for Cyprus I attended Best Man Larry Kinloch's surprise 60th birthday party in Dunstable. Louise and I had a fab night, with Dave Ventris joining us on our table. Larry didn't know a thing about the party and the look on his face as he walked into the hired Dunstable church hall to see dozens of family and friends, was priceless.

I attended a couple of home preseason Luton friendlies versus Premiership Leicester (0–1) and League One Scunthorpe (2–1) before watching my third Rangers game of the month, in Sheffield.

I drove Bob and Gary Rumble up on the Friday to meet the Kilsyth lads Duncan, Tam and Ian Adams and Co and we met Gus Watson too. A great Friday night ending up in a club that were mainly Sheff Utd lads.

The Rangers support at Hillsborough of NINE THOUSAND for a FRIENDLY, were given that massive side stand opposite the cameras. I believe this is the only time that occurred for a Sheff Wed FC match. Great day, great Rangers win 0–2.

Unbeknown to me, on the day a professional photographer had snapped a picture of the Rangers crowd. I was slap bang in the middle of it. It then appeared in betting shops and Ian Adams spotted it, took a picture and sent me it – then at my 60th party in 2018 he and the Kilsyth friends presented me with a full-sized fantastic canvas of the pic, which today takes pride and place on my wall in my man cave dining room/office as I type this amusingly looking at it.

I also met up first time that day with a Facebook Sheff Wed/Rangers pal Danny McGhie.

Then the LTFC season began in earnest and WHAT a start. At home to Yeovil. I wondered what sort of reaction/start there would be following the latest play off heartbreak versus Blackpool a few months prior?

The answer was emphatic – Luton 8 (EIGHT) Yeovil 2! with us even coming from 0–1 behind and James Collins scoring a hat-trick on his debut. The pick of the goals was another debutant, when Alan McCormack hit an absolute screamer. It turned out to be his only Town goal in 39 LTFC appearances – but what a goal!

This was/is only the second time I've seen us score eight in a match after the 8–0 versus Hayes and Yeading in 2010 (plus the 0–9 away friendly at Bedford).

I used my Diamond free voucher to see us knock out Championship side Ipswich 3–1 in the League Cup before travelling to Barnet days later.

As per usual Regal Litho sponsored at the Hive and Louise joined me as guests of owner Alan and his wife Kim. What happened in the bar enjoying pre-match drinks is another of those never to be forgotten experiences.

I took a phone call from old mate Magnet and had to sit down at the terrible news he was giving me. Louise and Kim immediately were concerned and later told me I went deathly ashen white.

Magnet had informed me that our mutual mate Steve Toyer had suddenly died in the L&D last night and that's all he knew at this point. It shook me to the bones and reminded me of when I got the call from cousin Richard Hines about Uncle Malcolm.

Louise was obviously concerned for me and to be honest I watched the match in a haze and couldn't wait to leave. Barnet won 1–0 and this might sound weird – but I was kind of GLAD! Had we scored/won I just do not think I'd have been capable of standing up happily cheering.

Apart from family, I had known big Steve longer than anyone else in my life. We had been friends since we first sat together in the same class at Stopsley Infants school in 1963 aged five.

I was sitting with Steve and his dad at his first LTFC match versus Southport (0–0) in 1967 just weeks and two games after my very first Town match versus Exeter. He was my companion at SO many football matches, one of us six Dunkirk 1975 veterans but not only Luton, also England and often we travelled to London to see ANY match at Arsenal, Chelsea, West Ham. He also shared my liking for Hartlepool, having a love for that club but especially it's people and town (like myself).

Steve was at my 21st party in 1979, summer holidays in Ibiza (84) and Portugal (85), the 1984 Munich Beer Festival, my 1985 Engagement party, both stag do's in Holland and Luton Flying Club and my 1986 wedding, as well as my 40th Birthday Party.

I was devastated, but one saving grace was that his last Hatters game he attended (Steve was still staunch to the end even in his wheelchair) was seeing us beat Yeovil 8–2.

Steve had been suddenly rushed to hospital on the Thursday night and died on Friday in the L&D of Septicaemia blood poisoning. He was 59.

His funeral the next month was going to be some event.

In the next home matchday programme versus Colchester (we won 3–0) I had written a nice piece in his memory that was printed in it.

At Steve's funeral the day after we beat Port Vale 2–0 at home, as expected, so many faces of our mutual past attended to pay their respects to this giant hearted man. I did a well-prepared epitaph speech at the service which I just about got through, before we saw him off in style at Stopsley WMC. A club just up the road from his house where we had jointly been members since 1974 when we were only 16 (my dad and granddad proposed and seconded us telling the club we were 18, lol).

Steve was truly loved by everyone who knew him. Mick Knight's Villa pals, but especially in Hartlepool. One of those Poolies particularly loved big Steve because when he first met him on the train going to Fulham versus Hartlepool, Steve befriended him and this Poolie never forgot that warmth. They became great lifelong friends and he drove all the way down to stay overnight for his funeral. Cap fucking Doffed Greg Swinbourne. RESPECT sir.

RIP big Steve – you will NEVER ever be forgotten by me or any other of your legions of friends!

A much happier occasion occurred on Sept 30th at Luton versus Newport.

On Facebook ex-Luton legend Peter Anderson and I were now friends. He has lived in Tampa Bay, Florida with his family for many years married to a lovely American lass Seretha.

As written previously, Peter literally saved LTFC from going out of business in December 1975 by agreeing to a transfer to Belgian side Royal Antwerp. That insulting £55,000 fee stopped us going bust the next day.

Peter was coming home on his own for a UK holiday and asked if it would be possible to get him and his sister and best mate ex-Town and Arsenal player David Court, tickets for this Newport game. 'Leave this with me Peter,' I replied and got in touch with my contacts at the club.

They were brilliant and came back to me with a fabulous proposal.

There would be a table for us all, including club historian Roger Wash, club photographer and friend Gareth Owen and some more ex-Luton players they contacted – John Moore, Ken Goodeve and Alan Garner. We would get the full treatment of meal, tour of the ground, photo's on the pitch and a special half time pitch introduction for the ex-players, which us old school Hatters lapped up with a massive round of applause.

I have to tell you that when I went to inform Chairman Nick Owen he might like to know that Peter Anderson is on my table, he was like a kid at Christmas.

SUCH excitement, evidently Peter was one of Nick's all time LTFC heroes.

We had a day to remember eternally with so many brilliant stories from Peter and the others. I learnt from Peter he was unaware (at the time) that in the summer of 1975 Aston Villa had offered LTFC £200,000 for him and the club turned it down without telling him. Pre-agent days in the main of course.

I was also told about how John Moore nearly caused a riot at Lazio in the 1973 Anglo Italian Cup 2–2 draw in Rome by getting sent off for punching an opponent and how there were problems for the whole team post-match in the dressing room as a result of big John's boxing, lol.

A personal highlight was a lovely personal gesture from Peter when he gave me a Luton versus Liverpool programme from the first game of 1974–75 (we lost 1–2). Inside it was a pic of Peter scoring at West Ham in our 1–2 Texaco Cup win (I was there naturally). He signed the pic, 'To Alan, Mr LTFC. Best Wishes Peter'. I was honoured.

We had a day to treasure – oh and Luton played brilliant for us, winning 3–1 with goals from Alan Sheehan and a Danny Hylton pair.

I also got to know Alan Garner well from that day on, having discovered he lived in Barton too. We often saw each other for a brief chat on his and my walks. Tragically, he died suddenly of a heart attack in July 2020, aged just 59. A lovely man and good defender he was too. RIP Alan.

Peter and I are still in regular contact and I will most certainly be posting him this book (signed) when it's published.

The next weekend Steve Odell and I had another fab overnight stay at the Accrington Dunkenhalgh Hotel. This time we were joined by Jesus, Phil Marlor and Bob Rumble. I took some stick from Gary Sweet and Chairman David Wilkinson there pre-match because of my sad stats.

As they walked by saying hello to us, I replied, "Morning chaps, today is my 1,794th Luton game and I want my 764th Hatters win please."

They amusedly looked at each other shaking heads and Gary Sweet said, "Adair you are one sad bastard." – I THINK he was joking?

We DID get my 764th win, 0–2 with Olly Lee and James Collins goals.

Our 13th game of the season was certainly not unlucky – Luton 7 (SEVEN) Stevenage 1 including a fine hat-trick by Luke Berry. I watched this in the Oak Road with mate Micky Dolan and over from Oz on holiday, ex-pat Hatter James Dobbin.

Our next game was at Exeter three nights later midweek and I took advantage of watching a live stream in the Eric Morecambe Lounge. We were utterly brilliant at SJP thrashing the Grecians 1–4 to go top for the first time since the opening day of the season.

I'm afraid there was more sad news on Nov 1st on the day after I was one of 98 Hats to see us win 1–2 at AFC Wimbledon in the EFL Trophy, with an Andrew Shinnie pair of goals.

My great friend and biggest work client Jane Hopkins, brother-in-law had died of cancer. He was Steve Kirkby, married to Jane's sister Debbie who worked with us both at CBC for many years. He was just 10 days short of his 58th birthday and a lovely, lovely guy, as well as a fellow mad Hatter. The church in Houghton Regis was a sea of Orange in his memory.

Then just nine days later, Debbie lost her and Jane's father too. Life can be SO, so cruel sometimes. RIP Steve and Christy.

After such joy seeing us demolish Stevenage (their official club record defeat) and Exeter, it was despair for my second love when I saw Rangers lose 2–0 versus Motherwell at Hampden Park in the Scottish League Cup Semi Final. Four days later the useless Pedro was sacked as Gers boss.

In the FA Cup first round we played League One side Portsmouth at home and I prearranged to meet up with Pompey pal Phil Hibbert and his Grandson in the Beech Hill Conservative Club. Joining us was Jesus and his lovely old mother-in-law. We deservedly won 1–0 with James Collins netting the only goal.

I saw us draw AGAIN at Cheltenham, 2–2 (all three of my visits there have been draws) before another Kenilworth Road avalanche versus Cambridge.

My 1,800th LTFC game attended was once again in the Oak Road.

Not only did we hammer them 7–0 with another Town hat-trick (the third so far this season) this one by Danny Hylton, but we also scored the goal of the season and DECADE!

Olly Lee made it 2–0 with a goal from INSIDE his own half and this was no fluke he meant it 100 per cent. Looking up and seeing their keeper off his line, Olly struck with perfection from fully 65 yards out. Sheer utter quality.

We had now inflicted official club record defeats to all of Yeovil, Stevenage and now Cambridge Utd.

In just nine home league games we had scored a staggering 31 goals – and two of those nine were 0–3 home defeats to Swindon and Coventry!

Next up was Adair Travel Blackpool trip number eight for our game at Crewe.

As previously explained the Claremont Hotel All Inclusive option only applied (then) after the Illuminations were over and this was the nearest fixture to Lancashire available. So Gresty Road it was.

I had a nightmare saga leading up to this trip as my regular coach company HL Travel went bust (without telling me) and I was in a panic about getting a replacement at such late notice. Fortunately, I managed to find one locally, the Barton Coach Company, but the owner told me no wonder they went bust charging those prices. He agreed to help me out of a hole by taking us (only not at the HL price) but it would cost us an extra £10 per person. I was grateful for them getting me out of the shite, but afraid I won't use them again. The driver was clueless (had no sat nav so we were stuck on the M6 for hours – but had a great laugh all doing a conga on the hard shoulder and even letting a couple of other stranded motorists use our loo, lol) oh and a window was also leaking soaking a lot of my passengers!

Other than that, the usual blinding weekend. This was the first time I met a married gay couple from Liverpool. Jan and Karen Lee. Absolute top wonderful girls who I'm great friends with to this day and have been back to join us on the last 3 trips also. I call them my LLLs – Liverpool, Lesbian, Legends! Oh and Luton beating Crewe 1–2 sealed the trip.

Eight days later on a Sunday early (very) a.m. I drove Richie Harding up to Newcastle where we booked a hotel for the night to see our FA Cup second round tie at Gateshead.

Pre-match in the great bar at Gateshead's Athletics Stadium, was when I first met some Scottish Hatters from Carnoustie, the lovely Tracey Leah and her Aussie born Scot Billy boy. What a fab couple they are (even if they're not Bears) and we would meet again more than once.

Three hundred and eighty-one Hats saw us demolish the Heed 0–5 then Richie and I would celebrate big time in the Toon that night meeting up with Northampton Hatter Tim Owen, who that night said – I'd love to come back here for the third round if we could get Newcastle and guess what? – we DID draw them!

From one 0–5 away Luton win, straight to ANOTHER on Boxing Day at Swindon in nonstop pouring rain. A fun day on the minibus ran by Freddie Dann/John Ashton from the Wheelwrights pub.

After a goalless first half we destroyed Swindon 0–5 getting ample revenge for our 0–3 home defeat in September. That was on the day when a mob of Swindon came to Luton early doors and bullied some outnumbered Luton youth in the Wheelies at opening time. They paid a price for that though post-match when taking a good doing by more equal

Luton numbers and our older chaps.

Four days later after the brilliant Swindon win and performance I drove Steve O'Dell up to Port Vale. This was only my second ever Vale Park visit. A great pre-match in the very welcoming Port Vale Social/Supporters' Club where I met Wrexham Hatter and mate Gary McPheat for the first time.

It was then ruined by our worst away performance of the season. Nathan Jones cocked up by 'resting' his entire midfield and we were deservedly slaughtered 4–0 by Vale.

Now just past the 2017–18 halfway stage, we had played 25 and were still top having won 15, drew 6 and lost only 4. Happy New Year.

We put the Vale result and performance to bed by winning a cracking New Year's Day game at home to Lincoln 4–2. Then prepared for a MASS exodus of Hats to Newcastle for our FA Cup third tie.

Us lads of course stayed in Hartlepool, with most Hats staying in the Toon and a few others elsewhere.

Newcastle were staggered at the demand from Hatters and gave us more, then more, then even MORE tickets – until in the end we had sold an astounding 7,477!!! Every Hatter was up for having a good time in this fabulous city and boy did we have some 'chaps' out that day/night/weekend.

Apart from Semi Final/Finals or Wembley, this is the biggest Luton away support we've ever taken. It's also the largest away support at St James' Park since it was modernised, with the exception of a 2004 friendly competition versus Rangers.

Fourth tier Luton lost to a full first team Premiership Magpies side. They did NOT want to lose this. Although we lost 3–1 (all three of their goals in a mad nine mins spell on 30 minutes) the Town did us proud. We were easily the better side in the second half. Danny Hylton pulled one back five minutes after the break and then cruelly as we were celebrating big time, had another disallowed for offside shortly after. It was a real close call. Had that gone in and Elliot Lee's rocket not hit the crossbar – who knows?

Yet a week later when I drove Steve and Richie up to another new ground for me, Chesterfield – we were rank PISH and easily lost 2–0!

Another long-distance trip 'oop north' occurred the following week in Cleethorpes for our game versus Grimsby.

The Mariners was another club who Regal Litho printed programmes for and so Alan Corkhill kindly invited myself and friends Steve O'Dell and Bob Rumble for an overnight hotel stay and corporate hospitality.

Joining us on our table (he paid separately) was Grimsby pal Graham Precious.

A great day/night topped off by us winning 0–1 with James Collins scoring the only goal. A personal highlight though was meeting ex-Luton player and Grimsby legend Matt Tees before the game in another bar.

He was sadly suffering with early dementia now but after I asked his sons if it was ok to have a wee chat with him, they were astounded when we discussed his time at Luton. I reminded Matt about a great goal he scored versus Bradford City when he scaled heights of which I'd never seen before or since, to head in a goal during our 1969 5–0 win. He came alive explaining how his partnership with Malcolm Macdonald was a thriving one. His sons at the end had tears in their eyes and thanked me profusely for in their words 'giving us back our dad for a few wonderful minutes' – no, the pleasure was MINE!

Matt Tees sadly succumbed to his dementia in Nov 2020. RIP Matt.

Three nights later we lost again (our third defeat in six) 2–3 at home to Wycombe. Then following two home victories over Exeter (1–0) and Crawley (4–1) I had another corporate day at home versus Cheltenham. This was because I had won the Diamond Player of the Month January competition in choosing Harry Cornick.

The prize was for two, meal in the Eric Morecambe Lounge and seats in the sponsors area etc., so I took father-in-law (ex) Alan with me.

Alan has always been a Hatters fan but had not been for a while so he was thrilled when I took him to this.

Though neither of us expected to see us 0–2 down with nearly an hour gone. But Luke Berry pulled one back and Alan Sheehan at least won us a point with his 92nd minute equaliser.

My next game was a crucial one versus fellow promotion challengers Accrington Stanley. I once again took Paul Keating and Christine in the Bobbers and Oak Road. Before I write this, credit must go to Accy Stanley for catching up and overtaking us to go top, the first time we had not been at the apex since mid-November – BUT!

We should have had an early penalty for the most blatant handball I'd seen in years. How the Referee Mr Drysdale and his female lino missed an Accy player practically CATCHING the ball in the area was astounding. The whole ground bar 205 Stanley fans, leapt up screaming handball, yet incredibly play was waved on to continue.

We then had 5 opportunities to score, including two Dan Potts headers cleared off the line.

Then the inevitable happened when Accy scored a minute before the break. We could/should have been at least three or four goals up at half time with that early pen not given and out of sight – instead we were LOSING!

But Elliott Lee equalised on the hour and as the match entered time added on, to be honest I'd have taken a point then to stay top. But cruelly in the 93rd min, the division's top scorer Billy Kee scored at the death to stun most of the 9,500 plus crowd, with and I have to say, a brilliantly well taken goal. His wild celebrations were understandable in front of the Accy fans, but out of order when he continued them right in front of our bench dugout.

This is one of only two times I've seen us lose (Pompey 2016 the other) when sitting in the Oak Road since we returned to our spiritual end in 2013.

Following our fourth defeat of 2018 in 13 games (we only lost 5/32 in the first half of the season) I then drove Steve and Phil Fensome up to Coventry – great, my bogey team who had won all SEVEN home games I'd seen the Sky Blues play in Coventry to date.

We had a couple of pre-match pints at the Ricoh in a nice bar there. It looked like same old same old when we found ourselves one down after just three minutes and then 2–0 at half time. Some Hats were beginning to ask questions is this going to be our eighth league defeat of the season (five since Christmas) and is Nathan Jones going to blow promotion AGAIN two years running?

Fear not you doubting Thomases – including me!

Scott Cuthbert pulled one back on 55 mins with his fourth and ultimately last LTFC goal.

Then with two minutes remaining Coventry born James Collins sent us 2,002 Hats into orbit to make it 2–2. AT LAST, my Coventry 100 per cent defeats in Coventry jinx – was over!

We enjoyed a post-match pint, with the added bonus of bumping into and chatting to ex-Hatters legends Brian Stein and Luton/Coventry (hence why he was there) Kirk 'Basher' Stephens, who as I might have previously mentioned brought my book in 2012.

Four days later Steve and I had another overnighter in Newport, where at a blowy (very) Rodney Parade we drew 1–1 and I nearly had a punch up – with a fellow Luton 'supporter' when Dan Potts equalised!

This bloke a few seats to my right was getting right on my tits, non-stop moaning from the minute we kicked off. Trailing to Newport after a second minute goal made him even worse.

When Dan Potts equalised we all naturally jumped up celebrating – except for this bloke! I was raging, shouting at him, "We've fucking SCORED! What's the matter with you? Why are you not cheering our goal!" He had to be held back and was livid and Steve also had to stop me from going over and lumping him one. We have some right fucking moany twats in our support sadly, but this bloke was no modern youngster. He was probably just a touch younger than me. I told Steve we have to move seats in the second half or I might get nicked, lol.

We won our first game in six beating Barnet at home 2–0 and returned to first place with seven games remaining. Unfortunately, that would be the last time we led the table in 2017–18.

Next up I drove Steve to a very rainy shitty day at Colchester with 1,940 other Hats at the Community Stadium. Unfortunately, a nightmare occurred in just the second minute when Luke Berry went down screaming in agony in an ordinary looking challenge with Col U's Lapsie. You could see how bad it really was because of the distress shown by both Luton players and our opponents. Referee (that tit Mr Kettle) took the players off the pitch for 11 mins as Luke received urgent medical treatment, before being stretchered off to hospital. Naturally, Luke's season was over and there was fear if he could ever return the same player from such a serious injury. He had suffered a horrible dislocated ankle – and fractured fibula! I'm delighted to write Luke did come back the next season and is still a Luton player as I write this.

To be honest the players hearts were not in this (no true excuse really) match. Colchester led 2–0 at half time and Danny Hylton's 88th minute penalty, following a foul on Luke Gambin, was just as a year prior, a 2–1 consolation goal.

We then hit a run of form when we most needed it. Beating Mansfield 2–1 at home on Easter Monday then thrashing Yeovil 0–3 away.

Three days after that I picked up my older sister Ann from Heathrow Airport. She was home to stay with me and various relations for a few weeks because it was my forthcoming 60th birthday and party (long since prior arranged) 11 days later.

This was only the second time (1999 the other) that Ann has been back in the UK since she left for her new life in Auckland, New Zealand in 1988.

We beat Crewe 3–1 at the Kenny and with just three games remaining, promotion was in touching distance.

Two nights before my big party I attended a music gig alone at St Albans Theatre. It was my first concert since Steve Toyer RIP and I went to see Ringo's Allstars band at Shepherds Bush Empire in 1999. Of course I was going to take my daughters to see Michael Jackson in 2009 as I had tickets at the O2, but Jacko went and bloody died on us. RIP.

The artist I went to see was Gilbert O'Sullivan and I have to write he was outstanding. Some stars from back in the day never know when to quit and their voices go. I put Rod Stewart, Elton John and sadly Paul McCartney in that group but Gilbert's voice is still there, he still rocks and sounds as good as he did in the 1970s. I'm so glad I went.

I had booked my 60th well in advance when the 2017–18 fixtures were out in the June, naturally having Stopsley WMC as the venue and Cali R legend Sid Hudson DJ'ing as my choices. The actual day of my birthday was a Thursday, so it was an option of either Saturday 21st when Luton were at Carlisle or the 28th at home to Forest Green Rovers. I chose the 21st so as not to be rushed after the home match and there was bound to be not that many Hatters going to Carlisle – er WRONG!

How on earth was I to know – that Luton could win PROMOTION on the actual day we played at Brunton Park FFS! if results went our way.

Some friends chose to go to Carlisle (totally understandable considering what was at stake) some elected to miss the match for my big night – and more than a few did both!

Naturally, I wasn't one of the 1,404 Hats who travelled to near Scotland and would have to settle watching Jeff Stelling's Sky Soccer Saturday for live updates at Louise's.

It goes without saying that I was desperate for the right result:

1) Because I wanted us up to be able to relax and

2) I just knew if we got the point probably needed and be promoted, I would have the party of all parties – especially as personal circumstances in 2008 dictated that it was inappropriate to have a 50th party.

After only 13 minutes I was in despair when Carlisle went 1–0 up with a penalty. Louise was screaming at me, "FFS calm down Alan otherwise you'll have a bloody heart attack and there will be no party."

It was still 1–0 after an hour then two minutes later it happened – Olly Lee equalised (little did I know this would be his ninth and penultimate LTFC goal) I leapt up what felt like 10 feet in the air and I think Louise would have heard me had she been at the bottom of her garden.

Jeff Stelling announced when Olly scored, "If it stays like this Luton will be automatically promoted with two games to spare." – It did and we were – let the party commence!

Moi, being the shy, bashful, retiring type, had long since ordered my party attire. Bright vivid orange suit, with tie and trilby hat to match and so off we walked the short distance to the Stopsley Working Men's Club.

The night went to plan with perfection, one of the greatest evenings in my entire life, of course Luton winning promotion on the same day was a dream climax and icing on the cake.

I had the big L-shaped dance hall, enough room/seats for the 250-plus guests, which included so many dear family and loyal friends. Folk from all over the place were there. Aunt Ann, Bob and cousin Nikki from Toronto, Canada. Sister Ann from New Zealand, the Rangers Kilsyth pals Duncan, Rab, Tam, Ian and their spouses from Scotland, old Windsor

Castle mates Dave Ventris, Eamon Taaffe and West Ham Rob and Kim Robinson. Best Man Larry Kinloch and Lynne, all my Domino team mates, SWMC member friends, close couple friends Bob and Kath Rumble, Paul Keating and Christine, Bobbers Club friends and naturally it goes without writing, my fellow Hatters family, too many to mention but Santa was there and Jesus – plus of course those who came straight from Carlisle. Naturally, most of my Blackpool Adair Travel regulars too.

I did invite Deb and she would have been more than welcome, but she declined, saying, "It's your big night Alan."

Her parents Julie and Alan, sister Liz and Del and Niece Lauren all came though (but not Lauren's then partner as he was a W**ford season ticket holder and he bottled it, lol).

Sid Hudson made sure the music played meant it could not have been a better night anywhere in the UK on April 21st 2018. With both my daughters there sharing the love, it was honestly the best night of my life.

There was one very, very sad part to the night though – but that's for the next chapter.

Five days later on my actual birthday came another special treat. For my present, sister Ann treated us both to a one night/two days in Liverpool, staying at the Beatles Hard Day's Night Hotel and going on the Magical Mystery Bus Tour, who's guide was the brother of Holly Johnson (Frankie Goes to Hollywood lead singer) seeing all the famous Beatles haunts like Penny Lane, Strawberry Fields, the fabs houses where they grew up and of course the Cavern which the ticket price included admission that night.

That evening we had dinner in the Hotel Restaurant which was amazing and they kindly laid on a 60th birthday cake for us. It's called Blake's after the famous artist who did the famous *Sgt Pepper* Album Cover.

Then in the evening at the Cavern mixing with such friendly local Scousers old and young, me with my huge 'I am 60' badge on, memories of a night I will take to my grave.

The Beatles tribute band were sensational and were so kind, they kept shouting out Big Al from Luton is 60 today and played all my requests.

Ann just could not believe the friendliness shown to us by the locals during the whole time we were in Liverpool.

The final home game was a 3–1 win versus Forest Green Rovers, followed by a grand finale party at Notts County.

Bob, Kath, Gary and Lois Rumble, Phil Fensome joined myself on the train to Nottingham, where we had all booked an overnight hotel for the Saturday night. Naturally, I wore my new orange suit, matching tie and trilby.

We started on the bevvy in the morning on the train, packed full of Hatters – and I finished the all day/night session walking into my hotel room at – 6 a.m. Sunday!

Notts County were brilliant giving us a whole side stand of 4,495 partying Hats. We drew 0–0 but nobody cared because we partied like it was 2018.

We ended this great season in second place, five points behind Champions Accrington Stanley. Full credit must be given to Accy as despite them losing 11 games (3 more than us) they put on such a brilliant final run of games to overtake us, they actually deserved the title.

Wycombe Wanderers joined us into League 1 (old division 3) by finishing third four points behind us and seventh placed Coventry won the Play-offs to complete the four promoted clubs.

Our Final 2017–18 stats were:

Played 46, Won 25, Drew 13, Lost 8. Goals scored 94 – by FAR the highest in the league, Goals against 46 – the equal lowest, Goal Difference +48 – easily the highest in the league.

Our home average league gate was 8,674 an increase of 548 on the last season and away average of 1,392, an increase of 330 on 2016–17.

Roll on August.

On May 9th I attended the LTFC end of season dinner celebrations at the Auction House. As you can imagine it was a brilliant night, with many of us suited and booted (*moi* naturally in my orange whistle and tit fer again).

Then five days later the tears flowed as Mollie and Lachlan said goodbye at Luton Parkway station. They had been with me for two wonderful years but Lachlan's working visa had run out and it was time for them to go back to Oz. But before arriving Down Under they would go on a holiday of a lifetime visiting lord knows how many continents and countries on route to Aussie. Oh to be young again.

It was farewell for now – but not Goodbye!

The day ended in further sad news when the lovely wife of an old friend Barry Dumpleton, passed away after her long brave fight battling cancer.

RIP Jacqui.

Melbourne Hatter Kevin Redmond and I in Sydney December 2018. This was on the night he and his company kindly treated me to Dinner by the Sydney Opera House. But while walking towards the restaurant, I was stunned when this young lad ran over and shouted 'OMG ALAN ADAIR' - it turned out he knew me by my previous book cover and that I sit behind his Dad in Enclosure D Block at LTFC – small world indeed!

2018–19

I could write a book on this season and chapter – ALONE!

On June 1st 2018 the new manager at Rangers started. His name – Steven Gerrard!

Now while more than a few Bears thought this was the wrong path, taking on a novice whose only experience was managing the Liverpool Under 18 Youth team for a short while, I and most other Gers fans were delighted at getting such a world-famous name/profile, who in my honest opinion would attract players to Rangers because of who he is, that we would never have a chance of attracting otherwise. Time would only tell, but I had good vibes and would make certain I'd be there for his first game in charge in July. There is no denying though it was a huge gamble.

On the very next night Louise and I attended long time mate Martyn 'Rasher' Bacon's 60th party at his Crawley Green Social Club. What a fab night it was too. His entrance was sheer class when wife Val had hired a Lambretta Scooter and driver to bring Rash down the drive at the club with him pillion passenger, dressed to the part with his Parka. Both he and the Purple Scoot looked the bollox.

Sitting on our table was old mate Phil O'Dell and a mutual pal Colin McPherson over on holiday from Adelaide. I first met Colin in Adelaide when I returned for a holiday there in 1994 (see Chapter 4).

Among the many, many guests celebrating Rash's big night was the Bacon's great friend and ex-Hatters legend Kirk 'Basher' Stephens. There was also big Di, a right female character from LTFC days of yore. I hadn't seen her in years.

Then exactly three weeks later at around 10 p.m. I took one of those telephone call life stopping moments, just like dad in 1976, Uncle Malc in 2005, Mum 2009 and big Steve Toyer only a year prior in 2017.

It was from Samantha Maguire, the daughter of my best mate Larry Kinloch. I'll never forget it as long as I shall live as she struggled to get the words out – 'Alan I'm really sorry to tell you that Dad suddenly DIED tonight'!! I was utterly stunned beyond belief, in shock and devastated.

Larry as you will have read throughout this book at times, was not only my best pal, but I was his Best Man at his wedding to Lynne in 1982, as was he at mine to Deb in 1986.

I had known Lol for 40 years having first met him in 1978 at Roydon Printers where we both worked, him initially as a van driver before retraining as a competent (very) machine minder, eventually running his own one-man business Kinloch Print.

We also had two unforgettable and such fun years when I was roadie and his assistant from 1980–82 at his San Fran Disco (WHAT a name) mobile disco.

Larry and Lynne owned a caravan in Cosgrove Park, Northants where they would spend every spare moment at weekends, bank holidays and summer holidays, before upgrading to a really nice plush mobile home there a year or so prior.

It was there on Friday June 22nd that after work, the Kinlochs as usual headed for their second home (where they had made an army of friends over the years). While Larry was in the bathroom, Lynne heard an almighty crash to enter and find him lying prone on the floor, he had suffered a heart attack. Screaming for help, neighbours/friends there came rushing to aid, one of their friends (a qualified nurse) did all she could with CPR as the 999 ambulance was on its way. Lol (as only a few elite close friends would he allow to call him that) was transferred to Northampton Hospital, where they were doing all they could to save him – only for him to suffer a second fatal heart attack and that was it, he was gone!

I never slept a wink that night and was meant to be going on mate Howie's Stag do the next day in Harpenden. I rang Howie to apologise telling him the situation and explaining no way could I go in the frame of mind I was in, he totally understood and was sympathetic.

That Saturday morning I drove round to Larry's house with a card and flowers for Lynne and family. Utter sheer heartache when I saw her and one of his daughters Kelly, but nothing compared to what was about to happen.

Larry's son Michael (my godson) was in Budapest, Hungary on a mate's stag weekend when he took the nightmare call. He naturally booked the first available flight home Sat a.m. and as I was there at the house, his cab from Luton Airport pulled up. That moment when he walked through the door I shall take with me to my grave. He utterly wailed into the arms of his mother and sister.

I felt horrific and helpless for these dearest friends. "I shouldn't be here, I must go and let you grieve as a family privately."

Michael roared, "Alan you ARE family. Fucking stay here with us please." Naturally I obeyed his wishes.

That week I was just in a daze at work, walking the dog, nonstop crying at a moment's notice, sick to the stomach with loss.

It was only two months prior we were having SUCH a brilliant time together at my 60th party – that was the last time I saw Larry!

He had bought me the most wonderful present which I will treasure forever, a beautiful canvas print of our shared love The Beatles.

I take solace and some comfort that at least the last time I saw him was a joyous occasion. RIP my lovely pal Larry. I miss you every day still.

His funeral would take place late the next month and I made sure I was as composed as best I could, to try and do him proud for his finale.

July 26th watch this space.

A happier occasion took place on July 7th when Louise and I attended an Adair Travel Blackpool regular, Tony Sussex's 80th birthday party at Harlington Village Hall. Him and his lovely wife Jean are good friends.

On the football front we were about to start our first season in the third tier since 2007–08. Ten years after the 2020 Board took over and purchased, saving the club in 2008.

At the end of June 2016, LTFC 2020 Board officially submitted a planning application for a new stadium in the town centre called Power Court. Documentation was made available for public viewing at various exhibitions locally and on line.

The stadium would have an initial capacity of 17,500, rising up to 22,500 optional and should we ever do a 'Leicester' even room for up to 40,000. Excitingly there was also an 1,800 seated music concert venue at the site. This is only the second official planning application ever submitted for a new Luton ground after the doomed Kohlerdome was rejected by Mr Prescott in 1998–99.

Two years on we were still awaiting a decision by the council, but this was mainly because the local Arndale Centre owners had constantly tried to block the move with various non-stop objections throughout – C**TS!

But during 2018–19 there would FINALLY be a council decision – watch this space!

On the playing front the usual comings and goings occurred pre- and during 2018–19.

Andrew Shinnie had signed a permanent deal from Birmingham on a free transfer after his season long loan. Other free signings were giant centre-half from Plymouth, Sonny Bradley and Kaz LuaLua from Sunderland. Two undisclosed fees went to Barnsley for defender Andrew Pearson and talented midfielder George Moncur.

We also had on loan from Nottm. Forest Jorge Grant and in January also from Forest, ex-Hibs/Rangers Scot, Jason Cummings.

Saying goodbye to Kenilworth Road were: Jordan Cook to Grimsby after five LTFC goals in 58 appearances, Scott Cuthbert to Stevenage 4/110 appearances, Johnny Mullins to Cheltenham (3/51), were all released.

Olly Lee whose equalising goal at Carlisle sealed the point that had won us promotion in April, chose to decline our contract offer and signed an out of contract bigger one on a free, at SPL club Hearts. Olly had scored 11 goals (including THAT one versus Cambridge) in 122 LTFC appearances.

Before Luton's season began, I had to be in Glasgow for Rangers new manager Stevie Gerrard's first official game in charge and so booked flights for his first two official games. I flew up on July 12 (how apt was that?) to see the Gers play at Ibrox in the Europa Cup first qualifying round first leg versus Macedonian side Shkupi, as well as the second leg too.

I was with Paisley Gers friends Claire and John Hanlon, as they kindly invited me to the Bar 72 Lounge and seats for the match, then I stayed the night at a hotel near Ibrox.

I first met the Hanlon's in Eindhoven in a bar (naturally) post-match versus PSV in 2011 and we have been friends ever since.

We watched Stevie G get off to a good winning start with a 2–0 Gers victory. The second leg in Macedonia I went with Duncan Angus for a two night/three day break and saw a 0–0 with us going through 2–0 on aggregate.

In the second qualifying Round Rangers would progress impressively by beating Croatian side Osijek, winning 0–1 over there after a 1–1 Ibrox draw. Thereby going through to Round three and facing Slovenian pedigree team Maribor, winning 3–1 at Ibrox, then Duncan and I would travel to the away leg in August for another 0–0.

Rangers created European history by becoming the first ever team to qualify for the Europa Cup group stages by going through all four qualifying Rounds with eight ties played. We beat Russian side UFA 2–1 on aggregate.

A very impressive start for Stevie G.

My first Luton game attended in the new season saw us well beaten by Championship side Norwich 1–3 at the Kenny in a pre-season friendly. This was the night before Larry's funeral.

A huge turnout packed the Lewsey Farm Church to the rafters on a very hot sunny day. I was one of the pall bearers and did a speech to my hugely missed best pal, JUST about holding it together without breaking down, throughout my epitaph. We saw Larry off in style at the United Services Club, a venue where Larry and Lynne joined me one brilliant night at one of the excellent Sid Hudson Cali R events.

Along with the family, I had arranged a large list of tunes that Larry was associated with and loved. Special memories of his favourites, some of which included his number one love 'Always and Forever' by Heatwave, closely followed by an eternal dance floor filler 'Heaven Must Have Sent You' the classic by the Elgins. He was most certainly sent by Heaven and is up there now partying. I miss him every day. RIP Larry.

Needing some happiness back in my life, I most certainly had it the very next day at the Putteridge Bury wedding of Anita Smyth and Howard 'Howie' Fossey.

Howie is a Yeovil Hatter who used to travel up as often as he could and I first met him in the Bobbers Club during our non-league Conference years. I think he supported Luton because of past family roots.

Howie met Anita on a coach at my very first Adair Travel Blackpool trip in April 2013 for the Southport versus Luton match. Anita was only there as a guest of a female mutual friend ex-schoolmate Elaine Beamon – nee Farr. I'm not even sure if she liked football then!

Well her and Howie immediately clicked and it would not be that long before he moved up from Somerset to live and work in Luton. They were an 'item' from that very day and are a lovely couple – Anita and her daughter are now with Howie, ardent LTFC season ticket holders in Enclosure J Block.

The gorgeous sunny day for the wedding service and then reception at the Coop Club in Round Green was perfect.

Sitting on our table next to Louise, was the immensely popular Nigel 'Santa is a Hatter' Martin. Lou, like EVERYONE loved Santa Nige.

The following weekend was the first league game of the new season at Portsmouth. Alas, I had to miss it (lightweight) because we were at another wedding, 'oop north' near Preston. This was for Louise's female northern cousin.

We stayed the weekend in a nearby hotel and had a fabulous day/night at the stunning venue.

While we were having such a good time, miles away down south Luton lost at Pompey 1–0 in front of 2,382 travelling Hats, but according to reports and all who attended, we played brilliant. Portsmouth fans evidently said to many Hats after the game, "I don't know how we won that? – Luton were outstanding!"

I had absolutely no idea or inclination, that this turned out to be the final time Louise and I stayed the night together.

The first home game saw a 1–1 draw versus Sunderland in which we were fortunate to get an equaliser with Matty Pearson's first LTFC goal.

I drove my regular Hatters partner Steve up to the Hawthorns to see us narrowly lose 1–0 to Premiership West Brom in the League Cup.

Pre-match we went in a fabulous pub that did Indian food, called the Vine. Packed with both Town and Albion fans freely mixing together.

A day after returning from my Rangers trip to Slovenia with Duncan, we played crap at Peterborough, losing 3–1 with all three Posh goals coming in the first 36 mins.

Next day was a bit of an informal celebration at the Sugar Loaf pub in town for ex-work colleague and good mate (I was his and wife Jane's Best Man in 1991) 60th birthday celebrations bash for Gary Hopkins.

Among the many there was a mutual friend who also used to work with us at CBC Print in the 1990s in the Bindery, Jean Kelly. I must be honest, I always used to fancy her back in those days but of course she was forbidden fruit, as both of us were married then. We were always friends but I had rarely seen her since I left CBC in 2000. Though we did see each other at her best friend Jane's Dad and Larry's funerals. "Nice to see you on a happy occasion for a change Jean," said I.

I didn't know she was going to be there and that she had been single for a long while. We got on fantastically well at Gary's birthday bash, like a house on fire. In short, we would relatively soon become an 'item' – but I must stress not getting it together until after I had ended my relationship with Louise!

I'm afraid by then I'd already nearly made up my mind to finish with Lou. To be frank I had never been the same since the rebuff at her daughter's wedding church service over two years previously.

When the time came for me to explain this was the main reason I wanted to call us quits after over five years, Lou thought I was a bit pathetic using that as an excuse and me being a bit of a drama queen.

I'm pleased to write though, we parted on good amicable terms, no nastiness at all. She will always be a lovely girl with a good heart and we are still friends today, with the odd mutual text/Facebook message.

I didn't start actually going out with Jean until after splitting with Lou.

More (much) drama though was soon to occur in this life of Adair on Friday Sept 7th 2018.

I had left Jane Hopkins with my latest print order from her office (Opel Ireland jobs) to take them to Regal Litho. On my way to collecting them I received a phone call from owner Alan Corkhill telling me to be at the Regal Litho office for an urgent meeting involving all staff. I told him I was on my way to McCann's to pick up two jobs and would go straight from there.

Upon arrival, the meeting was about to start and I was totally stunned when we were all informed that Regal Litho has ceased trading – as of TODAY!!!

I was both horrified and angry too. Having worked with them as a self-employed print farmer since 2011 (and using them for three years before that when I was at Russell Press too) – I was now officially jobless for only the second time in my entire working life since 1973.

Because I wasn't directly employed by Regal Litho there would be no redundancy package.

My immediate thought and duty though was to tell Jane. Here I was with two orders that I couldn't produce for her. I had to ask her to urgently place these (and all the other orders I had coming) – elsewhere!

Thankfully, she managed to do so by getting one of her other suppliers The Print Centre (TPC) in Berkhamsted to match our prices and produce all those jobs. Now I had to urgently concentrate on getting another job. ASAP.

Because it was a Friday and I had already pre-booked the train, I still reluctantly went to Doncaster versus Luton the next day, really not feeling up to it. But what was the point of moping around at home upset, knowing I wouldn't be able to do anything about the work situation on a weekend.

We lost 2–1 at Donny but frankly, that was the least of my concerns.

At the match I saw old ex-CBC colleague Pete Morris at half time, the first time in ages, as he had moved to Cambridgeshire a while back. Pete was very sorry when I told him of my plight, then mortified after I asked him if he heard about Larry. He hadn't and was shocked to the core. Pete used to live in the same Lewsey Farm close as Lol.

On Monday I sprang into action with my contacts in the print trade. The only other time I had been jobless back in 2008, I was working again just two days later with Mark Filmer at Russell Press in Ampthill.

Within days this time I quickly had offers of two positions, both doing the same as at Regal, as a self-employed print farmer placing the work directly with the printer. One was in Dunstable and the other was TPC in Berkhamsted. It was at Jane's suggestion to both TPC and myself, it would be best for me to take the TPC one as they were already on the Vauxhall Suppliers list. She could not guarantee getting another printer on the list, certainly not in terms of speed. For that very reason, it was a no brainer to take the TPC offer, where they would hand over the Vauxhall contract to me, to enable it to grow more than it had previously done prior. I was very grateful to both TPC and Jane and would start the very next Monday after another Blackpool weekender.

No Adair Travel trip for Blackpool versus Luton on this one.

Although the Claremont had now decided on a trial basis to include their All-Inclusive packages all year round, it was too late when the fixtures were announced to organise one, so instead just Steve and I went. We drew 0–0 after another fab Castle Bar pre match session (but it could never match the previous sensational craic) and the usual Soul Suite late nights.

Our 10th game of the season saw us draw 2–2 at home versus Charlton and if I'm honest we were lucky to get a point. Luton might have even undeservedly won it but for a 95th minute Addicks equaliser.

At that stage we were exactly halfway 12th/24 with three wins, four draws and three defeats, not bad for the higher step up.

Little did any of us Hats know what was soon to be coming up.

Three successive wins 1–2 at Oxford, 3–2 at home versus Scunthorpe (in the Bobbers and Oak Road again with Paul Keating and Christine) and a 3–0 home Checkatrade Trophy win versus Milton Keynes.

A game that most Hatters including myself, boycotted because under FL and FA rules the Bletchley Stealers were entitled to a share of the gate receipts in cup competitions.

The LTFC 2020 Board wisely decided to charge Adult Cat C £18 league prices and as a result only 875 attended (the lowest EVER official KR non-friendlies attendance) – of which this gate included 208 from MK! So only 667 home fans scabbed.

I watched us live on Sky TV at my house lose 3–2 at Barnsley. The live TV curse had struck again.

But I bet not one single Hatter of the 807 at Oakwell, or all of us other viewers, could envisage this would be our last league defeat until – mid-APRIL, creating a new LTFC record of 28 league games unbeaten!!!

The day after we beat Walsall 1–0 at home we had a wonderful family occasion at the Swan Hotel in Bedford.

It was to celebrate my Aunt Joan Hines' 70th Birthday. A fab time was had by all as we had a Sunday meal in a room exclusively to ourselves, with more than 20 of us Hines/Roberts/Adairs there including Georgina, who had now recently started a new career, working for British Airways as an Air Hostess. I was so proud as after the dinner she changed into her smart BA uniform and drove off to Heathrow.

Four days later I flew up to see my latest Rangers game, a midweek Europa Cup Group stage match at Ibrox versus Russians Spartak Moscow. The result was me seeing my third successive Gers 0–0. This was the halfway stage of the group having drew 2–2 at Villarreal and beat Rapid Vienna 3–1 at Ibrox. Unfortunately, we lost 4–3 in the return Moscow game, drew 0–0 at home versus Villarreal and narrowly lost 1–0 in Vienna to Rapid who overtook us into second place. We finished third, just a point behind but it was a great European journey for the Bears.

Jean and I were now officially an 'item'. We had one very special night out of the blue on a midweek evening when she came round and stayed at mine in Barton for the first time.

I have not been a home drinker for nearly all of my life. But that night was special, as I played non-stop YouTube tunes from back in our days and we danced – as well as cracked open every bottle of drink I had received for my 60th six months previous! Champagne, Sparkling wine, white wine, red wine – we downed the lot and went to bed VERY, very merry, lol!

It was the start of a very happy time for me and I will freely admit I actually changed my lifestyle because of Jean, in a good way.

I was generally looking after my health better, went walking with Clyde more, did more knee exercises, even took up weekly swimming and no doubt, I was also dramatically shedding the pounds.

We even went to MK on a clothes shopping spree for me one Saturday (while Luton were winning 0–2 at AFC Wimbledon). I purchased two new smart suits, a £100 pair of Italian leather designer shoes FFS, a nice pair of leather boots, three lovely long sleeved designer shirts, two pairs of Levi Jeans, one denim the other black and also two pairs of Adidas Trainers. As one who has never been a great shopper (apart from when I was a teenager) I reckon I spent more on clothes that day than in the last decade.

We had a nice lunch in MK then that night went out wearing some of my new gear and had a great session in the Wheelies and Brewery Tap in Town. No doubt, Jean and I were definitely clicking and getting on so well with each other.

I even gave up drinking beer when I started going out with Jean, to join her in large Rosé wine with Soda and Ice as my new tipple.

Changed man was Adair, lol.

The following weekend I drove Steve up to Rochdale for our 0–0 draw, where we stayed overnight in a lovely suburban hotel right in rural countryside.

We were a touch fortunate to earn a point, mainly thanks to keeper James Shea. Post-match and that night we had a great evening with old school Luton lads Micky Dolan, Denis Edwards and Tony Bojko. One of Tony's Rochdale ex-hoolie pals was DJing a fireworks party at a cricket club and we went in there for a blinding craic.

The next morning after breakfast and my usual morning walk in the country hills to exercise, I drove Steve home. Life was sweet.

We beat Wycombe Wanderers 2–0 at home knocking them out of the FA Cup first round, then the next week destroyed Plymouth 5–1 at KR in a sublime Town performance, with James Collins netting a hat-trick. I didn't know about this, but pre-match at the Brewery Tap in town there had been a massive Luton MIG's/old school Luton lads reunion. I wished I'd have known, as hundreds turned out to reminisce. Some squad of chaps attended by all accounts.

The following Friday Jean and I flew up to Glasgow to stay in a Greenock Holiday Inn Express Hotel.

Greenock and Port Glasgow was where Jean's family originated from and one of her brothers was still staying in Port Glasgow. Everything went ok, in the main.

I met her brother and other relations (all Celtic) and I have to write they were absolutely fine with me, knowing I'm a staunch Rangers man.

But a couple of things with Jean and I did occur that weekend (which will remain private) where for the very first time in our short relationship, we had 'words' after we arrived home.

For me it was the first time I had felt any seeds of doubt whether this would last long term. I was definitely at fault in part, but one thing I will reveal that she did not like at all and that was while in Scotland, I naturally took in the opportunity to see the Gers play at Ibrox (beating Livingston 3–0. On a sad, separate note, this was the very last time I saw my good Kilsyth friend Tam Adams alive, sitting next to him at the game)

Jean took exception to that saying I could go and watch Rangers any bloody time, but didn't like it while we were up visiting HER family. Did she have a point – was I so wrong? I didn't think so.

I actually pre-arranged to go to Ibrox with the Greenock Rangers Supporters Club and went on their bus to the game and straight back.

While I was in Scotland we beat Gillingham 1–3 at Priestfield.

We then stuffed Bradford City 4–0 at home. This was our 12th goal in the last three games. The Bradford game on Nov 27th would be the last Luton match I would attend until New Year's Day.

One of my 60th birthday presents from my daughters were return flight tickets London – Sydney with a Hong Kong stop over both ways, so that I could stay with Mollie and Lachlan in Oz for Christmas 2018.

Because I was due to fly shortly after, I missed our FA Cup second round tie at Bury, where we won 0–1. Sadly, the Shakers would go out of business the following summer, thanks once again to YET another crooked, bent owner. It's truly a crying shame and I desperately feel for my Bury mates Carl Mason and Phil Lyons that they no longer have their beloved club to support.

On Dec 5th I flew from Heathrow, excitedly alone and had two nights stop over en route.

I had originally planned to stay with my cousin, the Hong Kong pro Golfer, Iain Roberts at his house, he regretfully had to tell me he was going to be away on those dates, but he was certain I'd be ok for the homeward bound stay on the return journey.

So I booked a hotel.

Hong Kong was now another country to tick off the list, but I will write I prefer Singapore (far) and Dubai.

Iain then blew me out for the return stay too at late (very) notice, saying he was going away again. I therefore had to pay premium festive rates to stay at the hotel once more – never again shall I ask him a favour!

The two-night stay did the trick giving my knees respite and I eagerly landed in Sydney on Dec 8th to be picked up by Mollie and Lachlan. It was only seven months since they left mine in Barton, but it was so great to see them again as we prepared for my three-week holiday, where we would cram so very much into this exciting adventure.

After sleeping off my jet lag the first full day we had in Sydney, taking a ferry over to Manly for the day in scorching hot weather – lovely for my knees!

Before I left the UK I was in touch with a Melbourne Hatter Facebook friend by the name of Kevin Redmond. He was coming to Sydney on a pre-Christmas business trip and we prearranged to meet up one night at Circular Quay on Dec 10th.

It was obvious how we could know who we were by our LTFC shirts worn. Kevin extremely kindly told me that I was a 'supplier' and that tonight's dinner was on his company. So after a couple of drinks at the bar opposite the train station we crossed the road on the way to a nice Seafood Restaurant he knew. But on the way there, the most startling occurrence happened.

A young lad maybe late teens/early 20s – screamed OMG ALAN ADAIR! I looked at Kevin, then him, "Do I know you son?"

"No Alan, but you know my dad, as he sits in front of you in Enclosure D Block at Luton."

Kevin asked, "But how did you know it was Alan?"

He told us, "By his book that I've read."

Absolutely astonishing, but not the first time I had met a fellow Lutonian who knew me in Australia, as something similar happened in Morphett Vale, Adelaide in 1994 with Mick Racher. I was still flabbergasted none the less.

We had a fab night and a delicious meal sitting outside with the Opera House to our right and facing Sydney Harbour Bridge. I thanked Kevin profusely and promised him a match ticket if he came over for when our new Power Court Stadium opens – if I'm still here Kevin, that's a deal!

The next trip on the itinerary was to fly to the Gold Coast for three nights and meet my younger sister Michelle, who was flying over from Auckland, New Zealand, as well as seeing my niece Rachael who was now living in the Gold Coast. A friend of Rachael's very kindly let us all stay at her house in Biggera Waters for the time we were there.

On the first day Mollie, Lachlan and I went with Michelle to Robina where she used to live and where I stayed for Christmas 2009. We had lunch at that great RQ's pub where the local ex-pat Poms used to meet up.

An amazing time was had by all. I think the Gold Coast is now my favourite part of Australia and could live there no problem.

Next up was a part of the holiday I was REALLY looking forward to.

I had prearranged in the UK a special personal favour for mate Colin Macpherson, who lived in Morphett Vale, Adelaide the town where the Adair family lived 1972–74. I had first met Colin during my 1994 visit back to Adelaide and a couple of times since then when he was in Luton, including at Rashers 60th that year in 2018.

Mollie and I only would fly out for a two night/three day stay in Adelaide and kindly stay with Colin and his lovely wife Sandra where I presented Colin with that extremely cherished highly personal favour.

Mollie got on SO well with them both.

We all had a special, special night at Noarlunga United Soccer Club, where I was to meet up with John Foy again my best friend from those 1970s days.

Michelle also flew to Adelaide from the Gold Coast alone to meet up with us, staying at the lovely hotel Deb, Georgina and I were in at old Reynella in 1994, the one at the winery.

I drove the three us around showing Mollie where I had two of the happiest years of my life as a 14- to 16-year-old. We visited and took pics of the old Wakefield Wanderers site where they used to play in Acre Avenue, both houses we lived in at Brodie Road then incredibly, the nice lady invited us in to have a look at 43 Timothy Road. The house that we had built to the Adair family spec back in 1972.

I had to laugh when Michelle quietly pointed out, "Alan look, it's still the SAME purple bath, tiles and suite with gold taps." Lol. We were both quite emotional that day.

In Port Noarlunga we had a delicious breakfast at old Stopsley High School mate and Hatter Mick Racher's son's café – where Mick so kindly treated us all. Top Man.

Then spent the afternoon in Adelaide city centre and later had dinner by the beach at Glenelg.

When we returned to Colin's that night I could not believe it when a committee man from NUSC had dropped off some Noarlunga Utd gifts for me. A track suit top, bottle of NU wine and two Soccer Club key rings. I was both touched and honoured at their kindness.

It was the first time Michelle had been back to Adelaide since we lived there over 44 years before. She then flew back directly to New Zealand while Mollie and I returned to Sydney.

I'm going to be honest here. Both Mollie and Michelle thought Adelaide was very quiet and perhaps somewhat dated. Perhaps they were right? and honestly, I do now prefer Sydney and the Gold Coast – but Adelaide will always have a permanent place in my heart and again, I could still live back there anytime no problem!

Another personal special blinding night occurred in Crow's Nest, North Sydney on Dec 20th, again prearranged before I left the UK.

There is another Luton fan who lives in Sydney by the name of Gary Mason. He organises a monthly LTFC Curry Night and of course I HAD to be there, with Lachlan. I was 'Guest of Honour' lol and presented them with my book. It was a special book though, the signed copy one that Larry RIP owned. It now has permanent place in Sydney, Australia for any exiled Hatters to read.

Then a night on the Rocks, well AT the Rocks in Sydney, occurred when the three of us joined one of Mollie's friends and her parents (the father a Scot and Rangers fan – hence why we were there lol) with me naturally wearing my Royal Blue Rangers top! We dined at a delicious Steak Restaurant where you chose your own joints and cooked it yourself – yummy!

One of the most special days of my entire holiday was when Gary Mason and his lovely wife Amanda took the three of us out for the day on Sydney Harbour – on their own yacht!

What a joyous experience this was – well apart from when Mollie very nearly fell off the fucking thing! Lol, after a wild boat had created mass waves.

These experiences truly were amazing and I had yet another one on Christmas Eve, a day at a place called Menai.

Another event prearranged in the UK when Dover Hatter mate, Peter Buckthorpe and his wife Carron, were also spending the festive season in Sydney, staying at their old friends house in Menai. I was kindly invited to the house for a pre-Christmas Barby and naturally – drinks!

Brilliant time with all four of those Kent folk.

Christmas Day itself was to be spent with Lachlan's family at his cousin's amazing property in Dural. Not just a stunning house, naturally with a big pool – but a fucking lake at the bottom of their vast land! It was the first time I met Lachlan's parents and we would visit them again at their home in Penrith on Boxing Day. That was after popping in on route to say hi to see another Sydney Hatter in Kirrawee.

When Georgina briefly worked in Sydney she befriended a girl called Shona from Coventry, whose partner by the name of Eddie Coughlan knew me. But the coincidences didn't end there – oh no sir!

His Irish mum was staying with them for Christmas and when we got chatting it only turned out she used to run the Stag pub in Luton and knew Jean and all the Kellys extremely well. In fact Jean once worked behind the bar at the Stag for her. When I told Jean this she replied, "FFS Adair, how many more people from Luton are going to know of you 10,000 miles away?"

It really was eerie.

I left for home via Hong Kong on Dec 27th after being made so welcome by Mollie and Lachlan. It was my absolute pleasure to stay and be with and see them again.

I crammed so much into such a short space of time, but also couldn't wait to get home and see 1) Jean, 2) my wee dog Clyde and last but not least of course LTFC – who while I was away the entire trip moved up to second, remained unbeaten winning four games – Fleetwood and Burton at home both 2–0 and even winning at Coventry FFS 1–2, as well as 0–2 at Scunthorpe on Boxing Day, before keeping the run intact at Walsall the day before I arrived home with a last minute Lua Lua equaliser in a 2–2 draw.

I saw my first game back on New Year's Day at home versus Barnsley – fucking 0–0! Lol.

My first away game since Rochdale on Nov 3rd was at Sheff Wednesday's Hillsborough where we drew the second tier side in the FA Cup third round and achieved a replay by drawing 0–0 in front of an astounding 4,219 Hats.

Then just four days later Nathan Jones sensationally quit to announce he was joining Championship side Stoke City – FUCKING HELL!!!

Now while not one person could blame anyone for reputedly earning nearly treble their wage to secure his and his family's lives, the actual manner in which he left us had a sour (very) bitter taste. You see the problem was we actually believed him when he used to kiss the LTFC badge, thump his chest and say he never wanted to leave Luton unless it was Barcelona or maybe his home boyhood club Cardiff – well Stoke are not fucking Barca! He was now known as Judas and the people who once loved him turned on him big time. Being pictured receiving his Manager of the Month Award wearing a Stoke top, sent many Hats over the edge. His bridges were burnt forever – or were they?

I am writing this piece on Feb 20th 2021 and am in tears after confirmation from the Vets laboratory tests yesterday, our darling wee Westie Clyde has lymphoma cancer and is now in the last stages of his long, precious 14 years three months life. He has given the entire Adair family so much joy, bliss and unconditional love. I am going to be lost when that inevitable time comes when we have to release him to Rainbow Valley. Until then, I am going to try and cherish every single day we have left with him, as long as he is pain free and still can/want his walkies and be able to eat/drink. This has hit me hard and truly will be like losing one of our family. I'm in pieces.

The LTFC 2020 Board turned to legend Mick Harford to take temporary charge after NJ's exit. He could easily have stuck two fingers up to a Board that sacked him in 2009, but Mick is class personified and is better than that. He willingly accepted the job as caretaker manager, keeping coach Steve Rutter as his number two, a key choice. Big Mick's first game in charge was at Sunderland, ironically his birthplace.

I had long since pre-booked another Hartlepool lads' weekender naturally. An astounding 3,081 Hats travelled to the Stadium of Light and backed us ferociously. Mick was given an almighty rousing reception from us all.

We started the game well and but for two excellent saves by the Makems' keeper McLoughlin from Andrew Shinnie and James Collins we would have led at half time instead of Sunderland, who scored through Maguire.

However we equalised midway through the second half with a James Collins penalty to send us Hats nuts in scenes. Danny Hylton then idiotically got himself sent off on 70 mins just three mins after we levelled, meaning we had to see out the last 20 mins or so with 10 men.

I absolutely loved Danny for his first 2½ seasons after he joined us in 2016 and he was an exceptional finisher at the third/fourth tier levels, but sorry, ever since his injury in 2019 he has not been the same player.

Sunderland were also down to 10 men deep into injury time after their goal scorer Maguire was shown a straight red for a stamp on Alan McCormack. A great point, celebrated in style at my favourite North East town Hartlepool.

In Mick Harford's first home game second time around, we narrowly exited the FA Cup third round replay losing 0-1 to Sheff Wednesday.

Then the following evening, January 16th 2019, came the ecstatic news watching live on stream, generations of Luton fans had been waiting for – in over 50 YEARS! LTFC were FINALLY at long last granted official planning permission. APPROVAL by the local council to build our new Power Court Stadium. The celebrations and sheer relief of Hatters all around the world cannot be explained enough here.

The site which 2020 had already purchased and owned, was a prime town centre location facing our iconic St Marys church and in between both Luton railway stations. It would have an initial 17,500 capacity, then once any teething roadwork network problems etc. were ironed out, would extend to 22,500 capacity with even more room for at a later date, should Luton ever do a Leicester, expansion possible anywhere up to 40,000.

Amongst all the exciting Power Court 20-acre site plans were – a new River Lea frontage facing the church, community facilities including Bars, Restaurants, a public plaza, affordable local housing and a real personal thrill – a music concert venue seating 1,800! Something we have not had in the local area since the good old days of the California Ballroom, Queensway Hall and Caesars Palace.

As I write, work will finally commence on clearing and cleansing the site of its toxic waste. One reason why it had remained derelict and empty for over 15 years was because the old power Stations (hence named Power Court) spewed so much poisonous toxic waste in 2022, nobody would touch it with a bargepole because of the sheer cost and scale of cleansing it. God willing, we hope and have recently been told by the club that PC will be open for business sometime in 2024.

Had it not been for the only objectors, the pig-headed obstinate owners of the Arndale (Mall) shopping centre, constantly nonstop opposing the project at every given moment, meaning we had to always go through things with great precision – we could well have moved into PC by now!

I just hope and pray I'm still alive and healthy enough to see us play there. Far too many wonderful great Hatters I know, sadly will not.

Big Mick had his first win when thrashing Peterborough at home 4–0, followed by a narrow 0–1 win at Roots Hall, Southend which I missed. Matty Pearson scored the only goal and as a result, Luton went top of League 1 for the first time this season. It was also the first time we topped the third tier since May 2005.

What followed three nights later was the stuff of legends. January 30th 2019 Luton versus Portsmouth.

This highly sought-after sell-out between the league's top two teams in my honest opinion was the best first half LTFC performance I had seen in decades and a game right up there with the 2006 Luton 3 Liverpool 5 FA Cup classic.

Thanks to a Facebook Hatters pal Martyn Urban Rat, I managed to use two of his kids' season tickets (naturally paying the club extra adult pricing) to let an old friend of mine Clive McEvoy's two grown up children in to see the game. They were Bognor Regis Hatters Darran McEvoy and his sister Vicky Austin. I've already touched base in the 1990s section about their father, ex-original Oak Road late 1960s/early 1970s Skinhead Clive 'Mac'.

We all watched the game from my Enclosure D Block seats in a snowstorm. Luton were simply utterly – BRILLIANT! We came close three times to scoring through Stopsley boy James 'one of our own' Justin, Luke Berry and Kaz Lua Lua, before James Collins finally gave us a deserved lead our play so richly deserved. Luton went off to a thunderous ovation at half time.

But 1–0 is often not enough and surely we could not maintain that extreme upbeat tempo and excellence in the second half.

It was indeed the case when a much-improved Pompey equalised on 51 minutes. Our keeper James Shea then made two excellent saves from Morris, as well as our JJ then having a superb 25 yarder tipped over by their keeper MacGillvray. The football quality of this brilliant end to end game was astounding.

Then on 77 minutes, scenes when James Collins restored our lead with his second from the penalty spot after Lua Lua was felled in the area. But a mere two mins later we Hats were totally gutted when the impressive Bogle made it 2–2. How the fuck were we not winning this – after playing so well!! Fear not Adair.

Ten mins from time substitute George Moncur replaced Lua Lua and with just five minutes remaining he won a direct free kick directly in front of the Oak Road end goal. A prime position for any number of Town players to try their luck. It looked like it was going to be JJ, only for him to step over the ball and leave it for George himself to take it – and take it he DID! The ball was hit low and hard with such force, directly through the wall into the bottom corner of the net – utter bedlam and SCENES all round most of Kenilworth Road.

That night and victory was when I first truly believed we could actually win a second successive promotion here. The key win took us five points clear.

The very next night even more elation when Luton Council also formally approved the vital second planning application for Newlands Park.

This was the 40-acre site (also owned by 2020) at Junction 10A off the M1.

It will include High Quality Retail, Offices, Hotel and Leisure facilities. It was absolutely essential to get official approval on this site too, as a major part of actually help financing Power Court, was to eventually lease and sell off part of this land.

The following weekend I went with Jean to stay at her daughter Mel and Villa supporting (and nice bloke) boyfriend's house in Birmingham for the Saturday and evening. We had a lovely time in Brum.

After me keeping an eye constantly on updates from Shrewsbury (we comfortably won 0–3) the evening in Birmingham centre was special.

Firstly the four of us having drinks in the exclusive chef Marco Pierre White's Steakhouse Grill Champagne Bar with panoramic views of the city skyline, then going onto having dinner at a Brazilian Restaurant, finally ending up clubbing it watching a great live band.

There is no doubt, that for the vast majority of my time with Jean, we had some absolutely brilliant joyful occasions. But sadly, this was about to soon come crashing to an end.

I saw us beat Wycombe comfortably 3–0 at home, then it was time for ADAIR Travel Blackpool trip number nine Feb 15th–17th for Fleetwood versus Luton.

The day after I personally hand delivered Valentine's Red Roses and her favourite Rosé wine to her workplace KH, we left on my coach for Blackpool.

Jean had been SO looking forward to this, as was I naturally. But without revealing too much personally, sadly it was the weekend that finished us as a couple. I will not go into much detail but, A) on the first night (admittedly with the All-Inclusive nonstop wine flowing) I took exception to her putting me down in front of my Scots friends (which she later claimed was just banter – it WASN'T) and B) later that night Jean started again with it and I flipped, resulting in us having a huge row. We saw out the rest of the weekend as amicably as it could be, but secretly I knew things had changed.

On Monday, the day after we returned from Blackpool, she finished with me. Oh and Luton beat Fleetwood 1–2 to create a new LTFC record of 20 unbeaten League games without loss.

The truth is I kind of knew this was coming with Jean and to be honest after this particular weekend which promised so much for our relationship, I felt that things could never be the same again anyway, as a result.

In defence of Jean, I am not perfect and will admit I was partly in the wrong too with some of the things I said/did during our time. But I'll always be grateful for the period we did share together. She WAS great for me and certainly sorted me out in many ways in terms of keeping myself more fit, more healthy (arthritis aside) and keeping both myself and my house more hygienic.

She was good for me – though I soon gave up that Rosé wine pish, lol.

On March 2nd I used my Diamond voucher to have a brilliant corporate day when we beat Rochdale 2–0 at home. Joining me in the John Moore Lounge were great mates Steve O'Dell, Phil Marlor and Jesus.

We had a good craic in there meeting some ex-footballers such as Spurs John Duncan, Celtic's Mick McCarthy (boo), Rob Lee, the great man John Moore himself and also a crowd of Dutch Feyenoord fans.

Luton around then had a few stuttering performances drawing 0–0 at Plymouth and at home to Coventry (no surprise there) 1–1 and Gillingham 2–2.

One very important work situation was about to develop, with my near 45 years in the print trade as a career, starting to come to an end.

While I was at Mollie's in Sydney for Christmas, Vauxhall had a meeting with Jane mid-December. As a result the recent new 2018 owners Peugeot, had decided that from early 2019 they were going to produce 90 per cent of their printed literature online. The Car/Van Brochures you saw in Car Showrooms that we used to produce for Vauxhall/Opel Ireland would very soon cease to exist. In one fell swoop I was going to lose over 70 per cent of my business. Dealing with Vauxhall directly/indirectly since 1988, thirty years of loyal service was about to go out of the window.

So from February 2019 while continuing at TPC trying to exist on my other clients' print, it soon became very clear there wasn't enough to earn a living with just print anymore. TPC realising my plight, very kindly offered to let me drive their van helping with deliveries etc to help make up some of the deficit in earnings, but even that avenue soon ran dry when I was beginning to earn next to nothing in print sales with my other clients and so therefore I knew sometime soon I was going to have to take the plunge and get out of print to take another job – any job!

I also at that time as needs must, decided to sell my rarest LTFC programme. The 1986 League Cup tie versus Cardiff that was never played when the FL kicked us out of the competition because Chairman Evans refused to follow FL rules in letting Cardiff fans in. As a result the club were ordered to shred all the programmes printed. I managed to get one later in time from a club official. There are a few dozen about as I'm led to a believe a staff member of the printers kept hold of a box.

I sold mine to a collector for a much needed £200.

The last game in March was at Bristol Rovers where Phil Marlor and I had a good day out on the train, meeting up with Welsh based Bob and Christine Cowley and Exeter Hatter Hugh O'Rourke. I discovered that day Hugh and Bob were both ex-Royal Navy and served together in the past.

An excellent 1–2 win at the Memorial Ground left us edging ever so nearer to a fantastic second successive promotion with just six games left.

Although we slipped up dropping another couple of points in a 2–2 home draw versus Blackpool, LTFC had now reached a staggering club record of 28 games without defeat, stretching back six months since losing 3–2 at Barnsley in mid-October. That fabulous never to be beaten in my time (IMHO) run came to an end at The Valley, Charlton on April 13th.

We had a great day out by train to London with a huge pre-match session in the city, us lads paying a fucking fortune in a black cab to take us from the pub to Charlton.

A massive 3,144 Hats – PLUS my great friend DJ Janet Betts! Our full allocation had long since sold out, but I managed to get her in free with a well worked out Adair plan. Janet had to pretend she was my Mrs and as we reached the turnstile had a 'row' as she had lost her ticket. With hundreds queueing behind us to get in I pleaded with the operator to let her in, the jobsworth was having none of it but when a senior steward came over and I explained our predicament I said, "Mate I can't leave my wife out here on her own with the masses," and he kindly let her in.

Harry Cornick gave us a 15th minute half time lead with a superb long-range strike. It was his eighth and last goal of the season. 29 unbeaten games in a row looked certain at half time but credit to Charlton who were great at Kenilworth Road too, then here at the Valley in the second half. They tore us to pieces with another pair from Lyle Taylor – who nearly ALWAYS scores against us no matter who he plays for! Andrew Shinnie also saw Red with his second booking two mins from time. 3–1 the brilliant run and record was over. All good things come to an end at some time.

This was also the first time we had lost a game after taking the lead, for 76 matches in all competitions.

It was back to winning ways the following Saturday when we thrashed Accrington Stanley 0–3 in front of the Sky live TV cameras. With a 5.30 p.m. kick off that meant most of the 1,319 travelling Hats were in fine voice (and vast alcohol intake) to see a James Collins first half penalty (after he had also missed one) and a fine second half Pelly pair. With just three games left we were now within touching distance of both promotion and the title.

Steve and I had naturally stayed at the Accy Dunkenhalgh Hotel again and celebrated long into the night there.

It was AFC Wimbledon next at the Kenny three nights later on St Georges' Day. My cousin Bill Roberts was over on holiday from the USA visiting his parents and desperately wanted to see the Town possibly win promotion. Every single Luton home game had been a sell out in home area seating for all of 2019. But thanks to a 'contact' I succeeded in getting Bill a ticket near mine.

We took an early eighth minute lead when Elliot Lee completed a wonderful Town move involving Jack Stacey. Then ex-2016 Town loan Joe Pigott equalised with the Dons first shot on goal on 28 minutes. He has and still is, certainly been prolific at AFC.

James Collins restored our lead with a thumping header from a James Justin free kick. Bill was hugely impressed with JJ that night and raved about how good he looked for one so young. He wasn't wrong – as we all now know!

Even in this season of seasons, football can be cruel. In the second half we failed to add to our lead despite Lee and JJ having efforts brilliantly saved by Wombles keeper Ramsdale and then Jack Stacey hitting the crossbar. KR was then stunned into silence (bar the 733 away fans in the Oak Road corner) when Seddon struck to make it 2–2 - in the 93rd minute, FFS!

Every Hatter left the ground disappointed, but we dusted ourselves down to get ready for a promotion party at Burton four days later, the day after my 61st birthday.

Steve and I, lovely Janet Betts and her brilliant man Paul, all booked a Saturday night Burton hotel stay. Match tickets were like gold dust with the full 1,721 hatters allocation LONG since sold out. More than a few Hats had managed to purchase tickets in the home Burton sections.

James Collins had us celebrating massively by opening the scoring on 30 mins with his 25th goal of the season. If the score finished as this we were PROMOTED, but in the windy conditions, we were not quite at the races for some reason and utter disaster struck in the second half. It came as no surprise at all when Burton equalised on 62 minutes, but when Akins added his and Burton's second eleven mins later to win it 2–1 for the Brewers, we were stunned beyond belief.

We had lost only our sixth game of the season at the penultimate match and it looked like it was going to have to go to a nerve-wracking last game versus Oxford United at the Kenny a week later on May 4th. Barnsley were now level with us, equal top, with us ahead on goal difference by 4.

The Tykes would have to better our result, or score line by five goals at Bristol Rovers if/when we beat Oxford.

I must write, despite being downhearted for a fair while immediately after the match, we all soon dusted ourselves down and had a blinding night in Burton town centre.

But incredibly we had won promotion in midweek a few nights later before even kicking a ball against Oxford following an incredible sequence of results.

The only sides who could catch us apart from Barnsley, were Sunderland and Portsmouth. They both played their game in hand on us.

Pompey at home to Peterborough and Sunderland at Fleetwood. Incredibly both teams LOST (thanks Posh for winning 2–3 at Fratton Park and thanks Fleets for beating the Makems 2–1). WE WERE UP!!!!!!!!!!!!!!!

This was the third promotion of the last four that Luton had been involved in where we went up without playing a game – 2005 when Tranmere lost at Brentford, 2014 after Cambridge had lost at Kidderminster and now this particular night. LET THE PARTY COMMENCE.

Luton Town FC were back where this club truly belongs, in the 2nd tier of English football where we have spent the most seasons playing at that level (36) in our near 135-year history.

It would be great if we could deservedly end as Champions (which in fairness we should have done in League 2 the previous season). All we had to do was beat Oxford at home and by a bigger margin than Barnsley if they won their final match.

Pre-match in the Bobbers Club was a special, special day. I got out the orange suit, tie and trilby again and remember being interviewed for a podcast made by California Hatter Dianne Clark Jolly, who came specially over from the States for this party, as well as Aussie Hatter from New South Wales Roger Tavener and the lovely Actor/Model/Singer/Friend

Jane Ledsom who had a LTFC single record released back in the day.

Also in the Bobbers were now regulars Angie and Ray Bradley and many of their Hull family/friends. They were the parents of our captain Sonny Bradley. My old work colleague Kevin Hawkes and Aussie Hatter Mike Jakins at the beginning of 2018–19, first brought the Bradleys into the Bobbers and they became good friends of our little crowd, joining in with us fans and Bobbers staff for every home game (also travelling to every away game too).

They preferred to come into the Bobbers with the real supporters, than in the more formal corporate areas. An absolutely lovely and genuine couple who would be struck down by utter personal tragedy in December 2020.

It was also great to see ex-Hatters legends (and friends) Kirk 'Basher' Stephens and Brian Stein in the Bobbers on this day too.

To cut a long story short, we beat Oxford 3–1 with a pair from George Moncur and a great Elliot Lee goal. Boy did we celebrate being Champions LONG into the night at the post match Bobbers Disco party DJ'd by dear friend Janet Betts.

I decided that after some deep thinking and for various reasons, 2018–19 is now officially my all time favourite LTFC season.

Even eclipsing (just) the famous Division Two 1981–82 title winning and 1987–88 League Cup versus Arsenal, as well as the 2004–05 League 1 title winning ones. Granted those teams probably had better quality on the pitch, but it is for these reasons below 2018–19 is now my numero uno:

1) We created LTFC history with a 28-league game unbeaten run stretching exactly six months from Oct 13th– Apr 13th.
2) For only the second time in my life of supporting Luton since 1966, we remained undefeated at home in all league games. 1968–69 the only other.
3) The clincher, we had FINALLY been granted official planning permission to build our new stadium. A holy grail that the club had been seeking for most of my life.

Our full record as 2018–19 League 1 (old Division 3) Champions was:

Played 46, Won 27, Drew 13, Lost 6, Goals scored 90, Goals against 42, Goal difference + 42, Points 94.

We averaged league home gates of 9,514, our highest since the last top flight season in 1991–92.

We had sold out every home seat ticket available to purchase since Dec 2018.

Away from home we averaged 1,565 – the highest EVER in our history!

To complete this memorable season of all seasons, three nights later I attended the LTFC End of Season Dinner and as you might well imagine, it was the parties of all parties ending with myself joining in with a host of players and the lovely compere, Hatters supporting media celeb Faye Carruthers and her husband at the local Casino.

The final joyous occasion took place on May 31st (what would have been my 33rd wedding anniversary had I not been such a dick).

It was the wedding reception at a Newport Pagnell Hotel where I stayed overnight, of old Windsor Castle West Ham pal Rob Robinson, marrying his lovely Kim. I've obviously known Rob since those Windsor days in the late 1970s, but got to know him and Kim even more when seeing them regularly in Blackpool's brilliant Soul Suite club, at my many Adair

Travel trips. Rob's sister lives in Blackpool and they nearly ALWAYS book a visit to stay with her when the AT Luton posse hits the Golden Mile. Old WC mates Eamon Taaffe and Dave Ventris were on my table and Cali R DJ friends of Robbo's legendary Sid Hudson, provided the brilliant music.

A very sad picture. Sorry about the quality but it's the best I have. This is Larry Kinloch and wife Lynne at my 60th party in April 2018. He was my Best Man in 1986 and I his in 1982. Sadly that night was the last time I saw him, for just a few weeks later in June, he tragically died of a fatal heart attack. GBNF. Rest in Peace Larry my dear mate.

CHAPTER SEVEN

A SEASON THAT WOULD EVENTUALLY LITERALLY

CHANGE THE WORLD – COVID-19!

On May 2nd 2019 the 32nd Manager of Luton Town FC was appointed. Graeme Jones was an ex-Wigan top striker and had a good name in the coaching world, working with Roberto Martinez as coach to the Belgian national team, then at WBA – though according to social media Baggies fans did not like him and told us Hatters fans in no uncertain terms, we would not like his style of football, insisting on playing out from the back.

I'll be honest here, I thought we had a bit of a coup attracting the 2018 coach of a World Cup Semi Finalist to Luton. Only time would tell.

Evidently there were two or three previous unsuccessful attempts at enticing him to Luton for his first managerial job after Nathan Jones had done his GABO to Stoke. It appeared to be third/fourth time 'lucky' for us?

Despite Mick Harford and Steve Rutter doing a brilliant job in continuing and actually bettering Nathan's good work to see us win promotion as League 1 Champions, big Mick said all along he did not want the job full time and evidently the role Steve Rutter was offered at the club was only a bit part under Graeme Jones, who wanted his own staff – which turned into a mini army! So Steve left LTFC to move to a job in Greece.

A pity, as I believe Rutter made a big difference in his role at Luton and brought out the best in both Nathan Jones and big Mick.

Mick was more than happy to go out on a high (staying at the club back in his Chief Recruitment role) after in his words 'righting a wrong from 2008-09 when we were at our lowest ebb' he felt he let down Luton by not keeping us up in the minus 30 points 2008–09 fiasco season. Though every Luton fan will tell you Mick Harford owes LTFC nothing.

Before the new season began our first in the second tier since 2006–07 I attended a couple of social occasions. On June 22nd I spent the Saturday and Sunday with Larry Kinloch's family at his beloved mobile holiday home retreat in Cosgrove, Northants where he tragically died exactly a year previously. Many of Lol's family and good friends who he met and loved at Cosgrove joined us in a celebration of his life and remembering the good times. Yes there were tears, but there were many laughs too. I compiled a list of all the music tunes that meant so much to Larry and we played, danced, smiled and wept accordingly. This man will NEVER be forgotten.

A week later I joined old Stopsley pals Mick Knight, Chris McEvoy and their wives to celebrate the 2nd marriage of old Sportsman chum Keith Muddle. We attended both the Register Office service in Stevenage, then Reception in a private country village hall near Letchworth, where most of us including the Bride and Groom, stayed overnight in a

Letchworth Hotel. Lovely day, lovely night, lovely happy couple. As a result of that wedding both Laura and Keith, his brother Colin and wife and a few other couples at the Reception would book my next Adair Travel Blackpool trip in December.

The wedding was the day after James Justin left LTFC for Premiership Leicester City. JJ had been with us since he was seven, a Stopsley lad who went to Putteridge High School and was a good friend of James Higgs aka the 'Major', my good mate Bob Rumble's grandson.

JJ could easily have left us the year prior but wanted to stay to help Luton go up to the Championship, but knowing his dad Mick I was not in the least surprised. James left for an undisclosed fee to the Foxes but definitely a record one for LTFC, in the region of £7m (more than double our previous) as well as the natural add-ons that Gary Sweet so expertly manages to achieve for us – a certain amount for Premier appearances, percentage of any future transfer fee, England call up etc., etc.

JJ 'one of our own' was brilliant at Luton one of the finest home-produced Hatters of the last generation. He left having scored six goals in his 114 LTFC appearances and would always be welcomed home. Naturally, his father Mick would still watch his son play every game he could, Mick also insisted on keeping his Luton Season Ticket and would still watch the Hatters whenever he could. Testimony to the man and the Justin family.

As I write this in March 2021, James very sadly has just been seriously injured last month rupturing his anterior Cruciate ligaments and will miss the remainder of 2021. He was doing so well at Leicester having started every single game this campaign and was performing better than ever. So good, he was literally on the verge of his first England full squad call up. Let's hope JJ makes a complete full recovery.

I'm also really sorry to write that during 2020–21 we lost Mick Justin to Cancer at a way too young age. A terrible loss. RIP Mick.

In early July 2019 Mollie came home again (by herself) for another holiday until January because she was still homesick and missed her family so much, especially her Nan and Granddad, as well as Clyde of course.

There would naturally be numerous changes to the LTFC squad for this higher and far tougher level, as well as GJ wanting his own signings and departures. Although the second tier I believe as a club IS our proper level having spent the most years of our history in it (36 as I write) I'm also honest enough to realise the modern-day Championship is far greater a level than it once was. So many ex-Premiership clubs with their £m's parachute payments etc, and huge names like Cardiff, Fulham, Leeds, Derby, Nottm. Forest, WBA, etc. All clubs whose player wages dwarf ours. Our budget would easily be the lowest, as would our ground capacity of only 10,000 – of which we sold a record (capped) 7,000 season tickets! Until we move into Power Court, just to stay in this league would be a result in 2019–20, with a possible gradual increase in our league position slowly rising until we move in. If that can occur I for one will be ecstatic. Sadly, modern day football fans and social media Hatters – that might not be good enough for them?

Along with JJ, also leaving for big money (in Luton terms) would be the other full-back Jack Stacey, to Premiership Bournemouth for another undisclosed fee (thought to be in the region of £4m). He like JJ went with our best wishes and thanks after scoring five goals in 95 LTFC appearances. These two brilliant attacking full-backs would be nigh on impossible to replace but you cannot stand in the way of letting them secure their families future lives for mind blowing salaries.

Also saying farewell pre-, during and post-2019–20 were:

Luke Gambin, Alan McCormack (to Northampton after a great two years, albeit with niggling injuries and one brilliant goal in 59 Town appearances), Lua Lua (although he would change his mind in both summers of 2019 and 2020) in the January of 2020 we were sorry to see Alan Sheehan released (but understandable) following a superb four year spell for LTFC with eight goals – mostly screamers from set pieces – in 128 Hatters appearances. I was also sad to see youngster Frankie Musonda leave for Raith Rovers in Scotland. Frankie came through the ranks with JJ at a young age, but was never truly given a long enough spell in the first team to prove himself, making only 14 appearances in all those years. He's a lovely lad too.

Coming in under Graeme Jones, were a raft of free transfers and players out of contract.

This was mainly the way we had to do business in this league, with one massive exception (I'll come to that soon).

He signed full-backs Martin Crainie from Sheff United and young Brendon Galloway from Everton, Calum McManaman from Jones old club Wigan. Lua Lua changed his mind after his agent couldn't get him a better GABO elsewhere, Jacob Butterfield, Ryan Tunnicliffe, then in January promising highly rated youngster Peter Kioso from Hartlepool and back from Leeds after a brief spell with us once was Eunan O'Kane.

But the biggest story of the 2019 summer was our new unheard of Croatian Goalkeeper Simon Sluga – for a club record £1.35 million! – smashing the 30-year-old LTFC record £850,000 deal we paid for Lars Elstrup. I honestly thought I'd never live to see the day when Luton Town spent over £1m on a player.

For us this was big time and a stratosphere away from when we were losing 5–1 to Gateshead in the Conference just six years prior.

We also had various season-long loans in Luke Bolton from Man City, Aston Villa's James Bree, highly rated Izzy Brown from Chelsea and in January a key loan centre-half Cameron Carter-Vickers from Spurs.

I saw a couple of pre-season friendlies, ticking off another ground at Welwyn Garden City where we won 1–3 and a rather humiliating 1–5 home defeat to newly promoted Premiership side Norwich. That did ring a few shocking alarm bells for some.

The 2019–20 season in earnest began – with me missing Luton's first game (lightweight) at home to Middlesbrough! This was because I had prior booked with Duncan Angus from Kilsyth, seeing my second love Rangers play in Luxembourg, back at old nemesis Progres Niederkorn in the second leg of the Europa Cup Third Qualifying Round. No repeat embarrassment this time I'm pleased to write, as we drew 0–0 to progress (pun intended) to QR4 2–0 on aggregate. For the second year running Stevie Gerrard had managed Rangers through to the Group stages and did even better in 2019–20 by becoming the first ever club to not only qualify for the group stages (again) after all the qualifying rounds, but this time actually proceeding from their EL Group even further – into the last 16!

Little did I have any idea that this as I write in December 2021, was actually the last time I saw Rangers play live. Sad face emoji thing. TO DATE!

A fab trip of course, topped off with me pulling a 28-year-old local primary school French teacher in a bar. The fact we were both steaming was irrelevant – Adair still had it!

The reason I missed the Middlesbrough game was because it was moved to a Friday night for live Sky TV and I was still in Luxembourg Airport for kick off. I missed an absolute belter of a game in a 3–3 draw.

I kept checking updates on my phone in a topsy-turvy cracker. Skipper Sonny Bradley finally scored his first LTFC goal on his 51st appearance with an absolute screamer to equalise at 1–1. We then led 2–1 with new boy Martin Crainie scoring on his debut, then trailed 2–3 before James Collins opened his account at this higher level to make it 3–3 late on with his 46th LTFC goal on 85 mins.

So the first 2019–20 Luton game I saw in the Championship was at Cardiff's new stadium. I pre-booked an overnight city hotel for the Saturday and drove down mate Steve O'Dell who lived in Wales for donkeys years, early morning. We met up with his son Welsh Hatter Richard in a Wetherspoons and then post-match his two daughters would join us for a night out also. I have to write Cardiff is now a lovely city with fine folk and we had absolutely not an ounce of Welsh malice all weekend – that did not used to be the case once upon a time in the capital back in the day!

I must share with you what happened in the Wetherspoons pre-match. There was a large crowd of females next to us and I naturally started chatting to one of them. They were from Bristol and celebrating one of the girls 50th Birthday. When the lady asked what we were doing in Cardiff I told her we were Luton football fans here for the Cardiff match.

"Oh my husband is from Luton and supports the Hatters."

"Really, what's his name?"

"Jeff Stott-Everett," she says.

"OMG I KNOW JEFF! I met him at Yeovil a couple of years ago and got him a ticket for the game."

"Wait a minute Mary." I got out my phone and rang Jeff in front of her. "Hi Jeff, it's Alan Adair, I'm in Cardiff for the match."

"Oh hello Alan, yes my wife Mary is there too with a crowd of girls for a 50th."

"Wait a sec Jeff I can't hear you." Then proceeded to hand the phone over to Mary.

"Hello darling, it's ME." LOL – what a small world!

Brilliant and lovely lady too by the way.

AS for the match, it was a glorious sunny hot day watched by 24,724 including a great away following of 2,064 Hats. We played well against a side who had just been relegated from the Premiership.

After a goalless 1st half, Adam Flint then volleyed Cardiff into a 52nd minute lead. But on 86 mins we erupted when Matty Pearson headed in a well-deserved equaliser from a Luke Berry corner. But drama and heartache occurred in time added on.

On the last day of the transfer window the Bluebirds had signed ex-Hatter Isaac Vassell from Birmingham City. He came on as sub for his debut and you just knew he would score. In the bloody 96th minute he did just that, heading in their winner. We were pig sick gutted and did not deserve to lose. A harsh reality check, but evidence on that game we could compete, if this ex-Premiership side was anything to go by. Vassell is still at Cardiff as I write, but played only once more for them since that August 10th 2019 day.

We soon forgot about it though and the five of us had a wonderful night.

Three nights later I used my Diamond free ticket cup voucher to see Luton Reserves versus Ipswich Reserves. I hate the way these modern managers disrespect cup ties so much now, even third/fourth Division clubs are at it too. Graeme Jones made eleven changes. However an impressive (very) Izzy Brown made his Luton debut and was Man of the Match in a very good performance as Luton won 3–1.

The following Saturday we faced another relegated Premiership side, WBA at home. Despite Harry Cornick giving us a 1–0 half time lead with a fantastic diving header, Albion upped a gear in the second half to come back and win 1–2. This ended our unbeaten home league record of 28 games stretching back to March 2018 when Accrington Stanley beat us, also 1–2.

My first personal Luton second tier win since beating Sheff Wed 3–2 in February 2007, came at Oakwell, Barnsley. As per usual I drove Steve up on a glorious scorching hot day to join 1,173 other travelling Hats. What we witnessed in the first half was in my opinion the best Luton performance of all 2019–20, certainly the best away from home. Incredibly we were three goals up in the first 31 mins!

After just two minutes Jacob Butterfield scored what turned out to be his one and only LTFC goal in his 17 appearances. This was followed just 120 seconds later when James Collins made it 0–2 and the third was rifled home by Harry Cornick on 31 mins. We could not believe what we were seeing as the Town players went off to a rousing reception at half time from the ecstatic Hats. Barnsley won the second half 1–0. We were up and running. This was my first victory seen at Oakwell at the 6th attempt, since 1992.

It was back to Cardiff for Steve, his son Richard and I for another overnight stay, midweek four nights later for our League Cup second round tie.

Again, sweeping changes by both Graeme Jones and Neil Warnock, but those changes were oh so good for Town as we hammered the Bluebirds 0-3. Only 232 Hatters this time in a crowd of just 4,111 – over 20,000 less than the league fixture 18 days prior. I'm oh so glad we went.

We saw an opening Cardiff own goal just before half time, a trademark Alan Sheehan free kick (which turned out to be his eighth and final LTFC goal) and a rare extremely well taken Jake Jervis goal to finish Cardiff off.

On the last day of August we made it three wins in a row by beating another relegated Premiership side Huddersfield, 2–1 at the Kenny. We came from behind to equalise with a Collins penalty and when Andrew Shinnie netted the 66th minute winner, this turned out to be Shiniesta's 10th and final LTFC goal.

Six games played including two against relegated Premiership sides, two wins, a draw and two defeats. 15th place/24. Not a bad start at all.

Then three successive defeats. I missed a 3–2 loss at QPR (lightweight) in which we found ourselves 3–0 down after less than half an hour, then a somewhat unjust score-line of 0–3 at home versus Hull and another reserve side put out by GJ to see us thrashed 0–4 by a Brendan Rodgers Leicester team who at least respected the League Cup by fielding a strong side.

It was a nice welcome home for our James Justin. He made his Foxes debut and was quite rightly given a rousing reception when his name was announced. However, what happened when he actually scored against us shocked me. The sight of hundreds/thousands of Luton fans standing up and applauding his goal was both embarrassing and utterly cringeworthy. Yes I loved/love JJ but to actually cheer him scoring against us? – no sorry, modern football fans fucking suck!

It was at the end of September 2019 and immediately after a Blackpool weekender for Blackburn versus Luton, that for the first time since 1973–74 when I was a painter with dad living in Australia, I was about to start the latest chapter in my working career and to start a new job away from the Print trade – after over 45 years!

I started at a company called BBS (Bedford Body Shop) Fleet Logistics in Milton Earnest, near Bedford.

Very grateful for a successful interview at my age I would begin my new job on Monday Sept 30th 2019 as a vehicle Car/Van delivery/collection driver all over the UK from our me base.

The money is shite, Minimum Wage, Zero Hours Contract (meaning if there is no work on any given day, there is no pay) but there were some benefits I had not had for over 12 years.

At least I would now get holiday pay, accruing up to 28 days per year. But I absolutely love this job, especially getting to travel to all the different places nationwide, sometimes driving some lovely motors.

I remember on my first day a colleague by the name of Leo showing me the ropes and while we were out locally near Bromham, he took me to a mate of his who lived nearby – it was ex-Hatter Phil 'No Surrender' Gray! I was chuffed that both Phil and his lovely wife both remembered me. His wife was one of the hen party who sat next to me on the plane for my cousin Tim Hines's Stag Party in 2011 going to Tenerife.

Immediately before I started this new job I had another Blackpool weekender at the Claremont Hotel.

In 2019 the Choice Hotels Group which the Claremont is part of, decided on a trial year basis to have their All-Inclusive package extended to run for the entire calendar year. Unfortunately, this news came too late for me to organise an Adair Travel Group booking but Steve and I did stay, with me just driving up for Friday to Sunday.

We saw Luton play Blackburn at Ewood Park for the first time since a David Moss penalty beat Rovers in 1981. I'm delighted to write we won again, beating Blackburn 1–2 in pouring rain.

Sadly, this would be our last away victory for a long, long time.

After drawing 1–1 at home to Millwall next up was a drive to Pride Park, Derby. 2,606 travelling Hats including Steve and I saw our new record signing goalkeeper Simon Sluga have an absolute nightmare game.

On 11 minutes Matt Pearson scored an own goal but in no way was it his fault. He calmly passed the ball back to Sluga, but in rainy wet conditions our keeper decided to try and control the ball by trapping it with his fucking studs – the ball ran straight under them into an open net and Rams fans were pissing themselves with laughter! It became 2–0 and game over on 70 minutes and he was at fault for that one too. A cross from Lawrence was totally misjudged by Simon and went flying straight over him into the net. To compound the shite day, it took an age to get away from the ground and there was traffic mayhem with road accident closures and I didn't get home until near 10pm.

But I must write, the next game was a joy to behold to watch.

I once again took Paul Keating and Christine in the Bobbers Club and Oak Road. Pre-match in the Bobbers I introduced them to our captain Sonny Bradley's parents Angie and Ray.

We needed a boost as Town had now slipped to 18th/24. The three of us witnessed without a shadow of doubt, the finest home performance of the entire season against Bristol City, a side who had not lost on their travels yet in 2019–20.

We thrashed City 3–0 (our first league clean sheet of the campaign). This included a stunning Pelly opener and on top of that I also had a couple of quid on with cousin Ken Adair at 28/1, Luton to win 3–0. Happy day all round.

I missed a midweek 3–2 defeat at Fulham (no disgrace at that result) as I had a trip to Birmingham by train all booked with my Senior Railcard three days later.

I had prearranged to meet Blues Facebook pal Pete Bevins in his city centre match day local. A good time in there was had by all. I'm afraid my first St Andrews visit since 1993 saw the same 2–1 Blues result. Great Town support in non-stop rain from the 2,676 travelling Hats.

After a superb Harry Cornick equaliser on 67 minutes, we lost to a late 82nd minute goal that in truth, should not have stood as their scorer was all over our defender when heading in their winner. Que sera.

I remember having a great session at a pub next to New Street station before the train home. I missed two trains, such was the craic with a Wolves fan, long time Hatters mate Dave Fielding and his lovely wife Claire. It was so funny, the Wolves lad's girl said, "Isn't it great how football has changed for the better? 30/40 years ago you two would have probably been battling each other rather than having fun like now." She was bang on correct. In that respect Football IS far better now.

After losing a third successive time 1–2 at home to Nottm. Forest, I was off on the choo choo again to Reading using my senior railcard, this time with Phil Marlor. Pissed down all day and I'm afraid we saw the worst Town performance of the season to date. Luton lost 3–0, believe me it could/should have been far worse. Another great away turnout of 2,097 were let down. We all knew this league was going to be tough but the absolute minimum we Hatters fans demand – at the very least – is effort! That day at the Madejski – saw none from Luton!

We were now fourth from bottom and definitely in a relegation battle.

Before a fifth defeat in a row 1–2 at home to Leeds, I attended a happy event at the Venue 360 club, a dinner and speech organised for Luton legend 'God' Ricky Hill who was promoting his new book. A fantastic, delightful evening at the old Vauxhall Recreation Club. I was actually a touch nervous when meeting Ricky (and Brian Stein) and wondered if he would remember me? It had been a long time since the last time at Crawley Green Social Club in 2010. No such problem, upon meeting and greeting the guests it was, "AL, great to see you, you look brilliant and not changed a bit, maybe a touch less on the barnet?"

The bloke is just a GOD.

Sitting next to me was Rocky Baptiste, one of Ricky's lads when Town boss in 2000 who made three LTFC apps. Nice polite lad.

Our first win in six was much needed and came when we beat Charlton 2–1 at KR. We came from behind to an early seventh minute Addicks goal. Pelly equalised before Izzy Brown netted a 53rd minute winner, which turned out to be his only LTFC goal in the 28 appearances he made with us.

The next day Bob and Gary Rumble and I headed for Amsterdam for a two nights/three-day trip to see Rangers play their latest Europa Group stage game versus Feyenoord. We stayed in Amsterdam, as all of us had absolutely no chance of obtaining match tickets for the game in Rotterdam because Rangers FC (annoyingly) had decided when we returned to European Competition, that the Travel Club, of which I had been a paid-up member since it began in 2002, was now only allowing Season Ticket holders as members – therefore we had lost all the points accumulated over those years between 2002–12.

I booked us into the same Lancaster Hotel opposite Amsterdam Zoo that we had stayed in twice before for Rangers trips to Holland in 2002 and 2004.

The night before the match in the hotel bar when talking to the staff, we discovered the lad serving us was none other than the son of the previous owner from all those years ago – the Mick Hucknall Simply Red lookalike! On the day/night of the game we met old Luton Loyal mucker Gus Watson and his mate and all had a great session with hundreds of other ticketless Bears. We watched the match in a bar as Rangers played really well to draw 2–2. This was the fifth game of six in the group stages and after completing the group with a 1–1 Ibrox draw versus Young Boys of Berne, Rangers qualified for the last 32 stage by finishing second in the group a point behind Porto.

Steven Gerrard in his second season in charge had definitely made progress as manager, reaching his first Cup Final and especially progress in Europe. Not only reaching the Europa Group stages again after starting from the first qualifying rounds, but this season going further by qualifying from the group to reach the last 32. We were drawn against Braga from Portugal with the first leg at Ibrox in February.

Back from Amsterdam Friday night and hungover to fuck, there was no way I was going to Brentford the next day – by God I'm glad I didn't too!

I'm sorry to write we were hammered 7 (SEVEN) –0 at what was our last ever appearance at Griffin Park.

This was the final Brentford season there as they became one of the latest clubs with an impending move to a new stadium (just down the road off the A4). AFC Wimbledon were another, as they would move back to near their old Plough Lane abode on the old Greyhound stadium site. I digress.

This was the worst Luton defeat since 1966 when 2nd bottom Luton in Division Four, lost 8–1 at bottom side Lincoln – just two days after my very first Town game attended!

Some social media Luton fans were calling for the head of Graeme Jones already after this debacle, our sixth defeat in the last seven. There is no doubt any popularity he had was beginning to wane. His constant public put downs of 'little' Luton were not going down too well with us Hats. His recent post-match comment after the Nottingham Forest game was ludicrous, 'Little Luton cannot be expected to compete against the likes of Forest, twice ex-European Cup Champions' – FFS Graeme that was fucking over 40 YEARS ago!

The next week at home to Wigan was already becoming a must not lose match. After less than five minutes on the clock and trailing 0–1, the natives were starting to get restless. While there was no actual getting on the players backs, I sensed that all around me were not happy with G.J. With less than five minutes remaining and still 0–1 the heat was on. Substitute Callum McManaman then equalised against his old club to at least win us a point, only for another substitute George Moncur, to score his first goal of the season and a 93rd minute winner amid unbridled scenes of Hatters joy.

Wigan were one of only two clubs whose fans did not sell out the 1,000+ away allocation. They only had 667 fans in the Oak Road. Middlesbrough were the other club with 960 on the opening game, but that can be excused as it was a Friday night live Sky TV match.

The vital win versus the Latics lifted us up a place to 20th/24.

I'm afraid we were hammered 3–0 at Stoke a few nights later. The away form was now reaching alarming status.

My tenth Adair Travel Blackpool weekender occurred on Dec 13th–15th for our game at nearby Preston. We unluckily lost 2–1 at Deepdale but really should have had a draw at the very least when Harry Cornick through on goal, one on one with the keeper, failed to score. I'm afraid this was not the first or last time this happened with Harry. I do like him, but when in situations like this he can be poor.

In all my ten AT Blackpool trips this was only the second Luton defeat, a draw and seven wins the other results.

The day after we lost 0–1 at home to Swansea we had a lovely family pre-Christmas Sunday lunch at the Hansom Cab in Stopsley. Mollie expertly organised it all with the Adairs, Bavisters, Hineses and Roberts family all having a ball in the room we had exclusive use of.

On Boxing Day I watched a thriller of a match when we drew 3–3 at home to promotion contenders Fulham. Even though we dropped to 22nd/24 and now in a relegation place, I saw enough quality to know if we could just sort our wretched away form out, we could still survive in this league.

Two nights later I had a bit of an awkward personal situation as two good female friends both had their 50th birthday parties – on the same night!

So the answer of course was to attend both. I drove to Markyate Cricket Club for fellow Bobbers Club member and Adair Travel past traveller Sharon Hayward's big night then after a few hours, drove back to Barton, parked up then attended neighbour Debbie Norman's 50th at Barton Rovers FC. A great night had by all at both events. Though I'm sorry to write it didn't end too well for Shaz as in the wee small hours at her house, she fell (down the stairs I believe?) – and broke her ankle, FFS!

The day after and last game of 2019, I drove Steve to Bristol City. We met up at Ashton Gate with Bristol Hatter Jeff Stott-Everett. I'm afraid Luton were absolutely appalling, against a city side who were in very poor form themselves. City thrashed us 3–0. The only good part of the day was that pre-match in an early kick off, Rangers had won 1–2 at Celtic. Our first win at Porkheid in donkeys years.

I saw out 2019 with ex Deb and her sister Liz at a blinding New Year's Eve Cali R night in Dunstable. Little did any of us three know that would be the last one we would attend – for nearly two years!

The day after on New Year's Day I watched us live on Sky timidly lose 3–1 to Millwall at the New Den. A rare Sonny Bradley goal had given us a 0–1 lead but the Lions came back with a roar to easily beat us.

Next up was a welcome change of scenery from the relegation fight. The FA Cup Third Round had paired us up with Premiership Bournemouth away. I drove Steve down to what was only my fourth Dean Court visit and first since we lost 1–0 there in 1999.

We had a pleasant few drinks with some nice AFC Bournemouth fans after I managed to blag our way into a local Boscombe Conservative Club. Then I'm afraid we watched the Cherries hammer us 4–0, but it could have been oh so different.

It was only 1–0 up to 67 mins and we had a great chance to equalise with a penalty. The recalled Alan Sheehan was making only his seventh appearance of the season and stepped up to take the penalty. Sadly, he slipped as he took it and the ball came crashing off the crossbar. Nobody could guess at that time but it turned out to be Alan's 135th and final LTFC appearance. This fine talented player had been great for us in his four years at Luton, scoring eight goals, most of them from excellent set pieces. He left us at the end of January for Lincoln before moving to Northampton.

The next Saturday I missed us losing 1–2 at home to Birmingham because sometimes family has to come first and this was one such example. Mollie was finally going back to Sydney and I took her to Heathrow Airport for her flight. As I write this in December 2021, this is the last time (to date) I've actually been with/seen her personally.

The very next morning I took another of those shocking phone calls. This time from mate James Sellars to tell me that incredibly, one of his best friends and our mutual pal, as well as a friend to literally hundreds of Hatters, Nigel 'Santa' Martin – was dead!!!

I was in a state of shock as recent memories came flooding back of Larry and big Steve. Evidently Nigel had been to see a local music gig with one of his sons and they booked an overnight hotel stay. His son went down for Sunday breakfast, leaving Nige after not waking him, thinking he was still asleep. But when he returned he found him still not awake and the dreadful reality had set in, Santa was gone.

He had died sometime early a.m. of a sudden fatal heart attack, like Larry.

Aged just 63 Santa was one of, if not the most popular and well-known Luton fans there was in the modern era. He was known to so many because of his role with the football club, dressing up as Santa Claus and visiting numerous local children's wards in hospitals like the L&D and at Bedford. Nigel was the absolute double of Santa with his pure white long hair and beard. His enthusiasm and dedication, giving up much of his free time on countless occasions in helping sick young children get some happiness, knew no bounds and must not be underestimated how much he gave and helped little kiddies and their families.

He was a lovely soft, sensitive gentle soul who lived and breathed for his sons, Luton Town FC, his music, his religious faith, church and especially helping others.

This was a major, major shock and the tributes on social media ran into pages and pages. The impact of this man's loss was massive. His passing was felt by many, including the owners, players and all staff at LTFC.

Not many 'regular' supporters of a football clubs passing that I know of, would make the front page headline of local papers like the *Luton News* and *Bedfordshire Today*, as well as on local radio.

At the next home game versus Wayne Rooney's Derby County, the club would pay their deep respects by announcing the sad news pre-match and bringing out his two sons pre kick-off, then on the 25th minute (Christmas Day) a minutes applause, the likes of which I'd never heard so loud at Kenilworth Road in my life, when all four sides (and big credit to Derby fans too) stood up joining in, along with chants of 'Santa is a Hatter' – there wasn't a dry eye in the ground!

Nigel 'Santa' Martin you most certainly left your mark in life and will never ever be forgotten. RIP Santa.

The match, well it was almost like he had written the script. After a goalless first half, Wayne Rooney scored his first Derby goal to give the Rams a 0–1 lead just after the hour.

We then turned the game on its head with a Pelly equaliser four mins or so later, then Donervon Daniels headed a 73rd minute goal to put us 2–1 ahead. Ex-Hatter loan Chris Martin then cruelly equalised on 85 mins for 2–2. But just a minute later the Kenny erupted in scenes when a Bogle own goal gave Town our first win of 2020 and in nine games, since beating Wigan 2–1 on December 7th.

I bet Santa was beaming down grinning like a Cheshire Cat.

Four days later we lost our 12th successive away game, 2–0 at West Bromwich Albion, before a close 0–1 home defeat versus Cardiff.

The Bluebirds defeat came two days after Nigel's funeral in Milton Keynes.

His family understandably wanted a close private funeral, not wanting to in any way turn it into some kind of circus, as well as folks' good intentions were. It was their wish and was well respected.

I was both honoured and privileged to be asked if I would read an epitaph for Nigel at the gathering in his church's Christian Centre following the service at MK Crematorium. This was my third such one in recent years after Steve and Larry and I just about held it together for Nige. No more for a wee while though please.

Two nights before a much-needed weekend break away the next weekend, Luton had a narrow home 1–0 win versus Sheffield Wednesday. James Collins scored the only goal, with his 10th of the season.

Then a whole crowd of us had a brilliant Hartlepool weekender for the Middlesbrough match. I drove Steve and Phil Fensome up and joining us in the Pool were Hartlepool veterans Richie Harding, Phil O'Dell (no relation to Steve), Paul Clark, Tom and Poolie virgin Jesus.

Naturally, we also met up with Pool's great mate Greg Swinbourne and he would also join us going to Boro the next day.

We took the train to the local short distance for what was Luton's first appearance in Smoggyland since the very last game at Ayresome Park in 1995.

More Luton mates like Tony Bojko and Micky Dolan and Co met us in the town centre boozer for a right session. The thought of us Luton fans drinking in Boro pubs pre- or post-match, would have been simply unthinkable in the 1970s/80s/90s. But times have changed (for the better I might add) in that respect and us old gits now prefer to have a good drink with the locals rather than have to defend ourselves. It really is best that way.

On a howling windy/rainy day I took a cab to the Riverside Stadium for what was both LTFC's and my first ever visit. For me it was now different ground (old and current) number 225, number 168 old and new, seeing Luton play on and I'm delighted to write, my 114th different ground that I've seen Luton win on.

Not only did we stop the rot of 12 successive away defeats and our first victory on our travels since winning at Blackburn in September, but even the sometimes unpopular (unfairly in my opinion) Ryan Tunnicliffe, scored the only goal of the game to win it for us.

His first LTFC goal after 33 appearances and we were also now off the bottom as a result. A perfect weekend after the sadness of losing Nigel recently.

Our poor away form returned the next week when we lost 3–1 at Charlton just as we did the previous season.

I'm sorry to write, I received even more bad news from Kilsyth pal Duncan Angus on the Monday to inform me our mutual Rangers pal Tam Adams had suddenly died that morning. Another fatal sudden heart attack, yet just the day previous Tam was pictured on Facebook on a table with the Kilsyth/Kirky Bears at St Johnstone versus Rangers in Perth, all suited and booted enjoying corporate hospitality and looked a picture of health FFS! Tam was 67.

It was Tam who picked me up from Glasgow Airport when I first flew up in 1992 for Rangers 2–1 Scots Cup win versus Airdrie in 1992. That was when I first really got to know him, having been friends with his son Ian too.

We shared many fun times following Rangers both at home, in England and abroad after that. Tam was at my 60th party in Stopsley, Luton with his wife Liz, son Ian and of course Duncan/Rab and their partners. Little did I know that when I sat next to Tam at Ibrox for Rangers versus Livingston in Nov 2018, it would be the last time I'd see him alive.

I would try and do my utmost to get up to Scotland for Tam's funeral in March.

The night after Tam died I saw Luton versus Brentford and us gain a tiny bit of payback revenge against a Bees side who hammered us 7–0 at Griffin Park (the last time Luton ever played there as Brentford were the latest of many clubs to move to a new ground). In 2020 they would move down the road off the A4 into a 17,000 all seater.

We beat the Bees 2–1 to move off the bottom again and were now only four points off safety with 11 games remaining. There is no doubt things were indeed slowly improving under Graeme Jones and we still had a chance of survival.

Four days later on Sunday February 29th (this is the only time I've seen Luton play on a leap year date) we drew 1–1 at home to Stoke with a late, late, late 91st minute James Collins penalty equaliser.

We were lucky to get a point to be honest. Not one of the 10,070 in attendance (our highest home gate of the season) would have had any inkling that for the vast majority, this would be the last time most of us would see a live home Luton game at KR – for the rest of 2020!

The next weekend 1,312 Hats travelled to Wigan's DW Stadium and see a 0–0. Our first away draw all season and only the fourth in total.

Steve and I were once again in Blackpool at the All-Inclusive Claremont Hotel for yet another weekender there. This one was different though. We also met Jesus in Blackpool who was staying in another hotel. A great weekend still, but there is no doubt the word was spreading about a global worldwide new pandemic heading our way.

This was a virus that had originated in China. The virus was called Covid-19 or Coronavirus and was growing everywhere by the day it seemed. Everywhere we went that weekend was much quieter than usual, be it in the Hotel (only half full), the Blackpool pubs and even Soul Suite. It felt weird.

The disease had only started around December in Wuhan, China.

Nobody in the UK when we were in Blackpool/Wigan early March 2020, had any idea what the entire world was facing and very soon, for all of 2020 and as I'm writing this in June 2021 – we are still having to deal with.

The very first UK death of Covid-19 was registered in March 2020. As I'm writing this now, in Jan 2022 the death rate in our nation alone has reached a tragic and utterly staggering – over 150,000 deaths and worldwide over 5.6 million!!!

After arriving back from Blackpool and with Arsenal Manager Mikel Arteta being the first high profile football person to catch Covid-19, it was announced the following weekend's football had been called off indefinitely, until further notice because of the growing pandemic.

There were daily government briefings that the nation would soon be going into a full lockdown to try and prevent the spread of the virus.

More and more of the working population were starting to work from home but I was still working (a bit difficult to deliver/collect vehicles working in my house) and came up with a plan so I could make Tam Adams funeral on March 17th in Scotland.

My female office colleagues let me take home a Vauxhall Insignia on the Sunday. I then delivered the car on the Monday to Portobello Beach near Edinburgh. Tam's son Ian my good friend, collected me from the house and took me to the Coachman Hotel in Kilsyth, where I had pre-booked an overnight stay to make the funeral on Tuesday, as well as also pre booking a flight home from Edinburgh in the evening.

A sign that things were very serious was that I was able to book the one-way flight a mere couple of days prior for just £40 – usually if you can still get a seat at that late notice it's around the £250 mark.

The train and tram to the airport were half empty, the terminal had only a few dozen folk and I counted a total of 28 people on the Luton flight!

I made it back just, as a mere three days later it was announced by Prime Minister Boris Johnson the country would be entering a full lockdown with immediate effect. All pubs, restaurants, public places like swimming pools, gyms, hairdressers, obviously sporting arenas, schools would remain closed for the foreseeable future. The only people allowed to work were NHS key workers, supermarkets, chemists, carers etc. Schools would only remain open for the children of key workers and folk like myself, drivers who could not work from home.

But even that did not last long and from April I like most of the workforce in the UK, would be put on furlough leave. Meaning the Government would pay 80 per cent of your wages, with the company making up the other 20 per cent, but on a voluntary basis – BBS did not pay the 20 per cent!

The company started back as early as May/June, but because of my acute Arthritis health issues I was classed as high risk/vulnerable and had an official letter instructing me not to return to work until August.

All football was suspended until further notice.

On a much happier note, in early April Mollie and Lachlan announced their engagement and were wanting to marry in the UK in 2021 – obviously Covid-19 permitting! Which sadly has been proven impossible and they had to change their original March date to June, then even cancel that date – watch this space, alas it's not good news on that front!

Tragic news arrived on April 6th with the announcement of the death after a long illness of Raddy Antic. He of course will always be remembered by us Hats for that legendary 1983 goal at Maine Road.

Raddy was our first ever foreign signing in 1980 and went on to make 108 LTFC apps scoring 10 goals until he left in 1984. He also as a manager, was the only person to ever manage both Madrid clubs Athletico and Real – and Barcelona too! RIP Raddy.

There was major shocking news from Kenilworth Road on April 24th. LTFC announced that because of the Pandemic and a cost cutting measure, they parted with Graeme Jones and his mini army of background staff with immediate effect. To be honest there were not too many Hatters fans upset, but the announcement on May 28th of his replacement made local headline news – of startling proportions!

Ten days prior to that though the SPFL in their wisdom decided that all Scottish football would be curtailed and ended with immediate effect on a points per match basis.

The Scottish Premiership title would be awarded by Zoom to Celtic with nine games still remaining and yes, although Rangers were 13 points behind, had they won their game in hand and beat Celtic in the two remaining Old Firm fixtures, that gap could have been cut to four points and who knows? Hearts were relegated as a result of this scandal.

The whole thing stank to high heaven and it turned out Scotland was one of very few (if any) of the leagues in Europe to end it prematurely.

Oh, but the authorities merely 'suspended' the Scottish Cup Final until sometime in the next season (eventually December 2020) – nothing to do with Celtic being allowed to and wanting to complete a 4th successive treble of course!

I can guarantee had it been Rangers 13 points clear – the season would not have been ended early!

Back to my number one love. Luton announced the next manager as NATHAN JONES! Sensational stuff.

My take on this, was while I was at first not ecstatic at the news (in fact like many quite angry) after a bit of time to reflect it actually made a lot of sense. Nathan Jones still knew most of the team, most certainly knew the way the club operated and once he publicly apologised about the manner in which he left us for Stoke a year and a bit prior, then it made total sense.

I personally was prepared to forgive him after the apology, though certainly not forget and would definitely give him shite if there was any repeat of the badge kissing/shirt hugging pish.

I publicly stated on social media that if Nathan Jones could somehow turn a nine-point deficit around with nine games remaining and keep us in the second tier, he would have his slate wiped clean and in my eyes, be a hero. I think 90 per cent of Hats agreed. Sadly, there will always be a tiny few who will never forgive Nathan and in my honest opinion, they are the few who want him (and therefore Luton) to actually fail. Life is too short for such bitterness.

The football authorities decided that amid all sorts of testing of players and 'bubbles' etc the Premiership and Championship would resume with the final fixtures all to be played behind closed doors. Leagues One and Two would end with immediate effect and promotions/relegations controversially awarded aka SPFL, on a points per game basis. Leaving only the Play-off fixtures to occur. Some clubs like Peterborough were absolutely livid, while others like Wycombe who took their place in the Play-offs were ecstatic – and eventually even won promotion to the Championship as a result!

One of the few benefits of lockdown and not being allowed to attend games was that LTFC had decided that any of the clubs 7,000 Diamond or Season Ticket Holders who did not request a refund (only a very tiny few did) for the five home games missed, would be allowed free ifollow stream access (normally £10 per match) to not only watch all those five home matches live – but also the four away games too!

Our fabulous 2020 Board came up trumps yet again.

Football resumed on June 20th and the first of these free streams was at home to Preston. We drew 1–1 with Calum McManaman equalising on 87 minutes for a vital point, even though it was wins we now needed. This turned out to be Calum's fourth and final LTFC goal.

The next day I went to Larry Kinloch's house to share with Lynne and family, his memory on the second anniversary of his tragic sudden passing.

On the next Saturday (Mollie's 26th birthday) we had an incredible fantastic 0–1 away win at Swansea with James Collins heading in the only goal on 72 minutes.

Of course the original fixture on March 18th, Steve and I were pre-booked in the Grand Hotel (same hotel as my 1981 weekender with Mick Tearle, his June and Graham Baker) but Covid-19 put pay to that and my first Liberty Stadium visit is still awaiting (as I write).

Three nights later we faced the daunting task at Elland Road to face leaders Leeds Utd. what an incredible Luton performance to draw 1–1. Harry Cornick gave us a treat with an astounding 50th minute goal in the top corner of the net. This vital strike turned out to be his ninth and last goal of 2019–20. The draw was the absolute minimum we deserved.

It was after these two great away results that I truly actually started to believe – that Nathan Jones might actually pull this off!

So what happened next game? – Luton 0 Reading 5!!!!! We all then thought, 'No, we're doomed.' This was our heaviest home defeat since Sunderland tanked us by the same score in 2007. But it turned out to be the only defeat of NJ's 2019-20 homecoming.

But we only drew 1–1 at home to Barnsley next and were running out of games for a great escape with only four remaining.

There was no doubt, football played with no fans was both horrific and actually having an impact on games, with far more away victories occurring everywhere. The next match on Friday July 10th at Huddersfield was a classic example.

Nathan Jones had brought back players into his squad he knew and trusted, the likes of Luke Berry and Elliott Lee, who wasn't getting a look in and long since discarded under Graeme Jones. It worked an absolute treat as Luke Berry scored the goal versus Barnsley and against the Terriers second half goals from Sonny Bradley and Elliott Lee gave us an utterly brilliant performance and 0–2 away win. Now I truly was beginning to believe. Three games left. At home to QPR, then an absolutely crucial away must win at fellow strugglers Hull and ending at the Kenny versus Blackburn.

We drew at home 1–1 versus QPR after a James Collins penalty on 20 minutes gave us a lead, but we just could not hold out to get Nathan a first home win on his return. This meant that in almost reality we had to win our final two games.

We should have been having a weekend in Hull seeing our skipper Sonny Bradleys family there. By now I was very good friends with his parents Angie and Ray and their plan was to lay on a marquee on the Saturday for us Hatters they knew from the Bobbers Club.

But of course COVID-19 lockdown put paid to those plans.

Against the struggling Tigers who had not won a game for ages and were hammered 8 (eight) – 0 at Wigan just a few nights prior, we were the better side on the day and in the second half only one side looked like winning, that was us. James Collins and Danny Hylton both missed good chances as we poured forward and then Pelly curled an effort narrowly wide. We just could not score and it was looking like 0–0, which in near reality would send us both down. Kaz Lua Lua had come on as sub for Harry Cornick and looked lively as he often did when coming on as an impact sub.

With only five minutes left it then happened. Kaz found a way to fire in a fizzing strike low into the bottom corner of the net. I absolutely erupted at home watching it live on I follow and gave the dog a fright; lol. We saw it out to all but relegate the Tigers. Luton had lost just once in the eight games since Nathan Jones returned and only two of the last 14.

Everything came down to the last match as it so often has done in the past for LTFC.

The next day Barnsley were at home to Nottm.. Forest and if they didn't win they would almost certainly be joining Hull.

They did beat Forest (1–0) so the last game scenario on Wed July 22nd was an almost impossible one to work out. It was so tight that Luton could even stay up by losing at home to Blackburn – or go down if we won! Eight teams could still possibly be relegated.

Added to all this was that Wigan had been docked 12 points for entering Administration, but this would only apply if they finished in the bottom three, if not the points would be deducted in 2020–21.

The final night games that mattered to us happened as follows:

Bottom placed Hull on 45 points were at Cardiff and lost 3–0 – Relegated.

Second bottom Barnsley on 46 points incredibly won 1–2 at promotion seeking Brentford with a 90th minute winner to finish 21st – Survived.

Third bottom Luton came from a goal down versus Blackburn at home, to lead 3–1 with a James Collins penalty and two own goals, Rovers pulled one back. It finished 3–2 Town and because of other results and the Wigan situation, we finished 19th on 51 points above the bottom three and Barnsley and Birmingham – we survived, by coming out of the last three relegation places for the first time since December!

Wigan could only draw 1–1 at home to promotion chasing Fulham and as a result fell into the relegation zone, second bottom on 47 points after their 12-point deduction – Relegated.

The final relegated place went to Charlton on 48 points. Rumours abounded that ex-Leeds hero Lee Bowyer was hoping his old team would do him a favour as they were already up as Champions – no chance! the Addicks were thrashed 4–0 at Elland Road – Relegated.

This was the only time all season they had been in a relegation place. I like Charlton as a club and their fans, but after the arrogant Bowyer dismissed both us and Barnsley in February as already down – I was delighted he suffered the drop and we both survived! He also criticised his player Joe Aribo for transferring to Rangers, stating he lacked ambition moving to a two horse race in Scotland. Well as I write this I know Joe will have had no regrets moving to Ibrox.

Nathan had done it. As far as most non bitter Hatters were concerned, he was now totally forgiven for his past sin.

We finished 2019–20 in 19th place sixth from bottom, level with Huddersfield (seventh bottom) on 51 points.

Luton had 14 wins, 9 Draws and 23 defeats. Scored only 54 goals (only 4 teams scored less) and conceded a hefty 82 – only Hull with 87 had let in more!

*Pre COVID-19 lockdown LTFC had sold every available home area match ticket since December 2018. We had an average home league gate of 10,047 – the highest since 1990–91 when we were in the top flight Division 1.

Luton also had an away* league average of 1,628 – our highest ever!

LTFC now truly are back where we belong, in the second tier of English football. A division where we have spent the most seasons (36 and counting) in our entire 136-year history.

My pal of many years Keith McEvoy and I, celebrating Luton beating Watford 1-0 in April 2021. Because of COVID, fans were not allowed for most of 2020-21. But it didn't stop us attending and celebrating the win at our local in Barton the Waggon & Horses. This was the first time we had beaten the Foe since 2002 and first at Kenilworth Road incredibly – since 1993!

2020–21 – The Present, Here and Now *

In the extraordinary 2020 year of COVID-19 and while furloughed off work at home from April to July, four months with 80 per cent wages, literally the only times I went out socialising was on Mother's Day June 21st when restrictions had been eased a touch and a maximum up to six people were allowed to gather and mix outside. Kath Rumble kindly came over to Barton to pick me up and I joined her and Bob Rumble, along with Gary and Lois Rumble for a fun packed afternoon in Kath and Bob's garden in Stopsley. I had six cans of Guinness, literally my first drop of alcohol since Tam Adams' funeral in Kilsyth, Scotland on March 17th.

I also had a couple of nights out in July and August with the lads, Barton Curry Club neighbours at the Waggon and Horses pub and then the Passage to India Restaurant. My consumption of alcohol, including three cans of Guinness at home on New Year's Eve tuning in to the Cali R stream that Sid Hudson had kindly brought to our homes every weekend since lockdown began in March 2020, was a total of 19 pints in ten months! I've had more than that in a day/night session at some of my Blackpool Adair Travel trips!

I also drove over to Aylesbury, where Georgina now lived on August 8th for her 30th birthday celebrations (the next day) in her back garden. She originally booked the back function room at the Bull pub in Barton, but COVID-19 put paid to that – in fact, the Bull has still remained shut since March 2020! There is local talk it might never reopen which is sad as I personally think it's the best of our three village pubs.

Upon returning to work in August, it was so good to be back.

The next few months was actually the busiest period at BBS since I joined in Sept 2019. I was getting plenty of long hours, meaning of course earning more and certainly more than the previous four months shortfall.

As for the football front, there were serious (very) issues facing LTFC and all FL clubs that they had to address. With no fans allowed to attend nationwide because of Covid-19, the clubs could not survive for much longer on TV revenue alone. At Luton like at many other clubs, non-playing staff had been furloughed since March (but with LTFC choosing to also top up the Government 80 per cent furlough wages to 100 per cent) but of course Players/Directors etc. still had to be paid.

It soon became clear that without our vital 7,000 Season Ticket revenue, the club had a very real prospect of entering a 4th Administration in our history, at best. This time through no fault of their own at all.

The worst-case scenario – even face closure FFS! So it was the vast majority of those 7,000 ST Hatters that literally helped LTFC survive. The Players and Directors including the owner, all agreed (a tiny few players (no names) taking longer to agree than most) to take a 50 per cent wage referral for the foreseeable future. Once that had been publicly announced, over 95 per cent of season ticket holders renewed and those who couldn't/didn't – were replaced by the waiting list! I will not criticise any one person who didn't renew as their personal circumstances may well have dictated during COVID-19.

Despite the ongoing COVID-19 situation I did naturally renew, but I'm afraid could not justify (or afford) anymore the extra £150 Diamond package and so cancelled that.

Everybody knew there was no chance of attending football for the foreseeable future.

Some folk (possibly tight arses) questioned my sanity of forking out £400 knowing there was a real chance I might not be able to actually attend any games all season. The answer was simple. I did it to help save the Club I LOVE. If every Hatter took the logical (finance wise) decision – we possibly wouldn't have even had a club left!

At the end of 2019–20 there was the usual player comings and goings at LTFC. Jacob Butterfield and Calum McManaman had been released and both joined clubs in the Australian A League.

Luke Berry, Danny Hylton (I must write surprisingly, but then again he was always Nathan Jones pet favourite) Elliot Lee, Kaz Lua Lua and Glen Rea were all retained with various new contract offers. Glen Rea actually turned down a much better contract deal offered by Millwall to stay loyal to Luton – a rare occurrence in modern football!

We made four pre-season signings, securing James Bree from Aston Villa following his season long loan, defender Tom Lockyer from Charlton, Rhys Norrington-Davies on a season loan from Sheff Utd (though he would leave for Stoke in December having had a GABO) and midfielder Jordan Clark from Accrington Stanley, who I rated when seeing him play previously.

During the course of the season we also signed midfielder Joe Morrell from Bristol City in October, Gabriel Oshu from Reading on a free the next month In January, plus two key (very) signings came in.

Kal Naismith (who I really rated as a youngster at Rangers) and was then successful at Accrington Stanley, Portsmouth and Wigan and also young striker Elijah Adebayo from Walsall for an undisclosed fee, whose fans were gutted at him leaving.

Three other loans would arrive at Kenilworth Road during 2020–21.

In October we signed midfielder Kiernan Dewsbury-Hall for the season from Leicester and striker Sam Nombe from Milton Keynes. Then in February we signed the famous Tom Ince from Nathan Jones's old club Stoke.

Of all the new signings at Luton, the best was easily KDH – class personified, with a cultured, sweet left foot, possibly the best LTFC loan signing in the modern era? He was easily our Player of the Season for me.

Both Jordan Clark and Kal Naismith were exactly as I thought they would be, class signings. The other two, Nombe and Ince I'm afraid hardly appeared. Although Nombe has been a success on loan at Exeter in 2021

We loaned out a lot of youngsters during the season too. The highly rated full-back Peter Kioso signed from Hartlepool, was a success at both League two promoted Bolton and League one relegated Northampton on loan. Keeper Harry Isted was lent to Wealdstone, another real talent Josh Neufville went to Yeovil, along with Gabriel Oshu to Yeovil too before he went to Rochdale. Elliott Lee as I write, just played in the League one (old Division three) Play-off Final for Oxford, losing 1–0 to Blackpool.

In October Andrew Shinnie was loaned to Charlton then signed for the Addicks on a free transfer in February. I really liked Andrew as a player. Shienesta was great for LTFC in his time with us since 2017. A very popular player with both teammates and fans. I met the Scot (started at Rangers) on a few occasions and he was delightful company also. Andrew Shinnie most certainly played his part in our two successive promotions at Luton, making a total of 106 Hatters appearances and scoring 10 goals.

As I write this, Charlton announced Shinnie has left the Valley. Evidently when Lee Bowyer was in charge there (he left for Birmingham in 2021) and who signed him, he rated Shins, but their new manager didn't.

We started the season, naturally playing behind closed doors as Covid-19 was far from going away until new vaccines could prove to be successful. Four away pre-season friendlies took place with Luton winning them all, 0–3 at both Northampton, Wealdstone, 0–1 at Stevenage and 0–9 (nine) at Berkhamsted.

The actual Championship campaign commenced on Sept 12th at Oakwell, Barnsley.

For most of the season to follow and to enable players to have a proper summer break in 2021, most fixtures all season would be Sat/Sun – Tues/Wed with very few midweek breaks.

Part of the deal with Hatters fans renewing/buying LTFC season tickets was that we were allowed to watch ALL 23 league home games live, as well as all midweek away fixtures – free of charge (worth £10 per game) on the I follow stream. A great deal.

Despite this though and for financial (lack of) reasons only, I decided not to pay the £10 per game to watch Sat away fixtures, making do with Jeff Stelling or the BT football scores updates. I also cancelled my Sky Sports subscription as the new job, as much as I loved it, pays shite money. Minimum Wage. As a result it would mean missing out seeing Rangers play on Sky, but needs must etc, although I would be able to see any Gers Europa Cup matches screened on BT.

Of which, Rangers began their Europa Cup 20–21 campaign second qualifying round on Sept 17th. Because of Covid-19, the qualifying rounds in 2020–21 would only be one legged.

The previous season 2019–20, Rangers had done magnificently well to reach the last 16 of the Europa Cup, before finally going out to a crack Bayer Leverkusen side 4–1 on aggregate. This season we once again qualified for the group stages after winning 0–5 at Lincoln Red Imps in Gibraltar then impressive wins 0–4 at Dutch side Willem II and a fine 2–1 Ibrox win versus Turkish crack side Galatasaray. This was the third successive season Steven Gerrard had got us through to the group stages. Brilliant.

In the group stages not only did we reach the last 32 for the third time running, but actually topped the group impressively and stayed unbeaten. Wins at Standard Liege (0–2) including a sensational Kemar Roofe goal – from inside his own half! Aka Olly Lee versus Cambridge United in 2017, 1–0 at Ibrox versus Lech Poznan, two draws versus Benfica 3–3 in Lisbon and 2–2 at home, 3–2 in the return Ibrox leg versus Standard Liege and winning 0–2 in Poznan.

Brilliant Gers went through to face Belgians Royal Antwerp in the last 32 in February.

My first love got off to an absolute dream start – winning our first FOUR competitive fixtures! James Collins netted a hat-trick to knock out Norwich at the Kenny in the League Cup first round. He also scored the only goal at Barnsley in the first league game. Then Jordan Clark scored his first LTFC goal, heading in a 0–1 winner at Reading in the League Cup second round. Before a Wayne Rooney led Derby County lost 2–1 at K.R. with Clark scoring our 87th minute winner after ex-Hatter Jack Marriott had equalised Luke Berry's goal.

Under Nathan Jones' second homecoming, we had won 8, drew 4 and lost just once in his 13 games. He was now forgiven by all but the most bitter Hats.

We were actually in second place in the table at this early stage.

It really hit home just how much we were all missing not attending our football as our next two fixtures were proof in the pudding at exactly how much it was hurting – Man Utd at home in the League Cup third round and relegated from the Premiership WATFORD away!!

Just two years prior we were a full three tiers below our old foe and in 2014, light-years away in the Conference not knowing if we'd ever play them again. Yet here we were now, despite all their Premiership finances and £45 million potential relegation parachute payments (SO unfair) and they would get another £30m, and £15m if they didn't get promoted within three years! It's easy money for paying/rewarding failure.

Yet, we were now playing on a same second tier level at least on the pitch, if not off it.

Before the allotments trip though, Man U visited us under the lights. It was chosen for live Sky TV coverage and I watched it at fellow Hatter and neighbour Tim Norman's house. We gave United a hell of a game holding them to 0–0 until a needless penalty given away a minute before half time.

It was only when they brought on their three substitute big guns with us going close to an equaliser, that they scored twice more on 88 and 92 minutes. Even the United boss, Ole Gunnar Solskjaer, said 0–3 was unfair on Luton and flattered Man Utd.

Before Mata's 44th minute penalty Luton were honestly the better side and we were also equals until those late substitutions.

The fixture at W**ford had social media wind ups all week about how a mob of Luton MIG's were going to still travel and cause disruption, with one wag warning 'watch your Graham Taylor statue'. Incredibly, WFC took this as a real threat – and actually erected fencing around the statue! How gullible/naïve could you get?

There actually WAS a tiny crowd of Luton who did travel, but were turned back by old bill as soon as they entered into Watford.

The first local derby fixture since a 1–1 draw at Vicarage Road in 2006, saw a disappointing (very) Town performance as we lost our first league game of the season – shame it was against them! Our players just didn't perform or appear to know the magnitude of what it meant to us Hats.

Yet we oh so nearly even got a result. On 35 minutes James Collins smashed a sitter against the crossbar when in truth it looked easier and he should have scored. Had that gone in who knows? Instead, they went up the other end of the pitch and scored the only goal of the game.

April 17th – watch this space!

We won our next game easily enough beating Wycombe at home 2–0 including a beauty from Pelly Ruddock-M'Panzu and Elliot Lee finished off the Chairboys with what turned out to be his 30th and probably as I write, his final LTFC goal.

Town lost both our next two games 2–0. At home to Stoke and away at Millwall. We were never in either match in poor performances.

Then a great 0–1 win at Hillsborough beating Sheffield Wednesday with Pelly scoring the only goal on 74 mins to lift us up a place to 9/24.

After a 1-1 home draw versus Nottm Forest we were well beaten by a very good Brentford side 0-3. At the ten game stage of the season we put in our best away performance to date, winning 0–1 at Rotherham with James Collins once again netting the only goal. It was richly deserved, just a real pity that we were not allowed to attend Luton's first ever visit to the Millers new 'New York City' stadium.

An extremely good start had us win 5/10 games – three of those 0–1 away victories in Yorkshire at Barnsley, Sheffield Wed and Rotherham!

It was back up to West Yorkshire three days later to take on Huddersfield. George Moncur had put us 0–1 up on 21 minutes, but this time we had to settle for a 1–1 draw against the Terriers. It was our first away draw of 2020–21.

There followed two more draws (both 1–1) at home to Blackburn and Birmingham, Matty Pearson equalising against Blues with his first goal of the season.

What followed was described by Manager Nathan Jones as 'easily our worst result and performance of this campaign' getting hammered 4–0 at Nathan's boyhood idols Cardiff.

There was finally a tiny snippet of good news regarding Covid-19 in December. It was announced by the government that a tiny amount of supporters would be allowed to attend sporting events, amid stringent contingency rules. For our home game versus Norwich on December 2nd, a test situation would take place and 1,000 lucky Hatters would be chosen to attend at Kenilworth Road.

If all went smoothly, then 2,000 Hats would be allowed to the following home match versus Preston and future home fixtures versus Bournemouth, then Bristol City. But only if it proved successful and more importantly SAFE with no COVID-19 cases as a result.

The club had the difficult task choosing who of only 1,000, could be selected for the trial against the Canaries. It was decided (correctly in my honest opinion) the club would contact those Season Ticket holders with the longest history period, who knew KR and how these procedures would work best. Of those lucky enough to be chosen, family members in the same bubble could also attend, then for the next few home games if successful, the next 2,000 would be picked versus Preston, then Bournemouth, Bristol City etc. and move forward from there.

I was lucky enough and delighted to be one of the 'elite' fortunate 1,000, but was not for Preston. It was more than likely either Bournemouth, if not Bristol City would be my next game after Norwich.

Let me write, it truly was brilliant to be back at the Kenny after so long – over nine months to be precise, for what seemed like an eternity!

We were notified that all sorts of Covid-19 procedures had to take place to enable this test match to go ahead with 1,000 fans. All supporters would have to wear masks throughout the night, show proof you were chosen, collect your ticket in a named envelope from outside the ticket office.

My ticket was for the Kenilworth Upper stand, with literally us fans having our own row of seats in social distancing.

Even though only a total of 1,000 Hats were in the Kenny, Oak Road and David Preece stands, there was still a match atmosphere like no other behind closed doors. It was brilliant to attend my 1,894th LTFC match and the 1,230th at KR.

The players thrived off the crowd noise and defeated league leaders Norwich handsomely for the second time this season. It was the Canaries first loss in 11 games.

George Moncur opened the scoring after 15 minutes with a sweet right foot curler in off the Oak Road end post. But just four minutes later it was 1–1 when keeper James Shea, in for the injured Simon Sluga, was judged by referee Mr England to have fouled Placheta for a Norwich penalty. The excellent Buendia sent Shea the wrong way for their leveller. However, just three minutes later we restored our lead when Matty Pearson headed home from a Rhys Norrington-Davies cross. It would be Matty's second and last Town goal of the season, turning out to be his 10th and final LTFC goal too.

Within a minute into the second half we were off our seats at the Kenny end when Mr England awarded another penalty. This time (again a bit harsh in my honest opinion as was Norwich's penalty) it was for Hanley bringing down James Collins. I'll be honest if it were reverse roles I'd be fuming, but at that time it was a case of DILLIGAF.

Collo dispatched it for his fourth home goal of the season – all four against Norwich! A great win and it was so good to be back.

On the night we noticed captain Sonny Bradley was missing from the starting line-up and just assumed he was probably injured. Tragically he was not injured – but in mourning!

The next day while driving somewhere near Huddersfield in Yorkshire, I took a phone call from good mate Kevin Hawkes with shocking sad news – so bad that I had to quickly pull over!

Our mutual friend (Kev was much closer to him) Sonny's dad Ray Bradley, had unbelievably became yet another Covid-19 victim and had tragically died of it, aged just 57.

Kevin had been in constant touch throughout lockdown with Ray. It had only been until the very recent past that Ray's wife Angie told Kev, Ray was very poorly having contracted COVID-19 and was in hospital in a bad way. He very sadly died on the day of the Norwich match.

Everyone at the football club, Bobbers Club and all over social media mourned this absolutely lovely gentleman and family man Ray.

Kevin was the person responsible for bringing in Ray and Angie Bradley into the Bobbers Club pre-match when Sonny first joined us from Plymouth in 2018.

The Bradley family including Sonny's wife and other relations would soon become regulars in the Bobbers at every home game, preferring it in there with the fans, rather than in the more private player's lounge etc. They would sit with us and get to know most of the Bobbers Club folk. An extremely popular man, who was loved by all of us Hats and who were privileged to know him. I shall miss seeing him in the Bobbers, as well as at every away game cheering on his son. My heart went out to Angie and all the Bradley family at the loss of one of life's good guys. It was particularly saddening that the Bradley family were originally going to welcome us into their Hull home for our final away game of 2019–20, with intentions of a big marquee in their back garden. But of course Covid-19 put paid to that – as it did indeed cost Ray his life! I miss him.

RIP Ray Bradley.

The next two games both away from home, were scoreless, rather unfortunately losing 2–0 at Swansea and a really poor 0–0 spectacle at St Andrews where Coventry had shared Birmingham's ground for the past couple of seasons. I'm delighted to write that Coventry have recently announced they have finally come to an agreement with their Ricoh ground owners Wasps RFC and will be returning there to Coventry in 2021–22, having signed a 10-year minimum lease agreement. Great that Cov are back in Coventry – they should never have left Highfield Road!

We then had what was easily our best performance of the season to date, thrashing Preston 3–0 at home with James Collins netting another hat trick for measure. It was his first Championship treble for us and his fourth in total for LTFC to date. This was Nathan Jones exact 200th match in charge of Luton and his 100th Town win.

There is absolutely no doubt that even with just 2,000 Hatters at KR, the players thrived off the atmosphere.

Very sadly, this would turn out to be the last time fans were allowed into FL games for the remainder of 2020–21.

The next day was an enjoyable one as I joined great friends Paul Keating and his partner Christine for Sunday Lunch at the King William pub in Mangrove Green. They very kindly treated me, as we had such joy seeing each other for the first time since February.

Sadly, more utterly depressing news came through that Covid-19 was spiralling out of control again.

It was soon announced that supporters could no longer attend public events for the foreseeable future and that matches would have to resume behind closed doors again. The UK had to prepare for a third lockdown in the New Year 2021 as this pandemic was now beginning to threaten everybody.

After the brilliant Preston win we lost 1–0 at Middlesbrough, but it really should have been 1–1. James Collins took a penalty and levelled, only for the Boro players at Neil Warnock's insistence to hound the Ref and Linesman, convincing them that Collo's spot kick had somehow been touched twice as he kicked the ball. The goal was disallowed.

I couldn't help but think it was because of the influence and who Boro Manager Neil Warnock is.

We then played really well in holding relegated and promotion chasing Bournemouth to a 0–0 home draw. An entertaining game that Luton definitely deserved to win.

For the first time in my life I spent Christmas Dinner eating alone (well apart from Clyde naturally) But Deb and Georgina did come to visit on Christmas morning to exchange gifts. Deb's sister Liz who lived round the corner, very kindly dropped off a Christmas Turkey dinner with the trimmings at the doorstep. This lockdown was effecting many with all sorts of mental health problems nationally and no end in sight as the daily death toll began to rise again at an alarming rate. In January it would reach its utter peak as the NHS very nearly collapsed, being overwhelmed with an alarming death rate of then over one thousand deaths per day!!!

On Boxing Day we lost 2–1 at Reading with Lua Lua scoring his first goal of the season, but it came too late to make any difference. Then the last game of what had been a horrid 2020 year was at home to Bristol City. On Dec 29th we beat City 2–1 at the Kenny. KDH scoring the winner with his first LTFC goal.

On New Year's Eve I cracked open three cans of Guinness for my first alcoholic drink since August to see out the horrible year of 2020 by listening to the brilliant Soul sounds of Sid Hudson's excellent Cali R. Sid and Jacqui helped many, many peoples mental health with their Cali R streams every weekend during the entire lockdown period.

Happy New Year! – Things would surely only get better – wouldn't they!!!

The one bit of good news coming through the horizon was that the vaccinations progress were proving to be winning the fight against Covid-19 as jabs were soon to be announced and made available throughout 2021. We were to receive two jabs, the second twelve weeks after the first. Initially, the most vulnerable, over 80s, then NHS workers, carers etc., over 70s and high risk (me). I had my first jab on February 15th at the Rufus Centre in Flitwick, then the second one booked there for May 9th.

On January 2nd it was the 50th anniversary of the tragic Ibrox Disaster when 66 Rangers fans sadly perished on Stairway 13 at the Copland Road exit after a 1–1 Old Firm draw in 1971. On this day 50 years later Rangers continued their fine unbeaten league season with a 1–0 victory over our fierce rivals. A 70th min Callum McGregor own goal was enough to secure a second out of two Old Firm wins to date and keep up Rangers 100 per cent 2020-21 home league record.

Meanwhile that day, my first love were losing 0–2 at home rather tamely to another Rangers side QPR. Another game we would have really looked forward to – if allowed to attend!

In the FA Cup Third Round George Moncur scored the only goal of the game to knock out Reading. This meant we had now eliminated the Royals from both League and FA Cups.

We followed up that with an excellent 0–1 win at Dean Court, beating promotion chasing Bournemouth with KDS scoring the only goal on 67 minutes. It was well deserved too and now our fourth 0–1 away victory to lift us up to 12th place, exactly halfway in the table just after the halfway stage of the season.

Although not playing the brilliant free flowing football of some previous LTFC teams back in the day, it really didn't matter that we had scored only six away league goals at that stage. The fact is that with our bottom three budget, we were fighting WAY above our weight and with four 0–1 away wins already, Nathan Jones was doing a sterling job at Luton.

We faced another promotion chasing side Brentford four nights later at their new stadium. Gutted not to have been there as this would have been 1,000 per cent a game I'd have attended, but for Covid-19 lockdown.

Of which, that week commencing Jan 17th I had to be furloughed again for a second time due to me being classed as high risk because of the acute Arthritis condition I have.

There was good news on that front though.

At the end of January after nearly four years of weekly injecting a drug called Abatacept (with no great improvement sadly) I was given a new drug to take orally daily by the name of Baricitinib. The specialist told me this new, very expensive drug (I have to personally sign for it special home delivery) had a very good success rate with something like 85 per cent of RA patients stating their quality of life had rapidly improved taking it.

I was willing to try anything new after over 13 years of daily torment and have to write that even within a few days, I noticed a huge difference – just getting out of bed, but my walking even, dramatically improved beyond belief – with no more limp! I truly have felt like a new man since.

We then had three successive away games and although lost all three, we played well in each game.

Luton lost 1–0 at Brentford very unluckily as we were by far the better team, especially in the second half and did everything but score.

Their manager Thomas Frank even stated post-match that he couldn't wait for the final whistle and had it been a draw he'd have had no complaints. He said Luton were a quality side and the difference between that night and our very last appearance at Griffin Park in Nov 2019 when Luton lost 7–0 was like chalk and cheese!

Also around this time at the end of January came the news from Mollie in Sydney, that she had decided to not only call off her wedding in the UK to Lachlan, but to actually end the relationship and move out! To say I was stunned beyond belief was an understatement of epic proportions. Mollie had been with Lachlan for nearly 10 years, but she is my daughter and I have to respect her wishes and naturally will back and stand by her 100 per cent, even though I truly feel for Lachlan. She had her own reasons which will remain private and Mollie also didn't want it to be public knowledge at that time.

January 2021 it was possibly our worst month of the season results wise (Bournemouth away win apart).

We failed to score or win any of our other three league games that month, having lost 1–0 at Blackburn to an Armstrong late 85th minute goal just as it looked like we'd done enough for a deserved point.

Even after the Rovers goal Harry Cornick looked like he had scored his first goal of the season, only for it to be cruelly and harshly disallowed for offside by a late linesman's flag.

Sunday January 24th live on BBC 1, Luton did not disgrace themselves in any way, losing 3–1 at Chelsea's Stamford Bridge – with Simon Sluga also saving a penalty. It might have been SO different if Harry Cornick had not had a shot well saved to stop it being 2–2. Tom Lockyer then had a shot saved by Kepa in our best spell. But when Tammy Abrahams completed his hat trick with Chelsea's third on 74 minutes, that was it. 3–1.

This turned out to be Chelsea Manager Frank Lampard's last game in charge of the Blues, getting sacked the very next day.

The horrible pandemic has caused us to miss out on such great occasions such as our first local derby at the Allotments since 2006, Man Utd at home in the League Cup and now Chelsea at the Bridge in the FA Cup – of which I'm confident we'd have taken as many Hats there as our allocation would have allowed, 7/8,000?

The following week we drew 1–1 at home to Huddersfield with James Collins netting his first goal of 2021 giving us an 11th minute lead.

Unfortunately and not for the first time under Nathan Jones Part two, we sat back on 1–0 more and more as the game developed. This was getting a bit too regular for some of our social media warriors and they were in their element when the Terriers eventually equalised.

We actually needed to get a result at Birmingham just to avoid being sucked into around the relegation zone above. We were 15th/24 going to St Andrews (a ground we had not won at since 1986) our lowest position since Boxing Day.

But Nathan Jones has a habit of pulling out results just when we need them and this was no exception with our FIFTH 0–1 away league win. Dan Potts scoring the all-important 31st minute only goal, his one and only Luton goal of the season and only his 11th in seven seasons with us. This deserved (well) Town win gave us a bit of breathing space, before losing 0–2 at home disappointingly to Cardiff three nights later.

On the eve of that Cardiff match came some absolutely crushing news to the Adair family.

Our beloved pet Westie dog Clyde, who had been SUCH a huge part of all our lives, but especially mine living on my own, had to be taken to the Vets as Deb and Georgina had recently noticed Clyde had lumps under his throat and rear legs. The Round Green Vets did tests and X-rays on Clyde and told us we'd have the results by the end of the week, but prepare ourselves – as the Vet thought it could well be Lymphoma Cancer!

On the Friday Deb rang me with the results and it was the worst. I was totally devastated and wept buckets of tears that weekend having little or no sleep. So upset, I never even joined in with the Cali R that night or could be bothered to watch a terrible 3–0 Luton performance and defeat at Stoke the next day. Football and other things meant absolutely fuck all to me that weekend.

We asked the Vet how long left we had with Clyde, but she refused to give an answer as she genuinely did not know how long Clyde's lumps had been there. I looked it up on the internet and it stated that with treatment, he could last until maybe 10 months from diagnosis.

But there was no way at just over 14, we were putting Clyde through any operations /chemotherapy.

Without treatment – it said 1 to 2 months! So we all decided there and then after the weekend to enjoy what time we had left with Clyde and give him even more love and affection than he had received all his life.

I must write that had it not been for those lumps, you would not know there was anything wrong with him, he was still lively, loved his walks so it was no change and so the dreaded act and ultimately correct decision – until he, A) stopped eating, B) didn't want to walk anymore or, C) was in any pain whatsoever. Although I did have to slowly reduce the portion size of his breakfast/dinner as he was now beginning to throw them up if I was giving him too large dinner portions.

Rangers in the last 32 of the Europa Cup had two incredible high scoring ties with Belgian side Royal Antwerp. We won the first away leg 3–4 and then a stunning 5–2 win at Ibrox to send us through 9–5 on aggregate and reach the last 16 for a second successive season. Rangers would face Czech side Slavia Prague in March, a team that very impressively had just knocked out Leicester – watch this space!

After the 3–0 Stoke debacle, we drew 1–1 at home to Millwall. This was another game where we had played really well and were well on top against the Lions. The young striker recently signed from Walsall Elijah Adebayo, scored his first LTFC goal on 55 mins but in a repeat of the Huddersfield game (only even more so) it was clear Luton had settled for 1–0 again with us cruising the game and in no danger at all. But Nathan Jones cocked up in my honest opinion by going too cautious with his substitutions.

He replaced the excellent Joe Morell with Glen Rea, then Collins and Cornick on for KDH and Adebayo. We were clearly time wasting in the last 20 mins and at LEAST six mins extra time was added on at 90 mins by referee Mr Scott. It came as no surprise at all when Millwall equalised on 95 mins. In my honest opinion Nathan did cock up here, but some of the social media stick he took – was way OTT! For the first time since his return and leading up to the next match – NJ was actually getting some stick FFS!

We saw out February with an incredible game against Sheffield Wednesday at the Kenny. Make no mistake had we lost this match some would have had their knives out for Nathan Jones. Unfortunately, we have a few 'supporters' who can just NEVER forgive/forget Nathan for the manner in which he left us for Stoke. They need to get a life.

It is no exaggeration to write that in the first half we were totally abysmal, trailing lowly Owls 0–2 at half time, with ex-Rangers player Dean Windass netting both goals and truth be known, had Wednesday been four or five goals up we could not have complained.

Pre-match, we had slipped down to 17th/24 our lowest league position all season and in real danger of getting sucked into a relegation battle. The social media nutters were out in force at half time, absolutely crucifying Nathan Jones and Luton.

But whatever Nathan said during the break, or put in the players drinks – most certainly worked! His substitutions also this time worked and deserves huge credit for them. This was Nathan's 'Sliding Doors' 2020–21 LTFC moment as he made triple half time substitutions, bringing on Rea, Pelly and Cornick for Cranie, Morell and Paul Ince, as well as changing formation and reverting back to his trusted diamond shape. This turned out to be Joe Morrell's 11th and last LTFC appearance. Despite being a full Welsh International and playing a role at the EURO 2020 finals in the summer, he clearly was never settled at Luton under Nathan Jones and would move on to Portsmouth pre-2021-22.

We came out second half a totally different side. Recent signing Kal Naismith reduced the deficit on 50 mins with his first LTFC goal.

But when even the much (unjustified in my opinion) panned Ryan Tunnicliffe equalised on 58 minutes with his first ever Luton goal at the Kenny and only his second in 58 LTFC apps at the time, the social media Keyboard warriors were all of a sudden – shutting right the fuck up!

Sheff Wed after total first half domination were now shell shocked and in freefall. Their fans watching on ifollow could not believe what they were seeing, a team who should have been out of sight at half, were now level and there only looked one winner – who were in ORANGE!

We completed a truly amazing comeback to win 3–2 with Elijah Adebayo majestically rising up like a salmon to power home a brilliant 86th minute headed winner.

This was the first time we had come back from 0–2 down at half time to win in the FL – since beating Sheff Wed 3-2 in May 2004!

Things got even better three nights later when Ryan Tunnicliffe scored again for the only goal on 64 minutes at Nottm Forest following a lovely enticing Pelly cross. This turned out to be Ryan's 3rd and last LTFC goal. It was our sixth away league win of the season – all of them 0–1! Also the end of another jinx, with us winning at the City Ground for the first time since I saw Ricky Hill score the only goal there in 1983.

We had only scored a total of seven away league goals to date, but had six great 0–1 victories on the road – to date!

Four days later we lost 3–0 at leaders Norwich, a score line that flattered the Canaries in all honesty. Had James Collins not hit the post early on when it looked easier to score and make it 0–1 – who knows how it might have turned out?

We then lost again to an early 3rd minute Swansea goal at the Kenny in another match in which we played well, dominating but as was often the case in this 2020–21 season, failed to put the ball in the onion bag.

Rangers had been a touch fortunate to get a 1–1 draw away in Prague versus Slavia, but we took the vital away goal with pleasure and looked forward to the second leg.

I'm afraid that turned into a disaster, losing 0–2 at Ibrox and also having two players sent off. Don't get me wrong the Slavia side were definitely the better team over both legs and deservedly went through – but their Joe C**T of a player Kudela disgustingly went out of his way, covering his mouth to then racially abuse our Glen Kamara (a milder, gentler person you could not find).

Amid all the hoo-ha, UEFA did their usual bottle job by banning Kudela for a pitiful 10 games and Kamara for three matches because of his alleged 'revenge' in the tunnel at FT – of which I can't comment on because of an ongoing investigation by Police Scotland.

The racist pigs at both the club and their supporters, then went into overdrive in denial on social media. I must be honest it shocked me as when I went to with Rangers in 2002 I found both the city and its Prague citizens wonderful folk.

But Rangers were very happy in other matters as just two days before the first leg in Prague, we had successfully won a 55th Scottish League title, but equally importantly – stopping Celtic from achieving their 'Terry Munro' (10* in a row)! A magnificent achievement by Steven Ge55ard in what let's be totally honest here – Celtic FC and their fans quest was all they had sung and gone on about since 2012!

Wonderful. Glasgow was truly BLUE again.

Back to my first love, we then had a most welcome two victories to Nil.

A 2–0 midweek home win versus Coventry, with James Bree scoring not only his first LTFC goal, but his only ever professional CAREER goal to date also. An Adebayo penalty three minutes before HT made sure of the three points and almost certain safety in the Championship with 10 games still left.

We made it an incredible 7th 0–1 away win with an historical victory at Deepdale, Preston.

James Collins's 83rd minute header was deflected into the net and credited as an own goal by their keeper Daniel Iverson. It was our first win at Preston since January 8th 1972 when Alan Slough, RIP, scored a screamer.

How uncanny that just two days later came the very sad news that Alan had passed away aged 73 following a long heroic battle against Parkinson's Disease. I was particularly saddened at this, having personally known many of the Slough family, including one of his brothers Bob and sister Jane, who is married to ex-Roydon Printers work colleague and mate Ian Bealey.

I was a junior member aged 10–11 of the Alan Slough fan club, having us kids attend his 21st house Birthday celebrations and also the church wedding of Anne and Alan, dressed in our full White and Black LTFC kits in the late 1960s. Alan was also a pupil (with Bruce Rioch) at the same Stopsley High (then Secondary Modern) School as myself.

In his eight seasons with us from 1965–73 Alan scored 32 goals in 312 Hatters appearances. He left to join ex-Town boss Alec Stock, RIP, at Fulham and was captain of their 1975 FA Cup Final side who lost 2–0 to West Ham.

I am proud to write that our beloved LTFC played their part and stepped up the mark, by providing a Luton white shirt for Alan's son to wear at his funeral. RIP Alan Slough.

On the dreaded Covid-19 front after a horrific spread in January when over 1,000 people a day were dying, some good news was finally happening. A first easing of restrictions happened on March 29th when groups of up to Six were able to meet up outside, as well as in pubs/restaurants – so long as you were outside. To celebrate on that Bank Holiday Monday, repeating their Father's Day treat from June, great friends Bob and Kath Rumble kindly picked me up and we joined Gary Rumble and Sally Hattle in the Rumble back garden for liquid celebrations and a fun afternoon. I enjoyed several cans of Guinness, my first alcoholic drinks since New Year's Eve.

I was also delighted to be able to finally return to work for BBS from April 1st after being furloughed twice – for a total of over SIX MONTHS FFS!

It's ok that you're getting paid 80 per cent for doing fuck all, but that 20 per cent difference (plus other hours on top I used to work) was having a big impact on me financially and I needed to return full time – as well as for the state of my mental health! Though I appreciate, I was far from alone in that situation.

Not for the first or last time, Luton had an awful Easter. Losing 2–0 at Derby and 1–2 at home to Barnsley, where we only truly started to play and make a game of it in the last 10 mins.

Five days later we faced bottom side Wycombe away.

The day before that I was driving in Birmingham when news was announced of the death of HRH Prince Philip, Duke of Edinburgh, RIP. He reached a grand age of 99, being the Royalist I am, was saddened at hearing the news.

There was a tiny bit of pressure on us for the Wycombe game for a couple of reasons. Having lost four of our previous six games and with seven games remaining, we were still in a very healthy 13th/24 position but not yet mathematically safe. Wycombe after a dreadful start to life in their first ever season in the second tier, were now starting to have a bit of belief. They were getting some results and had won their previous two matches. There was also added on pressure to us – having never lost at Adams Park in 14 clashes since 1996!

We had also not lost three successive league games since Nathan Jones returned. If we did versus Wycombe and lose our unbeaten record at A.P., there definitely would have been a certain amount of pressure on us.

In fact during Nathan's entire time in charge at Luton, we have only lost three in a row once, losing to Accrington Stanley, Stevenage and Barnet back in March/April 2016 when he first joined.

We did not want to give Wycombe Wanderers any remote hope of catching us.

Pre-match a national two minutes' silence in honour of Prince Philip was observed.

I'm afraid the first half saw a woeful Luton display, fortunate to only be 1–0 down following a 37th minute penalty after Kal Naismith had clumsily brought down Muskwe with a clear foul.

I'd like to write the game changed in the second half when NJ made the necessary substitutions at half time and on 54 minutes he replaced Tunnicliffe, Berry and Pearson for KDH, Harry Cornick and Kaz Lua Lua and although they did make a difference to our play as we upped our performance, truth be told the REAL turning point came on both 57 and 76 minutes.

Wycombe's Josh Knight was shown a straight red card by referee Mr Langford for a bad challenge on Jordan Clark, though I have to write it looked far worse to the naked eye in normal time, than when seeing it again. But of course (mercifully) there is no hated VAR in the FL.

From that moment onwards (though we were the better side from 45–57 minutes), it was one way traffic after the dismissal, but still 1–0.

The key moment came when NJ replaced Matty Pearson for George Moncur.

It was only the second time Moncur had played any part since January. I like George and he is very popular with us Hats fans, but it is clear he is not one of Nathan Jones favourite players. It also has to be stated that his two previous managers at Luton and Barnsley, also appeared not to rate him enough to regularly start games. George has an abundance of skill, but it's a mystery why certain managers just do not 'fancy' him.

Within just four minutes of him coming on he scored a terrific 25-yard free kick low into the bottom corner to equalise. We now had the ascendency.

On 85 minutes Kaz Lua Lua gave us a 1–2 lead with an excellent curled effort into the top corner of the net at the end which Luton fans would have been at but for COVID-19. It was only his second goal of the season.

Kaz appears to be another player who is not a NJ favourite. These actually turned out to be both George Moncur (11th) and Kaz Lua Lua's (8th) final LTFC career goals.

To round off a wonderful final 10 minutes of the game, Elijah Adebayo, from a great Harry Cornick cross, rose majestically aka Matt Tees, RIP 1969, to head home our third.

This EIGHTH away league victory was now the first time we had scored more than one goal on our travels – this entire season! But it was also the first time we had come back from 1–0 down to win 1–3 away since Sheffield Utd at Brammall Lane – in 1994!!!

A new FL record had also occurred with this 14th unbeaten away league game (+ one FA Cup tie) at Wycombe Wanderers. The best such record in all four English tiers.

On the same day in Scotland the SPFL announced a two minutes silence for Prince Philip at all their games pre-kick off too.

At Celtic Park versus Livingston, not only did the club refuse to fly their flags at half-mast (no great surprise there to be honest) but when the silence began, within 20 seconds loud fireworks were set off by a group of Celtic fans outside Parkhead – they were set off from these dicks standing in a fucking cemetery! It is no wonder I and so many others despise this club and many of their supporters. Slowly, but surely, the rest of the UK is beginning to suss out and are aware more and more of what that club and its fans are all about.

Prince Philip's funeral took place on Saturday April 17th. As a mark of respect all football matches that day had either early lunchtime or evening kick offs to avoid clashing with the funeral at Windsor Castle.

It was a mightily important football weekend, with both of my loves having local derbies. Luton versus Watford on the Saturday and the next day in the Scottish Cup at Ibrox, Rangers versus Celtic.

We hosted our first Kenilworth Road derby since Jan 2nd 2006 and it was eagerly anticipated. Just such a shame we were not allowed in to attend it.

The foe were flying high in second place and on the brink of a straight return to the Premiership. To be brutally honest, with a first season parachute payment of £45 million (+ a further £30m and £15m for two more seasons if they did not get promoted) reward for failing to survive top flight football – so they fucking should be!

That morning I took Clyde for a haircut, knowing it would probably be (and sadly WAS) his last one.

I honestly would have taken beating Watford and losing our last remaining five games, not knowing when we might play them again?

Then on Sunday at Ibrox was the latest Old Firm clash in the Scottish Cup. Celtic had only two chances left this season in this final month of 2020–21 to:

A) beat Rangers for the first time this campaign.

B) Stop Rangers winning a double and

C) soon in the SPL have their final chance to prevent Rangers remaining unbeaten in the entire league season.

Well the two derby weekend results both went to perfection.

We beat Watford with a thoroughly deserved 1–0 victory. It was a truly super Town performance in which we dominated throughout, but had to wait until the 78th minute for our glorious moment and the breakthrough. Their keeper Bachmann brought down Elijah Adebayo for a blatant penalty. Elijah had to leave the field such was the extent of his injury, to be replaced by Substitute James Collins. With his first touch of the ball after an age in delaying stalling tactics by Shitford, Collo scored his 12th goal of the season. As far as we Hats were concerned it was the most important James Collins LTFC goal of the 72 he scored in his entire Town career!

In a frantic final 10 minutes plus, Watford finally woke up and had a go. But their Femenia was sent off on 88 minutes for his second yellow and then right at the death – Watford scored!

To make matters worse it was substitute and ex-Hatters hero Andre Gray who scored it – no bloody 'muted' goal celebrations from him either! He disappointed me with that to be honest.

But seeing the linesman flag him for offside was both a relief, then an almighty celebration. This win mattered so much to us Hats.

It was our first against the foe since beating them 1–2 in the 2002 League Cup tie at the Allotments, but incredibly – our first derby win at Kenilworth Road since the opening day of season 1993–94!

Even the most ardent Hornet on social media that night, all agreed Luton were the better team and we deserved the win.

I then watched the funeral of HRH Prince Philip. One thing is certain, this country certainly knows how to 'do' pomp correctly. It was both wonderful and very moving. I then had to go out and celebrate our win. So had my first drink since March 29th and for the first time since August 2020, my first pub visit.

Since March 29th pubs were allowed to open provided you sat outside in groups of no more than six. When I arrived my old mucker and fellow Barton resident Keith McEvoy was there. I naturally joined him to sink a few pints of Guinness as we celebrated beating the enemy big time.

The weekend was rounded off perfectly with Rangers knocking Celtic out of the Scottish Cup. Also a 1–0 victory with veteran Steve Davis netting a spectacular only goal with an overhead kick.

But on that very evening came a news announcement that would shake the football world to a core.

The so called 'big six' English clubs: Man City, Man Utd, Liverpool, Chelsea, Arsenal and Tottenham (how the fuck are Spurs classed as one of the big six with just TWO trophies (FA Cup and League Cup) in the last near 40 years and no top flight title – since 1961 FFS! – all announced they were leaving English football immediately to set up a new European Super League along with Juventus, Athletico and Real Madrid, Barcelona, Inter and AC Milan.

It would be a league – with no relegation! This was all about money and sheer greed, with zero consultation with any of the clubs' supporters.

Well they made a huge mistake in underestimating the power of English football fans. There was an immediate outrage by the six English clubs' fans – as well as the Premiership, UEFA and FIFA. With the threat of immediate expulsion from the Champions League/Europa Cup, but mostly the sheer outrage by clubs' fans, who threatened to boycott their clubs, refusing to buy season tickets, merchandise etc. – within just TWO days the ESL was dead on its feet and all over before it even began.

One by one every English club withdrew after pressure by their supporters.

Our next game was an entertaining 0–0 home draw versus Reading. Then on Sunday April 25th, history occurred at Ashton Gate, Bristol City.

50 years ago on Good Friday 1971, Luton had led 0–2 at HT and went on to lose the game 3–2. This time the exact roles were reversed.

In what was a poor (extremely) first half Town showing, we trailed 2–0 at half time a score line that actually flattered us. It really looked like Bristol City were easily heading for their first win in eight games. For the second half Nathan Jones had replaced Ryan Tunnicliffe with Harry Cornick and James Collins came on for Kaz Lua Lua.

A minute before the hour Collo scored his 13th goal of the season to reduce the deficit. Nobody had any idea at the time that this would be his 72nd and last LTFC career goal.

Then Elijah Adebayo equalised on 68 minutes with his fifth Town goal in 13 appearances. Both our goals were set up by player of the season and Leicester season long loanee, the magnificent Kiernan Dewsbury-Hall.

But the icing on the cake came on 74 minutes when Harry Cornick scored what proved to be our 2–3 winner – incredibly, it was Harry's FIRST and only goal of 2020–21! having made 39 apps (11 coming on as sub).

This was a first Luton victory at Ashton Gate since Enoch Showunmi scored our 1–2 winner in December 2004.

The historical side to this brilliant victory was that this was the first time (certainly post-WW2) that we had come back from trailing 2–0 at half time away from home, to win 2–3 in a league match.

We had previously twice away, come back from losing 2–0 at half time to win, but the scores were 3–4 at Cambridge in the Conference 2009 and also 3–4 (Joe Payne hat-trick) division two at Gigg Lane, Bury – in 1938!

This brilliant result lifted Town up a place to 11th/24, our highest position since mid-December with just three games remaining.

On May 1st we made it five league games unbeaten (easily our best run of the season) by drawing 1–1 at home to Middlesbrough. A fair result in which Glen Rea put us ahead on 19 minutes only for Boro to equalise a mere 120 seconds later via the head of Duncan Whatmore.

To be honest it came from a cross that Simon Sluga really should have dealt with. Sluga is a good keeper who had a much better second season at Luton after failing to settle early on in 2019–20 and made a host of errors.

But his weakness is definitely not dealing with crosses. He really does have a tendency to stay on his line.

Luton really should have won this though as on 73 minutes, KDH was fouled by McNair for a penalty. This after we were denied a more obviously blatant pen when Adebayo was tripped, only for the hopeless referee Mr Simpson not to give it, as he had denied Elijah ANY decision all game.

Up stepped James Collins who was having a (very) poor game and had his penalty saved. He also had a penalty goal ruled out at the away fixture versus Boro when adjudged to have struck the ball twice when scoring from it.

In the end though Middlesbrough might have even won it, but for a George Smith effort deflecting off our crossbar.

With just two games remaining we lay exactly halfway 12th/24.

The very next day my second love Rangers completed our Old Firm dominance over Celtic by thrashing them 4–1 at Ibrox Park. We had played them five times this season, winning four (including a Scottish Cup tie) and drawing one.

Two nights later came Luton's penultimate game of 2020–21 and our final Kenilworth Road fixture, a rearranged game at home to struggling Rotherham who needed at least a point, but preferably three in their relegation battle. How lovely it was that on this rare occasion we could relax with no fear. It has to be written though, Luton played with respect for other clubs against the Millers and although it ended 0–0, this was no end of season stroll.

Week commencing May 3rd was a harrowing time for my family. Our darling beloved wee Westie dog Clyde, was now very suddenly starting to go downhill rapidly. He had still been walking (all be it a bit slower mainly down to his 14+ years age) and still eating without any apparent pain. But the four of us all immediately agreed when Clyde was diagnosed with lymphoma cancer in February, that when he stopped doing any of those above – the correct humane decision would have to be made!

Tuesday was when Clyde stopped eating his food. We all agreed to book him into the Vets for Saturday morning to discuss exactly when the moment we had all been dreading was the right time to do it.

On the Tuesday night while watching Luton versus Rotherham. All of a sudden football truly was not all that important to me at that moment in time.

By Wednesday Clyde did not want to walk and we now agreed that Clyde would need to be put to sleep on Saturday – not just to discuss as to when!

But his condition rapidly worsened on Thursday May 6th. By the time I arrived home from work early, poor Clyde was now lying on Mollie's bedroom floor – shaking!

My niece Lauren had been in at lunchtime to let him into the garden, but she had to carry him there.

The sight of Clyde upon my arrival was destroying me and I had to act immediately. I rang Deb and Georgina to tell them to get over as quickly as possible because we NEEDED to put Clyde out of any pain on the NIGHT now, rather than wait for Saturday. I managed to book an immediate emergency euthanasia at the nearby Barton Vets for 6.30 p.m.. Deb was on her way and Georgina coming from Aylesbury, would meet us straight in the Vets Car Park.

Due to COVID-19 restrictions, only one person could be with Clyde when he was to be put to sleep, but mercifully they also had a rule that if the weather was ok up to three people could be with him, in the car park.

I had now been comforting Clyde the best I could by putting him in his bed, brought him down to the lounge and constantly giving him the love and affection HE had given us all his entire life. When Deb arrived, by now Clyde was having convulsions, it was truly horrible to see.

We drove to the Vets, he had another convulsion in the car. When we arrived I immediately ran to the Reception and pleaded for a vet to come out and end any discomfort/pain Clyde was in. I had turned my phone to silent in reception. Unbeknown to me, Deb had frantically been ringing me.

They promised a vet would be with us in minutes to inspect and inject Clyde. But tragically, when I was in Reception Clyde had one last fatal convulsion and died right in front of Debbie as she was comforting him.

I came back to the most awful of sights.

The vet had rushed out and arrived and took Clyde out of the car in his bed – at this very point Georgina had arrived at 18.28!

Having checked Clyde's pulse, the Vet confirmed what we already knew – our beloved wee darling Clyde was gone! I do take some comfort in that Clyde went in HIS time when he was ready and not by an injection being put to sleep, as well at least that when he took his very last breath, he was not alone and was with someone (Deb) who adored him.

The three of us wept buckets of tears as he lay there peacefully (FFS I'm crying my eyes out again writing this over four weeks later) but I have to write, the image of Clyde lying there in his bed dead – will go with me to my grave!

The entire Adair family was utterly distraught and broken-hearted.

We had lost such a character who was loved and adored by all, but none more so than Mollie in Australia – we had bought Clyde for her in 2007–08 when he was just a fluff of a white ball puppy!

It was the middle of the night and too early to tell Mollie in Sydney, it was imperative that we informed her before announcing to anyone else.

We all knew the dreaded moment had been coming since he was diagnosed in February, but I was astounded at just how quickly Clyde had deteriorated, a matter of mere days. Not even a week prior, while although Clyde had slowed down with his walking/eating etc., he still had his energy. IMHO the Tues/Wed/Thurs Clyde knew he was ready to go, but waited until either myself/Deb/Georgina was there with him before his final goodbye and go to Rainbow Bridge.

I am writing this a few weeks after his passing and although still raw, time is a good healer and I am beginning to get used to no Clyde, slowly but surely. For ages after he left us I could still feel his presence all around the house, but going for my daily walks is the most difficult, that's when I still constantly think of him.

I shall miss this bundle of fun excitingly running down the stairs to greet me with his little tail wagging and barking ten to the dozen. He lived with me for his 14 and a half years, the majority of that time just the two of us.

We have lost a unique character who gave us all undying unconditional love and such bliss/joy. He was the glue that kept the Adair family together. We are going to miss him enormously. As I write this, there is absolutely no way in the world I can go through this again and will definitely not have another dog. Therefore Clyde will be the first and last Adair family pet dog.

Since writing this, we have had Clyde cremated on his own and Georgina has created his own little Clyde's Corner in the kitchen. There lies his ashes in a beautiful urn, a plant that Georgina bought with his blue name collar tag and a couple of his white feathers with the plant, as well as the most truly heart wrenching, but amazing Westie condolence card sent from Mollie.

RIP our darling wee Clyde.

Luton completed the season at QPR on May 8th. Coming just two days after Clyde dying, I just didn't have the heart to watch it – nor be involved in the Cali R live stream on the Friday!

For the record we lost 3–1, our first defeat in seven games.

2020–21 turned out to be a magnificent campaign for LTFC.

In this weird full Covid-19 season where most football fans have not attended games, I was at least lucky enough to be one of the fortunate 1,000 Hatters selected to see us beat the eventual Champions Norwich 3–1 on Dec 2nd.

We ended 2020–21 in 12th/24 place.

Played 46, Won 17, Drew 11, Lost 18, Goals scored 41, Goals conceded 52, Goal Difference minus 11 and with 62 points.

This was our highest FL finish since 2005–06 in the Championship second tier when we ended in 10th place.

It has been a campaign that has exceeded WAY and beyond all but the most bitter or blind faith Luton fans dreams. To finish halfway in the second tier of English football with our tiny, miniscule budget in comparison with nearly all the other Championship clubs, is exceptional and a major achievement.

The only possible minus? Is that we didn't maybe score enough goals. The 41 we did score was our lowest at this level since scoring just 40 in a 1995–96 relegation season under Terry Westley/Lennie Lawrence.

Just eight seasons ago we finished 7th/24 in the FIFTH tier Football Conference – the lowest finish in our entire 136-year history!

We have now risen exactly 66 places up the football pyramid since 2013 and have improved our league position season on season, with the exception of 2015–16 when we ended up 11th/24 in the 4th tier, League 2.

Huge credit must go to the LTFC 2020 Board, manager Nathan Jones and his staff, naturally the Players, but especially LTFC legend Micky Harford, for having the vision and foresight to convince the 2020 Board to bury any hatchet in the spring of 2020, talk to Nathan Jones and bring him back to a club he knows. A club that NJ saved from almost certain relegation in 2019–20 and now to finish 12th/24 in 2020–21.

But none of this would have been able to occur without the magnificent loyal support of us Luton fans. We renewed/sold out our maximum 7,000 Season Tickets (with a waiting list too) all paying out despite knowing there was a good chance of the vast majority not being able to actually attend games during 2020–21.

Without that unwavering support where the vast majority also waived their rights to any season ticket refunds for missing the final five home games of 2019–20, we may well have suffered FAR worse consequences and in my honest opinion, would have struggled financially to compete.

By renewing with absolutely vital essential revenue, we were in a position to at least compete – albeit at a disadvantage to most other Championship clubs.

Cap well and truly doffed fellow Hatters.

We also finished with a fantastic NINE away league victories (the first seven winning 0–1) our most in the second tier since that brilliant 1981–82 division two title winning campaign, when we also won nine on the road then.

The season end has seen departures and retained list of Hatters players.

Significant exits at the end of their contracts are: James Collins with 72 goals in 183 LTFC appearances. Collo now only has 12 players above him in LTFC history who have scored more Town goals than him.

He leaves for Cardiff City with our grateful thanks and best wishes. Bluebirds manager Mick McCarthy, gave Collo his Ireland full international debut when in charge of the men in green. As I write this in early Dec 2021 – he has only just recently scored his first goal for Cardiff!

Defender Matty Pearson also exercised his right to leave at the end of his contract, by signing for Huddersfield and doubling his wage. Matty scored 10 goals in 136 LTFC appearances.

It was no great surprise either to see both George Moncur and Kaz Lua released too. Both players were very popular with us Hatters supporters, but clearly not enough for NJ. George made 59 LTFC apps, scoring 11 goals including that memorable free kick in 2019 at home to Portsmouth in the 3–2 Town thriller.

Kaz Lua Lua must also never be forgotten for playing his part, with eight goals in 87 LTFC apps. One of those goals at Hull in 2020 was definitely his most important one in a Luton shirt.

Pelly Ruddock M'Panzu surprised many Hatters by signing a new contract with Luton when it appeared and was reported, he had evidently received an offer from another Championship club – allegedly offering him an extra 7k a week wages! He is definitely our Marmite player. Many Luton fans idolise him and think he is brilliant & makes us tick – but more than a few Hatters think he is nowhere near good enough for the Championship. They say he can't tackle, has too many passes go astray and would be happy for him to move on. I personally am in the middle, but would prefer him to be a Luton player than not.

Ryan Tunnicliffe however turned down our contract offer and moved to 3rd tier Portsmouth.

We sadly have to accept that until Luton are in Power Court, we cannot compete with Championship clubs paying WAY over £10,000 a week to players.

Definitely signing new deals are Dan Potts and captain Sonny Bradley.

As for my second love Rangers, this has been a season to remember forever, with all sorts of brilliant achievements, most notably winning our first SPL title since 2010–11 and a record breaking 55th in total.

This was the first and only objective with Celtic's Terry Munro (10* (*9.75) titles in a row).

Some critics of Rangers have criticised Steven Ge55ard for 'only' winning one trophy out of nine in his three seasons to date. But 99.99 per cent will take with pleasure, he won THE title that mattered and stopped their holy grail – one that their fans and media had been banging on about and singing non-stop since 2012!

In Rangers two final league games we won 0–3 at Livingston to remain undefeated away from home, dropping just 12 points in six draws on our travels and after thrashing Aberdeen 4–0 have now won – EVERY single 2020–21 league game at Ibrox with a perfect 100 per cent 19 wins out of 19!

Also once again finishing in the last 16 of the Europa Cup.

A major achievement, even if being knocked out of both domestic cups by St Mirren and St Johnstone, left a wee touch of 'if only'?

The final 2020–21 SPL title standings make good reading:

Played 38, Won 32, Drew 6, Lost NIL, Goals scored 92, Goals conceded just 13, Goal Difference plus 79!, Points 102.

There were records set by equalling 26 clean sheets in any campaign and a new record of conceding just 13 league goals.

As for my first love, in all my 55+ years of supporting Luton I have experienced many, many highs and sadly many lows too. Pre-2021-22 I have seen a total of 1,894 Luton matches, of which attending 1,230 of those at Kenilworth Road. Of all those matches attended: 813 were Luton wins, 493 draws and 588 defeats.

I do wonder when and who will be our very last opponents for our final game at our beloved (but decrepit and antiquated) Kenilworth Road.

As I go to press in the winter of 2021 we have been told that officially we will hopefully play our first home game at Power Court some time in 2024-25?

Hopefully God willing, I shall still be around to see the last KR game and first at PC.

Of the 664 LTFC away games I've attended since 1968 (at W**ford), they have been on 168 different grounds old and new and of those, I've seen 114 Luton victories.

Of the CURRENT 92 Premiership/FL grounds, I have seen a game at 80 of them. Only Arsenal and Milton Keynes of those, not seeing Luton play.

Only twice have I seen Luton play abroad. Dunkirk (Battle of Part 2) in 1975 and Genoa, Anglo Italian Cup 1995.

Among the many, many highs I can choose from following Luton since 1966 are:

Championship winning seasons 1967–68 Division 4, 1981–82 Division 2, 2004–05 League 1 (old Division 3), 2013–14 Conference and 2018–19 League 1 (old Division 3). As well as other promotions as Runner Up in 1969–70 Division 3, 1973–74 Division 2, 2001–02 Division 3 (old Division 4) and 2017–18 League 2 (old Division 4).

Great Division 1 relegation last day escapes at Maine Road, Man City in 1983 and Derby's Baseball Ground 1990.

2009 JPT Trophy Wembley win versus Scunthorpe in front of 42,000 Hatters fans is right up there too, along with Conference side Luton creating history by becoming the first non-league club to win at a Premiership ground in the FA Cup, (since equalled by Lincoln winning at Burnley) 0–1 at Norwich in the 2013 FA Cup 4th Round.

But there can only be one numero uno high – My all time favourite LTFC occasion simply HAS to be April 24th 1988, League Cup Final at Wembley, Arsenal 2 Luton 3, to give us still to date, our only ever major honour and in front of the biggest crowd I'll ever attend watching the Town – 95,732.

The lows – there are many of those too. We must always have to take the lows with the highs:

FA Cup Semi Final heartaches from 1985, 1988 and 1994 – though the last two were frankly deserved!

Relegations in 1975, 1992, 1996, 2001, 07,08 and the minus 30 points fiasco of 2008–09.

100 per cent Play Off campaign failures in 1997, 2010, 2011, 2012 and 2017.

Losing 0–4 at home to W**ford in that 1997 game. Losing at home to Stevenage, a local side who I fondly used to look out for their results as I did Barton Rovers, Dunstable and Hitchin. Losing to Braintree four times, losing at home to Hyde, losing out on a return to the FL in 2011 via a penalty shoot-out at the Etihad in Manchester versus AFC Wimbledon.

But I still think my all time LTFC nadir is on April 6th 2013 at Carlisle's Brunton Park ground in front of just 382 (126 Mad Hats) – Gateshead 5 Luton 1.

My final piece writing this third publication, is that I have been a total idiot many times in my life and if I could turn the clock back I would have changed some of my many fuck ups. I will write though, that the good times do far outweigh the bad, a bit similar to LTFC's fortunes.

I like to think I'm a decent bloke in the main, possibly a bit too loud/ maybe too outspoken/opinionated for some, but one who has never intentionally hurt any one person and has nearly always tried to look on the good side of folk – and life in general.

One thing is absolutely 100 per cent certain and that is how proud I am of my two daughters Georgina and Mollie. All of their lives they have never given me any trouble. Many people have told me they are an absolute credit to both Deb and myself, along with the name Adair too. That is good enough for me.

It is therefore to both of them – that I dedicate this book!

COME ON YOU HATTERS – AND GERS!

FOOTNOTE

Since sending the Publisher this 3rd updated version and receiving the initial proofs to edit in the summer of 2021 – more drama came into the life of Alan Adair!

On Saturday July 10th I attended my first night out in Luton town centre since pre-lockdown prior to March 2020. It was for the COVID-delayed 50th Birthday party of mate Ian Warboys. Originally going to be held at the Crawley Green Social Club, Ian had to cancel and moved it to this date, while only being allowed to hold it outside in the Brewery Tap pub back garden due to ongoing restrictions then.

A fabulous night with many old school Hatters lads (& lasses) there, I continued after the party for a drunken completion at Luton Casino, before old Windsor Castle pal Eamon Taaffe put me in a cab to get me home to Barton.

I'm sorry to write - but there was an extremely heavy personal price to pay for attending the party!

Having been so careful during this entire COVID pandemic, always wearing a mask in public places like shops, buses, trains etc., at work in the office, in the vehicles I was delivering/collecting to/from clients, being double vaccinated in Feb & May, as a result of entering the Brewery Tap - I was pinged on Tues July 13th by my NHS App to inform me that as a result of being in contact with someone who had tested COVID Positive, I must self-isolate for 8 days. It could only have been at the garden party as the Tap was the only place I had applied my NHS app to in the months of June/July.

To cut a very long story as short as possible, despite being double jabbed I tested COVID positive at home on the Thursday and had the same result from the official test at Luton Airport on Sat July 17th.

With a worsening condition by the time Sat July 24th arrived and me feeling very ill – Deb & Georgina rang NHS COVID 111 and I was admitted by ambulance to the Luton & Dunstable Hospital COVID Ward 11, where I remained until they told me I was fit to go home (I didn't feel like I was) on the Tuesday afternoon.

By the next Saturday July 31st I was feeling so ill – my bed on the Thurs/Fri literally soaking wet with sweat, that Deb & Georgina this time had to ring 999 as they were extremely concerned I was getting worse by the hour. I was taken by ambulance again to the L& D Saturday pm, only this time admitted into Intensive Care Unit ASAP. I was in there until the Tuesday night before being moved back to COVID Ward 11 – but this time in a side ward on my own 24/7 with no visitors allowed (same for all the Covid wards, to be fair) and the only time allowed out of my room was to go to the toilet next door in the mornings.

During the Doctor's round on Wed morning I was told a few startling things. I was informed that not only did I have COVID & Pneumonia – but had also been the only patient in the L&D with a Legionella bug! Hence the reason I was in a side ward on my own. They told me a few more startling details, like any one of the three illnesses could have proven fatal and that had I not been A) double vaccinated & B) not admitted into Intensive Care on the

Saturday – I certainly would have died that July 31st night!!

Christ, when Adair is ill – I am ill!

The first two hospital spells lasted a total of 19 days before I was released again on Aug 16th.

Everybody in the medical team was intrigued to know where I could have caught the Legionella from and it was only when Georgina sent me a news report that Thameslink Trains had traces of Legionella found in the toilet areas on four of their trains – I was on the Thameslink Brighton train on my last day at work and the Tuesday before. It could only be there that I caught it from.

Within a week although the Legionella had gone during my 2nd hospital stay, I was back in for a third time on Aug 23rd because of ongoing breathlessness issues. Although the Covid had also officially gone, it had left me with scarred lung tissue that caused me to catch a Bacterial chest infection.

Released on the Friday night Aug 27th when my oxygen levels were at the minimum rate they should be (96) I came home again.

I can honestly write that it was only week commencing Sept 6th before I started to feel comfortable and I was beginning to actually feel like I was slightly improving. Before then I secretly wondered if I'd ever get back to 'normal'.

Here I am now nearly a month later definitely on the mend, to the point that if the Doctor at the L&D agrees when I see him on Oct 15th – I will be allowed to return to work on Monday Oct 18th – nearly a full 3 months since I last worked!

Well it is now December I'm writing this and the specialists did agree my return to work on Oct 18th and touch wood – I'm still delivering/collecting vehicles now.

There is no doubt this has been a nightmare harrowing ordeal, one I wouldn't wish on my worst enemy. To be told I actually could easily have died hits home and there is no doubt, this warning/scare is going to make me change my lifestyle when I'm eventually fully back to 'normal'.

Moderation is now the name of the game and key to my new life.

My final piece on this COVID etc. ordeal is this: A massive Thank You goes out to my dear friend of 35-plus years, Jane Hopkins.

She organised (eventually, as at first I was totally uncomfortable with the idea – until realising pride doesn't pay the Mortgage and Bills etc.) a crowdfunding page, to try and help me financially. The truth is, end of December was my first full wage at BBS - since the end of July!

Those wonderful friends, family & even strangers, who rallied to the cause know who they are and know how grateful I am for their help. I am utterly 100% convinced Jane and their actions gave me the mental strength in the recovery process. I also must importantly stress that Deb & my girls would never have seen me struggle either.

Sadly though, I have to write that not everybody was happy at the crowdfund page.

On one of the LTFC fans forums recently (called Outlaws) I was informed and looked to see that I had received horrific, vile personal abuse by more than a few Trolls. So shocked and upset, that I barely slept a wink that night – now I knew how Internet trolls can send so many folk over the edge!

This particular forum allows anyone to register, but only having user names. Leaving them free to abuse folk without knowing who the Trolls actually are. I probably even personally know some of them – boy I'd like to find out who & look forward to 'meeting' up one day!

Well they did not, nor never will destroy me and my last words to them is: GIRFUY's. They were at the abuse again in the first weekend of December when I ran my 11th ADAIR Travel Blackpool trip for our match at Bloomfield Road and are STILL at it, making even worse vile accusations/lies against my name and character. I also have no doubt they will again when this 3rd book is published. I don't see why I feel the need to defend myself when I haven't done anything wrong, but one of the many abuse messages was 'no doubt that's his Blackpool trip in Dec now all paid for with the crowdfunding' – when just for the record the actual truth is I had paid in full before I even fucking had COVID!

On a much happier note and the main subject matter of this 3rd and final book of mine, Luton Town FC.

We have started 2021-22 well and at this just past half-way point after 27 league games as I write, stand in a very respectable 10th/24 position. I'm more than happy with this and will be pleased if we end up there on May 7th. Sept 18th was when I finally attended my first Luton game since beating Norwich 3-1 at the Kenny on Dec 2nd 2020 – and only my 2nd game attended since 7/3/2020!

I couldn't have wished for a better opening 1st half. On 25 mins we led 3-0 against Swansea, playing scintillating football. But of course this IS Luton and the Swans came back strongly in the second half to draw 3-3. This is only the 4th time I've ever seen Luton blow a three-goal lead – 1992 at Cambridge Utd 3-3, 2000 at home v Wrexham 3-4 and 2009 FA Cup home v Rochdale 3-3. We did also lead 0-3 at Stamford Bridge in 1991, only for Chelsea to come back and draw 3-3 but I missed that one.

My 2nd game was SENSATIONAL – AND against my jinx team Coventry! There would be no adding to the Sky Blues' 16 wins I've seen against us – as we destroyed them 5-0!!!!!

The last time we won 5-0 at this level was v Barnsley at home 28 years prior in 1993.

This was easily our best display since returning to our rightful 2nd tier place in 2019.

5-0 flattered Cov, who I might add have made a great start to the campaign. In fact had they beaten us they could have gone top.

Every single one of Town's starting 11 and even the Subs were on their game. In fact Elijah Adebayo, James Bree, Jordan Clark, Harry Cornick and Glen Rea – all had their best ever LTFC game to date! IMHO.

Next up was a home 0-0 draw v Huddersfield 3 days later in non-stop rain. The same starting eleven were the better side 1st half when Amari Bell hit the post and a fresher Terriers side were the better team 2nd half. Definitely a fair result.

We had a fabulous 0-2 win at Millwall and 2-2 draw away to Derby following this, before I saw us narrowly beat Hull 1-0 to rise to the heights of 5th place! I drove buddies Steve Odell and Bob Rumble to finally see my 665th and first Luton away game since March 7th 2020 at Wigan. Sadly we were shite and lost 2-0 at Deepdale v Preston. Then on November 2nd a milestone achieved when we beat Middlesbrough 3-1 at home (after losing 0-1at HT) in front of the live Sky TV cameras. This was exactly my 1,900th Hatters match attended and we played superb with three goals in 5 second half minutes between 57-62.

Since then I've seen us lose 2-0 at QPR on another live Sky match on a Friday night. We actually played ok but R's took their chances and we simply didn't. Sadly a regular Luton fan by the name of Brian Rourke was cowardly attacked from behind by a local QPR thug. After being hit, he fell onto the kerb and smashed his head open! Brian is till in hospital now and far from out of the woods. Thankfully, there has been a crowd funder (hope the Trolls left well alone on that one) and benefit night organised by Loyal Luton Supporters Club– both raising many of £000's for him and his family to help deal with this nightmare. He was literally just walking back to the station.

My 2nd love Rangers, with nowhere near as good performances as last season – disappointingly exiting the Champions League Qualifiers to Malmo, losing home and away, then losing both our opening two Europa Cup group games to a fab Lyon side at Ibrox 0-2 and 1-0 at Sparta Prague (with more Racism issues there, as kids booed Glen Kamara's every touch of the ball). But came back magnificently in the Group by beating both Brondby and Sparta 2-0 at Ibrox, and drawing 1-1 away to Brondby and Lyon to finish 2nd and qualify again to the last 32 stage – for a 4th successive season. We play Borussia Dortmund. It will however be under a new Rangers Manager - as Stevie Gerrard sensationally quit Ibrox on November 11th for Aston Villa! I knew this day would come but the way in which he left us had touches of Nathan going to Stoke. The truth and my personal feelings, was one of being gutted but I could see the angle from SG too… he managed a big club in a poor league well – stopping the Celtic holy grail of *(9.75) 10 titles in a row, will mean he'll be forever remembered by most Bears with gratitude. If he ever wants the Liverpool job he will now have to prove himself in a big league with Villa. The Gers also lost an SPL game (1-0 first game at Dundee Utd) but still remain top after 23 games – just two points clear of Celtic!

Rangers new boss is ex Gers and Arsenal player Gio Van Bronkhorst, so no complaints from us Bears on that appointment. He has started well, undefeated with 9 SPL wins and 3 draws, along with a draw at Lyon in Europe.

Time will tell if it's title no. 56.

The situation with COVID worsened again as I close this book at the start of 2022. I saw a brilliant 3-0 win at Bloomfield Road on my Blackpool AT trip. Luton didn't play for nearly 3 weeks after Dec 11th and Celtic managed to bring the SPL winter break forward – nothing to do of course with them having a bad injury list!

In 2022 we have knocked out Harrogate in the FA Cup 3rd round 4-0 at home (my first time seeing the Yorkshire side – now leaving only Salford and Sutton remaining of the other 91 teams for me to see Luton play). We face Cambridge Utd away in Round 4. Our 4th Championship away win occurred at Reading 2-0. Then I paid my first visit to Bramall Lane since 1994 to see us deservedly lose 2-0 v Sheff Utd. Before two Kenny games, beating Bristol City 2-1 and drawing 0-0 v 2nd place Blackburn – who STILL have never won a league match at our shrine in something like 21 clashes!

I'm FINALLY booked to visit the Liberty Stadium, Swansea (3rd time lucky) in two nights time, which will be my 226th different ground, 169th with Luton and 81st/92. Hopefully I'll see my 115th different ground Luton win?

COYH and Gers.

Two more massive losses – Nigel 'Santa' Martin tragically died of a sudden heart attack (just like Larry) soon before Covid erupted in 2020 and then our beloved wee Westie Clyde, died aged 14 and ½ in May 2021.

ABOUT THE AUTHOR

Alan Adair has been a football fan for over 50 years, following his late Father who took him to his first game at Kenilworth Road in December 1966. He has spent his life supporting Luton Town Football Club, whilst working in the Print industry and travelling the World.

A father to his two Daughters Georgina and Mollie, Alan lives in Bedfordshire and still attends nearly every Hatters game.

Printed in Great Britain
by Amazon

85278114R00276